# Contents

OPPOSITE SÁMI WOMAN IN TRADITIONAL DRESS **PREVIOUS PAGE** DAWN AT PREIKESTOLEN

# Introduction to

# Norway

Quiet for a thousand years since the marauding days of the Vikings, Norway often seems remote to outsiders, even mysterious – remarkable given its geographical position close to the heart of Europe. Beyond Oslo and the famous fjords, the rest of the country might as well be blank on the map for all many visitors know. Yet it's out of the cities and off the major roadways that you'll experience Norway at its most magical: vast stretches of serene, postcard-perfect landscapes where it is at times possible to travel for hours without seeing a single soul. There is nothing tame – and precious little tamed – in this wilderness where everything is on a grand scale, from the deep, blue-black fjords and rearing snowy peaks to jagged forested hills and seemingly limitless expanse of Arctic tundra.

Norway stretches north in a long, slender band from the Skagerrak, the choppy channel that separates the country from Denmark, its coastline battered and buffeted by the Atlantic as it juts up towards the Arctic Sea. Behind this rough and rocky coast are spectacular mountain ranges, harsh upland plateaux, plunging river valleys, rippling glaciers, deep forests and mighty fjords of unsurmounted beauty – an exhilarating landscape begging to be explored by car, boat or bike, on skis or even husky-drawn sled. Perhaps inevitably, the fjords are the apple of the tourist industry's eye – with the infrastructure to prove it – though when well-heeled English and German gentlemen travellers arrived here in the late nineteenth century on the hunt for the Scandinavian exotic, Norwegians were so poor that you could hire a gillie or two for next to nothing. It is this stark contrast – between a severely impoverished past and an astoundingly wealthy present – that, for locals at least, remains a salient characteristic of life up here. Since the country happened upon vast oil and gas reserves under the Norwegian Sea in the 1960s, Norway has managed to assemble one of the most civilized, educated and tolerant societies in the world – one that its population maintains a deep loyalty for and pride in.

**ABOVE** SIGNPOST AT LONGBYEAREN AIRPORT; AQUAVIT; WALRUSES IN ISFJORD, SVALBARD **RIGHT** KAYAKING IN THE LOFOTEN ISLANDS

Norway may have a clutch of attractive, cosmopolitan cities, appealing destinations in their own right, but where the country really shines is not in its urban culture, but rather in the low-key, amiable small-town feel that pervades throughout its settlements. This is not to say that Norway suffers from provincialism – Munch, Ibsen, Grieg and Amundsen, to name but four, were all Norwegians of international importance, to say nothing of the many millions of Norwegian descent today successfully making their way somewhere off in the greater world. But one thing is for certain: every Norwegian you ever meet will at some point make their way back to this remarkable country, put on a pair of old hiking shoes and head off on foot for yonder mountain, reminding themselves how lucky they are to have one of the world's most ravishing landscapes right at their back door.

# Where to go

Though for the most part its people live in small towns and villages, Norway's five largest cities are the obvious – and the most popular – initial targets for a visit. They begin with urbane, vivacious **Oslo**, one of the world's most prettily sited capitals, with a flourishing café scene and a clutch of outstanding museums. Beyond Oslo, in roughly descending order of interest, are **Trondheim**, with its superb cathedral and charming, antique centre; the beguiling port of **Bergen**, gateway to the western fjords; gritty, bustling **Stavanger** in the southwest; and northern **Tromsø**. All are likeable, walkable cities worthy of time in themselves, as well as being within comfortable reach of some startlingly handsome scenery. Indeed, each can serve as a starting point for further explorations or as a

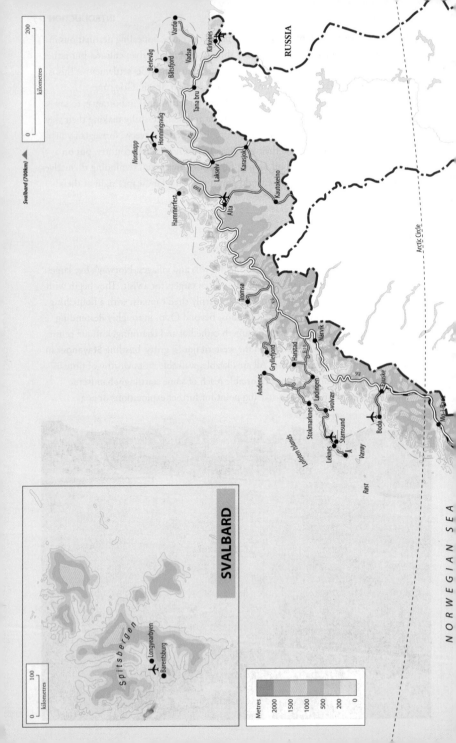

Svalbard (700km) ▲

| | | |
|---|---|---|
| 0 | | 200 |
| kilometres | | |

RUSSIA

Varde
Kirkenes
Vadse
Berlevåg
Båtsfjord
Tana bru
Honningsvåg
Nordkapp
Lakselv
Karasjok
Kautokeino
Alta
E6
E69
Hammerfest

Arctic Circle

Tromsø

Narvik

Gryllefjord
Harstad
Andenes
E10
Stokmarknes
Lødingen
Svolvær
Lofoten Islands
Leknes
Stamsund
Å
Værøy
Bodø
Fauske
E6
Mo i Rana

Røst

NORWEGIAN SEA

## SVALBARD

| | | |
|---|---|---|
| 0 | | 100 |
| kilometres | | |

Spitsbergen

Longyearbyen
Barentsburg

| Metres | |
|---|---|
| 2000 | |
| 1500 | |
| 1000 | |
| 500 | |
| 200 | |
| 0 | |

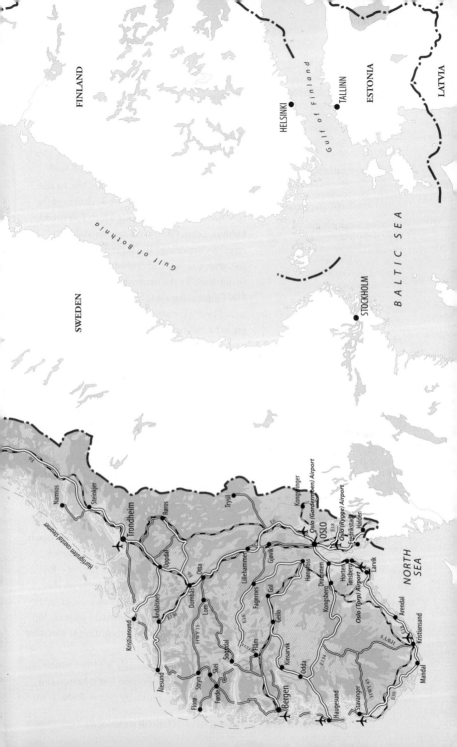

## FACT FILE

Norway's **population** numbers just under 5 million, of whom 600,000 or so live in Oslo, the capital. Bergen, Norway's second city, clocks up about 250,000 residents, while around 40,000 indigenous Sámi (Lapps) live mostly in the north of the country.

Norway has a **surface area** of 386,000 square kilometres, of which half is mountain and a further third forest, lake and river.

Norway is a **constitutional monarchy** and the present king, Harald V, came to the throne in 1991. The parliament – the Storting – sits in Oslo, but many functions are devolved to a complex network of local authorities.

Forget the seafood – **frozen pizza** can lay claim to being Norway's national dish: Norwegians eat over 20 million of them each year.

Norway is not a member of the **EU**, but has signed up to the EEA (European Economic Agreement) free-trade deal.

The Lutheran **Church of Norway** is the official state church and over eighty percent of the population belong to it, however nominally. Lutheran jokes are legion: one shipwrecked sailor to another "Don't worry: I make 50,000kr a week and I tithe; my Lutheran Pastor will find us."

weekend destination in their own right. And wherever you arrive, the trains, buses and ferries of Norway's finely tuned public transport system will take you almost anywhere you want to go, although services are curtailed in winter.

Outside of the cities, the perennial draw remains the **western fjords** – a must, and every bit as scenically stunning as the publicity suggests. Dip into the region from Bergen or **Ålesund**, both accessible by public transport from Oslo, or take more time to appreciate the subtle charms of the tiny, fjordside villages, among which **Balestrand**, **Lofthus**, **Loen**, **Flåm**, **Ulvik** and **Mundal** are especially appealing. This is great hiking country too, with a network of cairned trails and lodges (maintained by the nationwide hiking association DNT) threading along the valleys and over the hills. However, many of the country's finest hikes are to be had further inland, within the confines of a trio of marvellous **national parks**: the **Hardangervidda**, a vast mountain plateau of lunar-like appearance; the **Rondane**, with its bulging mountains; and the **Jotunheimen**, famous for its jagged peaks. Nudging the Skagerrak, the **south coast** is different again. The climate is more hospitable, the landscape gentler and the coast is sprinkled with hundreds of little islands. Every summer, holidaying Norwegians sail down here to explore every nautical nook and cranny, popping into a string of pretty, pint-sized ports, the most inviting being **Arendal** and **Mandal**, the latter the proud possessor of the country's finest sandy beach.

Hiking remains the most popular summer pastime in Norway, but there are alternatives galore, from whitewater rafting – for example at **Sjoa** and **Voss** – sea-kayaking at **Flåm**, and guided glacier walks on the **Jostedalsbreen**. In winter, it's all change when the Norwegians take to cross-country skiing in their droves, shooting off across the Hardangervidda mountain plateau, for example, from **Finse**, though some prefer Alpine skiing and snowboarding at specialist ski resorts like **Geilo** and Oslo's **Holmenkollen**.

Away to the **north**, beyond Trondheim, Norway grows increasingly wild and austere – two traits that make it perfect for off-the-beaten-track adventurers – as it humps and lumps across the Arctic Circle on the way to the modern, workaday port of **Bodø**. From

## NEW NORWEGIAN CUISINE

Upon tasting a piece of Norwegian flatbread, a Parisian woman in the mid-1800s described it as having "the shape and size of a plate, and the same consistency". With images of dried mutton, potato dumplings, cabbage stew and *lutefisk*, Nordic food has rarely been anything to write home about. That all changed in 2010, when Copenhagen's *Noma* was named the world's top restaurant by a panel of 800 chefs and critics, sending the foodie world into shock and turning tastebuds towards Scandinavian kitchens.

Even before this time, though, Norway had begun to reinvent its culinary identity, with new foodie movements, celebrity chefs and a series of government initiatives, such as the Arctic Menu Scheme (see box, p.300) and Taste of the Coast –aimed at supporting **local food producers**, preserving local farming traditions and championing the rich heritage of Norwegian ingredients. The country is now in the middle of a kitchen renaissance, returning to its long-standing local food traditions; once again, Norwegians are consulting their grandmothers' recipe books.

Given nearly 25,000 kilometres of rugged coastline, 150,000 lakes and some of the world's best angling rivers, it is no surprise that a huge variety of locally caught **fish and seafood** predominate in Norwegian kitchens. Norway's diverse landscape also provides habitat to a range of sheep, elk, reindeer and woodland fowl that graze on some of the greenest, most unpolluted grasses in the world, lending their **meat** a rich, succulent taste. And the country's temperate summers allow plants to ripen at a slower pace than elsewhere, infusing **fruits and vegetables** with a supple flavour that you can taste the instant they hit your tastebuds. Below is our pick of places to sample the best of Norwegian cuisine.

here, ferries shuttle over to the rugged **Lofoten** islands, which hold some of the most ravishing scenery in the whole of Europe – tiny fishing villages of ochre- and red-painted houses tucked in between the swell of the deep blue sea and the severest of grey-green mountains. Back on the mainland, it's a long haul north from Bodø to the iron-ore town of **Narvik**, and on to **Tromsø**, a delightful little city huddled on an island and with plenty of Arctic charm. These towns are, however, merely the froth of a vast wilderness that extends up to **Nordkapp** (North Cape), one of the northernmost points of mainland Europe, and the spot where the principal tourist trail peters out. Yet Norway continues east for several hundred kilometres, round to remote **Kirkenes** near the Russian border, while inland stretches an immense and hostile upland plateau, the **Finnmarksvidda**, one

# Author picks

Our two authors have combed Norway to prepare this new edition. Here are some of their personal favourites:

**Mountain roads** Not for the faint-hearted, or for the poor-of-steering, Norway's mountain roads boast some of the most imposing scenery imaginable – the Sognefjellsveg (p.235) and the Trollstigen (p.251) are two of the best.

**Stave churches** If there is one architectural symbol of Norway that stands out, it's the stave church: ornate and delicate outside; dark, pine-scented and mysterious within. Borgund is the most elegiac (p.173), Urnes (p.233) the wildest and Eidsborg the most idiosyncratic (p.178).

**Historic hotels** Finding a lovely country hotel in Norway is rarely difficult, but three of the best are the expansive *Alexandra* in Loen (p.242), the antique and remote *Union Hotel* in Øye (p.245) and the stylish, fin-de-siècle *Edvardas Hus* on Tranøy (p.296).

**Great hikes** Norway offers the adventurous hiker some wonderful experiences: the hike up from Lofthus to the lunar-like Hardangervidda plateau (p.212), the jaunt along the Besseggen ridge in the Jotunheimen Nasjonalpark (p.166) and the remote, fjord-and-mountain trek from Vinstad to Bunes (p.325) are three such favourites.

**Prettiest villages** Not all of Norway's villages match the beauty of their setting but tiny Mundal (p.230), with its pocket of fjordside houses, Ulvik (p.216), set 'twixt fjord and mountain, and quainter than quaint Å (p.326), certainly do.

**Skiing** Blanketed in snow for several months a year, skiing – be it downhill, cross-country or Telemark – in Norway is more a way of life than a sport. Join in, whether it's on the outskirts of Oslo (p.104), in rural Lillehammer (p.154), or even up the Lofoten coast setting off from Kabelvåg (p.320).

> Our author recommendations don't end here. We've flagged up our favourite places – a perfectly sited hotel, an atmospheric café, a special restaurant – throughout the guide, highlighted with the ★ symbol.

**FROM TOP** THE TROLLSTIGEN; BORGUND STAVE CHURCH; CROSS-COUNTRY SKIING

of the last haunts of the Sámi reindeer-herders. And finally, a short flight away, there is the wondrous chill of **Svalbard**, rising remote in the Arctic seas, islands of rolling glaciers and ice-glazed mountains where the snowmobile or Zodiac is more useful than a car.

# When to go

In the popular imagination, Norway is commonly regarded as remote and cold – spectacular but climatically inhospitable. There is some truth in this, of course, but when to go is not, perhaps, as clear-cut a choice as you might imagine with other seasons other than summer offering particular bonuses. There are, for example, advantages to travelling during the long, dark **winters** with their reduced everything: daylight, opening times and transport services. If you are equipped and hardy enough to reach the north, seeing the phenomenal **northern lights** (aurora borealis) is a distinct possibility and later, once the days begin to lighten, the **skiing** – and for that matter the dog-sledging, ice fishing and snowmobiling – is excellent. There are skiing packages to Norway from abroad, but perhaps more appealing – and certainly less expensive – is the ease with which you can arrange a few days' skiing wherever you happen to be. As the year advances, **Easter** is the time of the colourful Sámi festivals, and **mid-May** can be absolutely delightful if your visit coincides with the brief Norwegian **spring**, though this is difficult to gauge. Springtime is particularly beguiling in the fjords, with a thousand cascading waterfalls fed by the melting snow, and wild flowers in abundance everywhere. **Autumn** can be exquisite too, with **September** often bathed in the soft sunshine of an Indian summer, but – especially in the far north – it is frequently cold, often bitterly so, from late September to mid- to late May. Nevertheless, most people travel during the **summer** season, when bus, ferry and train connections are at their most frequent. This is the time of the **midnight sun**: the further north you go, the longer the day becomes, until at Nordkapp the sun is continually visible from mid-May to the end of July (see box below). Something worth noting, however, is that the summer season in Norway is relatively short, stretching roughly from the beginning of June to the end of August. Come in September and you'll find that many tourist offices, museums and other sights have cut back their hours and buses, ferries and trains have already switched to reduced schedules.

## THE MIDNIGHT SUN

The **midnight sun** is visible at the following places on the following dates, though climbing the nearest hill can – trees and clouds permitting – extend this by a day or two either way:
**Bodø**: June 2 to July 10
**Hammerfest**: May 14 to July 28
**Longyearbyen** April 19 to Aug 23
**Nordkapp**: May 12 to July 29
**Tromsø**: May 20 to July 21

**RIGHT FROM TOP** LINDESNES FYR; ISFJORD, SVALBARD

# 24

# things not to miss

It's not possible to see everything Norway has to offer in one trip – and we don't suggest you try. What follows is a selective take on the country's highlights, including outstanding scenery, picturesque villages and dramatic wildlife safaris. Each entry has a page reference to take you straight into the Guide, where you can discover more.

### 1 GEIRANGERFJORD
Page 245

Shadowed by rearing mountains, the S-shaped Geirangerfjord is one of Norway's most stunningly beautiful fjords.

### 2 CROSS-COUNTRY SKIING
Page 45

Norway's meadows, moors and mountains boast thousands of kilometres of powdered runs just waiting for adventuresome skiers. You might choose to start at Lillehammer (see p.154).

### 3 WILDLIFE SAFARIS IN SVALBARD
Page 374

From polar-bear spotting to birdwatching to husky driving, the vast, glaciated landscapes of this gorgeous Arctic archipelago present a spectacular range of wildlife safaris.

### 4 VIGELANDSPARKEN
Page 86

Before his death in 1943, Gustav Vigeland populated Oslo's favourite park with his fantastical, phantasmagorical sculptures.

### 5 THE FLÅMSBANA
Page 220

A ride on the Flåm railway from high up in the mountains to the fjords way down below is one of the most dramatic train journeys in the world.

10

### 6 THE OSLOFJORD
The islands of the Oslofjord are great for swimming, sunbathing and walking – and they are just a short ferry ride from the city centre.

### 7 VÆRØY'S SEA-BIRD COLONIES
This remote Lofoten island is renowned for its profuse bird life, which includes puffins, cormorants, kittiwakes, guillemots and rare sea eagles.

### 8 HJØRUNDFJORD
Wild and windswept, the deep, dark waters and icy peaks of this remote fjord make it one of Norway's most elegiac.

### 9 BERGEN
Norway's second city is an eminently appealing place with a clutch of fine old buildings, great restaurants and top-notch art galleries.

### 10 ÅLESUND
Nudging the ocean, beguiling Ålesund boasts a wonderful coastal setting and a platoon of handsome Art Nouveau buildings.

### 11 THE NORSK FISKEVAERSMUSEUM, Å
Hanging on for dear life between the mountains and the sea, the tiny village of Å has preserved its nineteenth-century buildings as the Norwegian Fishing Village Museum.

11

**WHALE-WATCHING, ANDENES**
Page 308

Pilots, minkes, humpbacks and sperm whales show themselves in all their glory during summertime scouting excursions off the Vesterålen coast.

 **NIDAROS DOMKIRKE, TRONDHEIM**
Page 268

Trondheim's vaunted gothic *domkirke* (cathedral) is the largest medieval building in Scandinavia – and one of the world's most awe-inspiring religious structures.

 **THE JOSTEDALSBREEN GLACIER**
Page 238

Take a guided walk out on to this mighty ice plateau as it grinds and groans, slips and slithers its way across the mountains behind the Nordfjord.

 **URNES STAVE CHURCH**
Page 233

Perhaps the finest of Norway's stave churches, Urnes is distinguished by the frenzied intricacy of its woodcarving.

**16** **THE HURTIGRUTEN**
Page 30

See Norway in all its scenic splendour on the Hurtiguten coastal boat, which sails north all the way from Bergen to Kirkenes.

**17** **STAY IN A LIGHTHOUSE**
Pages 38 & 130

Glued to a storm-battered islet, *Feisten Fyr*, near Stavanger (see p.138), is one of several lighthouses that make for fabulous places to stay.

**18** **THE OSEBERG LONGBOAT**
Page 82

Of the handful of Viking longboats that have survived, the *Oseberg* is the best preserved – and was unearthed complete with a rich treasure-trove of burial goods.

15

16

17

18

19

 **JUVET LANDSCAPE HOTEL**
Page 251

Scandinavia's most enchanting hotel, with freestanding rooms carved out of spruce, is set smack in a verdant river canyon – staying here is like watching an IMAX documentary from your bedroom.

 **THE NORTHERN LIGHTS**
Page 341

At once eerily disconcerting and bewitchingly beautiful, the aurora borealis flicker across northern Norway's winter firmament at irregular, unpredictable intervals.

 **EDVARD MUNCH**
Pages 68 & 79

Munch's unsettling, highly charged paintings appear in several of the country's museums, most memorably at the Nasjonalgalleriet in Oslo.

 **ALTA ROCK CARVINGS**
Page 347

Simple in design but complex in their symbolism, Alta's hillside prehistoric rock carvings offer insight into the beliefs of the region's earliest inhabitants.

 **WALKING IN THE JOTUNHEIMEN MOUNTAINS**
Page 163

One of Norway's most celebrated hiking areas, the Jotunheimen National Park is crisscrossed with trails and includes northern Europe's two highest peaks.

 **HENNINGSVÆR**
Page 320

The Lofoten islands are strewn about with scores of picture-postcard fishing villages, of which Henningsvær is among the most arresting.

# Itineraries

These three itineraries will give you a taste of Norway's astounding variety. Our Grand Tour mixes urban charm with stunning scenery while The Western Fjords will help you plan a route through these majestic lands. Real adventure junkies, however, will want to head north to the Arctic wilds for some of the most exhilarating thrills anywhere on Earth.

## GRAND TOUR

Spend two weeks – though three would be ideal – following the country's invigorating, surf-battered coast, experiencing its laidback cities and wild landscapes en route.

**❶ Oslo** Allow yourself a few days in the Norwegian capital, taking in its parks, museums, seafood restaurants and bars. **See p.60**

**❷ Stavanger** Stroll the atmospheric old town, visit the canning museum, boat out to an 1800-era lighthouse, then climb up to Pulpit Rock. **See p.133**

**❸ Bergen** This lovely old port is celebrated for its handsome coastal setting and fine wooden architecture. Time your stay to coincide with a festival – Nattjazz, for instance. **See p.187**

**❹ Bergen to Trondheim by boat** No Norwegian holiday would be complete without a sea cruise – sit back and enjoy the views from the Hurtigruten. **See p.30**

**❺ Trondheim** Trondheim features a magnificent cathedral, a charming old district and is a great springboard for points north. **See p.266**

**❻ Lofoten** With its rearing peaks and turbulent ocean, this archipelago is Norway at its most beautiful. **See p.312**

**❼ Tromsø** Home to lively restaurants and simmering bars, this "Paris of the north" is the

perfect spot to spend a few days gearing up for an excursion into the Arctic hinterlands. **See p.336**

**❽ Nordkapp** The northern end of mainland Europe, this jagged promontory pokes a knobbly finger out into the Arctic Sea. **See p.357**

## THE WESTERN FJORDS

Starting from Bergen (see p.187), this fjord itinerary will take about ten days – fourteen if you add a hike or two – at a comfortable pace by car, and a little longer by public transport.

**❶ Lofthus** Snuggling the Sørfjord, this lovely little village sits amid fruit orchards – and is within a day's hike of the Hardangervidda mountain plateau. **See p.212**

**❷ Trolltunga** Hike up to this remarkable overhang – the "Troll's Tongue" – for a truly incredible view. **See p.211**

**❸ Balestrand** Loveable village with an exquisite setting, its huddle of houses pressing up against the mountains. **See p.229**

**❹ Solvorn** From this quaint hamlet, which ambles up from the Lustrafjord, you can visit the remarkable Urnes stave church. **See p.233**

**❺ Mundal, Fjærlandsfjord** Isolated until the 1980s, the Fjærlandsfjord is gloriously wild. From Mundal you can hike up into the hills to long-abandoned mountain farms. **See p.230**

**ABOVE** OSLO; LOFTHUS; KIRKENES SNOWHOTEL

**❺ Jostedalsbreen glacier** A guided walk on this groaning, creaking glacier, one of the largest in Europe, is a must. **See p.238**

**❼ Cruise the Geirangerfjord** Hemmed in by mountains, this fjord is truly spectacular, and the boat cruise along it a real treat. **See p.246**

**❽ Ålesund** Draped around its pretty, little harbour, this delightful town boasts a confetti of Art Nouveau buildings. **See p.252**

## ARCTIC NORWAY

The more northerly stretches of Norway's beguiling coast beckon with gorgeous indigo light, a distinctly warm camaradarie and limitless outdoor activities – perfect for a couple of weeks' heart-pounding adventure.

**❶ Maelstrom in Saltstraumen** Experience the world's strongest tidal whirlpool, which sends some 400 million tonnes of water through the coastline's narrow fjords, producing an uncanny yelping sound. **See p.294**

**❷ Cross-country skiing in Kabelvåg** Spend a day or two skiing across the powdered marshes

and soaring mountains of this up-and-coming destination. **See p.320**

**❸ Polar Light Center in Laukvik** This specially designed centre gets you closest to the elusive northern lights – bright, fiery tapestries of light that flicker across the heavens. **See p.317**

**❹ Whale-watching in Vesterålen** Pilots, minkes and humpbacks seek out Vesterålen's nutrient-rich waters, turning the region into a hub for scouting excursions. **See p.308**

**❺ Dog-sledding outside Karasjok** Harness, rig, and prep your pack of snow-white Siberian huskies and head off on the Arctic's Formula 1 – a day-long sledging safari. **See p.354**

**❻ Sleep in an igloo, Kirkenes** Jump into an expedition-strength sleeping bag and drift off to sleep in a room made out of blocks of snow and ice. **See p.368**

**❼ Explore the ends of the earth on Svalbard** Ride the fjords in a rugged Zodiac or snowmobile out to an abandoned satellite station-turned-guesthouse, the perfect base for snowy wilderness exploration. **See p.374**

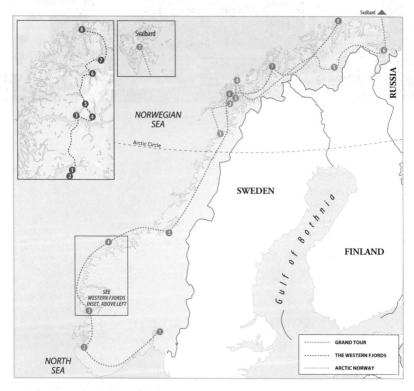

FERRY IN THE FJORDS

# Basics

# Getting there

**There is a good range of inexpensive flights to Norway from London, though from the UK's regional airports the choice is poorer. Oslo Gardermoen airport is the main point of arrival. Flights are almost invariably much less expensive than the long and arduous journey from the UK to Norway by train or car. There are currently no ferry services direct from the UK to Norway, but this situation may change and it's worth checking out if you're considering taking your car.**

From **Ireland**, there is much less choice, but there are regular flights to Oslo Gardermoen airport. For travellers arriving from **North America**, the main decision is whether to fly direct to Oslo – though the options are limited – or via another European city, probably London. **Australians**, **New Zealanders** and **South Africans** have to fly via another country – there are no nonstop, direct flights. Finally, getting to Norway **from the rest of Scandinavia** (Denmark, Sweden and Finland) is quick, easy and relatively inexpensive, whether you travel by plane, bus or train.

## Flights from the UK

From the UK, there's a good choice of **direct, nonstop flights** from London to Oslo as well as a scattering of flights there from the UK's **regional airports**. Norway's main international airport is Oslo Gardermoen, 45km north of the city, but several budget airlines use the deceptively named Oslo (Torp) airport, which is actually just outside Sandef-

jord, 110km from Oslo, and Oslo (Rygge) airport, 60km south of the city near the little town of Moss. There are also a handful of nonstop, direct flights from the UK to other Norwegian cities, including Stavanger, Ålesund, Bergen and Trondheim, but for the likes of Tromsø you'll have to change planes. Scandinavian Airlines (SAS) and its subsidiary Widerøe has the largest number of routes.

**Prices** vary enormously, but Norwegian Airlines often offers the least expensive tickets with a return from London Gatwick or Manchester to Oslo costing from as little as £140. **Flying times** are insignificant: Aberdeen to Stavanger takes just one hour, London to Oslo a little over two.

## Flights from Ireland

Flying from Ireland to Norway, there's not much choice, but Ryanair (w ryanair.com) has flights from Dublin to Oslo (Rygge) and Norwegian Airlines (w norwegian.com) flies between Dublin and Oslo Gardermoen. As sample fares, Norwegian charges anywhere between €70 and €160 for the flight from Dublin to Oslo with a **flying time** of just over two hours.

## Flights from the US and Canada

From the **US**, you can fly direct/nonstop to Oslo Gardermoen from New York City with United Airlines (w united.com) but otherwise you'll have to change at a hub airport with London being an obvious choice. Return fares from major cities in the US to London start at around US$800, but otherwise reckon on spending around US$1500–2000 return for a nonstop New York–Oslo return flight with Continental. There are no direct flights to Norway

---

## AIRLINES AND ROUTES

The following airlines currently cover nonstop routings from the UK to Norway. Note that some of these routings only operate during the summertime.

**bmi** (w flybmi.com). London Heathrow to Bergen, Oslo and Stavanger.
**British Airways** (w britishairways.com). London to Oslo Gardermoen.
**Eastern Airways** (w easternairways.com). Aberdeen, Glasgow and Newcastle to Stavanger.
**Norwegian Airlines** (w norwegian.com). London Gatwick to Ålesund, Bergen, Oslo Gardermoen and Trondheim; Edinburgh to Oslo Gardermoen; Manchester to Oslo Gardermoen.

**Ryanair** (w ryanair.com). London Stansted to Haugesund; Edinburgh, Liverpool and London Stansted to Oslo (Torp); Liverpool, Manchester, London Stansted and Gatwick to Oslo (Rygge).
**Scandinavian Airlines** (**SAS**; w flysas.com) and its subsidiary **Widerøe** (w wideroe.no). London Heathrow to Bergen, Oslo Gardermoen and Stavanger; Aberdeen to Bergen and Stavanger; Manchester to Oslo Gardermoen; Newcastle to Stavanger.

## A BETTER KIND OF TRAVEL

At Rough Guides we are passionately committed to travel. We believe it helps us understand the world we live in and the people we share it with – and of course tourism is vital to many developing economies. But the scale of modern tourism has also damaged some places irreparably, and climate change is accelerated by most forms of transport, especially flying. All Rough Guides' flights are carbon-offset, and every year we donate money to a variety of environmental charities.

from the west coast, but plenty of carriers will get you to Oslo with one stop, for as little as US$1500 return.

From **Canada**, the best deals are usually offered by Air Canada (W aircanada.com), which flies nonstop to London Heathrow, with onward connections to Norway. From Toronto to Oslo, expect to pay around Can$2000 in high season and Can$1500 in low season, while typical fares from Vancouver are around Can$2200 in high season and, likewise, Can$1500 in low season.

The **flying time** on a direct, nonstop flight from the east coast of North America to Norway is just over seven hours.

## Flights from Australia and New Zealand

There are no direct/nonstop flights from **Australia** or **New Zealand** to Norway. Most itineraries will involve two changes, one in the Far East – Singapore, Bangkok or Kuala Lumpur – and then another in the gateway city of the airline you're flying with – most commonly Copenhagen, Amsterdam or London. You can get tickets to Oslo from Sydney, Melbourne or Perth for Aus$1500–2500, NZ$2000–3000 from Auckland.

## Flights from South Africa

There are no direct/nonstop flights from South Africa to Norway, but several airlines will get you to Oslo with one stop via a European hub city. For example, KLM (W klm.com) fly from Cape Town to Amsterdam with onward connections to Oslo for a return fare of between ZAR9500 and ZAR12,500.

## By train from the UK

**Eurostar** (W eurostar.com) services running through the Channel Tunnel to Brussels put Norway within reasonable striking distance of the UK by **train**, but the whole journey from London to Oslo, which is usually routed via Brussels and Copenhagen, still takes about 22 hours and costs about £300 one-way (£350 return), though special

deals and concessionary rates can reduce these fares considerably.

### Rail passes

If you're visiting Norway as part of a longer European trip, it may be worth considering a **pan-European rail pass**. There are lots to choose from and **Rail Europe** (W raileurope.com and W raileurope.co.uk), the umbrella company for all national and international passes, operates a comprehensive website detailing all the options with prices. Note in particular that some passes have to be bought before leaving home, others can only be bought in specific countries. Note also that **Inter-Rail Pass** (W interrailnet.com) and **Eurail Pass** (W eurail.com) holders get discounts on some internal ferry and bus journeys within Norway.

## Driving from the UK

To reach Norway by **car or motorbike** from the UK, the best bet is to use **Eurotunnel**'s (W eurotunnel.com) shuttle train through the Channel Tunnel. Note that Eurotunnel only carries cars (including occupants) and motorbikes, not cyclists and foot passengers. From the Eurotunnel exit in Calais, it's a somewhat epic journey of around 1400km or so to Oslo.

## By ferry from the UK

There are currently no **car ferries** from the UK to Norway; the nearest you'll get is **Esbjerg** in Denmark, about 900km (around 10hr) by road from Oslo, with DFDS Seaways (W dfdsseaways.co.uk) from **Harwich**. **Tariffs** vary enormously, depending on when you leave, how long you stay, what size your vehicle is and how many passengers are in it; on overnight sailings, there is also the cost of a cabin to consider. As a sample fare, a seven-day, peak season return fare for two adults in an ordinary car costs around £250. Reservations are strongly recommended. There are three or four Harwich-to-Esbjerg sailings every week and the journey time is about eighteen hours.

## By train, bus and ferry from the rest of Scandinavia and Russia

**By train** you can reach **Oslo** from both Stockholm (2–3 daily; 6hr) and Copenhagen (2 daily; 8hr). There are also regular services from Stockholm to **Narvik** (1–2 daily; 21hr), operated by the Swedish company SJ (☏00 46 771 75 75 75, Ⓦsj.se). For online tickets, go to Ⓦraileurope.com.

Several **bus** companies provide services into Norway from other parts of Scandinavia. These include **Eurolines** (Ⓦeurolines.co.uk) buses from London to Oslo, which pass through several Danish and Swedish towns, notably Copenhagen, Malmö and Gothenburg; the Swedish company **GoByBus** (Ⓦgobybus.se), which has services to Oslo from Stockholm, Copenhagen, Malmö and Gothenburg among others; and **Swebuss** (Ⓦswebus.se), which operates an express bus from Stockholm to Oslo. In the far north, **Eskelisen Lapin Linjat** (Ⓦeskelisen-lapinlinjat.com) runs a number of bus services from Finland to Norwegian destinations, including Tromsø, Kirkenes and Nordkapp.

A number of **car ferries** shuttle across the Skagerrak **from Denmark** to Norway (see box below).

As for **border crossings**, there is (usually) little formality at either the Norway–Sweden or Norway–Finland borders, but the northern border with **Russia** is a different story. Border patrols (on either side) won't be overjoyed at the prospect of you nosing around. If you have a genuine wish to visit Russia from Norway, it's best to sort out the paperwork – visas and so forth – before you leave home. Kirkenes (see p.369) is the main starting point for tours into Russia from Norway.

## Tours and organized holidays

Tourism in Norway is a multi-million-dollar industry that has spawned a small army of tour operators. Some provide generic bus tours of parts of the country, but there are many more specialist companies too, featuring everything from skiing and walking through to whale-watching and cycling. Most of the better companies offer a choice of escorted and independent tours. Additional, domestic tour operators are detailed throughout the Guide.

### TOUR AND HOLIDAY OPERATORS

**Anglers' World Holidays** UK ☏01246 221 717, Ⓦanglers-world .co.uk. Sea- and river-fishing holidays in Norway.

**Brekke Tours & Travel** US ☏1 800 437 5302, Ⓦbrekketours .com. A well-established company offering a host of sightseeing and cultural tours of Scandinavia in general and Norway in particular.

**Discover the World** UK ☏01737 214 251, Ⓦdiscover-the-world .co.uk. Specialist adventure tours including whale-watching in Norway, wildlife in Spitsbergen and dog-sledging in Lapland. Independent, tailor-made tours too.

**Exodus** UK ☏0845 508 4197, Ⓦexodus.co.uk. Large, activity-holiday specialist offering cross-country skiing and all sorts of other winter sports plus whale-watching, hiking and Spitsbergen excursions.

**Headwater** UK ☏0845 564 7148, Ⓦheadwater.com. Limited but well-chosen selection of winter fun holidays in Geilo and Venabu, where punters choose anything from skiing to reindeer safaris.

**High & Wild** UK ☏0845 004 7801, Ⓦhighandwild.co.uk. Adventure holiday specialist through whose services you can join a Sámi reindeer migration.

**Hurtigruten Norway** ☏00 47 81 00 30 30, Ⓦhurtigruten.com. The Hurtigruten coastal voyage is Norway's most celebrated sea cruise (see p.30).

**Inntravel** UK ☏01653 617 001, Ⓦinntravel.co.uk. Outdoor holidays in Norway including skiing, walking, dog-sledging, fjord cruises, and whale- and reindeer-watching.

**North South Travel** UK ☏01245 608 291, Ⓦnorthsouthtravel .co.uk. Friendly, competitive travel agency, offering discounted fares worldwide. Profits are used to support projects in the developing world, especially the promotion of sustainable tourism.

**Saddle Skedaddle** UK ☏0191 265 1110, Ⓦskedaddle.co.uk. Highly recommended company organizing a couple of cycling tours of Norway each year, usually one to the Lofoten islands and another round the western fjords.

**Scandinavian America World Tours** US ☏1 800 545 2204, Ⓦscandinaviantravel.com. Scandinavian specialist offering an extensive programme of group and individual tours and cruises within Norway.

---

### INTERNATIONAL CAR FERRIES

**Copenhagen** (Denmark) to: Oslo (1 daily; 16hr; Ⓦdfdsseaways.no).
**Frederikshavn** (Denmark) to: Oslo (1 daily; 9hr to 12hr; Ⓦstenaline.no).
**Hirtshals** (Denmark) to: Kristiansand (2–3 daily; 2hr 15min–3hr 30min; Ⓦcolorline.com and Ⓦfjordline.com); Larvik (1–2 daily; 4hr; Ⓦcolorline.com); Stavanger/Bergen (3–5 weekly; 10hr/17hr; Ⓦfjordline.com).
**Strömstad** (Sweden) to: Sandefjord (4–6 daily; 2hr 30min; Ⓦcolorline.com).

## FJORD TOURS AND THE FJORD PASS

Perhaps the best non-specialist tour operator in Norway is Bergen's **Fjord Tours** (☎815 68 222, ✆ fjordtours.com). The company manages the first-rate **Fjord Pass** scheme (see p.36) and organizes a creative menu of Norwegian tours. It is the main organizer of the much-vaunted **Norway in a Nutshell** excursion (see box, p.207), and they also offer **Sognefjord in a Nutshell** (1250kr return from Bergen); **Hardanger in a Nutshell** (820kr return from Bergen); and a wonderful four-day tour from Oslo to Trondheim followed by a Hurtigruten cruise along the coast to Bergen (3280kr). There are no tour guides on any of these excursions, which suits most independent travellers just fine, and all use public transport – bus, train and ferry. Fjord Tours also offer **adventure packages** – cycling on the Rallarvegen (see box, p.221) or winter skiing for example – and, if you're travelling by car, they will book accommodation on your behalf with Fjord Pass hotels and advise on itineraries.

**Scand-America** US ☎ 1 727 415 5088, ✆ scandamerica.com. A wide variety of packages – everything from dog-sledging to garden tours – throughout Scandinavia. Florida based.

**Scantours** US ☎ 1 800 223 7226 ✆ scantours.com. Huge range of packages and tailor-made holidays to every Scandinavian nook and cranny.

# Getting around

**Norway's public transport system – a huge mesh of trains, buses, car ferries and passenger express ferries – is comprehensive and reliable. In the winter (especially in the north) services can be cut back severely, but no part of the country is unreachable for long.**

Bear in mind, however, that Norwegian villages and towns usually spread over a large distance, so don't be surprised if you end up walking a kilometre or two from the bus stop, ferry terminal or train station to get where you want to go. It's this sprawling nature of the country's towns and, more especially, the remoteness of many of the sights, that encourages visitors to **rent a car**. This is an expensive business, but costs can be reduced if you rent locally for a day or two rather than for the whole trip, though in high season spare vehicles can get very thin on the ground.

## By train

With the exception of the Narvik line into Sweden, operated by SJ (see p.298), all Norwegian **train** services are run by Norges Statsbaner (NSB; ☎815 00 888, ✆ nsb.no). Apart from a sprinkling of branch lines, NSB services operate on **three main domestic routes**, which link Oslo to Stavanger in the southwest, to Bergen in the west and to Trondheim and on to Bodø in the north. The nature of the country has made several of these routes engineering feats of some magnitude, worth the trip in their own right – the tiny **Flåm line** (see box, p.220) and the sweeping **Rauma line** (see box, p.165) from Dombås to Åndalsnes are exciting examples.

NSB have two main types of train – **Lokaltog** (local) and **Regiontog** (regional). There is one standard class on both, but certain regional trains have a "**Komfort**" (read more spacious and with electrical plugs) carriage, for which you pay a supplement of 90kr per person. All Regiontog have **internet access**, for which you'll need to register beforehand on the NSB website. It's also worth noting that on many long-distance intercity trains and on all overnight and international services, an advance **seat reservation** is compulsory. In high season, it's wise to reserve a seat on main routes anyway, as trains can be packed. General **NSB timetables** are available free at every train station and there are individual route timetables too. In the case of the more scenic routes, there are also leaflets describing the sights as you go.

### Fares and discounts

**Fully flexible, standard-fare prices** are bearable, with the popular Oslo–Bergen run, for example, costing around 800kr one-way, Oslo–Trondheim 870kr – a little less than twice that for a return. Both journeys take around six and a half to seven hours. NSB also offers a variety of **discount fares**. The main discount ticket scheme is the **Minipris** (mini-price), under which you can cut up to sixty percent off the price of long-distance journeys. In general, the further you travel, the more economic they become. The drawback is that Minipris tickets must be purchased at least one day in advance, are not available at peak periods and on certain trains, and stopovers are not permitted. NSB also showboats a variety of special deals and discounts – check the

NSB website or enquire locally (and ahead of time) for details on any specific route. For overnight trains, two-berth **sleepers** (*sove*) are reasonably priced at 850kr, especially if you consider you'll save a night's hotel accommodation.

In terms of **concessionary fares** on standard-price tickets, there are group and family reductions; children under 4 travel free; 4–15-year-olds pay half-fare, and so do senior citizens (67+) and the disabled. Pan-European **Inter-Rail** and **Eurail passes** can include the Norwegian railway system (see p.26) and there's also a **Norway Eurail Pass**, which entitles the holder to between three and eight days unlimited rail travel within one month. Prices for three days are 1500kr (1133kr for 12–25-year-olds), eight days 2277kr (1716kr). The rules and regulations regarding all these passes are complicated – consult the website of the umbrella company, **Rail Europe** (W raileurope .com). Note that some passes have to be bought before leaving home.

## By bus

Both supplementing and on occasion duplicating the train network, **buses** reach almost every corner of the country. The principal long-distance carrier is **Nor-Way Bussekspress** (T 815 44 444, W nor-way .no), whose services operate in conjunction with a dense network of local buses, some of which only run in the summertime. **Tickets** are usually bought on board, but on long-distance routes there are sometimes substantial discounts for advance purchase – check the Nor-Way Bussekspress website for details or inquire at the local bus station. Bus travel is almost invariably less expensive than the train, and prices are passable – especially as all tolls and ferry costs are included in the price of a ticket – but costs are still fairly high. For instance, the nine-hour Nor-Way Bussekspress trip from Oslo to Haugesund costs 650kr (490kr in advance), the

seven-hour journey from Ålesund to Trondheim 570kr (no advance discount).

As for **concessionary fares**, children under 4 travel free and both youngsters (under 16) and seniors (over 67) are entitled to discounts of up to fifty percent. Rail-pass holders and students are sometimes eligible for a fifty-percent reduction on the full adult rate too – ask and you may receive.

## By ferry

Using a **ferry** is one of the highlights of any visit to Norway – indeed, among the western fjords and around the Lofotens they are all but impossible to avoid. The majority are roll-on, roll-off **car ferries**. These represent an economical means of transport, with **prices** fixed on a nationwide sliding scale: short journeys (10–20min) cost foot passengers 25–35kr, whereas a car and driver will pay 60–100kr. The maximum tariff on this national scale (for sea journeys of up to 15km) is currently 43kr for foot passengers, 130kr for car and driver. **Ferry procedures** are straightforward: foot passengers walk on and pay the conductor, car drivers pay when the conductor appears at the car window either on the jetty or on board – although some busier routes have a drive-by ticket office. One or two of the longer car ferry routes – in particular Bodø–Moskenes – take advance reservations, but the rest operate on a **first-come, first-served** basis. In the off season, there's no real need to arrive more than twenty minutes before departure – with the possible exception of the Lofoten island ferries – but in the summer allow two hours to be really safe.

### Hurtigbåt passenger express boats

Norway's **Hurtigbåt** passenger express boats are catamarans that make up in speed what they lack in enjoyment: unlike the ordinary ferries, the landscape whizzes by and in choppy seas the ride can be disconcertingly bumpy. Nonetheless, they

## TIMETABLES

**Timetables** for almost all train, bus and ferry services are available online. **Train** details are easy to find on Norges Statsbaner's (Norwegian State Railways) all-encompassing website (W nsb.no), but **bus and ferry** timetables can be bothersome: there are lots of different carriers and, although most of their websites are in Norwegian and English, services are often divided up by county (commune) rather than alphabetically. Fortunately, Norway's principal **long-distance bus company**, Nor-Way Bussekspress, have an easy-to-use website (W nor-way .no), but the websites of the two biggest **ferry and local bus** operators, Norled (W norled.no) and fjord1 (W fjord1.no) are much complex. Alternatively, almost every Norwegian tourist office carries a comprehensive range of free local and regional public transport timetables, which they will help you decipher if necessary.

are a convenient time-saving option: it takes just four hours on the Hurtigbåt service from Bergen to Balestrand, for instance, and the same from Narvik to Svolvær. There are Hurtigbåt services all along the west coast, with a particular concentration in and around Bergen; the majority operate all year. There's no fixed tariff table, so **rates** vary considerably, though Hurtigbåt boats are significantly more expensive per kilometre than car ferries – Bergen–Flåm, for instance, costs 685kr for the five-and-a-half-hour journey, 800kr for the four-hour trip from Bergen to Stavanger.

There are **concessionary fares** on standard fares on all routes, with infants up to the age of 4 travelling free, and children (4–15) and senior citizens (over 67) getting a fifty-percent discount. In addition, rail-pass holders and students are often eligible for a fifty-percent reduction on the full adult rate and on most routes you get a similar discount for advance reservations on the internet.

## The Hurtigruten

Norway's most celebrated ferry journey is the long and beautiful haul up the coast from Bergen to Kirkenes on the **Hurtigruten** (literally, "rapid route" ⓦhurtigruten.com) **coastal boat** or steamer. To many, the Hurtigruten remains the quintessential Norwegian experience, and it's certainly the best way to observe the drama of the country's extraordinary coastline. Eleven ships combine to provide one daily service in each direction, and the boats stop off at over thirty ports on the way.

The whole round-trip lasts thirteen days (and twelve nights), and the **fare** per person in a two-berth cabin including breakfast, lunch and dinner ranges from 8000kr in the depths of winter to 1900kr at the height of the summer. The shorter, one-way cruise costs a lot more heading north than south: north ranges from 7800kr to 13000kr, south 4400kr to 10500kr, again per person in a two-berth cabin including breakfast, lunch and dinner. There

---

## HURTIGRUTEN SAILING SCHEDULE

**Northbound** Hurtigruten schedules fluctuate according to season: the summer timetable runs from mid-April to mid-September, winter from mid-September to mid-April.
**Southbound** the service sticks to the same timetable throughout the year. Below is a list of departure times from principal ports.

### NORTHBOUND
**Summer schedule**

| | |
|---|---|
| Bergen 8pm | Stamsund 7.30pm |
| Florø 2.15am | Svolvær 10pm |
| Ålesund 9.30am | Harstad 8am |
| Geiranger 1.30pm* | Tromsø 6.30pm |
| Ålesund 6.45pm | Hammerfest 6.45am |
| Trondheim noon | Honningsvåg 3.15pm |
| Bodø 3pm | Arrive Kirkenes 9.45am |

**Winter schedule**

| | |
|---|---|
| Bergen 10.30pm | Svolvær 10pm |
| Florø 4.45am | Harstad 8am |
| Ålesund 3pm | Tromsø 6.30pm |
| Trondheim noon | Hammerfest 6.45am |
| Bodø 3pm | Honningsvåg 3.15pm |
| Stamsund 7.30pm | Arrive Kirkenes 9.45am |

### SOUTHBOUND

| | |
|---|---|
| Kirkenes 12.45pm | Stamsund 10pm |
| Honningsvåg 6.15am | Bodø 4am |
| Hammerfest 12.45pm | Trondheim 10am |
| Tromsø 1.30am | Ålesund 00.45am |
| Harstad 8.30am | Florø 8.15am |
| Svolvær 8pm | Arrives Bergen 2.30pm |

*Note that northbound the service only stops at Geiranger during summertime; southbound it never stops at Geiranger.

are, however, all sorts of special deals for early reservations and so forth – see the website for details. Making a Hurtigruten booking within Norway is easy too, either on the website, by phone (☎810 03 030), or via most west-coast tourist offices.

A **short or medium-sized hop** along the coast on a portion of the Hurtigruten route is also well worth considering. **Port-to-port fares** are not particularly cheap, especially in comparison with the bus, but they are affordable providing you do not have a cabin. For example, the standard, mid-season (spring or autumn) one-way passenger fare from Trondheim to Bodø (26hr) is 1000kr without meals or cabin, about the same from Ålesund to Trondheim (22hr), again without meals or cabin. Last-minute bargains, however, can bring the rates down to amazingly low levels and there are often substantial one-off discounts in winter too. All the tourist offices in the Hurtigruten ports have the latest details and should be willing to telephone the captain of the nearest ship to make a reservation on your behalf. Most – but not all – of the Hurtigruten boats carry **cars**, but advance reservations are recommended.

As for specifics, there is a restaurant and a 24-hour cafeteria supplying coffee and snacks on all Hurtigruten boats; the restaurants are very popular, so reserve a table as soon as you board.

## By plane

**Internal flights** can prove a surprisingly inexpensive way of hopping about Norway, and are especially useful if you're short on time and want to reach the far north: Tromsø to Kirkenes takes the best part of two days by bus, but it's just an hour by plane. Domestic air routes are serviced by several companies, but the major carrier is **SAS** (Ⓦsas.no), a conglomerate with many (airline) subsidiaries. A one-way fare with SAS from Oslo to Trondheim costs from about 620kr, 900kr from Oslo to Kirkenes; return fares are about double. In terms of **concessionary fares**, SAS permits infants under 2 to travel free, while children under the age of 11 receive a 25 percent discount; there are also discounted rates for young people aged 11 to 25 years old.

You might also want to check out Widerøe (Ⓦwideroe.no), a subsidiary of SAS, which specializes in internal flights – they fly between 35 Norwegian airports – and **Norwegian Airlines** (Ⓦnorwegian.com), which operates flights between fifteen domestic airports at what can be staggeringly low prices – Oslo to Alta, for example,

from just 600kr. There's also the up-and-coming **Danish Air Transport** (Ⓦdat.dk), who operate 15 internal routes, most importantly several from the mainland to the Lofotens.

## By car

Norway's **main roads** are excellent, especially when you consider the rigours of the climate, and nowadays, with most of the more hazardous sections either ironed out or tunnelled through, driving is comparatively straightforward. Nonetheless, you still have to be careful on some of the higher sections and in the longer (fume-filled) tunnels. Once you leave the main roads for the narrow **mountain byroads**, however, you'll be in for some nail-biting experiences – and that's in the summertime. In winter the Norwegians close many roads and concentrate their efforts on keeping the main highways open, but obviously blizzards and ice can make driving difficult to dangerous anywhere, even with winter tyres (which are compulsory), studs and chains. At any time of the year, the more adventurous the drive, the better equipped you need to be, especially in the sparsely inhabited north: on remote drives you should pack provisions, have proper hiking gear, check the car thoroughly before departure, carry a spare can of petrol and take a mobile phone.

Norway's main highways have an **E prefix** – E6, E18, etc. The E roads are the nearest thing Norway has to motorways, but only rarely are they dual carriageways and they are often interrupted by roundabouts and even traffic lights. All the country's other significant roads (**riksvei**, or **rv**) are assigned a number and, as a general rule, the lower the number, the busier the road. In our guide, we've used the E prefix, but designated other roads as **Highways**, followed by the number. In an effort to boost tourism, around twenty routes or roads have been designated **Nasjonale Turistveger** (National Tourist Routes; Ⓦnasjonaleturistveger.no) with more to follow. Each is equipped with strategically positioned visitor centres and viewpoints.

---

### TOP 5 DRIVES

**Filefjell** See p.172
**Haukelifjell** See p.180
**Sognefjellsveg** See p.235
**Ørnevegen** See p.246 & p.250
**Trollstigen** See p.251

## OPENING/CLOSING DATES OF MAJOR MOUNTAIN PASSES

Obviously enough, there's no preordained date for the opening of **mountain roads** in the springtime – it depends on the weather, and the threat of avalanche is often much more of a limitation than actual snowfalls. The dates below should therefore be treated with caution; if in doubt, seek advice from a local tourist office. If you do head along a mountain road that's closed, sooner or later you'll come to a barrier and have to turn round.

**E6**: Dovrefjell (Oslo–Trondheim). Usually open all year.

**E69**: Skarsvåg–Nordkapp. Closed late October to April.

**E134**: Haukelifjell (Oslo–Bergen/Stavanger). Usually open all year.

**Highway 7**: Hardangervidda (Oslo–Bergen). Usually open all year.

**Highway 51**: Valdresflya. Closed December to early May.

**Highway 55**: Sognefjellet. Closed November to early May.

**Highway 63**: Grotli–Geiranger–Åndalsnes (Trollstigen). Closed early October to mid-May.

### Toll roads

**Tolls** are imposed on certain roads to pay for construction projects such as bridges, tunnels and motorway improvements. Once the costs are covered the toll is normally removed. The older projects levy a fee of around 15–30kr, but the tolls for the newer works may run to well over 100kr per vehicle. There's a toll on entering the country's larger cities (15–30kr), but whether this is an environmental measure or a means of boosting city coffers is a moot point.

There are **automatic toll stations** (*automatisk bomstasjon*) on every toll road. Here, signs indicate the amount of the toll to be levied and cameras read the **electronic tag** – officially the "AutoPASS On-Board Unit (OBU)" – that has, by law, to be attached to the windscreen of every Norwegian vehicle. Drivers do not need to stop, but the owner of the vehicle is billed in due course (usually within a week). All Norwegian car rental vehicles have one of these tags and the car rental companies are billed like everyone else – but predictably they pass on the charge to their customers (and that's why you can never wrap up the car rental bill completely when you return your vehicle). If you are taking your **own vehicle** to Norway, you can purchase a tag at or near your point of entry, but it is much easier to set up an online credit-card **Visitors' payment account**, in which the cameras read your number plate and invoice you accordingly. For further details, consult Ⓦ autopass.no.

Entirely separate from the state-run system are the modest tolls of 20–40kr levied on privately maintained country/mountain roads; drivers are expected to deposit their money in a roadside **honesty box**; they are easy to spot.

### Fuel

**Fuel** is readily available, even in the north of Norway, though here the settlements are so widely separated that you'll need to keep your tank pretty full; if you're using the byroads extensively, remember to carry an extra can. Current fuel prices are 12–15kr a litre, and there are four main grades, all unleaded (*blyfri*): 95 octane, 98 octane, super 98 octane and diesel.

### Documentation

All EU/EEA **driving licences** are honoured in Norway, but other nationals will need – or are recommended to have – an **International Driver's Licence** (available at minimal cost from your home motoring organization). No form of provisional licence is accepted. If you're bringing your own car, you must have vehicle registration papers, adequate insurance, a first-aid kit, a warning triangle and a green card (available from your insurers or motoring organization). Extra insurance coverage for unforeseen legal costs is also well worth having, as is an appropriate **breakdown policy** from a motoring organization. In Britain, for example, the AA charges members and non-members about £170 for a month's Europe-wide breakdown cover, with all the appropriate documentation, including green card, provided.

### Rules of the road

Norway has strict **rules of the road**: you drive on the right, with dipped headlights required at all times; seat belts are compulsory for drivers and front-seat passengers, and for back-seat passengers too, if fitted; and winter tyres are compulsory in winter. There's a **speed limit** of 30kph in residential areas, 50kph in built-up areas, 80kph on open roads and 80kph, 90kph or sometimes 100kph on motorways. Speed cameras monitor hundreds of kilometres of road – watch out for the **Automatisk Trafikkontroll** warning signs – and they are far from popular with the locals: there are all sorts of folkloric (and largely

## NORWAY: DISTANCE CHART (DISTANCE IN KILOMETRES)

| | Ålesund | Bergen | Bodø | Hamar | Hammerfest | Kirkenes | Kristiansand | Lillehammer | Narvik | Nordkapp | Oslo | Røros | Stavanger | Tromsø | Trondheim |
|---|---|---|---|---|---|---|---|---|---|---|---|---|---|---|---|
| Ålesund | 0 | 378 | 1010 | 441 | 1844 | 2218 | 811 | 382 | 1191 | 1913 | 533 | 430 | 621 | 1519 | 287 |
| Bergen | 378 | 0 | 1380 | 471 | 2214 | 2588 | 492 | 439 | 1561 | 2283 | 478 | 637 | 170 | 1844 | 657 |
| Bodø | 1010 | 1380 | 0 | 1108 | 962 | 1392 | 1534 | 1065 | 304 | 1059 | 1217 | 936 | 1560 | 562 | 723 |
| Hamar | 441 | 471 | 1108 | 0 | 1942 | 2316 | 443 | 59 | 1279 | 2011 | 123 | 289 | 575 | 1606 | 385 |
| Hammerfest | 1844 | 2214 | 962 | 1942 | 0 | 494 | 2368 | 1899 | 652 | 181 | 2051 | 1810 | 2394 | 549 | 1567 |
| Kirkenes | 2218 | 2588 | 1392 | 2316 | 494 | 0 | 2742 | 2273 | 1027 | 517 | 2425 | 2185 | 2768 | 944 | 1931 |
| Kristiansand | 811 | 492 | 1534 | 443 | 2368 | 2742 | 0 | 471 | 1715 | 2437 | 320 | 753 | 245 | 2054 | 811 |
| Lillehammer | 382 | 439 | 1065 | 59 | 1899 | 2273 | 471 | 0 | 1246 | 1968 | 167 | 282 | 587 | 1562 | 342 |
| Narvik | 1191 | 1561 | 304 | 1279 | 652 | 1027 | 1715 | 1246 | 0 | 721 | 1398 | 1123 | 1741 | 251 | 904 |
| Nordkapp | 1913 | 2283 | 1059 | 2011 | 181 | 517 | 2437 | 1968 | 721 | 0 | 2120 | 1869 | 2463 | 609 | 1626 |
| Oslo | 533 | 478 | 1217 | 123 | 2051 | 2425 | 320 | 167 | 1398 | 2120 | 0 | 423 | 452 | 1733 | 494 |
| Røros | 430 | 637 | 936 | 289 | 1810 | 2185 | 753 | 282 | 1123 | 1869 | 423 | 0 | 740 | 1352 | 166 |
| Stavanger | 621 | 170 | 1560 | 575 | 2394 | 2768 | 245 | 587 | 1741 | 2463 | 452 | 740 | 0 | 1852 | 837 |
| Tromsø | 1519 | 1844 | 562 | 1606 | 549 | 944 | 2054 | 1562 | 251 | 609 | 1733 | 1352 | 1852 | 0 | 1205 |
| Trondheim | 287 | 657 | 723 | 385 | 1567 | 1931 | 811 | 342 | 904 | 1626 | 494 | 166 | 837 | 1205 | 0 |

Ferry crossings not included in distances quoted.

apocryphal) tales of men in masks appearing at night with chain saws to chop them down. **Speeding fines** are so heavy that local drivers stick religiously within the speed limit. If you're filmed breaking the limit in a rental car, expect your credit card to be stung by the car rental company to the tune of at least 600kr and a maximum of 7800kr (yes, that's right). If you're stopped for speeding, large spot fines are payable within the same price range and, if you are way over the limit (say 60kph in a 30kph zone) you could well end up in jail; rarely is any leniency shown to unwitting foreigners. **Drunken driving** is also severely frowned upon. You can be asked to take a breath test on a routine traffic-check; if you're over the limit, you will have your licence confiscated and may face a stretch in prison. It is also an offence to drive while using a hand-held mobile/cell phone. **On-street parking** restrictions are rigorously enforced and clearly signed with a white "P" on a blue background; below the "P" are the hours where parking restrictions apply – Monday to Friday first and Saturday in brackets afterwards; below this are any particular limits – most commonly denoting the maximum (*maks*) number of hours (*timer*) – and then there's *mot avgift*, which means there's a fee to pay at the meter.

### Breakdown

If you **break down** in a rental car, you'll get roadside assistance from the particular repair company the car rental firm has contracted. This is a free service, though some car rental companies charge you if you need help changing a tyre in the expectation that you should be able to do it yourself. The same principles work with your own vehicle's breakdown policy. Two major vehicle **breakdown companies** in Norway are Norges Automobil-Forbund (NAF; 24hr; ☎08 505) and Viking Redningstjeneste (24hr; ☎06000). There are emergency telephones along some motorways, and breakdown trucks patrol all major mountain passes between mid-June and mid-August.

### Car rental

All the major international **car rental** companies have outlets in Norway, especially at the country's airports. To rent a car, you'll need to be 21 or over (and have been driving for at least a year), and you'll need a credit card. Rental **charges** are fairly high, beginning at around 3500kr per week for unlimited mileage in the smallest vehicle, but include collision damage waiver and vehicle (but not personal) insurance. To cut costs, watch for special local deals – a Friday to Monday weekend rental might, for

example, cost you as little as 800kr. If you rent from a local company rather than one of the big names, you should proceed with care. In particular, check the policy for the excess applied to claims and ensure that it includes collision damage waiver (applicable if an accident is your fault). There are lots of these local car rental companies in Norway, listed in the *Yellow Pages* under *Bilutleie*. Bear in mind, too, that one-way car-rental **drop-off charges** are almost always wallet-searing: if you pick up a car in Oslo and drop it in Bodø, it will cost you 6000kr – nearer 8000kr in Tromsø.

## By bike

Despite the difficulty of much of the terrain, **cycling** is popular in Norway in the summertime. Cycle lanes and tracks as such are few and far between, and are mainly confined to the larger towns, but there's precious little traffic on most of the minor roads and cycling along them is a pleasure. Furthermore, whenever a road is improved or rerouted, the old highway is often redesigned as a cycle/walking route. At almost every place you're likely to stay in, you can anticipate that someone will **rent bikes** – whether the tourist office, a sports shop, hostel, hotel or campsite. Costs are pretty uniform: reckon on paying between 120kr and 200kr a day for a seven-speed bike, plus a refundable deposit of up to 1000kr; mountain bikes are about thirty percent more.

A few tourist offices have maps of recommended **cycling routes** but this is a rarity. It is, nonetheless, important to check your itinerary thoroughly, especially in the more mountainous areas. Cyclists aren't allowed through the longer tunnels for their own protection (the fumes can be life-threatening), so discuss your plans with whoever you hire the bike from. With regard to **bike carriage**, bikes mostly go free on car ferries and attract a nominal charge on passenger express boats, but buses vary: sometimes they take them free, sometimes they charge and sometimes they do not take them at all. Nor-Way Bussekspress (see p.29) accepts bikes only when there is space and charges a child fare, while taking a bike on an NSB train (see p.28) costs half the price of your ticket up to a maximum of 175kr. Advance reservations are advised.

If you're planning a **cycling holiday**, your first port of call should be the Norwegian Tourist Board's website (🔵visitnorway.com), where you can get general cycling advice, information on roads and tunnels inaccessible to cyclists and a list of companies offering all-inclusive cycling tours. Obviously enough, tour costs vary enormously, but as a baseline reckon on about 6500kr per week all-inclusive.

## CYCLING CONTACTS

**Syklistenes Landsforening** Storgata 3, Oslo ☎ 22 47 30 30, ⓦ slf.no. The Norwegian Cyclists' Association has an excellent range of cycling books and maps, some of which are in English.

**Syklist Velkommen** ⓦ cyclingnorway.no. The website of "Cyclists Welcome" lists ideas for a dozen routes around the country from 100km to 400km, plus useful practical information about road conditions, repair facilities and places of interest en route.

# Accommodation

**Inevitably, accommodation is one of the major expenses you will incur on a trip to Norway – indeed, if you're after a degree of comfort, it's going to be the costliest item by far. There are, however, budget alternatives, principally guesthouses (*pensjonater*), rooms in private houses (broadly this is bed and breakfast, often arranged via the local tourist office), campsites and cabins, and last but certainly not least, an abundance of HI-registered hostels. Also bear in mind that many hotels offer myriad special deals as well as substantial weekend discounts of 25–40 percent.**

Almost everywhere, you can **reserve ahead** easily enough as English is nearly always spoken. Most tourist offices also operate an on-the-spot service for same-night accommodation for free or at minimal charge.

## Hotels

Almost universally, Norwegian **hotels** are of a high standard: neat, clean and efficient. Special bargains and impromptu weekend deals also make many of them, by European standards at least, comparatively economical. Another plus is that the price of a hotel room always includes a **buffet breakfast** – in mid- to top-range hotels especially, these can be sumptuous banquets. The only negatives are the size of the rooms in the larger cities, especially Oslo, where they tend to be small, and their sameness: Norway abounds in mundanely modern, concrete-and-glass, sky-rise chain hotels. though thankfully most of the country's more distinctive hotels are gathered together under the **De Historiske Hoteller** banner (see box, p.36). For a comprehensive list of hotels – along with special bargains and

> ## ACCOMMODATION PRICES
> Throughout this Guide we give a headline price for every accommodation reviewed. This indicates the **lowest price for a double/twin room during high season** (usually June to mid-August), barring regularly offered weekend discounts and special deals, which are signified **sp/r**. Single rooms, where available, usually cost between 60 and 80 percent of a double or twin. At **hostels**, we have given two prices – the price of a double room and of a dormitory bed – and at **campsites**, the cost of two people and a tent pitch.

a booking online facility – consult the tourist board's principal website, ⓦ visitnorway.com.

Predictably, **prices** are very sensitive to demand – a double room that costs 1000kr when a hotel is slack, soon hits the 2000kr mark if there's a rush on. Generally speaking, however, 1500kr should cover the cost of two people in a double room at most hotels most of the time, nearer to 1200kr at the weekend, slightly more in Oslo. The stated price will include breakfast unless stated otherwise.

### Hotel and guesthouse passes

One way to cut costs is to join one of Norway's **hotel discount and pass schemes**, though this may well put paid to any idea you might have of a flexible itinerary as advance booking can be a prerequisite. Most Norwegian hotels are members of one discount/pass scheme or another – there are half a dozen to choose from – and you can usually join the scheme at any one of them or in advance on the internet. The majority of schemes are tied to a particular hotel chain, which obviously affects the variety of your accommodation. Among the hotel chains, **Rica** (ⓦ rica-hotels.com) has a particularly varied portfolio of around seventy hotels, making their loyalty programme more appealing than most, though it's hardly bountiful: after joining the scheme, you earn 500 bonus points for every night you stay at a Rica – and with 5000 points you get one night free; you also get the best rate available on weekday nights at any of their hotels. With only ten properties in Norway, **Scandic Hotels** (ⓦ scandichotels.com) cannot offer the range of accommodation provided by some of their rivals, but their hotels are often especially good and they do have a "Frequent Guest Programme" in which points received for staying with them are exchanged for discounts and/or free nights.

Much more enticing, however, is the **Fjord Pass** (☎815 68 222, ⓦfjord-pass.com), which offers discounts of around 20 percent at 150 hotels, guesthouses, cottages and apartments all over Norway with a particular concentration in the western fjords. The Fjord Pass card costs just 140kr and is valid for two adults and children under the age of fifteen for the whole year in which it is purchased. Under the scheme, you can either book online with the place you want to stay at or leave it to the booking service of the company who run the scheme, the exemplary **Fjord Tours** (see p.28 for more details). The discount card itself can be bought direct from Fjord Tours or at the sales outlets detailed on the website.

## Pensions, guesthouses and inns

For something a little less anonymous than the average hotel, **pensions** (*pensjonater*) are your best bet – small, sometimes intimate guesthouses, which can usually be found in the larger cities and more touristy towns. Rooms go for 650–750kr single, 700–800kr double, and breakfast is generally extra. Broadly comparable in price and character is a *gjest-giveri* or *gjestehus*, a **guesthouse** or **inn**, though some of these offer superb lodgings in historic premises with prices to match. Facilities in all of these establishments are usually adequate and homely without being overwhelmingly comfortable; at the least expensive places you'll share a bathroom with others. Some pensions and guesthouses also have

kitchens available for the use of guests, which means you're very likely to meet other residents – a real boon (perhaps) if you're travelling alone.

## Hostels

For many budget travellers, as well as hikers, climbers and skiers, the country's **HI hostels**, run by Norwegian hostelling association, **Norske Vandrerhjem** (☎23 12 45 10, ⓦhihostels.no), are the accommodation mainstay. There are around seventy in total, with handy concentrations in the western fjords, the central hiking and skiing regions and in Oslo. Oslo-based Norske Vandrerhjem maintains an excellent website, which details hostel locations, opening dates, prices, facilities and telephone numbers; hostel bookings can be made online too. The hostels themselves are almost invariably excellent – the only quibble, at the risk of being churlish, is that those occupying schools (during the summer holidays) tend to be rather drab and institutional.

**Prices** for a single **dorm bed** per night range from 250kr to 400kr, which almost always includes breakfast, often a lavish buffet at the more expensive hostels. Almost all hostels have at least a few regular **double and family rooms**, too: at 500–900kr a double including breakfast, these are among the least expensive rooms you'll find in Norway. There's usually a choice of en-suite or shared facilities for both rooms and dorms with the en suite costing 70kr–100kr more per person. Bed-sheet rental will rush you a further 50kr, towels 20kr.

If you're not a **member** of Hostelling International (HI) you can still use the hostels, though there's a surcharge of around 15 percent – so, considering the low cost of annual membership, it's better to join up either before you go to Norway or at the first hostel you stay at. It cannot be stressed too strongly that **reserving** a hostel bed will save you lots of unnecessary legwork. Many hostels are only open from mid-June to mid-August and many close between 11am and 4pm. There's sometimes an 11pm or midnight curfew, though this isn't a huge drawback in a country where carousing is so expensive.

Many hostels serve a hot evening **meal** at around 110–140kr. Hostel meals are nearly always excellent value, though of variable quality, ranging from the bland and filling to the delicious. Most, though not all, hostels have small **kitchens**, but often no pots, pans, cutlery or crockery, so self-caterers should take their own. Inexpensive **packed lunches** are often available as well, which

**TOP 5 HI HOSTELS**
Oslo Vandrerhjem Haraldsheim
  See p.95
**Preikestolen Vandrerhjem** See p.142
**Kongsberg Vandrerhjem** See p.176
**Åndalsnes Vandrerhjem** See p.252
**Stamsund Vandrerhjem** See p.322

can be particularly useful if you are heading off into the great outdoors.

## Rooms in private houses

Tourist offices in the larger towns and the more touristy settlements can often fix you up with a **private room** in someone's house, possibly including kitchen facilities. Prices are competitive – from 350 to 400kr per single, 400 to 600kr per double – though there's usually a small reservation fee on top, and the rooms themselves are frequently some way out of the centre. Nonetheless, they're often the best bargain available and, in certain instances, an improvement on the local hostel. Where this is the case, we've said so in the Guide. If you don't have a sleeping bag, check the room comes with bedding – not all of them do; and if you're cooking for yourself, a few basic utensils may not go amiss.

## Camping

**Camping** is a popular pastime in Norway, and there are literally hundreds of sites to choose from – anything from a field with a few tent pitches to extensive complexes with all mod cons. The Norwegian tourist authorities detail several hundred campsites online at ⓦ camping.no, classifying them on a one- to five-star grading depending on the facilities offered (and not on the aesthetics and/or the location). Most sites are situated with the motorist (rather than the cyclist or walker) in mind, and a good few occupy key locations beside the main roads, though in

summer these prime sites can be inundated by seasonal workers. The vast majority of campsites have at least a few cabins or chalets, called *hytter* (see below).

Most campsites are two- and three-star establishments, where charges are usually per tent, plus a small fee per person and then for vehicles; on average expect to pay around 200–350kr for two people using a tent and with a car, though four- and five-star sites average around twenty percent more. During peak season it can be a good idea to **reserve ahead** if you have a car and a large tent or trailer; contact details are listed online and, in some cases, in this guide. The **Camping Key Europe Card** (ⓦ www.campingkeyeurope.com) brings faster registration at many Norwegian campsites and often entitles the bearer to special/discounted camping rates. It is valid for one year, costs 120kr and can be purchased from participating campsites or online.

## Cabins

The Norwegian countryside is dotted with thousands of timber **cabins/chalets** (called *hytter*), ranging from simple wooden huts through to comfortable lodges. They are usually two- or four-bedded affairs, with full kitchen facilities and often a bathroom, even TV, but not necessarily **bed linen**. Some hostels have them on their grounds, there are nearly always at least a handful at every campsite, and in the Lofoten islands they are the most popular form of accommodation, occupying refurbished fishermen's huts called *rorbuer* (or their modern replicas). **Costs** vary enormously, depending on location, size and amenities, and there are significant seasonal variations, too. However, a four-bed *hytter* will rarely cost more than 850kr per night – a more usual average would be about 650kr. If you're travelling in a group, they are easily the cheapest way to see the countryside – and in some comfort. Hundreds of *hytter* are also rented out as holiday cottages by the week.

## ROUGH CAMPING

**Camping rough** in Norway is a tradition enshrined in law. You can camp anywhere in open areas as long as you are at least 150m away from any houses or cabins, though certain restrictions apply in a limited number of circumstances – for example in sea-bird sanctuaries. As a common courtesy, you are also expected to ask the landowner/farmer for **permission** to use their land if feasible – and it is rarely refused. **Fires** are not permitted in woodland areas or in fields between April 15 and September 15, and camper vans are not allowed (ever) to overnight in lay-bys. A good sleeping bag is essential, since even in summer it can get very cold, and, in the north at least, mosquito repellent is absolutely vital.

## Mountain huts

One great option for hikers is the **mountain hut** (again called *hytter*). These are strategically positioned on every major hiking route and although some are privately run, the majority are operated by **Den Norske Turistforening** (DNT; Ⓦ turistforeningen.no; see p.45) and its affiliated regional organizations. There are three types of mountain hut/lodge – staffed, self-service and unstaffed. **Staffed** mountain lodges, found mostly in the southern part of the country, provide meals and lodging and are often quite large, accommodating a hundred guests or more. They are characteristically clean, friendly and well run, usually by DNT staff. **Self-service** huts, with twenty to forty beds, are also concentrated in the mountains of southern Norway and offer lodging with bedding, a shop selling groceries and a well-equipped kitchen. **Unstaffed** huts, often with fewer than twenty beds, are mostly in the north. They provide bedding, stoves for heating and cooking and all kitchen equipment, but you must bring and prepare your own food. **Reservations** are accepted at staffed lodges for stays of more than two nights, though the lodges are primarily for guests in transit. Otherwise, beds are provided on a first-come, first-served basis. During high season, lodges occasionally get full. If beds are not available, you are given a mattress and blankets for sleeping in a common area. DNT members over 50 years of age are always guaranteed a bed. No one is ever turned away.

You don't have to be a DNT member to use these huts, but **annual membership** only costs 550kr (less with concessions) and you'll soon recoup your outlay through reduced hut charges. For members staying in staffed huts, a bunk in a dormitory costs 135kr (non-members 195kr), a family or double room 240kr per person (315kr); meals start at 100kr (130kr) for breakfast, 260kr (290kr) for a three-course dinner. At unstaffed huts, where you leave the money for your stay in a box provided, an overnight stay costs 195kr (300kr).

## Lighthouses

The **Norsk Fyrhistorisk Forening** (Norwegian Lighthouse Association; Ⓦ lighthouses.no) is an umbrella organization that has taken the lead in preserving and conserving the country's **lighthouses**. Norway's coastal waters are notoriously treacherous and in the second half of the nineteenth century scores of lighthouses were built from one end of the country to the other. Initially, they were manned, but became mechanized from the 1950s onwards and the old lighthousemen's quarters risked falling into decay. The Norsk Fyrhistorisk Forening is keen for new uses to be found for these quarters and already around sixty are open to the public for overnight stays or day-trips – and more will follow. Some of these sixty lighthouses can be reached by road, but others can only be reached by boat and, with one or two lavish exceptions, the **accommodation** on offer – where it is on offer – is fairly frugal and inexpensive, with doubles averaging around 600kr. The reward is the scenery – almost by definition these lighthouses occupy some of the wildest locations imaginable.

## Farm holidays

In Norway, rural tourism is coordinated by **Norsk Bygdeturisme og Gardsmat** (Ⓦ norsk-bygdeturisme.no), whose assorted members, spread from one end of the country to the other, offer accommodation, local food, hunting and fishing. NBG's compendious website details everything that's on offer and costs do vary enormously, but for a night's bed and breakfast on a farm you can expect to pay around 450kr per person.

# Food and drink

**At its best, Norwegian food can be excellent: fish is plentiful and carnivores can have a field day trying meats like reindeer and elk or even, conscience permitting, seal and whale. Admittedly it's not inexpensive, and those on a tight budget may have problems varying their diet, but by exercising a little prudence in the face of the average menu (which is almost always in Norwegian and English), you can keep costs down to reasonable levels.**

**Vegetarians**, however, will have slim pickings (except in Oslo), and **drinkers** will have to dig very deep into their pockets to maintain much of an intake. Indeed, most drinkers end up visiting the supermarkets and state off-licences (Vinmonopolet) so that they can sup away at home (in true Norwegian style) before setting out for the evening.

## Food

There are scores of great places to eat in Norway, but because of the cost many travellers exist almost entirely on a mixture of picnic food and self-catering, with the odd café meal thrown in to boost morale. Frankly, this isn't really necessary (except on the tightest of budgets), as there are a number of ways to eat out inexpensively. To begin with, a good self-service **buffet breakfast**, served in almost every hostel and hotel, goes some way to solving the problem, while special **lunch deals** will get you a tasty hot meal for 150kr or so. Finally, alongside the regular restaurants – which are expensive – there's the usual array of budget pizzerias, cafeterias, hot-food stands and café-bars in most towns.

### Breakfast, picnics and snacks

More often than not, **breakfast** (*frokost*) in Norway is a substantial self-service affair of bread, crackers,

## NORWEGIAN SPECIALITIES

**brun saus** gravy served with most meats, rissoles, fishcakes and sausages.

**fenalår** marinated mutton that is smoked, sliced, salted, dried and served with crispbread, scrambled egg and beer.

**fiskeboller** fish balls, served under a white sauce or on open sandwiches.

**fiskekabaret** shrimps, fish and vegetables in aspic.

**fiskesuppe** fish soup.

**flatbrød** a flat unleavened cracker, half barley, half wheat.

**gammelost** a hard, strong smelling, yellow-brown cheese with veins.

**geitost/gjetost** goat's cheese, slightly sweet and fudge-coloured. Similar cheeses have different ratios of goat's milk to cow's milk.

**gravetlaks** salmon marinated in salt, sugar, dill and brandy.

**juleskinke** marinated boiled ham, served at Christmas.

**kjøttkaker med** home-made burgers with *surkål* cabbage and a sweet and sour sauce.

**koldtbord** – a midday buffet with cold meats, herrings, salads, bread and perhaps soup, eggs or hot meats.

**lapskaus** pork, venison (or other meats) and vegetable stew, common in the south and east, using salted or fresh meat, or leftovers, in a thick brown gravy.

**lutefisk** fish (usually cod) preserved in an alkali solution and seasoned; an acquired taste; see box, p.40.

**multer** cloudberries – wild berries mostly found north of the Arctic Circle and served with cream (*med krem*).

**mysost** brown whey cheese, made from cow's milk.

**nedlagtsild** marinated herring.

**pinnekjøtt** western Norwegian Christmas dish of smoked mutton steamed over shredded birch bark, served with cabbage; or accompanied by boiled potatoes and mashed swedes (*kålrabistappe*).

**reinsdyrstek** reindeer steak, usually served with boiled potatoes and cranberry sauce.

**rekesalat** shrimp salad in mayonnaise.

**ribbe, julepølse** eastern Norwegian Christmas dish of pork ribs, sausage and dumplings.

**spekemat** various types of smoked, dried meat.

### BREAD, CAKE AND DESSERTS

**bløtkake** cream cake with fruit

**fløtelapper** pancakes made with cream, served with sugar and jam

**havrekjeks** oatmeal biscuits, eaten with goat's cheese

**knekkebrød** crispbread

**kransekake** cake made from almonds, sugar and eggs, served at celebrations

**lomper** potato scones-cum-tortillas

**riskrem** rice pudding with whipped

cream and sugar, usually served with *frukt saus*, a slighly thickened fruit sauce

**tilslørtbondepiker** stewed apples and breadcrumbs, served with cream

**Trondhjemsuppea** kind of milk broth with raisins, rice, cinnamon and sugar.

**trollkrem** beaten egg whites (or whipped cream) and sugar mixed with cloudberries (or cranberries)

**vafle** waffles

cheese, eggs, preserves, cold meat and fresh and pickled fish, washed down with tea or ground coffee. It's usually first-rate at HI hostels, and often memorable in hotels, filling you up for the day and almost universally included in the price of the room – where it isn't, we have indicated in the Guide.

For **picnic food**, bread, cheese, yoghurt and local fruit are all relatively good value, but other staple foodstuffs – rice, pasta, meat, cereals and vegetables – can be way above the European average. Anything tinned is particularly dear (with the exception of fish), but coffee and tea are quite reasonably priced. **Supermarkets** are ten-a-penny.

As ever, **fast food** offers the best chance of a hot, bargain-basement takeaway snack. The indigenous Norwegian stuff, served up from a thousand and one street kiosks and stalls – **gatekjøkken** – consists mainly of rubbery hot dogs (*varm pølse*), while pizza slices and chicken pieces and chips are much in evidence too. A better choice, if a shade more expensive, is simply to get a sandwich, a **smørbrød** (pronounced "smurrbrur"), normally a slice of bread heaped with a variety of garnishes. You'll see them groaning with meat or shrimps, salad and mayonnaise in the windows of bakeries and cafés, or in the newer, trendier sandwich bars in the cities.

A standard cup of **coffee** is bitter and strong and served black with cream on the side, but lots of places – especially city coffee shops – have moved up a notch, serving mochas, cappuccinos and so forth. **Tea** is just as popular, but the local preference is for lemon tea or a variety of flavoured infusions; if you want milk, ask for it. All the familiar **soft drinks** are available, too.

## Lunch

For the best deals, you're often going to have to eat your main meal of the day at lunchtime, when **kafeterias** (often self-service restaurants) lay on daily specials, the *dagens rett*. This is a fish or meat dish served with potatoes and a vegetable or salad, often including a drink, sometimes bread, and occasionally coffee, too; it should go for 150–200kr. You'll find *kafeterias* hidden above shops and offices and adjoining hotels in larger towns, where they might be called *kaffistovas*. Most close at around 6pm, and many don't open at all on Sunday. As a general rule, the food these places serve is plain (though there are exceptions), but the same cannot be said of the much more up-to-date **café-bars** which abound in all of Norway's larger towns and cities. These affordable establishments offer much tastier (and sometimes more adventurous) meals like pasta dishes, salads and vegetarian options with main courses in the region of 160–220kr. They are also open longer – usually till late at night. **Restaurants** are worth investigating at lunchtimes too, as it's then that many of them cut their prices to pull in extra trade.

## Dinner

They may now share the gastronomic laurels with the nation's café-bars (see above), but there are first-class **restaurants** in every Norwegian city and most towns, though the villages can lose out if the local hotel(s) doesn't cut the mustard. Apart from exotica such as reindeer and elk, the one real speciality is the **seafood**, simply prepared and wonderfully fresh – whatever you do, don't go home without treating

## STOKFISK, KLIPPFISK AND LUTEFISK

The Vikings were able to sail long distances without starving to death because they had learnt how to dry white fish (mostly cod) in the open air. This dried fish, **stokfisk**, remained edible for years and was eaten either raw or after soaking in water – chewy and smelly no doubt, but very nutritious. In time, *stokfisk* became the staple diet of western Norway and remained so until the early twentieth century, with every fishing port festooned with massive wooden A-frames holding hundreds of drying white fish, headless and paired for size. Only in the 1690s did the Dutch introduce the idea of salting and drying white fish, again usually cod, to the Norwegians. The fish was decapitated, cleaned and split, then heavily salted and left for several weeks before being dried by being left outside on rocky drying grounds, *klipper* in Norwegian, hence **klippfisk** – or **bacalao** in Spanish. The Norwegians never really took to eating *klippfisk*, but their merchants made fortunes exporting it to Spain, Portugal, Africa and the Caribbean. The Norwegians did, however, take to eating **lutefisk**, in which either *stokfisk* or *klippfisk* is soaked in cold water and, at certain stages, lye, to create a jelly-like substance that many Norwegians regard as a real delicacy, though it is very much an acquired taste. The American storyteller and humourist Garrison Keillor would have none of it, suggesting in *Pontoon: A Lake Wobegon Novel* that "Most lutefisk is not edible by normal people." Most will find it hard to disagree.

**TOP 5 NORWEGIAN RESTAURANTS**
**Solsiden, Oslo** See p.98
**Hanne På Høyden, Bergen** See p.205
**Walaker Hotell, Solvorn** See p.234
**Sjøbua Fiskerestaurant, Ålesund**
See p.257
**Huset, Longyearbyen** See p.374

yourself at least once. Main courses begin at around 220kr, starters and desserts at around 110kr. Smoked salmon comes highly recommended, as does catfish, halibut and monkfish. The best deals are often at lunchtime, though some restaurants don't open till the evening. In the western fjords, look out also for the help-yourself, all-you-can-eat **buffets** available in many of the larger hotels from around 6pm; go early to get the best choice and expect to pay around 500kr to be confronted by mounds of pickled herring, salmon (*laks*), cold cuts of meat, a feast of breads and crackers, and usually a few hot dishes too – meatballs, soup and scrambled eggs.

In the towns, and especially in Oslo, there is also a sprinkling of **non-Scandinavian restaurants**, mostly Italian with a good helping of Chinese and Indian places. Other cuisines pop up too – Japanese, Moroccan and Persian to name but three.

Most restaurants have bilingual menus (in Norwegian and English), but we have provided a **menu reader** (see p.424).

### Vegetarians

**Vegetarians** are in for a hard time. Apart from a handful of specialist restaurants in the big cities, there's little option other than to make do with salads, look out for egg dishes in *kafeterias* and supplement your diet from supermarkets. If you are a **vegan** the problem is greater: when the Norwegians are not eating meat and fish, they are attacking a fantastic selection of milks, cheeses and yoghurts. At least you'll know what's in every dish you eat, since everyone speaks English. If you're self-catering, look for **health food shops** (*helsekost*), found in some of the larger towns and cities.

## Drink

One of the less savoury sights in Norway – and especially common in the north – is the fall-over **drunk**: you can spot one at any time of the day or night zigzagging along the street, a strangely disconcerting counter to the usual stereotype of the Norwegian as a healthy, hearty figure in a wholesome woolly jumper. For reasons that remain obscure – or at least culturally complex – many Norwegians can't just have a drink or two, but have to get absolutely wasted. The majority of their compatriots deplore such behaviour and have consequently imposed what amounts to alcoholic **rationing**: thus, although booze is readily available in the bars and restaurants, it's taxed up to the eyeballs and the distribution of wines, strong ales and spirits is strictly controlled and is in the hands of a state-run monopoly, Vinmonopolet (see below). Whether this paternalistic type of control makes matters better or worse is a moot point, but the majority of Norwegians support it.

You can get a drink at most outdoor cafés, in restaurants and obviously at bars, pubs and cocktail bars, but only in the towns and cities is there any kind of "European" bar life. Wherever you go for a drink, half a litre of beer should **cost** around 60kr, and a glass of wine from 50kr.

### What to drink

If you decide to splash out on a few drinks, you'll find Norwegian **beer** is almost universally lager-like and uninspiring; Carlsberg owns the country's largest brewer, Ringnes. That said, recent modifications to the alcohol laws have tried to stir the microbrewery pot and although this has made little headway so far, things may pick up. One notable star-turn is the Ægir microbrewery at the *Flåmsbrygga* in Flåm (see p.225). There has also been a minor boom in farmhouse **cider-making** across the western fjords: Ulvik, for example, has several producers. As regards **wine**, there's no domestic production to speak of and most **spirits** are imported too, with the principal exception being **aquavit** (*akevitt*), a bitter concoction served ice-cold in little glasses and, at forty percent proof or more, real head-banging material; it's more palatable with beer chasers. **Linie aquavit**, made in Norway from potatoes, is one of the more popular brands.

### Where to buy alcohol

**Weaker beers** (below 4.75% ABV) are sold in supermarkets and shops all over Norway, though generally (for all but the weakest) not after 8pm on weekdays and 6pm on Saturday, and some local communities, particularly in the west, have their own rules and restrictions. Stronger beers, along with **wines and spirits**, can only be purchased from state-run **Vinmonopolet** stores (Ⓦ vinmonopolet.no). There's generally one branch in each medium-sized town and many more in each of Norway's cities. Characteristically, these stores are open Monday to Friday 10am–4/6pm and Saturday 10am–1/3pm, but they all close on public holidays. At Vinmonopolet stores, wine is quite a bargain, from 80kr a bottle, and there's generally a wide choice.

# The media

**You can buy British and some American daily newspapers, plus the occasional periodical, in any major Norwegian city, but elsewhere things are very patchy. The most likely outlets are the Narvesen kiosks at train stations and airports. Most hotels have cable or satellite TV access.**

## Newspapers and magazines

**British newspapers** – from tabloid through to broadsheet – as well as the more popular **English-language magazines** are widely available either on the day of publication or the day after in all major Norwegian cities, along with internationally distributed **US newspapers** – principally the *Wall Street Journal*, *USA Today* and the *International Herald Tribune*.

As for the **Norwegian press**, state advertising, loans and subsidized production costs sustain a wealth of smaller papers that would bite the dust elsewhere. Most are closely linked with political parties, although the bigger city-based titles tend to be independent. The most popular newspapers in Oslo are the independent *Verdens Gang* (Ⓦ vg.no) and the independent-conservative *Aftenposten* (Ⓦ aftenposten.no); in Bergen it's the liberal *Bergens Tidende* (Ⓦ bt.no). One reliable and independent source of Norwegian news in English is online at Ⓦ norwaynews.com.

## TV and radio

Norway's **television** network has expanded over the last few years in line with the rest of Europe. Alongside the national channels, NRK1, NRK2, NRK3 and TV2, there are satellite channels like TV Norge and TV3; you can also pick up Swedish TV in many parts of the country. Many of the programmes are English-language imports with Norwegian subtitles, so there's invariably something on that you'll under-stand, though much of it is pretty average stuff. The big global cable and satellite channels are routinely accessible in hotel rooms too.

Local tourist **radio**, giving details of events and festivals, is broadcast during the summer months; watch for signposts by the roadside and tune in. Shortwave frequencies and schedules for the BBC World Service (Ⓦ bbc.co.uk/world service), Radio Canada (Ⓦ rcinet.ca) and Voice of America (Ⓦ voanews.com) are listed on their respective websites.

# Festivals and events

**Almost every town in Norway has some sort of summer shindig. There are winter celebrations too, though for the most part at least, these are worth attending if you are already in the area rather than meriting a special trip. Festivals fall broadly into two types, one focusing on celebrations of historical or folkloric events, the other based around music, whether jazz, pop or classical.**

As you might expect, most tourist-oriented events take place in summer and, as always, national and local tourist offices can supply details of exact dates, which tend to vary from year to year. Below we have listed the more important festivals, some of which are also mentioned in the Guide.

### JANUARY

**Nordlysfestivalen** (Northern Lights Festival), Tromsø. Late Jan. Ⓦ nordlysfestivalen.no. This week-long festival of classical and contemporary music coincides with the return of the sun, hence its name.

### MARCH/APRIL

**Birkebeinerrennet** Lillehammer. Late March. Ⓦ birkebeiner.no. Famous 58km cross-country ski race from Rena to Lillehammer, which celebrates the dramatic events of 1206, when the young prince Håkon Håkonsson was rushed over the mountains to safety. The race follows what is thought to have been the original route.

**Easter Festivals** Finnmarksvidda. Easter. Ⓦ festival.karport.no. Finnmark's largest festival, held in the town of Karasjok, is something of a Sámi New Year. Sámis prepare by fashioning new *gáktis* (Sámi dress), polishing their silver and cooking large meals, while during the festival there are snowmobile, reindeer and cross-country-skiing races, lassoing contests and art exhibitions and concerts.

### MAY

**Nasjonaldagen/Grunnlovsdagen** (National Day/Constitution Day). Nationwide. May 17. Many processions and much flag-waving with cheering crowds celebrating the signing of the Norwegian constitution on May 17, 1814.

**Festspillene i Bergen** (Bergen International Festival), Bergen. Late May until early June. Ⓦ fib.no. Much-praised festival of contemporary music that puts a real spring in Bergen's summer step. Venues across the city. See p.206.

## JUNE

**Norwegian Wood** Oslo. Mid-June. Ⓦ norwegianwood.no. Three-day, open-air rock festival, arguably Norway's best, that takes place in Frogner Park; showcases big-name international artists as well as up-and-coming local bands.

**Ekstremsportveko** (Extreme Sport Week). Voss. Late June. Ⓦ ekstremsportveko.com. Every reckless sport imaginable and then some – from paragliding and base jumping through to rafting and bungee jumping.

**Midnight Sun Marathon** Tromsø. Late June. Ⓦ msm.no. Taking advantage of 24hr daylight, this "night-time" run attracts hundreds of athletes. You can opt for shorter distances too.

## JULY

**Kongsberg Jazz Festival** Kongsberg. Four days in early July. Ⓦ kongsberg-jazzfestival.no. Large-scale jazz festival, one of the country's biggest, where the emphasis is on Norwegian musicians.

**Molde Jazz** Molde. Mid-July. Ⓦ moldejazz.no. Held over a six-day period in the middle of the month, this is one of the best festivals of its type, attracting big international names.

**Olsokdagene** (St Olav Festival), Stiklestad. Late July. Ⓦ stiklestad .no. St Olav, Norway's first Christian king, was killed at the battle of Stiklestad in 1030 (see p.281). Historical pageants and plays honouring him are staged on the King's feast day (July 29) as well as during the six days before.

**Rauma Rock** Åndalsnes. Late July to early Aug. Ⓦ raumarock.com. Two-day knees-up showcasing the talents of a wide range of local and international acts from the likes of the Bare Egil Band to the Raga Rockers and the Toy Dolls.

## AUGUST

**Oslo Jazzfestival** Oslo. Mid-Aug. Ⓦ oslojazz.no. A six-day event attracting a veritable raft of big international names.

**Norwegian International Film Festival** Haugesund. One week in late August. Ⓦ filmweb.no. Norway's most prestigious film festival, with a wide selection of the latest releases from across Scandinavia.

## SEPTEMBER

**Ultima** Oslo. Ten days in early to mid-Sept. Ⓦ ultima.no. Much-vaunted festival showcasing the talents of contemporary classical musicians from Scandinavia and beyond. Various venues.

## OCTOBER

**UKA** Trondheim. Three and a half weeks in Oct. Ⓦ uka.no. Prestigious cultural festival, one of Norway's largest, featuring a battery of international and domestic artists in everything from classical music to rock, theatre to wrestling, juggling and crime writing.

**Bergen Internasjonale Filmfestival (BIFF)** Bergen. Mid- to late Oct. Ⓦ biff.no. Week-long international film festival, one of the best of its type in the country. Various venues across the city centre.

# Outdoor activities

**Most Norwegians have a deep and abiding love of the great outdoors. They enjoy many kinds of sports – from dog-sledging and downhill skiing in winter, through to mountaineering, angling and whitewater rafting in the summer – but the two most popular activities are hiking and cross-country skiing.**

## Hiking

Norway boasts some of the most beautiful mountain landscapes in the world, its soaring peaks accentuated by icy glaciers, rocky spires and deep green fjords. Great chunks of this wild terrain have been incorporated into a string of **national parks**, 41 in total with 34 on the mainland and seven in Svalbard. These parks, especially the more accessible, are magnets for **hikers** in search of everything from easy rambles to full-scale expeditions along clearly marked trails, served by an excellent network of mountain cabins, which provide the most congenial of accommodation (see p.38).

The short **hiking season**, loosely defined by the opening and closing of the mountain lodges, runs from early July (mid-June in some areas) through to late September. This coincides with mild weather – daytime mountain temperatures of between 20°C and 25°C – ideal for hiking. And, of course, it's daylight for most of the time – beyond the Arctic Circle, all the time – so you're unlikely to be searching for a mountain lodge after dark.

### Hiking trails and maps

Norway's **hiking trails** are typically marked at regular intervals by cairns (piles of stones). Most junctions are marked by signposts, some of which are small and hard to spot. There are also red "T" symbols painted on rocks – especially useful when visibility is poor. Although waymarking is good, you'll always need a **hiking map**. The classic map range, with red and white covers and covering every part of the country, is the **Statens Kartverk M711 Norge 1:50,000 series**, though in recent years many of these maps have been updated and upgraded with red or blue covers and made waterproof and tear-resistant; many of the new maps in the series are also co-productions between Statens Kartverk (the Norwegian Mapping Authority) and a commercial publisher. To complicate matters, Statens Kartverk became part of the Nordeca group in 2011 and Nordeca has now produced

## TOP 5 NATIONAL PARKS

**Dovrefjell-Sunndalsfjella Nasjonalpark** Reached via the E6 and the Dombås–Trondheim railway, the eastern reaches of this large park are rugged and severe, but as you hike west the terrain gets even wilder as the serrated alpine peaks of the Romsdal hove into view. See p.168.

**Hardangervidda Nasjonalpark** Europe's largest mountain plateau, stretches east from the Hardangerfjord to Finse in the north and Rjukan in the east, its bare, almost lunar-like rocks and myriad lakes make for some spectacular hiking. The Hardangervidda begins about 130km east of Bergen. See p.215 .

**Jotunheimen Nasjonalpark** Norway's most famous hiking area has a heady concentration of towering, ice-tipped peaks, more than two hundred rising above 1900m, including northern Europe's two highest. The park is near the east end of the Sognefjord, about 300km from Oslo. See p.163 & p.235.

**Rondane Nasjonalpark** The Rondane comprises both a high alpine zone, with ten peaks exceeding the 2000-metre mark, and a much gentler upland area punctuated by rounded, treeless hills. It is on the E6 between Oslo and Trondheim and is especially popular with families. See p.161.

**Nordre Isfjorden Nasjonalpark, Svalbard** One of the archipelago's largest protected areas, this coastal tundra stretches across the Isfjorden north of Barentsburg. It comprises wetlands, lake and pond complexes, and is great for light day-hikes and wildlife-spotting; wildlife includes eider ducks, pink-footed geese, ringed seals, arctic fox and the Svalbard rock ptarmigan. See p.376.

For a list of all of Norway's national parks, consult Ⓦdirnat.no/nasjonalparker.

top-quality, GPS-compatible maps – **Turkart** – for all the key hiking areas at three scales – 1:25,000, 1:50,000 and 1:100,000. These are the best hiking maps on the market, and are on sale at DNT outlets, many tourist offices and some bookshops; you would, however, be well advised to buy before you go – Stanfords (Ⓦstanfords.co.uk), in London, is as good a source as any.

### Guided glacier hiking

**Guided glacier hikes** can be terrific – and the widest selection are available in the western fjords on the **Jostedalsbreen** glacier (see box, p.238). Glaciers are in constant if generally imperceptible motion, and are therefore potentially dangerous. People, often tourists, die on them nearly every year. Never hike on a glacier without a guide, never walk beneath one and always heed local instructions.

## Skiing

Norway has a strong claim to be regarded as the home of **skiing**: a 4000-year-old rock carving found in northern Norway is the oldest-known illustration of a person on skis; the first recorded ski competition was held in Norway in 1767; and Norwegians were the first to introduce skis to North America. Furthermore, one of the oldest cross-country ski races in the world, the 55km **Birkebeinerrennet**, is

held annually in late March, attracting several thousand skiers to participate in the dash between Rena and Lillehammer. The race follows the route taken by Norwegian mountain-men in 1206 when they rescued the two-year-old Prince Håkon. The rescuers wore birch-bark leggings known as Birkebeiners, hence the name of the race.

Although you may be tempted to go on a **ski package** via a tour operator (see p.27) remember that in most places you should find it easy (and comparatively inexpensive) to go **skiing independently**. Even in Oslo, there are downhill and cross-country ski runs within the city boundaries as well as convenient places from which to rent equipment. As a halfway house between independence and the package tour, DNT, the Norwegian Trekking Association (Ⓦturistforeningen.no), arranges a limited range of guided skiing excursions – see their website for details.

In terms of **preparation**, lessons on a dry slope are useful in so far as they develop confidence and balance, but cross-country skiing needs stamina and upper body as well as leg strength.

### Downhill skiing and snowboarding

**Downhill skiing** and **snowboarding** conditions in Norway are usually excellent from mid-November through to late April, though daylight hours are at a premium around the winter solstice. Otherwise, Norway scores well in comparison with the

## DNT

**Den Norske Turistforening** (The Norwegian Trekking Association; ⓦ turistforeningen.no) manages all aspects of hiking in Norway. It organizes all-inclusive tours and, in conjunction with a small army of local hiking associations, takes care of trails and waymarking. It also operates several hundred mountain lodges. DNT has outlets in all of Norway's largest cities, including Oslo, Bergen, Stavanger and Trondheim, which stock hiking maps and give advice on equipment. They also sell DNT **membership**, which confers, among much else, substantial discounts at its mountain huts (see p.37), though you can also join at any staffed DNT lodge. Neither is annual membership expensive at 550kr, 295kr for 19–26-year-olds, 175kr for 13–18 years, 67-plus 425kr, under 12 110kr.

better-known skiing regions of southern Europe: temperatures tend to be a good bit colder and the country has, in general terms at least, a more consistent snowfall; Norway's resorts tend to be less crowded, have smaller class sizes, shorter lift queues, and are at a lower altitude. Three main centres for downhill skiing are Voss (see p.218), Lillehammer (see p.154) and Geilo (see p.174).

### Cross-country skiing

**Cross-country skiing** is a major facet of winter life in Norway. Approximately half the population are active in the sport, and many Norwegians still use skis to get to work or school. Wherever you are in wintertime Norway, you're never far from a **cross-country ski route** and at major ski resorts sets of parallel ski tracks called *loipe* are cut in the snow by machine with the cross-country skier in mind: they provide good gliding conditions and help keep the skis parallel; some *loipe* are floodlit.

Cross-country skis can be **waxed** or **waxless**. Waxless skis have a rough tread in the middle called "fishscales", which grips adequately at temperatures around zero. Waxed skis work better at low temperatures and on new snow. Grip wax is rubbed onto the middle third of the ski's length, but a sticky substance called *klister* is used instead in icy conditions. All skis benefit from hard glide wax applied to the front and back thirds of the base.

All the main skiing centres, including Oslo's Holmenkollen, have designated cross-country skiing areas with at least some floodlighting.

### Telemarking

In the Telemark region of southern Norway a technique has been developed to enable skiers to descend steep slopes on free-heel touring skis. This technique, known as **Telemarking**, provides a stable and effective turning platform in powder snow. Essentially the skier traverses a slope in an upright position, but goes down on a right knee to execute a right turn and vice versa.

### Summer skiing

**Summer skiing** on Norway's mountains and glaciers – both alpine and cross-country – is very popular. Lots of places offer this, but one of the largest and most convenient spots is the **Folgefonn Sommar Skisenter** (ⓦ folgefonn.no; see p.211), not far from Bergen, which has ski rental, a ski school, a café and a ski lift to the slopes.

## Fishing

Norway's myriad rivers and lakes offer some of Europe's finest **freshwater fishing**. Common species include trout, char, pike and perch, not to mention the salmon that once brought English aristocrats here by the buggy load. In the south of the country, the fishing is at its best from June to September, in July and August in the north. **Seawater fishing** is more the preserve of professionals, but (amateur) sea angling off the Lofoten Islands is a popular pastime.

Sea- and freshwater fishing are both tightly controlled. The first does not require a national **licence**, but is subject to national and local restrictions regarding the size of the fish you can land and so forth. The second, freshwater fishing, needs both a local licence, which costs anything from 50kr to 400kr per day, and a national licence if you're after salmon, sea trout and char – while, that is, these fish are in fresh water. National licences are available at any post office and online (ⓦ inatur.no) for 235kr and local licences (*fiskekort*) are sold at sports shops, a few tourist offices, some hotels and many campsites. If you take your own fishing tackle, you must have it disinfected before use.

A number of **tour companies** specialize in Norwegian fishing trips and holidays (see p.27), but if you're just after a day or two's fishing, it's easy enough to get fixed up locally – start off by asking down at the nearest tourist office.

## Whitewater rafting

Norway has literally dozens of top-notch **whitewater rafting** runs. Two of the best places are Voss (see p.218) and Sjoa (see p.160). For a full list of **tour operators** offering rafting trips, consult the Norges Padleforbund (the Norwegian Canoe Association) website, Ⓦ padling.no.

## Fjord and sea-kayaking

**Fjord and sea-kayaking** are increasingly popular in Norway with a small army of tour operators concentrated in the western fjords. Local tourist offices have the details of what's on offer, and there's more information on the website of the Norges Padleforbund (the Norwegian Canoe Association; Ⓦ padling.no), but one place to aim for is Flåm, which is home to the sea-kayaking specialists, **Njord Flåm** (❶91 32 66 28, Ⓦ njord.as).

# Shopping

**Norway has a flourishing retail sector and all the large towns and cities are jammed with department stores and** international chains. There are a handful of obvious Norwegian goods – cheese, knitted pullovers and dried fish (*klippfisk*; see box, p.40) are three that spring to mind – but it's the Norwegian flair for design that is the country's most striking feature, especially as reflected in its fine art and interior design. You will, however, have to dig deep to bring any of it home – Norway is not a land of bargains. If you're visiting the far north, resist the temptation to bring back reindeer antlers – they really are naff.

Taking advantage of their decision not to join the EU, the Norwegians run a **tax-free shopping scheme** for tourists. If you spend more than 315kr at any of the three thousand outlets in the tax-free shopping scheme, you'll get a tax refund cheque voucher for the amount of VAT you paid. On departure at an airport, ferry terminal or frontier crossing, present the goods, the voucher and your passport and – provided you haven't used the item – you'll get 12–19 percent refund, depending on the price of the item. There isn't a reclaim point at every exit from the country, however – pick up a leaflet at any participating shop to find out where they are – and note that many of the

## CLOTHING AND SHOE SIZES

**WOMEN'S CLOTHING**

| | | | | | | | | |
|---|---|---|---|---|---|---|---|---|
| American | 4 | 6 | 8 | 10 | 12 | 14 | 16 | 18 |
| British | 6 | 8 | 10 | 12 | 14 | 16 | 18 | 20 |
| Continental | 34 | 36 | 38 | 40 | 42 | 44 | 46 | 48 |

**WOMEN'S SHOES**

| | | | | | | | | |
|---|---|---|---|---|---|---|---|---|
| American | 5 | 6 | 7 | 8 | 9 | 10 | 11 | |
| British | 3 | 4 | 5 | 6 | 7 | 8 | 9 | |
| Continental | 36 | 37 | 38 | 39 | 40 | 41 | 42 | |

**MEN'S SHIRTS**

| | | | | | | | | |
|---|---|---|---|---|---|---|---|---|
| American | 14 | 15 | 15.5 | 16 | 16.5 | 17 | 17.5 | 18 |
| British | 14 | 15 | 15.5 | 16 | 16.5 | 17 | 17.5 | 18 |
| Continental | 36 | 38 | 39 | 41 | 42 | 43 | 44 | 45 |

**MEN'S SHOES**

| | | | | | | | | | |
|---|---|---|---|---|---|---|---|---|---|
| American | 7 | 7.5 | 8 | 8.5 | 9.5 | 10 | 10.5 | 11 | 11.5 |
| British | 6 | 7 | 7.5 | 8 | 9 | 9.5 | 10 | 11 | 12 |
| Continental | 39 | 40 | 41 | 42 | 43 | 44 | 44 | 45 | 46 |

**MEN'S SUITS**

| | | | | | | | | |
|---|---|---|---|---|---|---|---|---|
| American | 34 | 36 | 38 | 40 | 42 | 44 | 46 | 48 |
| British | 34 | 36 | 38 | 40 | 42 | 44 | 46 | 48 |
| Continental | 44 | 46 | 48 | 50 | 52 | 54 | 56 | 58 |

## NORWEGIAN SWEATERS

No single item is more emblematic of Scandinavian tradition, heritage, workmanship and attention to detail as the Norwegian **wool sweater**. These beautiful items, many of which are handcrafted, have defined the Scandi look at home and abroad for centuries.

Knitting has a strong tradition in Norway, and the stitching techniques used in the wool sweaters of today had already been put into place by the ninth century, when the garments were the simple colours of natural wool. The best-known traditional design – the bespeckled black, grey and white **lusekofte sweater** – dates from the nineteenth century and hails from the Setesdal region. This sweater, traditionally worn by men, translates as "lice jacket" on account of the black and white diagonal check pattern.

Today, a number of shops in Oslo sell everything from poor-quality, machine-made discount sweaters to hand-knitted gems; the best ones are the hand-made items from the **Dale of Norway** brand (see p.102), the best known in the country. Other respected names include Devold, Norway's oldest knitwear producer, and Nordstrikk, a company based out of Ålesund whose products employ a combination of durable Norwegian and soft, nimble Australian wools.

smaller reclaim points keep normal shop hours, closing for the weekend at 2/3pm on Saturday. The downside is the shops themselves: the bulk are dedicated to selling souvenir goods you can well manage without.

# Travel essentials

## Addresses

Norwegian addresses are always written with the number after the street name. In multi-floored buildings, the ground floor is always counted as the first floor, the first the second and so on.

## Alphabet

The letters Æ, Ø and Å come at the end of the Norwegian alphabet, after Z (and in that order). Note that for convenience – rather than linguistic accuracy – we have alphabetized Æ as ae, Ø as O and Å as A throughout this guide.

## Climate

The Gulf Stream keeps all of coastal Norway temperate throughout the year. Inland, the climate is more extreme – bitterly cold in winter and hot in summer, when temperatures can soar to surprising heights. January and February are normally the coldest months in all regions, July and August the warmest. Rain is a regular occurrence throughout the year, particularly on the west coast, though there are significant local variations in precipitation (see box, p.48).

## Costs

Norway has a reputation as one of the most expensive of European holiday destinations, and in some ways (but only some) this is entirely justified. Most of what you're likely to need – from a cup of coffee to a bottle of beer – is very costly, but on the other hand certain major items are reasonably priced, most notably **accommodation** which, compared with other North European countries, can be remarkably inexpensive: Norway's (usually) first-rate youth hostels, almost all of which have family, double and dormitory rooms, are particularly good value. **Getting around** is reasonably good news too, as the relatively high cost of normal bus, boat and train tickets can be offset by a number of passes and there are myriad discounts and deals. Furthermore, **concessions** are almost universally available at attractions and on public transport, with infants (under 4) going everywhere free, plus children (up to 15 years) and seniors (over 67, sometimes 60) paying – on average at least – half the standard rate. **Food** is, however, a different matter. With few exceptions – such as tinned fish – it's expensive, while the cost of alcohol is enough to make even a heavy drinker contemplate abstinence.

Travelling by bicycle, eating picnics bought from supermarkets and cooking your own food at campsites, it's possible to keep **average costs** down to 400kr a day per person. Moving up a notch, if you picnic at lunch, stick to less expensive cafés and restaurants, and stay in cheap hotels or hostels, you could get by on around 850kr a day. Staying in three-star hotels and eating out in medium-range restaurants, you should reckon on about 1500kr a

## AVERAGE DAYTIME TEMPERATURES AND RAINFALL

| | Jan | Feb | Mar | Apr | May | June | July | Aug | Sept | Oct | Nov | Dec |
|---|---|---|---|---|---|---|---|---|---|---|---|---|
| **OSLO** | | | | | | | | | | | | |
| °C | -3.7 | -2.8 | 1.3 | 6.3 | 12.6 | 17.0 | 18.2 | 17.2 | 12.8 | 7.5 | 1.5 | -2.6 |
| °F | 25.3 | 26.9 | 34.3 | 43.3 | 54.6 | 62.6 | 64.7 | 62.9 | 55 | 45.5 | 34.7 | 27.3 |
| mm | 49 | 36 | 47 | 41 | 53 | 65 | 81 | 89 | 90 | 84 | 73 | 55 |
| **BERGEN** | | | | | | | | | | | | |
| °C | 1.5 | 1.6 | 3.3 | 5.9 | 10.5 | 13.5 | 14.5 | 14.4 | 11.5 | 8.7 | 4.6 | 1.6 |
| °F | 34.7 | 34.8 | 37.9 | 42.6 | 50.9 | 56.3 | 58.1 | 57.9 | 52.7 | 47.66 | 40.2 | 34.9 |
| mm | 190 | 152 | 170 | 114 | 106 | 132 | 148 | 190 | 283 | 271 | 259 | 235 |
| **TRONDHEIM** | | | | | | | | | | | | |
| °C | -3.3 | -1.8 | 1.9 | 5.4 | 10.9 | 13.8 | 15.1 | 14.8 | 11.2 | 7.0 | 1.1 | -1.8 |
| °F | 26 | 28.7 | 35.4 | 41.7 | 51.6 | 56.8 | 59.2 | 58.6 | 52.2 | 44.6 | 34 | 28.7 |
| mm | 63 | 52 | 54 | 49 | 53 | 68 | 84 | 87 | 113 | 104 | 71 | 84 |
| **TROMSØ** | | | | | | | | | | | | |
| °C | -4.7 | -4.1 | -1.9 | 1.1 | 5.6 | 10.1 | 12.7 | 11.8 | 7.7 | 2.9 | -1.5 | -3.7 |
| °F | 23.5 | 24.6 | 28.58 | 34 | 42 | 50.2 | 54.8 | 53.2 | 45.8 | 37.2 | 29.3 | 25.3 |
| mm | 95 | 87 | 72 | 64 | 48 | 59 | 77 | 82 | 102 | 131 | 108 | 106 |

day, the main variable being the cost of your room. On 2400kr a day and upwards, you'll be limited only by time, though if you're planning to stay in a five-star hotel and have a big night out, this still won't be enough. As always, if you're **travelling alone** you'll spend more on accommodation than you would in a group of two or more: most hotels do have single rooms, but they're usually around sixty to eighty percent of the price of a double.

## Crime and personal safety

Norway is one of the least troublesome corners of Europe, so there's little reason why you should ever come into contact with the Norwegian police. You will find that most public places are well lit and secure, most people genuinely friendly and helpful, and street crime and hassle relatively rare even late at night. It would be foolish, however, to assume that problems don't exist. Oslo in particular has its share of **petty crime**, fuelled – as elsewhere – by drug addicts and alcoholics after easy money. But keep tabs on your possessions and use the same common sense you would use at home and you should have little reason to visit the police. If you do, you'll find them courteous, concerned, and usually able to speak English. If you have something stolen, make sure you get a copy of the police report or its number – essential if you are to make a claim against your insurance.

As for offences *you* might commit, drinking alcohol in public places is not permitted, and being drunk on the streets can get you arrested. Drinking and driving is treated especially rigorously. Drugs offences, too, are met with the same attitudes that prevail throughout most of Europe.

## Customs

**Duty-free limits** at points of entry into Norway are: one litre of spirits and 1.5 litres of wine and two litres of beer. Or three litres of wine and two litres of beer. Or five litres of beer if no other duty-free alcoholic drink is brought in. For tobacco, it's 200 cigarettes or 250g tobacco and 200 cigarette papers. For further details, go to ⓦ toll.no.

## Electricity

The current is 220 volts AC, with standard European-style two-pin **plugs**. British equipment needs only a plug adaptor; American apparatus requires a transformer and an adaptor.

## Entry requirements

Citizens of the EU/EEA, US, Canada, Australia and New Zealand need only a valid passport to enter Norway for up to ninety days. All other nationals should consult the relevant embassy or consulate about visa requirements. For longer stays, including periods of paid employment in Norway, there are different rules for different nationals with EU/EEA citizens having greater ease of access than non-EU/EEA citizens. For further information, contact the relevant embassy in your country of origin, referring first to Ⓦudi.no.

## NORWEGIAN EMBASSIES AND CONSULATES ABROAD

**Australia** Ⓦ norway.org.au
**Canada** Ⓦ emb-norway.ca
**Ireland** Ⓦ norway.ie
**New Zealand** Ⓦ norway.org.au
**South Africa** Ⓦ norway.org.za
**UK** Ⓦ norway.org.uk
**US** Ⓦ norway.org

## Gay and lesbian travellers

In 1981, Norway was one of the first countries in the world to pass a law making discrimination against homosexuals and lesbians illegal. Twelve years later, it followed this up by becoming only the second country to pass legislation giving lesbian and gay couples the same rights as married couples, while retaining a bar on church weddings and the right to adopt children. Further legislation in 2002 and 2003 relaxed the restrictions on gay adoption, and same-sex marriages became legal in 2009. All this progressiveness, however, has more to do with respect for the rights and freedoms of the individual than a positive attitude to homosexuality – Norway remains, in essence at least, very much a (heterosexual) family-oriented society. Nevertheless, the general attitude to gays is so tolerant that few feel the need to disguise their sexuality. The age of consent for both gays and straights is sixteen.

It's commonplace for bars and pubs to have a mixture of straights and gays in their clientele. There is something of a separate scene in Bergen, Trondheim and especially Oslo (see p.104), but it's pretty low-key stuff and barely worth seeking out – and the same applies to the weekly gay and lesbian nights held in some small-town nightclubs. The best source of information on the **Oslo scene** is **Ungdomsinformasjonen** or **Use-it**, a youth information shop near Oslo S train station (☎24 14 98 20, Ⓦ use-it.no; see p.92). They produce a free annual booklet, *Streetwise*, also available online, which includes a "gay guide" to the city. The main gay event in the Oslo calendar, the **Skeive Dager** (Queer Days; Ⓦ skeivedager.no), takes place over ten days each June and includes the city's Gay Pride celebrations.

**Landsforeningen for Lesbisk og Homofil frigjøing** (LLH; Ⓦ llh.no), Norway's strong and effective gay and lesbian organization, has its national office in Oslo (see p.104)

## Health

Under **reciprocal health arrangements**, all citizens of the EU and EEA (European Economic Area) are entitled to discounted medical treatment within Norway's public health-care system. Non-EU/EEA nationals are not entitled to discounted treatment – though some of the countries concerned, for example Australia, do have limited mutual agreements – and should, therefore, take out their own medical insurance to cover them while travelling in Norway. EU/EEA citizens may want to consider private health insurance (see p.50) too, in order to cover the cost of the discounted treatment as well as items not within the EU/EEA's scheme, such as dental treatment and repatriation on medical grounds. Note also that the more worthwhile policies promise to sort matters out before you pay (rather than after) in the case of major expense; if you do have to pay upfront, get and keep the receipts.

Health care in Norway is of a very high standard and widely available: even the remotest communities are within relatively easy – or well-organized – reach of medical attention. Rarely will **English speakers** encounter language problems – if the doctor or nurse can't speak English themselves (which is unlikely) there will almost certainly be someone at hand who can. Your local pharmacy, tourist office or hotel should be able to provide the address of an English-speaking doctor or dentist. For **medical emergencies**, call ☎113.

If you're seeking treatment under EU/EEA **reciprocal public health agreements**, double-check that the doctor/dentist is working within (and seeing you as) a patient of the relevant public health-care system. This being the case, you'll receive reduced-cost/government-subsidized treatment just as the locals do; any fees must be paid upfront, or at least at the end of your treatment, and are non-refundable. Sometimes you will be asked to produce documentation to prove you are eligible for EU/EEA health care, sometimes

## EMERGENCY NUMBERS
**Ambulance** ☎113
**Fire** ☎110
**Police** ☎112

## MOSQUITOES

These pesky blighters thrive in the myriad lakes and lochs of northern Norway, though they can be a handful (or mouthful) in the south too. They are especially bothersome if you are camping. An antihistamine cream such as Phenergan is the best antidote, although this can be difficult to find – in which case preventative sticks like Autan or Citronella are the best bet.

no one bothers, but technically at least you should have your passport and your **European Health Insurance Card** (**EHIC**) to hand. If, on the other hand, you have a travel insurance policy covering medical expenses, you can seek treatment in either the public or private health sectors, the main issue being whether – at least in major cases – you have to pay the costs upfront and then wait for reimbursement or not.

## Insurance

Prior to travelling, you'd do well to take out an insurance policy to cover against theft, loss and illness or injury. Before paying for a new policy, however, it's worth checking whether you already have some degree of cover: for instance, EU/EEA health-care privileges apply in Norway (see p.49), some all-risks home insurance policies may cover your possessions when overseas, and many private medical schemes include cover when abroad.

After exhausting the possibilities above, you might want to contact a travel insurance company. A typical **travel insurance policy** usually provides cover for loss of baggage, tickets and – up to a certain limit – cash or cheques, as well as cancellation or curtailment of your journey and medical costs. Most of them exclude so-called dangerous sports – climbing, horseriding, rafting, windsurfing

and so forth – unless an extra premium is paid. Many policies can be chopped and changed to exclude coverage you don't need – for example, sickness and accident benefits can often be excluded or included at will. If you do take medical coverage, ascertain whether benefits will be paid as treatment proceeds or only after your return home, and whether the policy has a 24-hour medical emergency number. When securing baggage cover, make sure that the per-article limit will cover your most valuable possessions. If you need to make a claim, keep receipts for medicines and medical treatment. In the event you have anything stolen, you should obtain a crime report statement or number.

## Internet

Almost all of the country's hotels, B&Bs and hostels provide **internet access** for their guests either free or at minimal charge and wi-fi is increasingly commonplace too. Most cafés offer internet access too, as does almost every library, though here services are free but time-limited.

## Left luggage

There are coin-operated lockers in most train and bus stations and at all major ferry terminals.

## Mail

Norway has a very efficient **postal system** (W posten.no). Most post offices are open from 8am/9am–4/5pm and Saturday 9am–1/3pm. **Postage** varies according to weight, size and urgency. Currently, a standard-size letter or postcard under 20g that is sent "Priority" class costs 9.50kr within Norway, 13kr to the EU, and 15kr to everywhere else. Mail to the US should take about a week, two to three days within Europe. **Stamps** are widely available from post offices, tourist offices and many hotels.

## ROUGH GUIDES TRAVEL INSURANCE

Rough Guides has teamed up with WorldNomads.com to offer great travel insurance deals. Policies are available to residents of over 150 countries, with cover for a wide range of adventure sports, 24hr emergency assistance, high levels of medical and evacuation cover and a stream of travel safety information. Roughguides.com users can take advantage of their policies online 24/7, from anywhere in the world – even if you're already travelling. And since plans often change when you're on the road, you can extend your policy and even claim online. Roughguides.com users who buy travel insurance with WorldNomads.com can also leave a positive footprint and donate to a community development project. For more information go to W roughguides.com/shop.

# Maps

The **maps** in this book should be adequate for most general purposes, especially as they can be readily supplemented by the free local maps given out by almost every tourist office. Drivers, cyclists and hikers will, however, require something more detailed. Buying before you go helps in planning, and often saves a bit of money too.

For **Scandinavia** as a whole, the AA (Ⓦtheaa .com) produces a good-quality **road map** with the southern part of the region at the 1:800,000 scale, the north at 1:1,500,000. As regards **Norway** itself, Hallwag's *Norge/Norwegen* road map (Ⓦswisstravel center.com) is excellent. It has two scales – one for the south (1:800,000) and one for the north (1:900,000) – an index and a handy distance calculator on the back. Michelin (Ⓦviamichelin.com) also publishes a widely available *Norway* map (1:1,250,000), but although this is very accurate and useful for route planning, the index is very scanty.

Currently, the most detailed **book of Norwegian road maps** is the *Stort bilatlas Norge* (1:325,000) produced by Cappelen Damm (Ⓦcappelendamm .no). It has a comprehensive index and includes 75 good-quality city and town maps, but it's expensive, hard to get hold of outside of Norway, and much too cluttered for clarity in the country's more populated areas. Best bet is to use it in conjunction with the Hallwag map (see above). Cappelen also produce excellent **city maps** covering Bergen, Oslo, Trondheim and so on; they are at a variety of scales (1:4000 to 1:10,000) and are on sale locally at any good bookshop.

**Cycling maps**, with route suggestions, are usually on sale at tourist offices in the more popular cycling areas. **Hiking maps** are covered under "Hiking trails and maps" (see p.43).

# Money

Norway has its own currency, the **kroner**; one krone (literally "crown"; abbreviated **kr** or NOK), is divided into 100 **øre**. Coins in circulation are 50 øre, 1kr, 5kr, 10kr and 20kr; notes are for 50kr, 100kr, 200kr, 500kr and 1000kr (though note that smaller retailers often look askance at this last, largest note). At time of writing the rate of exchange for 1kr is £0.11, €0.13, US\$0.17, Can\$0.17, Aus\$0.16, NZ\$0.20, ZAR1.34. For the most up-to-date rates, check the currency converter website Ⓦoanda.com.

**ATMs** are liberally distributed around every city, town and large village in Norway, and accept a host of debit cards without charging a transaction fee.

Credit cards can be used in ATMs too, but in this case transactions are treated as loans, with interest accruing daily from the date of withdrawal. All major **credit/debit cards**, including American Express, Visa and MasterCard, are widely accepted. Typically, Norwegian ATMs give instructions in a variety of languages.

You can change **foreign currency** into kroner at most banks, which are ubiquitous; banking hours are usually Monday to Friday 9am–3.30pm, sometimes till 5/6pm on Thursdays. All major **post offices** also change foreign currency and they generally have longer opening hours.

# Opening hours and public holidays

**Business hours** (ie office hours) normally run from Monday to Friday 9.30/10am to 4.30/5pm. Normal **shopping hours** are Monday through Friday 10am to 5pm, with late opening on Thursdays till 6pm, 7pm or 8pm, plus Saturdays 10am to 1pm, 2pm or 3pm. Most supermarkets stay open much longer – from 9am until 8pm in the week and from 9am to 6pm on Saturdays, but close on Sundays. In addition, many kiosks-cum-newsstands open from 8/9am or so till 9pm or 10pm every day of the week (including Sun), but much more so in the cities and towns than in the villages. Many fuel stations sell a basic range of groceries and stay open till 11pm daily. Vinmonopolet, the state-run liquor chain, has outlets in almost every town and large village, but they operate limited opening hours; each store fixes its own schedule, but generally they're open

---

## NORWAY'S PUBLIC HOLIDAYS

**New Year's Day**
**Palm Sunday** week before Easter
**Maundy Thursday** Thursday before
    Easter
**Good Friday**
**Easter Sunday**
**Easter Monday**
**Labour Day** May 1
**Ascension Day** early to mid-May
**National (or Constitution) Day** May 17
**Whit Sunday** seventh Sunday after Easter
**Whit Monday**
**Christmas Day**
**Boxing Day** day after Christmas Day

Note that when a public holiday falls on a Sunday, then the next day becomes a holiday as well.

Monday to Friday 10am–4/6pm and Saturday 10am–1/3pm. Norway has literally hundreds of **museums**. The more important open all year, but many close for winter from October or November to April, May or even mid-June. Opening hours usually 9.30/10am–5pm every day, including Saturday and Sunday, but some limit their hours on the weekend and many more close on Mondays.

There are thirteen national **public holidays** per year, most of which are keenly observed and, although much of the tourist industry carries on regardless, almost every museum and gallery in the land is closed. The result is that Easter, when four of these public holidays fall, is not a good time for museum-lovers to visit. Otherwise most businesses and shops close, and the public transport system operates a skeleton or Sunday service. Some of these public holidays are also **official flag-flying days**, but there are additional flag days as well – for example on Queen Sonja's birthday (July 4).

## Phones

Given the sheer size of the country and its wide wilderness spaces, it's amazing just how much of Norway has **mobile phone** (**cell phone**) coverage – it's around 80 percent and counting. Norway is on the mobile phone (cell phone) network at GSM900/1800, the band common to the rest of Europe, Australia and New Zealand. Mobile/cell phones bought in North America need to be of sufficient specification to adjust to this GSM band. If you intend to use your mobile/cell phone in Norway, note that call charges can be excruciating – particularly irritating is the supplementary charge you often have to pay on incoming calls – so check with your supplier before you depart. You might also consider buying a **Norwegian SIM card**, though this can get complicated: many mobiles/cells will not permit you to swap SIM cards and the connection instructions for the replacement SIM card can be in Norwegian only. If you overcome these problems, there are myriad deals on offer beginning at about 100kr per SIM card; larger 7-Eleven and Narvesen kiosks sell them. **Text messages/SMS**, on the other hand, are normally charged at ordinary or at least bearable rates – and with your existing SIM card in place.

### USEFUL TELEPHONE NUMBERS

Domestic directory enquiries ☎ 1881
International directory enquiries & Operator assistance ☎ 1882

## Smoking

**Smoking** is prohibited in all public buildings, including train and bus stations, as well as in restaurants, clubs, bars and cafés. Nonetheless, one in five Norwegians still puffs away.

## Time

Norway is on **Central European Time** (**CET**) – one hour ahead of Greenwich Mean Time, six hours ahead of US Eastern Standard Time, nine hours ahead of US Pacific Standard Time, nine hours behind Australian Eastern Standard Time and eleven hours behind New Zealand. There are, however, minor variations during the changeover periods involved in **daylight saving**. Norway operates daylight saving time, moving clocks forward one hour in the spring and one hour back in the autumn.

---

### INTERNATIONAL CALLS

#### PHONING HOME FROM NORWAY

To make an international phone call from within Norway, dial the appropriate international access code as below, then the number you require, omitting the initial zero where there is one.

**Australia** ☎ 0061
**Canada** ☎ 001
**New Zealand** ☎ 0064
**Republic of Ireland** ☎ 00353

**South Africa** ☎ 0027
**UK** ☎ 0044
**US** ☎ 001

#### PHONING NORWAY FROM ABROAD

To call a number in Norway, dial the local international access code, then ☎ 47, followed by the number you require, omitting the initial zero where there is one. There are **no area codes** in Norway and the vast majority of Norwegian telephone numbers have eight digits; where this isn't the case, it's probably a premium-rated line, except those numbers beginning ☎ 800, which are toll-free.

# Tipping

Cafés and restaurants often add a service charge to their bills and this is – or at least should be – clearly indicated. Otherwise, few Norwegians **tip** at cafés, restaurants or bars and, given the country's high prices, you'll probably be disinclined as well, though restaurant waiters and taxi drivers may be disappointed not to get a tip of 10 per cent. Rounding your bill up by a few kroner to make a round number is, on the other hand, pretty standard and considered polite.

# Tourist information

The **Norwegian Tourist Board** operates an all-encompassing website, covering everything from hotels and campsites to forthcoming events. It also publishes a wide range of glossy, free booklets of both a general and specific nature, which for the most part at least are available at all the larger tourist offices throughout the country. Inside Norway, every town and most of the larger villages have their own **tourist office**; we've given their addresses, opening hours, websites and telephone numbers throughout the Guide. Staff almost invariably speak good to fluent English and dispense, among much else, free local maps, local brochures and public transport timetables; many will also help arrange last-minute/ in person accommodation. In addition, Norway is spectacularly well represented on the internet in terms of everything from activity holidays through to bus timetables; we've listed a few general websites below – many more are in the Guide.

## SOME USEFUL WEBSITES

Ⓦ **goscandinavia.com** The official website of the joint Scandinavian Tourist Boards in North America, offering a general introduction to Scandinavia, latest travel deals and links to the Norwegian Tourist Board website.

Ⓦ **kulturnett.no** Comprehensive information on the country's museums, culture and current exhibitions.

Ⓦ **regjeringen.no** Government site which, despite its plain presentation, has everything you ever wanted to know about contemporary Norway and then some. Especially good on political/ contemporary issues.

Ⓦ **visitnorway.com** The official site of the Norwegian Tourist Board, with links to all things Norwegian and good sections on outdoor activities and events.

# Travelling with children

In general terms at least, Norwegian society is sympathetic to its **children** and the tourist industry follows suit. Extra beds in hotel rooms are usually easy to arrange, baby-changing stations are commonplace, and highchairs for young children are usually at hand in cafés, if not so much in restaurants. Furthermore, **concessionary rates** are the rule, from public transport through to museums, and pharmacists carry all the kiddie stuff you would expect – nappies, baby food, and so forth – but this being Norway they cost a lot, so try to bring the gubbins with you. As far as **breastfeeding** in public is concerned, the *Journal of Human Lactation* states that in Norway "there is no problem with breastfeeding almost anywhere at any time. A mother might get an ugly glance once in a while, but restaurants, shopping centres, and even government offices allow breastfeeding without any discussion". As for things to do, Norway's many adventure activities can be ideal for kids, from kayaking to fishing, horseriding to skiing. Big-city Oslo has perhaps more **child-friendly attractions** than anywhere else (see box, p.103).

# Travellers with disabilities

There are decent facilities for travellers with disabilities across the whole country. An increasing number of hotels, hostels and campsites are equipped for disabled visitors, and are credited as such in the tourist literature by means of the standard wheelchair-in-a-box icon. Furthermore, on most main routes the trains have special carriages with wheelchair space, hydraulic lifts and disabled toilets; domestic flights either cater for or provide assistance to disabled customers; and the latest ships on all ferry routes have lifts and cabins designed for disabled people.

In the cities and larger towns, many restaurants and most museums and public places are wheelchair-accessible, and although facilities are not so advanced in the countryside, things are improving rapidly. Drivers will find that most motorway service stations are wheelchair-accessible and that, if you have a UK-registered vehicle, the disabled car parking badge is honoured. Note also that several of the larger car rental companies have modified vehicles available. On a less positive note, city pavements can be uneven and difficult to negotiate and, inevitably, winter snow and ice can make things much, much worse.

Getting to Norway should be relatively straightforward too. Most airlines and shipping companies provide assistance to disabled travellers, while some also have specific facilities, such as DFDS Scandinavian Seaways ferries' specially adapted cabins.

# Oslo and the Oslofjord

DEN NORSKE OPERAHUSET

**1**

# Oslo and the Oslofjord

No argument, Oslo is one of Europe's most amenable capitals, a vibrant, self-confident city with a relaxed and easy-going air, its handsome centre set between the rippling waters of the Oslofjord and the green, forested hills of the interior. Yet Oslo's confidence is new-found: for much of its history, the city was something of a poor relation to the other Scandinavian capitals, Stockholm and Copenhagen especially, and it remained dourly provincial until well into the 1950s. Since then, however, Oslo has transformed itself, forging ahead to become an enterprising and cosmopolitan commercial hub with a population of about half a million. Oslo is also the only major metropolis in a country brimming with small towns and villages – its nearest rival, Bergen, is less than half its size. This gives the city a powerful voice in the political, cultural and economic life of the nation and it's pulled in all of Norway's big companies, as a rash of concrete and glass tower blocks testifies.

Fortunately, these monoliths rarely interrupt the stately Neoclassical lines of the late nineteenth-century **city centre**, Oslo's most appealing district, which boasts a lively restaurant and bar scene as well as a clutch of excellent museums. Indeed, Oslo's biggest single draw is its **museums**, which cover a hugely varied and stimulating range of topics: the fabulous Viking Ships Museum, the Munch Museum, which showcases a good chunk of the painter's work, the sculpture park devoted to the stirring bronze and granite works of Gustav Vigeland, and the moving historical documents of the Resistance Museum, are, to name just four, enough to keep even the most jaded visitor enthralled for days. There's also a first-rate **outdoor scene**, with Oslo rustling up a good range of parks, pavement cafés, street entertainers and festivals, especially in summer when virtually the whole population seems to live outdoors – and visiting is a real delight. Winter is also a good time to be here, when Oslo's position amid hills and forests makes it a thriving, convenient and (surprisingly) affordable **ski centre**.

Although Oslo's centre is itself compact, its outer districts spread over a vast 453 square kilometres, encompassing huge chunks of forest, beach and water. Almost universally, the city's inhabitants have a deep and abiding affinity for these wide-open spaces and, as a result, the waters of the **Oslofjord** to the south and the forested hills of the **Nordmarka** to the north are tremendously popular for everything from boating and swimming to hiking and skiing. On all but the shortest of stays, there's ample opportunity to join in – the open forest and **cross-country ski** routes of the Nordmarka and the **island beaches** just offshore in the Oslofjord are both easily reached by metro or ferry.

# Highlights

**❶ Ibsenmuseet** See exactly where Norway's greatest dramatist, Henrik Ibsen, spent his last years and breathed his last breath. **See p.66**

**❷ Nasjonalgalleriet** Norway's most ambitious collection of fine art, the National Gallery has a bit of everything, from Munch to Manet, Dahl to Kittelsen. **See p.68**

**❸ Munch-museet** An extraordinary collection of paintings, woodcuts and lithographs by Norway's most extraordinary artist. **See p.79**

**❹ Vikingskipshuset** The world-famous Viking Ships Museum exhibits a trio of Viking longships

preserved in clay since they were interred at the height of the Viking period. **See p.82**

**❺ Vigelandsparken** Take a stroll round the fantastical creations of Gustav Vigeland in this wonderful open-air sculpture park. **See p.86**

**❻ Hovedøya** You can swim, walk through woods or laze on the beach on this charming Oslofjord island, just a short ferry ride from the city centre. **See p.89**

**❼ Stratos** Oslo has some great places to drink, but this laidback, infinitely groovy rooftop bar is hard to beat. **See p.100**

HIGHLIGHTS ARE MARKED ON THE MAP ON PP.58–59

1

Holmenkollen, Voksenkollen & Frognerseteren ▲ ▲ Emanuel Vigeland ▲ Sognsvann
Museum & Nordmarka

0 |_____| 400
metres

Frøen Ⓣ

**Barnekunstmuseet**

Borgen

**Frognerparken**

SØRKEDALSVEIEN

LLH

**Vigelandsparken**
❺

Majorstuen Ⓣ

**Oslo
Bymuseet**

**Vigeland-museet**

❺

Gimle Cinema

**Det Kongelige
Slott**

**Kulturhistorisk
Museum**

❼

Nationaltheatret Ⓣ

❶ **Nationaltheatret**

HENRIK IBSENS GATE

**Rådhus**

MUNKEDAMSVEIEN

**BYGDØY**

Dronningen
dock

Hjortneskai
(International
ferries)

*SEE CENTRAL OSLO MAP*

**Norsk
Folkemuseum**

❹

**Kon-Tiki
Museet**

Bygdøynes
dock

**Frammuseet**

*OSLOFJORD*

**Norsk Maritimt
Museum**

Lille
Herbern

Hovedøya

**Kunstverket**

❻

| ● RESTAURANTS | |
|---|---|
| Brasserie Blanche | 1 |
| Ekebergrestauranten | 2 |

| ■ BAR | |
|---|---|
| Oslo Mikrobryggeri | 1 |

| ■ HOTELS | | ■ HOSTELS, B&BS | |
|---|---|---|---|
| Clarion Collection | | & GUESTHOUSES | |
| Hotel Gabelshus | 7 | Ellingsens Pensjonat | 3 |
| Rica Hotel Bygdøy Allé | 5 | Oslo Vandrerhjem | |
| Saga Hotell Oslo | 4 | Haraldsheim | 1 |
| | | Oslo Vandrerhjem | |
| ■ CAMPING & CABINS | | Holtekilen | 6 |
| Bogstad Camping | 2 | | |
| Ekeberg Camping | 8 | | |

Gressholmen ▼

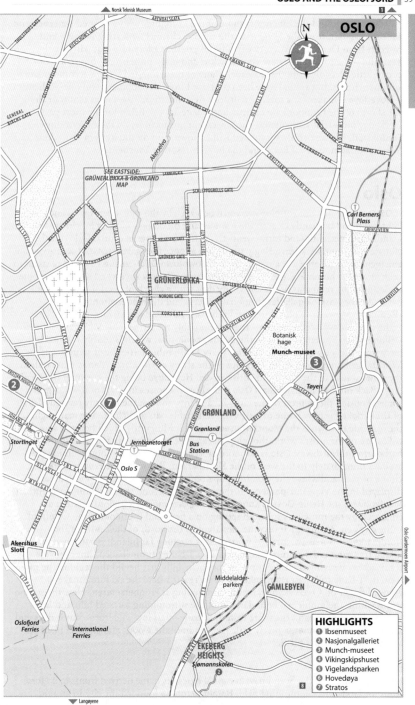

Norsk Teknisk Museum

N

**OSLO**

SEE EASTSIDE:
GRÜNERLØKKA & GRØNLAND
MAP

Carl Berners
Plass

Akerselva

GRÜNERLØKKA

NORDRE GATE

KORSGATA

Botanisk
hage
**Munch-museet**

❸

Tøyen

❷

GRØNLAND

Stortinget

Jernbanetorget

Grønland

Bus
Station

❼

Oslo S

Akershus
Slott

DRONNING EUFEMIAS GATE

SCHWEIGÅRDSGATE

Middelalder-
parken

**GAMLEBYEN**

NYDERES VEI

Oslofjord
Ferries

International
Ferries

**EKEBERG
HEIGHTS**

Sjømannskolen

Oslo Gardermoen Airport

**HIGHLIGHTS**
❶ Ibsenmuseet
❷ Nasjonalgalleriet
❸ Munch-museet
❹ Vikingskipshuset
❺ Vigelandsparken
❻ Hovedøya
❼ Stratos

Langøyene

**1**

Oslo curves round the innermost shore of the Oslofjord, whose tapered waters extend for some 100km from the Skagerrak, the choppy channel separating Norway and Sweden from Denmark. As Norwegian fjords go, the Oslofjord is not particularly beautiful – the rocky shores are generally low and unprepossessing – but scores of pretty little islets diversify the seascape. Many of these forested bumps accommodate summer chalets, but several have been protected from development and one of them – **Hovedøya** – makes for a lovely excursion. By comparison, the towns that trail along the shores of the Oslofjord are of little immediate appeal, being for the most part workaday industrial settlements. The few exceptions include, on the eastern shore, **Fredrikstad**, Norway's only surviving fortified town, and on the western shore, the Viking burial mounds of **Borre** and the holiday resort of **Tønsberg**.

# Oslo

If **OSLO** is your first taste of Norway, you'll be struck by the wide-open spaces and by the light – soft and brilliantly clear in the summer and broodingly gloomy in winter. The grand, late nineteenth- and early twentieth-century buildings of central Oslo suit the climate well – and look reassuringly sturdy just as once they gave a sense of security to an emergent nation. Largely as a result, most of **downtown Oslo** remains easy and pleasant to walk around, a humming, good-natured place whose breezy streets and squares combine these appealing remnants of the city's early days with a clutch of good museums – in particular the **Nasjonalgalleriet** (National Gallery) and the **Hjemmefrontmuseum** (Resistance Museum) – plus dozens of lively bars, cafés and restaurants.

The city's showpiece museums – most memorably the remarkable **Vikingskipshuset** (Viking Ships Museum) – are on the **Bygdøy peninsula**, which is readily reached by ferry from the jetty behind the Rådhus (City Hall); other ferries head south from the Vippetangen quay behind the Akershus to the string of rusticated **islands** that confetti the inner waters of the Oslofjord with wooded **Hovedøya** being the cream of the scenic crop. Back on the mainland, **east Oslo** is the least prepossessing part of town, a gritty sprawl housing the poorest of the city's inhabitants, though the recently revived district of **Grünerløkka** is now home to a slew of fashionable bars and clubs. The main sight on the east side of town is the **Munch-museet** (Munch Museum), which boasts a superb collection of the artist's work, though plans are afoot to move the museum to the harbourfront. **Northwest Oslo** is far more prosperous, with big old houses lining the avenues immediately to the west of the Slottsparken. Beyond is the **Frognerparken**, a chunk of parkland where the wondrous open-air sculptures of Gustav Vigeland are displayed in the **Vigelandsparken**. Further west still, beyond the city limits in suburban Høvikodden, the **Henie-Onstad Kunstsenter** displays more prestigious modern art, enhanced by the museum's splendid setting on a headland overlooking the Oslofjord.

The city's enormous reach becomes apparent to the north of the centre in the **Nordmarka**. This massive forested wilderness, stretching far inland, is patterned by hiking trails and cross-country ski routes. Two T-bane (Tunnelbanen) lines provide ready access, weaving their way up into the rocky hills that herald the region. The more westerly T-bane rolls past **Holmenkollen**, a ski resort where the ski jump makes a crooked finger on Oslo's skyline, before terminating at **Frognerseteren**. Here the station is still within the municipal boundaries, but the surrounding forested hills and lakes feel anything but urban. The more easterly T-bane offers less wilderness, but it does end up close to **Sognsvannet**, a pretty little lake set amid the woods and an ideal place for an easy stroll and/or a picnic.

### Brief history
Oslo is the oldest of the Scandinavian capital cities, its name derived from *Ås*, a Norse word for God, and *Lo*, meaning field. **Harald Hardrada** founded the city in around

### SAVING MONEY: THE OSLO PASS

The useful and money-saving **Oslo Pass** gives free admission to almost every museum in the city, unlimited free travel on the whole municipal transport system (see p.91) and free parking in municipal car parks. It also provides some discounts in shops, hotels and restaurants, though in winter, when opening hours for many sights and museums are reduced, you may have to work hard to make the card pay for itself. Valid for 24, 48 or 72 hours, it costs 230kr, 340kr or 430kr respectively, with children aged four to fifteen charged 100kr, 120kr or 160kr. It's available at the city's two tourist offices and at most hotels and hostels. The card is valid for a set number of hours (rather than days) starting from the moment it is first used, at which time it should either be presented and stamped or franked in an automatic machine, though you can always fill in the date and time yourself. A booklet detailing every advantage the Oslo Pass brings is issued when you purchase one.

1048, but it wasn't until Harald's son, **Olav Kyrre**, established a bishopric and built a cathedral here that the city really began to take off. Despite this, the kings of Norway continued to live in Bergen – an oddly inefficient division of state and church considering the difficulty of communication. At the start of the fourteenth century, **Håkon V** rectified matters by moving to Oslo, where he built himself the Akershus fortress, and the town boomed until 1349, when bubonic plague wiped out almost half the population. The slow decline that followed this catastrophe accelerated when Norway came under Danish control in 1397. No longer the seat of power, Oslo became a neglected backwater until its fortunes were revived by the Danish king **Christian IV**. He moved Oslo lock, stock and barrel from its marshy location at the mouth of the River Alna west to its present site, modestly renaming it **Christiania** in 1624. The new city prospered, and continued to do so after 1814, when Norway broke away from Denmark and united with Sweden. In the event, this political realignment was a short-lived affair, and by the 1880s, Christiania – and the country as a whole – was clamouring for independence. This was achieved in 1905, though the city didn't revert to its original name for another twenty years – and Oslo has hardly looked back since, except during the dark days of the German occupation of World War II. All seemed set fair until July 22, 2011, when a car bomb exploded on Akersgata, in the city centre, the work of a right-wing extremist – a cruel jolt to a city that is undoubtedly one of the most civilized in the world.

## Central Oslo

Despite the mammoth proportions of the Oslo conurbation, the **city centre** has remained surprisingly compact, and is easy to navigate by remembering a few simple landmarks. From the Oslo S train station, at the eastern end of the centre, the main thoroughfare, **Karl Johans gate**, heads directly up the hill, passing the **Domkirke** (Cathedral) and cutting a pedestrianized course until it reaches the **Stortinget** (Parliament building). From here it sweeps down past the **University** to **Det Kongelige Slott**, or Royal Palace, situated in parkland – the **Slottsparken** – at the western end of the centre. South of the palace, on the waterfront, stands the ever-expanding **Aker Brygge** shopping and leisure complex, across from which rises the distinctive twin-towered **Rådhus** (City Hall). South of the Rådhus, on the lumpy peninsula overlooking the harbour, rises the severe-looking castle, **Akershus Slott**. The castle, the Stortinget and Oslo S form a rough triangle enclosing a tight grid of streets that was originally laid out by Christian IV in the seventeenth century, but now holds many of the city's most imposing early twentieth-century buildings. For many years this was the city's commercial hub, and although Oslo's burgeoning suburbs undermined its position in the 1960s, the district is currently making a comeback, reinventing itself with specialist shops and smart restaurants.

1

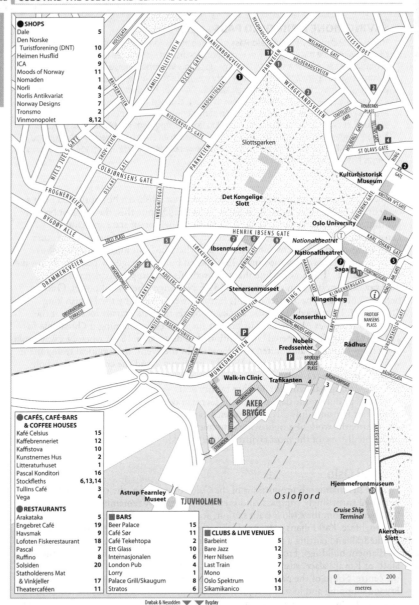

● **SHOPS**

| | |
|---|---|
| Dale | 5 |
| Den Norske Turistforening (DNT) | 10 |
| Heimen Husflid | 6 |
| ICA | 9 |
| Moods of Norway | 11 |
| Nomaden | 1 |
| Norli | 4 |
| Norlis Antikvariat | 3 |
| Norway Designs | 7 |
| Tronsmo | 2 |
| Vinmonopolet | 8,12 |

● **CAFÉS, CAFÉ-BARS & COFFEE HOUSES**

| | |
|---|---|
| Kafé Celsius | 15 |
| Kaffebrenneriet | 12 |
| Kaffistova | 10 |
| Kunstnernes Hus | 2 |
| Litteraturhuset | 1 |
| Pascal Konditori | 16 |
| Stockfleths | 6,13,14 |
| Tullins Café | 3 |
| Vega | 4 |

● **RESTAURANTS**

| | |
|---|---|
| Arakataka | 5 |
| Engebret Café | 19 |
| Havsmak | 9 |
| Lofoten Fiskerestaurant | 18 |
| Pascal | 7 |
| Ruffino | 8 |
| Solsiden | 20 |
| Statholderens Mat & Vinkjeller | 17 |
| Theatercaféen | 11 |

■ **BARS**

| | |
|---|---|
| Beer Palace | 15 |
| Café Sør | 11 |
| Café Tekehtopa | 2 |
| Ett Glass | 10 |
| Internasjonalen | 6 |
| London Pub | 4 |
| Lorry | 1 |
| Palace Grill/Skaugum | 8 |
| Stratos | 6 |

■ **CLUBS & LIVE VENUES**

| | |
|---|---|
| Barbeint | 5 |
| Bare Jazz | 12 |
| Herr Nilsen | 3 |
| Last Train | 7 |
| Mono | 9 |
| Oslo Spektrum | 14 |
| Sikamikanico | 13 |

Drøbak & Nesodden ▼   ▼ Bygdøy

## Domkirke

Karl Johans gate • Mon–Thurs, Sat & Sun 10am–4pm, Fri 4pm–midnight • Free • ⓦ oslodomkirke.no

Presiding over its surroundings a stone's throw from Oslo S, the chunky mass of the **Domkirke** (Cathedral) mostly dates from the late seventeenth century, though its heavyweight tower was remodelled in 1850. From the outside the cathedral may appear a little plain and dour, but the elegantly restored interior is a delightful surprise, its homely, low-ceilinged nave and transepts awash with maroon, green and

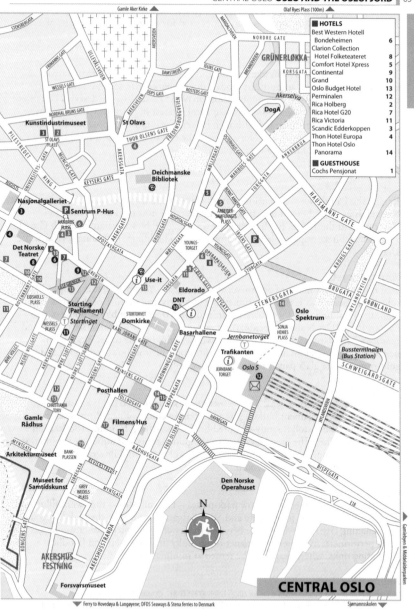

**HOTELS**

| | |
|---|---|
| Best Western Hotell Bondeheimen | 6 |
| Clarion Collection Hotel Folketeateret | 8 |
| Comfort Hotel Xpress | 5 |
| Continental | 9 |
| Grand | 10 |
| Oslo Budget Hotel | 13 |
| Perminalen | 12 |
| Rica Holberg | 2 |
| Rica Hotel G20 | 7 |
| Rica Victoria | 11 |
| Scandic Edderkoppen | 3 |
| Thon Hotel Europa | 4 |
| Thon Hotel Oslo Panorama | 14 |

**GUESTHOUSE**

| | |
|---|---|
| Cochs Pensjonat | 1 |

**CENTRAL OSLO**

gold paintwork. At the central crossing, the flashy Baroque pulpit, where cherubs frolic among the foliage, faces a royal box that would look more at home at the opera. The high altar is Baroque too, its relief of the Last Supper featuring a very Nordic-looking sacrificial lamb. To either side are stained-glass windows created by Emanuel Vigeland (see p.87) in 1910. The brightly coloured ceiling paintings are also modern, with representations of God the Father taking precedence in the Holy Trinity above the high altar, Jesus in the north transept and the Holy Spirit in the

**1**

south. Down below, the **crypt** is sometimes used for temporary exhibitions of religious fine and applied art.

## Stortorvet

The front doors of the Domkirke face out onto **Stortorvet**, once the main city square, but no longer of much account, its modest flower market overseen by a nineteenth-century **statue** of a distinctly chubby **Christian IV** (1577–1648). He deserves better: one of the few Dano-Norwegian kings to take a real interest in Norway, Christian was a hard-working diligent ruler and, although his reign was ultimately scarred by military failure, he remained popular in Norway until the end of his days – quite a tribute considering he ruled for almost six decades.

## Basarhallene

Dronningens gate

Edging the Domkirke is the curious **Basarhallene**, a circular, two-tiered structure whose brick cloisters once housed the city's food market, but now hold shops and cafés. Completed in the 1850s, the Basarhallene was designed by Christian Heinrich Grosch, a prolific architect responsible for a platoon of Oslo buildings, including several at the University.

## Youngstorget

Two minutes' walk north of Stortorvet along Torggata, **Youngstorget** is a large, split-level square that is enjoying something of a revival as a centre of the city's nightlife. Presiding over the square is a splendid **Art Deco tower block**, home of the Labour Party (Det Norske Arbeidpartiet) and two great bars – *Stratos* (see p.100) and *Internasjonalen* (see p.99). The covered passageway linking the tower block with neighbouring Storgata is an Art Deco delight, from the iron-bowl wall lights and gold-trim opaque glass panels up to the mosaic ceiling.

## Stortinget

Karl Johans gate • Guided tours: late June to mid-Aug 3 daily; Sept to late June Sat 3 daily • Free • ☎ 23 31 35 96, ⓦ stortinget.no

The **Stortinget** (Parliament building) is an imposing chunk of neo-Romanesque architecture, whose stolid, sandy-coloured brickwork, dating from the 1860s, exudes bourgeois certainty. The Stortinget is open for guided tours and although the interior is notably unexciting, the parliamentary chamber is of some mild interest for its informality – it looks like a ballroom.

## Eidsvoll plass

In front of the Parliament, a narrow park-piazza – **Eidsvoll plass** – runs west, filling out the space between Karl Johans gate and Stortingsgata. In summer, the park brims with promenading city folk, who dodge between the jewellery hawkers, ice-cream kiosks and street performers; in winter the magnet is the dinky little open-air and floodlit **ice-skating rinks**, where skates can be rented at minimal cost.

## Nationaltheatret

Stortingsgata • Guided tours: ask for details at the box office • Tickets ☎ 815 00 811, ⓦ nationaltheatret.no

Lurking at the western end of the Eidsvoll plass is the Neoclassical **Nationaltheatret** (National Theatre), built in 1899 and fronted by statues of Henrik Ibsen and Bjørnstjerne Bjørnson. The **Ibsen statue** went up during the great man's lifetime, which pleased him no end. Inside the theatre, the 800-seater red-and-gold main hall has been restored to its turn-of-the-twentieth-century glory and can be savoured during a performance – though these are usually in Norwegian – or by taking one of the occasional **guided tours**.

The Nationaltheatret is also a useful **transport interchange**. A pair of tunnels round the back – one for points west, the other east – give access to NSB trains, the T-bane and the Flytoget, the airport express train. In addition, many city buses and trams stop behind the Nationaltheatret, on Stortingsgata.

## The University Aula

Karl Johans gate • Usually late June to mid-Aug Tues–Thurs 10am–2pm • Free

Opposite the Nationaltheatret, at the western end of Karl Johans gate, stand three of the **University**'s main buildings, grand nineteenth-century structures whose classical columns, pilasters and imperial pediments fit perfectly with this monumental part of the centre. The middle of the trio is the **Aula**, where the imposing, deeply recessed entrance leads to a hall decorated with **murals by Edvard Munch**. The controversial result of a competition held by the university authorities in 1909, the murals weren't actually unveiled until 1916, after years of heated debate. Munch had just emerged (cured) from a winter in a Copenhagen psychiatric clinic when he started on the murals, and they reflect a new mood in his work – confident and in tune with the natural world they trumpet. All three main pieces feature a recognizably Norwegian landscape, harsh and bleak and painted in ice-cold blues and yellowy whites. *History* focuses on an old, bearded man telling stories to a young boy, and *Alma Mater* has a woman nourishing her children, but it is *The Sun* which takes the breath away, a searing globe of fire balanced on the horizon to shoot its laser-like rays out across a rocky landscape.

## Det Kongelige Slott and Slottsparken

Karl Johans gate • English-language guided tours of the palace: late June to mid-Aug 3 daily; 1hr • 95kr • Tickets in advance from any Norwegian post office or at the entrance at the beginning of the tour, but note that ticket demand often exceeds supply • ☎ 815 33 133, ⓦ kongehuset.no

Stuck on the hill at the west end of Karl Johans gate, **Det Kongelige Slott** (The Royal Palace) is a monument to Norwegian openness. Built between 1825 and 1848, when the monarchs of other European nations were nervously counting their friends, it now stands without railings and walls, its grounds – the **Slottsparken** (Palace Park) – freely open to the public, who can get up close to a snappy **changing of the guard**, which takes place outside the palace daily at 1.30pm. Directly in front of the palace is an equestrian statue of king **Karl XIV Johan**, inscribed with his motto (see box below). In the summertime, there are hour-long **guided tours** of parts of the palace, though you really have to be a fan of Norway's royal family to find these of much interest.

### JEAN-BAPTISTE BERNADOTTE AND THE ROYAL PALACE

The toings and froings of Scandinavian royalty can be befuddling, but few accessions were as unusual as that of **Karl XIV Johan** (1763–1844), king of Norway and Sweden. Previously, Karl Johan had been the Napoleonic Marshal Jean-Baptiste Bernadotte, a distinguished military commander who had endured a turbulent relationship with his boss, Napoleon, who sacked and reinstated him a couple of times before finally stripping him of his rank for alleged lack of military ardour at the battle of Wagram, outside Vienna, in 1809. In a huff, Bernadotte stomped off back to Paris, where – much to his surprise – he was informed that the **Swedish court** had elected him as the heir to their king, the childless Charles XIII. This was not, however, a quixotic gesture by the Swedes, but rather a desire to ensure that their next king was a good soldier able to protect them from their enemies, especially Russia. In the event, it worked out rather well: Bernadotte successfully steered the Swedes through the tail end of the Napoleonic Wars, firstly as Crown Prince to a decrepit King Charles XIII from 1810 and then, on Charles's death, as the Swedish king, adding Norway to his future kingdom in 1818. Not content, seemingly, with the terms of his motto, "The people's love is my reward", Karl Johan had the whopping **Kongelige Slott** built for his further contentment, only to die before it was completed.

**1**

## Ibsenmuseet

Henrik Ibsens gate 26 • Daily: mid-May to mid-Sept 11am–6pm; mid-Sept to mid-May 11am–4pm • 85kr • ⊕ norskfolkemuseum.no
/ibsenmuseet

The grand, nineteenth-century mansions bordering the southern perimeter of the Slottsparken once housed Oslo's social elite. It was here, in a fourth-floor apartment at Arbins gate 1, on the corner of what is now Henrik Ibsens gate, that Norway's most celebrated playwright, **Henrik Ibsen** (see box below), spent the last ten years of his life, strolling down to the *Grand* (see p.93) every day to hold court. Admirers did their best to hobnob with the great man as he took his daily walk, but Ibsen was unenthusiastic about being a tourist attraction in his own lifetime and mostly ignored all comers – no one could ever accuse him of being overly sociable. Ibsen's old apartment is now incorporated within the **Ibsenmuseet** (Ibsen Museum), which begins with a well-considered introduction to Ibsen and his plays, exploring, over two small floors, the themes that underpinned his work and his uneasy relationship with his home country. Beyond, **Ibsen's apartment** has been restored to its appearance in 1895, including

### IBSEN

**Henrik Johan Ibsen** (1828–1906), Norway's most famous and influential playwright, is generally regarded as one of the greatest dramatists of all time, and certainly his central themes have powerful modern resonances. In essence, these concern the alienation of the individual from an ethically bankrupt society, loss of religious faith and the yearning of women to transcend the confines of their roles as wives and mothers. Ibsen's central characters often speak evasively, mirroring the repression of their society and their own sense of confusion and guilt, with venomous exchanges – a major characteristic of the playwright's dialogue – appearing whenever the underlying tensions break through. Ibsen's protagonists do things that are less than heroic, often incompetent, even malicious. Nevertheless, they aspire to **dåd** – acting with heroism – arguably a throwback to the old Norse sagas. These themes run right through Ibsen's plays, the first of which, *Catalina* (1850), was written while he was employed as an apothecary's assistant at Grimstad on the south coast (see p.123).

The alienation the plays reveal was undoubtedly spawned by Ibsen's troubled **childhood**: his father had gone bankrupt in 1836, and the disgrace – and poverty – weighed heavily on the whole family. More humiliation followed at Grimstad, where the shy, young Ibsen worked for a pittance and was obliged to share a bed with his boss and two maids, which resulted in one of them bearing him a child in 1846. Ibsen escaped small-town Norway in 1850, settling first in Oslo and then Bergen. But he remained deeply dissatisfied with Norwegian society, which he repeatedly decried as illiberal and small-minded. In 1864, he **left the country** and spent the next 27 years living in Germany and Italy. It was during his exile that Ibsen established his literary reputation – at first with the rhyming couplets of **Peer Gynt**, featuring the antics of the eponymous hero, a shambolic opportunist in the mould of Don Quixote, and then by a vicious attack on provincial values in *Pillars of Society*. It was, however, **A Doll's House** (1879) that really put him on the map, its controversial protagonist, Nora, making unwise financial decisions before walking out not only on her patronizing husband, Torvald, but also on her loving children – all in her desire to control her own destiny. **Ghosts** followed two years later, and its exploration of moral contamination through the metaphor of syphilis created an even greater furore, which Ibsen rebutted in his next work, *An Enemy of the People* (1882). Afterwards, Ibsen changed tack (if not theme), firstly with *The Wild Duck* (1884), a mournful tale of the effects of compulsive truth-telling, and then *Hedda Gabler* (1890), where the heroine is denied the ability to make or influence decisions, and so becomes perverse, manipulative and ultimately self-destructive.

Ibsen **returned to Oslo** in 1891. He was treated as a hero, and ironically – considering the length of his exile and his comments on his compatriots – as a symbol of Norwegian virtuosity. Indeed, the daily stroll he took from his apartment to the *Grand Hotel* on Karl Johans gate became something of a tourist attraction in its own right – not that Ibsen, who was notoriously grumpy, often wanted to talk to anyone. Ibsen was incapacitated by a heart attack in 1901 and died from the effects of another five years later.

many of the original furnishings, but it can only be visited on a guided tour (hourly; no extra charge). Both Ibsen and his wife died here: Ibsen breathed his last as he lay paralysed in bed, but his wife, unwilling to expire in an undignified pose, dressed herself to die sitting upright in a chair in the library. Ibsen was argumentative to the end – famously, his final words were "To the contrary" in reply to his poor old maid, who had tried to cheer him up by suggesting he was looking better.

## Stenersenmuseet

Munkedamsveien 15 • Tues & Thurs 11am–7pm, Wed, Fri, Sat & Sun 11am–5pm • 75kr, but free Oct–March • Ⓦ stenersen.museum.no •
The museum is a little hard to find: the gallery is above and beside Munkedamsveien, the ring road, up a concrete stairway

The **Stenersenmuseet** (Stenersen Museum) is home to an eclectic collection of modern art, the bulk of which was gifted to the gallery in 1936 by the author and art collector Rolf Stenersen (the same man who gave a second collection to Bergen; see box, p.195). The museum's first-floor entrance, set beside the ugly concrete stairway at the back of the city's principal concert hall, leads straight into the main exhibition area, which holds an enjoyable sample of early to mid-twentieth-century Scandinavian paintings. The paintings are rotated regularly, but look out for the charming *Small Girl on a Sofa* by **Axel Revold** (1887–1962) and the aloof but finely observed *Two Children, Actress* and *Dressmaker* by **Per Krohg** (1889–1965). Both Krohg and Revold were one-time pupils of Matisse and Revold spent a few months teaching **Arne Ekeland** (1908–94), though this later artist was much more influenced by German Expressionism and Cubism, which suited his leftist, class-conscious politics perfectly. The gallery also holds a large sample of the work of **Jakob Weidemann** (1923–2001), who did much to popularize abstract paintings in Norway in the 1950s and 1960s. Curiously, it was Weidemann's eyesight – or rather the loss of it – which seems to have propelled him into abstraction: a member of the Resistance during World War II, he was blinded by an explosion and although he regained sight in his left eye, the experience left him keen to experiment with bold flashes of colour in a lyrical, abstract style that had many Scandinavian admirers.

The Stenersenmuseet also offers a lively programme of **temporary exhibitions**, but the Munch paintings that were once exhibited here were put in cold storage during the security panic that followed the theft of two of his paintings in 2004 (see p.79) – and there's no sign they will ever be returned.

## Kulturhistorisk Museum

Frederiks gate 2 • Tues–Sun: May–Sept 9am–6pm; Oct–April 10am–4pm • 50kr • Ⓦ khm.uio.no
Just north of Karl Johans gate, Oslo's **Kulturhistorisk Museum** (Cultural History Museum) occupies a handsome neo-Romanesque structure of imposing proportions. The capacious interior holds the university's hotchpotch historical and ethnographical collections, among which the undoubted highlight is the **Viking and early medieval section**, on the ground floor in the rooms to the left of the entrance.

### Viking and early medieval section

The museum's **Viking and early medieval section** features several magnificent portals from twelfth- and thirteenth-century **stave churches** (see box, p.173), alive with dragons and beasts emerging from swirling, intricately carved backgrounds, plus weapons, coins, drinking horns, runic stones, religious bric-a-brac and bits of clothing. The special highlight is, however, a superb **vaulted ceiling** dating from the late thirteenth century and retrieved from the stave church in Ål, near Geilo. The room's brightly coloured wooden planks are painted in tempera – a technique in which each pigment was mixed with glue, egg white and ground chalk – and feature a complicated biblical iconography, beginning at the apex with the Creation and Adam and Eve, followed, as you work your way down, by depictions of Christ's childhood and ultimately his death and resurrection. English-language information panels give the full

1

lowdown, but it's the dynamic forcefulness of these naive paintings, as well as the individuality of some of the detail, that really impresses – look out, in particular, for the nasty-looking Judas at the Last Supper, and the pair of amenable donkeys peeping into Christ's manger.

## Viking Age exhibition

The rest of the ground floor is taken up by a pretty average **Viking Age exhibition** geared towards school parties. The tiny dioramas are downright silly, and detract from the exhibits, which attempt to illustrate various aspects of early Norwegian society, from religious beliefs through to military hardware, trade and craft. More positively, there is a good sample of Viking decorative art, including several pieces illustrating the intensely flamboyant, ninth-century Oseberg and Borre styles and continuing into the Jellinge style, where greater emphasis was placed on line and composition. There's also a **skattkammeret** (treasure room) of precious objects – finger rings, crucifixes, pendants, brooches, buckles and suchlike – illustrating the sustained virtuosity of Norse goldsmiths and silversmiths.

## Etnografiske utstillingene (Ethnographic exhibition)

On the floor above, the beginning of the **etnografiske utstillingene** has an enjoyable collection of ancient Egyptian artefacts, but is mostly devoted to the Arctic peoples with an illuminating section on the Sámi, who inhabit the northern reaches of Scandinavia. Incongruously, there's a **myntkabinettet** (coin collection) here as well, while the top two floors contain a diverse collection of African and Asiatic art and culture, from Samurai suits to African masks.

## The Nasjonalgalleriet

Universitetsgata 13 • Tues, Wed & Fri 10am–6pm, Thurs 10am–7pm, Sat & Sun 11am–5pm • 50kr • ⓦ nasjonalmuseet.no/en/

Norway's largest and most prestigious art gallery is the **Nasjonalgalleriet** (National Gallery). Housed in a whopping nineteenth-century building, the collection may be short on internationally famous painters – apart from a fine body of work by **Edvard Munch** – but there's compensation in the oodles of Norwegian art, including work by all the leading figures up until the end of World War II. The only irritation is the way the museum is organized: the kernel of the collection is displayed on the **first floor**, which is convenient enough, but individual artists' works tend to be displayed across several different rooms, which can be very frustrating. The **free plan** available at reception helps illuminate matters; the text below mentions room numbers where it may be helpful, but note that locations are regularly rotated.

## Johan Christian Dahl and Thomas Fearnley

Near the top of the main staircase, rooms L and M feature the work of the country's most important nineteenth-century landscape painters, **Johan Christian Dahl** (1788–1857) and his pupil **Thomas Fearnley** (1802–42). The Romantic Naturalism of their finely detailed canvases expressed Norway's growing sense of nationhood after the break-up of the Dano–Norwegian union in 1814. In a clear rejection of Danish lowland civil-servant culture, Dahl and Fearnley asserted the beauty (and moral virtue)

---

### THE NATIONAL MUSEUM

Norway's Nasjonalmuseet (National Museum; ⓦ nasjonalmuseet.no) is the collective name for four separate collections, the **Nasjonalgalleriet** (National Gallery; see above), the **Kunstindustrimuseet** (Museum of Applied Art; see p.71), the **Museet for Samtidskunst** (Contemporary Art Museum; see p.74) and the **Arkitekturmuseet** (Museum of Architecture; see p.74). Plans are also proceeding with a fifth museum, a brand new edifice to be constructed down on the harbourfront, beside the Aker Brygge.

of Norway's wild landscapes, which had previously been seen as uncouth and barbaric. This reassessment was clearly influenced by the ideas of the Swiss-born philosopher Jean-Jacques Rousseau (1712–78), who believed that the peoples of mountain regions possessed an intrinsic nobility precisely because they were remote from the corrupting influences of (lowland) civilization. Dahl, who was a professor at the Academy of Art in Dresden for many years, wrote to a friend in 1841:

*Like a true Poet, a Painter must not be led by the prevailing, often corrupt Taste, but attempt to create … a landscape [that] … exposes the characteristics of this Country and its Nature – often idyllic, often historical, melancholic – what they have been and are.*

As for the **paintings** themselves, Dahl's large 1842 canvas *Stalheim* is typical of his work, a mountain landscape rendered in soft and dappled hues, dotted with tiny figures and a sleepy village. His *Hjelle in Valdres* (1851) adopts the same approach, although here the artifice behind the Naturalism is easier to detect. Dahl had completed another painting of Hjelle the year before; returning to the subject, he widened the valley and heightened the mountains, sprinkling them with snow. Fearnley often lived and worked abroad, but he always returned to Norwegian themes, painting no fewer than five versions of the moody *Labrofossen ved Kongsberg* (The Labro Waterfall at Kongsberg); his 1837 version is displayed in Room M.

### Adolph Tidemand and Hans Frederik Gude

A third Norwegian artist to seek out is **Adolph Tidemand** (1814–76), if not so much for the quality of his painting as for its content. Born in Mandal on the south coast, Tidemand went to art college in Denmark and taught art in Düsseldorf, but was firmly attached to his homeland, making a series of long research trips to study rural Norwegian folk customs and costumes. Tidemand's drawings were so precise that they are still used as a reference by students of traditional Norwegian dress, but his paintings are absurdly Romantic, reflecting the bourgeois nationalism that swept Norway in the middle of the nineteenth century. The museum displays a whole batch of Tidemand's paintings, but his most famous work is the *Bridal Voyage on the Hardanger Fjord* (Room N), in which **Hans Frederik Gude** (1825–1903) painted the landscape and Tidemand filled in the figures. Gude was a great friend of Tidemand, sharing his Romantic nationalism and being a fellow lecturer at the art academy in Düsseldorf.

### Gerhard Munthe, Erik Werenskiold and Christian Krohg

In the 1880s, Norwegian landscape painting took on a mystical and spiritual dimension. Influenced by French painters such as Théodore Rousseau, Norwegian artists abandoned the Naturalism of an earlier generation for more symbolic representations. **Gerhard Munthe** (1849–1929), for one, dipped into lyrical renditions of the Norwegian countryside, and his cosy, folksy scenes were echoed in the paintings of **Erik Werenskiold** (1855–1938), who is well represented by *Peasant Burial*. Of a similar ilk was the work of the novelist, journalist and artist **Christian Krohg** (1852–1925), whose highly stylized paintings of the poor and destitute pricked many a middle-class conscience. It was, however, his sympathetic paintings of prostitutes that created the real brouhaha, as exemplified by his tongue-in-cheek *Albertine at the Police Doctor's Surgery*.

### Theodor Kittelsen

Also during the late nineteenth century, **Theodor Kittelsen** (1857–1914) defined the appearance of the country's trolls, sprites and sirens in his illustrations for Asbjørnsen and Moe's *Norwegian Folk Tales*, published in 1883. Four of Kittelsen's original paintings are displayed in Room U – and a splendid sample they are too, especially the one of a princess delousing a troll, a time-consuming job if ever there was one. Here as well are

1

examples of Kittelsen's other work: a self-portrait and a landscape; a wooden cabinet whose shelves hold several dozen Kittelsen sketches; and several panels illustrating a traditional folk song, completed in an ersatz medieval style by Gerhard Munthe.

### Harald Sohlberg and Halfdan Egedius

In Room S, you encounter the works of **Harald Sohlberg** (1869–1935), who clarified the rather hazy vision of many of his Norwegian contemporaries, painting a series of sharply observed Røros streetscapes and expanding into more elemental themes with such stunning works as *En blomstereng nordpå* (A Northern Flower Meadow) and *Sommernatt* (Summer Night). These paintings are comparable with those of **Halfdan Egedius** (1877–99), as in *Opptrekkende uvær* (The Approaching Storm), again in Room S, though Egedius also touched on darker, gloomier themes as in his unsettling *Spill og dans* (Play and Dance).

### Edvard Munch

The Nasjonalgalleriet's star turn is its **Munch collection**, with representative works from the 1880s up to 1916 gathered together in Room T. His early work is very much in the Naturalist tradition of his mentor Christian Krohg, though by 1885 Munch was already pushing back the boundaries in *The Sick Child*, a heart-wrenching evocation of his sister Sophie's death from tuberculosis. Other works displaying this same sense of pain include *The Dance of Life*, *Madonna* and *The Scream*, a seminal canvas of 1893 whose swirling lines and rhythmic colours were to inspire the Expressionists. Munch painted several versions of *The Scream*, but this is the original, so it is hard to exaggerate the embarrassment felt by the museum when, in 1994, someone climbed in through the window and stole it. The painting was eventually recovered, but the thief was never caught. Consider Munch's words as you view it:

*I was walking along a road with two friends. The sun set. I felt a tinge of melancholy. Suddenly the sky became blood red. I stopped and leaned against a railing feeling exhausted, and I looked at the flaming clouds that hung like blood and a sword over the blue-black fjord and the city. My friends walked on. I stood there trembling with fright. And I felt a loud unending scream piercing nature.*

The gallery's sample of Munch's work serves as a good introduction to the artist, but for a more detailed appraisal – and a more comprehensive selection of his work – check out the Munch Museum (see p.79).

### Norwegian paintings from 1910 to the 1940s

Munch aside, the general flow of Norwegian art was reinvigorated in the 1910s by a new band of artists who had trained in Paris under Matisse, whose emancipation of colour from Naturalist constraints inspired his Norwegian students. Among this group, **Henrik Sørensen** (1882–1962) is the outstanding figure. Sørensen summed up the Frenchman's influence on him thirty years later: "From Matisse, I learned more in fifteen minutes than from all the other teachers I have listened to" – lessons that inspired Sørensen's surging, earthy landscapes of the lowlands of eastern Norway. **Axel Revold** (1887–1962) was trained by Matisse too, but also assimilated Cubist influences as in *The Fishing Fleet leaves the Harbour*, while **Erling Enger** (1899–1990) maintained a gently lyrical, slightly whimsical approach to the landscape and its seasons. Look out also for the work of **Arne Ekeland** (1908–94), whose various World War II paintings are bleak and powerful in equal measure – as evidenced by the fractured, mosaic-like composition of *The Last Shots*.

### International art

Finally, the museum holds an enjoyable sample of work by the **Impressionists** and **Post-Impressionists**, with assorted bursts of colour from Manet, Monet, Degas and

Cézanne, as well as a distant, piercing Van Gogh self-portrait. There is also a light scattering of early twentieth-century paintings by the likes of Picasso and Braque, but it must be said that for a national gallery there are few works of international significance, reflecting Norway's past poverty and its lack of an earlier royal or aristocratic collection to build upon.

## The Kunstindustrimuseet

St Olavs gate 1 • Tues, Wed & Fri 11am–5pm, Thurs 11am–7pm, Sat & Sun noon–4pm • Free, but admission charged for some exhibitions • ⓦ nasjonalmuseet.no/en/

The compendious **Kunstindustrimuseet** (Museum of Decorative Arts & Design) occupies a large and forceful nineteenth-century building some five minutes' walk from the Nasjonalgalleriet. Founded in 1876, it can lay claim to being one of the earliest applied-art museums in Europe, with a multifaceted permanent collection that's particularly strong on **furniture**: all the major styles – both domestic and imported – that have been popular in Norway from the medieval period to the present day are represented.

### The collection

The museum spreads over **four floors** with part of the ground floor devoted to a lively programme of temporary exhibitions. The next floor up focuses on the development of **Modernism**, casting a wide net to start in 1905 and end a century later. There are keynote displays on Art Deco, Pop Art and post-World War II Scandinavian design. The next floor up is devoted to the **History of Style 1100– 1905**, and here, in the first room to the right of the stairs, an especially engaging hotchpotch of **medieval** paraphernalia – from brooches and crosses through to portable altars – has been crammed into a glass cabinet. In the same room is the museum's most celebrated exhibit, the **Baldishol Tapestry** (see box below), plus a charming selection of **woven coverlets** decorated with religious and folkloric motifs. Using skills distantly inherited from Flemish weavers, the Norwegians took to pictorial coverlets in a big way, their main modification being the elimination of perspective in the attempt to cover the seams. Of ceremonial significance, these items were brought out on all major occasions – weddings and festivals in particular. The coverlets began as fairly crude affairs at the start of the seventeenth century, but achieved greater precision and detail throughout the eighteenth century, after which the art went into a slow decline. The two most popular subjects were the arrival of the Magi, and the Wise and Foolish Virgins, a suitably didactic subject – so it was thought – for any newlyweds. Next up on this floor is a sequence of **period interiors** illustrating foreign fashions from Baroque through to Rococo, Neoclassical and Art Nouveau.

The top floor holds a **fashion gallery**, one highlight being the collection of extravagant **costumes** worn by Norway's royal family at the turn of the twentieth

---

## THE BALDISHOL TAPESTRY

Remarkably beautiful, the Kunstindustrimuseet's intricate and brightly coloured **Baldishol Tapestry** is Norway's only surviving early medieval tapestry, which has prompted much speculation as to whether it was woven here at all. Carbon dated to between 1040 and 1190, its survival is a minor miracle: tucked away in a country church in Hedmark for many centuries, it ended up being a draught excluder before being retrieved and cleaned in the 1870s. It's actually a fragment of a larger tapestry, just two panels – representing April and May – surviving from the original twelve, one for each month of the year. It's woven out of Norwegian sheep's wool, its colours – primarily red, yellow, green and several shades of blue – produced with vegetable dye. Of the two panels, the bearded man with the birds represents April, the knight May, and the edging features that medieval favourite, acanthus leaves.

**1**

century. Dresses is too prosaic a word for the fairy-tale affairs favoured by Queen Maud, daughter of England's Edward VII and wife of Håkon VII, not to mention Crown Princess Sonja's priest-like consecratory robe from 1991.

## Gamle Aker Kirke

Akersveien • Mid-June to mid-Sept Mon, Tues, Thurs & Fri noon–4pm • Free • The church is a 10min walk along Akersveien from the Kunstindustrimuseet, and a 15min walk from Nordre gate in the Grünerløkka

The **Gamle Aker Kirke** (Old Aker Church) is a sturdy stone building still in use as a Lutheran parish church. It dates from around 1100, which makes it the oldest stone church in Scandinavia, although most of what you see today is the result of a heavy-handed nineteenth-century refurbishment. Curiously, the grassy hillock beneath the church is riddled with the workings of an old **silver mine**, which pumped up Oslo's economy in Viking times. Flooding closed the mines in the twelfth century, but legend had it that would-be prospectors were driven away by a gang of dragons – and on old city maps the silver workings are marked as "Dragehullene" (dragon holes).

## Damstredet

Branching off Akersveien, **Damstredet** is a steep cobbled lane that is flanked by early nineteenth-century clapboard houses built at all kinds of odd angles. These are some of the few wooden buildings to have survived Oslo's developers and they make the street a picturesque affair, a well-kept reminder of how the city once looked. From the bottom of Damstredet, you can stroll south along Fredensborgveien to regain the city centre in around fifteen minutes or you can stroll east to Grünerløkka (see p.77).

## The Rådhus

Fridtjof Nansens plass • Daily 9am–6pm • Free • Guided tours: June–Aug Mon–Sat 3 daily, Sun 1 daily; Sept–May Wed 3 daily; 45min; free • ☎ 23 46 12 00, ⓦ rft.oslo.kommune.no

Rearing high above the waterfront, and twenty years in the making, Oslo's **Rådhus** (City Hall) finally opened in 1950 to celebrate the city's nine-hundredth anniversary. Designed by Arnstein Arneberg and Manus Poulsson, this firmly Modernist, twin-towered building of dark brown brick was intended to be a grandiose statement of civic pride. At first, few locals had a good word for what they saw as an ugly and strikingly un-Norwegian addition to the city, but with the passing of time the obloquy has fallen on more recent additions to the skyline – such as Oslo S – and the Rådhus has become one of the city's more popular buildings.

Initially at least, the ornamentation was equally contentious. Many leading Norwegian painters and sculptors contributed to the decoration, which was designed to celebrate all things Norwegian, but the pagan themes chosen for much of the work gave many of the country's Protestants the hump. The **main approach** to the Rådhus is on its landward side via a wide ramp, whose **side galleries** are adorned by garish **wood panels** illustrating pagan Nordic myths with several featuring the Tree of the World, Yggdrasil or Yggdrask (see p.403).

### The interior

Inside, the principal hall – the **Rådhushallen** – is decorated with vast, stylized and very secular murals. On the north wall, Per Krohg's *From the Fishing Nets in the West to the Forests of the East* invokes the figures of polar explorer Fridtjof Nansen (on the left) and dramatist Bjørnstjerne Bjørnson (on the right) to symbolize, respectively, the nation's spirit of adventure and its intellectual development. On the south wall is the equally vivid *Work, Administration and Celebration*, which took Henrik Sørensen a decade to complete. The self-congratulatory nationalism of these two murals is hardly attractive, although the effect is partly offset by the forceful fresco in honour of the Norwegian Resistance of World War II, which runs along the east wall.

**The rear**

Outside, at the back of the Rådhus, a line of six muscular **bronzes** represents the trades – builders, bricklayers and so on – who worked on the building. Behind them, four massive, granite female sculptures surround a fountain with four more figures, and beyond is the busy central **harbour**, with the bumpy Akershus peninsula on the left and the islands of the Oslofjord filling out the backdrop. This is a delightful spot, one of the city's happiest moments, and from here you can catch a ferry to the museums of the Bygdøy peninsula (see p.80) or stroll over to the Nobels Fredssenter.

## Nobels Fredssenter

Brynjulf Bulls plass 1 • Mid-May to Aug daily 10am–6pm; Sept to mid-May Tues–Sun 10am–6pm • 80kr • ⓦ nobelpeacecenter.org

The **Nobels Fredssenter** (Nobel Peace Centre) was founded to celebrate and publicize the Nobel Peace Prize. Born in Sweden, **Alfred Nobel** (1833–96) invented dynamite in his thirties and went on to become extraordinarily rich with factories in over twenty countries. In his will, Nobel established a fund to reward good works in five categories – physics, chemistry, medicine, literature and peace. The awards were to be made annually, based on the recommendations of several Swedish institutions, with the exception of the Peace Prize, the recipient of which was to be selected by a committee of five, itself appointed by the Norwegian parliament.

Inside, the Peace Centre's **ground floor** features a series of temporary displays designed to get visitors into thinking about conflict and peace, poverty and wealth, refugees and asylum. **Upstairs**, there's a small display on the Nobel family; "wall papers" (broadly, information sheets) on all things to do with peace; and the so-called "**Nobel Field**", where each of the past holders of the Peace Prize is represented by a celebratory plaque attached to a light bulb on a wispy stalk. With the overhead lights dimmed down, the stalks make a sort of miniature electrical forest, which really looks both effective and very engaging. As for the winners of the Peace Prize themselves, there are many outstanding individuals – Martin Luther King, Desmond Tutu, Nelson Mandela and Willy Brandt to name but four – but some real surprises too, notably Theodore Roosevelt, who was part of the American invasion of Cuba in the 1890s, and the USA's **Henry Kissinger**, who was widely blamed for destabilizing Cambodia in the 1970s, his award prompting a leading comedian of the day to announce that political satire was dead. Indeed, despite its current exemplary image, the Nobel Prizes are in fact steeped in controversy: the writer and playwright Johan August Strindberg (1849–1912) was the pre-eminent literary figure in Sweden for several decades, but he was much too radical for the tastes of the prize givers and in 1911, after he had again failed to get one, the Swedish trades union movement organized a whip-round and gave him a "Nobel Prize" themselves.

## Aker Brygge

Behind the Peace Centre, the old Aker shipyard has been turned into the swish **Aker Brygge** shopping-cum-office complex, a gleaming concoction of walkways, circular staircases and glass lifts, all decked out with neon and plastic; the bars and restaurants here are some of the most popular in town.

## Astrup Fearnley Museet for Moderne Kunst

Tjuvholmen • Consult website for opening times • ⓦ afmuseet.no

By late 2012, the **Astrup Fearnley Museet for Moderne Kunst** (Astrup Fearnley Modern Art Museum), which was formerly housed on Dronningens gate, was scheduled to have moved into glitzy new premises at Tjuvholmen, at the west end of Aker Brygge. The new building, designed by Renzo Piano, is meant to impress – and will be a suitably posh setting for a prestigious programme of temporary exhibitions. The museum also possesses an extravagantly well-endowed permanent collection, including examples of the work of most major postwar Norwegian artists, as well as a smattering of foreign works by such celebrated figures as Francis Bacon, Damien Hirst, Jeff Koons and Anselm Kiefer.

## Rådhusgata to Bankplassen

**Rådhusgata** runs southeast from the Rådhus, cutting off the humpy spur of land dominated by the Akershus Castle (see p.76). At the foot of Øvre Slottsgate, it bisects an elegant cobbled square, **Christiania torv**, where attractively designed modern buildings jostle for space with older structures, including the courtyard complex holding the *Kafé Celsius* (see p.96) and Oslo's old town hall, the pint-sized, half-timbered **Gamle Rådhus**, which was badly damaged by fire in 1996 and now holds a restaurant.

Beyond the square, Rådhusgata cuts through what was once the commercial heart of the city, a role it shared with neighbouring Tollbugata and Prinsens gate. It was here that Oslo's late nineteenth-century business elite built a string of imposing, heavy-duty buildings, usually of roughly dressed stone in a sort of Romanesque Revival meets Second Empire style. There are lots of examples, but pride of architectural place goes to the old postal sorting office, the **Posthallen**, a slightly later building at Dronningens gate 15. Erected between 1914 and 1924, and part of an enormous complex that occupies a whole city block in between Tollbugata, Kirkegata, Prinsens gate and Dronningens gate, the Posthallen is a transitional structure, part Art Nouveau, part Art Deco, which is framed by a pair of imposing clock towers and encloses a large courtyard. Neighbouring **Bankplassen**, a pretty little square one block south of Rådhusgata, holds a further fine example of these proud commercial buildings in the former **Norges Bank headquarters** of 1907, a redoubtable Art Nouveau-meets-Romanesque edifice that has been refurbished to house the Museet for Samtidskunst.

## Museet for Samtidskunst

Bankplassen 4 • Tues, Wed & Fri 11am–5pm, Thurs 11am–7pm, Sat & Sun noon–5pm • Free • ⓦ nasjonalmuseet.no/en/

The enterprising **Museet for Samtidskunst** (Contemporary Art Museum) owns work by every major post-World War II Norwegian artist and many leading foreign figures too, for the most part displaying its wares in the form of a series of temporary, thematic exhibitions spread over two main floors. The works, some of which are massive, are each allowed a generous amount of space, so – given that the museum also hosts prestigious international exhibitions – only a fraction of the permanent collection can be shown at any one time. Nonetheless, Norwegian names to look out for include Bjørn Carlsen, Frans Widerberg, Erik Killi Olsen, Knut Rose, Snorre Ytterstad, Per Kleiva and Bjørn Ransve (see box opposite).

The museum's exhibits hang from every wall and offset every corner and stairwell, but it's still difficult not to be just as impressed by the building itself, its echoing halls resplendent with gilt and marble, ornamental columns and banisters. The museum also does a good line in T-shirts – a recent offering was inscribed "Welcome tourists – don't leave us alone with the Danes".

## The Arkitekturmuseet

Bankplassen 3 • Tues, Wed & Fri 11am–5pm, Thurs 11am–7pm, Sat & Sun noon–5pm • 50kr • ⓦ nasjonalmuseet.no/en/

One of Oslo's four national museums, the **Arkitekturmuseet** (Architecture Museum) is a lavish development in which keynote architectural displays are laid out in a handsome modern pavilion at the back of an older structure, which dates from 1830. Opened in 2008, the exhibitions usually focus on Norwegian architects – and Norwegian design – with detailed models and photos of new buildings constructed in every part of the country, increasingly with emphasis given to eco themes. Some of the new buildings are singularly impressive, though the write-ups can verge on the pretentious: the town of Halden (see p.109) has a new prison, but to describe its design as encouraging "freer movements between various activities" can't but help raise a smile.

## MODERN ART IN NORWAY

Norway has a well-organized, high-profile body of **professional artists** whose long-established commitment to encouraging artistic activity throughout the country has brought them respect, as well as state subsidies. In the 1960s, abstract and conceptual artists ruled the roost, but at the end of the 1970s there was a renewed interest in older art styles, particularly Expressionism, Surrealism and Cubism, plus a new emphasis on technique and materials. To a large degree these opposing impulses fused, or at least overlapped, but by the late 1980s several definable movements had emerged. One of the more popular trends was for artists to use beautiful colours to portray disquieting visions, a dissonance favoured by the likes of **Knut Rose** (1936–2002) and **Bjørn Carlsen** (b.1945), whose ghoulish *Searching in a Dead Zebra* has been highly influential. Other artists, the most distinguished of whom is **Tore Hansen** (b.1949), have developed a naive style. Their paintings, apparently clumsily drawn without thought for composition, are frequently reminiscent of Norwegian folk art, and constitute a highly personal response often drawn from the artist's subconscious experiences.

Both of these trends embody a sincerity of expression that defines the bulk of contemporary Norwegian art. Whereas the prevailing mood in international art circles encourages detached irony, Norway's artists characteristically adhere to the view that their role is to interpret, or at least express, the poignant and personal for their audience. An important exception is **Bjørn Ransve** (b.1944), who creates sophisticated paintings in constantly changing styles, but always focused on the relationship between art and reality. Another exception is the small group of artists, such as **Bjørn Sigurd Tufta** (b.1956) and **Sverre Wylier** (b.1953), who have returned to non-figurative Modernism to create works that explore the possibilities of the material, while the content plays no decisive role.

An interest in materials has sparked a variety of experiments, particularly among the country's artists, whose **installations** incorporate everyday utensils, natural objects and pictorial art. These installations have developed their own momentum, pushing back the traditional limits of the visual arts in their use of many different media including photography, video, textiles and furniture. Leading an opposing faction is the painter **Odd Nerdrum** (b.1944), who has long spearheaded the figurative rebellion against the Modernists, though some artists straddle the divide, such as **Astrid Løvaas** (b.1957) and **Kirsten Wagle** (b.1956), who work together to produce flower motifs in textiles. The most prominent Norwegian sculptor today is Bergen's own **Bård Breivik** (b.1948), who explores the dialogue between nature and humankind. With similarly ambitious intent are the much-lauded installations of **Jørgen Craig Lello** (b.1978) and the Swede **Tobias Arnell** (b.1978), who claim to "utilize logically broken trains of thought, false statements and fictional scenarios in their examination of how the world is interpreted and understood". Good luck to them, then.

## The Akershus complex

Outdoor areas daily 6am–9pm • Free • ⓦ forsvarsbygg.no

Though very much part of central Oslo by location, the thumb of land that holds the sprawling fortifications of the **Akershus complex** is quite separate from the city centre in feel. Built on a rocky knoll overlooking the harbour in around 1300, the original **Slott** (castle) was already the battered veteran of several unsuccessful sieges when **Christian IV** (1596–1648) took matters in hand. The king had a passion for building cities and took a keen interest in Norway – during his reign he visited the country about thirty times, more than all the other kings of the Dano-Norwegian union together. So, when old Oslo was badly damaged by fire in 1624, he took his opportunity and simply ordered the town to be moved round the bay and rebuilt in its present position, modestly renaming it Christiania – a name which stuck until 1925 – and transformed the medieval Akershus castle into a Renaissance residence. Around the castle he also constructed a new fortress – the **Akershus Festning** – whose thick earth-and-stone walls and protruding bastions were designed to resist artillery bombardment. Refashioned and enlarged on several later occasions, and now bisected by Kongens gate, parts of the fortress have remained in military use until the present day. There are several **entrances** to the Akershus complex, but the most appealing is at the west end of Myntgata.

**1**

### Besøkssenteret

Mon–Fri 10am–5pm, Sat & Sun 11am–5pm • Free

From the west end of Myntgata, a footpath leads up to a side gate in the perimeter wall. Just beyond the gate is a **Besøkssenteret** (Visitor Centre), which explores the history of the castle, especially its use as a prison, a role it performed until 1950. There are several interesting displays on notable prisoners, including **Christian Jensen Lofthus** (1750–97), a farmers' leader from the south coast who petitioned the government over excessive taxation and corruption in the civil service. He managed to meet the Crown Prince, who seemed to be sympathetic, but was subsequently arrested and imprisoned – and the armed revolt that broke out in his support was suppressed. Lofthus died in prison here in the Akershus. Back outside the Besøkssenteret, follow the signed **footpath** that twists its way up to the castle and the Resistance Museum, offering the possibility of heady views over the harbour on the way.

### Hjemmefrontmuseum

June–Aug Mon–Sat 10am–5pm, Sun 11am–5pm; Sept–May Mon–Fri 10am–4pm, Sat & Sun 11am–4pm • 50kr

The **Hjemmefrontmuseum** (Resistance Museum) occupies a distinctive old building just outside the castle entrance, an apt location given that the Gestapo had the habit of executing captured Resistance fighters a few metres away – after torturing them inside the castle first. Labelled in English and Norwegian, the displays detail the history of the war in Norway, from defeat and occupation through resistance to final victory. There are tales of extraordinary heroism here – notably the determined resistance of hundreds of the country's **teachers** to Nazi instructions – plus a section dealing with Norway's **Jews**, who numbered 1800 in 1939; the Germans captured 760, of whom 24 survived. There's also the moving story of a certain **Petter Moen**, who was arrested by the Germans and imprisoned in the Akershus, where he kept a diary by using a nail to pick out letters on toilet paper; the diary survived, but he didn't. Other acts of resistance included the sabotaging of German attempts to produce heavy water for an atomic bomb deep in southern Norway, at Rjukan (see p.179), but there's also an impressively honest account of Norwegian **collaboration**: fascism struck a chord with the country's petit bourgeois, and hundreds of volunteers joined the Wehrmacht. The most notorious collaborator was **Vidkun Quisling**, who was executed by firing squad for his treachery in 1945. When the German army invaded in April 1940, Quisling assumed he would govern the country and made a radio announcement proclaiming his seizure of power, though in the event the Germans soon sidelined him, opting for military control instead.

### Akershus Slott

May–Aug Mon–Sat 10am–4pm, Sun 12.30–4pm; Sept–April Sat & Sun noon–5pm • 70kr

Next door to the Resistance Museum, the severe stone walls and twin spires of the medieval **Akershus Slott** (Akershus Castle) perch on a rocky ridge high above the zigzag fortifications added by Christian IV. The castle is approached through two narrow tunnel-gateways, which lead to a cobbled courtyard at the heart of the fortress. So far so good, but thereafter the interior is a bit of a disappointment as you are arrowed round a string of sparsely furnished rooms linked by bare-brick passageways. Nevertheless, there are one or two items of interest, primarily the **royal crypt**, holding the sarcophagi of Norway's current dynasty – not that there have been many of them, just two in fact, Håkon VII (1872–1957) and Olav V (1903–91) – and the **royal chapel**. Among the castle's assorted halls, the pick are the **Romerikssalen**, worth a few moments for its Baroque fireplace and Flemish tapestries, and the grand neo-Gothic **Olavshallen**.

Near the end of a visit, it's a real surprise to stumble across the well-preserved office of **Henrik Wergeland** (1808–45), who worked in the castle as a royal archivist for the last four years of his life. Wergeland was one of the most prominent Norwegian poets and dramatists of his day and also an ardent campaigner for greater Norwegian independence. He was, therefore, roundly mocked for accepting the archivist's job – and pension – from the regime he had disparaged and ended up a bitter man: he kept a (fang-less) adder in his office to disconcert the unwary visitor, a not-so-playful reminder of one of his last works, *Vinaegers Fjeldeventyr*, in which the cruellest critic of a poet is so poisonous that a snake dies after it has bit him – and hence the plastic snake in the office today.

### The castle walkway

Back in the castle courtyard, walk through the first of the tunnel-gateways and then turn left along the **walkway** running down the side of the castle with the walls pressing in on one side and views out over the harbour on the other. At the foot of the castle, the path swings across a narrow promontory and soon reaches the **footbridge** over Kongens gate. Cross the footbridge for the Forsvarsmuseet (see below), or keep straight for the string of ochre-coloured barrack blocks that lead back to Myntgata.

### Forsvarsmuseet

May–Aug Mon–Fri 10am–5pm, Sat & Sun 11am–5pm; Sept–April Mon–Fri 11am–4pm, Sat & Sun 11am–5pm • Free

The **Forsvarsmuseet** (Armed Forces Museum), on the far side of the army parade ground, tracks Norwegian military history from the early Middle Ages to postwar UN peace-keeping. The first floor sets a hectic pace, beginning with a surprisingly cursory look at the Vikings before ploughing on as far as the German invasion of 1940. There's a mildly interesting section on the country's early use of ski troops, but otherwise it's hard to get enthralled by the innumerable wars fought between the Scandinavian countries for obscure dynastic reasons. By contrast, the section on **World War II** is much more detailed and the photographs chosen to illustrate the invasion and occupation are first-rate.

### Den Norske Operahuset

Kirsten Flagstads pl. 1 • Mon–Fri 10am–11pm, Sat 11am–11pm, Sun noon–10pm • Free • ⓦ operaen.no

**Den Norske Operahuset** (Opera House) is one of the city's proudest and newest buildings. Completed in 2008, and home to the city's opera and ballet companies, it's a glassy, cuboid structure with exterior ramps that look like extended ski slopes – all to a loquacious design by the Norwegian company, Snøhetta. It's meant to impress, with no expense spared with the interior, and since its opening Norwegians have visited in their thousands. The Operahuset is a key part of an ambitious, long-term project to transform the city's waterfront, which will probably include – though the plans have yet to be agreed – the re-housing of the Munch-museet here beside the opera house in another glossy, glassy building.

# East Oslo: Grünerløkka and the Munch-museet

East Oslo is not nearly as prosperous as the west half of the city with Akersgata/ Akersveien the rough divider. The area does, however, have one prime attraction, the **Munch-museet**, featuring the wondrous works of Edvard Munch, and one especially groovy neighborhood, the **Grünerløkka**, though some swear hard-edged, dishevelled **Grønland** is groovier still – and, true or not, no one could say it was pretentious.

### Grünerløkka

Trams #11, #12 & #13 run along Thorvald Meyers gate back and forth to the city centre

Formerly a run-down working-class district, **Grünerløkka** has recently been revived, its regeneration turning it into one of the most fashionable parts of the city, particularly among artists and students. The main drag, **Thorvald Meyers gate**, is

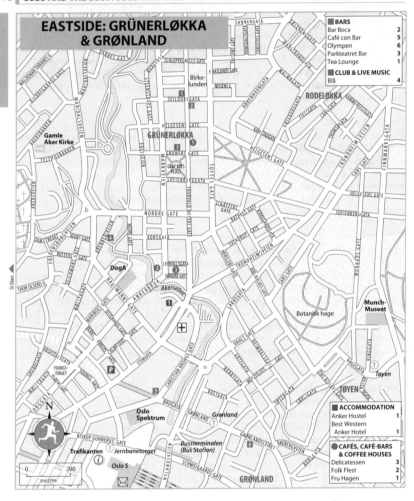

# EASTSIDE: GRÜNERLØKKA & GRØNLAND

**BARS**
| | |
|---|---|
| Bar Boca | 2 |
| Café con Bar | 5 |
| Olympen | 6 |
| Parkteatret Bar | 3 |
| Tea Lounge | 1 |

**CLUB & LIVE MUSIC**
| | |
|---|---|
| Blå | 4 |

**ACCOMMODATION**
| | |
|---|---|
| Anker Hostel | 1 |
| Best Western | |
| Anker Hotel | 1 |

**CAFÉS, CAFÉ-BARS & COFFEE HOUSES**
| | |
|---|---|
| Delicatessen | 3 |
| Folk Flest | 2 |
| Fru Hagen | 1 |

dotted with boho cafés, shops, bars and restaurants plus a couple of pocket-sized city parks; Grünerløkka is a great place to eat (see p.96) and drink (see p.100). Of the several entrances to the area, the prettiest is across the pedestrianized **Ankerbrua** (Anker bridge), which spans the **River Akerselva** to link Markveien with Torggata. The bridge sports sculptures by Norwegian sculptor Per Ung – look out for Peer Gynt and his reindeer.

## DogA Norsk Design og Arkitektursenter

Hausmanns gate • Mon, Tues & Fri 10am–5pm, Wed & Thurs 10am–8pm, Sat & Sun noon–5pm • Free • ☎ 23 29 28 70, ⊛ doga.no

Housed in a former electricity station, the **DogA Norsk Design og Arkitektursenter** (Norwegian Design and Architecture Centre) shunts up against the south bank of the River Akerselva, a short walk from the Ankerbrua. There's no permanent collection here, but rather temporary displays that trumpet contemporary Norwegian design. One popular theme is climate – and the various efforts the Norwegians are making to combat global warming, from insulation to wind farms.

# The Munch-Museet

Tøyengata 53 • June–Aug daily 10am–6pm; Sept–May Tues–Fri 10am–4pm, Sat & Sun 11am–5pm • 95kr • ⓦ munch.museum.no •
T-bane to Tøyen station, from where it's an easy 5min walk – just follow the signs

Nearly everyone who visits Oslo makes time for the **Munch-museet** (Munch Museum)
– and with good reason. In his will, **Edvard Munch** (1863–1944) donated all the works in
his possession to Oslo city council, a mighty bequest of several thousand paintings,
prints, drawings, engravings and photographs, which took nearly twenty years to
catalogue and organize before being displayed in this purpose-built gallery. The museum
has, however, had its problems: in August 2004, two armed **robbers** marched into the
museum and, in full view of dozens of bemused visitors, lifted two Munch paintings
– the *Madonna* and *The Scream*, his most famous work (though fortunately Munch
painted several versions – the earliest is in the Nasjonalgalleriet; see p.68). As if this wasn't
bad enough, further embarrassments followed: it turned out that the paintings were not
alarmed and neither were they especially secure, only being attached to the wall by a cord.
The two works of art were finally recovered two years later and, in a classic case of closing
the stable door after the horse has bolted, the gallery has beefed up its security, though
tentative plans are afoot to close it down and move the collection to central Oslo.

The Munch-museet's **permanent collection** is huge, and only a small – but always
significant – part can be shown at any one time, so the paintings are frequently rotated.
The museum also sources a lively programme of temporary exhibitions concentrating
on various aspects of Munch's work. Naturally, all this means that you can't be certain
what will be displayed and when, but the key paintings mentioned below are most
likely to be on view. At the start of the museum, an illustrated, potted **biography** of
Munch and a short **film** on his life and times sets the scene.

## EDVARD MUNCH

Born in 1863, **Edvard Munch** had a melancholy **childhood** in what was then Christiania
(Oslo). His early years were overshadowed by the early deaths of both his mother and a sister
from tuberculosis, as well as the fierce Christian piety of his father. After some early works,
including several self-portraits, he went on to study in **Paris**, a city he returned to again and
again, and where he fell (fleetingly) under the sway of the Impressionists in general and
Gauguin in particular, responding to the French painter's simplified forms and non-naturalistic
colours. In 1892 Munch moved to **Berlin**, where his style developed and he produced some of
his best and most famous work, though his first exhibition there was considered so
outrageous it was closed after only a week – his painting was, a critic opined, "an insult to art":
his recurrent themes, notably jealousy, sickness, alienation and the awakening of sexual desire,
all of which he had extrapolated from his childhood, were simply too much for his early
audience. Nevertheless, despite the initial criticism, Munch's work was subsequently exhibited
in many of the leading galleries of the day.

Generally considered the initiator of the **Expressionist** movement, Munch wandered
Europe, painting and exhibiting prolifically. Meanwhile overwork, drink and problematic love
affairs were fuelling an instability that culminated, in 1908, in a **nervous breakdown**. Munch
spent six months in a Copenhagen clinic, after which his health improved greatly, and though
his paintings lost the hysterical edge characteristic of his most celebrated work he never
dismissed the importance of his mental frailness to his art, writing, for example, "I would not
cast off my illness, for there is much in my art that I owe to it."

Munch **returned to Norway** in 1909 and was based there until his death in 1944. He
wasn't, however, a popular figure in his homeland despite – or perhaps because of – his high
international profile and he was regularly criticized in the press for all manner of alleged faults,
from miserliness to artistic arrogance. Neither was his posthumous reputation enhanced by
the **state funeral** organized for him by the occupying Germans, his coffin paraded up Karl
Johans gate in a cortege of guns, eagles and swastikas. To be fair, Munch had certainly not
wanted a fascist funeral and neither was he sympathetic to the Germans, who he feared would
end up confiscating his paintings and burning them as "degenerate" art – as they nearly did.

1

**1**

### Early and 1890s paintings

The landscapes and domestic scenes of Munch's **early paintings**, such as *Tête à Tête* and *At the Coffee Table*, reveal the perceptive if deeply pessimistic realism from which Munch's later work sprang. Even more riveting are the great works of the **1890s**, which form the core of the collection. Considered Munch's finest achievements, several of these key paintings are grouped together in the so-called *Frieze of Life*, whose preoccupations were love, anxiety and death. Among the wonderful paintings from this period come *Dagny Juel*, a portrait of the Berlin socialite Ducha Przybyszewska, with whom both Munch and Strindberg were infatuated; the searing representations of *Despair* and *Anxiety*; the chilling *Red Virginia Creeper*, a house being consumed by the plant; the deeply unsettling *Eye in Eye*; and, of course, *The Scream* – of which the museum holds several versions.

### Later paintings

Munch's style was never static and a batch of his **later paintings**, produced after he had recovered from his breakdown and withdrawn to the tranquillity of the Oslofjord, reflect a renewed interest in nature and physical work – *Workers On Their Way Home* (1913) is a prime example. His technique was also changeable: in works like the *Death of Marat II* (1907) he began to use streaks of colour to represent points of light. Later still, paintings such as *Garden in Kragerø* and *Model by the Wicker Chair*, with skin tones of pink, green and blue, begin to reveal a happier, if rather idealized, attitude to his surroundings, though this is most evident in works like *Spring Ploughing*, painted in 1916. But for Munch, the unsettling and the perturbing were never far away and so he returned to the themes of the 1890s again and again as in the *Dance of Life*, first painted in 1900 with another version appearing twenty-five years later.

### Self-portraits

Throughout his life, Munch had a penchant for **self-portraits** and these provide a graphic illustration of the artist's state of mind at various points in his life. There's a palpable sadness in his *Self-Portrait with Wine Bottle* (1906), along with obvious allusions to his heavy drinking, while the telling perturbation of *In Distress* (1919) and *The Night Wanderer* (1923) indicates that he remained a tormented, troubled man even in his later years. One of his last works, *Self-Portrait by the Window* (1940), shows a glum figure on the borderline between life and death, the strong red of his face and green of his clothing contrasting with the ice-white scene visible through the window.

### Lithographs and woodcuts

Munch's **lithographs and woodcuts**, of which the museum owns several hundred, are a dark catalogue of swirls and fogs, technically brilliant pieces of work and often developments of his paintings rather than just simple copies. In them, he pioneered a new medium of expression, experimenting with colour schemes and a huge variety of materials, which enhance the works' rawness: his wood blocks, for example, show a heavy, distinct grain, while there are colours like rust and blue drawn from the Norwegian landscape. The hand-coloured lithographs tend to be, by comparison, more sensuous with many focusing on the theme of love (taking the form of a woman) bringing death.

## The Bygdøy peninsula

Other than the city centre, the place where you're most likely to spend any time in Oslo is the **Bygdøy peninsula**, across the bay to the southwest of the main harbour, where **five museums** make for an absorbing cultural and historical excursion. It's possible to cram all of them into a day's sightseeing, but it's better to spread a visit over a couple of mornings or afternoons.

## ARRIVAL AND DEPARTURE                                    BYGDØY PENINSULA

**By ferry** The most enjoyable way to reach the Bygdøy is by ferry #91. This leaves from the Rådhusbrygge (pier 3) behind the Rådhus every 20–30min (April to mid-May & Sept to early Oct daily 8.45am–6pm; mid-May to Aug daily 8.45am–8.45pm; 40kr), returning to a similar schedule. All ferries to the peninsula perform a loop, calling first at the Dronningen dock (10min from Rådhusbrygge) and then the Bygdøynes dock (15min) before returning to the Rådhusbrygge; note that the ferries only go one-way – so there is no service from Bygdøynes to Dronningen. The two most popular attractions – the Viking Ships and Folk museums – are within easy walking distance of the Dronningen dock; the other three are a stone's throw from Bygdøynes. If you decide to walk between the two groups of museums, allow about 15min: the route is well signposted but dull.

**By bus** The alternative to the ferry is bus #30 (every 15–30min; 20min), which runs all year from Jernbanetorget and the Nationaltheatret to the Folk Museum and Viking Ships Museum.

## Norsk Folkemuseum

Museumsveien 10 • Mid-May to mid-Sept daily 10am–6pm; mid-Sept to mid-May Mon–Fri 11am–3pm, Sat & Sun 11am–4pm • 100kr • ⓦ norskfolkemuseum.no • The museum is about 700m up from the Dronningen dock – just follow the signs

The **Norsk Folkemuseum** (Norwegian Folk Museum) combines indoor collections on folk art, furniture, dress and customs with an extensive open-air display of reassembled buildings, mostly wooden barns, stables, storehouses and dwellings from the seventeenth to the nineteenth centuries. Look out also for the imaginative temporary exhibitions, for which the museum has a well-deserved reputation. Pick up a free **map** of the museum at the entrance. The complex of buildings just beyond the entry turnstiles holds the museum's **indoor collections**, both permanent and temporary.

### Folk art

The permanent **folk art** section on the lower level of the main exhibition building (building B) is delightful, exhibiting samples of handsome carved and painted furniture from the sixteenth century onwards plus examples of the coverlets (see p.71) that were once the pride and joy of many a Norwegian family. It's here you'll also spot the occasional fancily carved mangle board, the significance of which is not at first apparent: these were given by boys to girls as **love gifts** – though quite how a mangle board could be construed as romantic requires a leap of the imagination – and, if the attraction was mutual, the girls gave the boys mittens or gloves. In rural Norway, it was considered improper for courting couples to be seen together during the day, but acceptable (or at least tolerated) at night – and to assist the process parents usually moved girls of marrying age into one of the farm's outhouses, where tokens could be swapped without embarrassment.

### Folk dress

On the next floor up from the folk art, the **folk dress** section is excellent too. Rural customs specified the correct dress for every sort of social gathering with variations in colour and design dependent on the area. Interestingly, Norway's age-old isolation meant that some items of dress imported and adopted in medieval times stayed in vogue for several centuries – the short **tunic** being a case in point. The most striking items are the **bridal headdresses**, at their most elaborate in the *bringesylv*, for which silver jewellery and other precious ornaments were attached to a red bib. Neither was the bridegroom ignored: in many areas, custom dictated they wore a *brudgomsduk*, a richly embroidered square of linen cloth fastened to the shirt.

### Church art

In Building C, a small but informative display on the Norwegian **clergy** serves as a preamble to a substantial collection of Norwegian **church art**, mostly wooden altarpieces, furniture and statues. There's some exquisite carving here with one of the finest items being a Buskerud birchwood altarpiece from 1697, in which a swirling undergrowth of acanthus leaves frames the story of Jesus from the Last Supper to the Resurrection.

**1**

Open-air collection

The **open-air collection** consists of more than 150 reconstructed buildings. Arranged geographically, they provide a marvellous sample of Norwegian rural architecture, somewhat marred by inadequate explanations. That said, it's still worth tracking down the **stave church** (see box, p.173), particularly if you don't plan to travel elsewhere in Norway. Dating from the early thirteenth century but extensively restored in the 1880s, when it was moved here from Gol, near Geilo, the church is a good example of its type, with steep, shingle-covered roofs, dragon finials, an outside gallery and fancily carved doorposts. The interior is cramped and gloomy, the nave preceding a tiny chancel painted with a floral design and sporting a striking if faded *Last Supper* above and behind the altar. Elsewhere, the cluster of buildings from **Setesdal** in southern Norway holds some especially well-preserved dwellings and storehouses from the seventeenth century, while the **Numedal** section contains one of the museum's oldest buildings, a late thirteenth-century house from Rauland whose doorposts are embellished with Romanesque vine decoration.

Many of the buildings are open for viewing and in the summertime **costumed guides** roam the site to both explain the vagaries of Norwegian rural life and demonstrate traditional skills, from spinning and carving to dancing and horn blowing.

## Vikingskipshuset

Huk Aveny 35 • Daily: May–Sept 9am–6pm; Oct–April 10am–4pm • 60kr • ⓦ khm.uio.no

The **Vikingskipshuset** (Viking Ships Museum) occupies a large, cross-shaped hall specially constructed to house a trio of ninth-century Viking ships, with viewing platforms to enable you to see inside the hulls. The museum's star exhibits are the Oseberg and Gokstad ships, named after the places on the west side of the Oslofjord where they were discovered in 1904 and 1880 respectively.

All three oak vessels were retrieved from ritual **burial mounds** in southern Norway, each embalmed in a subsoil of clay, which accounts for their excellent state of preservation. The size of a Viking burial mound denoted the dead person's rank and wealth, while the possessions buried with the body were designed to make the afterlife as comfortable as possible. Implicit was the assumption that a chieftain in this world would be a chieftain in the next, a belief that would subsequently give Christianity, with its alternative, less fatalistic vision, an immediate appeal to those at the bottom of the Viking pile – slaves, for example, were frequently killed and buried with their master or mistress. Quite how the Vikings saw the transfer to the **afterlife** taking place is less certain. The evidence is contradictory: sometimes the Vikings stuck the anchor on board the burial ship in preparation for the spiritual journey, but at other times the vessels were moored to large stones before burial. Neither was ship burial the only type of Viking funeral – far from it. The Vikings buried their dead in mounds and on level ground, with and without grave goods, in large and small coffins, both with and without boats – and they practised cremation too.

### Oseberg ship

The first vessel you see as you enter the museum is the **Oseberg ship**, which is, at 22m long and 5m wide, representative of the type of vessel the Vikings used to navigate fjords and coastal waters. The ship has an ornately carved prow and stern, both of which rise high above the hull, where thirty oar-holes indicate the size of the crew. It is thought to be the burial ship of a Viking chieftain's wife and much of the treasure buried with it was retrieved and is now displayed just behind it. The **grave goods** reveal an attention to detail and a level of domestic sophistication not traditionally associated with the Vikings. There are marvellous decorative items like the fierce-looking animal-head posts and exuberantly carved ceremonial pieces, including a sled and a cart, plus a host of smaller, more mundane household items such as shoes, rattles, agricultural tools and cooking pots.

OSEBERG SHIP, VIKINGSKIPHUSET >

**1**

## ANNE STINE AND HELGE INGSTAD – OR HOW THE NORSE BEAT CHRISTOPHER COLUMBUS

Often unnoticed, a modest **monument** beside the entrance to the Vikingskipshuset honours **Helge Marcus Ingstad** (1899–2001) and his wife **Anne Stine** (1918–1997), explorer-archeologists who spent years looking for Norse settlements on the North Atlantic seaboard. Their efforts were inspired by two medieval Icelandic sagas, which detailed the establishment of the colony of **Vinland** somewhere along the American coast in about 1000 AD. Many academics were sceptical, but Ingstad and Stine were proved right when, in 1960, they discovered the remnants of a **Norse village** at L'Anse aux Meadows in Canada's Newfoundland. These remains comprised the foundations of eight turf and timber buildings and a ragbag of archeological finds, including a cloak pin, a stone anvil, nails, pieces of bog iron and an oil lamp. Ingstad and Stine concluded that these were left behind by a group of about one hundred sailors, carpenters and blacksmiths who probably remained at the site for just one or maybe two years – and several hundred years before Columbus reached the Americas.

### The Gokstad and Tune ships

Mixed in among the treasure from the Oseberg ship are finds from the **Gokstad ship**, most memorably an ornate bridle and two dragon-head bedposts, though the Gokstad burial chamber was ransacked by grave robbers long ago and precious little has survived. The Gokstad ship itself is slightly longer and wider than the Oseberg vessel and is quite a bit sturdier too. Its seaworthiness was demonstrated in 1893 when a replica sailed across the Atlantic to the USA. The third vessel, the **Tune ship**, is the smallest of the nautical trio and only fragments survive; these are displayed unrestored, much as they were discovered in 1867 on the eastern side of the Oslofjord.

### The Frammuseet

Bygdøynes • Late Feb to April & Oct daily 10am–4pm; May & Sept daily 10am–5pm; June–Aug daily 9am–6pm; Nov to early Jan Mon–Fri 10am–3pm, Sat & Sun 10am–4pm; closed early Jan to late Feb • 60kr • ⓦ frammuseum.no

Just up from the Bygdøynes dock stands the **Gjøa**, the one-time sealing ship in which **Roald Amundsen** (1872–1928) made the first complete sailing of the Northwest Passage in 1906. The fulfilment of a nautical mission that had preoccupied sailors for several centuries, this was by any measure a remarkable achievement. It took three years, with Amundsen and his crew surviving two icebound winters deep in the Arctic, but this epic journey was soon eclipsed when, in 1911, the Norwegian dashed to the South Pole famously just ahead of the ill-starred Captain Scott. Scott's main mistake was to rely on Siberian ponies to transport his tackle. The animals were useless in Antarctic conditions and Scott and his men ended up pulling the sledges themselves, whereas Amundsen wisely brought a team of huskies.

The ship that carried Amundsen to within striking distance of the South Pole, the **Fram**, is displayed inside the mammoth triangular display hall that is the **Frammuseet** (Fram Museum). Designed by Colin Archer, a Norwegian shipbuilder of Scots ancestry, and launched in 1892, the *Fram*'s design was unique, its sides made smooth to prevent ice from getting a firm grip on the hull, while inside a veritable maze of beams, braces and stanchions held it all together. Living quarters inside the ship were necessarily cramped – as visitors can observe as they wander through the bowels of the vessel, clambering up and down its steep and narrow stairways. It may have been cramped, but – in true Edwardian style – the Norwegians still found space for a piano.

### Frammuseet galleries

The walls of the **three walkway-galleries** surrounding the *Fram* are lined with display cases devoted to polar exploration with one section, on the middle of the three galleries, holding copies of the fascinating hand-coloured **lantern slides** made during the Amundsen expedition to the South Pole. Up above, on the uppermost of the three galleries, are some of the assorted knick-knacks Amundsen and his men took with them, including rifles, snowshoes and surgical instruments. On this uppermost gallery also is an intriguing display on one of Norway's most remarkable men, **Fridtjof Nansen** (1861–1930), an all-rounder who clocked up an extraordinary range of achievements. In 1895, Nansen made an unsuccessful attempt to reach the North Pole having previously hiked across Greenland. He then proceeded to publish six volumes of scientific observations on the Arctic before championing the cause of an independent Norway – and the break-up of the Norway–Sweden union. Later, he became a leading figure in the League of Nations, running their High Commission for Refugees and organizing the vital supplies that saved literally millions of Russians from starvation during the famine of 1921–22. He was awarded the Nobel Peace Prize in 1922.

### The Kon-Tiki Museet

Bygdøynes • Daily: March & Oct 10am–4pm; April, May & Sept 10am–5pm; June–Aug 9.30am–5.30pm; Nov–Feb 10.30am–3.30pm • 65kr • ⓦ kon-tiki.no

Across from the Frammuseet, the **Kon-Tiki Museet** (Kon-Tiki Museum) displays the eponymous balsawood raft on which, in 1947, the Norwegian **Thor Heyerdahl** (1914–2002) made his famous journey across the Pacific from Peru to Polynesia. Heyerdahl wanted to prove the trip could be done: he was convinced that the first Polynesian settlers had sailed from pre-Inca Peru, and rejected prevailing opinions that South American balsa rafts were unseaworthy. Looking at the flimsy raft, you could be forgiven for agreeing with Heyerdahl's doubters – and for wondering how the crew didn't murder each other after a day, never mind several weeks in such a confined space, especially as – horror upon horror – one of them brought his guitar. The whole saga is outlined here in the museum, and if you're especially interested, the story is also told in his book *The Kon-Tiki Expedition*.

Heyerdahl went on to attempt several other voyages, sailing across the Atlantic in a papyrus boat, **Ra II**, in 1970, to prove that there could have been contact between Egypt and South America. *Ra II* is also displayed here and the exploit is recorded in another of Heyerdahl's books, *The Ra Expeditions*. Preoccupied with transoceanic contact between prehistoric peoples, Heyerdahl organized two major archeological expeditions to **Easter Island**, one in 1955–56 and again in 1986–88. Heyerdahl was keen to demonstrate that there had been contact between the island and the mainland of South America and, although many still dispute his theory, it has now received a degree of acceptance. Perhaps more importantly, Heyerdahl undertook invaluable work in restoring the island's giant statues – the Moai – and the museum gives the lowdown.

### Norsk Maritimt Museum

Bygdøynes • Mid-May to Aug daily 10am–6pm; Sept to mid-May Tues–Fri 10am–3pm, Sat & Sun 10am–4pm • 60kr • ⓦ marmuseum.no

Across from the Kon-Tiki Museet, the **Norsk Maritimt Museum** (Norwegian Maritime Museum) fills out two buildings, the larger of which is a modern brick structure holding a varied collection of all things nautical. In the museum's basement, there are regular showings of a twenty-minute film on the Norwegian coast and up above, on the ground floor, are temporary exhibitions and a display of old sailing boats and ships' figureheads. The bulk of the permanent collection is shown on the two floors above, beginning on the first floor with pinpoint-accurate ship models, a peculiar-looking fog cannon dating to 1900, a section on shipwrecks, old passenger-ferry cabins and even part of the deck of an old sailing ship from 1893. Here also is the so-called **Gibraltar boat**, a perilously fragile, canvas-and-board home-made craft on which a bunch of Norwegian sailors fled Morocco for British Gibraltar after their ship had been impounded by the Vichy French authorities in World War II. Up above, the top floor chimes in with more models and what is reputed to be the **oldest surviving Norwegian boat**, a carved-out tree trunk about two thousand years old.

The museum's second building, the **Båthallen** (boat hall), holds an extensive collection of small and medium-sized wooden boats from all over Norway, mostly inshore sailing and fishing craft from the nineteenth century, though, frankly, non-sailors may find it all of limited interest.

## Henie-Onstad Kunstsenter

Sonja Henies vei 31, Høvikodden • Tues–Fri 11am–7pm, Sat & Sun 11am–5pm • 80kr • ☏ 67 80 48 80, Ⓦ hok.no • Bus #151 from Oslo S bus terminal (every 15–30min; 25min), and ask to be let off at the Høvikodden bus stop (or else you'll go whistling past), from which it's a 5–10min walk from the Kunstsenter; by car the Kunstsenter is close to – and signposted from – the E18 road to Drammen

Overlooking the Oslofjord, some 15km west of the city centre in Høvikodden, the **Henie-Onstad Kunstsenter** (Henie-Onstad Art Centre) is one of Norway's most prestigious modern art centres. There's no false modesty here – it's all about art as an expression of wealth – and the low-slung, modernistic building is a glossy affair located on a handsomely landscaped, wooded headland. The gallery was founded in the 1960s by ice-skater-cum-movie-star **Sonja Henie** (1910–69) and her third husband, the shipowner-cum-art-collector Niels Onstad. Henie won three Olympic gold medals (1928, 1932 and 1936) and went on to appear in a string of lightweight Hollywood musicals. Many of her accumulated cups and medals are displayed in a room of their own, and they once prompted a critic to remark: "Sonja, you'll never go broke. All you have to do is hock your trophies." Despite her successes, Henie was not universally admired – far from it, not least because of her links with the Nazi elite both before and during World War II.

The wealthy couple accumulated an extensive collection of **twentieth-century painting and sculpture**. Matisse, Miró and Picasso, postwar French abstract painters, Expressionists and modern Norwegians all feature, but these now compete for gallery space with **temporary exhibitions** of contemporary art, making it impossible to predict what part of the permanent collection will be on display at any one time. After the museum, be sure to spend a little time wandering the surrounding **Skulpturparken** (Sculpture Park), where you'll see work by the likes of Henry Moore and Arnold Haukeland; plans of the park are available at reception.

## Frognerparken

Take tram #12 (central stops include Oslo S and Aker Brygge); get off at Vigelandsparken, the stop after Frogner plass

The green expanse of **Frognerparken** (Frogner Park), to the northwest of the city centre, incorporates one of Oslo's most celebrated and popular cultural targets, the open-air **Vigelandsparken**. This, along with the nearby **museum**, commemorates a modern Norwegian sculptor of world renown, **Gustav Vigeland** (1869–1943), displaying a good proportion of his work, including over two hundred figures in bronze, granite and cast iron. These were all presented to the city in return for favours received by way of a studio and apartment during the years 1921–30. The park is also home to Frogner Manor, which now houses the **Oslo Bymuseet**.

### The Vigelandsparken

Kirkeveien • Daylight hours • Free

A country boy, raised on a farm just outside Mandal, on the south coast, **Gustav Vigeland** began his career as a woodcarver but later, when studying in Paris, he fell under the influence of Rodin, and switched to stone, iron and bronze. He started work on the **Vigelandsparken** in 1924, and was still working on it when he died almost twenty years later. It's a literally fantastic concoction, medieval in spirit and complexity, and it was here that Vigeland had the chance to let his imagination run riot. Indeed, when the place was unveiled, many city folk were simply overwhelmed – and no wonder. From the monumental wrought-iron gates on Kirkeveien, the central path

## EMANUEL VIGELAND

Gustav Vigeland (see opposite) enthusiasts may be interested in the work of the great man's younger and lesser-known brother, **Emanuel Vigeland** (1875–1948), a respected artist in his own right. His stained-glass windows can be seen in Oslo's Domkirke (see p.63), while the **Emanuel Vigeland Museum** (Sun only noon–4pm; 40kr; Ⓦ emanuelvigeland.museum.no), 10km or so northwest of the city centre at Grimelundsveien 8 (T-bane #1 to Slemdal and a 10min walk), has a collection of his frescoes, sculptures, paintings and drawings.

takes you to the **footbridge** over the river and a world of frowning, fighting and posturing bronze figures – the local favourite is *Sinnataggen* (The Angry Child), who has been rubbed smooth by a thousand hands. Beyond, the **central fountain** is an enormous bowl representing the burden of life, supported by straining, sinewy bronze Goliaths; a cascade of water tumbles down into a pool flanked by figures engaged in play or talk, or simply resting or standing.

Yet it is the 20m-high **obelisk** up on the stepped embankment just beyond the central fountain that really takes the breath away. It's a deeply humanistic **work**, a writhing mass of sculpture that depicts the cycle of life as Vigeland saw it: a vision of humanity playing, fighting, teaching, loving, eating and sleeping – and clambering on and over each other to reach the top. The granite sculptures grouped around the obelisk are exquisite too, especially the toddlers, little pot-bellied figures who tumble over muscled adults, providing the perfect foil to the real children who crawl all over them, giggling and screaming.

### The Vigeland-museet

Nobels gate 32 • June–Aug Tues–Sun 10am–5pm; Sept–May Tues–Sun noon–4pm • 50kr, but free Oct–Dec • Ⓦ vigeland.museum.no

The distinctive dark-red-brick **Vigeland-museet** (Vigeland Museum), on the southern edge of the Frognerpark, was Gustav Vigeland's studio and home during the 1920s. It was built for him by the city, who let him live here rent-free on condition that the building – and its contents – passed back to public ownership on his death. It's still stuffed with all sorts of items related to the sculpture park, including photographs of the workforce, discarded or unused sculptures, woodcuts, preparatory pieces, and scores of plaster casts. Vigeland was obsessed with his creation during his last decades, and you get the feeling that given half a chance he would have had himself cast and exhibited. As it is, his ashes were placed in the museum tower.

### The Oslo Bymuseet

Frognerveien 67 • Tues–Sun: June–Aug 11am–5pm; Sept–May 11am–4pm • Free • Ⓦ oslomuseum.no

The mildly diverting **Oslo Bymuseet** (Oslo City Museum) is housed in the expansive, eighteenth-century **Frogner Manor**. The buildings are actually rather more interesting than the museum: a central courtyard is bounded on one side by the half-timbered Manor House, complete with its dinky little clocktower, and by antique agricultural buildings on the other three – and if the weather is good the courtyard is a pleasant spot for a cup of tea. The **Bymuseet** is in one of the old agricultural buildings – the renovated barn – and holds a sequence of displays exploring the history of the city. Among many others, there are sections on medicine, prisons, kitchens, the fire brigade and the police, but it's the paintings and photos of old Oslo and its people that catch the eye.

## The Nordmarka

Crisscrossed by **hiking trails** and **cross-country ski routes**, the forested hills and lakes that comprise the **Nordmarka** occupy a tract of land that extends deep inland from central Oslo, but is still within the city limits for some 30km. A network of byroads, as well as two T-bane lines (#1 and #3), provides dozens of access points to this wilderness, which is extremely popular with the capital's outdoor-minded citizens. **Den Norske Turistforening**

**1**

(DNT), the Norwegian hiking organization, maintains a handful of staffed and unstaffed huts here – and its Oslo branch has detailed **maps** and sells DNT membership (see p.92).

## Holmenkollen Skimuseet and ski jump

Kongeveien 5 • **Skimuseet** Daily: June–Aug 9am–8pm; Sept 9am–5pm; Oct–May 10am–4pm • 100kr • Ⓦ holmenkollen.com
**Ski Simulator** Daily: May & Sept 10am–5pm; June–Aug 10am–8pm; Oct–April 10am–4pm • 55kr • Ⓦ skisimulator.no • T-bane #1 to Holmenkollen; the Skimuseet and ski jump are about 1km from the T-bane station

**Holmenkollen** is one of Norway's busiest ski resorts, its popularity bolstered by its international **ski jump**, a gargantuan affair that dwarfs its surroundings. A mountain of metal steps leads up to the top of the ski jump from where the view down is, for most people, horrifyingly steep. It seems impossible that the tiny bowl at the bottom could pull the skier up in time – or that anyone could possibly want to jump off in the first place. When competition skiers aren't hurling themselves off it, the ski jump can be visited as part of the **Skimuseet** (Ski Museum), whose various exhibits explore the history of skiing at some length, and there's a **Ski Simulator** here as well.

## Frognerseteren and Ullevålseter lodges

**Frognerseteren** Mon–Sat 11am–10pm, Sun 11am–9pm • Ⓦ frognerseteren.no **Ullevålseter** Tues–Sun 9am–5pm; July Tues–Sun 10am–4pm • ☎ 22 14 35 58, Ⓦ ullevalseter.no

Five stops on from Holmenkollen, a thirty-minute ride north of the city centre, **Frognerseteren** is the terminus of T-bane #1. From the station, it's just a couple of hundred metres to Frognerseteren's large and good-looking wooden **lodge**, where the views from the terrace out over Oslo and the Oslofjord are much more enjoyable than the food. From the T-bane terminus, there's also a choice of **signposted trails** across the surrounding countryside. Forest footpaths link Frognerseteren with **Sognsvannet** to the east (see below), an arduous and not especially rewarding trek over the hills of about 5km. Locals mostly shun this route in summer, but it's really popular in winter with parents teaching their children to cross-country ski. A better alternative, at least in summer, is the longer but more interesting hike to Sognsvannet via **Ullevålseter**, where the lodge has a very good café serving excellent home-made apple cake. The whole route is about 9km long, and takes about three hours to complete.

## Sognsvannet

T-bane #3 to Sognsvann terminus (15min from central Oslo), from where it's a 5min walk straight ahead down the slope to the lake

The T-bane trip to the **Sognsvann terminus** is not as pleasant a journey as the T-bane trip to Frognerseteren (see above) – the landscape is flatter and you never really leave the city behind – but Sognsvann is but a brief walk from **Sognsvannet**, an attractive lake flanked by forested hills and encircled by an easy four-kilometre hiking trail. The lake is iced over until the end of March or early April, but thereafter it's a perfect spot for a picnic or a swim, though Norwegian assurances about the warmth of the water should be treated with caution (or mirth). Forest footpaths link Sognsvannet with Frognerseteren.

# The islands of the inner Oslofjord

The archipelago of low-lying, lightly forested **islands** to the south of the city centre in the **inner Oslofjord** is the capital's summer playground, and makes going to the **beach** a viable option, especially on warm summer days when the less populated islands become favourite party venues for the city's youth.

**ARRIVAL AND DEPARTURE**      **THE ISLANDS OF THE INNER OSLOFJORD**

**By ferry** Passenger ferries to the islands leave from the Vippetangen quay, at the foot of Akershusstranda – a 20min walk or 5min ride on bus #60 from Jernbanetorget. Ferry tickets cost 27kr each way, though the Oslo Pass and all other transport passes are valid and there's also a ferry day-pass (*Øybilletten*) allowing unlimited inter-island travel (45kr). There are automatic ticket machines on the quayside.

## Hovedøya

Ferry #92 daily: mid-March to late May & Sept to mid-Oct every 1hr–1hr 30min 7.30am–6.30pm; late May to Aug hourly 7.30am–11.30pm; mid-Oct to mid-March 5 daily; 5min

Conveniently, **Hovedøya**, the nearest island to the city centre, is also the most interesting and probably the prettiest, its rocky, rolling hills decorated with woods and pastures. There are several specific attractions too, beginning with the **Kunstverket** (early July to late Aug Wed–Sun 1–5pm; free), a little art gallery housed in an old building just up from the jetty, where there are displays of contemporary art. There are also the substantial ruins of a **Cistercian monastery**, built by English monks in the twelfth century, and incidental **military remains**, reminders of the time when the island was garrisoned and armed to protect Oslo's harbour. Maps of the island are displayed here and there – there's one at the jetty – and these help with orientation, but on an islet of this size – it's just ten minutes' walk from one end to the other – getting lost is pretty much impossible. There are plenty of **footpaths** to wander, you can swim at the shingle **beaches** on the south shore, and there's a seasonal **café** opposite the monastery ruins. Camping, however, is not permitted as Hovedøya is a protected area, which is also why there are no summer homes.

## Langøyene

Ferry #94 late May to Aug hourly 9am to 6.30/9pm; 15min

After Hovedøya, the pick of the other islands is **Langøyene**, a pint-sized, H-shaped islet, just ten minutes' walk or so from one side to the other, where a central meadow is flanked on either side by low, lightly forested rocky hills. There are no houses on the island and no roads to speak of, but there is a long and narrow sandy(ish) **beach**, plus a rudimentary café. Most visitors, however, bring their own supplies, especially those who camp here – there's no campsite as such but **wilderness camping** is permitted and quite a few visitors do just that.

## ARRIVAL AND DEPARTURE
OSLO

Downtown Oslo lies at the heart of a superb public transport system, which makes arriving and departing convenient and straightforward. The principal arrival hub is **Oslo Sentralstasjon** (usually shortened to **Oslo S**), a large complex that includes the main train and bus stations, city tram, metro and bus stops, and exchange facilities; it is at the eastern end of the main thoroughfare, Karl Johans gate. The other if less comprehensive transport hub is **Nationaltheatret**, at the west end of Karl Johans gate, which is handier for most city-centre sights and Oslo's main harbour. There are two **tourist information offices** – one at Oslo S and another close to Nationaltheatret, on Fridtjof Nansens plass (see p.92).

### BY PLANE

#### OSLO GARDERMOEN AIRPORT

**Oslo Gardermoen airport** (Ⓦosl.no) is 45km north of the city centre, just off the E6 motorway. It's a lavish affair designed in true pan-Scandinavian style, with high ceilings and acres of lightly varnished pine. Departures is on the upper level, Arrivals on the lower, where there are also currency exchange facilities, car rental offices (see p.91) and a visitor information desk. There are three ways to get from the airport to the centre of Oslo by public transport – express train, local train and airport bus.

**By train** The fastest and most expensive way (barring taxis) to get to central Oslo is the FlyToget (Airport Express train; daily every 10–20min 5.30am–12.30pm; 170kr one-way, 340kr return; Ⓦflytoget.no), which takes 20min to reach Oslo S with some trains continuing onto Nationaltheatret. Alternatively, several NSB (Norwegian Railway) regional trains – including the hourly

Lillehammer to Skien service – stop at the airport before proceeding on to Oslo S and usually Nationaltheatret (around 30min; 110kr one-way, 220kr return). Note also that there are express trains north from Gardermoen to a number of destinations, including Trondheim; long-distance services often require a reservation – details and reservations at the train ticket office in Arrivals.

**By bus** Flybussen (Mon–Fri 4am–10pm, Sat & Sun 4am–9pm; every 15–30min; 150kr one-way, 250kr return; Ⓦflybussen.no/oslo) depart from outside the Arrivals concourse for the main downtown bus station, Oslo Bussterminalen, part of the Oslo S complex; the journey takes about 55min, traffic depending. These buses then continue onto the Radisson *Blu Scandinavia Hotel* on Holbergs gate with a couple of stops in between – one is outside the *Hotel Bondeheimen* (see p.93). For Gardermoen departures, the Flybussen follows the same route in the opposite direction. In addition, Flybusseksspressen (☎177

**1**

from within Oslo, ☎815 00 176 from without; ⓦflybussekspressen.no) operates a variety of bus services from the airport direct to the small towns surrounding Oslo at regular intervals and at reasonable rates.

**By taxi** The taxi fare from Gardermoen to the city centre is a wallet-singeing 700kr. There's a taxi rank immediately outside Arrivals.

### OSLO (TORP) AIRPORT

Oslo second largest airport, **Oslo (Torp)** (ⓦtorp.no), is just outside the town of Sandefjord, about 110km southwest of Oslo.

**By bus** The Torp-Ekspressen bus (ⓦtorpekspressen.no) links this airport with the main downtown bus station, Oslo Bussterminalen, part of the Oslo S complex, about six times daily; the bus schedule, both to and from Torp, links with flight arrivals and departures. The bus journey takes a little under two hours and costs 200kr one-way, 340kr return; you buy tickets from the driver. There is also a train service to Oslo S (see p.118).

### OSLO (RYGGE) AIRPORT

The third airport, **Oslo (Rygge)**(ⓦen.ryg.no), is 8km southeast of Moss, a small town about 60km south of Oslo.

**By bus** The Rygge-Ekspressen bus (☎177, ⓦrygge -ekspressen.no) runs to the main bus terminal at Oslo S. The bus schedule links with flight arrivals and departures and you buy tickets from the driver. A one-way fare is 140kr, return 250kr, and the journey time is about 45min.

### BY TRAIN

**Oslo S** Operated by NSB (Norwegian State Railways; ☎815 00 888, ⓦnsb.no), both international and domestic trains use Oslo Sentralstasjon, known as Oslo S, which is beside Jernbanetorget, the square at the eastern end of the main drag, Karl Johans gate. There are money exchange facilities and a post office here, and just outside – in the distinctive Trafikanten clock tower – is one of the city's two tourist offices. Reservations are compulsory on most long-distance trains heading out of Oslo. Note that almost all trains heading north from Oslo S stop at Oslo Gardermoen airport.

**Nationaltheatret station** Many domestic trains also pass through the Nationaltheatret station, at the west end of Karl Johans gate, which is slightly more convenient for the city centre.

Destinations Åndalsnes (3 daily, change at Dombås; 5hr 30min); Arendal (4–5 daily, change at Nelaug; 4hr 10min); Bergen (4 daily; 6hr 50min); Dombås (3–5 daily; 4hr); Fredrikstad (hourly; 1hr 10min); Geilo (3–4 daily; 3hr 30min); Halden (hourly; 1hr 50min); Hamar (hourly; 1hr 30min); Hjerkinn (2–3 daily; 4hr 30min; request stop only); Kongsberg (2–4 daily; 1hr 10min); Kongsvoll (2–3 daily; 4hr 30min; request stop only); Kristiansand (2–4 daily; 4hr

30min); Kvam (1–2 daily except Sat; 3hr 40min; request stop only); Lillehammer (hourly; 2hr); Myrdal (4 daily; 4hr 50min); Otta (2–4 daily; 3hr 30min); Røros (4–6 daily, change at Hamar; 5hr); Sandefjord (hourly; 1hr 50min); Stavanger (2–4 daily; 8hr); Tønsberg (hourly; 1hr 30min); Trondheim (2–4 daily; 6hr 40min); Voss (4 daily; 5hr 30min).

### BY BUS

**Bussterminalen** Part of the Oslo S complex, the central Bussterminalen (bus terminal) is a short, signposted walk northeast from the train station on Schweigårdsgate. International and domestic long-distance buses arrive at and depart from here, as do the SAS Flybussen (for Oslo Gardermoen airport), the Torp-Ekspressen (for Oslo Torp airport), and the Rygge-Ekspressen (for Oslo Rygge airport). There is a general bus station information desk.

**Bus companies** Nor-Way Bussekspress (☎815 44 444, ⓦnor-way.no) is the largest domestic carrier. Among the other bus companies using the bus station, Swebus (☎800 58 444, ⓦswebus.se) operates a number of international buses to Sweden and Denmark, including Copenhagen, Gothenburg and Stockholm. Another major carrier is Lavprisekspressen (☎67 98 04 80, ⓦlavprisekspressen .no), which concentrates on long-distance Norwegian routes.

Lavprisekspressen to: Stavanger (1–2 daily; 9hr); Trondheim (2–3 daily; 8hr 30min).

Nor-Way Bussekspress to: Ålesund (2 daily; 10hr); Åndalsnes (2 daily; 8hr); Balestrand (3 daily, change at Sogndal; 8hr 30min); Bergen (3 daily; 12hr); Dombås (2 daily; 6hr); Haugesund (3 daily; 8hr 45min); Kongsberg (6 daily; 1hr 30min); Kristiansand (6 daily; 5hr); Lillehammer (6 daily; 3hr); Lom (3 daily; 6hr 40min); Måløy (3 daily; 11hr); Mundal, Fjærland (3 daily; 7hr 50min); Otta (4 daily; 5hr 30min); Rjukan (6 daily, change at Notodden; 3hr 30min); Sogndal (3 daily; 7hr); Stavanger (5 daily, change at Kristiansand; 10hr); Stryn (3 daily; 8hr 40min).

### BY CAR FERRY

**DFDS Seaways and Stena Line** DFDS Seaways (☎21 62 13 40, ⓦdfds.no) and Stena Line (☎02010, ⓦstenaline .no) operate car ferries from Denmark to Oslo – Stena Line from Fredrikshavn, DFDS from Copenhagen. The ferries of both companies dock at the Vippetangen quay, a 15min walk (1200m) south from Oslo S: take Akershusstranda/ Skippergata to Karl Johans gate and turn right. Alternatively, catch bus #60 marked "Jernbanetorget" (Mon–Fri 6.30am to midnight, Sat from 8.30am, Sun from 9am; every 20–30min; 5min).

**Color Line** On Color Line (☎810 00 811, ⓦcolorline.no) services from Kiel, you'll arrive at the Hjortneskaia, some 3km west of the city centre. From here, bus #33 runs to the Nationaltheatret, bang in the centre of the city (every

30min: Mon–Fri 7am–8pm, Sat 10am–5pm) – but not to Oslo S.

## BY CAR

Driving into Oslo by car, you'll have to proceed through one of the **automatic toll-points** that encircle the city; the toll for ordinary cars is 26kr. All number plates are read electronically and an invoice is sent to either the car rental company concerned or the registered owner of the vehicle. Oslo's ring roads encircle and tunnel under the city; if you follow the signs for "Ring 1" you'll be delivered right into the centre and emerge (eventually) at the multistorey Sentrum P-hus car park (see below).

**Car rental** Bislet Bilutleie, Pilestredet 70 (☎ 22 60 00 00, ⓦ bislet.no); Europcar, several downtown locations and at Gardermoen airport (☎ 64 81 05 60, ⓦ europcar .no); Hertz, several Oslo locations including Holbergs gate 30 (☎ 22 21 00 00), and at Gardermoen airport (☎ 64 81 05 50, ⓦ hertz.no); Sixt, at Gardermoen airport (☎ 66 69 99 00, ⓦ sixt.no). See also under "Bilutleie" in the *Yellow Pages*.

**Parking** You won't need your car to sightsee in Oslo, so you'd do best to use a designated car park. There are half a dozen multistorey car parks in the centre, though some of them operate restricted hours: both the Sentrum P-hus at CJ Hambros Plass 1, two blocks north of Karl Johans gate, and Aker Brygge P-hus, Sjøgata 4, are open 24hr. Charges begin at 27kr for 30min during the daytime (Mon–Sat 7am–7pm), up to a maximum of 240kr for 24hr; Sun evening (after 7pm) and overnight rates are heavily discounted. Alternatively, you can park in pay-and-display car parks and at on-street metered spaces around the city. Identified by blue "P" signs, these metered spaces are owned and operated by the municipality, and are usually free of charge from Mon to Fri between 5pm and 9am and over the weekend after 3pm on Saturday. There is usually a maximum 2hr stay in pay periods. Charges vary considerably: a prime on-street parking spot (if you can get one) costs 70kr for 2hr, half that further out. Oslo Pass (see p.61) holders get free parking in all municipal parking spaces, but have to abide by the posted regulations. Pass holders must be sure to write the vehicle registration number, date and time on the card in the space provided.

**Car breakdown** Both of the two major national breakdown companies have a 24hr helpline. They are Falck (☎ 02222) and Viking Redningstjeneste (☎ 06000).

## GETTING AROUND

Oslo's safe and efficient public transport system consists of buses, trams, a small underground rail system (the Tunnelbanen, or T-bane) and local ferries, run by Oslo Sporveier.

**Information** The main transport information office, Trafikanten, is at the foot of the distinctive, transparent clocktower in front of Oslo S, on the Jernbanetorget (Mon–Fri 7am–8pm, Sat & Sun 8am–6pm; ☎ 177, ⓦ trafikanten.no). The office, which shares its premises with one of the city's two tourist offices, sells tickets and passes, has racks of free timetables and gives away a useful visitor's transit map, the *Besøkskart*, though this is also available at the tourist office. Route plans for the buses and trams are also posted at most central stops. There's a second, smaller Trafikanten information office on the harbourfront at the start of Aker Brygge (Mon–Fri 7am–7pm, Sat 10am–6pm).

**Tickets** Flat-fare tickets for all forms of city transport cost 28kr if purchased before the journey, or 44kr if purchased from a bus or tram driver or on a ferry. There are automatic ticket machines at all T-bane stations, most tram stops and some bus stops. Tickets are valid for unlimited travel within the city boundaries for 1hr including transfers; seniors (67+) and children 4 to 15 years old travel half-price, babies and toddlers free. All tickets and passes must be stamped or electronically read when they are first used: buses, trams and T-bane stations all have automatic stamping machines, but on ferries there's usually a conductor. Ticket inspectors roam around checking up on things and if you haven't got a valid, stamped pass or ticket you will receive a hefty on-the-spot fine.

**Passes** There are several ways to cut costs. The best is to buy an Oslo Pass (see box, p.61), which is valid on the whole network and on certain routes into the surrounding *kommunes* – but not on trains or buses to the airport. If you're not into museums, however, a straight travel pass might be a better buy. A 24hr pass (*Dagskort*) is valid for unlimited travel within the city limits and costs 75kr, while a seven-day pass costs 220kr. Passes and tickets can be bought at the automatic ticket machines (see opposite), as well as from the Trafikanten office, which also sells discounted electronic travel cards – *Reisekortet* – for frequent travellers.

## BY BUS

Many **city bus services** originate at – or pass through – Jernbanetorget, the square in front of Oslo S, while most suburban services depart from the Bussterminalen nearby. A second common port of call is Nationaltheatret further to the west near the harbour. Most buses stop running at around midnight, though on Fri and Sat nights **night buses** (*nattbussen*) take over on certain major routes.

**1**

## BY TRAM

The city's trams run on six routes through the city, crisscrossing the centre from east to west, and sometimes duplicating the bus routes. They are a bit slower than the buses, but are a rather more enjoyable and relaxing way of getting about. Major stops include Jernbanetorget, Nationaltheatret and Aker Brygge. Most operate regularly – every 10–20min (6am–midnight).

## BY T-BANE

The **Tunnelbanen** – T-bane – has six lines which converge to share a common slice of track crossing the city centre from Majorstuen in the west to Tøyen in the east, with Nationaltheatret, Stortinget, Jernbanetorget/Oslo S and Grønland stations in between. From this central section, lines run west (*Vest*) and east (*Øst*) out into the suburbs. The system mainly serves commuters, but you may find it useful for hopping around the centre and for trips out into the forested hills of the Nordmarka. Outside the central section, trains travel above ground. The system runs from around 6am until 12.30am.

## BY COMMUTER TRAIN

Several NSB commuter trains link Oslo with satellite towns like Moss and Drammen; departures are from Oslo S, with many also stopping at Nationaltheatret.

## BY FERRY

**To Bygdøy** As far as the average visitor is concerned, the most popular services are the summertime ferries (mid-March to mid-Oct) that leave from Pier #3, immediately behind the Rådhus, bound for the museums of the Bygdøy peninsula (see p.80).

**To Oslofjord** There are all-year ferry services to a number of Oslofjord islets, including Hovedøya, and a late May to Aug service to Langøyene, which depart from the Vippetangen quay, 1200m south of Oslo S. To get to the Vippetangen quay by public transport, take bus #60 from Jernbanetorget.

## BY TAXI

**Fares** The speed and efficiency of Oslo's public transport system means that you should rarely have to resort to a taxi, which is probably just as well as they are very expensive. Taxi fares are regulated, with the tariff varying according to the time of day – night-times are about 25 percent more expensive than daytime – though on many longer routes there is a fixed tariff: central Oslo to Gardermoen airport, for instance, costs 700kr.

**Taxi ranks** There are taxi ranks dotted all over the city centre and outside all the big hotels. You can also telephone Oslo Taxi on ☎02323 or Norgestaxi on ☎08000.

## BY BIKE

Renting a bicycle is a pleasant way to get around Oslo, particularly as the city has a reasonable range of cycle tracks and many roads have cycle lanes – and, furthermore, central Oslo is not engulfed by traffic thanks to its network of motorway tunnels.

**Bike rental** There is a municipal bike rental scheme (Easter to Nov; ⓦoslobysykkel.no) in which bikes are released like supermarket trolleys from racks all over the city. Visitors can join the scheme (and receive the appropriate smartcard) at the tourist office by paying 90kr for a 24hr cycling pass plus a substantial refundable deposit. Bikes can be used for up to 3hr before they have to be dropped off (or swapped) at one of the bike racks; otherwise cyclists get penalized. A map showing you the location of the racks and cycle lanes is provided by the tourist office, and is also available on the website.

## INFORMATION

### CITY TOURIST OFFICES

**Main tourist office** Fridtjof Nansens plass 5, across from the Rådhus (April, May & Sept Mon–Sat 9am–5pm; June–Aug daily 9am–7pm; Oct–March Mon–Fri 9am–4pm; ☎815 30 555, ⓦvisitoslo.com). Oslo's main tourist information office has a full range of information about Oslo and its environs, and issues both free city maps and maps of the public transport system. They also sell the Oslo Pass (see p.61), supply free copies of both the very thorough *Oslo Guide* and the listings brochure *What's On in Oslo*, and can also make accommodation reservations.

**Trafikanten tourist office** Trafikanten tower, Jernbanetorget (Mon–Fri 7am–8pm; Sat & Sun: Oct–April 8am–6pm; May–Sept 8am–8pm; ☎815 30 555, ⓦvisitoslo.com). At the base of the Trafikanten tower in front of Oslo S, the city's second tourist office offers the same services as at the Fridtjof Nansens plass branch and shares its premises with the city's main public transport information centre (see p.91).

### YOUTH INFORMATION OFFICE

**Ungdomsinformasjonen** (**Use-it**) Møllergata 3, a brief walk from Oslo S (July & Aug Mon & Wed–Fri 9am–6pm, Tues 11am–6pm; Sept noon–5pm; Sept–June Mon–Fri 9.30am–5pm; ☎24 14 98 20, ⓦuse-it.no). Oslo has a youth information shop, which produces a free annual booklet, *Streetwise*, giving a roundup of local bars and clubs and providing all sorts of advice and information about inexpensive food and accommodation. They also offer free internet access and carry all manner of fliers for gigs and concerts.

### HIKING INFORMATION OFFICE

**Den Norske Turistforening (DNT)** Storgata 3 (Mon–Fri

10am–5pm, Thurs 10am–6pm, Sat 10am–3pm; ☏ 22 82 28 22, Ⓦ dntoslo.no). The Norwegian hiking organization's city-centre office stocks a full range of Norwegian hiking maps, books and equipment. Also sells DNT membership (530kr per annum), which confers substantial discounts at DNT huts.

## ACCOMMODATION

Oslo has the range of **hotels** you would expect of a capital city, though surprisingly few of them are independents – most are chain hotels with Thon and Rica the two big players. The city also has a light smattering of **B&Bs** and **guesthouses** plus a trio of **youth hostels**.

**Where to stay** To appreciate the full flavour of the city, you're best off staying on or near the western reaches of Karl Johans gate – between the Stortinget and the Nationaltheatret – though noise can be a real problem here in the summertime when Oslo's youth take to the streets in numbers, peaceable but loud: be sure to take a room away from the street unless you are a heavy sleeper. Most of the city's less expensive lodgings are further to the east in the vicinity of Oslo S, traditionally a rather glum district but one that is slowly improving.

**How to get a good deal** Accommodation prices are firmly pegged to demand and consequently there are often good deals to be had in the summertime when most of the country's business folk are on holiday, leaving many chain hotels struggling for custom. As ever, advance online booking can save you substantial sums, but both tourist offices (see opposite) do provide a same-day and in-person accommodation booking service, and they often get discounted rates too.

## HOTELS

At all but the busiest of times, you should be able to get a fairly small and simple, en-suite double room in a hotel in central Oslo for about 1000kr. You hit the comfort zone at about 1200kr, and luxury from around 1500kr. However, **special offers**, summer specials and weekend deals often make the smarter hotels more affordable than this, with discounts of 30–40 percent commonplace. Also, most room rates are tempered by the inclusion of a good to excellent self-service buffet **breakfast**. The tourist office keeps lists of the day's best offers, or try the places in the following list – but always ring ahead first.

### DOWNTOWN

★ **Best Western Hotell Bondeheimen** Rosenkrantz gate 8 ☏ 23 21 41 00, Ⓦ bondeheimen.com; map pp.62–63. One of Oslo's most enjoyable hotels, dating from 1913, the *Bondeheimen* is handily placed just 2min walk north of Karl Johans gate. Both the public areas and the comfortable bedrooms are attractively decorated in a modern, pan-Scandinavian style, with polished pine everywhere. The inclusive buffet breakfast, served in the *Kaffistova* (see p.96), is substantial, and there's free internet access plus free coffee and tea in the evenings. The rooms towards the back are much quieter than those on the front. **1000kr**

**Clarion Collection Hotel Folketeateret** Storgata 21 ☏ 22 00 57 00, Ⓦ clarionhotel.com; map pp.62–63. In the delightful Art Deco passageway connecting Youngstorget with Storgata, this brand-new, deluxe hotel has 160 slick, modern bedrooms and a rooftop terrace bar. Some of the hotel's original features have been kept, but most have been swept away in a decorative rush. **1900kr**

**Comfort Hotel Xpress** Møllergata 26 ☏ 22 03 11 00, Ⓦ comforthotelxpress.no; map pp.62–63. Opened in 2011, and aimed firmly at the youth/clubbing market, this chain hotel in a seven-storey block does its best to create a cool/relaxed vibe, beginning with the striking Pop Art decor in the foyer. There are few formalities at reception – you check in at the electronic kiosks – and the 180 guest rooms beyond (modernism-meets-spartan) are similarly hi-tech. **695kr**

★ **Continental** Stortingsgata 24–26 ☏ 22 82 40 00, Ⓦ hotelcontinental.no; map pp.62–63. Arguably the classiest hotel in town, family-owned and with swish public areas that ooze an easy comfort – all pastel shades, flowers, and even some Munch paintings (or at least near-perfect copies of them). The bedrooms beyond are extremely comfortable and decorated in a fetching, modern style with delicate patterned wallpaper setting the tone. The hotel is also ideally located, a stone's throw from Karl Johans gate, though the rooms overlooking the street can be noisy. Wonderful, banquet-like breakfasts too. **2400kr** sp/r **1600kr**

**Grand** Karl Johans gate 31 ☏ 23 21 20 00, Ⓦ grand.no; map pp.62–63. Once Norway's most prestigious hotel, its café the haunt of Ibsen and his chums, the *Grand* remains Oslo's most famous hotel, but its 300-odd guest rooms vary enormously: the ones at the front, complete with balconies overlooking Karl Johans gate and all sorts of period touches, are a delight, the ones at the back much more mundane. Hefty weekend and summertime discounts make it much more affordable than you might perhaps expect. Now a Rica hotel. **2000kr**, sp/r **1400kr**

**Oslo Budget Hotel** Skippergata 19; entrance Prinsens gate 6 ☏ 22 41 36 10, Ⓦ budgethotel.no; map pp.62–63. This modest but pleasant hotel, a long-time favourite with budget travellers, is located above shops in a typical Oslo apartment block near Oslo S. The surroundings are a little seedy, but the hotel is cheerful enough, with small but perfectly adequate rooms. **600kr**

**1**

**Perminalen** Øvre Slottsgate 2 ☎ 24 00 55 00, ⓦ perminalen.no; map pp.62–63. This hostel-like hotel has two things going for it – a central location and budget prices: a bed in a four-berth room costs just 370kr, a single 620kr. At these rates, it's hardly surprising that the guest rooms are frugal to positively spartan, though at least all the doubles and singles are en suite. Popular with the Norwegian military. 840kr

**Rica Holberg** Holbergs plass 1 ☎ 23 15 72 00, ⓦ rica .no; map pp.62–63. This grand nineteenth-century building has been thoroughly refurbished both inside and out, but still retains fragments of its historic atmosphere. The public rooms, with their slender pillars and skylight, are appealing, while the bedrooms are spick, span and modern, though one or two of them might be considered a tad small. Overlooks Holbergs plass, a pint-sized square about 500m from the Slottsparken. 1900kr, sp/r 1600kr

**Rica Hotel G20** Grensen 20 ☎ 22 01 64 00, ⓦ rica.no; map pp.62–63. New Rica hotel with a handy central location and 96 modern rooms decorated in shades of white with grey furnishings. They all have iPod docks, flat-screen TVs and floor-to-ceiling windows. There's also a bar lounge and a restaurant. 1800kr

**Rica Victoria** Rosenkrantz gate 13 ☎ 24 14 70 00, ⓦ rica.no; map pp.62–63. A large, modern hotel, just south of Karl Johans gate. Its two hundred spacious rooms have every convenience, and it's justifiably popular with visiting business folk. 1400kr, sp/r 1000kr

**Scandic Edderkoppen** St Olavs plass 1 ☎ 23 15 56 00, ⓦ scandichotels.com; map pp.62–63. Overlooking one of the city's more pleasant, semi-pedestrianized squares, this Scandic hotel occupies a straightforward modern block, but the interior has been creatively remodelled in a bright and stylish modern manner – all spotlights, distinctive curved furniture and patterned carpets. Unusually, it shares its premises with a theatre. 1300kr

**Thon Hotel Europa** St Olavs gate 31 ☎ 23 25 63 00, ⓦ thonhotels.no; map pp.62–63. In a substantial brick tower block, this large and well-maintained chain hotel has 168 briskly decorated modern rooms and a central location – overlooking a mini-square. 1400kr

★ **Thon Hotel Oslo Panorama** Rådhusgata 7b ☎ 23 31 08 00, ⓦ thonhotels.no; map pp.62–63. Barely a 5min walk from Oslo S and the Operahuset, this is one of Oslo's more affordable chain hotels. The foyer is routinely modern, but the spacious rooms occupy an imaginatively converted 1960s tower block just behind – the key selling point being the wide views over the harbour from the upper floors. 1500kr

### WESTSIDE

**Clarion Collection Hotel Gabelshus** Gabels gate 16 ☎ 23 27 65 00, ⓦ clarionhotel.com; map pp.58–59. In a good-looking, ivy-covered building dating from 1912, this attractive, medium-sized hotel stands in a smart residential area a couple of kilometres west of the city centre, off Drammensveien. The public areas are kitted out with antique furnishings, while the bedrooms are smart, very modern and well appointed. Tram #13 from the centre. 1700kr

**Rica Hotel Bygdøy Allé** Bygdøy allé 53 ☎ 23 08 58 00, ⓦ rica.no; map pp.58–59. With its forest of spiky, late nineteenth-century towers, this Rica possesses the most imposing hotel facade in the city. The guest rooms don't quite live up to the exterior – how could they – but they are bright and cheerful and most have pleasant retro touches. The hotel is situated in a busy residential area about 2km west of the centre; to get there, take bus #30 or #31 from Nationaltheatret. 1400kr

**Saga Hotell Oslo** Eilert Sundts gate 39 ☎ 22 55 44 90, ⓦ sagahoteloslo.no; map pp.58–59. West of the centre, in a pleasant and quiet residential area, this 47-room hotel occupies a tastefully updated late nineteenth-century, three-storey block. The decor is mostly charcoal, black and grey and all the guest rooms are well appointed. The nearest tram stop, a 5min walk away, is Rosenberg. 1400kr

### EASTSIDE

**Best Western Anker Hotel** Storgata 55 ☎ 22 99 75 00, ⓦ anker-hotel.no; map p.78. This large budget hotel occupies a high-rise block beside the Akerselva River at the east end of Storgata. The clientele is mainly Norwegian, and the facilities are adequate, if somewhat frugal, though there is free internet access and all the rooms are en suite. Very handy for Grünerløkka, the trendiest part of the city, and just 15min walk from Oslo S, or 5min by tram; the same block also houses the *Anker Hostel* (see opposite). 1800kr, sp/r 850kr

### HOSTELS, B&BS AND GUESTHOUSES

Oslo has three very popular **hostels**, two of them members of the HI-affiliated **Norske Vandrerhjem** (Norwegian Hostelling Association; ⓦ hihostels.no). The city also possesses a handful of **guesthouses**, or *pensjonater*, which offer basic but generally adequate accommodation, either with or without en-suite facilities, though breakfast is not included in the price, and at some places you may need to supply your own sleeping bag. The tourist office has the details of rooms in **private houses**, which are sometimes referred to as **B&Bs**. These can only be booked in person at either of the city's two tourist offices on the day you need the accommodation and there's usually a minimum two-night stay. They cost in the region of 500kr for a single room, and 600–900kr for a double, less off-season, which is something of a bargain especially as many of them have cooking facilities (breakfast is not included), but they are rarely en suite and tend to be well away from the city centre.

**Anker Hostel** Storgata 55 ☎22 99 72 00, ⓦankerhostel.no; map p.78. In the same large modern block as the *Anker Hotel* (see opposite), this hostel has 50 rooms – and 250 beds – all year and extra space in the summertime. The rooms are plain and simple, but perfectly adequate. Bed linen and towels are for rent, or bring your own; sleeping bags are not allowed. The least expensive dorm beds are in 6-bedded rooms, costing 30kr more in a 4-bedded room; singles cost the same as doubles. Breakfast is not included in the price. The hostel is 15min walk from Oslo S or 5min by tram. Dorms 220kr, doubles 580kr

**Cochs Pensjonat** Parkveien 25 ☎23 33 24 00, ⓦcochspensjonat.no; map pp.62–63. Friendly and engaging guesthouse occupying the upper floors of an old apartment block, in a handy location behind the Slottsparken. There are 88 rooms (with 205 beds), each decorated in a frugal modern style – wood laminate floors and so on. There are three different types of room: those with shared facilities cost 700kr for a double (490kr single), en suite 760kr (590kr) and those with a kitchen unit 860kr (640kr). Breakfasts (60kr extra) are served just along the street at *KafeCaffé*, Parkveien 21. 700kr

**Ellingsens Pensjonat** Holtegata 25 ☎22 60 03 59, ⓦellingspensjonat.no; map pp.58–59. Inexpensive accommodation in a large, late nineteenth-century house on the west side of the city centre, just beyond the Slottsparken. Rooms are spacious and those with en suite cost 670kr, 580kr without. Guests have access to a small garden. 580kr

★ **Oslo Vandrerhjem Haraldsheim** Haraldsheimveien 4, Grefsen ☎22 22 29 65, ⓦharaldsheim.no; map pp.58–59. The pick of Oslo's HI hostels, 4km northeast of the centre, has public areas that are comfortable and attractively furnished in brisk, modern style and frugal but clean bedrooms. There are 270 beds in 70 rooms, most of which are four-bedded, and a good number have their own showers and WC. The hostel also has self-catering facilities, a restaurant, internet access and washing machines. The only downside can be parties of noisy schoolchildren. It's a very popular spot, so advance

reservation is essential throughout summer. To get there, take tram #17 from Storgata, near the Domkirke, northeast to the Sinsenkrysset stop, from where it's a 5min (signposted) walk. By road, the hostel is close to – and signed from – Ring 3. The basic en-suite dorm bed price including breakfast is 270kr; singles cost 415kr (en suite 470kr), en-suite doubles 625kr. Open all year except Christmas week. Dorms 245kr, doubles 540kr

**Oslo Vandrerhjem Holtekilen** Micheletsvei 55, Stabekk ☎67 51 80 40, ⓦhihostels.no; map pp.58–59. Much smaller than *Haraldsheim*, this HI hostel occupies part of a college building in its own grounds some 9km west of the city centre off the E18. There are kitchen facilities, an outdoor area and a laundry. Open mid-May to late Aug. Rates, including breakfast, are singles 350kr (en suite 475kr); en-suite doubles 630kr. To get there from Oslo Bussterminalen, take bus #151, #153, #161, #162 or #252 to the Kveldsroveien bus stop, from where it's a 200m walk. Dorms 220kr, doubles 500kr

### CAMPING AND CABINS

The peripheries of Oslo are dotted with **campsites** – a dozen or so are within a 50km radius and the nearest is just 3km away. If you're out of luck with rooms in town, most sites also offer **cabins** (*hytter*), but be sure to ring ahead to check availability.

**Bogstad Camping** Ankerveien 117 ☎22 51 08 00, ⓦbogstadcamping.no; map pp.58–59. Massive campsite on the edge of the Nordmarka, about 9km north of the city centre, with a good range of facilities including self-catering, plus access to the Nordmarka's walking trails and ski slopes. They have fifty or so cabins – from simple to deluxe – with prices starting at 1000kr/night to accommodate two adults. The campsite is open all year. To get there, take bus #32 from Oslo S or the Nationaltheatret; the journey takes about 35min. Tent, car and up to 4 people 270kr, cabins 1000kr

**Ekeberg Camping** Ekebergveien 65 ☎22 19 85 68, ⓦekebergcamping.no; map pp.58–59. Large campsite in a rocky, forested slice of parkland just 3km east of the city centre that's somewhat rudimentary but still popular. To get there, take bus #34 from Oslo S; it's a 10min journey. Open June–Aug. Tent, car and up to 4 people 260kr

## EATING

At the top end of the market, Oslo possesses several dozen fine **restaurants**, the most distinctive of which feature Norwegian cuisine and ingredients, especially fresh North Atlantic fish, but also more exotic dishes of elk, caribou and salted-and-dried cod – for centuries Norway's staple food. There is a reasonable selection of less expensive, non-Scandinavian restaurants too – everything from Italian to Vietnamese. More affordable – and more casual – are the city's **cafés and café-bars**. These run the gamut from homely places offering traditional Norwegian stand-bys to student haunts and ultra-trendy joints. Nearly all serve inexpensive lunches, and many offer excellent, competitively priced evening meals as well, though some cafés close at around 5 or 6pm as do the city's many **coffee houses**, where coffee is, as you might expect, the main deal alongside maybe a light snack. Finally, those carefully counting the kroner will find it easy to buy bread, fruit, snacks and sandwiches from stalls, **supermarkets** and kiosks across the city centre, while

**1**

fast-food joints offering hamburgers and *warme pølser* (hot dogs; 20–25kr) are legion. **Smoking** is forbidden inside every Norwegian bar, café and restaurant – hence the smoky huddles outside.

## CAFÉS, CAFÉ-BARS AND COFFEE HOUSES

### DOWNTOWN

★ **Kafé Celsius** Rådhusgata 19 ☎22 42 45 39, ⓦkafecelsius.no; map pp.62–63. Smashing café-bar occupying imaginatively refurbished old premises just off the cobbled square at the junction of Rådhusgata and Øvre Slottsgate. Especially attractive courtyard seating too – for either a drink or a light meal: a home-made burger, for instance, costs 160kr. Tues–Sat 11.30am–1am, Sun 1–10pm.

**Kaffebrenneriet** Akersgata 45, cnr Grensen ☎24 20 17 28, ⓦkaffebrenneriet.no; map pp.62–63. One of the most central branches of this popular Norwegian coffee-house chain. Serves particularly good espressos and cappuccinos, as well as snacks and fresh, tasty cakes. Bright, modern decor. Mon–Fri 7am–7pm, Sat 9am–5pm.

**Kaffistova** Rosenkrantz gate 8 ☎23 21 41 00, ⓦbondeheimen.com; map pp.62–63. Part of the *Hotell Bondeheimen* (see p.93), this spick-and-span self-service cafeteria serves reasonably tasty, traditional Norwegian cooking in large portions and at very fair prices – reckon on 150kr for a main course. Meatballs, gravy and potatoes are the house speciality. There's usually a vegetarian option, too. Mon–Fri 10am–9pm, Sat & Sun 11am–7pm.

**Kunstnernes Hus** Wergelandsveien 17 ☎22 85 34 10, ⓦkunstnerneshus.no; map pp.62–63. This contemporary art gallery, whose charming Art Deco facade faces the Slottsparken, hosts exhibitions, lectures and concerts upstairs and a fashionable but unpretentious café-bar-cum-restaurant down below on the ground floor and adjoining terrace. Offers good-quality food with a Norwegian slant, with main courses around 220kr. Daily 11am–6pm.

★ **Litteraturhuset** Wergelandsveien 29 ☎22 95 55 30, ⓦlitteraturhuset.no; map pp.62–63. Opposite the tail end of the Slottsparken, this amenable café-bar-cum-bookshop spreads its net wide with poetry readings, public debates and book signings as well as a café and outside terrace. Light meals here – the salads are good – will cost you around 180kr. Café-bar Mon & Tues 10am–midnight, Wed–Sat 10am–3am, Sun noon–8pm; kitchen closes Mon–Sat at 10pm, Sun at 6pm; reduced hours in July.

★ **Pascal Konditori** Tollbugata 11 ☎22 42 11 19, ⓦpascal.no; map pp.62–63. Lovely little café-patisserie comprising two rooms – one pleasantly modern, the other, in the original bakery, decorated with antique, ceramic tiles of cherubs and fruit. Mouthwatering pastries, great coffee and delicious, freshly prepared lunches – the salads (170kr) are delicious and the fish soup (165kr) first-rate. Also at Henrik Ibsen's gate (see p.98). Mon–Sat 10am–5pm.

★ **Stockfleths** Lille Grensen, off Karl Johans gate; C.J. Hambros plass; Prinsens gate 6; ⓦstockfleths.as; map pp.62–63. With good reason, many locals swear by the coffee served at this small chain, which regularly wins awards for its brews. All branches Mon–Fri 7am–7pm, Sat 10am–6pm, Sun noon–6pm.

**Tullins Café** Tullins gate 2 ☎22 20 46 16, ⓦtullins.no; map pp.62–63. The building may be glum – it's a dull modern high-rise – but this ground-floor café-bar is painted in an attractive modern style and furnished with an idiosyncratic mix of bygones. A wide-ranging, notably inexpensive menu covers everything from salads and burgers to pizzas and Indian dishes – reckon on 120kr per main course. There's inexpensive beer here too as the place morphs into a late-night bar. Mon–Thurs 10am–2am, Fri 10am–3.30am, Sat noon–3.30am, Sun noon–1am.

**Vega** Akersgata 74, cnr Thor Olsens gate ☎47 92 12 14, ⓦvegafairfood.no; map pp.62–63. Simple and straightforward vegetarian café sited in an old Oslo apartment block a short walk north of the centre. Has a good range of vegan dishes too. Help-yourself lunchtime buffet for 100kr. Sun–Thurs noon–8pm, Fri noon–8pm in summer (11am–4pm in winter); plus Nov–Jan Sat 4.30–9pm.

### EASTSIDE

★ **Delicatessen** Søndre gate 8, Grünerløkka ☎22 71 45 46, ⓦdelicatessen.no; map p.78. Lovely, boho café-bar with large, push-back windows and a fine line in authentic tapas (70–140kr) as well as the freshest of salads (150kr). Be prepared to wait for a table at the weekend. Mon–Thurs 11am–midnight, Fri & Sat noon–2am, Sun noon–midnight.

**Folk Flest** Markveien 67, Grünerløkka ☎22 38 19 47, ⓦfolk-flest.no; map p.78. Bijou brasserie down by the river at the south end of Grünerløkka, with outdoor seating when the sun is out. A Mediterranean-inspired menu has salads at around 130kr, main dishes 200kr. Mon–Fri 4–11pm, Sat & Sun noon–11pm.

**Fru Hagen** Thorvald Meyers gate, Grünerløkka 40 ☎45 49 19 04, ⓦfruhagen.no; map p.78. Long-standing, colourful joint that's still trendy, serving tasty snacks and meals from an inventive menu with a Mediterranean slant. Filling sandwiches, salads and wok-cooked dishes too. Main courses around 150kr. The kitchen closes at 9.30pm, after which the drinking gets going in earnest, plus DJ guest spots Fri and Sat. Very popular so go early to be sure of a seat. Mon & Tues 11am–midnight, Wed 11am–2am, Thurs–Sat 11am–3am, Sun noon–11pm.

1

## TOP 5 BEST FOR FISH

All restaurants are listed below.

Arakataka
Brasserie Blanche
Havsmak
Lofoten Fiskerestaurant
Solsiden

## RESTAURANTS

Dining out at one of Oslo's restaurants can make a sizeable dent in your wallet unless you exercise some restraint. In most places, a main course will set you back between 160kr and 240kr – not too steep until you add on a couple of beers or a bottle of wine. Advance **reservations** are a good idea almost everywhere, especially at the weekend, and note that many restaurants have summer holidays, usually in July.

### DOWNTOWN

**Arakataka** Mariboes gate 7 ☎ 23 32 83 00, ⓦ arakataka.no; map pp.62–63. This smart, modern restaurant serves excellent food, mostly fish and meat, at reasonable prices with à la carte mains averaging 190kr. Highly recommended, and a good place to sample that old Norwegian favourite, salted cod (*bacalao*), when it is on the menu. Located a 10min walk north of the Domkirke on the way to Grünerløkka. Mon–Thurs 4–10pm, Fri & Sat 4–11pm, Sun 4–9pm.

**Engebret Café** Bankplassen 1 ☎ 22 82 25 25, ⓦ engebret-cafe.no; map pp.62–63. Across from the Contemporary Art Museum, this comparatively formal restaurant occupies a fetching old building with oodles of wood panelling and old oil paintings on the walls. Specializes in Norwegian delicacies such as reindeer and fish, including *bacalao*, with main courses in the region of 230–300kr, less at lunchtime. Attracts an older clientele. In summer, there's outside seating on the square. Mon–Fri 11am–11pm, Sat 3–11pm.

**Havsmak** Henrik Ibsens gate 4 ☎ 24 13 38 00, ⓦ havsmak.no; map pp.62–63. Smart, specialist seafood restaurant kitted out in cool modern style with oodles of blue paint. First-rate range of fresh fish, albeit of minimalist portions, with main courses averaging 200kr. Set meals too – two courses for 350kr, 580kr with wine. Mon–Sat 11am–1am, kitchen till 10pm.

**Lofoten Fiskerestaurant** Stranden 75, Aker Brygge ☎ 22 83 08 08, ⓦ lofoten-fiskerestaurant.no; map pp.62–63. This smart, modern restaurant offers an excellent selection of fish and shellfish, all immaculately prepared and served. It's beside the harbour at the far end of the Aker Brygge complex, which makes it popular with locals and tourists alike. Mains kick off at around 270kr, but some of the more unusual fish – including the wonderfully

textured catfish (*steinbit*) – cost another 50kr or so. Mon–Sat 11am–11pm, Sun noon–10pm.

**Pascal** Henrik Ibsens gate 36 ☎ 22 55 00 20, ⓦ pascal .no; map pp.62–63. An offshoot of the *Pascal Konditori* on Tollbugata, this bright and breezy restaurant-cum-café offers tasty salads, cakes and pasties plus more substantial meals from around 180kr. Mon–Sat 10am–5pm, Sun noon–5pm.

**Ruffino** Arbins gate 1 ☎ 22 55 32 80, ⓦ ruffino.no; map pp.62–63. Bright, modern and cheerful, this first-rate Italian restaurant has a well-chosen menu featuring fresh pastas (165–200kr) and a handful of meat and fish dishes (260–300kr). Exemplary service; delicious, unpretentious food; and no pizzas. On the corner of Henrik Ibsens gate. Mon–Sat 3–11pm.

★ **Solsiden** Søndre Akershus Kai 35 ☎ 22 33 36 30, ⓦ solsiden.no; map pp.62–63. Tucked in below the Akershus castle, right on the harbourside in a smart hangar-like structure, this lively and relaxed restaurant specializes in seafood (it has its own lobster tank), which is generally reckoned to be as good as anywhere in Oslo – try the turbot in a mustard purée. The emphasis is on natural, organic ingredients. Mains start at 140kr, but average twice that. May–Aug only, daily 5–10pm.

**Statholderens Mat & Vinkjeller** Rådhusgata 11 ☎ 22 41 88 00, ⓦ statholdergaarden.no; map pp.62–63. Distinctive, top-of-the-range restaurant in lovely period rooms dating back to the eighteenth century. The house speciality is a ten-course menu (600kr) with a theme – fish and shellfish, Tuscan food and so on – and there's à la carte too, with mains averaging 280kr. No one could say they don't think about the menu: lamb served with orange pickled tomato, spinach, cauliflower purée, lentils and bay leaves gives the flavour. Every attempt is made to use local, seasonal ingredients. Tues–Fri 11.30am–midnight, Sat 12.30pm–midnight; dinner served 4–9.30pm, Sat from 5pm.

**Theatercaféen** Hotel Continental, Stortingsgata 24–26 ☎ 22 82 40 50, ⓦ hotelcontinental.no; map pp.62–63. This handsome restaurant, with its long mirrors, vaulted ceiling and marble pillars, has been pulling in the city's movers and shakers for decades. The imaginative menu features such delights as halibut in a cream and crab sauce with beet and pickled onions. Mains cost around 280kr. Mon–Sat 11am–11pm, Sun 3–10pm; closed most of July.

### WESTSIDE

**Brasserie Blanche** Josefines gate 23 ☎ 23 20 13 10, ⓦ blanche.no; map pp.58–59. With its whitewashed, bare-brick walls and beamed ceiling, this Franco-Norwegian restaurant has a distinctly rustic charm. Offers a well-considered menu – try, for example, the sole with salad and almond butter (280kr). Tues–Fri 3pm–1am, Sat noon–1am, Sun 3pm–1am; kitchen till 10pm.

**1**

## EASTSIDE

**Ekebergrestauranten** Kongsveien 15 ☎23 24 23 00, ⓦ ekebergrestauranten.com; map pp.58–59. On the Ekeberg heights, to the southeast of the centre, this combined café, lounge-bar and restaurant occupies a splendid Art Deco building dating from the 1920s. There are panoramic views over the Oslofjord from inside as well as from the spacious terrace-veranda. The food is international meets Norway with the likes of halibut served with new cabbage, petit pois and bacon. Mains average 200kr at the restaurant, less in the café. To get there by public transport, take tram #18 or #19 from outside Oslo S and get off at the old marine academy, the Sjømannskolen, from where it's a steep 10min walk up through the woods along Kongsveien. Restaurant Mon–Sat 11am–midnight, Sun noon–10pm; bar Mon–Sat 5pm–1am, Sun 5–10pm.

## DRINKING AND NIGHTLIFE

Downtown Oslo boasts a vibrant **bar scene**, boisterous but generally good-natured and at its most frenetic at summer weekends, when the city is crowded with visitors from all over Norway. There's an infinitely groovy string of bars out of the centre too, in the Grünerløkka district. With the city's bars staying open till the wee hours, Oslo's **nightclubs** struggle to make themselves heard – indeed there's often little distinction between the two – though there is still a reasonably good and varied scene. **Live music** is not Oslo's forte, and Norway's domestic rock and pop is far from inspiring, but **jazz** fans are well served, with a couple of first-rate venues in the city centre.

## BARS

**Bar-hopping** in Oslo is an enjoyable affair. The more mainstream (meat-market) bars are in the centre along and around Karl Johans gate, while the sharper, more alternative spots are concentrated on and around Youngstorget and, further out, in the Grünerløkka district to the northeast or in the rougher/tougher Grønland to the east. The westside of the city has its chic spots too, mostly along and around Hegdehaugsveien and Bogstadveien. Most city bars stay **open** until around 1am on weekdays, often 3–4am at the weekend, and almost all of them are open daily. Drinks are uniformly expensive, so if you're after a big night out, it's a good idea to follow Norwegian custom and have a few warm-up drinks at home before you set out (*vorspiel* in Norwegian). A number of bars feature **live music**, blurring the lines between the bars listed here and the dedicated live venues (see p.100).

### DOWNTOWN

**Beer Palace** Holmensgata 3, Aker Brygge ☎22 83 71 55, ⓦ beerpalace.no; map pp.62–63. One of the old shipyard buildings down on the Aker Brygge has been turned into this large, split-level bar where there is – as you might expect from the name – a wide range of domestic and international beer, mostly bottled. Heaves on the weekend. Daily 1pm–1am, till 3am on Fri & Sat.

**Café Sør** Torggata 11 ☎41 46 30 47, ⓦ cafesor.no; map pp.62–63. This groovy daytime café, with its funky music and modern art on the walls, turns into a late-night bar with a good line in cocktails. Mon–Wed 11am–12.30am, Thurs–Sat 11am–2am, Sun noon–12.30am.

**Café Tekehtopa** St Olavs plass 2 ☎22 20 33 23, ⓦ tekehtopa.no; map pp.62–63. *Tekehtopa* is *Apoteket* (pharmacy) spelt backwards – an appropriate little verbal play as this busy bar, which attracts a student crew, occupies a former pharmacy, complete with the original wooden fittings. There's a wide range of beers on draft and in bottles, plus inexpensive pizzas, salads, omelettes and so forth. Mon–Thurs 10am–1am, Fri 10am–3am, Sat & Sun noon–1am; kitchen closes at 11pm.

**Ett Glass** Karl Johans gate 33, entrance just up Rosenkrantz gate ☎22 33 40 79, ⓦ ettglass.no; map pp.62–63. Dark and intimate, split-level café-bar with an inexpensive menu – burgers plus – and a good line in drinks. Guest DJs on Sat nights. Popular with a mixed clientele, but notably gay-friendly. Daily 11am till the wee hours, kitchen till 11pm.

**Internasjonalen** Youngstorget 2 ☎40 00 42 77, ⓦ internasjonalen.no; map pp.62–63. On the ground floor of the 1930s tower block overlooking Youngstorget, this super-cool bar specializes in cocktails served up in stylish retro surroundings: Pop Art meets Eastern Europe. Live bands too. Daily noon–3am.

**London Pub** C.J. Hambros plass 5 ☎22 70 87 00, ⓦ londonpub.no; map pp.62–63. The best – and certainly the busiest – gay bar in town with a pool table, jukeboxes and guest DJs on Fri and Sat nights. Daily 3pm–3.30am.

**Lorry** Parkveien 12, cnr Hegdehaugsveien ☎22 69 69 04, ⓦ lorry.no; map pp.62–63. Popular and enjoyable bar with a cranky mix of fixtures and fittings from maquettes to stuffed animals. There's a wide choice of beers – well over a hundred – and outdoor seating in the summer. Also serves food. Mon–Sat 11am–3.30am, Sun noon–1.30am.

**Palace Grill/Skaugum** Solligata 2 ☎23 13 11 40, ⓦ palacegrill.no; map pp.62–63. A real rabbit warren of a place, this popular New Age-meets-alternative café-bar has a roots, rock and jazz soundtrack, and serves filling food too. There's also a heaving outside bar, *Skaugum*, in the

**1**

## CITY LISTINGS AND TICKETS

For entertainment **listings** it's worth checking out *What's On Oslo*, a monthly English-language freebie produced by the tourist office. One other useful free publication is *Streetwise*, which is produced annually by Use-It, the city's youth information shop (see p.92); among much else, it carries descriptions of the city's best bars and clubs. For **tickets** contact the venue direct or try Billettservice (☎815 33 133, ⊛billettservice.no), who use some Narvesen kiosks as outlets – details are on the website.

yard behind and beside the *Palace*. Palace Grill Mon–Sat 3pm–3am, Sun 3pm–1am. Skaugum May–Sept Tues–Sat 6pm–3am; Oct–April Fri & Sat 10pm–3am.

★ **Stratos** Youngstorget 2 ☎21 04 64 00, ⊛stratos .as; map pp.62–63. At the top of the large and distinctive Art Deco tower dominating Youngstorget, this outstanding rooftop bar offers great views and great cocktails from amid its decorative brickwork. Accessible by lift. Late June to mid-Aug only Tues–Sat 3pm–3am, Sun 8pm–3am.

### WESTSIDE

**Oslo Mikrobryggeri** Bogstadveien 6, entrance on Holtegata ☎22 56 97 76, ⊛omb.no; map pp.58–59. Dark, almost gloomy bar with loud music and a dartboard plus a tasty range of ales, the pick of which are brewed on the premises. Sun–Fri 3pm–1am, Sat noon–1am.

### EASTSIDE

**Bar Boca** Thorvald Meyers gate 30, Grünerløkka ☎22 04 13 77; map p.78. Tiny 1950s retro-style bar serving some of the best cocktails in town. The bartenders take their work very seriously, and you need to get there early to avoid the crush. Live jazz once or twice weekly. Mon–Thurs 11am–1am, Fri & Sat 11am–3am, Sun noon–1am.

**Café con Bar** Brugata 11, Grønland ☎22 05 02 00, ⊛cafeconbar.no; map p.78. Hip-as-you-like place with a retro interior and a long bar that can make buying a drink hard work. Good atmosphere, loungy decor and unisex toilets for those surprise meetings. Mon & Tues 11am–midnight, Wed–Sat 11am–2am, Sun noon–midnight.

**Olympen** Grønlandsleiret 15, Grønland ☎24 10 19 99, ⊛olympen.no; map p.78. A rare survivor, this old beer hall, dating from the 1890s, has kept many of its antique furnishings and fittings, from the chandeliers down to the oil paintings and the wooden benches, and sells a good range of specialist beers at reasonable prices. Familiarly known here in the Grønland as "Lompa" (sausage wrap), rather than its grand official name. Mon–Thurs 11am–1am, Fri 11am–2am, Sat noon–3am, Sun noon–1am.

**Parkteatret Bar** Olaf Ryes plass 11, Grünerløkka ☎93 28 80 02, ⊛parkteatret.no; map p.78. Choose a brew from the extensive beer menu at this boho bar,

which occupies the foyer of a disused cinema – hence the old cinema seats. Sandwiches are supplied by an excellent local deli, and Scandinavian indie rock is pumped up round the clock. Live acts too. Daily 11am–1am, till 3am on Fri & Sat.

**Tea Lounge** Thorvald Meyers gate 33c, Grünerløkka ☎22 37 07 05; map p.78. Lounge-type café-bar with velvety red couches and big windows. As you might guess from the name, tea is a big deal here – all sorts are on offer, served to a soft house backtrack. Cocktails too. Mon–Wed 11am–1am, Thurs–Sat 11am–3pm, Sun noon–3am.

## CLUBS AND LIVE MUSIC

At the city's **nightclubs**, nothing much gets going before 11pm with venues generally closing around 3.30am. Most clubs focus on DJ events and special party or theme nights, but some also host a variety of **live music**, ranging from local home-grown talent to big-name bands. Some clubs charge an entrance fee, but many don't, depending on what's on and who is performing. At the smarter places there's an informal dress code – go scruffy and you will be turned away. Oslo has a strong **jazz** tradition, as evidenced by its jazz festival (see box opposite); otherwise, check out *Bare Jazz* or *Herr Nilsen* for regular jazz acts.

**Barbeint** Henrik Ibsens gate 60a ☎95 06 46 86, ⊛barbeint-oslo.no; map pp.62–63. If you're familiar with Scandinavian bands and films, you may recognize a few faces in this jam-packed, infinitely groovy bar. Loud sounds – primarily soul, funk, disco and house – great cocktails, and all sorts of party nights. On the west side of the city centre, close to Parkveien. Thurs–Sat 11pm–3am.

**Bare Jazz** Grensen 8 ☎22 33 20 80, ⊛barejazz.no; map. pp.62–63. Split-level joint with a superb selection of jazz CDs for sale on the ground floor and a jazz café up above with frequent live sounds, both home-grown and imported. Courtyard café too. Mon & Tues 10am–6pm, Wed–Sat 10am–midnight.

**Blå** Brenneriveien 9c ☎40 00 42 77, ⊛blaaoslo.no; map p.78. Creative, cultural nightspot in Grünerløkka, featuring everything from live jazz and cabaret through to poetry readings. Also features some of the best DJs in town, keeping the crowd moving until 3.30am at the weekend. In summer, there's a riverside terrace too. Usually daily from 10pm, though depends on events.

**Herr Nilsen** C.J. Hambros plass 5 ☎ 22 33 54 05, ⓦ herrnilsen.no; map pp.62–63. Small and intimate jazz club whose brick walls are decorated with jazz memorabilia. Live jazz – often traditional and bebop – most nights. A/c and in a central location. Mon–Sat noon–3am, Sun 3pm–3am.

**Last Train** Karl Johans gate 45 ☎ 22 41 52 93, ⓦ lasttrain.no; map pp.62–63. Long-established (heavy) rock pub/club that prides itself on the quality of its live music – and its refusal to be upgraded into minimal-chic. Convenient downtown location too, though note the entrance is on Universitetsgata. It's a good place to check out up-and-coming (sometimes going nowhere) Norwegian bands. Mon–Fri 3pm–3.30am, Sat 6pm–3.30am.

**Mono** Pløens gate 4 ☎ 22 41 41 66, ⓦ cafemono.no; map pp.62–63. Darkly lit bar, with retro fixtures and fittings, that attracts a student crowd. Showcases a wide range of pop/rock music with elements of folk, country, electronica and jazz and featuring (mostly Norwegian) live acts several nights a week. Pløens gate is off Torggata, north of Oslo S. Mon–Sat 11am–3am, Sun 6pm–3am.

**Oslo Spektrum** Sonja Henies plass 2 ☎ 815 11 211, ⓦ oslospektrum.no; map pp.62–63. Major venue, close to Olso S, showcasing big international acts, as well as smaller-fry local bands.

**Sikamikanico** Møllergata 2 ☎ 22 41 44 09, ⓦ sikamikanico.net; map pp.62–63. Café during the day, but morphs into a heaving club at night with hip-hop, drum'n'bass, jazz and house. Near Oslo S. Wed & Thurs 9pm–3.30am, Fri & Sat 2pm–3.30am, Sun 10am–3.30am.

## ENTERTAINMENT

### CLASSICAL MUSIC AND OPERA

**Classical music** enthusiasts benefit from an ambitious concert programme. In the summertime, in addition to the Konserthus (see below) there are also classical concerts at a variety of other venues, including the Domkirke; for details of the summer programme, contact the tourist office (see p.92). In Sept, the ten-day **Ultima Contemporary Music Festival** (☎ 22 40 18 90, ⓦ ultima.no) gathers together Scandinavian and international talent in an ambitious programme of concerts featuring everything from modern contemporary music to opera, ballet, classical and folk. The performances take place in a variety of venues throughout the city; for full details check Ultima's website or contact the tourist office.

**Konserthus** Munkedamsveien 14 ☎ 23 11 31 00, ⓦ oslokonserthus.no. Opened in 1977, Oslo's main concert hall has two auditoria – one large and one small. The city's principal orchestra, the Oslo Filharmonien (☎ 23 11 60 60, ⓦ oslofilharmonien.no), gives regular concerts here. As you might expect, the orchestra's programme often includes works by Norwegian and other Scandinavian composers. Tickets for most performances cost around 400kr.

**Operahuset** Kirsten Flagstads plass 1; tickets ☎ 21 42 21 21, ⓦ operaen.no. Oslo's spanking new Operahuset (Opera House) is home to Den Norske Opera & Ballett, Norway's prolific opera and ballet company, which offers a popular repertoire – Mozart, R. Strauss and the Italians – but also undertakes a number of contemporary works each year. The Operahuset is on the waterfront near Oslo S.

## MUSIC FESTIVALS

From rappers to rock, big-name bands and artists often include Oslo on their tours with many of them appearing at Oslo Spektrum (see above). The most prestigious annual event is **Norwegian Wood** (ⓦ norwegianwood.no), a five-day, open-air rock festival held in June in the outdoor amphitheatre at Frogner Park, a ten-minute ride from the city centre on tram #12. Previous years have attracted the likes of Iggy Pop, Patti Smith, Ringo Starr, The Kinks and Van Morrison, and the festival continues to pull in major international artists, supported by a variety of Norwegian acts. The arena holds around six thousand people, but tickets (around 580kr/day) sell out well in advance.

Oslo also hosts the rather more adventurous **Øyafestivalen** (ⓦ oyafestivalen.com), a four-day event held in August that showcases a wide range of artists, mostly Scandinavian but with a string of imports too – Pulp and Kanye West for instance. A club night traditionally kicks the whole thing off in style. The festival takes place in venues across the city with major performances in the open air in Middelalderparken, a large slab of greenery, off Bispegata, a ten-minute walk east from Oslo S – or take tram #18 or #19 from Jernbanetorget. Finally, in early or mid-August, Oslo's week-long **Jazz Festival** (ⓦ oslojazz.no) attracts internationally renowned artists as well as showcasing local talent, who perform at a variety of venues, both inside and out.

**Tickets** for all three festivals are available from Billettservice (☎ 815 33 133, ⓦ billettservice.no).

**1**

## CINEMA

The ease with which most Norwegians tackle other languages is best demonstrated at the **cinema**, where films are shown in their original language with Norwegian subtitles. Given that American (and British) films are the most popular, this has obvious advantages for visiting English-speakers. Oslo has its share of mainstream multi-screens, as well as a good art-house cinema. Prices are surprisingly reasonable with tickets averaging 85–100kr. Cinema **listings** – including information on late-night screenings – appear daily in the local press, and the tourist office has details too.

**Eldorado** Torggata 9 ☎820 50 001, ⓦoslokino.no. Mainstream cinema showing the usual blockbusters. Near the Domkirke.

**Filmens Hus** Dronningens gate 16, cnr Tollbugata ☎22 47 45 89, ⓦnfi.no. Art-house cinema with a varied and extremely enjoyable programme mixing mainstream and alternative/avant-garde films.

**Gimle** Bygdøy Allé 39 ☎820 50 001, ⓦoslokino.no. A sympathetically revamped old cinema with some of the most comfortable seats in town. Varied programme, mostly mainstream. One screen only.

**Klingenberg** Olav V's gate 4 ☎820 50 001, ⓦoslokino .no. Mainstream cinema with four screens in a central location, metres from the Nationaltheatret.

**Saga** Stortingsgata 28, cnr Olav V's gate ☎820 50 001, ⓦoslokino.no. Mainstream cinema with six screens metres from the Nationaltheatret.

## THEATRE

Nearly all of Oslo's **theatre** productions are in Norwegian, making them of limited interest to (most) tourists, though there are occasional English-language performances by touring theatre companies.

**Nationaltheatret** Stortingsgata ☎815 00 811, ⓦnationaltheatret.no. Oslo's principal theatre has a lively programme of classics and modern works and also hosts the prestigious, annual Ibsen Festival.

**Det Norske Teatret** Kristian IV's gate 8 ☎22 42 43 44, ⓦdetnorsketeatret.no. An inventive progamme of modern works is the hallmark here, with many plays commissioned specially.

## SHOPPING

Make no mistake, shopping in Oslo is expensive and, like so much else in western Europe, it's the big multinational chains that ring the changes. The city's most individual offering is its **bookshops**, but for many travellers the key search is for the nearest **supermarket** to stock up for picnics and so forth. Fortunately, there are lots of small supermarkets in the city centre – Rimi, ICA and Kiwi are three of the larger chains – and all of them sell at least a small selection of fresh fruit and veg.

## CLOTHING AND DESIGN

**Dale** Karl Johansgate 45 ☎97 48 12 07, ⓦdale.no; map pp.62–63. The flagship storefront to Norway's most famous clothing brand, where you can pick up everything from classic, colourful handknit sweaters to mittens and hats – some in strikingly modern interpretations of traditional knitwear patterns. Dale's sweaters are always pricey, but you'll only ever have to buy one in your life. Mon–Fri 10am–6pm, Sat 10am–4pm.

**Heimen Husflid** Rosenkrantz gate 8 ☎23 21 42 00, ⓦheimen.net; map pp.62–63. Norwegian handicrafts are not cheap – you wouldn't expect them to be – but this long-established shop does have the city's most extensive range of tradional Norwegian clothing – the pullovers are perhaps the most appealing items. Mon–Fri 10am–6pm, Sat 10am–3pm.

**Moods of Norway** Akersgata 18 ☎46 62 77 96, ⓦmoodsofnorway.com; map pp.62–63. This small Norwegian chain has created quite a stir with its offbeat T-shirts and design logo – the good, old Norwegian tractor in all sorts of weird and wonderful colours. Concentrates on clothing for the young and the young at heart. Mon–Fri 10am–7pm, Sat 10am–6pm.

**Norway Designs** Stortingsgata 28 ☎23 11 45 10, ⓦnorwaydesigns.no; map pp.62–63. From ties to cutlery, this large shop sells a wide range of high-spec Scandinavian goods. The clocks and watches are especially stylish. Mon–Fri 9am–5pm, Thurs till 7pm, Sat 10am–4pm.

## FOOD AND DRINK

**ICA** Akersgata 45 ☎22 42 01 94; map pp.62–63. Small but central, standard-issue supermarket near the corner of Grensen. Has a better than average selection of fruit and vegetables. Mon–Fri 9am–9pm, Sat 9am–6pm.

**Vinmonopolet** Oslo S; Rosenkrantz gate 11; ⓦvinmonopolet.no; map pp.62–63. There are lots of branches of Vinmonopolet, the state-run liquor and wine store, in Oslo, and the Oslo S outlet is one of the largest. There's another downtown branch at Rosenkrantz gate. For a complete list of stores, with opening hours, check the website. Oslo S branch Mon–Fri 9am–6pm, Sat 9am–3pm; Rosenkrantz gate branch Mon–Fri 10am–6pm, Sat 10am–3pm.

## MAP AND BOOKSHOPS

**Den Norske Turistforening (DNT)** Storgata 3 ☎22 82 28 22, ⓦdntoslo.no; map pp.62–63. The Norwegian hiking organization's city-centre office stocks a full range of Norwegian hiking maps. Mon–Fri 10am–5pm, Thurs till 6pm, Sat 10am–3pm.

**Nomaden** Uranienborgveien 4 ☎ 23 13 14 15, ⓦ nomaden.no; map pp.62–63. Located just behind the Slottsparken, this medium-sized bookshop sells the city's widest selection of Norwegian road maps, both national and regional, as well as travel guides to scores of countries. The clearest and most accurate Norwegian road maps are produced by Michelin. Sells Norwegian hiking maps too. Mon–Fri 10am–6pm, Thurs till 8pm, Sat 10am–4pm.

**Norli** Universitetsgata 20–24 ☎ 22 00 43 00, ⓦ norli .no; map pp.62–63. This particular branch of Norli, a bookshop chain, has a competent range of English fiction as well as a separate – and especially interesting – section

devoted to English translations of Norwegian writers. Mon–Fri 9am–7pm, Sat 10am–5pm.

**Norlis Antikvariat** Universitetsgata 18 ☎ 22 20 01 40; map pp.62–63. Oslo does a good line in secondhand bookshops and Norlis is perhaps the best among them. Most of their stock is Norwegian, but there is a good smattering of English titles too. Opposite the National Gallery. Mon–Fri 10am–4pm, Sat 10am–3pm.

★ **Tronsmo** Kristian Augusts gate 19 ☎ 22 99 03 99, ⓦ tronsmo.no; map pp.62–63. The best independent bookshop in town, especially if you are politically left of centre, where great care has been taken to select the best books on a wide range of subjects – both Norwegian and English titles. Mon–Wed 9am–5pm, Thurs & Fri 9am–6pm, Sat 10am–4pm.

## SPORTS

Surrounded by forest and fjord, Oslo is very much an outdoor city, offering a wide range of sports and outdoor pursuits. In summer, locals take to the hills to **hike** the network of trails that lattice the forests and lakes of the Nordmarka, where many also try their hand at a little freshwater **fishing**, while others head out to the offshore islets of the Oslofjord to sunbathe and **swim**. In winter, the cross-country **ski** routes of the Nordmarka are especially popular, as is downhill skiing. Indeed skiing is such an integral part of winter life here that the T-bane carriages all have ski racks. Every winter, from November to March, a floodlit **skating rink**, Narvisen, is created in front of the Stortinget, beside Karl Johans gate. Admission is free and you can rent skates on the spot at reasonable rates. The

## OSLO WITH CHILDREN

There's no shortage of things to do with young (pre-teen) children in Oslo, beginning with the enchanting, open-air **Vigelandsparken** (see p.86) and, if the weather is good, the **beaches** of the Oslofjord islands (see p.88). In wintertime, ice-skating, tobogganing and horse-drawn sleigh rides (see above) are also almost bound to appeal.

Few children will want to be dragged round Oslo's main museums, except perhaps for the **Frammuseet** (see p.84), but there are a couple of museums geared up for youngsters (see below). Another bit of good news is that **discounts** for children are commonplace. Almost all sites and attractions let babies and toddlers in free, and charge half of the adult tariff for children between 4 and 16 years of age. It's the same on public transport, and hotels are usually very obliging too, adding camp beds of some description to their rooms with the minimum of fuss and expense.

### NORSK TEKNISK MUSEUM

The most popular museum with children is the **Norsk Teknisk Museum**, at Kjelsåsveien 143 (Technology Museum; late June to late Aug daily 10am–6pm; late Aug to late June Tues–Fri 9am–4pm, Sat & Sun 11am–6pm; 90kr, children 50kr; ⓦ tekniskmuseum.no). Out to the north of the city, this is an interactive museum *par excellence*, equipped with working models and a galaxy of things to push and touch, as well as a café and picnic area. To get there from the city centre, take bus #54 from the Aker Brygge to Kjelsås station alongside the museum.

### BARNEKUNSTMUSEET

Rather more creative is the **Barnekunstmuseet** at Lille Frøens vei 4 (Children's Art Museum; mid-Jan to late June Tues–Thurs 9.30am–2pm, Sun 11am–4pm; late June to mid-Aug Tues–Thurs & Sun 11am–4pm; mid-Sept to early Dec Tues–Thurs 9.30am–2pm, Sun 11am–4pm; closed mid-Aug to mid-Sept; 60kr, children 40kr; ⓦ barnekunst.no). This has an international collection of children's art – drawings, paintings, sculpture and handicrafts – along with a children's workshop where painting, music and dancing are frequent activities; call ahead for details on ☎ 22 46 85 73 or check out the website. To reach the museum take the T-bane to Frøen station.

**1**

tourist office also has the details of all sorts of other winter fun in the Nordmarka – from **tobogganing** and **horse-drawn sleigh rides** to guided **winter walks**.

## SKIING

**Information** Both cross-country and downhill enthusiasts might begin by either calling in at the tourist office or contacting Skiforeningen (Ski Association; ☎ 22 92 32 00, ⊚ skiforeningen.no). They both have lots of information on Oslo's floodlit trails, cross-country routes, downhill and slalom slopes, ski schools (including one for children) and excursions to the nearest mountain resorts.

**Equipment rental** Most Norwegians have their own skiing gear, but equipment rental is available – among several suppliers – from Skiservice, Tomm Murstadbakken 2, beside the Voksenkollen T-bane station (☎ 22 13 95 00, ⊚ skiservice.no).

**Tryvann Vinterpark** Oslo's largest and best downhill ski area is Tryvann Vinterpark (Tryvann Winter Park; ⊚ tryvann .no), where there are fourteen ski slopes and seven ski lifts. Its facilities include a ski school and ski equipment rental and, snow permitting, the park is open from Dec to April. It's also easy to reach by public transport – take T-bane #1 to Voksenkollen station and catch the shuttle bus.

## DIRECTORY

**Dentist** Municipal dental information on ☎ 22 67 30 00. Otherwise, see under "Tannleger" in the *Yellow Pages*.

**Embassies and consulates** Canada, Wergelandsveien 7 (☎ 22 99 53 00); Ireland, Haakon VII's gate 1 (☎ 22 01 72 00); Netherlands, Oscars gate 29 (☎ 23 33 36 00); Poland, Olav Kyrres plass 1 (☎ 22 43 00 15); South Africa, Drammensveien 88 (☎ 23 27 32 20); UK, Thomas Heftyes gate 8 (☎ 23 13 27 00); US, Henrik Ibsens gate 48 (☎ 21 30 85 40). For others, look under "Ambassadeur og Legasjoner" in the *Yellow Pages*. There is no Australian or New Zealand consulate or embassy.

**Emergencies** Ambulance & medical assistance ☎ 113. Police ☎ 112. Fire brigade ☎ 110.

**Gay Oslo** There's not much of a scene as such, primarily because Oslo's gays and lesbians are mostly content to share pubs and clubs with heteros. That said, gay men do congregate at the *London Pub* (see p.99), and at *Ett Glass* (see p.99). The main gay event is the Skeive Dager (Queer Days; ⊚ skeivedager.no) festival usually held over ten days in late June with parties, parades, political meetings and a film festival; it also incorporates Gay Pride. Norway's national gay and lesbian organization is LLH (Landsforeningen for lesbisk og homofil frigjøring; ⊚ llh.no); their Oslo office is at Valkyriegaten 15a, 5th floor (☎ 22 60 68 60, ⊚ llh.no/oa).

**Internet** Almost all city hotels and hostels provide internet access for their guests either free or at (fairly) reasonable rates. Internet access is also available for free at the main city library, the Deichmanske bibliotek, at Arne Garborgs plass 4 (June–Aug Mon–Fri 10am–6pm, Sat 11am–2pm; Sept–May Mon–Fri 10am–7pm, Sat 10am–4pm; ⊚ deichman.no), and, if you are under 26, at Oslo's youth information shop, Use-it, Møllergata 3 (see p.92).

**Laundry** (*Vaskerier*) Majorstua Myntvaskeri, Vibes gate 15 (☎ 22 69 43 17); Snarvask, Thorvald Meyers gate 18, Grünerløkka (☎ 22 37 57 70), but entrance on Sannergata.

**Left luggage** Coin-operated lockers (24hr) at Oslo S.

**Lost property** (*Hittegods*) Trams, buses and T-bane at the Nationaltheatret station (☎ 22 08 53 61); NSB railways at Oslo S (☎ 815 68 340); police, call ☎ 22 66 90 50.

**Medical treatment** For medical emergencies, call ☎ 113. For lesser problems, either head for the nearest pharmacy (see below) or the Walk-In Clinic, to the rear of the Aker Brygge complex at the corner of Munkedamsveien and Sjøgata (☎ 22 83 10 83, ⊚ walk-in-clinic.com). The clinic is fast, efficient, friendly – and expensive. For cheaper treatment, stick to Oslo Legevakt, the A&E department of the nearest hospital, which is located at the north end of Storgata, beside the river.

**Pharmacy** Oslo has scores of pharmacies (*Apotek*), including the 24hr Vitusapotek, in front of Oslo S at Jernbanetorget 4 (☎ 23 35 81 00). See also "Medical treatment".

**Police** In an emergency, phone ☎ 112.

**Post offices** There are lots of post offices dotted across the city, including a branch in Oslo S (Mon–Fri 9am–6pm, Sat 9am–3pm). All post offices exchange currency and cash travellers' cheques at very reasonable rates.

# Around Oslo: the Oslofjord

Around 100km from top to bottom, the narrow straits and podgy basins of the **Oslofjord** link the capital with the open sea. This waterway has long been Norway's busiest, an islet-studded channel whose sheltered waters were once crowded with steamers shuttling passengers along the Norwegian coast. The young **Roald Dahl**, who spent his summer holidays here from 1920 to 1932, loved the area, writing in his autobiography, *Boy*: "Unless you have sailed down the Oslofjord … on a tranquil

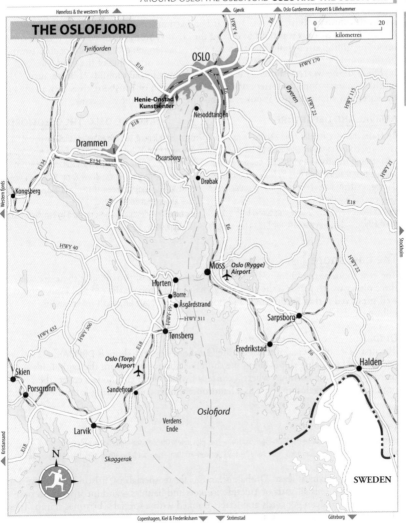

# THE OSLOFJORD

Hønefoss & the western fjords ▲  
Gjøvik ▲  
▲ Oslo Gardermoen Airport & Lillehammer

0 — 20  
kilometres

**1**

*Tyrifjorden*

HWY 4

**OSLO**

E16

HWY 170

Øyeren

HWY 22

HWY 115

**Henie-Onstad Kunstsenter**

E18

**Nesoddtangen**

E6

**Drammen**

E134

E134

*Oscarsborg*

Western fjords ◀

E18

**Kongsberg**

E18

● **Drøbak**

E18

HWY 40

E6

HWY 22

Stockholm ▶

**Moss** ● *Oslo (Rygge) Airport* ✈

**Horten** ● **Borre**
● **Åsgårdstrand**

HWY 19

—HWY 311

**Sarpsborg** ●

HWY 432

HWY 306

E18

**Tønsberg**

**Fredrikstad**

E6

**Halden**

*Oslo (Torp) Airport* ✈

**Skien** ●

**Porsgrunn** ●

**Sandefjord** ✈

*Oslofjord*

Kristiansand ◀

E18

● **Larvik**

*Verdens Ende*

**N**

*Skagerrak*

**SWEDEN**

Copenhagen, Kiel & Frederikshavn ▽  ▽ Strömstad

Göteborg ▽

summer's day, you cannot imagine the sensation of absolute peace and beauty that surrounds you." Even now, though cars have replaced the steamers, the Oslofjord makes for delightful sailing, and in good weather you can spy dozens of tiny craft scuttling round its nooks and crannies. The ferry ride from Oslo to **Drøbak**, a pretty village on the fjord's east shore, provides a pleasant introduction to these nautical pleasures, though it's not quite the same as having your own boat.

Today, both shores of the Oslofjord are dotted with humdrum industrial towns, and frankly, apart from the fjord itself, there's not much to tempt you out of Oslo if your time is limited – especially as several of the city's major sights are half-day excursions in themselves. But if you have more time, there are several places on the train and bus routes out of the city that do warrant a stop. The pick of the crop is the town of **Fredrikstad**, down the fjord's **eastern shore** on the train route to Sweden – or rather the old part of Fredrikstad, which consists of an immaculately preserved fortress whose late

1

sixteenth-century gridiron streets and earthen bastions snuggle up to the River Glomma. The fortress was built to defend the country from the Swedes, as was the imposing hilltop stronghold that rears up above **Halden**, an otherwise innocuous town further southeast, hard by the Swedish border. On the other side of the fjord, the highlight of the **western shore** is the cluster of Viking burial mounds at **Borre**, just outside the ferry port of Horten, while the breezy town of **Tønsberg** gives easy access to the shredded archipelago that pokes a rural finger out into the Skagerrak.

## ARRIVAL AND DEPARTURE

**By train** There's a regular train service from Oslo S serving both sides of the Oslofjord. On the east side, the train stops at Fredrikstad and Halden, but not Drøbak, which is best reached from Oslo by ferry (see opposite). On the western side, trains run to Drammen and Tønsberg, but not Horten

**By car** Motorways leave Oslo to strip along both sides of the Oslofjord – the E6 in the east, the E18 to the west. To

## AROUND OSLO: THE OSLOFJORD

cross the Oslofjord, you can either use the 7km tunnel that runs west from Drøbak, or catch the car ferry (every 30min, 45 min at the weekend: Mon–Fri 5.30am–midnight, Sat & Sun 7am–midnight, 30min; driver & car 80kr each way; ⓦ basto-fosen.no) between Horten and Moss, which is itself about 60km south of Oslo.

**By boat** One destination best reached by ferry is Drøbak (see opposite).

## The east shore

The **east shore** of the Oslofjord may be Norway at its most prosaic, but there are still three places worth a visit – the pretty little hamlet of **Drøbak**, the old and especially well-preserved fort at **Fredrikstad**, and border-town of **Halden**, with its sprawling hilltop citadel.

## Drøbak

The first place of any real interest on the Oslofjord's eastern shore is **DRØBAK**, a pocket-sized port that slopes along the shoreline about 40km from the capital. It's at its prettiest round the **harbour**, where a cluster of white clapboard houses covers the headland and straggles up towards a handsome timber **church** dating from the early eighteenth century.

### Tregaarden's Julehus

Havnebakken 6 • March–Oct Mon–Fri 10am–5pm, Sat 10am–3pm, plus June to Oct Sun noon–4pm; Nov to early Dec Mon–Fri 10am–7pm, Sat 10am–3pm, Sun noon–4pm; early Dec to 23 Dec Mon–Fri 10am–8pm, Sat & Sun 10am–4pm; Dec 24 9am–midnight • ⓣ 64 93 41 78, ⓦ julehus.no

Among Norwegians at least, Drøbak is famous for its specialist Christmas shop, the **Julehus**, which sells all sorts of Yuletide trinkets and baubles – and incorporates a post office, where you can get cards and letters franked with a special Christmas stamp. The shop's popularity is such that many Norwegian kids believe that Father Christmas actually lives here; he doesn't, of course, because his reindeer prefer Lapland.

### Oscarsborg island

Hourly passenger ferries run from Drøbak harbour (10min; 80kr return)

Drøbak witnessed one of the few Norwegian successes during the German invasion of 1940, when the cruiser *Blucher* was sunk by artillery as it steamed towards Oslo. The gunners, who were stationed just offshore on the island-fortress of **Oscarsborg**, had no way of realizing just how important this was – the delay to the German flotilla gave the Norwegian king, Håkon VII, just enough time to escape the capital and avoid capture. Few commented upon it at the time, but the gun that did the damage was made in Germany by Krupp, a rich irony if ever there was one. The gun is long gone, but you can now wander round the fortress, one of a series built in the nineteenth century to defend the seaward approaches to Oslo; decommissioned several years ago, no one was quite sure what to do with it until it was turned into a hotel (see opposite).

## ARRIVAL AND DEPARTURE

**By boat** The most enjoyable way to get to Drøbak from Oslo is by boat. From mid-May to Aug, passenger ferries (❶177) depart Oslo's Aker Brygge pier for Drøbak five times weekly, stopping off at a couple of small islands on the way. The journey takes just over an hour and costs 100kr each way. The boat's timetable often makes it possible to complete the return trip on the same day, though this isn't crucial as you can always take the bus.

**By bus** There's a fast and frequent bus service between Drøbak and Oslo (#541; every 30min to Jernbanetorget; 1hr).

## ACCOMMODATION AND EATING

**Oscarsborg Hotel & Spa** Oscarsborg fortress ❶64 90 40 00, ⓦoscarsborghotel.no. Oscarsborg fortress is a little sombre, especially in poor weather, but it has a great setting in the Oslofjord and has been creatively converted into a spa hotel. There are 89 rooms here, many of which have fjord views, though with each occupying a former military premises they can seem somewhat severe. There's a regular passenger service to and from Drøbak on the mainland (hourly; 10min; 80kr return). **1600kr**

**Skipperstuen** Havnebakken 11 ❶64 93 07 03. In the wooden house on the knoll next to the harbour, this likeable café-restaurant offers a wide-ranging menu from local seafood to Spanish-style tapas. At lunchtimes, main courses average 160kr. Mon–Sat noon–10pm, Sun noon–8pm.

## Fredrikstad

An ideal day-trip from the capital, it's an hour-long, ninety-kilometre train journey south from Oslo to **FREDRIKSTAD**, a modest little town of around 70,000 people that fills out a thumb of land just across the river from a superbly preserved seventeenth-century **fortress**, now known as the **Gamlebyen** (Old Town).

Danish kings ruled Norway from 1387 to 1814 and, with rare exceptions, the country's interests were systematically neglected in favour of Copenhagen. A major consequence was Norway's involvement in the bitter rivalry between the Swedish and Danish monarchies, which prompted a seemingly endless and particularly pointless sequence of wars lasting from the early sixteenth century until 1720. The eastern

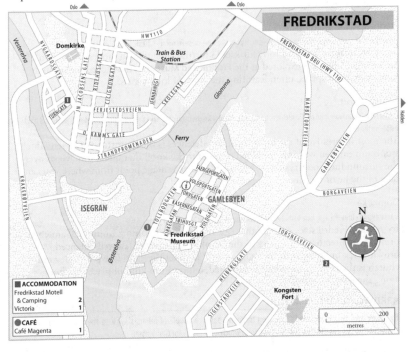

FREDRIKSTAD

**ACCOMMODATION**
Fredrikstad Motell & Camping ... 2
Victoria ... 1

**CAFÉ**
Café Magenta ... 1

**1**

approaches to Oslo (then Christiania), along the Oslofjord, were especially vulnerable to attack from Sweden, and to thwart the Swedes the Danish king **Frederik II** had a fortified town built here at the mouth of the River Glomma in 1567, modestly naming it after himself. In the event, Frederik II's fort only lasted three years before it was burnt to the ground, though it didn't take long for a replacement to be constructed – and for the whole process to be repeated again. Finally, in the middle of the seventeenth century, Fredrikstad's **fortifications** were considerably strengthened: the central gridiron of cobbled streets was encircled on three sides by zigzag bastions, which allowed the defenders to fire across and into any attacking force. In turn, these bastions were protected by a moat, concentric earthen banks and outlying redoubts. Armed with 130 cannon, Fredrikstad was by 1685 the strongest fortress in all of Norway – and it long remained in military use, which partly accounts for its excellent state of preservation. The fort was also unaffected by the development of **modern Fredrikstad**, which grew up as a result of the timber industry: the new town was built on the west bank of the Glomma while the old fort is on the east. Fredrikstad's other claim to fame is as the place where the last woman to be executed in Norway met her untimely end: the year was 1876 and the woman was a certain Sophie Johannesdatter, who had poisoned her husband.

## Gamlebyen

The Byfergene (passenger ferry; Mon–Thurs 5.30am–11pm, Fri 5.30am–1am, Sat 7am–1am, Sun 9.30am–11pm; 5min; 10kr) shuttles over every 15–30min from the modern town to the Gamlebyen's gated back wall

The pastel-painted timber and stone houses of the **Gamlebyen**, just three blocks deep and six blocks wide, make for a delightful stroll, especially as surprisingly few tourists venture this way except at the height of the season. It's the general appearance of the place that appeals rather than any specific sight, although the main square, **Torvgaten**, does hold an unfortunate **statue of Frederik II**, who appears to have a serious problem with his pantaloons.

## Fredrikstad Museum

Tøihusgaten 41 • Late June to Aug daily 11am–4pm, Sept to late June Tues–Fri noon–3.30pm, Sat & Sun 11am–4pm • 50kr

The historical background to Fredrikstad's fortress, including a modest collection of archeological finds, is explored at the **Fredrikstad Museum**. The museum also holds temporary art displays, often featuring the work of local artists.

## Kongsten fort

The fort is a 10min walk from the Gamlebyen: go straight ahead from the main gate, take the first right along Heibergsgate and it's clearly visible on the left

The most impressive of the town's outlying defences is the **Kongsten Fort**. Here, thick stone and earthen walls are moulded round a rocky knoll that offers wide views over the surrounding countryside – an agreeably quiet vantage point from where you can take in the lie of the land.

## Domkirke

Nygaardsgata • Tues–Fri: late June to mid-Aug 11am–3pm, rest of year 11am–2pm • Free

In modern Fredrikstad, on the other side of the River Glomma from the Gamlebyen, pride of architectural place goes to the **Domkirke** (Cathedral), a well-balanced, brown-brick building with stained glass by Emanuel Vigeland (see p.87). Beyond the church is the centre of modern Fredrikstad, a humdrum kind of place that nudges up along the river.

## ARRIVAL AND INFORMATION
FREDRIKSTAD

**By train and bus** Fredrikstad's adjoining train and bus stations are located in the new part of town, from which it's a couple of minutes' walk to the River Glomma and the ferry for Gamlebyen.

**Tourist office** Torvgaten 59, Gamlebyen (June to late Aug Mon–Fri 8.30am–5pm, Sat 10am–4pm, Sun 11am–4pm; late Aug to May Mon–Fri 9am–4.30pm; ☎ 69 30 46 00, Ⓦ fredrikstad-hvaler.no). They have oodles of local information and a comprehensive list of places to stay.

## ACCOMMODATION AND EATING

**Café Magenta** Tolldbodgaten 105 ☎ 98 63 91 49. Pleasant old-town haunt offering an especially good line in waffles, though they serve up tasty salads and omelettes too. Salads from 85kr, soups from 95kr. Daily 11am–5pm.

**Fredrikstad Motell & Camping** Torsnesveien 16 ☎ 99 22 19 99, Ⓦ fredrikstadmotel.no. This bargain-basement place is about 400m straight ahead outside the main gate of the Old Town; it provides tent space as well as inexpensive rooms. Rooms 500kr, tent pitch 170kr

**Victoria** Turngata 3 ☎ 69 38 58 00, Ⓦ hotelvictoria .no. Overlooking the park next to the Domkirke, this is the most recommendable among the town's handful of hotels: a comfortable, medium-sized, family-owned place with period trimmings that dates back to the 1880s. 695kr

## Halden

Just 3km from the Swedish border – and 40km from Fredrikstad – the workaday wood-processing town of **HALDEN** is bisected by the River Tista and hemmed in by steep forested hills, the closest of which is crowned by the commanding **Fredriksten Festning** (fortress), Halden's star turn and the main reason to visit. Work began on the fortress in 1661 at the instigation of Frederik III during a lull in the fighting between Sweden and Denmark. The stakes were high: the Swedes were determined to annihilate the Dano–Norwegian monarchy and had only just failed in their attempt to capture Oslo and Copenhagen. Consequently, Frederik was keen to build a fortress of immense strength to secure his northerly possessions. He called in Dutch engineers to design it and, after a decade, the result was a labyrinthine citadel whose thick perimeter walls, heavily protected gates, bastions and outlying forts were perfectly designed to suit the contours of the two steep, parallel ridges on which they were built. The proof of the pudding was in the eating. The Swedes besieged Fredriksten on several occasions without success, though the town itself suffered badly. In 1716, the Norwegians razed it to the ground, a scorched-earth policy that later prompted some nationalistic poppycock from the writer Bjørnstjerne Bjørnson: "We chose to burn our nation, ere we let it fall."

### Fredriksten Festning

Mid-May to Aug daily 10am–5pm • Guided tours (1hr) run throughout the season • 60kr • Ⓦ halden.museum.no

Ingenious and impregnable, **Fredriksten Festning** (Fredriksten Fortress) is on the south side of the River Tista, its forested slopes climbed by several steep footpaths, the most enjoyable of which begins on **Peder Colbjørnsens gate** and leads up to the main gatehouse. Allow at least an hour for a thorough exploration. Although most of the buildings are labelled, only a handful are open to the public, most notably the **Krigshistorisk Utstilling** (Military History Exhibition) in the old prison in the eastern curtain wall. Guided tours are available, but you shouldn't require any help to absorb the obvious and powerful atmosphere.

On the far side of the fortress, where the terrain is nowhere near as steep, you'll find a **monument** to the **Swedish king Karl XII**, who was killed by a bullet in the temple as he besieged the fort in 1718. An inveterate warmonger, Karl had exhausted the loyalty of his troops, and whether the bullet came from the fortress or one of his own men has been a matter of considerable Scandinavian speculation.

## ARRIVAL AND INFORMATION                                                    HALDEN

**By train** Halden train station abuts the south bank of the River Tista.

**By bus** The bus station is close to the train station on Jernbanegata.

**Tourist office** Torget 2, midway between the train station and the fortress (Mon–Fri: mid-June to mid-Aug 9am–4.30pm; mid-Aug to mid-June 9am–3.30pm; ☎ 69 19 09 80, Ⓦ visithalden.com).

**1**

## ACCOMMODATION

Despite its sterling fortress, Halden is too routine a place to spend the night, but if you're marooned there is a reasonable range of accommodation – and the tourist office (see p.109) has a full list.

**Park Hotel** Marcus Thranes gate 30 ☎69 21 15 00, ⓦpark-hotel.no. The pick of Halden's hotels, this neat and trim establishment occupies a mostly modern complex on the northwest edge of the town centre. 1430kr, sp/r 1090kr

# The west shore

West of the city centre, Oslo's rangy suburbs curve round the final basin of the Oslofjord before bubbling up over the hills almost as far as **DRAMMEN**, a substantial industrial settlement some 40km southwest of the capital. Built on an arm of the Oslofjord, the town handles most of the vehicles imported into Norway. This is hardly a reason to visit, however, and nor do the modern office blocks and stuffy late nineteenth-century buildings of its centre conjure up much interest. From here, there's a **choice of routes**, with the E134 wriggling west through Kongsberg (see p.174) bound for the western fjords, while the E18 presses on south down the Oslofjord.

Beyond Drammen, the **E18** soon shoots past **HORTEN**, a small port and naval base from where a **car ferry** shuttles across the Oslofjord to Moss (see p.106). Horten is also just to the north of the Viking burial mounds at Borre (see opposite). After the Horten turning, the E18 zips on down to the old port of Tønsberg, by some measure the most interesting town on this side of the Oslofjord.

## Tønsberg

The last town of any size on the Oslofjord's western shore, **TØNSBERG**, some 100km from Oslo, was founded by Harald Hårfagre in the ninth century, and rose to prominence in the Middle Ages as a major ecclesiastical and trading centre: its sheltered sound made a safe harbour, the plain behind it was ideal for settlement, and the town's palace and castle assured the patronage of successive monarchs. All of which sounds exciting, and you might expect Tønsberg to be one of the country's more important historical attractions, but sadly precious little survives from the town's medieval heyday. On the other hand, the recently upgraded waterfront makes for a particularly pleasant stroll, zeroing in on a handsome set of renovated, nineteenth-century warehouses, the **Tønsberg Brygge**, where the narrow lanes are dotted with bars and restaurants.

### Slottsfjellet

Mid-June to late Aug daily noon–5pm; late Aug to mid-Sept Sat & Sun noon–4pm • Free

Of Tønsberg's medieval castle, the **Slottsfjellet** (castle), only the foundations have survived, fragmentary ruins perched on a steep, wooded hill immediately to the north of the centre – though it is easy to appreciate the castle's strategic and defensive virtues. The Swedes burned it down in 1503 and the place was never rebuilt: today's watchtower, the clumpy **Slottsfjelltårnet**, was plonked on top in the nineteenth century.

## ARRIVAL AND INFORMATION

TØNSBERG

**By train** From Tønsberg train station, it's a 5–10min walk south to the main square, Torvet, and just a couple of hundred metres more – along Rådhusgaten – to the waterfront's Tønsberg Brygge.

**Tourist office** Storgaten 38, just off Torvet (late June to mid-Aug Mon–Fri 9.30am–4.30pm, plus July Sat 10am–2pm; ☎48 06 33 33, ⓦvisittonsberg.com). They issue free town maps and carry all sorts of local information.

## ACCOMMODATION AND EATING

### HOTELS AND HOSTEL

**Quality Hotel Tønsberg** Ollebukta 3 ☎33 00 41 00, ⓦchoicehotels.no. Right on the waterfront, this is the most stylish of Tønsberg's several central hotels, handsomely built in the shape of a ship's bow and as such a striking addition to the town's skyline. Part conference

centre and even including a concert hall, the hotel has over four hundred comfortable rooms with all mod cons, most with harbour views. **1395kr**, sp/r **1095kr**
**Thon Hotel Brygga** Nedre Langgate 40 ☎ 33 34 49 00, ⓦ thonhotels.no. This pleasant waterfront hotel holds seventy cheerful guest rooms in a modern building that has been constructed in the style of an old warehouse. **1600kr**
**Tønsberg Vandrerhjem** Dronning Blancasgate 22 ☎ 33 31 21 75, ⓦ hihostels.no. Tønsberg's well-kept HI hostel occupies a chalet-like structure in a residential area

beneath (and to the east of) the Slottsfjellet: turn right out of the train station and follow the signs for the 5min walk. Dorms **350kr**, doubles from **675kr**

**RESTAURANT**
**Restaurant Havariet** Nedre Langgate 30 ☎ 33 35 83 90. One of the better waterfront options, this popular and informal spot offers a wide menu with seafood and salads to the fore. Mains from 120kr. Mon–Sat 11am–1am, Sun noon–1am; kitchen till 10pm.

## Verdens Ende

The low-lying **islands and skerries** that nudge out into the Skagerrak to the south of Tønsberg are a popular holiday destination. By and large, people come here for the peace and quiet, with a bit of fishing and swimming thrown in, and the whole coast is dotted with summer homes. To the outsider, this is not especially stimulating, but there is one wonderfully scenic spot, **Verdens Ende** – "World's End" – about thirty minutes' drive from Tønsberg, right at the southernmost tip of the southernmost island, **Tjöme**. In this blustery spot, rickety fishing jetties straggle across a cove whose blue-black waters are surrounded by bare, sea-smoothed rocks and miniature islets. It would be nice to think a wandering Viking gave the place its name, but in fact it was a romantic gesture by a visiting Victorian.

## Åsgårdstrand

A short drive north from Tønsberg on Highway 311 is the seaside village of **ÅSGÅRDSTRAND**, where **Edvard Munch** spent many of his summers. Munch avoided the mountains of Norway whenever he could, sticking firmly to the country's flattest parts on account of his agoraphobia – and the lightly forested shoreline here at Åsgårdstrand suited him just fine.

### Munchs Hus

Edvards Munchs gate 25 • May & Sept Sat & Sun 11am–6pm; June–Aug Tues–Sun 11am–6pm • 25kr • ☎ 33 08 21 31
Perhaps surprisingly, the old, ochre-painted fisherman's **cottage** Munch purchased in 1897 has survived and, renamed the **Munchs Hus** (Munch House), it has been returned to its appearance when the artist lived and painted here; the adjoining studio has been repaired and refurbished too. There are no Munch paintings on display, but there are a few Munch prints and bits and bobs of period furniture.

## Borre's Viking burial mounds

Midgard Historisk Senter: May to mid-Sept daily 11am–4pm; mid-Sept to April Wed–Fri 11am–2pm & Sun 11am–4pm • 60kr • ⓦ midgardsenteret.no • From Åsgårdstrand, take Highway 311 to Highway 19 and turn right (for Horten)
A short distance north of Åsgårdstrand, 4km south of Horten and about 14km north of Tønsberg, **BORRE** is a scattered hamlet that boasts one of the largest ensembles of extant **Viking burial mounds** (600–900 AD) in all of Scandinavia, the **Borrehaugene**. There are seven large and 21 small mounds in total, with the best preserved being clustered together in the woods by the water's edge, a five-minute walk from the car park. These grassy bumps date from the seventh to the tenth century, when Borre was a royal burial ground and one of the wealthiest districts in southern Norway. The mounds are interesting in themselves but the setting is even better – in springtime wild flowers carpet the woods making this a perfect spot for a picnic. The area has been designated a national park and a visitor centre, the **Midgard Historisk Senter** (Midgard Historical Centre) stands beside the car park, though there's precious little actually in it – save yourself the entrance fee.

# The South

FEISTEIN FYR, NEAR STAVANGER

# The South

2

Arcing out into the Skagerrak between the Oslofjord and Stavanger, Norway's south coast may have little of the imposing grandeur of other, wilder parts of the country, but its eastern half, running down to Kristiansand, is undeniably lovely. Speckled with islands and backed by forests, fells and lakes, it's this part of the coast that attracts Norwegians in droves, equipped not so much with bucket and spade as with boat and navigational aids – for these waters, with their narrow inlets, islands and skerries, make for particularly enjoyable sailing.

Hundreds of Norwegians have summer cottages along this stretch of the coast and camping on the offshore islands is very popular too, especially as there are precious few restrictions: you can't stay in one spot for more than 48 hours, nor light a fire either on bare rock or among vegetation, and you must steer clear of anyone's home, but other than that you're pretty much free to go and come as you please. Leaflets detailing further coastal rules and regulations are available at any local tourist office.

The first part of the south coast, down to Kristiansand, is within easy striking distance of Denmark and as such has always been important for Norway's international trade. Many of the region's larger towns, Larvik and Porsgrunn for instance, started out as timber ports, but are now humdrum, industrial centres in their own right. In contrast, several of their smaller neighbours – **Risør**, **Lillesand** and **Grimstad** are the prime examples – have dodged (nearly) all the industry to become pretty, pocket-sized resorts, their white-painted clapboard houses providing an appropriately nautical, almost jaunty, air. Larger **Arendal** does something to bridge the gap between the resorts and the industrial towns and does so very nicely. There's also amenable **Sandefjord**, which may well be the first stop on your itinerary as it has its own international airport – Oslo Torp (see p.118).

Anchoring the south coast is Norway's fifth largest city, **Kristiansand**, a bustling port and lively resort with enough sights, restaurants, bars and beaches to while away a night, maybe two. Beyond Kristiansand lies **Mandal**, an especially fetching holiday spot with a great beach, but thereafter the coast becomes harsher and less absorbing, and there's precious little to detain you before **Stavanger**, a burgeoning oil town and port with a clutch of historical sights and a full set of first-rate restaurants. Bergen may lay claim to being the "Gateway to the Fjords", but actually Stavanger is closer with the splendid **Lysefjord** and its famous **Preikestolen** rock leading the scenic charge.

Right along the south coast, **accommodation** of one sort or another is legion, with all the larger towns having at least a couple of hotels, but if you're after a bit of social bounce bear in mind the **season** is short, running from the middle of June to August; outside this period many attractions are closed and local boat trips curtailed.

## GETTING AROUND                                                    THE SOUTH

**By train** There are regular NSB trains (ⓦnsb.no) from Oslo to Kristiansand and Stavanger, but the rail line runs inland for most of its journey, only dipping down to the coast at the major resorts, which makes for a disappointing ride with the

Ibsen cuts his teeth in Grimstad p.123
Cruising the Blindleia p.124
Staying in a lighthouse p.130

Antony Gormley in Stavanger p.133
Stavanger to Bergen p.138

# Highlights

**❶ The Clarion Hotel Tyholmen** Occupying a brace of handsome wooden buildings looking out to sea, Arendal's top-flight hotel is one of the finest places to stay on the whole of the south coast. **See p.122**

**❷ M/B Øya** Take a delightful three-hour cruise along the coast between Lillesand and Kristiansand on this pocket-sized ferryboat. **See p.124**

**❸ Mandal** One of the prettiest ports on the south coast, Mandal boasts the country's finest beach, a long and wide sandy expanse with forested dunes immediately behind. **See p.129**

**❹ Gamle Stavanger** The prettiest part of the city, comprising a network of lovely old clapboard houses with picket fences and immaculate gardens. **See p.135**

**❺ Stay in a lighthouse** A string of south-coast lighthouses offer simple lodgings in wild locations. Best of all is probably storm-battered Feistein. **See p.138**

**❻ Preikestolen** A geological oddity near Stavanger, this great hunk of rock offers staggering views down to the Lysefjord on three of its sides. **See p.141**

**❼ Kjeragbolten** Not for the faint-hearted, this rock is snagged between cliffs high above the Lysefjord – walk on it if you dare. **See p.141**

**HIGHLIGHTS ARE MARKED ON THE MAP ON P.116**

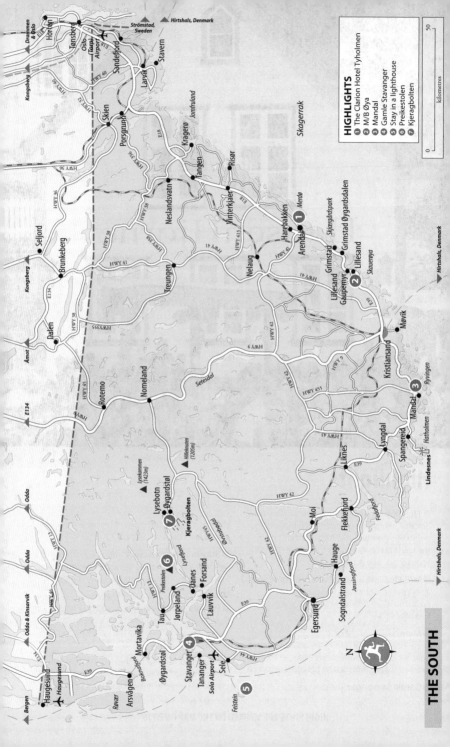

HIGHLIGHTS
1 The Clarion Hotel Tyholmen
2 M/B Øya
3 Mandal
4 Gamle Stavanger
5 Stay in a lighthouse
6 Preikestolen
7 Kjeragbolten

0 ———— 50
kilometres

N

sea mostly shielded from view. Note also that many main-line train stations are some way inland, meaning you'll need to take another connecting journey by local bus or train to get to the smaller seaside resorts. Kristiansand, on the other hand, has its own main-line bus and train stations.

**By bus** The main long-distance bus company is Nor-Way Bussekspress (Ⓦ nor-way.no), whose express buses connect Oslo with Kristiansand and Kristiansand with Stavanger. As with the train, long-distance buses tend to take inland routes, dropping passengers at rural bus stops from where connecting local buses run to the smaller resorts – Risør is a case in point.

**By car** Like the train line, the main road– the E18/E39 – sticks stubbornly inland for most of the 330km from Oslo to Kristiansand (E18) and again for the 240km on to Stavanger (E39). You're much better off with your own vehicle if you're after visiting most of the smaller places unless you are infinitely diligent with bus and rail timetables.

**2**

# Sandefjord to Lillesand

The fretted **shoreline** that stretches the 200km southwest from Tønsberg (see p.110) to Lillesand is home to a series of small resorts that are particularly popular with weekenders from Oslo. The most interesting is **Grimstad**, with its Ibsen connections, the liveliest is **Arendal**, and the prettiest are **Lillesand** and **Risør**. All four have decent places to stay, but only a fifth resort, pint-sized **Kragerø**, has an HI hostel. Many of the resorts, including Lillesand, Kragerø and Arendal, offer **boat trips** out to the myriad islets that dot this coast, with trippers bent on a spot of swimming and beach – or at least rock – combing. The islands were once owned by local farmers, but many are now in public ownership and zealously protected from any development. Most of the resorts also offer longer cruises along the coast during the summer, the prettiest being the delightful three-hour trip from Lillesand to Kristiansand.

## GETTING AROUND
SANDEFJORD TO LILLESAND

**By bus** Fast and frequent express buses scuttle along the E18 from Oslo and/or Tønsberg to Kristiansand and these connect with local buses that run from the main road to individual resorts.

**By train** A train line runs just inland from the coast, but it's not a particularly useful service – of the places described here only Arendal and Sandefjord have their own train stations.

## Sandefjord

**SANDEFJORD**, some 120km south of Oslo, is best known as an international ferry port and as the site of **Oslo (Torp) airport**. It's an amiable, low-key kind of place, whose wide and open waterfront culminates in a spectacular water fountain – the **Hvalfangstmonumentet** (Whalers' Monument) – in which, amid the billowing spray, a slender rowing boat and its crew ride the tail fluke of a whale. This is perhaps as good as it gets, but the town does rustle up a quartet of other/lesser attractions.

### Kurbadet
Thor Dahls gate • Ⓦ sandefjordkurbad.no
Sandefjord's former thermal baths, the **Kurbadet**, are housed in a distinctive wooden complex built in a Viking-inspired dragon style in 1899; the baths closed at the beginning of World War II and have come close to being demolished on several occasions, but they have managed to hang on and are now in use as a cultural centre. The complex is located a couple of minutes' walk from the Hvalfangstmonumentet – to the right as you face inland.

### Hvalfangstmuseet and the Southern Actor
**Hvalfangstmuseet** Museumsgata 39 • May–Aug daily 11am–5pm; Sept daily 11am–4pm; Oct–April Mon–Sat 11am–3pm, Sun noon–4pm • 75kr **Southern Actor** Late June to Aug daily 11am–5pm • Same ticket as Hvalfangstmuseet • ☎ 94 79 33 41, Ⓦ hvalfangstmuseet.no
The town's best museum is the **Hvalfangstmuseet** (Whaling Museum) which, like the Hvalfangstmonumentet, also trumpets the town's whalers. The local whaling industry

built up a head of steam at the end of the nineteenth century, peaking in the early 1950s, when as many as three thousand local men were dependent on whaling for their livelihoods. The museum's forte is its large collection of photographs of whalers at work, rest and play.

If the museum whets your interest, there's more whaling paraphernalia back down on the waterfront in the **Southern Actor**, a 1950s' whaling vessel that managed to end up moored in the harbour.

## Bjerggata

Running roughly parallel to – and one block east of – Museumsgata is the oldest and prettiest part of town, a narrow wedge of old clapboard buildings which ramble along the narrow confines of **Bjerggata**. Here you get the real flavour of what Sandefjord was like until the 1950s, with many of the houses built around rocks that were too difficult to move or extract.

### North of the centre: Gokstadhaugen
Open access • Free

It's just a couple of kilometres northeast from the town centre along Highway 303 to the **Gokstadhaugen**, the grassy mound which marks the spot where the **Gokstad Viking longship** was unearthed in 1880. The vessel is now on display in Oslo (see p.84), but information plaques displayed here add some context.

### ARRIVAL AND INFORMATION                                                    SANDEFJORD

**By plane** Oslo (Torp) airport is about 10km northeast of Sandefjord. The Torp-Ekspressen bus (see p.90) links the airport with Oslo and there are also airport buses to Sandefjord Torp train station, just one stop along the line from Sandefjord station (hourly; 7min) – and a little under 2hr from Oslo S.

**By train and bus** From Sandefjord's train and neighbouring bus station, it's about 900m to the waterfront, straight down Jernbanealleen. Destinations by train from Sandefjord include Oslo (every 1–2hr; 1hr

50min) and Tønsberg (every 1–2hr; 20min); there are also buses to Oslo (5–7 daily; 4hr; change at Skien).

**By ferry** Regular Color Line car ferries (ⓦ colorline.com) link Sandefjord with Strömstad in Sweden. The ferry dock is at the foot of the town, close to the centre.

**Tourist office** In the Kurbadet at Thor Dahlsgate 7, just back from the waterfont (July to late Aug Mon–Fri 9am–5.30pm, Sat 10am–5pm, Sun 12.30–5pm; rest of year Mon–Fri 9am–4pm; ☎ 33 46 05 90, ⓦ visitsandefjord.com).

### ACCOMMODATION AND EATING

#### HOTELS AND B&BS

**Hotel Kong Carl** Torggata 9 ☎ 33 46 31 17, ⓦ kongcarl .no. This is Sandefjord's most distinctive hotel, located in an old timber building right in the centre of town. The 25 guest rooms are each kitted out with a potpourri of old furnishings – pleasant if not exactly stunning. **1495kr**, sp/r **1095kr**

**Lisbet's Guesthouse** Bjerggata 33 ☎ 45 24 00 02, ⓔ lisbe-ti@online.no. There are a couple of attractive B&Bs in the old part of town, notably this homely little place where there is one room to rent in the annexe with a two-bed bunk and a shower. **450kr**

**Rica Park Hotel** Strandpromenaden 9 ☎ 33 44 74 00,

ⓦ rica.no. This large, chain hotel in a big, modern tower block just back from the waterfront is one of Sandefjord's more appealing places to stay. The rooms lack distinction, but they are proficiently modern. **1300kr**

#### RESTAURANT

**Mathuset Solvold** Thor Dahlsgate 9 ☎ 33 46 27 41, ⓦ smak.no. This well-turned-out café-restaurant, located between the tourist office and the main square, offers a wide-ranging menu – from pasta to mussels – with main courses averaging around 250kr. Mon–Sat 5pm–1am, kitchen till 10pm.

# Kragerø

Around 70km south of Sandefjord along the E18 you reach the first of several turns that lead down to the seashore at **KRAGERØ**, one of the busiest resorts on the coast, whose narrow harbour is spanned by a dinky little bridge. Kragerø has a tiny centre, its cramped lanes and alleys rising steeply from the harbourfront, and makes a good living as a supply depot for the surrounding coves and islets, where the Norwegians hunker down in their summer cottages. Kragerø was founded as a timber port in the seventeenth century and later boomed as a shipbuilding centre, its past importance recalled by its clutch of handsome old houses. The port was also a fashionable watering hole in the late nineteenth and early twentieth centuries, and it was here that **Edvard Munch** produced some of his jollier paintings.

### Kittelsenhuset

Theodor Kittelsens vei 5, off Storgata • Mid-June to mid-Aug Mon–Sat noon–5pm • 70kr • ⓦ telemarkmuseum.no/museum
/kittelsenhuset

A middling painter but superb illustrator, **Theodor Kittelsen** (1857–1914) defined the popular appearance of the country's folkloric creatures – from trolls through to sirens – in his illustrations for Asbjørnsen and Moe's *Norwegian Folk Tales*, published in 1883. A native of Kragerø, Kittelsen spent many of his summers here and his family home, in the centre of town just west of the harbour, is now the bright and breezy **Kittelsenhuset**. The lively little museum celebrates the artist's life and times with a smattering of his paintings and a few family knick-knacks.

### Jomfruland

Ferries: 4 daily; 1hr; 70kr each way; ☎ 40 00 58 58, ⓦ fjordbat.no

The most popular jaunt out from Kragerø is the ferry to **Jomfruland**, a long and slender island stuck out in the Skagerrak beyond the offshore skerries. The island, which is just 8km long and never more than 900m wide, is very different from its rocky neighbours, its fertile soils supporting deciduous woodland and providing good pastureland. The flatness of the terrain, plus the abundant bird life, attracts scores of **walkers**, who wander the island's network of footpaths. For many, the **beach** is the main target, rough and pebbly on the island's sea-facing side, more shingle and sand on its sheltered side with the best bit generally reckoned to be **Øitangen** in the north. The ferry docks about halfway along the island, an easy stroll from the island's two **lighthouses** – one old, from 1839, the other new, from 1937 – which stand side by side.

### ARRIVAL AND INFORMATION                                              KRAGERØ

**By bus** Long-distance express buses linking Oslo and Kristiansand stop at Tangen, from where there is a connecting local bus service on to Kragerø; the journey from Tangen takes 25min. Kragerø bus station is a stone's throw from the northern tip of the harbour. Sørlandsekspressen services (#190; ⓦ nor-way.no) run from Tangen to Kristiansand (every 2hr; 2hr) and Oslo (every 2hr; 3hr).

**By train** The nearest train station is at Neslandsvatn, on the Oslo–Kristiansand line. There is a connecting bus service from Neslandsvatn to Kragerø (1hr), but note that

buses do not meet all the trains – check with NSB before you set out. There are services from Neslandsvatn to Kristiansand (2–4 daily; 1hr 50min) and Oslo (2–4 daily; 2hr 40min).

**Tourist office** Torvgata 1 (mid-June to mid-Aug Mon–Fri 9am–7pm, Sat 9am–6pm, Sun 10am–5pm; rest of year Mon–Fri 9am–4pm; ☎ 35 98 23 88, ⓦ visitkragero.no). The tourist office is a stone's throw from the northern tip of the harbour, and also just a couple of minutes' walk from the Jomfruland ferry dock.

### ACCOMMODATION AND EATING

**Tollboden Restaurant** P. A. Heuchs gate 4 ☎ 35 98 90 90, ⓦ tollboden.org. Popular waterfront café-restaurant with a large open-air terrace that spreads a wide gastronomic net from pizzas through to seafood. Pizzas begin at 170kr; main courses – both meat and fish – are around 250kr in the evening, less at lunchtime. June–Aug Mon–Sat noon–9pm, Sun 1–9pm; check website for out-of-season hours.

**Victoria Hotel** P.A. Heuchs gate 31 ☎ 35 98 75 25, ⓦ victoria-kragero.no. This is Kragerø's most agreeable hotel, occupying a good-looking, brightly painted harbourside building right in the centre of town. Each of the hotel's 33 guest rooms are individually decorated in browns and creams and the best have balconies overlooking the harbour. They also offer massage sessions and bike rental. **1050kr**

# Risør

**RISØR**, spreading round the head of a gentle promontory about 45km from Kragerø, is a good-looking town, its genial array of old and white timber houses winkling back from its wide and deep harbour. The town rustles up a string of summer festivals, from bluegrass in July (⊚risorbluegrassfestival.no) to chamber music in June (⊚kammermusikkfest.no), and is something of a centre for arts and crafts, but it's the general flavour of the place that appeals rather than anything specific.

Risør started out as a small fishing village, but the Dutch fleet began dropping by for timber in the 1570s and the port boomed until, by the 1880s, one hundred sailing vessels – and one thousand seamen – called the place home. A fire destroyed the bulk of the town in 1861 but it was quickly rebuilt, and most of the wooden houses that survive date from this period. Risør's marine economy collapsed in the 1920s and today it looks like a rather conservative small town, but – surprise, surprise – in 2007 its citizens elected Knut Henning Thygesen, a member of the Red Party, a fusion of the Workers' Communist Party (AKP) and the Red Electoral Alliance (RV), as their mayor.

## ARRIVAL AND INFORMATION                                        RISØR

**By bus** Long-distance express buses linking Oslo and Kristiansand stop at Vinterkjaer, from where there is a connecting local bus service on to Risør (25min). Risør bus station is on the main street just a few metres from the harbour. Sørlandsekspressen services (#190; ⊚nor-way.no) run from Vinterkjaer to Kristiansand (every 1–2hr; 1hr 40min) and Oslo (every 1–2hr; 3hr 20min).

**Tourist office** Torvet 1, down by the harbour (early June & late Aug Mon–Sat 10am–4pm; late June to mid-Aug Mon–Fri 10am–6pm; rest of year Mon–Fri 11am–3pm; ☎37 15 22 70, ⊚risor.no). Can advise on all things local.

## ACCOMMODATION AND EATING

**Bakgården** Kragsgate 3 ☎90 17 79 90. In the town centre just back from the harbour, this cosy little café serves tasty salads and snacks. It also doubles up as an art gallery and performance venue for theatre and live music. Core hours: Tues–Fri 11am–5pm, Sat 11am–6pm.

**Det Lille Hotel** Storgata 5 ☎37 15 14 95, ⊚detlillehotel.no. Among the town's several hotels and guesthouses, the most individual is this hotel whose twelve suites, each of which is decorated in a pleasing rendition of period style, are distributed between two old buildings, one in the centre, one by the harbour. **1800kr**

# Arendal

South from Risør, it's about 45km to the bustling town of **ARENDAL**, one of the most appealing places on the coast, its sheltered harbour curling right into the centre, which is further crimped and cramped by the forested hills that push in from behind. The town's heyday was in the eighteenth century when its shipyards churned out dozens of the sleek wooden sailing ships that then dominated international trade. The shipyards faded away in the late nineteenth century, but there's an attractive reminder of the boom times in the striking medley of old timber buildings that make up the oldest part of town, **Tyholmen**, which rolls over the steep and bumpy promontory just to the southwest of the modern centre. To explore Tyholmen's every nook and cranny, sign up for one of the tourist office's guided walking tours.

## Gamle Rådhus

Rådhusgaten

Tyholmen's architectural highlight is the **Gamle Rådhus** (Old Town Hall), Norway's tallest wooden house, a handsome, four-storey structure, whose classical symmetries overlook the Tyholmen waterfront. The house was built as a private residence in 1815, but the Danish merchant who owned the place died twelve years later and his widow sold it to the council, who turned it into the town hall, a role it performed until 2004.

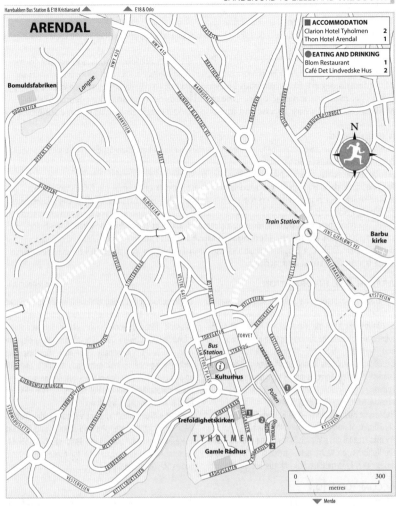

## Trefoldighetskirken

Kirkebakken

Perched on a rocky knoll overlooking the town centre at the northern edge of Tyholmen, the massive and massively ugly red-brick **Trefoldighetskirken** (Church of the Trinity) was meant to celebrate the town's economic success as well as its godliness. Instead, it almost ended up in farce and fiasco: Arendal hit the financial skids in 1886 and, although the church had been finished, there was no money left to equip the interior and the altar was only installed twenty years later.

## Kulturhus and Pollen

The town centre's most conspicuous building is the glassy, modern **Kulturhus**, on Sam Eydes plass (ⓦarendalkulturhus.no), which hosts conferences, public meetings and concerts to suit (almost) every musical taste. From here, it's a couple of minutes' walk east to **Pollen**, the short, rectangular inner harbour, which is flanked by pavement cafés and bars.

**2**

## The Bomuldsfabriken

Oddenveien 5 • Tues–Sun noon–4pm • Free • ☎ 37 01 31 43, ⓦ bomuldsfabriken.no • Signposted off Highway 410, one of the main approach roads into Arendal from the E18

The district's largest contemporary arts gallery, the **Bomuldsfabriken**, is housed in a former textile factory around 2km north of the centre. The gallery hosts half a dozen exhibitions of contemporary art every year with Norwegian work to the fore, though Swedes and Danes get regular outings here too. One recent exhibition featured the talented **Sverre Malling** (b.1977), whose precise and intricate work is magic realism at its unsettling best.

## Merdø island

Passenger ferries (30min) leave from Pollen • June to late Aug daily every hour, on the hour (10am–5pm); rest of year sporadic service – details from the tourist office • 50kr

Among the scattering of islands lying just offshore from Arendal, the most diverting is **Merdø**, a fairly flat, lightly wooded islet, whose safe anchorages, orchards and fresh water made it a popular haven for sailing ships right up until the end of the nineteenth century. Footpaths network the island, and there's a shingle beach and a summertime café. Merdø's one and only village is a pretty affair that spreads along the foreshore, and it's here that you'll find the **Merdøgaard Museum** (late June to mid-Aug Mon–Fri noon–4pm; 20kr), a brightly painted eighteenth-century sea captain's house, complete with original fixtures and fittings.

### ARRIVAL AND INFORMATION

ARENDAL

**By train** On a branch line from Nelaug train station, Arendal train station is on the north side of town, a 5–10min walk from the main square, Torvet: go to the roundabout close to the station and then either proceed up and over the steep hill along Iuellsklev and then Bendiksklev, or (more easily) stroll through the tunnel (signed: P-Torget). Torvet is metres from the inner harbour, Pollen.

Arendal to: Nelaug (2–4 daily; 35min).

Nelaug to: Kristiansand (2–4 daily; 1hr); Oslo (2–4 daily; 3hr 20min); Stavanger (2–4 daily; 4hr 30min).

**By bus** Arendal bus station is in the centre of town beside the Kulturhus on Vestre gate, just west of Torvet. Local buses (☎ 177, ⓦ nettbuss.no) link the bus station with neighbouring points along the coast, including Grimstad (hourly; 30min), Kristiansand (hourly; 1hr 30min) and Lillesand (hourly; 50min). For places further afield, including Oslo (every 2hr; 3hr 45min), long-distance express buses, principally Nor-Way Bussekspress's Sørlandsekspressen (#190; ⓦ nor-way.no), drop and pick up passengers on the edge of town, just off the motorway at the Harebakken kiosk and bus station, from where you'll need to take a local bus into town.

**Tourist office** Kulturhus complex, Sam Eydes plass 1 (Mon–Fri 8.30am–4pm, plus mid-June to mid-Aug Sat 11am–4pm & July Sun 11am–4pm; ☎ 37 00 55 44, ⓦ arendal.com). They issue free town maps and have oodles of local information.

### ACCOMMODATION

★ **Clarion Hotel Tyholmen** Teaterplassen 2 ☎ 37 07 68 00, ⓦ choicehotels.no. This smashing hotel occupies a matching pair of warehouse-style buildings right on the Tyholmen quayside: full marks to the architects, who designed the second, newer block to blend in seamlessly with its older neighbour. The guest rooms are resolutely modern, with blues and whites throughout, and most have splendid sea views. **1400kr**, sp/r **1000kr**

**Thon Hotel Arendal** Friergangen 1 ☎ 37 05 21 50, ⓦ thonhotels.com. This straightforward, modern chain hotel is in the centre just off the west side of Pollen. Browns and creams predominate and there are wooden floors throughout. **1300kr**, sp/r **1000kr**

### EATING AND DRINKING

In the summertime, Arendal hums at night with a clutter of busy cafés, bars and restaurants lining up along and around **Pollen** – quite enough to keep the punters going till the wee hours of the morning each and every weekend.

**Blom Restaurant** Langbryggen 9 ☎ 37 00 14 14, ⓦ blomrestaurant.no. Smart, modern restaurant with an outside terrace overlooking Pollen. An inventive menu features the likes of grilled reindeer with pear cooked in cassis, creamed celeriac and rosemary sauce (325kr). Daily 4–11pm.

**Café Det Lindvedske Hus** Nedre Tyholmsvei 7b ☎ 37 02 18 38. Upstairs in an old building just to the south of Pollen, the grooviest place in town is a laidback, arty sort of place serving light meals – pastas, salads and so forth. Mains start at around 80kr and the kitchen closes at 9pm, whereupon it's over to the drinking. Mon–Fri 11am–11pm, Sat & Sun 1–11pm.

# Grimstad

Some 20km south from Arendal along the E18, **GRIMSTAD** is a brisk huddle of white timber houses with orange- and black-tiled roofs stacked up behind the harbour. Nowadays scores of yachts are moored in the harbour, but at the beginning of the nineteenth century the town had no fewer than forty shipyards and carried on a lucrative import–export trade with France – an economic boom that hooked in a young **Henrik Ibsen**.

**2**

## Ibsen-museet

Henrik Ibsens gate 14 • Early June & late Aug Sat 11am–5pm, Sun noon–5pm, plus guided tours Mon–Fri – contact Grimstad tourist office; mid-June to mid-Aug Mon–Sat 11am–5pm, Sun noon–5pm • 80kr

The small house where Henrik Ibsen lived and worked as a pharmacist is now the **Ibsen-museet**, located just up from the harbour in the centre of town. The alley that serves as the entrance to the museum and much of the ground floor beyond has been returned to an approximation of its appearance when Ibsen lived here, complete with creaking wooden floors and narrow-beamed ceilings. Upstairs, there's a detailed display on Ibsen the dramatist plus an assortment of original letters and documents and, best of all, a glass cabinet of Ibsen memorabilia – his glasses and their case, an inkstand, a ruler and even a piece of the great man's hair.

## Reimanngården

Vestregate

Signposted off Storgata, once the town's main street, near the harbourfront is the **Reimanngården**, four replica eighteenth-century buildings. One of these is a reconstruction of another pharmacy where Ibsen worked – the original building was demolished in the 1950s. The Reimanngården is now home to the town's art society.

## Grimstad Kirke

Kirkegata • No fixed opening times • The church is a short, steep hike north of the Ibsen House

The **Grimstad Kirke** is a large, late nineteenth-century wooden church on a high hill above the harbour. Many of its original fittings have survived, including some heavy-duty wrought-iron lamps and candelabras, plus a tapestry of the Resurrection by the font.

## Skjærgårdspark

Contact the tourist office for information and advice on boats

Many of the myriad islands that guard the seaward approaches to the town are protected within the **Skjærgårdspark**, and have public access moorings, as well as picnic and bathing facilities. One or two of them can be reached by water taxi, but mostly you'll have to rent a boat.

### IBSEN CUTS HIS TEETH IN GRIMSTAD

Born in the hamlet of Skien, **Henrik Ibsen** (1828–1906) left his home at the tender age of sixteen, moving to Grimstad, where he worked as an apprentice pharmacist for the next six years. The ill-judged financial dealings of Ibsen's father had impoverished the family, and Henrik's already jaundiced view of Norway's provincial bourgeoisie was confirmed here in the port, whose worthies Ibsen mocked in poems like *Resignation*, and *The Corpse's Ball*. It was here too that Ibsen picked up first-hand news of the Paris Revolution of 1848, an event that radicalized him and inspired his paean to the insurrectionists of Budapest, *To Hungary*, written in 1849. Nonetheless, Ibsen's stay on the south coast is more usually recalled as providing the setting for some of his better-known plays, especially his *Pillars of Society*.

**2**

## ARRIVAL AND INFORMATION                                      GRIMSTAD

**By bus** Local buses (☎ 177, ⓦ nettbuss.no) link Grimstad bus station, at the south end of the harbour, with neighbouring points along the coast, including Arendal (hourly; 30min), Kristiansand (hourly; 1hr) and Lillesand (hourly; 1hr). For places further afield, including Oslo (every 2hr; 4hr 15min), long-distance express buses, principally Nor-Way Bussekspress's Sørlandsekspressen (#190; ⓦ nor-way.no), drop and pick up passengers on the edge of town, just off the motorway at Grimstad Øygardsdalen.

**Tourist office** Storgata 1, by the harbour in the centre of town around 200m from the bus station (late June to late Aug Mon–Fri 9am–6pm, Sat & Sun 10am–4pm; rest of year Mon–Fri 8.30am–4pm; ☎ 37 25 01 68, ⓦ visitgrimstad.com). They supply free town maps and have lots of information on the Skjærgårdspark.

## ACCOMMODATION AND EATING

**Apotekergården** Skolegata 3 ☎ 37 04 50 25, ⓦ apotekergaarden.no. The liveliest place in town, this informal café-restaurant has a wide-ranging menu, featuring everything from pizzas and burgers to meat and fish dishes – try the braised beef (245kr). Mon–Thurs & Sun 11am–midnight, Fri & Sat 11am–2am.

**Rica Hotel Grimstad** Kirkegaten 3 ☎ 37 25 25 25, ⓦ rica-hotels.com. The best hotel in town, occupying an old and cleverly converted clapboard complex among the narrow lanes near the Ibsen Museum. One hundred well-appointed guest rooms. 1900kr, sp/r 1300kr

# Lillesand

Bright and cheery **LILLESAND**, just 20km south of Grimstad, is one of the most popular holiday spots on the coast, the white clapboard houses of its tiny centre draped prettily round the harbourfront. One or two of the buildings, notably the sturdy **Rådhus** of 1734, are especially fetching, but it's the general appearance of the place that appeals, best appreciated from the terrace of one of the town's waterfront café-bars.

## ARRIVAL AND INFORMATION                                      LILLESAND

**By bus** Local buses (☎ 177, ⓦ nettbuss.no) pull into the centre of Lillesand, pausing at the bus station at the southern end of the harbour, footsteps from the tourist office; local buses serve Arendal (hourly; 1hr 30min), Kristiansand (hourly; 30min) and Grimstad (hourly; 1hr). However, long-distance express buses, principally Nor-Way Bussekspress's Sørlandsekspressen (#190; ⓦ nor-way.no) to Oslo (every 2hr; 4hr 30min), drop and pick up passengers on the edge of town, just off the E18 motorway at Lillesand Gaupemyr.

**Tourist office** Havnegata 10, in the centre (late June & early Aug Mon–Sat 10am–6pm & Sun noon–4pm; July daily 10am–6pm; ☎ 37 26 17 50, ⓦ lillesand.kommune.no).

## ACCOMMODATION AND EATING

★ **Hotel Norge** Strandgata 3 ☎ 37 27 01 44, ⓦ hotelnorge.no. Lillesand's one first-rate hotel occupies a grand old wooden building metres from the harbour.

Refurbished in attractive vintage style, the interior holds some charming stained-glass windows with rooms named after some of the famous people who have stayed

---

## CRUISING THE BLINDLEIA

Lillesand's nautical highlight is the three-hour cruise aboard **M/B Øya** (July to early Aug Mon–Sat daily at 10am; 255kr one-way, 420kr return; ☎ 95 93 58 55, ⓦ blindleia.no), a dinky little passenger ferry which wiggles its way south to Kristiansand (see opposite) in part along a narrow channel separating the mainland from the offshore islets. Sheltered from the full force of the ocean, this channel – the **Blindleia** – was once a major trade route, but today it's trafficked by every sort of pleasure craft imaginable, from replica three-mast sailing ships and vintage tugboats to the sleekest of yachts. Other, faster, boats make the trip too, but the M/B Øya is the most charming.

If the sailing schedule of the M/B Øya does not suit, contact Lillesand tourist office for details of a wide variety of local boat trips, from fishing trips and cruises along the coast to the summertime **badeboot** (bathing boat), which shuttles across to Hestholm bay on the island of **Skauerøya**, where swimmers don't seem to notice just how cold the Skagerrak actually is.

here – the novelist Knut Hamsun and the Spanish king Alfonso XIII for starters. It also has the town's best restaurant (June–Aug daily noon till 11pm; out of season, call ahead for hours), a smart affair where they serve delicious meat and fish dishes (mains around 250kr) – try the butter-roasted halibut with seasonal vegetables. 1500kr, sp/r 1200kr

**Tingsaker Familiecamping** Øvre Tingsaker ❶ 37 27 04 21, ⓦ tingsakercamping.no. Well-equipped and very popular lakeside campsite with self-catering facilities, canoe rental, a pool and cabins with en-suite facilities, two bedrooms and a mini-veranda. About 1km northeast of the centre – to get there, take Storgata and keep going. May–Sept. Tents 185kr, cabins 990kr

# Kristiansand

With 82,000 inhabitants, **KRISTIANSAND**, some 30km west along the E18 from Lillesand, is Norway's fifth-largest town and a part-time holiday resort – altogether a genial, energetic place which thrives on its ferry connections with Denmark, busy marinas, passable **sandy beaches** and, last but not least, its offshore oil industry. In summer, the seafront and adjoining streets are a frenetic bustle of bars, fast-food joints and flirting holidaymakers, and even in winter Norwegians come here to live it up.

Like so many other Scandinavian towns, Kristiansand was founded by – and named after – **Christian IV**, who saw an opportunity to strengthen his coastal defences here. Building started in 1641, and the town has retained the spacious quadrant plan that characterized all of Christian's projects. There are few specific sights as such, but the place is well worth a quick look around, especially when everyone else has gone to the beach and left the central pedestrianized streets relatively empty. The main historic attraction, however, is a few kilometres out of town at the **Kristiansand Kanonmuseum**, the forbidding remains of a large coastal gun battery built during the German occupation of World War II.

KRISTIANSAND

**ACCOMMODATION**
| | |
|---|---|
| Centrum Budget Hotel | 3 |
| Frobusdalen Rom | 2 |
| Rica Hotel Norge | 5 |
| Roligheden Camping | 1 |
| Scandic Kristiansand | 4 |

**EATING & DRINKING**
| | |
|---|---|
| Drømmeplassen | 1 |
| FRK Larsen | 3 |
| Glipp | 2 |
| Sjøhuset | 4 |
| Vaertshuset Pieder Ro | 5 |

## Domkirke

Kirkegata • Sept–June Mon–Sat 11am–2pm, plus Fri 9.30pm–midnight; July Mon–Sat 10am–4pm; closed Aug; services only on Sun • Free

Neat and trim, the gridiron streets that make up Kristiansand's compact centre hold one architectural highlight, the **Domkirke** (Cathedral), an imposing neo-Gothic edifice dating from the 1880s, whose spire pokes high into the sky at the corner of Kirkegata and Rådhusgaten. The interior of the cathedral is sombre-serious, but there is one notable decorative feature, the large **painting** above the main altar showing a post-Resurrection scene – the breaking of bread at Emmaus – by Eilif Petterssen (1852–1928), a prominent portrait-painter and illustrator.

## Sørlandets Kunstmuseum

Skippergaten 24 • Tues–Sat 11am–5pm, Sun noon–4pm • 60kr • Ⓦ skmu.no

The pick of the town's several museums is the **Sørlandets Kunstmuseum** (Sørlandet Art Museum), whose well-appointed premises are used for a lively programme of temporary exhibitions with contemporary art to the fore. The museum's permanent collection is quite small – though there are ambitious plans to expand it – but it does hold examples of the work of many of Norway's leading nineteenth-century painters, including two works by Johan Dahl (see p.68), a Munch, and Christian Krohg's earthy *Admonition*. There are also several paintings by Amaldus Nielsen (1838–1932), a largely forgotten Norwegian Romanticist whose smooth and glossy landscapes are best exemplified by the beatific *Morgen i Ny-Hellesund*.

## Christiansholm Festning

Strandpromenaden • Mid-May to mid-Sept daily 9am–9pm • Free

As a point of interest, the cathedral's main rival is the **Christiansholm Festning** (Christiansholm Fortress), a squat fortress whose sturdy circular tower and zigzagging earth-and-stone ramparts overlook the marina in the east harbour. Built in 1672, the tower's walls are 5m thick, a defensive precaution that proved unnecessary since it never saw action. These days it houses various arts and crafts displays.

## Galgebergtangen

If you fancy a **swim**, one option is to head off to **Galgebergtangen** (Gallows' Point), an attractive rocky cove with a small sandy beach, 2km east of the town centre. To get there, go over the bridge at the end of Dronningens gate, take the first major right at the lights – Kuholmsveien – and follow the signs.

## Kristiansand Kanonmuseum

Feb to mid-May, Oct & Nov Sun only noon–4pm; mid-May to mid-June & mid-Aug to Sept Mon–Wed 11am–3pm, Thurs–Sun 11am–5pm; mid-June to mid-Aug daily 11am–6pm • 60kr • Ⓦ kanonmuseet.no • Take Highway 456 out of Kristiansand, then Highway 457 for the last 3km

Despite the inveigling of the German admiralty, who feared the British would occupy Norway and thus trap their fleet in the Baltic, **Hitler** was lukewarm about invading Norway until he met **Vidkun Quisling** (see p.395) in Berlin in late 1939. Hitler took Quisling's assurances about his ability to stage a coup d'état at face value, no doubt encouraged by the Norwegian's virulent anti-Semitism, and was thereafter keen to proceed. In the event, the invasion went smoothly enough – even if Quisling was soon discarded – but for the rest of the war Hitler overestimated both Norway's strategic importance and the likelihood of an Allied counter-invasion in the north. These two errors of judgement prompted him both to garrison the country with nigh on half a million men and to build several hundred **artillery batteries** round the coast – a huge waste of resources even by his standards.

Work began on the coastal battery that is now conserved as the **Kristiansand Kanonmuseum**, at **MØVIK** 10km south of Kristiansand along the coast, in 1941, using – like all equivalent emplacements in Norway – the forced labour of POWs. Around 1400 men worked on the project, which involved the installation of four big guns and the construction of protective concrete housings. The idea was to make the Skagerrak impassable for enemy warships at its narrowest part, and so complementary batteries were also installed opposite on the Danish shore; only a small zone in the middle was out of range, and this the Germans mined. The Kristiansand battery once covered 220 acres, but today the principal remains hog a narrow ridge, with a massive, empty **artillery casement** at one end, and a whopping **38cm-calibre gun** in a concrete well at the other. The gun, which could fire a 500kg shell almost 55km, is in pristine condition, and visitors can explore the loading area, complete with the original ramrods, wedges, trolleys and pulleys. Below is the underground command post and soldiers' living quarters, again almost exactly as they were in the 1940s – including the odd bit of German graffiti.

## ARRIVAL AND DEPARTURE

### KRISTIANSAND

Note the distinction between Kristiansund in the north and Kristiansand in the south: to make things easier, on timetables and in brochures they are often written as Kristiansund N and Kristiansand S.

**By train** The train station is beside Vestre Strandgate, on the edge of the central town grid.

Destinations Arendal (2–4 daily, change at Nelaug; 2hr); Kongsberg (3–5 daily; 3hr 20min); Oslo (2–4 daily; 4hr 30min); Stavanger (4–6 daily; 3hr).

**By bus** Buses, like international ferries, arrive close to the train station by Vestre Strandgate. Nor-Way Bussekspress's Sørlandsekspressen (#190) runs to Oslo (7 daily; 5hr) and the Sør-vest ekspressen (#300) to Flekkefjord (3–4 daily; 2hr) and Stavanger (3–4 daily; 4hr). Local buses link Kristiansand with Mandal (3–4 daily; 50min).

**By car** The main car parks are along Vestre Strandgate and,

although spaces can be hard to find at the height of the season, they remain your best bet as on-street parking in the rest of the town centre is strictly limited. Moving on from Kristiansand, the most obvious – as well as most pleasant – journey is to Stavanger (see p.133); it's certainly a lot more pleasant than the dreary 240km haul north up Setesdal on Highway 9 to the E134.

**By boat** If you're travelling north towards Oslo in July and early Aug, it might be worth considering the 3hr cruise up to Lillesand on the M/B Øya (see box, p.124). Boats depart from Quay 6, down on the waterfront.

## INFORMATION

**Tourist office** Rådhusgaten 6 (mid-June to Aug Mon–Fri 8.30am–6pm, Sat 10am–6pm, Sun noon–6pm; Sept to mid-June Mon–Fri 8.30am–4.30pm; ☎38 12 13 14, ⓦ visitkrs.no). The main regional tourist office, in the

centre of town, will issue free town maps and public transport timetables, assist with accommodation and has information on local boat cruises, island bathing and beaches.

## GETTING AROUND

**By foot** The best way to explore the town centre is on foot – it only takes about 10min to walk from one side to the other.

**By bike** For outlying attractions, including the best

beaches, you might want to rent a bike at Kristiansand Sykkelsenter, about 800m northwest of the tourist office, just off Highway 9 at Grim Torv 3 (☎38 02 68 35, ⓦ sykkelsenter.no).

## ACCOMMODATION

Kristiansand has a good range of accommodation with a fair sprinkling of hotels, a guesthouse or two, and a nearby campsite. Note, however, that vacant rooms can be thin on the ground in high season, when you should reserve ahead.

**Centrum Budget Hotel** Vestre Strandgate 49 ☎38 70 15 65, ⓦ budgethotel.no. Hard by the train station, this hostel-like hotel provides frugal, modern and very clean

lodgings at budget prices. Doubles are in the form of bunk beds, and all rooms are en suite. Breakfasts are served close by in a neighbouring café. <u>**550kr**</u>

**2**

**Frobusdalen Rom** Frobusdalen 2 ☎91 12 99 06, ⓦgjestehus.no. Undoubtedly the best place in town, this delightful guesthouse is a family-run affair occupying a good-looking mansion built for a ship-owner in 1917. The interior has been sensitively restored, with individually decorated, en-suite rooms and public areas sprinkled with period antiques. It's just a 5–10min walk from the train station, but is a little hard to find: on foot, head north up Vestre Strandgate, go straight on at the roundabout by the flyover (signed Evje), then take the path immediately to your right; Frobusdalen is 10m along on the left. Drivers should head north along Festningsgata; turn left onto Tordenskjolds gate; and then watch for the short right turn that leads to a narrow bridge spanning the E18; the far side of the bridge is a few metres from the guesthouse. Breakfast is not provided, but there are self-catering facilities. **600kr**

**Rica Hotel Norge** Dronningens gate 5 ☎38 17 40 00, ⓦrica.no. No prizes for architectural charm, but this large chain hotel is right in the centre of town and its 170 guest rooms are decorated in attractive modern style. Has its own spa too. **1600kr**, sp/r **1300kr**

**Roligheden Camping** Framnesveien ☎38 09 67 22, ⓦroligheden.no. Large campsite 3km east of the town centre behind a car park, which itself edges a yacht jetty. To get there, drive over the bridge at the end of Dronningens gate, turn right along Marviksveien, then right again near the end, following the signs. Open June–Aug. Pitch **140kr**

**Scandic Kristiansand** Markensgate 39 ☎21 61 42 00, ⓦscandic-hotels.com. The enterprising Scandic group, with its first-rate environmental policy, has about a dozen hotels in Norway and this one occupies a large modern block in the heart of downtown. The rooms are immaculate, all pastel shades and unfussy furnishings and fittings, and the breakfasts are top-notch. **1400kr**, sp/r **1000kr**

### EATING AND DRINKING

There are lots of cafés and restaurants in the centre of Kristiansand, with a particular concentration in the **Fiskebrygga**, a huddle of mostly modern timber houses set around a small harbour just off the eastern end of Vestre Strandgate. Standards are, however, very variable, so it pays to be selective. Kristiansand also has a fairly active **nightlife** based around a handful of downtown bars, which stay open until 2 or 3am.

**Drømmeplassen** Cnr Skippergaten/Kirkegata ☎38 04 71 00, ⓦdrommeplassen.no. Part clothes shop, part bakery, part café, this attractive little place sells an excellent range of bread as well as tasty coffee and the freshest of snacks. Mon–Fri 7am–6pm, Sat 9am–5pm, Sun 10am–5pm.

**FRK Larsen** Markensgate 5, cnr Kongens gate ☎38 07 14 13. It's something of a surprise that this resolutely alternative café-bar has survived for so long – but here it is in all its retro-New Age glory. Cocktails from 8pm and occasional live acts. Mon–Thurs & Sun 11am–midnight, till 3am Fri & Sat.

**Glipp** Rådhusgaten 11 ☎38 02 96 20, ⓦglipp.com. Popular, sometimes slick café-bar that does a reasonably good line in pastas and pizzas, though its main pull is its outside terrace, which looks out over the spacious main square. Daily 11am–11pm.

★ **Sjøhuset** Østre Strandgate 12a ☎38 02 62 60, ⓦsjohuset.no. In an old converted warehouse by the harbour at the east end of Markensgate, this excellent restaurant serves superb fish dishes at 250–350kr – less if you stick to the bar menu. Nautical fittings and wooden beams set the scene and there's an attractive outside terrace with sea views too. Mon–Sat 3–11pm, plus (as café-bar) April–Aug daily from 11am.

★ **Vaertshuset Pieder Ro** Gravane 10 ☎38 10 07 88, ⓦpieder-ro.no. Many locals swear this is the best seafood restaurant in town – and it certainly does have a lively atmosphere. It occupies an ersatz traditional timber building down in the Fiskebrygga complex, and it's so popular that reservations are advisable at all times. Main courses average 250kr, less at lunchtimes. Lunch Mon–Fri 11.30am–6pm; dinner daily 4–11pm.

# Mandal to Stavanger

West of Kristiansand lies a sparsely inhabited region, where the rough uplands and long valleys of the interior bounce down to a shoreline pierced by a string of inlets and fjords. The highlight is undoubtedly **Mandal**, a fetching seaside resort with probably the best sandy **beach** in the whole of Norway, but thereafter it's a struggle to find much inspiration. The best you'll do is the old harbour town of **Flekkefjord**, though frankly there's not much reason to pause anywhere between Mandal and Stavanger.

The **E39** weaves its way west for 240km from Kristiansand to Stavanger, staying a few kilometres inland for the most part and offering only the odd sight of the coast.

The **train line** follows pretty much the same route – though it does, unlike the E39, bypass Flekkefjord – until it reaches **Egersund**, where it returns to the coast for the final 80km, slicing across long flat plains with the sea on one side and distant hills away to the east.

## Mandal

Pint-sized **MANDAL**, just 40km from Kristiansand along the E39, is Norway's southernmost town. This old timber port had its salad days in the eighteenth century, when pines and oaks from the surrounding countryside were much sought after by the Dutch to support their canal houses and build their trading fleet. The timber boom fizzled out decades ago, but Mandal has preserved its quaint **old centre**, a narrow strip of white clapboard buildings spread along the north bank of the Mandalselva River just before it rolls into the sea, and it also possesses an enjoyable **museum**.

### Vest-Agder Museum i Mandal

Store Elvegate 5 • Late June to mid-Aug Mon–Fri 11am–5pm, Sat & Sun noon–5pm • 50kr

Occupying an antique merchant's house overlooking the river, Mandal's rambling **Vest-Agder Museum** (Town Museum) holds a varied collection, from agricultural implements to seafaring tackle, as well as a small but enjoyable collection of nautical paintings. Outside in the garden there's also a statue of the Viking chieftain Egil Skallagrimsson by the town's most famous son, **Gustav Vigeland** (see p.86). The central character of *Egil's Saga*, Skallagrimsson is a complex figure, sometimes wise and deliberate, at other times rash and violent. Vigeland has him putting on a horse's head, presumably a reference to his family's reputation as shape-shifters or shape-changers, with the ability to change form: it was a power that the Skallagrimssons shared with several Norse gods, including Odin himself.

### Sjøsanden and Furulenden

Mandal's popularity as a holiday spot is down to its fine beach, **Sjøsanden**. An 800m stretch of golden sand, backed by pine trees and framed by rocky headlands, it's touted as Norway's best beach – and although this isn't saying a lot, it's a very enjoyable place to unwind for a few hours. The beach is about 1km from the town centre: walk along the harbour, past the tourist office to the end of the road and keep going through the woods on the signed footpath.

You can also explore **Furulunden**, a tiny wooded peninsula directly to the west of the beach, where a network of paths winds through the trees and rocks to reveal hidden sand and shingle coves; pick up a map at the tourist office.

### ARRIVAL AND DEPARTURE                                                                                           MANDAL

**By bus** There are no trains to Mandal, but there are regular local buses to and from Kristiansand (3–4 daily; 50min) and Stavanger (3–4 daily; 3hr 30min), which pull in at the bus station by the bridge on the north bank of the Mandalselva River. From the bus station, it's a brief walk west along the riverbank to the old town centre and around 200m more to the tourist office.

**Tourist office** Bryggegata 10, facing the river (June–Aug Mon–Fri 9am–7pm, Sat & Sun 10am–4pm; Sept–May Mon–Fri 9am–4pm; ☎38 27 83 00, ⟨w⟩lindesnesregionen.com).

### ACCOMMODATION

**First Hotel Solborg** Neseveien 1 ☎38 27 21 00, ⟨w⟩firsthotels.com. Medium-sized chain hotel in an odd-looking but somehow rather fetching modern structure with every mod con, including a pool; it's on the west side of the town centre, a good 10min walk from the bus station, tight against a wooded escarpment. **1300kr**

**Kjøbmandsgaarden Hotel** Store Elvegate 57 ☎38 26 12 76, ⟨w⟩kjobmandsgaarden.no. Handy and affordable hotel which occupies an old timber house in a street of antique buildings across from the bus station. All the dozen or so rooms here are spick-and-span and the decor is bright and cheerful, albeit a little staid. **1200kr**

**Ryvingen Fyr** Ryvingen ☎ 95 73 16 86, ⓦ ryvingenfyr .no. There's been a lighthouse out in in the Skagerrak on the rocky islet of Ryvingen since 1867, though the first version was far from universally popular – local fishermen wrote to the local newspaper by the dozen complaining that it was so bright it scared the fish. The present lighthouse, a sturdy red and white structure, is glued to a large shank of rock with the churning ocean down below. The old lighthouse keeper's quarters have been pleasantly modernized and a handful of cheerfully bright rooms can be rented from late June to late Aug. Guests are responsible for their own food, water and bed linen. From Mandal, the return boat trip costs about 1600kr and the tourist office will make all the necessary arrangements. Per person per night: 200kr

**Sjøsanden Feriesenter** Sjøsandvei 1 ☎ 38 26 10 94, ⓦ sjosanden-feriesenter.no. You can camp very close to the western end of the Sjøsanden beach at this holiday centre, though note that the access road to the camp detours round the back of the woods, which back onto the beach; it's well signposted. They also rent out two-bedroom cabins that can sleep 6. Pitch 100kr; cabins 1250kr, sp/r 950kr

## EATING AND DRINKING

**Hr.Redaktor** Store Elvegate 23A ☎ 38 27 15 30, ⓦ red.no. In the centre of town, this groovy restaurant-cum-bar has a lively and inventive menu – fried redfish with tomato fennel and olive compote as a main, for example (300kr). After 10pm, the place morphs into a busy bar. Mon–Thurs noon–midnight, Fri & Sat noon–2.30am; kitchen closes at 10pm.

**Jonas B Gundersen** Store Elvegate 25 ☎ 38 27 15 00, ⓦ jbg.no. Popular pizzeria and bar in the town centre across from the old water fountain. Serves filling food at affordable prices with pizzas from 120kr. Mon–Fri 11am–11pm, Sat 11am–3am, Sun 1–10pm.

# Lindesnes

To the west of Mandal Highway 460 leaves the E39 to snake its way the 15km south to **Spangereid** at the start of **Lindesnes** (literally "where the land curves round"), a chubby promontory that juts out into the Skagerrak. Formidable seamen they may have been, but the Vikings feared the cape's treacherous waters to such an extent that they cut a canal across the base of the promontory at Spangereid to avoid the vagaries of the open sea. In honour of this nautical achievement, a new canal was cut here in 2007.

### Lindesnes Fyr

Mid-April to mid-June & mid-Aug to mid-Oct daily 11am–5pm; mid-June to mid-Aug daily 10am–8pm; rest of year Sat & Sun 11am–5pm • 50kr • ☎ 38 25 54 20, ⓦ lindesnesfyr.no

At Norway's most southerly point, 10km south of Spangereid, a sturdy red-and-white lighthouse – **Lindesnes Fyr** – perches on a knobbly, lichen-stained headland. There has been a lighthouse here since the seventeenth century, but today's structure and its assorted outhouses mostly date from 1916. The history of the lighthouse and its keepers is explored in a modest **museum**, which has been cut into the rock of the headland, and the **tower** is open to the public too. The most dramatic time to visit is during bad weather: the headland is exposed to extraordinarily ferocious storms, when the warm westerly currents of the Skagerrak meet cold easterly winds.

## STAYING IN A LIGHTHOUSE

The rocks and reefs of the south coast prompted the Norwegians to construct a string of **lighthouses** and now, with the lighthouse keepers long gone, a number of them offer simple, hostel-like **accommodation** during the summertime. Lighthouse lodging is inexpensive (averaging around 200kr per person per night), though you're almost always responsible for your own food, water and bed linen – and getting there and back can cost anything up to 2000kr. Furthermore, arranging it all can be difficult unless you speak Norwegian, though the local tourist office will help fix things up. Of the lighthouses offshore from Mandal offering summer accommodation, **Ryvingen Fyr** (see above) is the most enticing, though best of all perhaps is **Feistein Fyr**, near Stavanger (see p.138).

**FROM TOP** SJØSANDEN BEACH, MANDAL (P.129); NORSK HERMETIKKMUSEET, STAVANGER (P.135); KJERAGBOLTEN (P.141) >

## Flekkefjord

With a population of 6000, **FLEKKEFJORD**, 70km from Mandal, has a tiny centre with old and picturesque timber houses strung along the banks of a short (500m) channel that connects the Lafjord and the Grisefjord. Flekkefjord boomed in the sixteenth century on the back of its trade with the Dutch, who purchased the town's timber for their houses and its granite for their dykes and harbours. Later, in the 1750s, the herring industry was the main money-spinner, along with shipbuilding and tanning, but the Flekkefjord economy had pretty much collapsed by the end of the nineteenth century when sailing ships gave way to steam.

The oldest and prettiest part of Flekkefjord – known as **Hollenderbyen** after the town's Dutch connections – is on the west side of the channel, and only takes a few minutes to explore, though you can extend this pleasantly enough by visiting the nearby nineteenth-century period rooms of the **Vest-Agder-museet Flekkefjord**, Dr Krafts gate 15 (Flekkefjord Museum; mid-June to Aug Mon–Fri 11am–5pm, Sat & Sun noon–5pm; 50kr).

### ARRIVAL AND INFORMATION
FLEKKEFJORD

**By bus** Buses pull in on Jernbaneveien, just south of the main drag and about 250m east of the central waterway. Nor-Way Busekspressen's Sør-Vest ekspressen services (#300; ⓦ nor-way.no) run to Kristiansand (3 daily; 2hr) and Stavanger (3 daily; 2hr 20min).

**Tourist office** Elvegata 3, on the waterway's west side (mid-June to mid-Aug Mon–Fri 10am–6pm, Sat 10am–4pm, plus Sun in July 11am–4pm; rest of year Mon–Fri 9am–4pm; ☎ 38 32 80 81, ⓦ regionlister.com).

### ACCOMMODATION

**Maritim Fjordhotell** Sundegata 9 ☎ 38 32 58 00, ⓦ fjordhotellene.no. There's no pressing reason to overnight in Flekkefjord, but if you do want to stay, the best bet is this unassuming, fifty-room hotel in a four-storey block overlooking the east side of the central waterway. **900kr**

## Jøssingfjord

At Flekkefjord, the E39 turns inland, threading its way over the hills and down the dales bound for Stavanger, 120km away. Alternatively, you can take the more southerly, but slightly longer (30km or so), Highway 44 which offers occasional glimpses of the sea, most memorably when it wiggles across the narrow **Jøssingford**, the scene of dramatic events in World War II. In February 1940, the German supply ship *Altmar* was transporting 300 Allied POWs to Germany, when it was spotted by a British destroyer, HMS *Cossack*. The destroyer gave chase, trapped the *Altmar* here in the Jøssingfjord and freed the prisoners. At this time in the war, this was a rare British success and it prompted those Norwegians who were opposed to the Germans – the vast majority of the population – to call themselves "Jossings" throughout hostilities.

## Sogndalstrand

From the Jøssingfjord, it's about 5km to Hauge, a modest little town which is itself just a couple of kilometres north of the sailing port of **SOGNDALSTRAND**, a lovely little spot, its narrow main street meandering down towards the pretty little harbour. If you want to break your journey hereabouts, this is a good place to do it – and there's an attractive hotel here too.

### ACCOMMODATION
SOGNDALSTRAND

**Sogndalstrand Kulturhotell** Strandgaten 22, Sogndalstrand ☎ 51 47 72 55, ⓦ sogndalstrand -kulturhotell.no. This appealing hotel occupies half a dozen old buildings, and has fifteen cosy and intimate guest rooms. There's also a very good restaurant (Mon–Sat 10am–10pm), where they feature local ingredients – try the salmon when it is in season. **1490kr**

## Egersund

Around 25km from Sogndalstrand, **EGERSUND** is a port and minor manufacturing centre that spreads over a jigsaw of bays and lakes at the end of a deep and sheltered ocean inlet. Apart from an assortment of old timber houses in the centre, along **Strandgaten**, there's no real reason to hang around and Egersund's transport links are the main reason why you might pass through – the town is on the Kristiansand to Stavanger train line.

**2**

# Stavanger and around

**STAVANGER** is something of a survivor. Unlike a flotilla of Norwegian coastal towns that have fallen foul of the precarious fortunes of fishing, Stavanger has diversified and is now the proud possessor of a dynamic economy, which has swelled the population to over 125,000. It was the herring fishery that first put money into the town, crowding its nineteenth-century wharves with coopers and smiths, net makers and menders. Then, when the fishing failed, the town moved into shipbuilding and now it makes its money through oil – Stavanger builds rigs for Norway's offshore oilfields and refines it as well – backed up by a profitable sideline in tourism as witnessed by the mammoth cruise ships that regularly pull into its harbour.

Much of central Stavanger is strikingly modern, a jingle and a jangle of mini- and not-so-mini tower blocks that spreads over the hilly ground abutting the main harbour and surrounding the decorative, central lake, **Breiavatnet**, the most obvious downtown landmark. None of this may sound terribly enticing, but in fact Stavanger is an excellent place to start a visit to Norway: all the town's amenities are within easy walking distance of each other; it has excellent train, bus and ferry connections; and it possesses an especially attractive harbour, a couple of enjoyable museums, a raft of excellent restaurants plus several lively bars. The town is also – and this comes as a surprise to many first-time visitors – nearer to the fjords than Bergen, the self-proclaimed "Gateway to the Fjords": within easy reach of Stavanger are the **Lysefjord** and the dramatic **Preikestolen** rock formation.

## Domkirke

Haakon VII's gate • June–Aug Mon–Sat 11am–7pm, Sun 1–7pm; Sept–May Tues–Sat 11am–4pm • Free

The principal relic of medieval Stavanger is the **Domkirke** (Cathedral), whose pointed-hat towers signal a Romanesque church dating from the early twelfth century, though it has been modified on several subsequent occasions. Inside, the squat pillars, dog-tooth arches and rough stonework of the narrow, three-aisled **nave** are the Romanesque heart of the church, but the **choir** beyond, with its curling tracery and pointed windows, is Gothic, the work of English masons who were brought here in the

### ANTONY GORMLEY IN STAVANGER

Stavanger has no fewer than 23 sculptures by the contemporary British sculptor **Antony Gormley** (best known for his *Angel of the North* in England) and together they constitute **Broken Column**, whose aim is to illustrate the many facets of the city and, for that matter, life (and death) itself. Each and every sculpture is a blank-faced human figure made of cast iron and 195cm high, the same height as – and apparently modelled on – Gormley himself, though some are partly sunk into the ground. This sinking is, as you might expect from Gormley, not at random: each location has a predetermined height quota and the last one in the series, which is stuck out on a rock in the harbour, is mostly (149cm) under water. One of the sculptures is beside the Domkirke, a second is beside Torget's covered fish market. Work began on *Broken Column* in 1999 and the project was completed four years later.

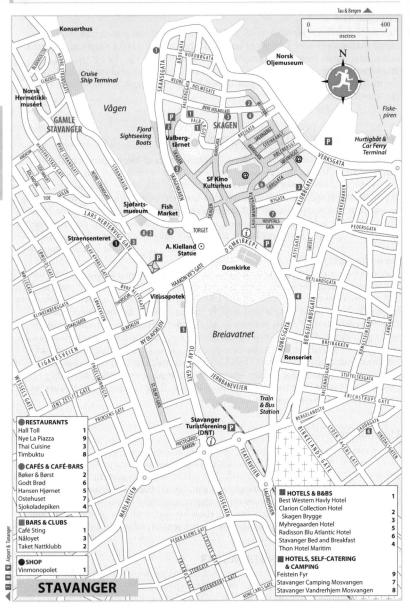

Tau & Bergen

0                    400
metres

N

Konserthus

Norsk
Oljemuseum

Cruise
Ship Terminal

Norsk
Hermetikk-
muséet

NORDBØGATA

SKANSEGATA

NEDRE    HOLMEGATA

ØVRE HOLMEGATA

Vågen

GAMLE
STAVANGER

Fjord
Sightseeing
Boats

Valberg-
tårnet

SKAGEN

LARS HERTERVIGS GATE

Sjøfarts-
museum

Fish
Market

SF Kino
Kulturhus

VERKSGATA

Hurtigbåt &
Car Ferry
Terminal

Fiske-
piren

NYGATA

HOSPITALS
GATA

Stræensenteret

TORGET

A. Kielland
Statue

DOMKIRKEPL

PEDERSGATA

Vitusapotek

HAAKON VII's GATE

Domkirke

HETLANDSGATA

Breiavatnet

Renseriet

BREIBAKKEN

STIFTELSESGATA

Train
& Bus
Station

Stavanger
Turistforening
(DNT)

ERICHSTRUPS GATE

PRESTEGÅRDS-
BAKKEN

TEATERVEIEN

MADLAVEIEN

SAUDAGATA

**STAVANGER**

● **RESTAURANTS**
| | |
|---|---|
| Hall Toll | |
| Nye La Piazza | 9 |
| Thai Cuisine | 3 |
| Timbuktu | 8 |

● **CAFÉS & CAFÉ-BARS**
| | |
|---|---|
| Bøker & Børst | 2 |
| Godt Brød | 6 |
| Hansen Hjørnet | 5 |
| Ostehuset | 7 |
| Sjokoladepiken | 4 |

■ **BARS & CLUBS**
| | |
|---|---|
| Café Sting | 1 |
| Nåløyet | 3 |
| Taket Nattklubb | 2 |

● **SHOP**
| | |
|---|---|
| Vinmonopolet | 1 |

■ **HOTELS & B&BS**
| | |
|---|---|
| Best Western Havly Hotel | 1 |
| Clarion Collection Hotel | 2 |
| Skagen Brygge | 3 |
| Myhregaarden Hotel | 5 |
| Radisson Blu Atlantic Hotel | 6 |
| Stavanger Bed and Breakfast | 4 |
| Thon Hotel Maritim | |

■ **HOTELS, SELF-CATERING & CAMPING**
| | |
|---|---|
| Feistein Fyr | 9 |
| Stavanger Camping Mosvangen | 7 |
| Stavanger Vandrerhjem Mosvangen | 8 |

1270s. This was far from unusual: the Norwegians had little experience of building in stone, so whenever they decided to build a stone church they imported skilled craftsmen, mainly from England and Germany. The ornate seventeenth-century **pulpit** is the most distinctive feature of the nave along with a set of conspicuous **memorial tablets** that hang on its walls – sombre-serious family portraits surrounded by a jumble of richly carved cherubs, angels, crucifixes and apostles.

# Torget

From the top of **Torget**, the main square, there is a fine view of Stavanger's principal harbour, **Vågen**, a tapering finger of water that buzzes with cruise ships, yachts, ferryboats and catamarans. Sharing the view is a **statue** of the author **Alexander Kielland** (1849–1906), one of the city's most famous sons, looking decidedly pleased with himself in his top hat and cape. Born into a rich merchant family, Kielland was a popular figure hereabouts, praised for his novels and plays and for his (relatively) generous treatment of the workers in his factory. He also set about building a political career, becoming burgomaster of Stavanger in 1891, but it was food – not his political rivals – that did for him: Kielland loved food and, to all intents and purposes, ate himself to death.

**2**

# Stavanger Sjøfartsmuseum

Nedre Strandgate 17 & 19 • Mid-June to Aug daily 11am–4pm; Sept to mid-June Sun 11am–4pm • 60kr • 📞 51 84 27 00, 🔤 stavanger .museum.no

The mildly diverting **Sjøfartsmuseum** (Stavanger Maritime Museum) occupies two former warehouses facing the west side of the harbour, metres from Torget. The museum's interior is jam-packed with all things nautical, from charts and drawings and replica workshops, through to archeological finds, paintings of ships, model boats and, perhaps best of the lot, scores of old photos drawn from a huge permanent collection.

# Gamle Stavanger

On the western side of the main harbour is the city's star turn, **Gamle Stavanger**. Though very different in appearance from the modern structures back in the centre, the buildings here were also the product of a boom. From 1810 until around 1870, herring turned up just offshore in their millions, and Stavanger took advantage of this slice of luck. The town flourished and expanded, with the number of merchants and shipowners increasing dramatically. Huge profits were made from the exported fish, which were salted and later, as the technology improved, canned. Today, some of the wooden stores and warehouses flanking the western quayside hint at their nineteenth-century pedigree, but it's the succession of narrow, cobbled lanes behind them – along and around **Øvre Strandgate** – that shows Gamle Stavanger to best advantage. Formerly home to local seafarers, craftsmen and cannery workers, the area has been maintained as a residential quarter, mercifully free of tourist tat: the long rows of white-painted, clapboard houses are immaculately maintained, complete with picket fences and tiny terraced gardens. There's little architectural pretension, but here and there flashes of fancy wooden scrollwork must once have had the curtains twitching among the staunchly Lutheran population.

## The Norsk Hermetikkmuseet

Øvre Strandgate 88 • Mid-June to Aug daily 11am–4pm; Sept to mid-June Tues–Sun 11am–4pm • 60kr • 📞 40 72 84 70, 🔤 stavanger.museum.no

In the heart of Gamle Stavanger, the **Norsk Hermetikkmuseet** (Norwegian Canning Museum) occupies an old **sardine-canning factory** and gives a glimpse of the industry that saved Stavanger from collapse at the end of the nineteenth century. When the herring vanished from local waters in the 1870s, the canning factories switched to imported fish, thereby keeping the local economy afloat. They remained Stavanger's main source of employment until as late as 1960: in the 1920s there were seventy canneries in the town, and the last one only closed down in 1983.

**2**

A visit to an old canning factory may not seem too enticing, but the museum is actually very good. Downstairs the assorted drying racks, canning trays, smokers and other paraphernalia set the scene, but the highlight is upstairs in the museum's collection of **sardine tin labels**, called *iddis* in these parts from the local pronunciation of *etikett*, the Norwegian for label. A couple of hundred labels have survived, in part because they were avidly collected by the town's children, though this harmless hobby seems to have worried the town's adults no end – "Label thefts – an unfortunate collection craze", ran a 1915 headline in the *Stavanger Aftenblad* newspaper. The variety of label design is extraordinary – anything and everything from representations of the Norwegian royal family to surrealistic fish with human qualities. Spare a thought also for a Scottish seaman by the name of William Anderson: it was his bearded face, copied from a photograph, that beamed out from millions of Skippers' sardine tins, a celebrity status so frowned upon by shipowners that Anderson couldn't find work, though fortunately the story ended happily: Anderson wrote to the cannery concerned to complain and they put him on the payroll for the remainder of his working life.

The museum smokes its own sardines on the first Sunday of every month and every Tuesday and Thursday from mid-June to August – and very tasty they are too.

## Skagen

After years in the doldrums, **Skagen**, the bumpy promontory on the east side of the main harbour, is on the up, its old, bright-white wooden houses now holding some of the city's best bars and cafés, though the clumsily modern **Kulturhus**, at the centre of affairs, is still a noticeable blotch. Skagen's mazy street plan is the legacy of the original Viking settlement, but there is nothing else to recall them and the only sight as such is the spiky **Valbergtårnet** (Valberg tower), a nineteenth-century firewatch sitting atop Skagen's highest point and offering sweeping views of the city and its industry.

## The Norsk Oljemuseum

Kjeringholmen • June–Aug daily 10am–7pm; Sept–May Mon–Sat 10am–4pm, Sun 10am–6pm • 100kr • ☎ 51 93 93 00, ⓦ norskolje.museum.no

The intricate workings of the offshore oil industry are explored in depth at the excellent **Norsk Oljemuseum** (Norwegian Petroleum Museum), a sleek modern building beside the waterfront on the far side of Skagen. The first tentative searches for oil beneath the North Sea began in the early 1960s and the first strike was made in 1969. Production started two years later and has continued ever since with Norway making an enormous fortune from its vast oil and gas reserves – easily enough to transform what had once been one of Europe's poorer countries to one of the richest. The museum is not especially large, but it is a little confusing unless you pick up a free plan at reception.

There are introductory displays on North Sea geology, explaining how the oil was created, and on how much money Norway is making from its oil and gas, but you're soon into the offshore section with scale models of oil rigs, explanations as to how oil wells are sunk, and a few mechanical bits and pieces – drill bits, diving bells and so forth. There's also a small section on the **Alexander Kielland disaster** of 1980, when the eponymous oil rig collapsed in heavy seas, killing 123 oil workers, Norway's worst offshore disaster by a mile. The museum has a mini-cinema, showing a film about the industry, plus several hands-on exhibits, notably a mock-up of a drilling platform with an emergency exit chute. Embedded in the museum are nuggets of social commentary: women were only allowed to work offshore from the late 1970s and soon after their arrival the oil companies had to bring in more toiletries for the men, who suddenly started to shower (more). A further section is devoted to the divers who work on the sea bed, their endeavours illustrated with a remarkable short film on the laying and repairing of a stretch of underwater pipeline.

Incidentally, the large yellow bridge-like **structure outside the museum** was retrieved from the Frigg oilfield, when it closed down in 2004 after 27 years of production. Frigg was a joint operation between the UK and Norway and this particular piece of kit, built to link two oil installations far out in the ocean, actually crossed the international frontier – as the surviving signage illustrates.

From the museum, the most agreeable way to return to the centre is by walking west along **Øvre Holmegate**, one of Skagen's prettiest streets, lined with old wooden buildings.

## ARRIVAL AND DEPARTURE

**By plane** Stavanger's international airport is 14km southwest of the city centre at Sola. A Flybussen (every 15–30min: Mon–Fri 8am–midnight, Sat 9am–11pm, Sun 10am–11pm; 20–30min depending on traffic; 95kr one-way, 150kr return; ⓦ flybussen.no) links the airport with the city centre, stopping at several downtown hotels, including the *Radisson Blu Atlantic*, as well as the Fiskepiren ferry terminal and the bus and train stations.

**By train** Stavanger's train station is on the southern side of Breiavatnet. For train information contact NSB (ⓣ 51 56 96 10, ⓦ nsb.no).

Destinations Egersund (hourly; 1hr 10min); Kristiansand (4–6 daily; 3hr); Oslo (2–4 daily; 8hr).

**By bus** Stavanger's bus terminal is adjacent to the train station. Inside the bus station, Kolumbus Rogaland Kollektivtrafikk operates an information centre (Mon–Fri 7am–7pm, Sat 10am–3pm; ⓣ 177, ⓦ kolumbus.no), which provides comprehensive details of buses, boats and trains in the city and surrounding area. Nor-Way Busekspressen (ⓦ nor-way.no) runs the following services: Sør-Vest ekspressen (#300) to: Flekkefjord (3 daily; 2hr 20min); Kristiansund (3 daily; 4hr 15min). Kystbussen (#400) to: Bergen (every 1–2hr; 5hr to 5hr 30min); Haugesund (every 1–2hr; 2hr)

**By domestic ferry** Most domestic ferries from the islands and fjords around Stavanger, including both Hurtigbåt

### STAVANGER AND AROUND

passenger express boats and car ferries, dock at the Fiskepiren terminal, a short walk to the northeast Breiavatnet – and about 800m from the train and bus stations. Kolumbus (see below) has a second information centre here (Mon–Thurs 7am–4.30pm, Fri 7am–6pm, Sat 8am–1pm & Sun 10am–noon & 3.30–5.30pm). You can also pick up Hurtigbåt passenger express boat tickets for the trip north to Haugesund (1–4 daily; 1hr 25min) and Bergen (1–2 daily; 4hr) at the Flaggruten information office here (ⓣ 055 05, ⓦ flaggruten.no).

**By international ferry** There are no international car ferries into Stavanger, but Fjordline (ⓣ 815 33 500, ⓦ fjordline.com) operates a car ferry service from Hirstals in Denmark to Tananger, about 12km west of the city.

**By car** There's a 20kr toll on all roads leading into Stavanger, but you won't be asked to stop as it's levied electronically. On-street parking is difficult, but not impossible; otherwise, there are several city-centre car parks, one of the more convenient of which is just a few metres to the west of the Fiskepiren ferry terminal. In the centre car rental is available from - Hertz/Europcar, Olav V's gate 13 (ⓣ 51 53 82 02). Also at Stavanger airport are Europcar (ⓣ 51 65 10 90) and Hertz (ⓣ 51 65 10 96).

## GETTING AROUND

**By taxi** Stavanger Taxi ⓣ 51 90 90 90.
**By bike** The tourist office rents bikes at 250kr/day, and

issues free cycling maps.

## INFORMATION AND TOURS

**Tourist office** Domkirkeplassen 3 (June–Aug daily 9am–8pm; Sept–May Mon–Fri 9am–4pm, Sat 9am–2pm; ⓣ 51 85 92 00, ⓦ regionstavanger.com). Stavanger tourist office publishes a useful and free guide to Stavanger, and provides local bus and ferry timetables.

**Tours** The tourist office can make bookings on guided tours both on land and sea. The most popular excursions are to the Lysefjord and Preikestolen (see p.140) with some trips departing from the Fiskepiren terminal, others from Skagenkaien, beside the main harbour, Vågen.

## ACTIVITIES

**Hiking** The DNT-affiliated Stavanger Turistforening in the underpass at the top of Olav V's gate (Mon–Wed & Fri 10am–4pm, Thurs 10am–7pm, Sat 10am–3pm; ⓣ 51 84 02 00, ⓦ stavanger-turistforening.no) will advise on local hiking routes and sells a comprehensive range of hiking

maps. They maintain around 900km of hiking trails and run more than thirty cabins in the mountains east of Stavanger, as well as organizing ski schools at winter weekends. They also offer general advice about local conditions, weather and so on, and you can obtain DNT membership here too.

**2**

## STAVANGER TO BERGEN

With great ingenuity, Norway's road builders have cobbled together the **E39** coastal road, the **Kystvegen** (ⓦ kystvegen.no), which traverses the west coast from Stavanger to Haugesund, Bergen and ultimately Trondheim with eight ferry trips breaking up the journey. The first part of the trek, the 180km haul up from Stavanger to Bergen, includes two ferry trips and sees the highway slipping across a string of islands, which provide a pleasant introduction to the scenic charms of western Norway – and hint at the sterner beauty of the fjords beyond. Perhaps surprisingly, this region is primarily agricultural: the intricacies of the shoreline, together with the prevailing westerlies, made the seas so treacherous that locals mostly stuck to the land, eking out a precarious existence from the thin soils that had accumulated on the leeward sides of some of the islands.

### ACCOMMODATION

There's no shortage of accommodation in Stavanger. A string of **hotels** is dotted around the town's compact centre and although prices are fairly high, all of them offer substantial weekend discounts. Alternatively, you can opt for a no-frills guesthouse, an HI **hostel** and a **campsite**, with a **lighthouse** as a further choice, though this is a good way out of town.

#### HOTELS AND B&BS

**Best Western Havly Hotel** Valberggata 1 ☎ 51 93 90 00, ⓦ havly-hotell.no. Neat and trim, medium-sized hotel occupying a rather bunker-like modern building squeezed into a narrow side street off Skagenkaien. Forty spick-and-span modern rooms. **1760kr**, sp/r **880kr**

★ **Clarion Collection Hotel Skagen Brygge** Skagenkaien 30 ☎ 51 85 00 00, ⓦ skagenbryggehotell .no. A pleasing quayside hotel, built in the style of an old warehouse but with lots of glass and great views over the harbour. The rooms are modern and unfussily decorated, the buffet breakfast very good and mid-afternoon nibbles are free. The only quibble concerns the noise from outside: if you are a light sleeper, either take potluck (summer weekends are noisiest) or a room at the back. Recently incorporated into the Clarion Collection chain, so the website may change. **1800kr**, sp/r **1100kr**

★ **Myhregaarden Hotel** Nygata 24 ☎ 51 86 80 00, ⓦ myhregaardenhotel.no/hotel-stavanger. Housed in part of a large and really rather grand late nineteenth-century building, this hotel has a handy location and 53 guest rooms with the comfiest of beds. The decor is bright if a tad spartan with the attic rooms especially pleasant. Great breakfasts too. **1900kr**, sp/r **1000kr**

**Radisson Blu Atlantic Hotel** Olav V's gate 3 ☎ 51 76 10 00, ⓦ radissonblu.com/atlantic-stavanger. There was a time when this was *the* place to stay in Stavanger, hosting every celebrity who ever set foot in the city from Paul Gascoigne to Fats Domino. The hotel looks a tad jaded now – and it certainly occupies a big bruiser of a modern block – but the rooms are large and spacious and most offer attractive views over the central lake. **2095kr**, sp/r **1200kr**

**Stavanger Bed and Breakfast** Vikedalsgaten 1a ☎ 51 56 25 00, ⓦ stavangerbedandbreakfast.no. This friendly, hostel-like B&B has 22 simple and straightforward modern rooms, most of which have showers and sinks (but shared toilets). Every night at 9pm, guests gather in the dining room for the complimentary coffee and waffles – and a very sociable affair it is too. The B&B is in a residential area just 5min walk from the train station. A real snip, even if some of the inter-room walls are paper-thin. **890kr**

**Thon Hotel Maritim** Kongsgata 32 ☎ 51 85 05 00, ⓦ thonhotels.com. No points for architectural style – this chain hotel occupies a glum-looking modern block – but the interior has been nicely remodelled. It's in a quiet, central location, and the upper floors overlook the city's dinky little central lake, Breiavatnet. **1800kr**, sp/r **1000kr**

#### HOSTEL, SELF-CATERING AND CAMPING

★ **Feistein Fyr** Feistein ☎ 51 42 98 00 or ☎ 95 00 94 74, ⓦ klepp.kommune.no/artikler/feistein-fyr. On a rocky, sea-buffeted offshore islet, the old lighthouse keeper's quarters of Feistein lighthouse have been turned into an appealing guesthouse with 15 beds and a self-catering kitchen. A wonderful setting it is – but *The Ritz* isn't: they provide pillows and duvets, but you bring your own sheets/sleeping bag; it can get very cold, so bring lots of warm clothes; and there's no hot water. Overnight accommodation is inexpensive but you also have to add on the price of the boat trip out to the island (250kr return). The ferry dock is at Sele marina, off Highway 510, beyond the airport and about 25km from Stavanger. Rate is per person per night. **250kr**

**Stavanger Camping Mosvangen** Tjensvollveien 1b ☎ 51 53 29 71, ⓦ stavangercamping.no. On the south side of lake Mosvatnet, just 3km from the centre – and not far from the HI hostel (see below) – this large and well-equipped campsite has space for tents and caravans as well as a selection of cabins for up to six people. Open April to Sept. Tent pitch **120kr**, cabin **450kr**

**Stavanger Vandrerhjem Mosvangen** Henrik Ibsens gate 19 ☎ 51 54 36 36, ⓦ hihostels.no. This no-frills, chalet-meets-barracks HI hostel stands on the south side of Mosvatnet lake, a 3km walk from the centre. The hostel has self-catering and laundry facilities, and the 45 rooms hold between one and five bunk beds each with en-suite doubles costing 645kr; advance reservations are advised.

The nearest you'll get by public transport is on bus #4 from the bus and train stations – get off at the start of Ullandhaugsveien (or at least ask the driver to put you off) on the southeast side of the lake. Open early June to late Aug. Dorms **225kr**, double **595kr**

## EATING

The centre of Stavanger's **restaurant and café-bar** scene is down by the harbour, where a gaggle of places line up along Skagen and neighbouring Skagenkaien. Standards vary enormously and you'll almost certainly pay top-dollar, so by and large you're better off in the more reasonably priced places in the narrow side streets of the Skagen district, on the promontory immediately to the east of the main harbour.

### CAFÉS AND CAFÉ-BARS

**Bøker & Børst** Øvre Holmegate 32 ☎51 86 04 76, ⓦbokerogborst.com. Charming café-bar where the decor really does set the tone – from the vintage posters and Oriental bric-a-brac through to the jam-packed bookshelves that seem to fill out every spare corner. There's a pavement terrace at the front and a mini-courtyard at the back plus an oh-so relaxing soundtrack. The drinks – both soft and alcoholic – are the main event, but they do sell snacks and there are live gigs here too. Daily 10am–2am.

**Godt Brød** Sølvberggata 51 84 40 80, ⓦbakeverksted.no. One of a large chain, this inexpensive, modern café sells a good range of freshly baked bread as well as inexpensive sandwiches. Opposite the Kulturhus in the middle of Skagen. Mon–Sat 7am–6pm, Sun 10am–5pm.

**Hansen Hjørnet** Skagen 18 ☎51 89 52 80, ⓦhansenhjornet.com. When the sun is out, this harbourside café-bar has the prettiest outside terrace in town – decorated with flowers and protected by a windbreak – though you my struggle to find an empty chair. Mon–Sat 11am–midnight, Sun 1–11pm.

★ **Ostehuset** Hospitalsgata 6 ☎51 86 40 10, ⓦostehuset.no. Attractive modern café in airy premises, where the speciality is pizza: the basic model costs 100kr and then you choose from a delicious range of extra toppings for 25–35kr each. There's also a daily menu featuring the freshest of local ingredients with mains from about 120kr plus sandwiches, baguettes and large-size salads (from 165kr). Mon–Fri 8am–9pm, Sat 8am–6pm.

★ **Sjokoladepiken** Øvre Holmegate 27 ☎47 20 19 84, ⓦsjokoladepiken.no. This lovely little place sells the best coffee in town, but the real highlights are the

chocolates and the cakes, all handmade and earth-shatteringly tasty. This tastiness doesn't come cheap – a slice of cake costs 90kr – but the pleasure easily outweighs the financial pain. Mon–Wed 11am–10pm, Thurs–Sat 11am–midnight & Sun noon–9pm.

### RESTAURANTS

**Hall Toll** Skansegata 2 ☎51 51 72 32, ⓦhall-toll.no. Down on the harbour, in the capacious former toll house, this restaurant-cum-bar and club is one of the busiest places in town, its restaurant combining a sushi bar with a more conventional area whisking up tasty Norwegian dishes. Mains average 200kr. Mon–Fri 4.30pm–1.30am, Sat 12.30pm–1.30am; kitchen till 11pm. Club Fri & Sat 11.30pm–3am.

**Nye La Piazza** Rosenkildetorget 1 ☎51 52 02 52, ⓦnyelapiazza.no. By the main harbour, just off Torget, this long-established Italian restaurant may be a tad staid, but the pizzas are large and tasty as are the meat, fish and pasta dishes. Pizzas begin at 150kr, other main courses 260kr. Mon–Sat noon–midnight, Sun noon–10pm.

★ **Thai Cuisine** Kirkegata 41 ☎51 86 07 88, ⓦthaicuisine.no. Sociable and very popular restaurant in trim modern premises that serves the best Thai food in Stavanger. The menu, which covers all the classics and then some, has main courses from around 200kr. Daily 11am–11pm.

**Timbuktu** Nedre Strandgate 15 ☎51 84 37 40, ⓦherlige -restauranter.no/timbuktu. Smooth and slick restaurant-bar down by the harbour with some striking 1960s-style design features. It does a great line in Asian fusion cuisine, with mains averaging around 220kr. Mon & Tues 6pm–midnight, Wed–Sat 6pm–3am; kitchen till 10pm.

## DRINKING AND NIGHTLIFE

Stavanger is lively at night, particularly at weekends when a rum assortment of oil workers, sailors, fishermen, executives, tourists and office workers gathers in the bars and clubs on or near the harbour to live (or rather drink) it up. Most places stay open until 2am or later, with rowdy – but usually amiable – boozers lurching from one bar to the next.

### BARS AND CLUBS

**Café Sting** Valberget 3 ☎51 89 38 78, ⓦcafe-sting.no. Right next to the Valbergtårnet tower, this laidback

café-bar attracts a youthful, vaguely arty crew. The food is filling and inexpensive and the place also doubles as an art gallery and live music venue, hosting anything from indie

**2**

to rock. Mon–Thurs noon–midnight, Fri & Sat noon–3am, Sun 3pm–midnight.

**Nåloyet** Nedre Strandgate 13 ☎ 51 84 37 00, ⓦ herlige-restauranter.no/naloyetbar. Dark and funky bar which heaves on the weekend with a wide range of domestic and foreign beers the main alcoholic pull. Daily 8pm–2am.

**Taket Nattklubb** Nedre Strandgate 15 ☎ 51 84 37 00, ⓦ herlige-restauranter.no/taket. The best club in town, strong on house music with great cocktails too; don't be surprised if you have to queue. It's above *Timbuktu* (see p.139), just west of Torget. Wed–Sun midnight–3.30am.

## ENTERTAINMENT

### CLASSICAL MUSIC

**Stavanger Konserthus** Nedre Strandgate 89 ☎ 51 53 70 00 (tickets), ⓦ stavanger-konserthus.no. The city's sparklingly new concert hall hosts regular performances by visiting artists, from pop to classical and theatre, and is home to the Stavanger Symphony Orchestra (ⓦ sso.no). It's located north of the centre, on the waterfront just beyond the main Cruise Ship terminal.

### CINEMA

**SF Kino Kulturhus** Sølvberggata 2 ☎ 820 00 100, ⓦ sfkino-stavanger.no. Stavanger has several cinemas and this one, inside the Kulturhus, is one of the handiest. Shows the latest blockbusters, both international and Scandinavian.

## SHOPPING

**Vinmonopolet** Lars Hertevigs gate 6. State-run liquor and wine outlet in the Straensenteret shopping centre, just west of Torget. Mon–Fri 10am–6pm, Sat 10am–3pm.

## DIRECTORY

**Internet** Internet access is free at the main library, inside the Kulturhus at Sølvberggata 2 (Mon–Thurs 10am–7pm, Fri 10am–5pm, Sat 10am–4pm, plus Sept–May Sun noon–4pm).

**Laundry** Renseriet, Kongsgata 40, on the east side of Lake Breiavatnet (☎ 51 89 56 53). Coin-operated machines.

**Left luggage** Coin-operated lockers at the Fiskepiren terminal (Mon–Fri 6.30am–11.15pm, Sat 6.30am–8pm,

Sun 8am–10pm); at the train station (Sun–Fri 6am–11pm, Sat 6am–6pm); and at the bus station (daily 7am–10pm).

**Pharmacy** Among many, there is a Vitusapotek at Olav V's gate 11 (Mon–Fri 8.30am–11pm, Sat 9am–11pm, Sun & hols 10am–11pm).

**Post office** The main post office is on Lars Hertevigs gate, just a few metres from Haakon VII's gate (Mon–Fri 9am–6pm & Sat 10am–3pm).

# Around Stavanger: Lysefjord and Preikestolen

Stavanger sits on a long promontory that pokes a knobbly head north towards the **Boknafjord**, whose wide waters form a deep indentation in the coast and lap against a confetti of islets and islands. To the east of Stavanger, longer, narrower fjords drill far inland, the most diverting being the blue-black **Lysefjord**, famous for its precipitous cliffs and an especially striking rock formation, the **Preikestolen**. This distinctive 25m-square table of rock boasts a sheer 600m drop to the Lysefjord down below on three of its sides.

Getting to Preikestolen by ferry and bus is comparatively straightforward, but cruising the Lysefjord by ferry requires a little forethought – best with the help of Stavanger tourist office (see p.137), who sell the boat tickets. Note also that no matter what the publicity hype says, you do not get a decent view of **Preikestolen** from the waters of the Lysefjord.

## GETTING AROUND
### LYSEFJORD

There are no roads along the length of the Lysefjord, so although the fjord can be reached by car at three points – one at the west end, one at the east and one in the middle – you'll need to take a **boat trip** to appreciate its full dimensions.

**Hurtigbåt passenger express boat** The fastest trips are by Hurtigbåt passenger express boat (May, June & Sept 1 daily; July & Aug 2 daily; Oct–April 1 weekly; 3hr; 390kr; ☎ 51 89 52 70, ⓦ rodne.no), but these round-trip excursions, which depart from Stavanger's Skagenkaien, only go halfway up along the Lysefjord and the views from the boat are not nearly as good as they are from a car ferry.

**Car ferry** A regular car ferry runs from the Fiskepiren terminal in Stavanger to Lysebotn, at the far end of the Lysefjord; advance booking is recommended (3 weekly; 1hr

45min; passengers 115kr, car and driver 400kr; ☎ 177, ⓦ kolumbus.no).

**Tourist car ferry** From late May to late June, Norled

tourist car ferries (4hr; passengers 210kr each way; driver & car 400kr each way; ☎ 51 86 87 80, ⓦ norled.no) run between the Fiskepiren terminal and Lysebotn (1 daily each way); from late June to late August they run to Lysebotn from Lauvvik, much closer to the west end of the Lysefjord (2 daily each way) – there's a connecting bus from Stavanger for foot passengers. From Lysebotn, drivers can head off into the mountains and/or return to Stavanger, but note that vehicle owners are strongly advised to make advance ferry reservations at least a day ahead. Passengers often hang around Lysebotn and then come back along the same route, though the return ferry journey can be a bit of a drag.

**Tours** You can liven up the standard Stavanger–Lysebotn itinerary by opting for the "Fjord and Mountain" excursion (late June to late Aug 1 daily; 8hr; 590kr) run by Norled (☎ 51 86 87 80, ⓦ norled.no), which involves a bus ride over the mountains from Stavanger to Øygardstøl, the dramatic hairpin drive down to Lysebotn and then the car ferry along the Lysefjord back to Stavanger. The brave can also ramp up the stakes by taking Norled's "Hiking tour to Kjerag from Stavanger" (late June to late Aug 1 daily, early Sept 3 weekly; 10hr; 490kr), which follows the same itinerary as the "Fjord and Mountain" trip except that you get off the bus at Øygardstøl for a guided hike to the Kjeragbolten (see below), after which you return to Stavanger.

## Stavanger to Lysebotn

Heading out from Stavanger, both the regular and the tourist **Lysefjord car ferries** (see opposite) chop through raggle-taggle islands before turning into the **Lysefjord** between **Oanes**, on its northern shore, and **Forsand** to the south. Before long the ferry passes the base of Preikestolen (see below), though from this angle the rock hardly makes any impression at all. It then nudges on up the fjord with mighty cliffs to either side before reaching **Flørli**, one of several request stops, where a scattering of houses hugs the shore in sight of the old power station – the new one is actually inside the mountain. A remarkably long wooden stairway leads up the mountainside here and, even more remarkably, the occasional visitor actually gets off the boat to clamber up it.

### Lysebotn

**Lysebotn**, at the far end of the Lysefjord, is the neatest of villages, a tiny little place built to house hydroelectric workers in the middle of the twentieth century. It's also extremely popular with base-jumpers, who hunker down here before heading off into the mountains nearby.

**ACCOMMODATION**                                                       **LYSEBOTN**

**Lysefjorden Vandrerhjem** ☎ 94 82 66 02, ⓦ hihostels.no. Housed in a modern building, this well-equipped hostel has a café serving breakfast, lunch and dinner, self-catering facilities, common rooms and an outdoor area. There are 49 beds in 22 rooms, with en-suite doubles available. Rates include breakfast. Mid-June to Aug. Dorms 260kr, doubles 815kr

## Lysebotn to Stavanger via Øygardstøl and Kjeragbolten

Leaving the Lysefjord behind, the narrow **road up from Lysebotn** (closed in winter) offers spectacular views as it wiggles and wriggles its way up the mountainside. Eventually, after 7km, just above the last hairpin, the road arrives at the **Øygardstøl café**, which has panoramic views back down towards the fjord. Øygardstøl is also the starting point for the **hiking trail** (see above) which leads west to the **Kjeragbolten**, a much-photographed boulder wedged between two cliff faces high above the ground. It's a tough route, so allow six hours for the round trip – and steel your nerves for the dizzying drops down to the fjord below.

Beyond Øygardstøl, the road crosses a stunningly beautiful mountain plateau, a barren, treeless expanse of boulder and loch whose wide vistas are intercepted by the occasional cabin. Eventually, the road meets Highway 45, which slices west between the bulging mountains of **Øvstabødal** on its way back to Stavanger.

## Preikestolen

Lysefjord's most celebrated vantage point, **Preikestolen** (Pulpit Rock), offers superlative views, though on sunny summer days you'll be sharing them with lots and lots of others. How much you enjoy it depends on your vertigo: the bold/foolhardy dangle the odd limb over the abyss, the more cautious stay away from the edge – and there are no fences or barriers. From the car park at the end of the road, where you'll also find a hostel and a mountain lodge, it's a four-hour **hike** there and back to Preikestolen along a clearly marked trail. The first half is steep in parts and paved with uneven stones, while the second half – over bedrock – is a good bit easier. The change in elevation is 350m and you should take food and water; the hike is not feasible in winter unless you really know what you are doing.

**2**

### Hikes from the Preikestolen car park

The DNT-affiliated Stavanger Turistforening (see p.137) have details of hikes around Preikestolen, and sell an excellent English-language hiking guide to the area

From Preikestolen car park, a short sharp hike leads down to **Refsvatn**, a small lake encircled by a footpath which takes three hours to negotiate, passing birch and pine woods, marshes, narrow ridges and bare stretches of rock. It also threads through **Torsnes**, an isolated farm that was inhabited until 1962. The lake footpath connects with a rough path that careers down to the **Refsa quay** on the Lysefjord.

---

### ARRIVAL AND DEPARTURE

### PREIKESTOLEN

**By ferry and car** To get to Preikestolen by car, take the ferry east from Stavanger to Tau (every 30min–1hr; 40min; passengers 43kr, car and driver 129kr; ⓦnorled .no) and then drive south along Highway 13 until, after about 14km, you reach the signed side road leading to Preikestolen.

**By ferry and bus** Ferry and bus deals covering the Stavanger–Tau–Preikestolen route are available throughout the season; timetables are available from Stavanger tourist office (mid-April to mid-May & late Sept Sat & Sun 6 daily; mid-May to mid-Sept 6 daily; bus journey 35min; 200kr return).

### ACCOMMODATION

**Preikestolenfjellstue** ⓪51 74 20 74, ⓦpreikestolenfjellstue.no. Operated by the Stavanger branch of DNT, the Norwegian hiking association, this large and comfortable mountain lodge is a handsome wood and glass structure that blends in well with its environs. It's well equipped too, with a restaurant and spacious common areas. The rooms, all of which are en suite, are priced according to the view – those offering panoramic views are the most expensive, those looking out into the forest are the cheapest. Substantial discounts for YHA and DNT members (doubles from 795kr). Located

close to the Preikestolen car park. Open all year. 995kr **Preikestolen Vandrerhjem** ⓪51 74 20 74, ⓦhihostels.no. Right by the Preikestolen car park, this first-rate HI hostel perches high on the hillside with great views over the surrounding mountains. Built on the site of an old mountain farm, it comprises a small complex of turf-roofed lodges, each of which has a spick-and-span pine interior. There are self-catering facilities, and a café serving breakfasts, lunches and simple evening meals; reservations are advised as the place is popular with school groups. Open April–Oct. Dorms 280kr, en-suite doubles 740kr

---

# Haugesund

There is no overpowering reason to break your journey between Stavanger and Bergen, but **HAUGESUND**, a lively industrial town 100km north of Stavanger – via the E39 and the Mortavika–Arsvågen ferry (see box, p.138) – has its moments. Now a major player in the North Sea oil industry, Haugesund once thrived on its herring fisheries, whose whopping profits funded the series of large and imposing, early twentieth-century stone buildings that dot **Smedasundet**, the bustling main harbour.

Specific sights are perhaps thin on the ground, but a stroll along the **harbourfront** is an amiable way to spend half an hour and the tumbling water fountains of adjacent **Torggata** lead up towards the town's prettiest church, **Vår Frelsers Kirke**, a slender brick affair of 1901 whose neo-Gothic design is enlivened by some *Jugendstil* flourishes. Haugesund may be light on sights, but it does well for festivals, the prime examples being the **Sildajazz Festival** (ⓦsildajazz.no) and the first-rate **Norwegian International Film Festival** (ⓦfilmweb.no/filmfestivalen), both of which are held in August. The town's other claim to fame is as the hometown of the baker Edward Mortenson, who emigrated to the USA, where he almost certainly fathered Norma Jean, otherwise **Marilyn Monroe**.

## Haraldshaugen

The first ruler of a united Norway, **Harald Hårfagre** (Harald Fair Hair; c.880–930), is thought to have been buried up along the coast just 2km to the north of Haugesund – and a grand granite obelisk, the **Haraldshaugen**, now marks his presumed resting place, sitting pretty just off Highway 47. Hårfagre defeated a coalition of local chieftains at the battle of Hafrsfjord just south of Stavanger in about 885, thereby cementing his control of the fjordland, an achievement that, according to legend, released him from a ten-year vow not to cut his hair until he had united the country. In a nationalist flush, the Norwegians erected the Haraldshaugen monument to celebrate Hårfagre in 1872, but very little is known about Hårfagre's rule or the extent of his real power. The most detailed evidence comes from several of the sagas, which insist that Harald "kept a sharp eye on the landed men and rich farmers", so much so that many fled west to settle in Iceland and the Faroes, though this does not entirely match with the facts – the move west began earlier.

### ARRIVAL AND DEPARTURE                                    HAUGESUND

**By plane** Haugesund's pocket-sized international airport is some 14km southwest of the centre. From the airport, there is a regular Flybussen service to Haugesund (25min; 70kr one-way, 110kr return; @ flybussen.no), with departure times linked to flight arrivals.

**By bus** Long-distance buses pull into Haugesund bus station, an inconvenient 20min walk from the harbourfront. The taxi fare from the station to the harbour is about 80kr.

Destinations Nor-Way Bussekspress's Kystbussen (#400) runs to Bergen (every 1–2hr; 3hr 15min) and Stavanger (every 1–2hr; 2hr), and its Haukeliekspressen (#180) to Oslo (1–2 daily; 9hr).

**By ferry** Hurtigbåt passenger express ferries from Bergen (2–3 daily; 3hr) and Stavanger (2–3 daily; 1hr 40min) stop on the harbourfront right in the centre of town.

**By car** Moving on up the coast from Haugesund, drivers can either continue north on the E39 to Bergen (see box, p.138), or branch off east along the E134 towards either Odda (see p.211) and the Hardangerfjord (see p.208) or Oslo via the wild and woolly Haukelifjell mountain pass.

**Tourist office** Strandgata 171, one block in from the main harbour (May–Aug Mon–Fri 9am–5pm, Sat & Sun 10am–3pm; Sept–April Mon–Fri 10am–4.30pm; ☎ 52 01 08 30, @ visithaugesund.no).

### ACCOMMODATION

**Clarion Hotel** Amanda Smedasundet 93 ☎ 52 80 82 00, @ choicehotels.no. On the main harbourfront, this medium-sized hotel occupies a good-looking, early twentieth-century stone building; the rooms are large and comfortable, and have benefited from a recent upgrade. An evening buffet meal is included in the price on weekdays. Sauna, steam room and bike rental too. 1800kr, sp/r 1000kr

**Rica Maritim** Åsbygaten 3 ☎ 52 86 30 00, @ rica.no. The town's plushest hotel is located in a large, ultramodern block on the harbourfront. All the rooms here are decorated in crisp, modern style and most have harbour views. 1600kr

**Røvær Vandrerhjem** Røvær, 10km to the west of Haugesund ☎ 52 71 80 35, @ vandrerhjem.no. For something more distinctive than Haugesund's chain hotels, take the ferry to the green, fairly flat and car-free little island of Røvær (@ visitrovar.no), where there's a no-frills HI hostel in a distinctive timber building metres from the ferry dock, as well as easy rambling and a beach or two. Passenger ferries leave from Haugesund's harbourfront (6–7 daily; 25min; 50kr each way) and dock a short walk from the main village. Open late June to late Aug. Dorms 220kr, doubles 590kr

### EATING AND DRINKING

**Café Moody** Strandgata 152 ☎ 52 72 74 20. One block up from the harbourfront, near the corner of Torggata, this is the best café in Haugesund by a long chalk, a laidback sort of place with secondhand furniture and modern art on the walls. The café attracts a student crew and serves up tasty, filling sandwiches and snacks from 70kr and up. Mon & Tues 11am–11pm, Wed–Fri 11am–1.30am, Sat noon–1.30am; closed Sun.

**Lothes Mat & Vinhus** Skippergata 4 ☎ 52 71 22 01. The pick of the town's several restaurants, located in a cosy huddle of old timber buildings just up from the harbourfront. The wide-ranging menu features a whole raft of Norwegian favourites, with main courses costing in the region of 300kr. When the kitchen closes at night, the place morphs into a bar till 1 or 2am. Kitchen Mon–Sat 11am–10pm.

# Central Norway

DALEN HOTEL

# Central Norway

Preoccupied by the fjords and the long road to Nordkapp, few tourists are tempted to explore central Norway. The Norwegians know better. This great chunk of land, trapped between Sweden and the fjords, boasts some of the country's finest scenery, with the forested dales that trail north and west from Oslo heralding the region's mountain passes and rearing peaks. And among much else, it's here, within shouting distance of the country's principal train line and the E6 – long the main line of communication between Oslo, Trondheim and the north – that you'll find three of Norway's prime hiking areas. These comprise a trio of mountain ranges, each partly contained within a national park – from south to north, Jotunheimen, Rondane and the Dovrefjell-Sunndalsfjella.

There are four main highways running from Oslo and its environs to the fjords. Whichever one you choose, allow a little time to appreciate the wonderful scenery and to muse on the ingenuity of Norway's road builders – and the difficulty of communication before they set to work: until well into the 1970s, a trip to Oslo from many a fjordland village could take at least a couple of days. Among these four major highways, the **E6** is the busiest, running up the **Gudbrandsdal valley** past several historic sights and within easy striking distance of a battery of **national parks**, most notably Jotunheimen, Rondane and Dovrefjell-Sunndalsfjella. Of the three, **Jotunheimen** is the harshest and most stunning, with its string of icy, jagged peaks; the **Dovrefjell-Sunndalsfjella** is more varied with severe mountains in the west and open moors and rounded ridges in the east; while **Rondane**, a high alpine zone, has more accessible mountains and low vegetation. Each of the parks is equipped with well-maintained walking trails and DNT huts, two of which – **Rondvassbu** and **Gjendesheim** – are ideal for hiking expeditions deep into Rondane and Jotunheimen respectively. For Dovrefjell-Sunndalsfjella, the easiest place to start is **Kongsvoll**, on both the E6 and the train line. The E6 also passes reasonably near to the intriguing old copper-town of **Røros** and, even better, it's the starting point for Highway 15 and the E136, two magnificent roads that thread through the mountains to the fjords (see Chapter 4).

On the other hand, the **E16** is the most direct route to the fjords, a 350km yomp up the Valdres valley and over the Filefjell mountain pass to **Lærdal**, firmly in fjord country and at the start of the series of long **tunnels** that enable the E16 to fast-track west to Flåm (see p.224) and ultimately Bergen. The long lakes and wooded hills of the **Valdres valley** make for a delightful drive and on the way you'll shoot past several **stave churches**, though the most beautiful and certainly the most famous is beyond the valley, over the Filefjell pass, at **Borgund**.

WHITEWATER RAFTING, RIVER SJOA

# Highlights

❶ **Whitewater rafting, Sjoa** Brave some of Norway's most exciting whitewater-rafting on the River Sjoa. **See p.160**

❷ **Lake Gjende** A boat trip along one of Norway's most beautiful lakes provides a scenic introduction to the mighty Jotunheimen mountains. **See p.163**

❸ **Hike the Besseggen ridge** Norway at its wildest: sample the magnificent scenery of the Jotunheimen Nasjonalpark on this classic walk, one of the country's most celebrated. **See box, p.166**

❹ **Kongsvold Fjeldstue** This lovely hotel occupies a tastefully restored complex of old timber buildings, and is convenient for exploring the Dovrefjell-Sunndalsfjella National Park. **See p.168**

❺ **Borgund stave church** One of the best preserved and most harmonious of Norway's 28 remaining stave churches: admire the intricacy of its construction and the intimacy of its decoration. **See p.173**

❻ **Kongsberg** This lovely little town is home to Norway's most imposing Baroque church. **See p.174**

❼ **Dalen Hotel** Immaculately restored 1890s hotel in a quiet country town halfway between Oslo and the fjords. **See p.179**

HIGHLIGHTS ARE MARKED ON THE MAP ON PP.148–149

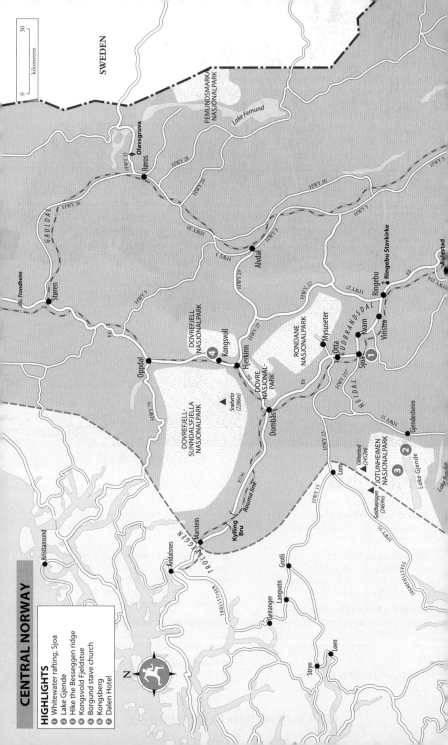

## CENTRAL NORWAY

**HIGHLIGHTS**

1. Whitewater rafting, Sjoa
2. Lake Gjende
3. Hike the Besseggen ridge
4. Kongsvold Fjeldstue
5. Borgund stave church
6. Kongsberg
7. Dalen Hotel

SWEDEN

N

FEMUNDSMARKA NASJONALPARK

Lake Femund

Olavsgruva

Røros

HWY 31

HWY 28

HWY 30

HWY 30

HWY 26

HWY 30

HWY 30

HWY 3

HWY 3

HWY 3

Alvdal

HWY 29

Aulestad

HWY 254

HWY 254

Ringebu Stavkirke

Trondheim

Støren

E6

HWY 3

HWY 3

HWY 27

Ringebu

E6

DOVREFJELL NASJONALPARK

Kongsvoll

Hjerkinn

Oppdal

HWY 70

RONDANE NASJONALPARK

Mysuseter

Otta

Vinstra

Sjoa

Kvam

GUDBRANDSDAL

DOVREFJELL-SUNNDALSFJELLA NASJONALPARK

Snøhetta (2286m)

DOVRE NASJONAL-PARK

Dombås

E6

E6

HEIDAL

HWY 257

Gjendesheim

HWY 51

Lom

Galdhøpiggen (2469m)

Glittertind (2452m)

JOTUNHEIMEN NASJONALPARK

Lake Gjende

Lake Bygdin

HWY 15

HWY 15

Rauma line

E136

Marstein

**Kylling Bru**

Andalsnes

Kristiansund

TROLLSTIGEN

TROLLVEGGEN

Grotli

Langvatn

Geiranger

Strynefjellsveg

HWY 55

Loen

Stryn

kilometres

0      30

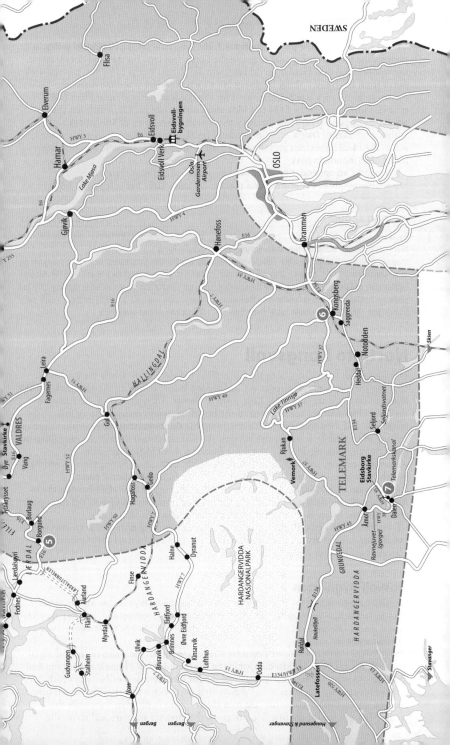

Further south, the first part of **Highway 7**, the long haul up the **Hallingdal valley**, is perhaps the least diverting way to get to the fjords, but later on the road does traverse the wonderfully wild Hardangervidda mountain plateau (see p.215). You can also fork north from Highway 7 along Highway 50, which thunders down the dramatic Aurlandsdalen valley (see p.225) bound for the fjords at Aurland, near Flåm (see p.224). Finally, there's the **E134** to Odda and Lofthus (see p.212), which has the advantage of passing through the attractive former silver-town of **Kongsberg** and within a whisker of **Dalen**, with its excellent hotel, before making a dramatic defile across the Hardangervidda and then proceeding up and over the wild and desolate **Haukelifjell mountain pass**.

In terms of **accommodation**, roadside campsites are commonplace, there's a reasonable supply of HI hostels, and every town and village has at least one hotel or guesthouse.

**GETTING AROUND**             **CENTRAL NORWAY**

**By train** Trains shuttle along the two main rail lines that cross central Norway: the Oslo–Bergen line shadows Highway 7 until just after Geilo, while the Oslo–Trondheim line passes through Hamar, Lillehammer and Dombås, the junction for the superbly scenic run down to the fjords at Åndalsnes on the Rauma branch line. An alternative train route from Oslo to Trondheim dodges Lillehammer and Dombås, but includes Røros.

**By bus** Nor-Way Bussekspress buses (Ⓦ nor-way.no) ply the E6 as well as most of the E16 and the E134, but once you get onto the minor roads, including Highway 7, the bus system thins out and travelling becomes much more difficult without your own vehicle.

# North to Kongsvoll

Heading north from Oslo, both the E6 and the railway thump across the lowlands, clipping the international airport at Gardermoen before following the east bank of **Lake Mjøsa** to skip past the amenable little town of **Hamar**. Thereafter, it's a short haul to ski-crazy **Lillehammer**, home to one of the best of Norway's many open-air folk museums, and then road and rail sweep on up the **Gudbrandsdal valley**, within sight of a string of modest little towns and villages, the first significant attraction being **Ringebu stave church**. Pushing on, it's just a few kilometres more to **Sjoa**, a centre for whitewater rafting, and then, a little further north, **Otta**, an undistinguished town but one that is within easy reach of two particularly magnificent **national parks**, **Jotunheimen** and **Rondane**. Further north still is the rugged **Dovrefjell-Sunndalsfjella Nasjonalpark**, which is most pleasingly approached from tiny **Kongsvoll**. All three parks are networked by an extensive and well-planned system of hiking trails.

From Kongsvoll, Trondheim is within comfortable striking distance; alternatively, you can detour east to **Røros**, a fascinating old copper-mining town on the mountain plateau that stretches across to Sweden.

## Eidsvoll-bygningen

House and visitor centre April & Sept Tues–Fri 10am–3pm, Sat & Sun noon–5pm; May–Aug daily 10am–5pm; Oct–March Wed–Fri 10am–3pm, Sat & Sun noon–5pm · House 75kr; visitor centre free · Ⓦ eidsvoll1814.no · Eidsvoll-bygningen is 2km off the E6 (just follow the signs), and about 1.5km from Eidsvoll Verk train station; trains run from Oslo S (hourly; 50min) and Hamar (hourly; 1hr), though you need to change at Eidsvoll

About 70km north of Oslo, in a countryside setting just to the south of the industrial town of Eidsvoll Verk, is **Eidsvoll-bygningen** (Eidsvoll Manor House), a charming and spacious old manor house that gives a real insight into the tastes of Norway's early nineteenth-century upper class. In its own little park with a river running down below, this two-storey timber house has just over thirty rooms, with what were once the owners' living areas on the first floor, beneath the servants' quarters and above the

## EIDSVOLL-BYGNINGEN AND THE CONSTITUTION OF 1814

**Carsten Ankers** (1747–1824) was a close friend and ally of the Danish crown prince **Christian Frederik**, a connection that has given Eidsvoll national importance. Towards the end of the Napoleonic Wars, the Russians and British insisted the Danes be punished for their alliance with the French, and proposed taking Norway from Denmark and handing it over to Sweden. In an attempt to forestall these territorial shenanigans, the Danes dispatched Christian Frederik to Norway, where he set up home in Carsten Ankers' house in 1813, and proceeded to lobby for Norwegian support. In April of the following year more than a hundred of the country's leading citizens gathered here near **Eidsvoll** to decide whether to accept union with Sweden or go for independence with Christian Frederik on the throne. The majority of this National Assembly chose independence, and set about drafting a **liberal constitution** based on those of France and the United States.

Predictably, the Swedes would have none of this. Four years earlier, the Swedes had picked one of Napoleon's marshals, **Jean-Baptiste Bernadotte** (see p.65), to succeed their previous king who had died without an heir. As **King Karl Johan**, Bernadotte was keen to flex his military muscles and, irritated by the putative National Assembly, he invaded Norway in July 1814. Frederik was soon forced to abdicate and the Norwegians were pressed into **union with Sweden**, though Karl Johan did head off much of the opposition by guaranteeing the Norwegians a new constitution and parliament, the Storting.

**3**

basement kitchens. The main entrance hall is in the Neoclassical style much favoured by the Dano–Norwegian elite, its columns a suitably formal introduction to the spacious suites that lie beyond. The library is well stocked, and there's a billiard room and a smoking room, as well as a string of elegant dining rooms and bedrooms. Oriental knick-knacks and English furniture appear throughout, and the occasional mural depicts Greek mythological figures. There's also an obsession with symmetry: doors were camouflaged and false windows created to avoid breaking up the architectural regularity whenever it was threatened. The house was owned by the **Ankers family**, who made their money from the local ironworks – hence the splendid cast-iron stoves.

It's a delightful ensemble, but the house owes much of its present appearance – perhaps even its survival – to its historical significance (see box above) rather than its aesthetics. One of the family, Carsten Ankers, converted the upper storey of his home into premises for the **National Assembly**, comprising a handful of administrative offices plus the Room for the Constitutional Committee, where the original wooden benches have survived along with various landscape paintings. There's a rusticated modesty to it all which is really rather charming, and a painting of Venus has been put back in the room after years of being shunted up and down the adjoining corridors: after prolonged discussion, it had originally been removed because the representatives considered it an erotic distraction. For more on the evolution of democracy in general and the Norwegian Constitution in particular, drop by the **visitor centre** just down from the house near the river.

# Hamar

Set midway around the eastern shore of **Lake Mjøsa**, some 130km from Oslo, **HAMAR** is a pleasant if undemanding town of 29,000 inhabitants, whose centre rustles up a scattering of substantial nineteenth-century buildings, including a large and really rather imposing train station. In fact, the rail line – and its embankment – currently sit between the town centre and the lake, though there are ambitious plans to re-route the railway further out on the lake. In the meantime, it's easy to unwind here in Hamar, which is at its prettiest in the little **park** in between Strandgata and the railway embankment, and on the old **jetty** where the vintage *Skibladner* docks during the summer (see box, p.153). The town also possesses one notable sight: the **Hedmarksmuseet**.

E6 & Oslo

Lake Mjøsa

Vikingskipet

E6 & Lillehammer

**HAMAR**

| ■ ACCOMMODATION | |
|---|---|
| Quality Hotel Astoria | 3 |
| Scandic Hamar | 1 |
| Vikingskipet motell og Vandrerhjem | 2 |

| ● EATING | |
|---|---|
| Hot & Spicy | 2 |
| Pepperværna | |
| Mat og Vinhus | 1 |

ESPERN

Lake Mjøsa

Tjuvholmen

RV156VEG

ÅKERSVIKAVEGEN

VANGSVEGEN

RINGGATA

Kulturhuset

DISENSTRANDVEGEN

Hamar Stadion

ST. OLAVS GATE

GRØNNEGATA

ØSTREGATA

STRANDGATA

BRYGGA

STORHAMARGATA

KIRKEGATA

FURNESVEGEN

SAGATUNVEGEN

Bus Station

Train Station

Skibladner Jetty

ESPERNGATA

STANGEVEGEN

FALSENS GATE

SVERDRUPS GATE

CHRISTIES GATE

WERGELANDS GATE

WELHAVENS GATE

ANDERS SANDVIGS GATE

P. SANDVIKS GATE

HÅKON GATE

TORGGATA

N

0          150
   metres

## DS SKIBLADNER

Hamar is as good a place as any to pick up the 130-year-old **paddle steamer**, the DS *Skibladner* (❶61 14 40 80, ⓦskiblander.no), which shuttles up and down **Lake Mjøsa** during the summer offering wide views over rolling forested hills to east and west. Travellers heading north may find the trip to Lillehammer tempting at first sight, but the lake is not particularly scenic, and after four hours on the boat you may well feel like jumping overboard. The best bet is to take the shorter ride to Eidsvoll instead.

Sailings run from late June to mid-August. On Tuesdays, Thursdays and Saturdays the boat makes the return trip across the lake from Hamar to **Gjøvik** and on up to **Lillehammer** (just under 8hr; 320kr); on Wednesdays, Fridays and Sundays it chugs south to **Eidsvoll** and back (4hr 30min; 280kr); there's no Monday service. Sailing times are available direct or at any local tourist office. Tickets are bought on board; one-way fares cost a little over half the return fare. In Hamar, the *Skibladner* jetty is handily located about 600m to the west of the train station along the lakeshore. In Lillehammer, it's on the west side of the lake, across the bridge from the centre of Lillehammer, beside the E6.

**3**

Before the railroad arrived in the 1880s, the lake was an important transport route, crossed by boats in summer and by horse and sleigh in winter. It's also halfway country: the quiet settlements around the lake give a taste of small-town southern Norway before the E6 plunges into the wilder regions further north.

## Hedmarksmuseet

Domkirkeodden • Late May to late June Tues–Sun 10am–4pm; late June to mid-Aug daily 10am–5pm; late Aug Tues–Sun 10am–4pm • 100kr • ⓦhedmarksmuseet.no

Unlikely though it may seem today, Hamar was once the seat of an important medieval bishopric, and the battered remains of its Romanesque-Gothic **Domkirke** (Cathedral), now protected by a glass and steel superstructure – the Hamardomen – are stuck out on the Domkirkeodden (Cathedral Point), a low, leafy headland about 2km west of the centre. The cathedral is thought to have been built by the "English pope" Nicholas Breakspear, who spent a couple of years in Norway as the papal legate before becoming Adrian IV in 1154, but the building, along with the surrounding episcopal complex, was ransacked during the Reformation, and local road-builders subsequently helped themselves to the stone.

The cathedral ruins have now been incorporated into the rambling **Hedmarksmuseet** (Hedmark Museum), which also contains an archeological section, the remains of the bishop's palace, a display of vintage photographs of the town and its surroundings, and an open-air folk museum. The latter holds around sixty buildings collected from across the region and, although it's not as comprehensive as the one in Lillehammer (see p.155), it does contain several particularly fine buildings, the oldest of which are clustered in the Hedmarkstunet section.

The most scenic approach to the **Hedmarksmuseet** is along the pleasant lakeshore footpath that stretches 2km north from the train station.

### ARRIVAL AND DEPARTURE                                          HAMAR

**By train** Hamar train station is near the lakeshore on the southeast corner of the downtown grid. It's the starting point of a branch line that leads to Røros (see p.168), a fine ride over hills and through huge forests.

Destinations Lillehammer (hourly; 40min); Oslo (hourly; 1hr 20min); Oslo Gardermoen (hourly; 1hr); Røros (3–6 daily; 3hr 30min); Trondheim (2–4 daily; 5hr 15min).

**By bus** The main bus station is a couple of minutes' walk away to the east of the train station. Nor-Way Bussekspress runs the following services:

Dag og Nattekspressen (#142) to: Lillehammer (2 daily; 1hr); Oslo (2 daily; 2hr); Oslo Gardermoen (2 daily; 1hr 20min); Otta (2 daily; 3hr 20min).

Gudbrandsdalekspressen (#148) to: Lillehammer (Mon–Fri 1 daily; 1hr); Oslo (Mon–Fri 1 daily; 2hr); Otta (Mon–Fri 1 daily; 3hr 20min).

## ACCOMMODATION

★ **Quality Hotel Astoria** Torggata 23 ☎ 62 70 70 00, ⓦ choicehotels.no. Plumb in the centre of town, with its best rooms overlooking the main square, this medium-sized and noticeably friendly chain hotel is decorated in bright and cheerful colours. Breakfast is taken in a mock-up of a *bondstua* (farmer's house) – all a little daft perhaps, but still somehow rather endearing. 1400kr, sp/r 1100kr

**Scandic Hamar** Vangsvegen 121 ☎ 21 61 40 00, ⓦ scandichotels.com. Located in a large modern block on the northeast edge of the town centre, this chain hotel may not be especially prepossessing from the outside, but the interior has been kitted out in a bright and well-conceived

modern/minimalist style as have the spacious bedrooms, some of which – on the top floors – have wide views over town. Breakfasts here are first-rate too. 1600kr, sp/r 1200kr

**Vikingskipet motell og Vandrerhjem** Åkersvikvegen 24 ☎ 62 52 60 60, ⓦ hihostels.no. Hamar's all-year HI hostel occupies a modern two-storey motel-style timber building about 1km east along the lakeshore from the train station. It's in the middle of nowhere, just across from the massive skating arena, the Vikingskipet, built for the 1994 Winter Olympics in the shape of an upturned Viking ship. There's a café, a laundry and self-catering facilities. All rooms are en suite. Dorms 410kr, doubles 840kr

## EATING

**Hot & Spicy** Torggata 21, cnr Enggata ☎ 62 52 02 60, ⓦ hot-andspicy.com. Handily located in the centre of town, this cheerfully decorated Chinese/Thai restaurant is an informal, family-run place, where the service is fast and efficient and main courses are priced 140–190kr. Mon & Wed–Sat 3–11pm, Sun 2–10pm; closed Tues.

**Pepperkvaerna Mat og Vinhus** Torggata 23 ☎ 62 70 70

30. Attached to the *Quality Hotel Astoria* (see above), this neatly turned-out restaurant does not look particularly outstanding but the food is absolutely delicious with the emphasis on traditional Norwegian dishes with added zip (and perfect sauces). They also try to source locally – try the mountain trout with potatoes, a veritable snip at 280kr. Mon–Thurs 5–11pm, Fri & Sat 6–11pm; kitchen till 10pm.

# Lillehammer and around

**LILLEHAMMER** (literally "Little Hammer"), 60km north of Hamar and 190km from Oslo, is Lake Mjøsa's largest settlement and, in winter at least, its most worthwhile destination. The town has become one of Norway's top ski centres (see box below), its semi-rural lakeside setting and extensive cross-country ski trails contributing to its selection as host of the **1994 Olympic Winter Games**. The Lillehammer area is a popular summer holiday spot too. As soon as the weather picks up, hundreds of Norwegians hunker down in their second homes in the hills that flank the town, popping into the centre for a drink or a meal. Cycling, walking, fishing and canoeing are popular pastimes at this time of year, but however appealing the area may be to Norwegians, the countryside hereabouts has little of the wonderful wildness of other parts of Norway, and unless you're someone's guest or bring your own family, you'll probably feel rather out on a limb.

Even though its centre does look a tad humdrum, Lillehammer is not a bad place to break your journey. Orientation couldn't be easier: pretty much everything that's happening is focused on the pedestrianized part of **Storgata**, which runs north from Bankgata to the tumbling River Mesnaelva, a five-minute stroll away; **Kirkegata**, another

## LILLEHAMMER: WINTER ACTIVITIES

In preparation for the 1994 Winter Olympics, the Norwegian government spent a massive two billion kroner on the town's sporting facilities, which are now among the best in the country. Spread along the hillsides above and near the town, they include several dozen downhill **ski trails** catering for everyone from beginner to expert, floodlit slopes for night skiing, ski-jumping towers and multiple chairlifts, an **ice hockey** arena, and a **bobsleigh** track. There is even a special stadium – the **Birkebeiner** – where skiers can hone their skills before setting off into the mountains, which are crisscrossed by 350km of cross-country ski trails. As you would expect, most Norwegians arriving here in winter come fully equipped, but it's possible to rent or buy equipment locally – the tourist office will advise, but note that advance booking is strongly recommended.

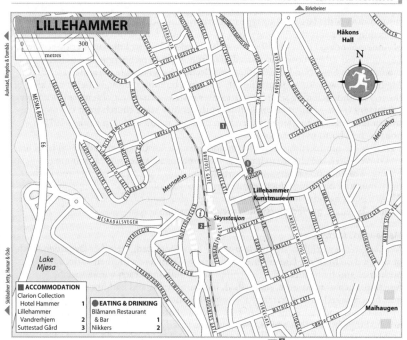

**3**

useful street, runs one block parallel to the west of Storgata (down the hill). Lillehammer's three top attractions are the **Kunstmuseum** (Art Museum), **Maihaugen** open-air museum, and **Aulestad**, the country home of Norwegian author Bjørnstjerne Bjørnson, about thirty minutes' drive away. It's also one of the ports of call of the antique **DS Skibladner** paddle steamer as it shuttles up and down Lake Mjøsa (see box, p.153).

## Lillehammer Kunstmuseum

Stortorget 2, Kirkegata • Late June to late Aug daily 11am–5pm; rest of year Tues–Sun 11am–4pm • 100kr; extra admission charge for temporary exhibitions • Ⓦ lillehammerartmuseum.com

Lillehammer's workaday modern centre has just one top-quality attraction, the **Kunstmuseum** (Art Museum), housed in two adjacent buildings – one a municipal structure from the 1960s, the other a newer, flashier edifice. The gallery is renowned for its temporary exhibitions, but the small permanent collection is also very worthwhile, comprising a representative sample of the works of most major Norwegian painters, from Johan Dahl and Christian Krohg to Munch and Erik Werenskiold. In particular, look out for the striking landscapes painted by one of the less familiar Norwegian artists, **Axel Revold** (1887–1962). A student of Matisse and an admirer of Cézanne, Revold spent years working abroad before returning home and applying the techniques he had learned to his favourite subject, northern Norway: his beautifully composed and brightly coloured *Nordland* is typical. Revold also dabbled in the bizarre, as in the bold Expressionism of *A Sailor's Dream*.

## Maihaugen

June–Aug daily 10am–5pm; Sept–May Tues–Sun 11am–4pm • Frequent guided tours in summertime; call ☎ 61 28 89 00 •110kr, June–Aug 150kr • Ⓦ maihaugen.no • From Storgata, walk up Bankgata, turn right onto Maihaugenvegen, and keep going, following the signs (20min)

The much-vaunted **Maihaugen** open-air folk museum, about 1.5km southeast of the town centre, is the largest of its type in northern Europe. Incredibly, the bulk of the collection represents the lifetime's work of one man, a magpie-ish dentist by the name of **Anders Sandvig** (1862–1950), who only ended up here in Lillehammer by accident: he contracted tuberculosis and moved here from Oslo to recuperate in the clear mountain air. Since Sandvig's death, the collection has gradually been increased and Maihaugen now holds approaching 200 relocated buildings, brought here from all over the region and including several real treasures such as a charming seventeenth-century **presbytery** (*prestegårdshagen*) and a thirteenth-century **stave church** from Garmo. The museum has also attempted to widen its range, one recent addition being a **1970s house** – bell-bottoms to the fore.

During the summertime, **costumed guides** give the lowdown on traditional rural life and there's often the chance to have a go at domestic activities such as spinning, baking, weaving and pottery – good, wholesome fun. You can spend time too in the main **museum** building, which features temporary exhibitions on folkloric themes. Allow a good half-day for a visit and you might also want to take advantage of the free English-language **guided tours** when they are scheduled.

### Maihaugen's farms

Maihaugen's key exhibits are two **farms**, one from **Bjørnstad**, the other **Øygarden**, both of which date from the late seventeenth century. Complete with their various outhouses and living areas, the two comprise 36 buildings, each with a specific function, such as food store, sheep-shed, hay barn, stable and bathhouse. This setup may have worked, and it certainly looks quaint, but it was, in fact, forced upon farmers by their tried-and-tested method of construction, **laft**. Based on the use of pine logs notched together at right angles, the technique strictly limited the dimensions of every building, as the usable part of the pine tree was rarely more than 8m long. Indeed, it seems likely that many farmers would have preferred to keep their winter supplies in the main farmhouse rather than in a separate store, as implied by a draconian medieval law that stated, "When a man discovers another in his storehouse … then he may kill the man if he so wishes."

## Around Lillehammer: Aulestad

Late May to Aug daily 10am–5pm; Sept to early Oct Tues–Sun 11am–4pm • 110kr • By car, head north from Lillehammer on the E6 and turn onto Highway 255 after about 4km; to get back onto the E6 heading north, follow Highway 255 from the Bjørnson house, then turn onto Highway 254, which brings you out on the E6 halfway between Lillehammer and the Ringebu church (see p.158)

In the hamlet of **Follebu**, 18km northwest of Lillehammer, is **Aulestad**, a good-looking villa perched on a leafy knoll that formerly belonged to **Bjørnstjerne Bjørnson** (see box below), who moved to Aulestad in 1875 and stayed there for the rest of his life. The house was gifted to the nation on the death of Bjørnstjerne's widow Karoline in 1934, and is jam-packed with family mementoes. An audiovisual display inside the house gives further details on the man and his times.

---

### BJØRNSTJERNE BJØRNSON

**Bjørnstjerne Bjørnson** (1832–1910) was a major figure in the literary and cultural revival that swept the country at the end of the nineteenth century. Bjørnson made his name with the peasant tales of *Synnøve Solbakken* in 1857 and thereafter he churned out a veritable flood of novels, stories, poems and plays, many of which romanticized Norwegian country folk and, unusually for the time, were written in Norwegian, rather than the traditional Danish. He also championed all sorts of progressive causes, from Norwegian independence through to equality of the sexes and crofters' rights, albeit from a liberal (as distinct from leftist) viewpoint. Nowadays, however, his main claim to fame is as author of the poem that became the **national anthem**.

## ARRIVAL AND INFORMATION

**By train** The Skysstasjon, on Jernbanetorget, at the foot of Jernbanegata, incorporates the train station and the bus terminal. It's just a couple of minutes' walk from Storgata, the main drag – walk up the hill.

Destinations Hamar (hourly; 40min); Oslo (hourly; 2hr); Oslo Gardermoen (hourly; 1hr 40min); Trondheim (2–4 daily; 4hr 30min).

**By bus** The bus station is housed in the Skysstasjon. Nor-Way Bussekspress run the following services:
Gudbrandsdalekspressen (#148) to: Hamar (Mon–Fri 1 daily; 1hr); Oslo (Mon–Fri 1 daily; 3hr); Otta (Mon–Fri 1 daily; 4hr 20min).
Nordfjordekspressen (#147) to: Langvatn (3 daily; 4hr

## LILLEHAMMER AND AROUND

50min); Lom (3 daily; 3hr 20min); Oslo (3 daily; 3hr); Otta (3 daily; 2hr 30min); Stryn (3 daily; 5hr 50min).

**By car** The E6 motorway cuts along the lakeshore about 500m below – and to the west of – the centre of Lillehammer. The town's one-way system is befuddling, but once you have reached the city centre, on-street parking is (usually) easy to find.

**Tourist office** In the Skysstasjon, Jernbanetorget (mid-June to mid-Aug Mon–Sat 9am–6pm, Sun noon–5pm; mid-Aug to mid-June Mon–Fri 8am–4pm, Sat 10am–2pm; ☎61 28 98 00, ⌨lillehammer.com). Staff have information on local events and activities, can issue a comprehensive town brochure, and will help with finding accommodation.

## ACCOMMODATION

**3**

**Clarion Collection Hotel Hammer** Storgata 108 ☎61 26 73 73, ⌨choicehotels.no. Gallant and largely successful attempt by this large chain to create a hotel with a cosy, traditional feel – from the open fireplaces and soft pastels of the public areas to the retro, high-gabled facade. The rooms are well equipped and comfortable and set round a courtyard with the quieter ones to the rear. Just west of the centre, about 5min walk from the train station. Rates include an evening buffet meal. **1270kr**, sp/r **970kr**

**Lillehammer Vandrerhjem** Jernbanetorget 2 ☎61 26 00 24, ⌨hihostels.no. All-year HI hostel in the same

recently revamped block as the train station. Has a good range of facilities, from a self-catering kitchen and a daytime café through to free parking and common rooms. The guest rooms – eighty bunk beds divided into thirty rooms – are fairly spartan, but they are perfectly adequate and all are en suite. Dorms **300kr**, doubles **780kr**

**Suttestad Gård** Suttestådveien 17 ☎61 25 04 44, ⌨lillehammer.com. Large former farmhouse with five modern guest rooms, most of which are en suite and have pleasant views down towards the lake. *Suttestad Gård* is 1.5km south of the train station: take Kirkegata and Suttestådveien is a turning on the right. **700kr**

## EATING AND DRINKING

In downtown Lillehammer, much of the gastronomic action – as well as the drinking – is focused towards the west end of pedestrianized **Storgata**, often to the sound of the River Mesna as it tumbles through town heading for Lake Mjøsa.

**Blåmann Restaurant & Bar** Lilletorvet 1 ☎61 26 22 03, ⌨blaamann.com. One of the better spots in town, this comparatively smart restaurant, off the pedestrianized part of Storgata, has a leafy terrace suspended over the cascading river below. The menu is probably more wide-ranging than is good for it, covering everything from Mexican to burgers, salads and pasta. Pasta dishes cost around 150kr, 250kr for the likes of reindeer. Mon–Sat noon–11pm, Sun 1–10pm; kitchen till about 9pm.

**Nikkers** Elvegata 18 ☎61 24 74 30, ⌨nikkers.no. Spread over two premises on short and sweet Elvegata, a lane off Storgata, *Nikkers* has a restaurant – including a riverside terrace – in one building, and a sports bar in the other. The restaurant premises are pleasantly traditional, all low ceilings and oodles of wood, and the food is filling and reasonably priced: their burger, for example, costs 179kr. Bar and restaurant Mon–Wed 11am–11pm, Thurs–Sat 11am–3am, Sun 1–10pm; restaurant kitchen till around 9pm.

# The Gudbrandsdal

Heading north from Lillehammer, the E6 and the railway leave the shores of Lake Mjøsa to run along the **Gudbrandsdal**, an appealing 160km river valley, which was for centuries the main route between Oslo and Trondheim. Enclosed by mountain ranges, the valley has a comparatively dry and mild climate, and its fertile soils have nourished a string of farming villages since Viking times; even today, despite the thunderings of the E6, the Gudbrandsdal remains predominantly – and distinctly – rural.

**By train and bus** All the larger towns in the valley are accessible by train and bus, and most of the smaller places can be reached on both the Gudbrandsdalekspressen (#148; Mon–Fri 1 daily) and the Nordfjordekspressen (#147; 3 daily), both operated by Nor-Way Bussekspress.

## Ringebu stavkirke

Daily: late May to June & early to mid-Aug 9am–5pm; July 8am–6pm • 40kr, 60kr including Weidemannsamlingen • The church is 1km off the E6

About 60km north of Lillehammer, the E6 swings past the turning to **Ringebu stavkirke** (Ringebu stave church), whose distinctive maroon spire stands on a hill a couple of kilometres south of Ringebu village. Dating from the thirteenth century, the original church was modified and enlarged in the 1630s, reflecting both an increase in the local population and the new religious practices introduced after the Reformation. At this time, the nave was broadened, the chancel replaced and an overlarge tower and spire plonked on top. The exterior is rather glum, but the western entrance portal sports some superb if badly weathered zoomorphic carvings from the original church. Inside, the highlights are mainly eighteenth-century Baroque – from the florid pulpit and altar panel through to a memorial to the Irgens family, complete with trumpeting cherubs and intricate ruffs.

### Weidemannsamlingen

Late May to mid-Aug Tues–Sun 10am–5pm • 40kr, 60kr including church

The old **vicarage** behind the church now holds the **Weidemannsamlingen** (Weidemann Exhibition), featuring a selection of thirty-or-so later paintings by the prolific **Jakob Weidemann** (1923–2001), one of Norway's most talented modern artists. Many of Weidemann's works were inspired by the Norwegian landscape, but he eschewed realism for deeply coloured abstract canvases of great emotional intensity. His liking for strong colours is often linked to an accident that befell him during World War II. Active in the Resistance, Weidemann was forced to escape to neutral Sweden, where he lost an eye when an explosive charge was accidentally detonated.

## Hundorp

About 12km northwest of the Ringebu church is the straggling village of **HUNDORP**, whose southern peripheries hold a neat little quadrangle of old farm buildings, sitting pretty beside the E6 and serving as a combined educational and cultural centre. There has been a farm here since prehistoric times, its most famous owner being a Viking warrior by the name of **Dalegudbrand**, who became a bitter enemy of St Olav after his enforced baptism in 1021.

Evidence of Hundorp's long history is easy to spot as there are half a dozen small but distinct **Viking burial mounds**, as well as a rough circle of **standing stones** close to the complex. The stones, which date from around 700 AD, mark the spot where freemen gathered in the *allting* to discuss issues of local importance – such meetings were nearly always held in the open air. The most powerful local chieftain presided over the *allting* with the assistance of a "law speaker", who was able to recite existing law and memorize new decisions. Theoretically at least, it was one man, one vote, but in practice the more powerful landowners usually had their own way with the assembled freemen showing their consent by brandishing their weapons and/or banging on their shields. A **display board** in the farm courtyard provides a general map of Hundorp, showing what is where, but it's rather hard to follow and the best bet is to take the grassy **track** that leads left from the farm entrance to the standing stones and the nearest burial mound. Thereafter, just follow your nose.

**By bus** There is no train station at Hundorp, but buses stop in front of the old farm beside the E6. Nor-Way Bussekspress runs the following services:
Gudbrandsdalekspressen (#148) to: Hamar (Mon–Fri 1

daily; 2hr 30min); Oslo (Mon–Fri 1 daily; 4hr 30min); Otta (Mon–Fri 1 daily; 45min).

Nordfjordekspressen (#147) to: Lillehammer (3 daily; 1hr

10min); Lom (3 daily; 2hr 30min); Oslo (3 daily; 4hr); Otta (3 daily; 1hr 30min); Stryn (3 daily; 4hr 30min).

## ACCOMMODATION

★ **Sygard Grytting** Sør-Fron ☎61 29 85 88, ⓦ grytting.com. This ancient farmstead, overlooking the E6 about 6km north of the Hundorp farmstead, provides some of the region's most distinctive lodgings. Nestling among the orchards, the eighteenth-century farm buildings are in an almost perfect state of preservation, a beautiful ensemble with the assorted barns, outhouses and main house facing onto a tiny courtyard. An even older building, dating from the fourteenth century, the upper storey of

which was used to shelter pilgrims on the long haul north to Trondheim cathedral, now houses dormitory accommodation; most of the double rooms though are in the main farmhouse, which has been superbly renovated to provide extremely comfortable lodgings amid antique furnishings, faded oil paintings and open fires. Breakfast (included) is splendid too – the bread is baked on the premises – and dinner is available by prior arrangement (at 7pm). Open July to mid-Aug. Dorms **335kr**, doubles **1400kr**

## Kvam

**KVAM**, about 20km north of Hundorp along the E6, is a modest chipboard-producing town that witnessed some of the worst fighting of World War II. Once the Germans had occupied Norway's main towns in the spring of 1940, they set about extending their control of the main roads and railways, marching up the Gudbrandsdal at the double. At Kvam, they were opposed by a scratch force of Norwegian and British soldiers, who delayed their progress for two weeks (April 14–30, 1940) despite being poorly equipped – the captain in charge of the British anti-tank guns had to borrow a bicycle to patrol his defences.

### Gudbrandsdal Krigsminnesamling and around

Late June to July daily 10am–5pm; early Aug Wed–Sun 10am–4pm • 40kr • ⓦ krigsminne.no

The battle for the Gudbrandsdal is commemorated at the **Gudbrandsdal Krigsminnesamling** (Gudbrandsdal War Museum), beside the E6 in the centre of Kvam. A series of excellent multilingual displays runs through the campaign, supported by a substantial collection of military mementoes and lots of fascinating photographs. There are also informative sections on the rise of Fascism and the Norwegian Resistance, plus a modest display on the role played by the villagers of Otta in the Kalmar War between Sweden and Denmark/Norway of 1611–13.

Across the main street from the museum, in the **church graveyard**, is a Cross of Sacrifice, honouring the 54 British soldiers who died here in Kvam while trying to halt the German advance.

### ARRIVAL AND DEPARTURE                                                    KVAM

**By train** Kvam train station, a request stop, is about 200m south of the museum. Trains run to Lillehammer (1 daily except Sun; 1hr 10min), Oslo S (1 daily except Sun; 3hr 30min) and Otta (2 daily except Sat; 15min).

**By bus** The Gudbrandsdalekspressen (#148; Mon–Fri 1 daily) and the Nordfjordekspressen (#147; 3 daily) travel through Kvam on the E6; there's a request stop metres from the museum.

## Sjoa and the Heidal valley

From Kvam, it's 9km further up the valley to **SJOA**, a scattered hamlet set beside the junction of the E6 and Highway 257. The latter cuts west along the **Heidal valley**, where the **River Sjoa** boasts some of the country's most exciting **whitewater rafting** (see p.160). Beyond the Heidal valley, Highway 257 continues west to meet Highway 51, the main access road to the east side of the Jotunheimen National Park at Gjendesheim (see p.163).

### ARRIVAL AND DEPARTURE                          SJOA AND THE HEIDAL VALLEY

**By bus** There's no longer a train station at Sjoa, but Nor-Way Bussekspress's Gudbrandsdalekspressen bus (Mon–Fri

1 daily; #148) stops beside the E6, near the Highway 257 intersection, a 1.5km walk from the hostel.

## ACTIVITIES

**Whitewater rafting** If you want to come to grips with the Sjoa River's gorges and rapids, contact the local specialists, Heidal Rafting (☎61 23 60 37, ⊛heidalrafting .no). An all-inclusive, one-day rafting excursion costs around 1090kr, 890kr for half a day. The season lasts from May to Oct and reservations are recommended, though there's a reasonably good chance of being able to sign up at the last minute. Heidal Rafting is based at the HI hostel, *Sjoa Vandrerhjem*.

## ACCOMMODATION AND EATING

**Sjoa Vandrerhjem** Sjoa ☎61 23 62 00, ⊛hihostels .no. Perched on a wooded hillside high above the river, the main building of this HI hostel is a charming log farmhouse dating from 1747 and, although visitors sleep in more modern quarters, this is where you eat. Breakfasts are banquet-like, and dinners (by prior arrangement only) are reasonably priced if rather less spectacular. The hostel offers two types of accommodation: a no-frills dormitory block at the bottom of the slope and a handful of spacious and comfortable chalets up above. Reservations are advisable for the chalets at weekends. The hostel is just off Highway 257, about 1500m west of the E6. Open mid-May to mid-Sept. Dorms **305kr**, doubles from **720kr**

## Otta

OTTA, just 11km beyond Sjoa, is an unassuming and unexciting little town at the confluence of the rivers Otta and Lågen. It may be dull, but Otta does make a handy base for hiking in the nearby Rondane National Park (see opposite), especially if you're reliant on public transport – though staying in one of the park's mountain lodges is much to be preferred. The town is also within easy driving distance (100km or so) of the Jotunheimen (see p.163). In Otta itself, everything you need is within easy reach: the E6 sweeps along the east bank of the Lågen, passing within 300m of the town centre, while Highway 15 bisects the town from east to west with the few gridiron streets that pass for the centre lying a few metres to the south.

### ARRIVAL AND INFORMATION                                        OTTA

**By train** Otta's train station is part of the Otta Skysstasjon, on the north side of Highway 15.
**Destinations** Hamar (2–4 daily; 2hr); Oslo (2–4 daily; 3hr 30min); Oslo Gardermoen (2–4 daily; 3hr); Trondheim (2–4 daily; 3hr).
**By bus** The bus terminal is located inside the Skysstasjon. Nor-Way Bussekspress runs the following services:
Gudbrandsdalekspressen (#148) to: Hamar (Mon–Fri 1 daily; 3hr 20min); Lillehammer (Mon–Fri 1 daily; 4hr 20min); Oslo (Mon–Fri 1 daily; 5hr).

Nordfjordekspressen (#147) to: Langvatn (3 daily; 2hr 10min); Lillehammer (3 daily; 2hr 30min); Lom (3 daily; 1hr); Oslo (3 daily; 5hr 30min); Stryn (3 daily; 3hr).
**Tourist office** Skysstasjon (July to mid-Aug Mon–Fri 8.30am–6pm, Sat 10am–4pm; mid-Aug to June Mon–Fri 8am–4pm; ☎61 23 66 50, ⊛rondane-dovrefjell.no). The tourist office can provide local bus timetables, book accommodation and reserve Lake Gjende boat tickets (see p.163); they also sell local hiking maps.

---

### PILLARGURI SAVES THE DAY

A **statue** outside Otta's Skysstasjon commemorates a certain **Pillarguri**, whose alertness made her an overnight sensation. During the Kalmar War of 1611–13, one of many wars between Sweden and Denmark, a band of Scottish mercenaries hired by the king of Sweden landed near Åndalsnes (see p.251), intent on crossing Norway to join the Swedish army. The Norwegians – Danish subjects at that time – were fearful of the Scots, and when Pillarguri spotted them nearing Otta she dashed to the top of the nearest hill and blew her birch-bark horn to sound the alarm. The locals hastily arranged an ambush at one of the narrowest points of the trail and all but wiped the Scots out – a rare victory for peasants over professionals. One of Pillarguri's rewards was to have a hill named after her, and today the stiff hike along the footpath up the forested slopes to the summit, **Pillarguritoppen** (853m), across the River Otta south of the centre, is a popular outing; free trail maps are available at the tourist office (see above).

## OTTA TO THE WESTERN FJORDS

Running west from Otta, **Highway 15** sweeps along wide river valleys bound for Lom (see p.236), where there's a choice of wonderful routes on into the western fjords. As regards **public transport**, Nor-Way Bussekspress (⍵ nor-way.no) operates the especially useful Nordfjordekspressen linking Oslo with Måløy (3 daily). This runs along Highway 15 west from Otta to Lom, Langvatn (see p.245) and Stryn (see p.242).

### ACCOMMODATION AND EATING

**Norlandia Otta Hotell** Ola Dahls gate 7 ☎ 61 21 08 00, ⍵ norlandia.no. In a modern block just a few minutes' walk west of the Skysstasjon, this chain hotel has 85 spick-and-span rooms. **1200kr**, sp/r **1000kr**

**Otta Camping** ☎ 61 23 03 09, ⍵ ottacamping.no. Convenient campsite located about 1500m from the town centre on the wooded banks of the River Otta. There are cabins and spaces for tents and caravans. To get there, cross the bridge on the southwest side of the centre, turn right and keep going. Open May to mid-Oct. Cabins fit 4–5 persons, and include facilities. Cabins from **350kr**, tents from **90kr**

**Pillarguri Café** Storgata 7 ☎ 61 23 01 04. Otta's selection of places to eat is constrained – and this is the best you'll do, a cosyish café-cum-restaurant and bar serving burgers, pizzas plus standard Norwegian dishes at around 210kr. It's bang in the centre of town, just south of Highway 15. Mon–Thurs 8am–8pm, Fri 8am–midnight, Sat 8am–2am, Sun 3–8pm. Kitchen: Mon–Thurs 10am–6pm, Fri 10am–9pm, Sat 11am–9pm & Sun 3–8pm.

3

# Rondane Nasjonalpark

Spreading north and east of Otta, **Rondane Nasjonalpark** was established in 1962 as Norway's first national park and is now one of the country's most popular hiking areas, its 963 square kilometres, much of which is in the high alpine zone, appealing to walkers of all abilities. The soil is poor, so vegetation is sparse – lichens, especially reindeer moss, predominate – but the views across this bare landscape are serenely beautiful, and a handful of lakes and rivers plus patches of dwarf birch forest provide some variety. Within the Rondane, the most obvious target is **Rondvatnet** lake, a lazy blue flash of water surrounded by wild mountain peaks. To the west of the lake are the wild cirques and jagged peaks of Storsmeden (2017m), Sagtinden (2018m) and Veslesmeden (2015m), while to the east of the lake rise Rondslottet (2178m), Vinjeronden (2044m) and Storronden (2138m). Further east still, Høgronden (2115m) dominates the landscape. The mountains in the vicinity of the lake, ten of which exceed the 2000m mark, are mostly accessible to any reasonably fit and eager walker, thanks to a dense network of trails and hiking huts/lodges. Note though that parts of the park are out of bounds during the reindeer calving season, from early May to the middle of June.

## Hikes in Rondane

There are score of **hikes** to choose from in the Rondane, but one popular choice is the haul up from **Rondvassbu mountain lodge** to the top of **Storronden** (2138m), the first peak to the right of Rondvatnet. This makes a fine excursion for the beginner, since – except for a short steep and exposed section just below the summit – there is no really difficult terrain to negotiate and the trail is clearly signed; the round trip takes about five hours – three up and two down. Neighbouring peaks involve more arduous mountain hiking, with the finest views over the range

## BOAT TRIPS ON LAKE RONDVATNET

If visibility is poor or you don't fancy a climb, you can take the delightful **summer boat service** (July & Aug 2–3 daily; 30min each way; 100kr each way) on the vintage *Rondegubben* from Rondvassbu to the far end of Rondvatnet, from where it takes about two and a half hours to walk back along the lake's steep western shore.

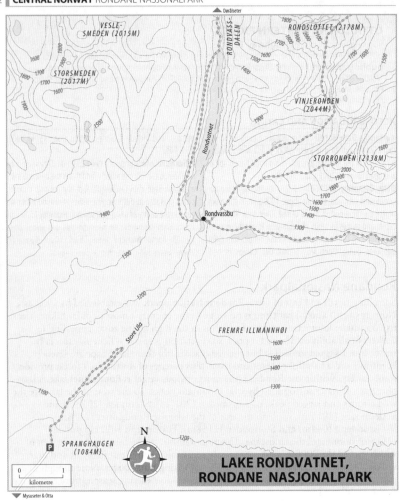

▲ *Dørålseter*

VESLE-
SMEDEN (2015M)

RONDVASS-
DALEN

RONDSLOTTET (2178M)

1800
1700
1600

STORSMEDEN
(2017M)

1900
1800
1700
1600

VINJERONDEN
(2044M)

1900

Rondvatnet

STORRONDEN (2138M)

2000
1900
1800
1700
1600
1500
1400

1400

Rondvassbu

1300

1300

Store Ula

FREMRE ILLMANNHØI

1600

1500
1400

1300

1200

N

1200

P

SPRANGHAUGEN
(1084M)

1100

0            1
kilometre

**LAKE RONDVATNET,
RONDANE NASJONALPARK**

▼ *Mysuseter & Otta*

generally reckoned to be from **Vinjeronden** and nearby **Rondslottet**, both to the north of Storronden.

## ARRIVAL AND DEPARTURE                                    RONDANE NASJONALPARK

**By car** Access to the park is by a series of narrow roads that thread their way either into or to the peripheries of the Rondane Nasjonalpark from pretty much every point in the compass. From Otta, the main access route is the 15km-long byroad leading first to the sprawling chalet settlement of Mysuseter and then the Spranghaugen car park, right on the edge of the national park itself, respectively 15km and 20km away. From the car park, it's a level walk northeast (1hr 30min) along the service road to the southern tip of Lake Rondvatnet; where the *Rondvassbu* lodge is located.

**By bus** Local buses link Otta bus station with Mysuseter – but not Spranghaugen, though it is a very limited service (#538; late Aug only, Sat & Sun 1–2 daily; 40min; ⓦ fjord1.no).

**By taxi** Taxis can be picked up at Otta train/bus station; reckon on 500kr for the trip to Spranghaugen.

**Tourist office** Otta tourist office, in the Skysstasjon (see p.160), sells a wide range of maps of Rondane Nasjonalpark, will advise on hikes and has local bus timetables.

## ACCOMMODATION

**Rondvassbu** ☎ 61 23 18 66, ⓦ rondvassbu.com. The most accessible of the Rondane's several huts and lodges, this large and popular DNT lodge has more than 100 beds and offers filling meals. For all but the briefest of hikes, it's best to arrive at the lodge the day before so that you can start first thing the next morning – either on foot or on the boat (see box, p.161). The lodge is staffed mid-June to early Oct, when you are also advised to make an advance reservation, and is open but unstaffed at certain periods during the rest of the year. There is a range of prices, with the smaller rooms (1–3 bunks) costing 230kr per person with non-members surcharged an extra 60kr or so. Dorms (DNT members) from ‾190kr‾

# Jotunheimen Nasjonalpark

Norway's most celebrated hiking area, **Jotunheimen Nasjonalpark** ("Home of the Giants" National Park), lives up to its name: pointed summits and undulating glaciers dominate the skyline, soaring high above river valleys and lake-studded plateaus. Covering no less than 1152 square kilometres, the park offers an amazing concentration of high peaks, more than two hundred of which rise above 1900m, including Norway's (and northern Europe's) two highest mountains, **Galdhøpiggen** (2469m) and **Glittertind** (2452m). Here also is Norway's highest waterfall, **Vettisfossen**, boasting a 275-metre drop and located a short walk from the Vetti lodge on the west side of the park. A network of **footpaths** and **mountain lodges** lattices the Jotunheimen, but be warned that the weather is very unpredictable and the winds can be bitingly cold – take care and always come well equipped.

## Gjendesheim and Lake Gjende

**Gjendesheim**, some 90km from Otta, has long been a popular base for exploring the Jotunheimen – the first mountain hut was built here in the 1870s – but it is still no more than a ferry dock and a couple of buildings, one of which is the excellent, staffed DNT lodge at the tip of **Lake Gjende**. Some 18km long and 146m deep, the lake itself is one of Norway's most beautiful, its glacially fed waters tinted green by myriad clay particles; it was also here that Ibsen had his Peer Gynt tumble into the water from the back of a reindeer. Every summer, the lake is a hive of activity with hikers stalking off into the mountains and up onto the Besseggen ridge (see box, p.166) or hopping into the **passenger boats** (see below) that whisk along the lake.

### ARRIVAL AND DEPARTURE                          JOTUNHEIMEN NASJONALPARK

**By car** There are no public/asphalted roads into Jotunheimen, but two well-maintained roads do trim the extremities – the Sognefjellsveg (Highway 55; see p.235) to the west and Highway 51 to the east; the latter passes within 2km of Gjendesheim.

**By bus** Nor-Way Bussekspress provides a half-reasonable bus service to Gjendesheim: their Valdresekspressen bus (#160; 4–6 daily), linking Oslo and Sogndal, runs through Fagernes, where you change for Beitostølen (3 daily; 45min), changing here again for Gjendesheim (late June to early Sept; 2 daily; 40min).

**By foot/skis** Hikers, mountaineers and skiers usually enter the Jotunheimen from the west, from the Sognefjellsveg (see p.235).

### GETTING AROUND

**By boat** Starting from Gjendesheim, boats (mid-June to mid-Sept 6 daily; ☎ 61 23 85 09, ⓦ gjende.no) travel the length of Lake Gjende, connecting with mountain trails and dropping by *Memurubu* (20min) and *Gjendebu* lodges (45min). A one-way fare from Gjendesheim to Memurubu costs 120kr, Gjendebu 180kr; returns are twice that unless you make the round trip on the same day, in which case fares are 140kr and 200kr respectively. Naturally, you get to see a slice of the Jotunheimen and avoid a hike by riding the boat and sleeping at the lodges – a prudent choice in bad weather.

### ACCOMMODATION

**Gjendebu** ☎ 61 23 89 44, ⓦ gjendebu.com. At the west end of Lake Gjende, this staffed DNT lodge, at an elevation of nigh on 1000m, has 120 beds. Open mid-June to mid-Sept. Dorms from ‾130kr‾, doubles ‾460kr‾

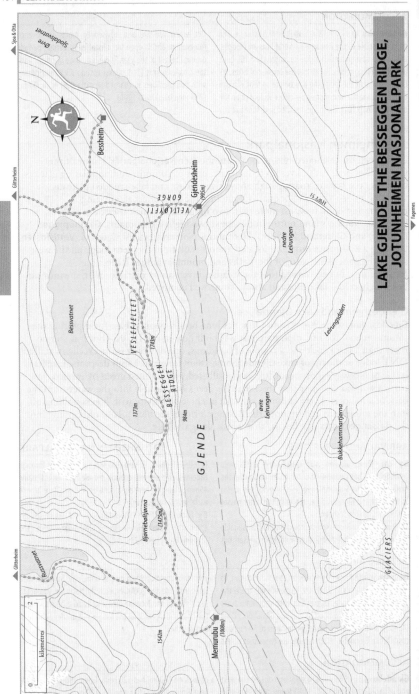

LAKE GJENDE, THE BESSEGGEN RIDGE, JOTUNHEIMEN NASJONALPARK

N

Sjoa & Otta
Øvre Sjodalsvatnet
Glitterheim
Bessheim
Gjendesheim (995m)
VELTLØYFTI GORGE
nedre Leirungen
Bessvatnet
VESLFJELLET
1743m
BESSEGGEN RIDGE
984m
1373m
øvre Leirungen
Leirungsdalen
GJENDE
Bjørnebolitjørna (1425m)
Russvatnet
Glitterheim
Bukkehammartjørna
1542m
Memurubu (1008m)
GLACIERS
HWY 51
Fagernes

0    2
kilometres

Gjendebu

**Gjendesheim ☎**61 23 89 10, **ⓦ**gjendesheim.no. At the eastern tip of long and slender Lake Gjende, this staffed DNT lodge, one of the organization's most famous, has 185 bunk beds in different permutations from three-bunk to six-bunk rooms. Open in both the summer and the winter seasons (late Feb to April & mid-June to early Oct). Dorms (members) **190kr**

**Memurubu ☎**61 23 89 99, **ⓦ**memurubu.no. In a relatively sheltered location, halfway along the lake's north shore, this privately owned lodge mostly dates from a recent rebuild following fire damage, though its origins are as a mountain farm. Open mid-June to mid-Sept. Dorms from **200kr**

# Dombås to Kongsvoll and beyond

From Otta, the E6 and the railway lead 45km north to **Dombås**, a mundane crossroads settlement, from where the dramatic Rauma train line (see box below) begins its dramatic defile west to the port of Åndalsnes (see p.251). North of Dombås, the E6 and the main train line push on through the mountains towards the wind-blasted uplands of **Hjerkinn** and then **Kongsvoll**, nothing much in itself but equipped with a great place to stay. Kongsvoll is also within comfortable striking distance of both Trondheim (160km) and Røros (210km), which is best reached along picturesque Highway 30.

## Dombås

Long an important crossroads, **DOMBÅS** manages to be almost without interest, its indeterminate ramble falling beside the junction of the E6 and the E136, though it can act as a base for **musk-ox safaris** (see box, p.166). It also has one minor claim to fame as the place where an American air attaché, Robert Losey, was killed by the bombs of the Luftwaffe in April 1940, making the unfortunate man one of the very first US military fatalities of World War II.

### ARRIVAL AND DEPARTURE                                                   DOMBÅS

**By train** Dombås train station is close to the junction of the E6 and the E136.
Destinations Åndalsnes (2–4 daily; 1hr 20min); Hjerkinn (2–4 daily; 20min; request stop only); Kongsvoll (2–4 daily; 30min; request stop only); Oslo (2–4 daily; 4hr); Trondheim (2–4 daily; 2hr 40min).

**By bus** The bus station is next to the train station. Nor-Way Bussekspress run the following services:
Dag og Nattekspressen (#142) to: Åndalsnes (2 daily; 1hr 50min); Oslo (2 daily; 6hr); Oslo Gardermoen (2 daily; 5hr); Otta (2 daily; 45min).
Fjordekspressen (#431) to: Trondheim (1 daily; 3hr).

### ACCOMMODATION

**Dombås Vandrerhjem** Skitrekkveien **☎**61 24 09 60, **ⓦ**hihostels.no. Chalet-style hostel way up on the hillside above the E6, with just thirteen rooms, all en suite, plus self-catering facilities and a café-restaurant. To get there, head north out of Dombås along the E6 for around 1km and follow the signs up the hill (a further 500m). Open all year. Dorms **325kr**, doubles **895kr**

---

### THE E136 AND THE RAUMA BRANCH LINE TO ÅNDALSNES

**Dombås** is where the **E136** and the **Rauma train line** spear west for the thrilling 110km rattle down to Åndalsnes. The journey begins innocuously enough with road and rail slipping along a ridge high above a wide, grassy valley, but soon the landscape gets wilder as both nip into the hills. After 65km, they reach **Kylling bru**, an ambitious stone railway bridge, 56m high and 76m long, which spans the River Rauma. Pressing on, it's a further 20km to the shadowy hamlet of **Marstein** with the grey, cold mass of the **Trollveggen** ("Troll's Wall") rising straight ahead. At around 1100m, the Trollveggen incorporates the highest vertical overhanging mountain wall in Europe and as such is a favourite with experienced mountaineers, though it wasn't actually scaled until 1967. Somehow, the E136 and the railway manage to squeeze through the mountains and soon afterwards they slide down to Åndalsnes (see p.231), the fjord glistening beyond.

As for **timetables**, there are 2–4 trains daily on the Rauma line and you can also cover pretty much the same ground on Nor-Way Bussekspress's Dag og Nattekspressen (see above).

## HIKING THE BESSEGGEN RIDGE

**Start**: Memurubu (1008m).
**Finish**: Gjendesheim (995m).
**Distance**: 15km.
**Time**: 6hr.
**Highest point**: Besseggen ridge (1743m).
**Maps**: DNT produces an excellent map of the Jotunheimen in its1:50,000 series.
**Transport**: Nor-Way Bussekspress operates the Valdresekspressen (#160; 4–6 daily), which runs from Oslo to Sogndal, passing through Fagernes on the way. At Fagernes, change to the Nor-Way Bussekspress bus to Beitostølen (3 daily), where you change again for Gjendesheim (late June to early Sept; 2 daily). The boat from Gjendesheim to Memurubu is also seasonal (mid-June to mid-Sept; 6 daily; ☏61 23 85 09, ⓦgjende.no).
**Accommodation**: *Gjendesheim*, full-service DNT hut (see p.165); *Memurubu*, full-service private hut (see p.165).

### THE HIKE

The one-day hike across the Jotunheimen's Besseggen ridge high above Lake Gjende is one of Norway's most popular excursions. Starting at the **Memurubu** jetty, the first part of the hike involves a stiff haul up to the base of the **Besseggen ridge** (2hr 30min), which is a good spot to take a break and enjoy the views over the surrounding wilderness before tackling the ridge itself. Thereafter, the thirty-minute scramble up to the peak of the ridge is very steep, with ledges that are, on occasion, chest high; you need to be moderately fit to negotiate them. In places, the ridge narrows to 50m with a sheer drop to either side, but you can avoid straying close to the edge by following the DNT waymark "T"s. The views are superlative, but the drops disconcerting – and a head for heights is essential. Beyond the peak of the ridge, the trail is less dramatic as you cross a couple of plateaus and clamber up the slopes in between before reaching the **Veltløyfti gorge**. Here, a slippery scramble with steep drops requires care, though the trail is well marked and the final destination, **Gjendesheim**, is clearly visible.

If you do the hike in the opposite direction to the route described here, you can return by boat to Gjendesheim in the evening, but you'll have to calculate your speed accurately to meet the boat at Memurubu – and that isn't easy. Whichever direction you take, be sure to confirm boat departure times before you set out, and check weather conditions too, as snow and ice can linger well into July.

### ACTIVITIES

**Musk-ox safaris** Several companies in the Dombås/Hjerkinn area offer musk-ox safaris, including the *Dombås Motel*, which is located beside the E136, a few hundred metres north of the E6/E136 crossroads at Romsdalsvegen 6 (☏45 67 19 95, ⓦdombasmotel.com). From late May to late Sept, there's one tour daily, lasting anywhere between five and seven hours at a cost of 300kr per person. You'll need warm, waterproof clothes and proper hiking boots.

## Hjerkinn

It's just 30km north from Dombås along the E6 to the outpost of **HJERKINN**, stuck out on bare and desolate moorland, its pint-sized military base battened down against the wind and snow of winter. Hjerkinn is no more than a light scattering of houses, but as a staging post on the long journey to and from Trondheim, 170km away, it's a handy place to break the long journey north: there's been a mountain inn on the site of *Hjerkinn Fjellstue* since medieval times.

If you're heading for Røros (see p.168), then you can branch off here along Highway 29, though this is a long-winded and (by Norwegian standards) a fairly dull drive – and Highway 30, further north, is a much more scenic approach.

### ARRIVAL AND DEPARTURE                                  HJERKINN

**By train** The train station is adjacent to the military base, overlooking the E6/Highway 29 junction. Note that trains only stop here by prior arrangement with the ticket inspector.

Destinations Dombås (2–4 daily; 20min); Kongsvold (2–4 daily; 10min; request stop only); Oslo (2–4 daily; 4hr 30min); Trondheim (2–4 daily; 2hr 15min).

## ACCOMMODATION

**Hjerkinn Fjellstue** ☎ 61 21 51 00, ⊛ hjerkinn.no. The modern incarnation of *Hjerkinn Fjellstue* is set on a hill overlooking the moors just over 2km east of the train station beside Highway 29. The hotel comprises two expansive wooden buildings featuring big open fires and breezy pine furniture, but their speciality is horseriding, which is available for guests at extra cost. The restaurant is good too – try the reindeer culled from local herds. **1190kr**

## Kongsvoll

North of Hjerkinn, the E6 slices across barren uplands before descending into a narrow ravine, the **Drivdal**. Hidden away here, just 12km from Hjerkinn, is **KONGSVOLL**, home to a tiny train station and the delightful *Kongsvold Fjeldstue*, which provides some especially charming accommodation and can serve as a great base for hikes into the neighbouring Dovrefjell-Sunndalsfjella Nasjonalpark (see below).

### ARRIVAL AND DEPARTURE                                          KONGSVOLL

**By train** Be aware that trains only stop here by prior arrangement with the conductor.
Destinations Dombås (2–4 daily; 30min); Hjerkinn (2–4 daily; 10min; request stop only); Oslo (2–4 daily; 4hr 30min); Trondheim (2–4 daily; 2hr).

### ACCOMMODATION AND EATING

★ **Kongsvold Fjeldstue** ☎ 72 40 43 40, ⊛ kongsvold.no. As at Hjerkinn, an inn has stood here at Kongsvoll since medieval times and the present complex, a huddle of tastefully restored timber buildings with sun-bleached reindeer antlers tacked onto the outside walls, dates back to the eighteenth century. Once a farm as well as an inn, its agricultural days are recalled by several outbuildings: there are the little turf-roofed storehouses (*stabbur*), the lodgings for farmhands (*karstuggu*) and the barn (*låve*), on top of which is a bell that was rung to summon the hands from the fields. The main building retains many of its original features and also holds an eclectic sample of antiques. The bedrooms, dotted round the compound, are of the same high standard (en suite 450kr extra) – and the old vagabonds' hut (*fantstuggu*), built outside the white picket fence that once defined the physical limits of social respectability, contains the cosiest family rooms imaginable. Dinner is served in the restaurant, with mains averaging 260kr, and the complex also includes a café. Located just off the E6 and 500m up the valley from the train station. **1350kr**

## Dovrefjell-Sunndalsfjella Nasjonalpark

Running west towards the coast from the railway and the E6, **Dovrefjell-Sunndalsfjella Nasjonalpark** comprises a great slab of wild wilderness, 1693 square kilometres in extent, its mountains becoming increasingly steep and serrated as they approach the jagged spires backing onto Åndalsnes. **Hiking trails** and **huts** are scattered across the park with Kongsvoll (see above) making an ideal starting point: it's possible to hike all the way from here to the coast, but this takes all of nine or ten days. A more feasible expedition for most visitors is the two-hour circular walk up to the mountain plateau, or a two-day, round-trip hike to one of the four ice-tipped peaks of mighty **Snøhetta**, at 2286m. There's accommodation five hours' walk west from Kongsvoll at the unstaffed **Reinheim hut** (all year). Further hiking details and maps are available at the *Kongsvold Fjeldstue*.

## Røros and around

**RØROS**, glued to a treeless mountain plateau some 160km northeast of Kongsvoll, is a blustery place even on a summer's afternoon, when it's full of day-tripping tourists surveying the old part of town, which is little changed since its days as a **copper-mining centre**. Mining was the basis of life here from the seventeenth century onwards and

**MUSK OXEN**

On the first part of any hike west from Kongsvoll into the **Dovrefjell-Sunndalsfjella Nasjonalpark**, you're quite likely to spot **musk ox**, the descendants of animals imported from Greenland in the late 1940s – which are also viewable on a musk-ox safari (see p.166). These hefty beasts have lived in the Arctic for thousands of years, protected from the cold by two coats of hair and using their hooves to dig through the snow to reach the roots, lichens and mosses on which they depend. So far so good, but their habit of herding together with the adults surrounding the young when faced with danger proved disastrous when they were hunted by rifle. By the mid-1940s, the future of the Greenland herd looked decidedly grim, so some were transferred to Norway to help preserve the species, and here in their new home they have prospered in a modest sort of way and now number about one hundred.

Conventional wisdom is that they will ignore you if you ignore them and keep at a distance of at least 200m. They are, however, not afraid of humans and will charge if irritated – retreat as quickly and quietly as possible if one starts snorting and scraping. Incidentally, there's no truth in the rumour, promulgated by the mockumentary film *Trolljegeren* ("Troll Hunter"; 2010) that the musk ox serve as a handy larder for local trolls; or is there?

although the mining company finally went bust in 1977, its assorted industrial remains were never bulldozed, making Røros a unique and remarkable survivor of the resource towns that once littered Norway's more isolated regions. Copper mining was dirty and dangerous work and even if the locals supplemented their incomes with a little farming and hunting, life for the average villager can't have been anything but hard.

Remarkably, Røros' **wooden houses**, some of them 300 years old, have escaped the fires which have devastated so many of Norway's timber-built towns, and as a consequence the town is on UNESCO's World Heritage list. Firm regulations now protect this rare townscape and changes to its grass-roofed cottages are strictly regulated. Film companies regularly use the town as a backdrop for their productions: as early as 1971, it featured as a Soviet labour camp in the film version of Alexander Solzhenitsyn's *One Day in the Life of Ivan Denisovich*, a choice of location that gives something of the flavour of the place.

Røros makes for a pleasant overnight stay, which is just as well given its solitary location. The uplands that encircle the town are good for **hiking**, with one of the more popular being the five-hour trek east to the self-service DNT hut at Marenvollen. In winter, the uplands are popular with **cross-country skiers**; the tourist office has a leaflet mapping out several possible skiing routes.

### Røros kirke

Kjerkgata • Early to mid-June & mid-Aug to mid-Sept Mon–Sat 11am–1pm; mid-June to mid-Aug Mon–Sat 10am–4pm, Sun 12.30–2.30pm; mid-Sept to May Sat 11am–1pm • 50kr, including English-language guided tour (1–2 daily most days; times from the tourist office) • ⓦ roroskirke.no

In the town centre, **Røros kirke** (Røros church) is the most obvious target for a stroll, its heavy-duty tower reflecting the wealth of the early mine-owners. Built in 1784, and once the only stone building in Røros, the church is a massive structure designed – like the church at Kongsberg (see p.175) – to overawe rather than inspire. The most notable feature of the interior, which looks more like a theatre than a place of worship, is the two-tiered gallery running around the nave. Mine labourers were accommodated in the gallery's lower level, while "undesirables" were compelled to sit above, and even had to enter via a separate, external staircase. Down below, the nave exhibited even finer distinctions: you moved a pew closer to the front as you climbed the social ladder and mine managers vied for the curtained boxes, each of which had a well-publicized annual rent. The monarch (or royal representative) had a private box commanding views from the back and the pulpit was placed directly over the altar to sanctify the priest.

## Slegghaugan

Immediately below the church, on either side of the river, lies the oldest part of Røros, a huddle of sturdy cross-timbered smelters' cottages, storehouses and workshops squatting in the shadow of the **slegghaugan** (slagheaps) – more tourist attraction than eyesore, and providing fine views over the town and beyond.

## Smelthytta

Malmplassen • Late April daily 11am–2pm; May & mid-Sept to late April Mon–Fri 11am–3pm, Sat & Sun 11am–2pm; early June Mon–Fri 11am–4pm, Sat & Sun 11am–3pm; mid-June to mid-Aug daily 10am–6pm; mid-Aug to mid-Sept Mon–Fri 11am–4pm, Sat & Sun 11am–3pm • 70kr • ⓦ roros.no

Next to the river are the rambling main works, the **Smelthytta** (literally "melting hut"), which has been tidily restored and turned into a museum. A large three-storey affair, the museum's most interesting section, housed in the cavernous hall that once contained the smelter, explains the intricacies of copper production. Dioramas illuminate every part of the process, and there are production charts, samples of ore and a potted history of the company – pick up the comprehensive English-language leaflet available free at reception. All that said, there's actually not that much to look at – the building was gutted by fire in 1975 – and so the museum is perhaps for genuine mining enthusiasts only.

## Malmplassen and around

The Smelthytta faces on to **Malmplassen** ("ore-place"), the wide earthen square where the ore drivers arrived from across the mountains to have their cartloads of ore weighed on the outdoor scales. In the square also, hung in a rickety little tower, is the **smelters' bell**, which used to be rung at the start of each shift. Malmplassen is at the top of **Bergmannsgata** which, together with parallel **Kjerkgata**, forms the heart of today's Røros. Conspicuously, the smaller artisans' dwellings, some of which have become art and craft shops, are set near the works, away from the rather more spacious dwellings once occupied by the owners and overseers, which cluster round the church.

## Olavsgruva copper mine

Guided tours: early June & mid-Aug to mid-Sept Mon–Sat 2 daily, Sun 1 daily; late June to mid-Aug 5 daily; mid-Sept to May Sat 1 daily • 90kr • ⓦ rorosmuseet.no • Reservations at Røros tourist office (see p.171)

Some 13km east of Røros off Highway 31, one of the old copper mines, the **Olavsgruva**, has been kept open as a museum, and there are guided tours of its workings throughout the summer. The temperature down the mine is a constant 5°C, so remember to take something warm to wear – you'll need sturdy shoes too.

| ARRIVAL AND INFORMATION | RØROS AND AROUND |
| --- | --- |

**By train** Røros train station is at the foot of the town centre, and has services to Hamar (3–6 daily; 3hr 30min); Oslo (4 daily; 5hr); Oslo Gardermoen (4 daily; 4hr 30min); and Trondheim (3 daily; 2hr 30min).

By bus Røros bus station is next to the train station. Nor-Way Bussekspress' Rørosekspressen (#611) runs to Otta (2–3 daily; 3hr, change at Støren on the E6) and Trondheim (2–3 daily; 3hr).

**Tourist office** Peder Hiortsgata (mid-June to mid-Aug Mon–Sat 9am–6pm, Sun 10am–4pm; rest of year Mon–Fri 9am–3pm, Sat 10.30am–12.30pm; ☎72 41 00 00, ⓦroros.no). The tourist office, a couple of minutes' walk from the stations, will supply a comprehensive booklet on Røros and the surrounding region, provide hiking information and has bus and train timetables.

## ACCOMMODATION

**Erzscheidergården Hotell** Spell-Olaveien 6 ☎72 41 11 94, ⓦerzscheidergaarden.com. The best deal in town, this small, family-run hotel has some especially charming rooms in its wooden main building. Some rooms also have fine views over town, and there's an attractive subterranean breakfast area as well as a cosy lounge. 1100kr

**Røros Hotel** An-Magrittsveien ☎72 40 80 00, ⓦroroshotell.no. Big, modern, independent hotel on the northern edge of the centre, 1.3km from the train station. Has made something of a bid for the conference trade, which partly explains the indoor pool and sauna. 1700kr, sp/r 1400kr

**Vertshuset Røros** Kjerkgata 34 ☎72 41 93 50, ⓦvertshusetroros.no. This appealing guesthouse has been dovetailed into an old timber building of 1914 and an adjacent former textile factory. There are about thirty guest rooms, half with their own kitchenette, and (at the same price) a handful of self-catering apartments 1750kr, sp/r 1200kr

## EATING AND DRINKING

**Galleri Thomasgaarden** Kjerkgata 48 ⓦthomasgaarden.no. This nifty little art gallery, tucked away on Kjerkgata, houses the cosiest café in town, where you can avoid the tourist crowds and get tasty home-cooked snacks. Tues–Sat 11am–4.30pm, Sun noon–4pm.

**Vertshuset Røros** Kjerkgata 34 ☎72 41 93 50, ⓦvertshusetroros.no. The unfussy homeliness of the restaurant at this hotel makes it a good spot to enjoy an evening meal – choose from traditional Norwegian dishes like *kjøttkaker i brun saus* (meatballs in brown sauce) at around 250kr. Every effort is made to source the food locally. Daily noon–10pm.

# Oslo to the western fjords

In almost any other country, the forested **dales and uplands** that fill out much of central Norway between Oslo and the western fjords would be prime attractions in their own right, but here in Norway they are overshadowed by the mountains and deep black-blue fjords of the north and west. One result is that the towns and villages hereabouts lack the concentration of tourist facilities found in the more popular areas, though the Norwegians themselves come here in their droves to savour the summer and explore the countryside from their mountain huts and second homes. Setting aside the E6 (see p.150), there are three main highways between Oslo and the western fjords – the **E16**, **Highway 7** and the **E134**: whichever one you choose, you'll encounter spectacular scenery, from wide sweeping valleys and plunging waterfalls to bare and bleak mountain passes, but if it's mainly speed you're after plump for the E16.

## GETTING AROUND | OSLO TO THE WESTERN FJORDS

**By train** The train is the quickest mode of transport to the western fjords, albeit more limited in its range of destinations: Oslo to Bergen by train takes about 7hr with stops at Finse on the Hardangervidda (see p.220), Myrdal (for the Flåmsbåna; see p.220) and Voss (see p.218), near the Hardangerfjord.

**By bus** Regular long-distance buses travel the E16 and the E134, but not Highway 7. The journey from Oslo to Bergen takes about 11hr on the Haukeliekspressen (#180), operated by Nor-Way Bussekspress.

## The E16

The **E16** is the fastest route from Oslo to the western fjords, a quick and handsome 350km gallop up from the capital to both the fjord ferry near Sogndal (see p.232) and the colossal 24.5km tunnel leading to Flåm (see p.224). It also shoots past half a dozen stave churches, the most remarkable of them being **Borgund**.

3

## Fagernes

Clipping along the E16 from Oslo, it's about 180km up through wide, wooded dales to **FAGERNES**, an amenable little town whose modern centre is sandwiched between a lake and a river. A handy pit stop, it possesses a couple of hotels and is just a couple of kilometres short of Highway 51, which branches north from the E16 to run along the eastern edge of the Jotunheimen Nasjonalpark, passing near Gjendesheim and its lodge (see p.163) before finally joining Highway 15 west of Otta (see p.160).

### ARRIVAL AND INFORMATION                                                        FAGERNES

**By bus** Buses to and from Fagernes pull into the Skysstasjon, bang in the centre of town on Jernbanegata, a few metres from the lake. Nor-Way Bussekspress's Valdreskspressen (#160/#161) services Bergen (1–2 daily; 6hr 30min, change at Tyinkrysset); Oslo (5 daily; 3hr); and Sogndal (2–3 daily; 3hr 30min, change at Tyinkrysset). There's also a summer service to Beitostølen (3 daily;

45min), where you change for Gjendesheim in the Jotunheimen (late June to early Sept 2 daily; 40min).

**Tourist office** Skysstasjon (late June to late Aug Mon–Fri 9.30am–6pm, Sat 10am–6pm, Sun 10am–4pm; late Aug to late June Mon–Fri 8.30am–4pm; ☏ 61 35 94 10, ⓦ valdres.com).

### ACCOMMODATION

**Quality Hotel Fagernes** ☏ 61 35 80 00, ⓦ choicehotels.no. Dominating the lakeshore, right in the centre of town opposite the Skysstasjon, this large chain hotel is built in the style of a lodge. Though the 1960s look and feel of its capacious public areas – down to the

gold-embossed wallpaper and the two stuffed bears – may not be to everyone's taste, the 138 bedrooms, many of which have recently been refitted, are mostly large and well appointed. **1235kr**

## Fagernes to Lomen

Beyond Fagernes, the E16 sweeps up the valley at the heart of the **Valdres district** with forested hills rising on either side of a string of lakes. It's lovely scenery, with none of the harshness of the mountains further west, where farmers have tilled the land and fished the lakes for many centuries as witnessed by the four **stave churches** dotted along – or at least near – this part of the E16. You'd have to be something of an ecclesiastical fanatic to want to see them all – especially as Borgund stave church beckons nearby (see opposite) – but Lomen stave church will do very nicely.

### Lomen stavkirke

Late June to early Aug daily 10am–4pm • 40kr

Dating from the late twelfth century, and in regular use until 1914, **Lomen stavkirke** (stave church) occupies a pretty, rural setting just above the E16 about 30km west of Fagernes. Its interior holds the finely decorated woodwork and cleverly interlaced joists typical of a stave church. There's also an unusual medieval chest inscribed with a spell-casting runic inscription.

### Vang

Around 25km west of the Lomen stave church, standing beside the road in the hamlet of **VANG**, is the curious **Vangsteinen** (Vang stone), a two-metre-high hunk of slate inscribed with runes and decorated with a lion-like animal, foliage and a tangle of braided ribbons. The carving dates from around 1000, a time when the Norwegians were abandoning paganism in favour of Christianity, and the stone once stood outside Vang stave church, but this was bought, lock, stock and barrel, by a Prussian royal and re-erected in Poland in the 1840s; apparently, it still stands there today.

### Filefjell and the Lærdal valley

Beyond Vang, it's just 11km to Øye, where the E16 begins its long climb up and over the **Filefjell mountain pass** amid a bare and treeless landscape dotted with lakes and sprinkled with mountain cabins. On the far side of the mountains, the E16 rips along

## STAVE CHURCHES: NORWAY'S PRIDE AND JOY

The majority of Norway's **28 surviving stave churches** (ⓦstavechurch.com) are inland in the south and centre of the country, but taken together they represent the nation's most distinctive architectural legacy. The key feature of their design is that their timbers are placed vertically into the ground – in contrast to the log-bonding technique used by the Norwegians for everything else. Thus, a stave wall consists of vertical planks slotted into sills above and below, with the sills connected to upright posts – or **staves**, hence the name – at each corner. The general design seems to have been worked out in the twelfth century and common features include external wooden galleries, shingles and finials. There are, however, variations: in some churches, nave and chancel form a single rectangle, in others the chancel is narrower than, and tacked onto, the nave. The most fetching stave churches are those where the central section of the nave has been raised above the aisles to create – from the outside – a distinctive, almost pagoda-like effect. In virtually all the stave churches, the **door frames** (where they survive) are decorated from top to bottom with surging, intricate carvings that clearly hark back to Viking design, most memorably fantastical long-limbed dragons entwined in vine tendrils.

The **origins** of stave churches have attracted an inordinate amount of academic debate. Some scholars argue that they were originally pagan temples, converted to Christian use by the addition of a chancel, while others are convinced that they were inspired by Russian churches. Pagan or not, each part of the stave church acquired a symbolic Christian significance with, for example, the corner posts representing the four Gospels, the ground beams God's apostles upon whom (literally in this case) the church was built.

In the nineteenth century, they also acquired symbolic importance as reminders of the time when Norway was independent. Many had fallen into a dreadful state of repair and were clumsily renovated – or even remodelled – by enthusiastic medievalists with a nationalist agenda. Undoing this repair work has been a major operation, and one that continues today. For most visitors, seeing one or two will suffice – and three of the finest are those at **Heddal** (see p.177), **Borgund** (see below) and **Urnes** (see p.233).

**3**

the **Lærdal valley** bound for Borgund stave church (see below), which is about 50km from Øye. For almost all of its long history, the church stood beside the main road, but not any longer: in 2003, a new set of tunnels bypassed the church as well as one of the most beautiful portions of the **old E16**, the twisting, 10km-long route through the rocky ravine trimming the River Lærdal. This ravine loop, now signed as an "**Historic Route**" with Borgund stave church at the east end, is an enjoyable detour that should only take about half an hour. From Borgund stave church, it's about 30km to the eastern end of the massive Lærdalstunnelen (see p.227), which links the Lærdal valley with Aurland, Flåm (see p.224) and points west to Bergen. The tunnel is part of the E16, but you can instead branch off here for the short trip north along Highway 5 to Lærdalsøyri (see p.227) and the Fodnes–Mannheller car ferry (for Sogndal; see p.232).

### Borgund stavkirke

May–Sept daily 10am–5pm • 75kr • ⓦ stavechurch.com • The church is 2km off the E16 – just follow the signs

The wooded slopes of the Lærdal valley shelter the stepped roofs and angular gables of **Borgund stavkirke** (stave church), one of the best-preserved stave churches in Norway, built beside what was one of the major pack roads between east and west until bubonic plague wiped out most of the local population in the fourteenth century. Much of the church's medieval appearance has been preserved, its tiered exterior protected by shingles and decorated with finials in the shape of dragons and Christian crosses, the whole ensemble culminating in a slender ridge turret. A rickety wooden gallery runs round the outside of the church, and the doors sport an intense swirl of carved animals and foliage. Inside, the dark, pine-scented nave is framed by the upright wooden posts that define this type of church. The **visitor centre**, just 100m away, fills in some of the historical and architectural background.

## Highway 7

The E16's nearest rival, the slower and equally pretty **Highway 7**, branches off the E16 at Hønefoss to weave its way up the Hallingdal valley before slicing across the wild wastes of the Hardangervidda plateau en route to the fjords at Eidfjord (see p.214) near Hardangerfjord, a distance of 340km from Oslo. If you need to break your journey, workaday **Geilo** is your best bet. Alternatively, 180km from Hønefoss at **Hagafoss**, you can pick up **Highway 50**, which splits off Highway 7 to descend the dales to reach, after 100km, the Aurlandsfjord just round the coast from Flåm (see p.224). For most of its length, Highway 7 is shadowed by the **Oslo–Bergen railway**, though they part company near Geilo when the train swings north for its spectacular traverse of the mountains, barrelling its way over to Finse, Myrdal (where you change for the scenic branch line down to Flåm (see p.224) and points to Bergen.

### Geilo

With mountains and hills to either side, sprawling **GEILO**, 250km from Oslo, is one of the largest winter ski resorts in Norway, its assorted chalets and second homes, some of which are exceedingly extravagant, spreading out along Highway 7. Despite its open aspect, Geilo struggles to make much of an impression outside of the skiing, but it does have good train connections to points both east and west and several inexpensive places to stay.

#### ARRIVAL AND INFORMATION                                    GEILO

**By train** Geilo train station is handily located in the town centre, with services running to Bergen (4 daily; 3hr); Myrdal (4 daily; 1hr 10min); and Oslo (4 daily; 3hr 30min).
**By bus** The bus station is close to the train station. The Hallingbussen (#175; 1–2 daily except Sat; 4hr 30min) runs to Oslo.

**Tourist office** Vesleslåttvegen 13 (July to mid-Aug Mon–Fri 8.30am–6pm, Sat 9am–3pm; rest of year Mon–Fri 8.30am–4pm, Sat 9.30am–2pm; ☎ 32 09 59 00, ⊚ geilo.no). The tourist office, just a few minutes' walk southwest of the train station has a complete list of accommodation.

#### ACCOMMODATION

**Geilo Vandrerhjem** Lienvegen 137 ☎ 32 08 70 60, ⊚ hihostels.no. This large hostel, which occupies two modern structures both built in the style of a mountain lodge, has a café and self-catering facilities plus dorms and doubles with shared facilities. The hostel is located just off Highway 7, about 2km east of both the town centre and the train and bus stations. Open all year. Dorms $\overline{290kr}$, doubles $\overline{685kr}$

## The E134

The third and most southerly route to the western fjords, the **E134**, covers the 417km from Drammen near Oslo to Haugesund, passing near Odda on the Sørfjord after 310km. Again, it's a slower route, but it has the advantage of passing through the attractive town of **Kongsberg** before threading its way across Telemark (⊚ visittelemark .no), a county that covers a great forested chunk of southern Norway. In a country where the fjords are the apple of the tourist industry's eye, Telemark is often neglected, but it can be stunningly beautiful, its deep valleys, blue-black lochs and bulging forested hills intercepted by tiny villages in a manner that resembles the Swiss Alps. The key targets here are **Heddal stave church** and **Dalen**, the site of the region's most enjoyable hotel. Beyond Telemark, the E134 nudges its way over the southern reaches of the Hardangervidda plateau (see p.215) to cross one of Norway's highest mountain passes, the storm-blasted **Haukelifjell**.

### Kongsberg

Stuck up in the hills some 90km from Oslo, **KONGSBERG** is a pretty little place with plenty of green spaces. The **River Lågen** tumbles and rumbles through its centre and merely wandering around the town is an enjoyable a way as any of spending an hour or two. Statues on the town **bridge**, at the foot of Storgata, commemorate various local activities, including foolhardy attempts to locate new finds of silver – one of which involved the use of divining rods – for Kongsberg's history has been pretty much defined by its **silver mines**.

A local story claims that the silver responsible for Kongsberg's existence was discovered by two goatherds, who stumbled across a vein of the metal laid bare by the scratchings of an irritable ox. True or not, Christian IV (1577–1648), with his eye on the main chance, was quick to exploit the find, sponsoring the development of mining here – the town's name means "King's Mountain" – at the start of a **silver rush** that boosted his coffers no end. In the event, it turned out that Kongsberg was the only place in the world where silver could be found in its pure form, and there was enough of it to sustain the town for a couple of centuries. By the 1750s, it was the largest town in Norway, with half its 8000 inhabitants employed in and around the 300-odd mine shafts that dotted the area. The silver works closed in 1805, but by this time Kongsberg was also the site of a royal mint, which still employs people to this day.

**3**

### Kongsberg kirke

Kirketorget • Mid-May to mid-Aug Mon–Fri 10am–4pm, Sat 10am–1pm, Sun 2–4pm; mid- to late Aug Mon–Fri 10am–noon; Sept to mid-May Tues–Thurs 10am–noon • 30kr

To appreciate the full economic and political clout of the mine owners, it's necessary to visit the church they funded – **Kongsberg kirke** (Kongsberg church), the largest and arguably most beautiful Baroque church in Norway. It dates from 1761, when the mines were at the peak of their prosperity, its ruddy-brown brickwork and

copper-green spire shadowing a large square, whose other three sides are flanked by period wooden buildings. The interior is a grand affair too, with its enormous and showy mock-marble western wall incorporating the altar, pulpit and organ. Unusually, the **pulpit** is actually above the altar to hammer home the point that the priest was expressing God's will. And it wasn't just the will of God: the mine owners looked on the priest as a sort of ex-officio member of the board, who could be relied upon to extol the virtues of hard work, sobriety and punctuality. The owners also prescribed the church's **seating arrangements**, which were rigidly and hierarchically defined. Facing the pulpit are the King's Box and boxes for the silver-works' managers, while other officials sat in the glass enclosures. The pews on the ground floor were reserved for their womenfolk, while the sweeping balcony was divided into three tiers to accommodate the Kongsberg petite bourgeoisie, the workers and, squeezing in at the top and the back, the lumpen proletariat.

## Norsk Bergverksmuseum

Hyttegata 3 • Mid-May to Aug daily 10am–5pm; Sept to mid-May Tues–Sun noon–4pm • 80kr • ⓦ norsk-bergverksmuseum.no

Mining enthusiasts will enjoy the **Norsk Bergverksmuseum** (Norwegian Mining Museum), housed in the old smelting works near the river. It shares its premises with a tiny ski museum and coin collection, which has examples of the silver coins minted here in town. Established in 1686, Kongsberg's mint – Det Norske Myntverket – was removed from state control and privatized in 2004.

## Sølvgruvene silver mine

Tours (1hr 30min): mid-May to Aug 3–7 tours daily, Sept & Oct 2 weekly; consult tourist office for schedule • 150kr, children under 16 90kr • Signposted to the right off the E134 towards Notodden

One set of Kongsberg's silver mines, the **Sølvgruvene**, in the hamlet of **Saggrenda**, about 8km west of Kongsberg, is open for tours and makes for a good excursion, especially if you have pre-teen children in tow. The entertaining tour includes a ride on a **miniature train** into the shafts through dark tunnels – take a sweater, as it's cold underground.

After you've finished the tour, you can explore the old ochre-painted workers' compound – the **Sakkerhusene** – just 350m or so down the hill from the mine. The compound has been carefully restored and contains a **café** as well as some rather half-hearted displays on the history of the mines.

## ARRIVAL AND INFORMATION    KONGSBERG

**By train** Kongsberg train station is on the north side of town, a 5min walk from the centre. There are services to and from Kristiansand (4 daily; 3hr 30min); Nelaug (for Arendal; 4 daily 2hr 30min); Oslo (every 1–2hr; 1hr 20min); and Oslo Gardermoen airport (every 1–2hr; 2hr 10min).

**By bus** The bus station is next to the train station. Nor-Way Bussekspress run the following services:

Haukeliekspressen (#80) to: Åmot (2–4 daily; 4hr);

Haugesund (2–4 daily; 5hr 40min); Oslo (2–4 daily; 1hr 15min). Change at Åmot for Dalen.

Rjukanekspressen (#185) to: Rjukan (2–3 daily; 2hr)

**Tourist office** Inside the train station (late June to mid-Aug Mon–Fri 9am–5pm, Sat 10am–2pm; mid-Aug to late June Mon–Fri 9am–4pm; ☎ 32 29 90 50, ⓦ visitkongsberg .no). They can help with accommodation – not that there's much to choose from.

## ACCOMMODATION

**Kongsberg Vandrerhjem** Vinjesgate 1 ☎ 32 73 20 24, ⓦ hihostels.no. This well-kept HI hostel occupies an attractive timber lodge close to the town centre, and has both dorms and en-suite doubles, a well-equipped self-catering kitchen, laundry and café serving breakfast, lunch and dinner. To get there, drivers need to follow the signs on the E134, whereas train and bus users should walk south from the station along Storgata, cross the bridge, walk

round the back of the church on the right-hand side, then head down the lane beside the bandstand and cross over the footbridge – a 15min walk in all. Dorms 350kr, doubles 900kr

**Quality Hotel Grand** Christian Augusts gate 2 ☎ 32 77 28 00, ⓦ choicehotels.no. Easily the most appealing hotel in the centre of Kongsberg, the *Grand* occupies a modern block down near the river. From the outside, the hotel is undistinguished, but the interior, which is decorated in crisp modern style, is well maintained and the 175 guest rooms are large and extremely comfortable; the best, on the top floors, offer wide views over the churning, tumbling River Lågen. **2000kr**, sp/r **1600kr**

## EATING AND DRINKING

**Circa** Storgata 13 ☎ 32 76 70 80, 🖥 circa-cafe.no. Serves the best coffee in town as well as sandwiches, snacks and light lunches; in the evening, it morphs into a very pleasant, laidback bar. Kitchen: Mon–Fri 9am–6pm, Sat 10am–6pm, Sun 11am–4pm.

**Opsahlgården** Kirkegata 10 ☎ 32 76 45 00, 🖥 opsahlgarden.no. The pick of the town's several restaurants is this smart and cosy little place near the church. They do a particularly good line in seafood with main courses averaging 250kr. Mon–Sat 5–10pm.

## Heddal stavkirke

Late May to late June & late Aug to mid-Sept Mon–Sat 10am–5pm, Sun 1–5pm; late June to late Aug Mon–Sat 9am–6pm, Sun 1–6pm • 60kr • 🖥 heddalstavkirke.no

Some 30km west of Kongsberg, and 5km beyond the workaday industrial town of Notodden, is **HEDDAL**, whose delightful **stave church** stands beside the road fronted by the neatest of cemeteries. The largest surviving stave church in Norway, it boasts a pretty tumble of shingle-clad roofs, each of which was restored to something like its medieval appearance in 1955, rectifying a heavy-handed nineteenth-century remodelling. The crosses atop the church's gables alternate with dragon-head gargoyles, a mix of Christian and pagan symbolism typical of many stave churches (see box, p.173). Inside, masks surmount the masts of the nave and there's some attractive seventeenth-century wall decoration in light blues, browns and whites, but pride of place goes to the ancient **bishop's chair** in the chancel. Dating from around 1250, the chair carries a relief retelling the saga of Sigurd the Dragonslayer, a pagan story that Christians turned to their advantage by recasting the Viking as Jesus and the dragon as the Devil.

Across from the church, there's a **café** and a modest museum illustrating further aspects of the church's history.

## Seljord

West of Heddal, the E134 rattles up the valley, passing the first (and quickest) turning to Rjukan (see p.179), before making a dramatic defile over the mountains on its way to **SELJORD**, a small but straggly industrial town at the head of **Seljordsvatnet lake**, about 55km from Heddal. Modest it may be, but Seljord seems to have attracted more than its fair share of "Believe It or Not" stories: a **monster** is supposed to lurk in the depths of the lake; elves are alleged to gather here for some of their soirees; and the **medieval stone church**, with its whitewashed walls and dinky little spire, was, so the story goes, built by a goblin. Beside the church are two more curiosities: the nearer is a large granite slab carved with a picture of the Norwegian pastor **Magnus Brostrup Landstad** (1802–80), shown mounted on his horse with an open hymn book in his hand. Landstad, who was briefly a minister here in Seljord, made his name among the Norwegian nationalists of his day by collecting traditional country ballads and by creating the *Landstad Hymnbook*, which discarded the Danish of its predecessors for Norwegian; it was in use until 1985. A few metres away, stuck in the ground, is the **570-kilogram stone**, which was lifted for the first and last time by a Telemark strongman, one **Nils Langedal** (1722–1800), who, according to local legend, was reared on mare's milk.

## South to Dalen

To the west of Seljord, there are two roads leading to Dalen (see p.178) south from the E134 – Highway 45 and, further to the west from the Åmot crossroads, Highway 38; both are around 20km long. **Highway 38** has the more imperious scenery as it inches its way along the edge of the **Ravnejuvet** (Raven Gorge), a severe gash in the landscape whose sheer dark walls are no less than 350m high. According to the local tourist brochure, the gorge's unusual air currents mean you can throw a banknote over the edge and it will come back to you – but most people experiment with ordinary bits of paper instead. The second road, the more subdued **Highway 45**, threads its way over forested hills before nipping through a series of alpine-like valleys, where old farmsteads hug the hillsides flanked by bright-green pastureland. This is fine scenery indeed and it's here you'll find Eidsborg stavkirke.

### Eidsborg Stavkirke

Late May to Aug daily 10am–5pm • 40kr

Just 5km north from Dalen along Highway 45 is **Eidsborg Stavkirke** (Eidsborg stave church), whose tightly packed roofs, decorative finials and cedar shingles date back to the thirteenth century. The church, which is now the prize exhibit among the old timber buildings of the **Vest-Telemark Museum** (West Telemark Museum), remains one of the best preserved in the country (albeit with several renovations), and its interior sports some fascinating if faded watercolour friezes of biblical scenes. Given its remote location, it's not surprising that the church has attracted more than its fair share of legend, one of the most charming of which relates to the adjacent graveyard: digging graves was so difficult in this rocky plot of land that a local magistrate offered mercy to a pair of condemned women if they could rectify matters; they solved the problem by carrying sand here in their aprons and were promptly pardoned. The church is dedicated to St Nicholas of Bari (aka Santa Claus) and, in an echo of a pagan past, a wooden image of the saint was carried round the lake below the church three times once every year and then ceremonially washed, right up until the 1850s.

### Dalen

Trailing along the valley between steep forested hills, the sleepy little town of **DALEN** is a pleasant place in a pleasant setting, its string of modern houses somewhat reminiscent of small-town USA. Dalen's four hundred inhabitants mostly work in the hydro and timber industries, but a fair few of them are reliant on the town's star turn, the *Dalen Hotel* (see opposite), right at the end of town facing the lake. In the 1890s, the opening of the Telemarkskanal (see box below) made Dalen an important transit point and it was then that a group of businessmen decided to build the hotel as the region's showpiece – as it remains today.

**ARRIVAL AND INFORMATION**                                   **DALEN AND AROUND**

**By bus** There are local buses to Dalen from Åmot, on the E134. Åmot can be reached on the Haukeliekspressen (#180), a Nor-Way Bussekspress bus which runs from Oslo to Haugesund (2–4 daily).
**By car** Heading west from Seljord on the E134, it's 30km to Highway 45, the first of the two turnings for Dalen, and

16km more to the Åmot crossroads at the start of the second turning, Highway 38.
**Tourist office** The tourist office is a few metres from the *Dalen Hotel* (May to mid-Aug Mon–Fri 9am–7pm, Sat & Sun 10am–5pm; rest of year Mon–Fri 9am–3.30pm; ☎ 35 07 56 56, ⓦ visitdalen.com).

---

### THE TELEMARKSKANAL

Dalen is the terminus of the passenger ferry that wends its way southeast along the **Telemarkskanal** to **Skien** (ferries mid-May to early Sept 3–6 weekly; 800kr one-way; ☎ 35 90 00 30, ⓦ telemarkskanalen.no), a journey that takes a little under nine hours, leaving around 8am. Extending 105km, the canal links a string of lakes and rivers by means of eighteen locks that negotiate a difference in water levels of 72m. Completed in 1892, the canal was once an important trade route into the interior, but today it's mainly used by pleasure craft and vintage passenger ferries. It's also possible to make shorter excursions out by boat and back by bus. The jetty is 750m beyond the *Dalen Hotel*.

## ACCOMMODATION AND EATING

**Dalen Bed & Breakfast ☎ 35 07 70 80, ⊕ dalenbb .com.** If your budget won't stretch as far as the *Dalen Hotel*, then this all-year B&B, which occupies an attractive, modern chalet-like house just a few metres away, is a good alternative; there are thirteen guest rooms here and most are en suite (100kr extra). 970kr

★ **Dalen Hotel ☎ 35 07 90 00, ⊕ dalenhotel.no.** Dating back to the 1890s, this lavish hotel was once one of the most fashionable spots in the country, but it hit the skids after World War II when the development of the road system began to undermine its importance. Luckily it was picked up and expertly restored in the 1990s. The hotel's main facade is an imposing affair, whose twin towers are topped by finials in a permutation of Viking style. Inside, pride of place goes to the galleried hall with its huge stained-glass ceiling, open fireplace and carved woodwork. The 42 very comfortable guest rooms, which are in the hotel's two wings, have been returned to an approximation of their original appearance too, and the pick have balconies overlooking the hotel gardens, which stretch down to the lake. The hotel dining room is also very grand with its acres of wood panelling and the food – traditional Norwegian – is top-notch with main courses averaging 300kr. Open mid-May to Oct. 2300kr, sp/r 1800kr

## Rjukan

**RJUKAN**, some 60km north of the E134, spreads out along the bottom of the Vestfjorddalen valley, its oldest buildings dating from its foundation as a saltpetre manufacturing centre at the start of the twentieth century. Saltpetre needed power and Rjukan had plenty of that in the form of the water that tumbles down into the valley from the harsh mountains up above – and this was harnessed to create a reliable source of electricity. Nowadays, the town still produces hydroelectricity, but it has diversified into tourism, taking advantage of its proximity to the **skiing and hiking trails** of the Hardangervidda mountain plateau (see p.215), while its first power station, **Vemork**, has become an industrial museum of some repute. Nonetheless, museum and mountain plateau aside, Rjukan is really rather humdrum, its four thousand inhabitants sharing a modest gridiron town centre originally assembled by the Norsk Hydro power company – for in essence this has always been a company town.

### The Norsk Industriarbeidermuseum

May to mid-June & mid-Aug to Sept daily 10am–4pm; mid-June to mid-Aug daily 10am–6pm; Oct–April Tues–Fri noon–3pm, Sat & Sun 11am–4pm • 75kr • ☎ 35 09 90 00, ⊕ visitvemork.com • Visitors have to park on the far side of the suspension bridge and walk the last 700m (15min); there is a minibus service in summer (late June to mid-Aug; 30kr)

Rjukan's key attraction is the **Norsk Industriarbeidermuseum** (Norwegian Industrial Workers' Museum), housed in the former **Vemork hydroelectric station**, some 7km to the west of Rjukan. When it was opened in 1911, Vemork had the greatest generating capacity in the world – its ten turbines provided a combined output of 108 megawatts – and it remains a fine example of industrial architecture pretending to be something else: with its high gables and symmetrical windows it looks more like a country mansion. Inside, the museum explores the effects of industrialization on what was then a profoundly rural region, has displays on hydroelectric power and the development of the trade unions, and features a gallery of propagandist paintings about workers and the class struggle by Arne Ekeland.

Yet, most foreigners come to the museum because of the plant's role in – and excellent displays on – **World War II**, when it was the site chosen by the Germans for the manufacture of **heavy water** – necessary for regulating nuclear reactions in the creation of a nuclear bomb. Aware of Vemork's importance, the Americans bombed it on several occasions and the Norwegian Resistance mounted a string of guerrilla attacks; as a result, the Nazis decided to move the heavy water they had made to Germany. The only way they could do this was by train, and part of the journey was across Lake Tinnsjø just east of Rjukan – ingeniously the ferry was fitted with a set of railway tracks. This was the scene of one of the most spectacular escapades of the war, when the Norwegian Resistance sunk ferry and train on January 20, 1944. All the heavy water was lost, but so were the fourteen Norwegian passengers – a story recounted in the 1965 film *The*

*Heroes of Telemark*, in which Kirk Douglas played the cinematic stereotype of the Norwegian: an earnest man with an honest face, wearing a big pullover.

### Krossobanen cable car

Daily: late June to mid-Aug 9am–8pm; mid-Aug to Sept 10am–6pm; rest of year 10am–4pm • 50kr each way • ☎ 35 09 00 27, ⓦ krossobanen.no

Easy access to the Hardangervidda is provided by Rjukan's **Krossobanen cable car**, which carries passengers up to the plateau from a station at the west end of town, about 2km from the bus station. Built in 1928, the Krossobanen was the first cable car to be built in northern Europe and Norsk Hydro stumped up the money, curiously enough because they wanted their workers to be able to see the sun in winter.

### Gaustabanen

Late June to mid-Oct daily 10am–5pm • 350kr return • ☎ 45 50 22 22, ⓦ gaustabanen.no

Built for the military in the 1950s Rjukan's **funicular railway**, the **Gaustabanen**, goes 860m into the heart of Mount Gausta, where you change for the 1km-long journey up to the top of the mountain. By means of the railway, Norwegian soldiers could maintain their mountain-top radio-listening gear with the greatest of ease and, now that the army has gone, it's open to tourists. The Gaustabanen terminal is 14km east of Rjukan.

### ARRIVAL AND DEPARTURE                                                     RJUKAN

**By bus** Long-distance buses to Rjukan pull in at the bus station on the south side of the river. From here, it's a couple of minutes' walk to the town centre, across the bridge on the north side of the river. Nor-Way Bussekspress's Rjukanekspressen (#185) runs to Kongsberg (2–3 daily; 2hr); Notodden (Mon–Fri 2 daily; 1hr 30min); and Oslo (via Notodden or Kongsberg; 2–5 daily; 3hr 30min).

**By car** From the E134, there are two roads to Rjukan – one from a point west of Heddal stave church (see p.177), the other from the Åmot crossroads (see p.177). The first is 55km long and fairly fast, the second is about 65km long and quite slow.

**Tourist office** Torget 2 (late June to early Sept Mon–Fri 9am–7pm, Sat & Sun 10am–6pm; early Sept to late June Mon–Fri 8am–3.30pm; ☎ 35 08 05 50, ⓦ visitrjukan.com). The tourist office, right in the centre of town, carries local bus timetables, sells maps and has details of local accommodation. They will also provide advice on hiking the Hardangervidda as well as other outdoor pursuits, from ice climbing to bungee jumping from the suspension bridge leading to the Industriarbeidermuseum.

### ACCOMMODATION AND EATING

**Rjukan Hytteby** Brogata 9 ☎ 35 09 01 22, ⓦ rjukan -hytteby.no. Rjukan is short of good accommodation, but one of the better bets is this batch of ten modern cottages, built in the style of the original workers' houses of the 1910s, which string along the south side of the river about 800m east of the centre. The straightforward café-restaurant (daily 11am–11pm) here sells filling basics like burgers and pizzas at affordable prices with mains starting at 120kr, though it can heave on the weekend. Linen costs an extra 100kr per person. **875kr**

## Åmot to Røldal

Continuing west from the **Åmot crossroads**, the E134 zigzags across hill and dale before beginning its long climb up to the bare and bleak wastes of the Hardangervidda plateau (see p.215) via the wild and storm-buffeted **Haukelifjell**, one of Europe's highest mountain passes. The road cuts a nervous course across the plateau, diving into a series of tunnels before slipping down into the hamlet of **RØLDAL**, a remote little place nestled in the greenest of valleys.

### Røldal stavkirke

Daily: June & late Aug 10am–4pm; July 9.30am–6.30pm; early Aug 10am–5pm • 40kr

Within shouting distance of the E134, **Røldal stavkirke** (stave church) is a trim, rusticated affair dating from the thirteenth century – and the only stave church still in religious use today. In medieval times, it was a major place of pilgrimage on account of the crucifix with healing powers that still hangs above the altar - and it was then that the elaborate wall paintings were added.

## Røldal to Odda

After Røldal, the E134 makes another stirring climb to reach its junction with Highway 13, the scenic but extremely long-winded road south to Stavanger (see p.133). From this crossroads, the combined E134/Highway 13 plunges on across the southwest edge of the Hardangervidda en route to another crossroads, where you either keep going on the E134 to Haugesund (see p.142), 130km away, or stay on Highway 13 as it drops down a severe, boulder-strewn river valley, passing, in 5km, the **Latefossen waterfall**, where two huge torrents empty into the river with a deafening roar. Beyond lie Odda (see p.211) and Lofthus (see p.212).

3

# Bergen and the western fjords

VIEW ACROSS THE FJÆRLANDSFJORD FROM MUNDAL

# Bergen and the western fjords

If there's one familiar and enticing image of Norway it's the fjords, giant clefts in the landscape running from the coast deep into the interior. Rugged yet serene, these huge, wedge-shaped inlets are visually stunning; indeed, the entire fjord region elicits inordinate amounts of purple prose from tourist-office handouts, and for once it's rarely overstated.

The fjords are undeniably beautiful, especially around early May, after the brief Norwegian **spring** has brought colour to the landscape; but **winter**, when all is unerringly quiet, has its charms too, the blue-black waters of the fjords contrasting with the blinding white of the snow that blankets the hills, valleys and mountains. In **summer**, the wilds are filled with hikers and the waters patrolled by a steady flotilla of bright-white ferries, but don't let that put you off: the tourists are rarely in such numbers as to be intrusive, and even in the most popular districts, a brief walk off the beaten track will bring solitude in abundance.

The fjords run all the way up the coast from Stavanger to the Russian border, but are most easily – and impressively – seen on the west coast near **Bergen**, the self-proclaimed "Gateway to the Fjords". Norway's second-largest city, Bergen is a welcoming place with an atmospheric old warehouse quarter, a relic of the days when it was the northernmost port of the Hanseatic trade alliance. It's also – as its tag suggests – a handy springboard for the nearby fjords, beginning with the gentle charms of the **Hardangerfjord** and the Flåmsdal valley, where the inspiring **Flåmsbana** mountain railway trundles down to the Aurlandsfjord, a small arm of the mighty **Sognefjord**. Dotted with pretty village resorts, the Sognefjord is the longest and deepest of the country's fjords and is perhaps the most beguiling, rather more so than the **Nordfjord**, lying parallel to the north. Between the Sognefjord and Nordfjord lies the growling and groaning **Jostedalsbreen glacier**, mainland Europe's largest ice-sheet, while east of the Nordfjord is the narrow, S-shaped **Geirangerfjord**, a rugged gash in the landscape that is perhaps the most beautiful of all the fjords. Further north still, the scenery becomes even more extreme, reaching pinnacles of isolation in the splendid **Trollstigen** mountain highway, a stunning prelude

URNES STAVE CHURCH

# Highlights

**❶ Bergen's Fløibanen** There are wonderful views over the city at the top of what must be Europe's quaintest funicular railway. **See p.193**

**❷ Troldhaugen** Visit the delightful fjordside home and studio of Edvard Grieg, Norway's foremost composer. **See p.199**

**❸ Hardangervidda** A mountain plateau of striking beauty, the Hardangervidda offers some of the country's finest hiking. **See p.215**

**❹ The Flåmsbana** The exhilarating Flåm railway, careers down the mountainside with the fjords waiting down below. **See p.220**

**❺ Balestrand** The relaxing charms of small-town Balestrand make it a fine base for

further Sognefjord explorations. **See p.229**

**❻ Urnes stave church** The oldest stave church in Norway is renowned for its exquisite, almost frenzied, Viking woodcarvings. **See p.233**

**❼ The Sognesfjellsveg** View the sharp, ice-tipped peaks of the Jotunheimen, Norway's most imposing mountain range, from the Sognefjellsveg mountain road. **See p.235**

**❽ Kjenndalsbreen** Inspect the mighty Jostedalsbreen glacier at close quarters on the Kjenndalsbreen, "nodule". **See p.241**

**❾ Ålesund** A beguiling ferry and fishing port, whose streets are flanked by handsome Art Nouveau buildings. **See p.252**

HIGHLIGHTS ARE MARKED ON THE MAP ON P.186

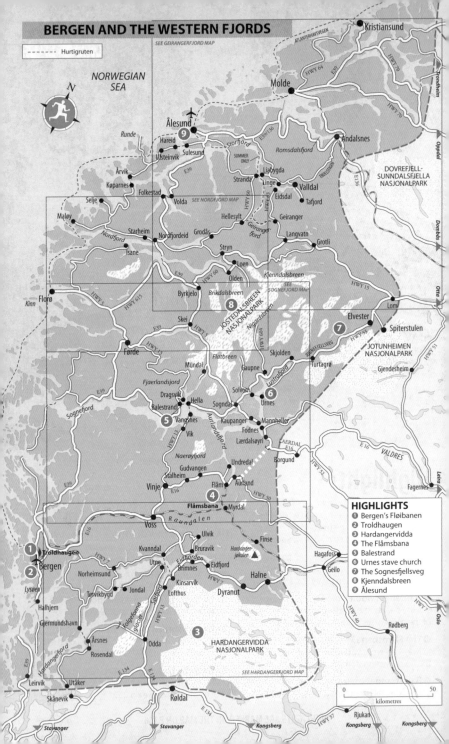

# BERGEN AND THE WESTERN FJORDS

- - - - Hurtigruten

NORWEGIAN SEA

SEE GEIRANGERFJORD MAP

Kristiansund

ATLANTERHAVSVEGEN

HWY 64

E39

HWY 70

Trondheim

Molde

HWY 70

Runde

Ålesund

Hareid

Sulesund

Ulsteinvik

SUMMER ONLY

Storfjord

Romsdalsfjord

Andalsnes

DOVREFJELL-SUNNDALSFJELLA NASJONALPARK

Oppdal

Liabygda

Stranda

Linge

Valldal

Eidsdal

Tafjord

TROLLSTIGEN

E136

Dombås

Arvik

Køparnes

Folkestad

E39

Volda

SEE NORDFJORD MAP

Geiranger

Geirangerfjord

Langvatn

Grotli

HWY 15

Otta

Selje

Maløy

Starheim

Nordfjordeid

Grodås

Hellesylt

Stryn

Loen

Olden

Kjenndalsbreen

SEE SOGNEFJORD MAP

Lom

Elvester

Spiterstulen

Nordfjord

Isane

E39

HWY 60

Byrkjelo

Brikdalsbreen

JOSTEDALSBREEN NASJONALPARK

Nigardsbreen

HWY 15

HWY 55

Florø

Kinn

HWY 5

HWY 615

Skei

HWY 5

Flatbreen

Skjolden

SOGNEFJELLSVEG

Turtagrø

JOTUNHEIMEN NASJONALPARK

HWY 51

Gjendesheim

Førde

E39

HWY 13

Mundal

Gaupne

Luster

Fjærlandsfjord

Dragsvik

Hella

Solvorn

Urnes

Sogndal

Kaupanger

Mannheller

Fødnes

HWY 13

Balestrand

Vangsnes

Vik

Aurlandsfjord

Lærdalsøyri

LÆRDAL E16

VALDRES

Leira

Sognefjord

Nærøyfjord

Gudvangen

Stalheim

Undredal

Borgund

E16

HWY 53

Fagernes

Vinje

E16

Flåm

Aurland

HWY 50

Flåmsbana

Myrdal

HIGHLIGHTS

1 Bergen's Fløibanen
2 Troldhaugen
3 Hardangervidda
4 The Flåmsbana
5 Balestrand
6 Urnes stave church
7 The Sognesfjellsveg
8 Kjenndalsbreen
9 Ålesund

Voss

Raundalen

Ulvik

Bruravik

Finse

Hardangerjøkulen

Hagafoss

Geilo

1 Troldhaugen

2 Bergen

Lysøen

HWY 7

E16

Kvanndal

Utne

Eidfjorden

Brimnes

Eidfjord

Halne

Dyranut

Oslo

Norheimsund

Torvikbygd

Jondal

Kinsarvik

Lofthus

HWY 13

HWY 7

Halhjem

Gjermundshavn

Folgefonna

HWY 13

Hardangervidda NASJONALPARK

Rødberg

Årsnes

Rosendal

Odda

HWY 40

HWY 7

Hardangerfjord

E134

Leirvik

Utåker

E39

E134

Røldal

SEE HARDANGERFJORD MAP

Skånevik

Stavanger

Stavanger

Kongsberg

Kongsberg

Kongsberg

HWY 37

Rjukan

0                    50
kilometres

N

to both the somewhat hang-dog town of **Åndalsnes** and the charming port of **Ålesund**, with its attractive Art Nouveau buildings.

# Bergen and around

As it has been raining ever since she arrived in the city, a tourist stops a young boy and asks if it always rains here. "I don't know," he replies, "I'm only thirteen." The joke isn't brilliant, but it does contain a grain of truth. Of all the things to contend with in **BERGEN**, the weather is the most predictable: it rains on average 260 days a year, often relentlessly even in summer, and its forested surroundings are often shrouded in mist. Yet, despite its dampness, Bergen is one of Norway's most enjoyable cities, boasting – amid seven hills and sheltered to the north, south and west by a series of straggling islands – a spectacular setting. There's plenty to see in town too, from sturdy old stone buildings and terraces of tiny wooden houses to a veritable raft of **museums**, while just outside the city limits are Edvard Grieg's home, **Troldhaugen**, as well as the charming open-air **Gamle Bergen** (Old Bergen) museum.

More than anything else, though, it's the general flavour of the place that appeals. Although Bergen has become a major port and something of an industrial centre in recent years, it remains a laidback, easy-going town with a firmly nautical air. Fish and fishing may no longer be Bergen's economic lynchpins, but the bustling main harbour, **Vågen**, is still very much the focus of attention. If you stay more than a day or two – perhaps using Bergen as a base for viewing the nearer **fjords** – you'll soon discover that the city also has the region's best choice of **restaurants**, some impressive **art galleries** and a decent nightlife.

### Brief history

Founded in 1070 by **King Olav Kyrre** ("the Peaceful"), a Norwegian survivor from the Battle of Stamford Bridge in 1066, Bergen was the largest and most important town in medieval Norway and a regular residence of the country's kings and queens. In the fourteenth century the town also became an ecclesiastical centre, supporting no fewer than thirty churches and monasteries, and a member of the **Hanseatic League**, as by

**4**

---

## BERGEN ORIENTATION

Very little of medieval Bergen has survived, although parts of the fortress, the **Bergenhus Festning** – which commands the entrance to the harbour – date from the thirteenth century. The rest of the city centre divides into several distinct parts, the most historically interesting being the harbourside **Bryggen**, which accommodates an attractive ensemble of stone and timber eighteenth- and nineteenth-century merchants' trading houses. The Bryggen ends at the head of the harbour, where Bergen's main square, the **Torget**, features an open-air fish market. East of here, stretching up towards the train station, is one of the older areas, a mainly nineteenth-century quarter that's at its prettiest along and around **Lille Øvregaten**. The main thoroughfare of this quarter, **Kong Oscars gate**, has been roughly treated by the developers, but it does lead to the city's most endearing museum, the **Lepramuseet** (Leprosy Museum). A stone's throw from here, the modern concrete blocks surrounding the central **lake**, Lille Lungegårdsvann, form the cultural focus of the city, holding Bergen's art galleries and main concert hall, while the chief commercial area is a few metres to the west along the wide and airy **Torgalmenningen**. The steep hill to the south of the central lake is topped by the **university.**

Most of the main sights and museums are concentrated in these areas, but no tour of the city is complete without a stroll out along the **Nordnes peninsula**, where fine timber houses pepper the bumpy terrain and the old USF sardine factory now contains a lively and very fashionable arts complex and café.

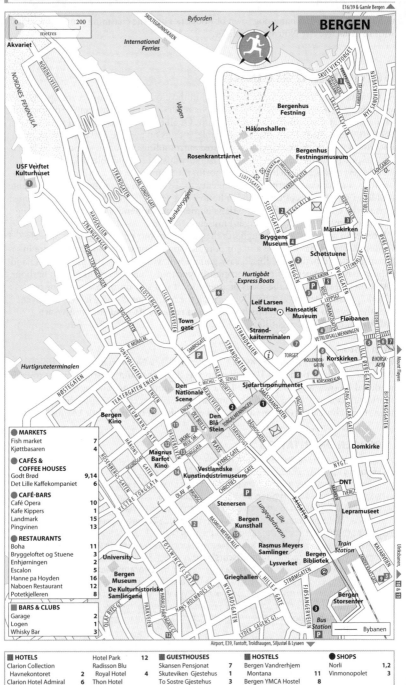

BERGEN

this time the town had become a prosperous port linked to other European cities by a vigorous trading life, with **fish** being the main commodity. The League was, however, controlled by German merchants and, after Hansa and local interests started to diverge, the Germans came to dominate the region's economy, reducing the locals to a state of dependency. Neither could the people of Bergen expect help from their kings and queens: rather, in return for easily collected taxes from the Hansa merchants, Norway's medieval monarchs compelled west-coast fishermen to sell their catch to the merchants – and at prices the merchants set themselves. As a result, the German trading station that flourished on the Bryggen, Bergen's main wharf, became wealthy and hated in equal measure, a self-regulating colony with its own laws and an administration that was profoundly indifferent to local sentiment.

In the 1550s, with Hansa power finally evaporating, a local lord – one **Kristoffer Valkendorf** – reasserted Norwegian control, but not out of the goodness of his heart. Valkendorf and his cronies simply took over the monopolies that had enriched their German predecessors, and continued to operate this iniquitous system, which so pauperized the region's fishermen, right up to the late nineteenth century. Bergen's merchants benefited from Norway's neutrality in World War I, developing their trade and expanding their fleets, but it was only after World War II that the town got into its stride, transforming itself from a fish-dependent backwater to the lively city of today.

## Torget

Fish market June–Aug daily 7am–7pm; Sept–May Mon–Sat 7am–4pm

In 1890, Lilian Leland, author of *Traveling Alone: A Woman's Journey Around the World*, complained of Bergen that "Everything is fishy. You eat fish and drink fish and smell fish and breathe fish." Those days are long gone, but now that Bergen is every inch a go-ahead, modern city, tourists in search of all things piscine flock to **Torget**'s open-air **fish market**. It's not a patch on the days when scores of fishing vessels crowded the quayside to empty their bulging holds, but the stalls still display mounds of prawns and crab-claws, dried cod, buckets of herring and a hundred other varieties of marine life on slabs, in tanks, under the knife, and in packets. Fruit, vegetables and flowers – as well as souvenirs – have a place in today's market too, and there's easily enough variety to assemble an excellent picnic lunch, so load up or eat up. At the end of the jetty behind Torget, also take a peek at the **statue** of Leif Andreas Larsen, aka Shetlands Larsen, one of Norway's most renowned World War II heroes (see p.280), now presiding over a semicircular war memorial.

## Bryggen

Spearing down the north side of Vågen, **Bryggen** is the obvious historical and cultural target after Torget. The site of the original settlement, the area recalls its medieval provenance by a string of wooden and stone warehouses, whose distinctive gable ends face out to the waterfront. The whole area between the Bryggen and Øvregaten just to the rear (see p.191) was once known as Tyskebryggen, or "German Quay", after the **Hanseatic** merchants who operated their trading station here, but the name was unceremoniously dumped after World War II. The **medieval buildings** of the Bryggen were destroyed by fire in 1702, to be replaced by another set of wooden warehouses. In turn, many of these were later demolished to make way for brick-and-stone warehouses built in a style modelled on – and sympathetic to – that of the Hansa period. Nevertheless, a significant number of early eighteenth-century timber buildings have survived, though the first you'll come to, the **Hanseatic Museum** (see p.190), at the north end of Torget, has brick-and-stone neighbours.

A few metres from here is the main block of old **timber buildings**, now housing souvenir shops, restaurants and bars. Despite the crowds of tourists, it's well worth

**4**

---

## SAVING MONEY: THE BERGEN CARD

The **Bergen Card** is a 24-hour (200kr; children 3–15 years 75kr) or 48-hour (260kr; children 3–15 years 100kr) pass that provides free use of all the city's public transport (except for the airport bus) and free or substantially discounted admission to most of the city's sights, plus reductions on many sightseeing trips. Discount details are given in the official *Bergen Guide* booklet. Obviously, the more diligent a sightseer you are, the better value the card becomes – doubly so if you're staying a bus ride from the centre. The card is sold online and at a wide range of outlets, including the tourist office and major hotels.

---

nosing around here, wandering down the passageways wherever you can. Interestingly, these eighteenth-century buildings carefully follow the original building line: the governing body of the Hansa trading station stipulated the exact depth and width of each merchant's building, and the width of the passage separating them – a regularity that's actually best observed from Øvregaten. The planning regulations didn't end there: trade had to be carried out in the front section of the building, with storage rooms at the back; above were the merchant's office, bedroom and dining room. Up above those, on the top floor, were the living quarters of the employees, grouped into rooms by rank – junior merchants, journeymen/clerks and foremen, wharf hands and, last (and least), errand boys. Every activity in this rigidly hierarchical, all-male society was tightly controlled – employees were forbidden to fraternize with the locals and stiff fines were imposed for hundreds of "offences" including swearing, waking up the master and singing at work.

### Hanseatisk Museum

Bryggen • Mid-May to mid-Sept daily 9am–5pm; mid-Sept to mid-May Tues–Sat 11am–2pm, Sun 11am–4pm • 60kr, including Schøtstuene • ☎ 55 54 46 90, 🌐 www.museumvest.no

The **Hanseatisk Museum** (Hanseatic Museum) may not be entirely authentic or original, but it is still a fine illustration of an early eighteenth-century merchants' dwelling, kitted out in late Hansa style. As per standard Hansa format, it was a real rabbit warren of a place in which the trading area occupied the ground floor and the junior staff the top, with the merchants in between. There was, predictably enough, a considerable difference in the comfort afforded to the juniors as distinct from the merchants, but everyone hunkered down in the panelled bunk beds that survive to this day. Also of particular interest is the building's **painted woodwork**, with broad, bold and colourful floral designs in many of the working areas and more formal, Italianate scenes in the merchants' quarters – though the exact provenance of these designs has been the subject of much debate. Dotted throughout the museum is an idiosyncratic assortment of bygones, including the possessions of contemporary families, a medley of indeterminate portraits, several fine pieces of furniture, and an ancient and much-used fish press.

### The Bryggens Museum

Dreggsallmenningen • Mid-May to Aug daily 10am–4pm; Sept to mid-May Mon–Fri 11am–3pm, Sat noon–3pm, Sun noon–4pm • 60kr • ☎ 55 30 80 30, 🌐 bymuseet.no

Just off the Bryggen, beside the *Radisson Blu Royal Hotel*, stands the lumpily modern **Bryggens Museum**. Visits begin in the basement, which exhibits all manner of things dug up in the archeological excavations of the Bryggen in the 1950s. A wide range of items was unearthed, from domestic implements like combs and pots through to shoes, buckles and trade goods plus several runic sticks – perhaps surprisingly, Norwegians were laboriously carving runes (see p.380) onto their sticks well into medieval times. The museum displays these finds thematically both to illustrate the city's early history and provide the backcloth to a set of twelfth-century foundations at the back of the basement, left in *situ* where they were discovered. The museum's two upper floors are given over to modest temporary exhibitions exploring other aspects of Bergen's past.

## Mariakirken

Dreggsallmenningen • Late June to late Aug Mon–Fri 9–11am & 1–4pm; late Aug to late June Tues–Fri 11am–12.30pm • 20kr, free in winter • ☎ 55 59 32 50 • Closed for repairs till 2015

Behind the Bryggens Museum, the perky twin towers of the **Mariakirken** (St Mary's Church) are the most distinctive feature of what is Bergen's oldest extant building, a Romanesque-Gothic church dating from the twelfth century. Still in use as a place of worship – or at least it will be again when the repairs are completed – Mariakirken is now firmly Norwegian, but from 1408 to 1706 it was the church of the Hanseatic League merchants, who purchased it lock, stock and barrel. The merchants installed the church's ostentatious Baroque pulpit and its gaudy North German altarpiece, a fifteenth-century triptych, whose exquisite framing is really rather wasted on the sentimental carvings of saints and apostles it surrounds. The walls of the Mariakirken are hung with old commemorative paintings, an insipid lot for the most part with the exception of a finely detailed portrait of *Pastor Lammer, his wife and six children,* looking suitably serious in their Sunday best. The painting is by Lambert von Haven, a seventeenth-century Dutch artist, who went on to greater things at the royal court in Copenhagen; it hangs above the side door on the right-hand side of the nave.

## Schøtstuene

Øvregaten 50 • March to mid-May & mid-Sept to Dec Tues–Sun 11am–2pm; mid-May to mid-Sept daily 9am–5pm • 60kr, including Hanseatisk Museum • ⓦ www.museumvest.no

The **Schøtstuene**, at the back of the Mariakirken, comprises the old Hanseatic assembly rooms, where the merchants would meet to lay down the law or just relax – it was the only building in the whole trading post allowed heating and so it was here that they held their feasts, ceremonies and celebrations. As you explore the comfortable and commodious rooms, it's hard not to conclude that the merchants cared not a jot for their employees shivering away nearby – though, to be fair, their bunk beds weren't much fun either.

## Øvregaten

The Schøtstuene is on **Øvregaten**, an attractive cobbled street that has marked the boundary of the Bryggen for the last eight hundred years and was once, despite the fulminations of the Hansa merchants, the haunt of the city's prostitutes. From Øvregaten, it's still possible to discern the layout of the old Bryggen **trading station**, a warren of narrow passages separating warped and crooked buildings surmounted by their hat-like, high-pitched roofs. On the upper levels, the eighteenth-century loading bays, staircases and higgledy-piggledy living quarters are still much in evidence, while the overhanging eaves of the passageways were designed to shelter trade goods.

# Bergenhus Festning

Overlooking the mouth of the harbour, **Bergenhus Festning** (Bergen Fortress) is a large and roughly star-shaped fortification now used mostly as a park. The fort's thick stone-and-earth walls date from the nineteenth century, but they enclose the remnants of earlier strongholds – or rather their copies: the Bergenhus was wrecked when a German ammunition ship exploded just below the walls in 1944.

## Rosenkrantztårnet

Bergenhus • Mid-May to Aug daily 10am–4pm; Sept to mid-May Sun noon–3pm • 60kr • ☎ 55 30 80 30, ⓦ bymuseet.no

Of the two main medieval replicas in the Bergenhus, the more diverting is the forbidding **Rosenkrantztårnet** (Rosenkrantz Tower), whose spiral staircases, medieval rooms and low rough corridors make an enjoyable gambol. It's also possible to walk out onto the rooftop battlements, from where there is a wide view over the harbour. The tower is named after **Erik Rosenkrantz** (1519–75), governor of Bergen in the 1560s,

## WITCHERY IN BERGEN: ANNE PEDERSDATTER

In 1590, **Anne Pedersdatter** was burnt as a witch here in Bergen and, remarkably enough, the court proceedings have survived. They reveal a strong-willed and sharp-tongued woman, who antagonized many of her neighbours, whose chosen course of revenge was to accuse her of being a **witch**. As far as the judge was concerned, the crucial bit of evidence came from Anne's maid, who said she had been used as a horse to transport her mistress to a Sabbat (Witches' Sabbath). Clearly, Anne's maid either had a grudge or was suborned, but no matter – and despite the objections of Bergen's bishop – she went to the flames. Anne was not alone: 300 "witches" were executed in Norway in the sixteenth and seventeenth centuries – 250 of them women – in a cruel mix of misogyny and superstition that had spread across most of Europe.

who turned his draughty medieval quarters into a grand fortified residence, equipping his own chamber with fine large windows and a handsome Renaissance chimneypiece, both of which have survived in good condition. This same room also has a copy of Rosenkrantz's gravestone, a somewhat ill-balanced but still strikingly realistic work depicting his wife in a long flowing dress and him in a suit of armour with a codpiece so tight it would bring tears to most men's eyes. Also within the tower are several other small but intriguing exhibits, principally one on the sophisticated penal codes instituted by King Magnus Lagabøter (Lawmender; 1238–80) and another on Anne Pedersdatter (see box above). As for Rosenkrantz himself, he was known principally as the architect of a new law under which anyone found guilty of an illegitimate sexual affair had to confess to a priest before being fined. The law applied initially to men and women in equal measure, but by the 1590s women bore the brunt of any punishment. In Bergen, for example, women who could not pay the fine had to stand naked at the entrance to a church before being thrown out of town – the men just got exiled.

### Håkonshallen

Bergenhus • Daily: mid-May to Aug 10am–4pm; Sept to mid-May noon–3pm (Thurs till 6pm) • 60kr • ☎ 55 30 80 30, ⊛ bymuseet.no

In the Bergenhus, metres from the Rosenkrantztårnet, is the entrance to a large cobbled courtyard, which is itself flanked by nineteenth-century officers' quarters and the **Håkonshallen**, a careful reconstruction of the Gothic ceremonial hall built for King Håkon Håkonsson in the middle of the thirteenth century. After Norway lost its independence, the capacious hall became surplus to requirements and no one knew quite what to do with it for several centuries, but it was revamped in 1910 and rebuilt after the 1944 explosion and is now in use once again for public ceremonies.

### Bergenhus Festningsmuseum

Øvre Dreggsallmenningen • Tues–Sun 11am–5pm • Free • ☎ 55 54 63 87

Often neglected, the **Bergenhus Festningsmuseum** (Bergenhus Fortress Museum) is one of the city's better museums, its first floor holding several well-composed displays exploring the effects of World War II on Bergen. There's a detailed account of the German naval attack on Bergen in 1940 and on the development of the Resistance thereafter. Bergen had long-standing seafaring links with Great Britain and had also suffered grievously from U-boat attacks on Norwegian shipping in World War I, as a result of which the Resistance to the occupation was particularly strong here. Unfortunately, the Germans proved adept at tracking down their enemies, and time and again they broke the back of the main Resistance groups, though they were flummoxed by the explosion that levelled much of the Bergenhus on Hitler's birthday in 1944: they thought it was sabotage, but in fact it was an accident. The museum's second floor is far less interesting, being given over to a detailed exploration of the history of the Bergenhus fortress; the ground floor is for temporary displays.

## THE FLØIBANEN FUNICULAR RAILWAY

Dating back to the 1910s, the distinctly Ruritanian lower terminus of the **Fløibanen funicular railway** on Vetrlidsallmenningen (departures every 15–30min: May–Aug Mon–Sat 8am–midnight, Sun 9am–midnight; Sept–April Mon–Sat 8am–11pm, Sun 9am–11pm; return fare 80kr, one-way 40kr; ☎ 55 33 68 00, ⓦ floibanen.com) is a delightful introduction to one of the city's major attractions, whose trains shuttle passengers up to the top of **Mount Fløyen** – "The Vane" – at 320m above sea level. When the weather is fine, you get a bird's-eye view of Bergen and its surroundings from the plateau-summit, and here also is a large and popular café-restaurant. Afterwards, you can walk back down to the city in about 45 minutes, or push on into the woods along several well-marked, colour-coded footpaths (pick up free trail maps of the summit at the lower terminal). The shortest and perhaps the most enjoyable is the 1.6km-loop trail to Skomakerdiket lake and back.

## Lille Øvregaten

Running east from the lower Fløibanen terminal, **Lille Øvregaten** is lined by an appealing mix of expansive nineteenth-century villas and dinky timber houses, mostly bright-white clapboard, but some deep red, ochre and light blue too. There are more old timber houses up above, and these are, if anything, even quainter, pressing in against the steep cobbled lanes that steer and veer around hunks of stone which were, at the time, simply too bothersome to move: to explore the area, take the first left up the hillside from Lille Øvregaten and follow your nose.

### Domkirke

Domkirkeplass • Late June to late Aug Mon–Fri 10am–4pm; late Aug to late June Tues–Fri 11am–12.30pm • Free • ☎ 55 59 32 70

Lille Øvregaten curves round to the **Domkirke** (Cathedral), a heavy-duty edifice whose stern exterior, with its whopping tower, has been restored and rebuilt several times since its original construction in the thirteenth century. The interior doesn't set the pulse racing, though there's a noticeable penchant for fancy wooden staircases – two leading to the organ and one to the pulpit – which can't help but seem a little flippant given the dourness of their surroundings.

## Lepramuseet

Kong Oscars gate 59 • Mid-May to Aug daily 11am–3pm • 60kr • ☎ 55 96 11 55, ⓦ bymuseet.no

The fascinating **Lepramuseet** (Leprosy Museum), housed in the charming, eighteenth-century buildings of **St Jørgens Hospital** (St George's Hospital), whose assorted dwellings are ranged around a paved courtyard, tells the tale of the Norwegian fight against leprosy. The disease first appeared in Scandinavia in Viking times and became especially prevalent in the coastal districts of western Norway, with around three percent of the population classified as lepers in the early nineteenth century. The hospital specialized in the care of lepers, assuming a more proactive role from 1830, when a series of Norwegian medics tried to find a cure for the disease. The most successful of them was **Armauer Hansen**, who in 1873 was the first person to identify the leprosy bacillus. The last lepers left St Jørgens in 1946 and the hospital has been left untouched, the small rooms off the central gallery revealing the patients' humble living quarters. Also on display are medical implements and a few gruesome sketches and paintings of sufferers alongside their desperate life stories. Dating from 1702, the adjoining hospital **chapel** is delightfully homely, its rickety, creaking timbers holding a domineering pulpit topped off by half a dozen folksy cherubs and an altarpiece decorated with yet more cherubs and some dainty scrollwork. The two altar paintings are crude but appropriate – *Jesus and the Ten Lepers* and *The Canaanite's Daughter Healed*.

## Lille Lungegårdsvann: Bergen's art galleries

Bergen's attractively landscaped central lake, **Lille Lungegårdsvann**, is a focus for summertime festivals and parades, and its southern side is flanked by no fewer than five art galleries, four of which comprise the excellent **Bergen Kunstmuseum**. Taken together, these four galleries hold an outstanding collection of Norwegian art and they have the same opening hours and a common admission fee; the other, separate gallery, the **Bergen Kunsthall** is devoted to temporary exhibitions of contemporary art.

Also on the southern side of the lake, behind the galleries on Nygårdsgaten, is the **Grieghallen** concert hall, a large modern edifice that serves as the main venue for the annual Bergen International Festival (see p.206).

### Bergen Kunstmuseum – Lysverket

Rasmus Meyers Allé 9 • Mid-May to mid-Sept daily 11am–5pm; mid-Sept to mid-May Tues–Sun 11am–5pm • Joint ticket 100kr • ☏ 55 56 80 00, ⓦ kunstmuseene.no

The easternmost of the lakeside galleries is **Lysverket**, which occupies a distinctive Art Deco/Functionalist building – complete with its own mini-rotunda – that started out as offices for a power company. The gallery spreads over **three floors** and is divided up both thematically and chronologically, which can be a tad confusing, and there's some rotation of the paintings on display too.

#### The ground floor

The ground floor is largely devoted to **temporary exhibitions**, though there is also a separate section on **Nikolai Astrup** (1880–1928), who is generally regarded as the last of the Norwegian Romantics – or at least neo-Romantics: sometimes Astrup's paintings portray a benign and strongly coloured rural idyll, at other times – as in *Kollen* – the Norwegian landscape appears dangerous and malevolent.

#### The first floor

The next floor up has a good sample of the work of **Johan Christian Dahl** (1788–1857; see p.68), one of Norway's finest landscape painters. Several of Dahl's early sketches are exhibited here, but these are crude affairs executed before he hit his artistic stride, whereas his *Bergen Harbour* and *Nordic Landscape with a River* reveal Dahl at his most accomplished. On this floor also are several examples of the work of **Adolph Tidemand** (1814–76) and **Hans Gude** (1825–1903), both of whom specialized in rural scenes populated by idealized versions of Norwegian country folk, and of the influential **Christian Krohg** (1852–1925), whose striking Realism is seen to fine advantage in his *Fight for Survival*, which rails against urban poverty. A final section on this floor holds the Kunstmuseum's modest selection of **old masters**, mostly Dutch and Italian paintings, plus an engaging miscellany of medieval Greek and Russian **icons**.

#### The top floor

The top floor is dedicated to the twentieth century and it's here you'll find a selection of watercolours and oils by the versatile Norwegian **Jakob Weidemann** (1923–2001), whose work was much influenced by French Cubists during the 1940s, though he is now associated with the shimmering, pastel-painted abstracts he churned out in the 1960s. There's also a delightful *Four Sisters* by **Alf Rolfsen** (1895–1979), the disturbing magic realism of **Bjarne Lund** (1896–1931), and a searing *Sisters of Liberty* by **Arne Ekeland** (1908–94). A self-taught painter from Eidsvoll, near Oslo, Ekeland was a committed leftist whose paintings either protest the oppression of the working class or portray a vision of a Socialist utopia – though some do both at the same time. A final section on the same floor displays a small selection of twentieth-century international works, most notably from Picasso, Braque, Ernst and the Bauhaus painter, Paul Klee.

## THE GREAT GIVER: ROLF STENERSEN

Many of the twentieth-century paintings in the Bergen Kunstmuseum collection were bequeathed to the city by **Rolf Stenersen** (1899–1978), one of Norway's most prominent men of letters. Stenersen donated his first art collection to his hometown of Oslo in 1936 (see p.67) and was in a similar giving mood 35 years later, the beneficiary being his adopted town of Bergen. He was something of a Renaissance man – one-time Olympic athlete, financier and chum of Munch – who seems to have had a successful stab at almost everything, even writing some highly acclaimed short stories in the 1930s.

### Bergen Kunstmuseum – Rasmus Meyers Samlinger

Rasmus Meyers Allé 7 • Mid-May to mid-Sept daily 11am–5pm; mid-Sept to mid-May Tues–Sun 11am–5pm • Joint ticket 100kr • ☎ 55 56 80 00, ⓦ kunstmuseene.no

Housed in a large and distinctive building with a pagoda-like roof, the **Rasmus Meyers Samlinger** (Rasmus Meyer Collection) boasts a superb survey of Norwegian art from 1815 to 1915, gifted to the city by one of its old merchant families – the Meyers – and now displayed broadly chronologically on two easily absorbed and well-organized floors. On the ground floor, a string of rooms concentrates on **Norwegian Romanticism**, with Dahl, Gude, Thomas Fearnley and Tidemand much in evidence. There are a couple of period rooms here too, most memorably the Rococo excesses of the **Blumenthal room**, whose fancy stucco work and allegorical wall and ceiling paintings were knocked up in the 1750s for a Bergen merchant by an itinerant Danish artist, one Mathias Blumenthal. The first floor holds examples of the decorative medievalism of Gerhard Munthe (1849–1929), the colourful landscapes of Nikolai Astrup (1880–1928), and the work of **Erik Werenskiold** (1855–1938), who is best known for his colourful illustrations of the folk stories collected by Asbjørnsen and Moe in rural Norway. The stories had already been published several times when Werenskiold and his accomplice **Theodor Kittelsen** (1857–1914) got working on them, but it was they who effectively defined the appearance of the country's various folkloric figures – from trolls onwards – in the popular imagination.

The Rasmus Meyers Samlinger is perhaps best known for its substantial sample of the work of **Edvard Munch** (1863–1944) – if you missed out in Oslo (see p.70 & p.79), this is the place to make amends. There are examples from all Munch's major periods, with the disturbing – and disturbed – works of the 1890s inevitably stealing the spotlight, especially the searing and unsettling *Jealousy*, the fractured *Woman in Three Stages* and the ghoulish *Evening on Karl Johan*.

### Bergen Kunsthall

Rasmus Meyers Allé 5 • Tues–Fri noon–6pm (Thurs till 8pm), Sat & Sun noon–5pm • 50kr • ☎ 55 55 93 10, ⓦ kunsthall.no

The **Bergen Kunsthall** has developed into the city's most imaginative contemporary arts venue with up to three separate exhibitions at any one time. It's all very hit and miss – banal at worst, stunning at best – but no one could say the exhibitions were predictable. Norwegian artists predominate, but there is a leavening of international stuff too.

### Stenersen

Rasmus Meyers Allé 3 • Mid-May to mid-Sept daily 11am–5pm; mid-Sept to mid-May Tues–Sun 11am–5pm • Joint ticket 100kr • ☎ 55 56 80 00, ⓦ kunstmuseene.no

In a glum concrete block, the **Stenersen** gallery specializes in temporary exhibitions of contemporary art, mostly international but with a strong Norwegian showing. The gallery occupies two smallish floors above the ground-floor shop and coffee bar.

### Vestlandske Kunstindustrimuseum

Nordahl Bruns gate 9 • Mid-May to mid-Sept daily 11am–5pm; mid-Sept to mid-May Tues–Sun 11am–5pm • Joint ticket 100kr • ☎ 55 56 80 00, ⓦ kunstmuseene.no

The **Vestlandske Kunstindustrimuseum** (West Norway Decorative Art Museum) occupies the Permanenten building, a whopping Neoclassical-meets-mock-Gothic structure built as a cultural centre in the 1890s. The museum offers a varied exhibition programme with the focus on contemporary craft and design, but the permanent collection seems to lack focus – no matter how it is badged up – being not much more than a hotch-potch of everything from chests, chairs and cupboards to textiles and porcelain.

## Torgalmenningen and the Sjøfartsmonumentet

The broad sweep of pedestrianized **Torgalmenningen** is a suitably handsome setting for the commercial heart of modern Bergen, lined with arcaded shops and department stores and decorated at its Torget end by the vigorous, large-scale granite and bronze **Sjøfartsmonumentet** (Seafarers' Monument), celebrating the city's seafaring traditions. Unveiled in 1950, it sports twelve sculptures on its lower section with two sets of reliefs up above. Its southeast side – nearest the Galleriet shopping centre – bears the inscription **Tiende Århundre** (Tenth Century), the theme being the Vikings' semi-legendary voyages to Vinland (North America). The reliefs depict a Viking ship with its sails hoisted and a meeting between the Norsemen and American Indians; down below there is a Norwegian chieftain with a spear, a *skald* (Norse bard) wearing sheepskin clothing, and a *berserker* (warrior) with a shield on his back. On the monument's southwest side, inscribed **Attende Århundre** (Eighteenth Century), the theme is the rediscovery of Greenland by Bergen seamen, with reliefs of the Norwegian missionary Hans Egede preaching to the Eskimos (Inuit) and a ship being launched while a huge sea serpent writhes in the water beneath it. The northwest side of the monument is dedicated to Bergen's mercantile success in the **Nittende Århundre** (Nineteenth Century). There are sculptures of a wealthy shipowner with a top hat, a rookie merchant seaman and a pilot; the reliefs above show whaling and a scene from a shipyard. The fourth side, facing the fish market, and inscribed **Tjuende Århundre** (Twentieth Century), has the theme of carrying oil and the sculptures depict a young deckhand, a first mate with binoculars and a ship's engineer with a spanner – respectively symbolizing daring, watchfulness and loyalty. One relief up above has a ship with the rising sun behind it (symbolizing hope) and the other depicts the Resurrection in which the drowned souls on the left are resurrected to eternal life by an angel.

## Ole Bulls plass

Pedestrianized **Ole Bulls plass** is the town's main meeting point: locals gather for all sorts of reasons, from first dates to commemorations, at **Den blå stein** (The Blue Stone), a 3m-long rectangular hunk of stone placed here on a cross-lying block by the sculptor Asbjørn Andersen in 1993. Ole Bulls plass also sports a rock pool and fountain, above which stands a jaunty statue of local lad **Ole Bull**, the nineteenth-century virtuoso violinist and heart-throb – his island villa just outside Bergen is a popular day-trip (see p.200). Ole Bulls plass stretches up to the municipal **theatre**, Den Nationale Scene, a curious Art Nouveau building from 1909 that hogs the brow of a hill guarded by a singularly fearsome, saucer-eyed statue of Henrik Ibsen.

## Bergen Museum: De Kulturhistoriske Samlinger

Håkon Sheteligsplass 10 · June–Aug Tues–Fri 10am–4pm, Sat & Sun 11am–4pm; Sept–May Tues–Fri 10am–3pm, Sat & Sun 11am–4pm · 50kr · ☏ 55 58 31 40, ⓦ uib.no/universitetsmuseet

Bergen University hogs the hill at the south end of Christies gate, its sprawling campus zeroing in on the several collections of the **Bergen Museum**. Pride of place here goes to **De Kulturhistoriske Samlinger**, whose large and rambling cultural historical collection includes excellent sections on stave churches, medieval woodcarvings, folk art – most memorably

BRYGGEN    HANDEL

---

**THE ULRIKSBANEN: A BIRD'S-EYE VIEW**

Providing panoramic views over Bergen and its surroundings, the **Ulriksbanen cable car** (daily: May–Sept 9am–9pm; Oct–April 9am–5pm – weather/wind permitting; 145kr return; ☎ 53 64 36 43, ⓦ ulriken643.no) whisks passengers up to the top of **Mount Ulriken**, where there are walks and a café. The cable car's lower terminal is behind the Haukeland Sykehus (hospital) about 6km east of the centre; to get there by public transport, take city bus #2 or #3 (Mon–Fri every 10–20min, Sat & Sun every 20–30min) from Småstrandgaten.

---

several charming coverlets – and St Olav, the patron saint of Norway. In the foyer, look out also for the **Eggjasteinen** (Eggja Stone), dated to between the seventh and ninth centuries and inscribed with one of the longest runes to have survived. Life must have been pretty gloomy – one verse reads: "Over my relatives the wild one cast a corpse wave".

## The Nordnes peninsula

On the south side of Vågen, the hilly **Nordnes peninsula** juts out into the fjord. It takes about fifteen minutes to walk there from Ole Bulls plass – via Klostergaten/Haugeveien – but the effort is perhaps better spent in choosing a different, more southerly, route along the peninsula. This takes you past the charming timber houses and nineteenth-century stone villas of **Skottegaten** and **Nedre Strangehagen** before it cuts through the bluff leading to the old, waterside United Sardine Factories, imaginatively converted into an arts complex, the **USF Verftet Kulturhuset** (see box, p.206); this incorporates a groovy, harbourside café-bar, *Kafe Kippers* (see p.204). From here, it takes about ten minutes more to get to the aquarium.

### Akvariet

Nordnesbakken 4 · Daily: May–Aug 9am–7pm; Sept–April 10am–6pm · May–Aug 200kr; Sept–April 150kr · ☎ 55 55 71 71, ⓦ akvariet.no · City bus #11

Perched on the western tip of the Nordnes peninsula, and set amid a pleasant park, Bergen's **Akvariet** (Aquarium) has penguin and seal hidey-holes as well two tanks packed with carp. The main items of interest are the large glass tanks which encircle a viewing area, each filled with North Sea fish of every conceivable species.

## Gamle Bergen

Nyhavnsveien 4 · Guided tours every hour on the hour: May to Aug daily 11am–3pm · 70kr · ☎ 55 39 43 00, ⓦ bymuseet.no · Take bus #3, #4, #5 or #18 from Torget and ask the driver to put you off

**Gamle Bergen** (Old Bergen), located just off the E16/39 about 4km north of the city centre, is an open-air complex comprising forty wooden houses representative of eighteenth- and nineteenth-century Norwegian architecture. Entry to the site as well as the adjacent park, which stretches down to the water's edge, is free and there's open access, but the **buildings** can only be visited on a **guided tour**. Immaculately maintained, the interiors give a real idea of small-town life, and the anecdotal tour is bound to make you grin. The enduring impression is one of social claustrophobia: everyone knew everyone else's business, grim or scandalous, mundane or bizarre. It was this enforced uniformity that Ibsen loathed and William Heinesen explored in *The Black Cauldron* (see p.419).

## Out from the centre

The lochs, fjords and rocky wooded hills surrounding central Bergen have channelled the city's **suburbs** into long ribbons, which trail off in every direction. These urban outskirts are not in themselves particularly appealing, though they are extraordinarily handsome when viewed from either **Mount Fløyen** (see p.193) or the highest of the

## EDVARD GRIEG

The composer of some of the most popular works in the standard orchestral repertoire, **Edvard Grieg** (1843–1907) was born in Bergen, the son of a saltfish merchant. It was, considering the region's historical dependence on the product, an appropriate background for a man whose romantic compositions have come to epitomize western Norway, or at least an idealized version of it: certainly, Grieg was quite happy to accept the connection, and as late as 1903 he commented that "I am sure my music has the taste of codfish in it." In part this was sincere, but the composer had an overt political agenda too. Norway had not been independent since 1380, and, after centuries of Danish and Swedish rule, its population lacked political and cultural self-confidence – a situation which the Norwegian nationalists of the day, including Ibsen and Grieg, were determined to change. Such was their success that they played a key preparatory role in the build-up to the dissolution of the union with Sweden, and the creation of an independent Norway in 1905.

Musically, it was Grieg's mother, a one-time professional pianist, who egged him on, and at the tender age of 15 he was packed off to the Leipzig Conservatory to study music, much to the delight of his mentor, **Ole Bull** (see p.200). In 1863, Grieg was on the move again, transferring to Copenhagen for another three-year study stint and ultimately returning to Norway an accomplished performer and composer in 1866. The following year he married the Norwegian soprano **Nina Hagerup** (1845–1935), helped to found a musical academy in Oslo and produced the first of ten collections of folk-based *Lyric Pieces* for piano. In 1868, Grieg completed his best-known work, the *Piano Concerto in A minor*, and, in 1869, his *25 Norwegian Folk Songs and Dances*. Thereafter, the composer's output remained mainly songs and solo piano pieces with a strong folkloric influence, even incorporating snatches of traditional songs.

During the 1870s Grieg collaborated with a number of Norwegian writers, including **Bjørnstjerne Bjørnson** and **Henrik Ibsen**, one of the results being his much acclaimed *Peer Gynt* suites and, in 1884, he composed the *Holberg Suite*, written to commemorate the Dano-Norwegian philosopher and playwright, Ludvig Holberg. It is these orchestral suites, along with the piano concerto, for which he is best remembered today. In 1885, now well-heeled and well known, Grieg and his family moved into **Troldhaugen**, the house they had built for them near Bergen. By that time, Grieg had established a pattern of composing during the spring and summer, and undertaking extended performance tours around Europe with his wife during the autumn and winter. This gruelling schedule continued until – and contributed to – his death in Bergen in 1907.

---

seven hills around town, the 642-metre **Mount Ulriken** (see box, p.198). Elsewhere, tucked away among the city's surroundings to the south of the centre, are three prime attractions: **Troldhaugen**, Edvard Grieg's former home; **Lysøen**, Ole Bull's fanciful island villa; and the composer Harald Sæverud's former home at **Siljustøl**. The fourth attraction hereabouts, **Fantoft stave church**, is not really in the same league, but it is a popular target. All four sights are accessible by **public transport** with varying degrees of ease and there are organized excursions too – the tourist office has the details and sells the tickets (see p.202).

## Troldhaugen

Troldhaugveien • Daily: early Jan to April & Oct to mid-Dec 10am–4pm; May–Sept 9am–6pm • 80kr • ☎ 55 92 29 92, ⓦ kunstmuseene.no • Bybanen to Hop station(every 10–20min; 23min; 27kr), from which it's a dull 30min walk along Troldhaugveien – double back from the station and you'll spot the sign to Troldhaugen on the left; by car take the E39 south from the centre and follow the signs

**Troldhaugen** (Hill of the Trolls), about 8km south of the city centre off Highway 580, was the lakeside home of **Edvard Grieg** (see box above) for the last 22 years of his life – though "home" is something of an exaggeration, as he spent several months every year touring the concert halls of Europe. Norway's only composer of world renown, Grieg has a good share of commemorative monuments in Bergen – a statue in the city park and the Grieghallen concert hall to name but two – but it's here that you get a sense of the man, an immensely likeable and much-loved figure of leftish opinions and disarming modesty: "I make no pretensions of being in the class with Bach, Mozart

> ### RECITALS AT TROLDHAUGEN
>
> Troldhaugen offers a top-ranking programme of **Grieg concerts**, held in the Troldsalen, throughout the summer both at lunchtimes (early June to Sept 1 daily; 30min; 100kr) and in the evening (mid-June to mid-Aug 2 weekly; 1hr; 220kr). For evening performances free buses leave from near the tourist office (see p.202) one hour before the concert begins. Tickets can be bought online (⦿ kunstmuseene.no) or from the tourist office, but are snapped up quickly.

and Beethoven," he once wrote, "Their works are eternal, while I wrote for my day and generation."

A visit begins at the **museum**, where Grieg's life and times are exhaustively chronicled, and a short film provides yet further insights. From here, it's a brief walk to the **house**, a pleasant and unassuming villa built in 1885, and still pretty much as Grieg left it, with a jumble of photos, manuscripts and period furniture. Grieg didn't, in fact, compose much in the house, but preferred to walk round to a tiny **hut** he had built just along the shore. The hut has survived, but today it stands beside a modern concert hall, the **Troldsalen**, where there are recitals of Grieg's works in the summer (see box above). The bodies of Grieg and his wife – the singer Nina Hagerup – are inside a curious **tomb** blasted into a rock face overlooking the lake, and sealed with twin memorial stones; it's only a couple of minutes' walk off from the main footpath, but few people venture out to this beautiful, melancholic spot.

## Ole Bull's villa

Lysøen • Villa: mid-May to Aug Mon–Sat noon–4pm, Sun 11am–5pm; Sept Sun noon–4pm • 40kr • ☎ 56 30 90 77, ⦿ lysoen.no • Bybanen to Nesttun station (every 10–20min; 25min; 27kr), then bus #62 (Mon–Fri every 1–2hr, Sat 2 daily, no Sun service; check times before you set out) to Buena, 100m from Buena Kai (quay); from here passenger ferries run to Lysøen (hourly on the hour when the villa is open; last ferry back from the island at 4.30pm, 5.30pm on Sun; 10min; 60kr return) • By car and ferry head south out of Bergen on the E39, then take Highway 580 to Lagunen followed by Highway 546 to Fanal; at Fanal fork onto Highway 163 to Buena Kai and catch the passenger ferry

Around 25km south of Bergen, the leafy, hilly little island of **Lysøen** boasts the eccentrically ornate summer **villa** of the violinist **Ole Bull** (1810–80), which, like Grieg's home, has been turned into a museum packed with biographical bits and pieces. With its onion dome and frilly trelliswork, Bull's villa was supposed to break with what the man felt to be the dour architectural traditions of Norway, but whether it works or not is difficult to say – for one thing, the arabesque columns and scrollwork of the capacious music hall-cum-main room look muddled rather than inventive. Bull may have chosen to build in a foreign style, but he was a prominent member of that group of nineteenth-century artists and writers, the **Norwegian Romanticists**, who were determined to revive the country's traditions – his special contribution being the promulgation of its folk music. He toured America and Europe for several decades, his popularity as a sort of nineteenth-century Mantovani dented neither by his fervent utopian socialism, nor by some of his eccentric remarks: asked who taught him to play the violin, he replied "The mountains of Norway". Then again, people were inclined to overlook his faults because of his engaging manner and stunning good looks – smelling salts were kept on hand during his concerts to revive swooning women, and were much in use. The hourly **guided tour** of the house is perhaps a little too reverential for its own good, but the island's wooded footpaths, laid out by Bull himself, make for some energetic walks afterwards. Maps of the island are given away free at the house, from where it's a stiff, steep but short walk over the hill to **Lysevågen**, a sheltered cove where you can go for a dip.

## Siljustøl Museum

Siljustølveien 50, Rådal • Late June to mid-Sept Sun noon–4pm • 60kr • ☎ 55 92 29 92, ⦿ kunstmuseene.no • Bybanen to Nesttun station (every 10–20min; 25min; 27kr), then bus #60, #61 or #62 to Rådalskrysset (ask the driver to put you off), from where it's a 15min walk

• By car drive south out of Bergen on the E39, then take Highway 580 to Lagunen, where you pick up Highway 179 at the roundabout; follow the signs from Highway 179

Bergen's own **Harald Sæverud** (1897–1992) was a classical composer of some European standing, whose oeuvre included a hatful of symphonies and concertos. Among Norwegians he was, however, more popular for the anti-Nazi music he wrote during the German occupation of World War II and his gallows humour. After his death, his old home and studio at Siljustøl, about 12km south of Bergen, were turned into the **Siljustøl Museum**, where you can nose around his life and musical times. Sæverud's music is showcased in a series of **summer concerts** (tickets from Bergen tourist office) and the house, a large stone structure dating from the 1930s, is surrounded by wooded parkland, crisscrossed by footpaths.

## Fantoft stavkirke

Fantoftvegen • Mid-May to mid-Sept daily 10.30am–6pm • 45kr • ☎ 55 28 07 10, ⌨ fantoftstavkirke.com • Bybanen to Paradis (every 10–20min; 21min; 27kr), then a 25min walk: from the station walk up Birkelundsbakken hill to the car park, from which a steep path leads up to the church • By car take Highway 582 south from the centre and follow the signs

**Fantoft stavkirke** (Fantoft stave church), about 5km south of downtown Bergen, was actually moved here from a tiny village on the Sognefjord in the 1880s. The first owner, a government official, had the structure revamped in the style of Borgund stave church (see p.173), complete with dragon finials, high-pitched roofs and an outside gallery, though in fact it's unlikely that the original church looked much like Borgund at all. This is, however, somewhat irrelevant as the Fantoft church was burnt to the ground in 1992 by a supposed Satanist. Extraordinarily, the then owner didn't surrender, but had a replica of the destroyed church built instead and it stands today, a finely carved affair with disconcertingly fresh timbers, set among beech and pine trees.

**4**

## ARRIVAL AND DEPARTURE
**BERGEN AND AROUND**

### BY PLANE
**Bergen airport** is 20km south of the city at Flesland and it's connected to the centre by Flybussen (every 15–30min: Mon–Fri 7.30am–11pm, Sat 10am–6pm, Sun noon–10pm; 45min; 100kr one-way, 160kr return; ⌨ flybussen. no). In the city centre, these Flybussen pull in at the bus station, on Ole Bulls plass, and at the tourist office before terminating at the harbourfront *Radisson Blu Royal Hotel*, on the Bryggen. Taxis from the rank outside the airport arrivals hall charge around 350–400kr for the same trip. Note that eventually the Bybanen (Light Railway) will be extended to the airport, though no definite date has yet been fixed.

### BY TRAIN
**Bergen train station** (⌨ nsb.no) is located on Strømgaten, from where it's a 5–10min walk west to Bergen's main harbour, Vågen, via the pedestrianized shopping street, Marken.
Destinations Finse (4 daily; 2hr 20min); Geilo (4daily; 3hr); Myrdal (4 daily; 1hr 50min); Oslo (4 daily; 6hr 30min); Voss (4 daily; 1hr 10min).

### BY BUS
**Bergen bus station** is inside the Bergen Storsenter shopping mall, on Strømgaten, metres from the train station and a 5–10min walk from Bergen's main harbour. Nor-Way Bussekspress runs the following services:

Fjordekspressen (#430) to: Ålesund (2 daily; 10hr); Førde (5 daily; 3hr 30min); Grotli (1 daily; 8hr); Loen (3 daily; 6hr 20min); Lom (1 daily; 9hr); Otta (1 daily; 10hr); Skei (5 daily; 4hr 30min); Stryn (3 daily; 6hr 30min).

Haukeliekspressen (#180) to: Norheimsund (2–3 daily; 1hr 30min); Odda (2–3 daily; 3hr 30min); Oslo (2–3 daily; 10hr 30min); Utne (2–3 daily; 2hr 50min).

Kystbussen (#400) to: Haugesund (every 2hr; 3hr); Stavanger (every 1–2hr; 5hr, 5hr 45min via Haugesund).

Sognebussen (#450) to: Flåm (4–5 daily; 3hr); Gudvangen (4–5 daily; 2hr 35min); Sogndal (4–5 daily; 4hr 30min); Voss (4–5 daily; 1hr 50min).

### BY BOAT
**Hurtigbåt passenger express boats** (⌨ fjord1.no or ⌨ norled.no) to and from Haugesund, Stavanger and the Hardangerfjord, as well as those from Sognefjord and Nordfjord, line up on the south side of the Vågen at the Strandkaiterminalen.

Destinations Ålesund (Mon–Fri 1 daily; 8hr 30min); Balestrand (2 daily; 4hr); Flåm (May–Sept 1 daily; 5hr 25min); Florø (1–2 daily; 3hr 30min); Haugesund (2–3 daily; 3hr); Rosendal (2 daily; 2hr); Sogndal (1 daily; 4hr 40min); Stavanger (2 daily; 4hr 30min).

**Hurtigruten** Bergen is the home port of the Hurtigruten coastal boat (☎ 810 30 000, ⌨ hurtigruten.com), which docks at the Hurtigruteterminalen, on the south side of the city centre, off Nøstegaten, about 900m due south of the main harbour. Hurtigruten sailing schedules are listed in Basics (see p.30).

**International ferries** Fjord Line (☎ 51 46 40 99, ⓦ fjordline.com) international car ferries from Stavanger and Hirsthals in Denmark dock at the Skoltegrunnskaien, near the tip of the main harbour, Vågen.

### BY CAR

**Driving** If you're driving into Bergen, note that a toll (15kr) is charged on all vehicles entering the city centre, but you don't have to stop – it's levied electronically with cameras reading number plates. There's no charge for driving out of the city. In an attempt to keep the city centre relatively free of traffic, there's a confusing and none-too-successful one-way system in operation, supplemented by rigorously enforced on-street parking restrictions.

**Parking** Outside peak periods, on-street parking is free but difficult to find, whereas during peak periods (Mon–Fri 8am–5pm, Sat 8am–10am) it's both hard to find and metered for a maximum of 2hr at 15kr/hr. Your best bet, therefore, is to make straight for one of the central car parks; the largest is the 24hr Bygarasjen, a short walk from the city centre, behind the Storsenter shopping mall and bus station. Charges here are heavily discounted – it costs just 130kr for 24hr. The 24hr Rosenkrantz P-Hus, on Rosenkrantzgaten, is much handier for the harbourfront, but charges are higher: 24hr costs 200kr. To get to the Rosenkrantz P-Hus, follow the international ferry signs until you pick up the car park signs.

**Car rental** All the major international car rental companies have offices in town and/or at the airport, including Avis at Lars Hilles gate 20 (☎ 55 55 39 55); and Europcar, at the airport (☎ 55 22 73 20). For the full list see under "Bilutleie" in the *Yellow Pages*.

### INFORMATION AND ACTIVITIES

**Tourist office** Torget (May & Sept daily 9am–8pm; June–Aug daily 8.30am–10pm; Oct–April Mon–Sat 9am–4pm; ☎ 55 55 20 00, ⓦ visitbergen.com). Handily located beside the harbour, the tourist office supplies free copies of the exhaustive *Bergen Guide*, sells the Bergen Card (see box, p.190), provides listings leaflets, changes foreign currency, and sells train, city-tour and fjord-tour tickets. They also have oodles of free information about the whole of the

western fjords and operate a last-minute, in-person accommodation reservation service. In high season, expect long queues.

**Hiking** The DNT-affiliated Bergen Turlag, Tverrgaten 4–6 (Mon–Wed & Fri 10am–4pm, Thurs 10am–6pm, Sat 10am–2pm; ☎ 55 33 58 10, ⓦ bergen-turlag.no), will advise on hiking trails in the region, sells hiking maps and arranges guided walks.

### GETTING AROUND

Most of Bergen's key attractions are located in the city centre, which is compact enough to be readily explored **on foot**. For outlying sights and accommodation, however, you may well need to use the city's public transport network, which is coordinated by **Skyss** (☎ 177, ⓦ skyss.no).

**By bus** Bergen's buses reach into every corner of the city and its environs. The hub of the network is the bus station, in the Storsenter shopping mall on Strømgaten. Flat-fare tickets for travel within the city limits cost 27kr; they are available from the driver.

**By Bybanen** Beginning in the city centre at the junction of Olav Kyrres gate and Kaigaten/Starvhusgate, Bergen's one-line Bybanen (Light Railway) stretches south into the suburbs as far as Nesttun, a distance of 10km. Flat-fare tickets cost 27kr and there are trains every 10min or so; tickets are

---

### GUIDED TOURS IN BERGEN

**Guided tours** of Bergen and its surroundings are big business and the tourist office (see above) has a flood of details. In the city itself, the most popular choice is City Sightseeing Bergen's **On&Off Sightseeing Bus**, which takes in all the central sights, including the aquarium and Torget (every 30min; 150kr; ☎ 97 78 18 88, ⓦ citysightseeing-bergen.net). Troldhaugen (see p.199) and Fantoft stave church (see p.201) are also on many guided tours, including those offered by **Norled** (May–Sept 1 daily; 350kr; ☎ 55 23 88 87, ⓦ norled.no).

There are lots of fjord sightseeing trips too, with **Fjord Tours** (ⓦ fjord-tours.com), one of the leading companies, offering a wide range of tours including "Norway in a Nutshell" (see box, p.207) and the whirlwind "Hardanger in a Nutshell" (May–Oct 1 daily; 10hr; 820kr). A further, rather more economical option is Rødne Fjord Cruise's Hurtigbåt passenger express boat excursion from Bergen to **Rosendal** (see p.212) and its manor house (May–Sept 1–2 daily; 7.5hr; 500kr; ☎ 51 89 52 70, ⓦ rodne.no). All tours can be **booked** either direct with the company concerned or at Bergen tourist office.

available from the automatic machines at every station. There are plans to extend the railway as far as the airport.

**By passenger ferry** Within Bergen, two passenger ferries offer useful short cuts: one bobs across Vågen between Munkebryggen, on Carl Sundts gate, and a point near the Bryggens Museum on the Bryggen (Mon–Fri 7am–4pm; 20kr); the second links Torget with the Nordnes peninsula, docking not far from the Akvariet (late May to Aug daily 10am–6pm; 70kr return, 45kr one-way).

**By taxi** The main taxi company is Bergen Taxi (☎ 07000).

## ACCOMMODATION

Finding **budget accommodation** in Bergen can be a bit of a problem at the height of the season, but is almost always straightforward during the rest of the year. There are three hostels, a choice of guesthouses, and some of the central hotels are surprisingly good value. Also among the better deals are the rooms in private houses – or **private rooms** – that can be reserved through the tourist office. The vast majority provide self-catering facilities and some are fairly central, though most are stuck out in the suburbs; prices are in the region of 500–700kr per double per night. They are popular, so in summer you'll need to arrive at the tourist office early to secure one for the night.

### HOTELS

★ **Clarion Collection Havnekontoret** Slottsgaten 1 ☎ 55 60 11 00, ⓦ choicehotels.no. Prestigious development in which Bergen's former harbour office has been imaginatively converted into a deluxe hotel. The public areas are capacious and although the emphasis is on the modern, the original 1920s main entrance, featuring vaulted ceiling and intricate murals, has been preserved. The best of the guest rooms, where browns and creams predominate, have harbour views. There are even wider views from the tower on top of the hotel, but guests need to get the key from reception. Rates (usually) include an evening buffet meal. 1600kr, sp/r 1200kr

**Clarion Hotel Admiral** Carl Sundts gate 9 ☎ 55 23 64 00, ⓦ clarionadmiral.com. Housed in a big old building that dates back to 1906, this substantial chain hotel is a popular spot: the rooms are fairly routine, but the pick look out over the harbour and have mini-balconies, which is a real plus. 1800kr, sp/r 1350kr

**Grand Hotel Terminus** Zander Kaaes gate 6 ☎ 55 21 25 00, ⓦ ght.no. There was a time when tweed-jacketed, salmon-hunting gentlemen from Britain headed straight for the *Grand* as soon as they arrived in Bergen – and not just because the hotel is next door to the train station. Those ritzy days are long gone, but the hotel, which opened in 1928, does make the most of its public areas, where quasi-baronial flourishes, notably the extensive wood panelling, chandeliers and stained glass, survive in good condition. Breakfasts are very good too, but the bedrooms vary considerably and some are rather tired and poky: if you can, have a look before you commit. Interestingly, Roald Amundsen spent his last night on land here at the *Grand* on Sunday 17 June, 1928: the next day he set out by flying boat on his ill-fated expedition to save a group of Italians who had become stranded in the Arctic; he never made it. 1790kr, sp/r 1290kr

★ **Hotel Park** Harald Hårfagres gate 35 ☎ 55 54 44 00, ⓦ hotelpark.no. This excellent hotel occupies two handsome, late nineteenth-century townhouses on the edge of the city centre near the university. The charming interior is painted in soft pastel colours and the public areas are dotted with antiques. The bedrooms are smart, neat and appealing. It's very popular, so reservations are advised. 1650kr

**Radisson Blu Royal Hotel** Bryggen ☎ 55 54 30 00, ⓦ radissonblu.com. Full marks here to the architects, who have built a smart hotel behind a brick facade that mirrors the style of the old timber buildings that surround it. All facilities – pool, health club and so forth – plus attractively appointed rooms in a great Bryggen location. 1800kr

**Thon Hotel Rosenkrantz** Rosenkrantzgaten 7 ☎ 55 30 14 00, ⓦ thonhotels.com. Proficient, mid-range chain hotel in an oldish building just behind the Bryggen. Has everything you'll need, including free coffee and internet access in the foyer, though the rooms could do with a refit (one is promised) and it's worth avoiding the ones that face the interior courtyard, insisting instead on a room that overlooks the Bryggen and, on the top floors, the harbour; there's no extra charge. Better-than-average buffet breakfast too. Shame about the aluminium window-frames stuck in the old facade. 1600kr, sp/r 1200kr

### GUESTHOUSES

★ **Skansen Pensjonat** Vetrlidsallmenningen 29 ☎ 55 31 90 80, ⓦ skansen-pensjonat.no. This pleasant little guesthouse occupies a nineteenth-century stone house of elegant proportions just above – and up the hairpins from – the terminus of the Fløibanen funicular railway, near Torget: it's a great location – one of the most beguiling parts of town. The pension has eight guest rooms, most of which have shared facilities, and all are very homely. A snip at 750kr

**Skuteviken Gjestehus** Skutevikens smalgang 11 ☎ 93 46 71 63, ⓦ skutevikenguesthouse.com. Set amid one of the oldest parts of town, a huddle of narrow, cobbled lanes and bright-white clapboard houses, this excellent guesthouse offers five tastefully renovated apartments, all wood floors, smashing modern bathrooms and neat modern furniture. Each apartment has a living room, kitchenette, bathroom and bedroom. Free wi-fi too. Parking near by on Skutevikstorget. A real snip at 450kr

**4**

★ **To Søstre Gjestehus** Nedre Stølen 4c ☎ 98 29 92 11, ⊕ tosostre.no. This delightful, family-run guesthouse – "The Two Sisters" – is really rather special, a lovingly renovated old timber house with three tastefully decorated, en-suite rooms in a modern rendition of period style – the Attic Room is just fantastically cosy. On a narrow cobbled lane among a small pocket of wooden houses close to the Bryggen. 1320kr

### HOSTELS

**Bergen Vandrerhjem Montana** Johan Blyttsveien 30, Landås ☎ 55 20 80 70, ⊕ montana.no. This large and comfortable HI hostel occupies lodge-like premises in the hills overlooking the city. Great views and great breakfasts, plus self-catering facilities, a café, a laundry and internet access. Has dorm accommodation, family rooms and doubles – almost all of which are en suite. The hostel is 6km east of the centre, 15min on local bus #12 from the bus station – ask the driver to put you off and it's a 200m walk from the bus stop. Popular with school parties, who are (usually) housed in a separate wing. Dorms (in 4/5-bunk rooms) 225kr, doubles 640kr

**Bergen YMCA Hostel** Nedre Korskirkealmenning 4 ☎ 55 60 60 55, ⊕ bergenhostel.com. Comparatively neat and trim hostel right in the centre of the city, a short walk from Torget. Has room for a couple of hundred guests, but fills up fast in summer. Facilities include self-catering and a laundry. Open all year. Dorms 190kr, doubles (all en suite) 400kr

**Intermission Hostel** Kalfarveien 8 ☎ 55 30 04 00, ⊕ intermissionhostel.no. Christian-run, private hostel in a two-storey, oldish wooden building, a 5min walk from the train station – just beyond one of the old city gates. There's a self-catering kitchen, laundry and limited parking. Open mid-June to mid-Aug. Breakfast costs 30kr. Dorms (mixed) 190kr

## EATING

Bergen has a first-rate supply of **restaurants**, the pick of which focus on seafood – the city's main gastronomic asset. The pricier tourist haunts are concentrated on the Bryggen, but these should not be dismissed out of hand – several are very good indeed. Other, marginally less expensive, restaurants dot the side streets behind the Bryggen and there's another cluster on and around Engen. Many locals, however, tend to eat more economically and informally at the city's many **café-bars** that are dotted all over the city centre – as are the city's coffee houses.

### MARKETS

**Fish market** Torget. For picnics, the fish market offers everything from dressed crab, prawn rolls and smoked-salmon sandwiches to pickled herring and canned caviar. June–Aug daily 7am–5pm; Sept–May Mon–Sat 7am–4pm.

**Kjøttbasaren** Vetrlidsallmenningen. A handful of stalls sell fresh produce and cooked snacks in the Kjøttbasaren (covered market), the long and narrow, fancily gabled building at the Torget end of the Bryggen. Mon–Fri 10am–5pm, Sat 9am–4pm.

### CAFÉS AND COFFEE HOUSES

**Godt Brød** Nedre Korskirkealmenning 12 ☎ 55 32 80 00; Vestre Torggata 2 ☎ 55 56 33 10, ⊕ bakeverksted .no. The Nedre Korskirkealmenning branch is an eco-bakery and café (in that order), with great bread plus coffee and made-to-order sandwiches; at the Vestre Torrgate branch the order is reversed – it's a café first and then a bakery. Both branches Mon–Fri 7am–6pm, Sat 8am–5pm, Sun 10am–5pm.

★ **Det Lille Kaffekompaniet** Nedre Fjellsmau 2 ☎ 55 32 92 72, ⊕ kaffekompaniet.no. Many locals swear by the coffee here, reckoning it to be the best north of the Alps. Great selection of teas too, plus delicious cakes and funky premises – just one medium-sized room in an old building, two flights of steps above the Fløibanen funicular terminal. Mon–Fri 10am–10pm, Sat noon–6pm, Sun noon–10pm.

### CAFÉ-BARS

**Café Opera** Engen 18 ☎ 55 23 03 15, ⊕ cafeopera.org. Inside a white wooden building with plant-filled windows, a fashionable crowd gathers to drink beer and good coffee. They also rustle up a good line in snacks and light meals from as little as 90kr. DJ sounds and live bands at the weekend too. Mon 11am–12.30am, Tues–Sat 11am–3am, Sun noon–12.30am.

**Kafe Kippers** USF Verftet Kulturhuset, Georgernes Verft ☎ 55 31 00 60, ⊕ usf.no. Part of the city's leading contemporary arts complex, this laidback café-bar on the Nordnes peninsula serves inexpensive, canteen-style food, with mains about 120kr; occasionally rustles up great barbecues too. With its sea views and terrace, this is *the* place to come on a sunny evening when the crowds gather, especially when there's some live music or DJ sounds. Also puts on an ambitious programme of concerts, art-house films and contemporary plays. Mon–Thurs 11am–11pm, Fri 11am–midnight, Sat noon–midnight, Sun noon–11pm.

**Landmark** Rasmus Meyers Allé 5 ☎ 55 55 93 10, ⊕ kunsthall.no. Café-bar with an arty atmosphere and a student vibe – dig that 1960s decor. Part of the Bergen Kunsthall gallery (see p.195) with regular exhibitions of contemporary art on the floor up above. Snacks and light meals Tues–Sat noon–5pm. Tues–Fri noon–6pm (Thurs till 8pm), Sat & Sun noon–5pm.

**Pingvinen** Vaskerelven 14 ☎ 55 60 46 46, ⊕ pingvinen .no. "The Penguin" is a lively and informal café-restaurant with a long bar, a battery of bar stools and bare-brick walls. The menu concentrates on traditional Norwegian food with such delights as fish pie, reindeer and meatballs costing from as little as 80kr. Kitchen closes down at 10pm, after which the place morphs into a bar. Sun–Fri 1pm–3am, Sat noon–3am.

### RESTAURANTS

★ **Boha** Vaskerelven 6 ❶55 31 31 60, ⓦboha.no. Smooth and polished restaurant kitted out in attractive modern style and offering a small(ish) but extremely well-chosen menu. Main courses – for example pan-fried skate with leek compote – hover around 260kr. Mon–Thurs 4–10pm, Fri 4–11pm, Sat 5–11pm.

**Bryggeloftet og Stuene** Bryggen 11 ❶55 30 20 70, ⓦbryggeloftet.no. A tourist favourite, this restaurant may be a little old-fashioned – the decor is too folksy for its own good – but they do serve a very good range of seafood: delicious, plainly served meals usually with a good wallop of potatoes. Elk, reindeer and other Nordic beasts too, plus occasional diversions into that old Norwegian favourite, *lutefisk*. Main courses around 250kr, less at lunchtime. Mon–Sat 11am–11.30pm, Sun 1–11.30pm.

**Enhjørningen** Bryggen ❶55 30 69 50, ⓦenhjorningen.no. Smart and fairly formal second-floor restaurant in wonderful premises – all low beams, creaking floors and old oil paintings on the walls. The prices match the decor, with most main courses approaching 300kr, but the seafood is indeed outstanding. A tourist favourite. Mon–Sat 4–11pm.

**Escalon** Vetrlidsallmenningen 21 ❶55 32 90 99, ⓦescalon.no. Cheery basement tapas-bar-cum-restaurant, where they serve authentic Spanish food at competitive prices – tapas cost 60kr and upwards. Metres from the lower terminus of the Fløibanen. Mon–Fri 3pm–1am, Sat 1pm–1am, Sun 3pm–1am.

**Hanne pa Hoyden** Fosswinckelsgate 18 ❶55 32 34 32, ⓦhannepaahoeyden.wordpress.com. Sleek and smart restaurant with a period-vintage look where the nouvelle food has garnered all sorts of rave reviews – try for example the chicken with celery heads and cherries (for 310kr). Mon–Sat 11.30am–midnight; kitchen closes at 10pm.

**Naboen Restaurant** Sigurdsgate 4 ❶55 90 02 90, ⓦgrannen.no. Easy-going, pleasantly presented restaurant featuring a lively, inventive menu – including Swedish specialities and, on occasion, the likes of kangaroo and ostrich. Offers a good range of fish dishes, including unusual offerings such as sea bass with blood-orange sauce; the cod is especially good. When you've finished eating, you can venture down to the basement bar. Reckon on 250kr for a main course. Restaurant Mon–Sat 4–11pm, Sun 4–10pm; bar Mon–Thurs & Sun till midnight, Fri & Sat till 1am.

**Potetkjelleren** Kong Oscars gate 1a ❶55 32 00 70, ⓦpotetkjelleren.no. In a cosy, vaulted basement, this smart little restaurant offers contemporary cuisine with lots of Norwegian flourishes – with the likes of Arctic char with petit pois and horseradish sauce costing in the region of 290kr. Mon–Sat 4pm–1am, kitchen till 10pm.

## DRINKING AND NIGHTLIFE

As a general rule, Bergen's café-bars (see opposite)– and indeed some of its restaurants – provide the city's more appealing drinking destinations, but there is a scattering of late-night bars and clubs too, the best of which attract an arty/boho crew.

### BARS AND CLUBS

**Garage** Christies gate 14 ❶55 32 19 80, ⓦgarage.no. Very busy place catering to a mixed crowd. Two bars on the ground floor, and a live music area in the basement – mostly rock and pop (and lots of hair). Packed at the weekend. At the corner of Nygårdsgaten. Mon–Sat 1pm–3am, Sun 5pm–3am.

**Logen** Øvre Ole Bulls plass 6 ❶55 23 20 15. Grooviest bar in the city centre: climb the stairs past the entrance to the Logen Teater, and you'll finally reach this pint-sized bar,

all subdued lighting and rickety fittings – plus a great view over Ole Bulls plass from the terrace. Über-cool clientele. Daily from 6pm till the wee hours, Sun from 8pm.

**Whisky Bar** Grand Hotel Terminus, Zander Kaaes gate 6 ❶55 21 25 00, ⓦght.no. With more whiskies than could possibly be good for you, this discrete/discreet bar is a sedate affair ensconced within the really rather fetching 1920s surroundings – stained glass, wood panelling and so forth – of the *Grand Hotel*. Mon–Sat 5pm to midnight.

## PERFORMING ARTS AND CINEMA

### CINEMA

**Bergen Kino** Neumanns gate 3 ❶55 56 90 50, ⓦbergenkino.no. The biggest cinema in town, with no fewer than thirteen screens, showing both mainstream and independent movies. Neumanns gate is a 5min

walk from Ole Bulls plass.

**Magnus Barfot Kino** Magnus Barfots gate 12 ❶55 56 90 50, ⓦbergenkino.no. This cinema works in tandem with Bergen Kino, just along the street, but it's smaller with just five screens.

## THE BERGEN INTERNATIONAL FESTIVAL

Bergen takes justifiable pride in its **performing arts**, especially during the **Festspillene i Bergen** (Bergen International Festival; ☎ 55 21 06 30, ⓦ fib.no), held over two weeks at the end of May and the beginning of June, and presenting an extensive programme of music, ballet, folklore and theatre. The principal venue for the festival is the **Grieghallen**, on Edvard Griegs plass (see below), where you can pick up programmes, tickets and information; these are also available from the tourist office. The city's contemporary arts centre, the **USF Verftet Kulturhuset**, down on the Nordnes peninsula (☎ 55 30 74 10, ⓦ usf.no), contributes to the festival by hosting **Nattjazz** (☎ 55 30 72 50, ⓦ nattjazz.no), a prestigious and long-established international jazz festival held over the same period.

### CLASSICAL MUSIC

**Grieghallen** Edvard Griegs plass; tickets ☎ 55 21 61 50, ⓦ grieghallen.no. The city's main concert hall offers a wide-ranging programme of performing arts – everything from rock concerts to theatre and dance. The Bergen Filharmoniske Orkester (ⓦ harmonien.no) performs here regularly too.

**Troldhaugen** Troldhaugveien ☎ 55 92 29 92, ⓦ kunstmuseene.no. Throughout the summer, Grieg concerts are performed at the composer's old home (see box, p.200).

### THEATRE

**Den Nationale Scene** Engen ☎ 55 23 40 08, ⓦ dns.no. Bergen's main theatre offers a wide range of performances on several stages. Most productions are, as you would expect, in Norwegian, but there are occasional appearances by English-speaking troupes.

### SHOPPING

**Norli** Torgalmenningen 7 ☎ 55 30 24 50; Torgalmenningen 8 ☎ 55 21 42 80; ⓦ norli.no. Easily the best bookshop in town, Norli has a competent range of English titles as well as a wide selection of Norwegian hiking and road maps. There's also a smaller branch across the street at no.8.

Both branches: Mon–Fri 9am–8pm, Sat 9am–4pm.

**Vinmonopolet** Bergen Storsenter, Strømgarten. There is a large branch of this state-owned liquor store in the city's main shopping mall. Mon–Thurs 10am–6pm, Fri 9am–6pm, Sat 9am–3pm.

### DIRECTORY

**Dentists** Emergency dental care is available at Vestre Strømkai 19 (Mon–Fri 6–8.30pm, Sat & Sun 3.30–8.30pm; ☎ 55 56 87 17).

**Internet** Free at the main city library, Bergen Bibliotek, on Strømgaten, immediately in front of the Bergen Storsenter shopping centre (☎ 55 56 85 00, ⓦ bergenbibliotek.no; Mon–Thurs 10am–8pm, Fri 10am–4.30pm, Sat 10am–4pm).

**Laundry** Coin-operated and service wash at Jarlens Vaskoteque, Lille Øvregate 17, near the funicular (Mon–Fri 10am–6pm, Sat 10am–3pm; ☎ 55 32 55 04).

**Pharmacy** Vitusapotek Nordstjernen, in Bergen Storsenter, by the bus station (Mon–Sat 8am–11pm, Sun 10am–11pm).

**Post office** Bergen's main post office is in the Xhibition shopping centre at the junction of Olav Kyrresgate and Småstrandgaten (Mon–Fri 9am–8pm, Sat 9am–6pm).

# The western fjords

From Bergen, it's a hop, skip and jump over the mountains to the **western fjords**. The most popular initial target is the **Hardangerfjord**, a delightful and comparatively gentle introduction to the wilder terrain that lies beyond, but similarly popular is **Voss**, inland perhaps, but still an outdoor sports centre of some renown. Voss is also a halfway house on the way to the Sognefjord by train, bus or car. By train, it's a short journey from Voss east to **Myrdal**, at the start of a spectacularly dramatic train ride down the Flåmsdal valley to **Flåm**, sitting pretty against the severe shores of the **Aurlandsfjord**, one of the Sognefjord's many subsidiaries; by road, you can head north direct to Flåm along the E16 or stick to Highway 13 as it careers over the mountains bound for **Vik** and **Vangsnes**. Both of these little towns are on the **Sognefjord** and it's this fjord, perhaps above all others, that captivates visitors, its stirring beauty amplified by its sheer size, stretching inland from the coast for some

200km, and including several magnificent arms, most memorably the **Lustrafjord** and the **Fjærlandsfjord**. Beyond, and running parallel, lies the **Nordfjord**, smaller at 120km long and less intrinsically enticing, though its surroundings are more varied with hunks and chunks of the **Jostedalsbreen glacier** visible and visitable nearby. From here, it's another short journey to the splendid **Geirangerfjord** – narrow, sheer and rugged – as well as the forbidding **Norangsdal** valley, with the wild and beautiful **Hjørundfjord** beyond. Skip over a mountain range or two, via the dramatic **Trollstigen**, and you'll soon reach the town of **Åndalsnes**, which boasts an exquisite setting with rearing peaks behind and the tentacular **Romsdalsfjord** in front. From here, it's another shortish journey west to the region's prettiest town, **Ålesund**, whose centre is liberally sprinkled with charming Art Nouveau buildings, partly paid for by Kaiser Wilhelm II.

A suggested western fjord itinerary is given in the Itineraries section (see p.22), which includes several specific targets: **Ulvik** and **Lofthus** are the most appealing bases in the Hardangerfjord; Sognefjord has Flåm and **Balestrand**; the Fjærlandsfjord has **Mundal**; and further north the cream of the crop are **Loen** and Ålesund. Perhaps above all, this is not a landscape to be hurried – there's little point in dashing from fjord to fjord. Stay put for a while, go for at least one hike or cycle ride, and it's then that you'll really appreciate the western fjords in all their grandeur. The sheer size is breathtaking – but then the **geological movements** that shaped the fjords were on a grand scale. During the Ice Age, around three million years ago, the whole of Scandinavia was covered in ice, the weight of which pushed the existing river valleys deeper and deeper to depths well below that of the ocean floor – the Sognefjord, for example, descends to 1250m, ten times deeper than most of the Norwegian Sea. Later, as the ice retreated, it left huge coastal basins that filled with sea water to become the fjords, which the warm Gulf Stream keeps ice-free.

**4**

## ARRIVAL AND GETTING AROUND | THE WESTERN FJORDS

The convoluted topography of the western fjords has produced a dense and complex **public transport** system that is designed to reach all the larger villages and towns at least once every weekday, whether by train, bus, car ferry, Hurtigruten coastal boat or Hurtigbåt passenger express boat. Bear in mind, however, that although there may be a transport connection to the town or village you want to go to, many Norwegian settlements are scattered and you may be in for a long walk after you've arrived – a particularly dispiriting experience if it's raining. We've covered the western fjords region from south to north – from the Hardangerfjord to Sognefjord, Nordfjord, Geirangerfjord, Åndalsnes and Ålesund. There are certain obvious connections – from Bergen to Flåm, and from Geiranger over the Trollstigen to Åndalsnes, for example – but otherwise routes are really a matter of personal choice; the text details the options.

**By train** The western fjords are not well served by train: NSB (ⓦ nsb.no) runs trains to Bergen, Finse and Flåm in the south and Åndalsnes in the north, but for everything in between you're confined to buses and ferries.

**By bus** Long-distance buses are the domain of Nor-Way Bussekspress (ⓦ nor-way.no). Three of their most useful services in the western fjords are the Nordfjordekspressen (#147), linking Lom, Langvatn and Styrn; the

### NORWAY IN A NUTSHELL

Of all the myriad excursions organized by fjordland tour operators, the most trumpeted is the whistle-stop **Norway in a Nutshell**, which can be booked at any tourist office in the region or online at ⓦ norwaynutshell.com. There are several possible itineraries to choose from, but the classic round trip from Bergen takes eight and a half hours, and is an exhausting but exhilarating romp that gives you a taste of the fjords in one day. The tour begins with a train ride to Voss and Myrdal, where you change for the dramatic Flåmsbana branch line down to Flåm. Here, a two-hour cruise heads along the Aurlandsfjord and then the Nærøyfjord to Gudvangen, where you get a bus back to Voss, and the train again to Bergen. You can pick up the tour (and shave an hour and a half off) in Voss for an affordable 705kr: the full excursion from Bergen costs 1045kr.

Haukeliekspressen (#180) linking Bergen and Utne; and the Sognebussen (#450) connecting Voss, Bergen, Gudvangen and Sogndal. A network of local buses supplements these long-distance routes; there are lots of different operators, but one of the largest is Fjord 1 (ⓦ fjord1.no), but not in and around the Hardangerfjord, which is pretty much the preserve of Skyss (ⓦ skyss.no).

**By car** Note the main road east from Bergen to the western fjords – the E16 – is prone to congestion and possesses over twenty tunnels, many of which are horribly noxious. Avoid the E16 east of Bergen if you can, and certainly aim to branch off onto the relatively tunnel-free and much more scenic Highway 7 the first chance you get – about 30km east of the city (see opposite). Bear in mind also that the E39, which cuts an ingenious north–south route across the western edge of the fjords, is potentially useful as a quick way of getting between Bergen and Ålesund.

**By car ferry** Many car ferries shuttle back and forth every hour or two, if not more often, from around 7am in the morning until 10pm at night every day of the week. Car ferry fares are priced according to a nationally agreed sliding scale, with 10min crossings running at around 25kr per person and 61kr per car and driver, 31kr and 85kr respectively for a 25min trip.

**By Hurtigbåt passenger express boat** Hurtigbåt

> **TOP 5 FJORDLAND HOTELS**
> Hotel Ullensvang, Lofthus See p.213
> Walaker Hotell, Solvorn See p.234
> Alexandra Hotel, Loen See p.242
> Union Hotel, Geirainger See p.249
> Brosundet Hotel, Ålesund See p.256

services are usually fairly infrequent – three a day at most. Hurtigbåt fares are fixed individually with prices starting at around 125kr for every hour travelled: the 4hr trip from Bergen to Balestrand, for example, costs 500kr, 685kr to Flåm. Rail-pass holders are often entitled to discounts of up to fifty percent and on some routes there are special excursion/return fare deals – always ask.

Boat timetables and companies Boat timetables are available on the internet, but the problem is that there's no guarantee the companies running the routes one year will be the same the next: the whole network is subject to competitive tendering. At time of writing, most car ferries and Hurtigbåt passenger boats are operated by either Fjord 1 (ⓦ fjord1.no) or Norled (ⓦ norled.no).

**By Hurtigruten** The Hurtigruten coastal boat (ⓦ hurtigruten.com) sails up the west coast from Bergen to Ålesund and beyond (see box, p.30).

## INFORMATION

Every significant village and all the towns in the western fjords has a tourist office and each of them concentrates on local information, usually including details of local hikes and public transport timetables. In addition, an extremely useful synopsis of all facilities, including

public transport services, is provided in the *Fjord Norway Travel Guide*, an annual publication that is available for free from almost every tourist office and is also online at ⓦ fjordnorway.com.

## ACCOMMODATION

**Reservations** At the height of the season, roughly late June to August, vacant rooms of any description can get very thin on the ground and prices start to climb. Therefore, both for peace of mind and to save money, you're far better making reservations either direct or through Fjord Tours, the company that operates the Fjord Pass scheme

(ⓦ fjord-pass.com; see p.28). At other times of the year, you can pretty much come and go as you please.

**Closing months** Note that many hotels and nearly all hostels close for winter – from October, sometimes November, to April or more likely May.

# The Hardangerfjord

To the east of Bergen, the most inviting target is the 180km-long **Hardangerfjord** (ⓦ hardangerfjord.com), whose wide waters are overlooked by a rough, craggy shoreline and a scattering of tiny settlements. At its eastern end the Hardangerfjord divides into several lesser fjords, and it's here you'll find the district's most appealing villages, **Utne**, **Lofthus** and **Ulvik**, each of which has an attractive fjordside setting and at least one an especially good place to stay. To the east of these tributary fjords rises the **Hardangervidda**, a mountain plateau of remarkable, lunar-like beauty and a favourite with Norwegian hikers. The plateau can be reached from almost any direction, but one popular starting point for the extremely fit is Lofthus, with this approach involving a stiff day-long climb up from the fjord.

## ARRIVAL AND DEPARTURE

### BY CAR

**From Bergen and the west** The fastest approach to the Hardangerfjord by bus or car from Bergen is along the E16 via Voss (see p.218), but this is not a particularly enjoyable journey and you're much better off forking onto Highway 7 after about 30km. This is a rattlingly good trip, with the road twisting over the mountains and down the valleys, gliding past thundering waterfalls and around tight bends before racing down to Norheimsund (see below).

**From the north** Arriving from the north, from Voss,

### THE HARDANGERFJORD

Highway 13 is the quickest route to the Hardangerfjord, though you can enliven the journey by turning off onto the old postal road – Highway 572 – which cuts a fine course over hill and dale before hairpinning down into Ulvik.

**From the east and south** Even more dramatic are the routes to the Hardangerfjord from the east and south: both Highway 7 and the E134 thread across the Hardangervidda plateau before sweeping down to the fjord with the latter negotiating the Haukelifjell, one of the region's bleakest and wildest mountain passes.

## GETTING AROUND

**By car and car ferry** Of the two principal car ferries negotiating the Hardangerfjord, one shuttles between Kvanndal, Utne and Kinsarvik, the other links Brimnes with Bruravik, though this will be replaced by a stupendous suspension bridge, which will be completed in the summer of 2013. Ferries are operated by Norled (⊕ norled.no).

**By bus** There are no trains in the Hardangerfjord area, but buses are fairly frequent, allowing you to savour the scenery and get to the three key villages without too much difficulty, except possibly on Sun when services are reduced. The buses are operated by Skyss (⊕ skyss.no).

## Norheimsund

A small-time port and former furniture-making town, **Norheimsund** makes a gallant effort to bill itself as a gateway to the fjords, but in truth it's a modest, middling sort of place and there's precious little reason to hang around: like many fjord settlements, it's the journey to get there that is the main attraction.

## Utne

The tiny hamlet of **UTNE** occupies a splendid location, its huddle of houses and perky country church overlooking the Hardangerfjord from the tip of the rearing peninsula that divides the Hardangerfjord from the Sørfjord. Utne was long dependent on the orchards that still trail along the Sørfjord's sheltered slopes, its inhabitants making enough of a living to support themselves in some comfort, especially when

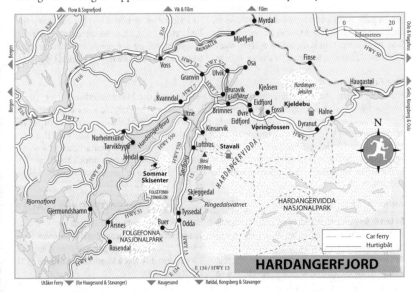

supplemented by fishing and furniture-making: the brightly painted furniture that once hailed from the district made a popular export.

### Hardanger Folkemuseum

May–Aug daily 10am–5pm; Sept–April Mon–Fri 10am–5pm • 70kr • ☎ 53 67 00 40, ⓦ hardangerogvossmuseum.no

Utne's heritage is celebrated at the **Hardanger Folkemuseum**, a five-minute walk north along the fjord from the ferry quay. One of the largest and best-appointed folk museums in the region, its collection features a wide range of displays on various aspects of traditional Hardanger life, from fishing and farming through to fruit-growing and trade. A particular highlight is the large display of local **folk costume** – the women's headdresses hereabouts were among the most elaborate in Norway and a popular subject for the Romantic painters of the nineteenth century, notably Adolph Tidemand and Hans Frederik Gude. There are also some fine examples of the Hardanger fiddle, an instrument much loved by both Ole Bull (see p.200) and Grieg. Outside, an assortment of old wooden buildings – farmhouses, cottages, store houses and so forth – rambles over the steep and rocky hillside behind the museum. The logic of this **open-air section** is hard to fathom, but in summertime, when there are demonstrations of farming and craft skills, things make much more sense. One of the more intriguing buildings is a sixteenth-century dwelling, known as an **Uglenesløa**, whose dark and dingy interior is encased by roughly hewn log walls. When the museum is closed, you can still wander round the open-air section as you please.

### ARRIVAL AND DEPARTURE                                        UTNE

**By car ferry** Utne is the Kvanndal ferry's midway point. The ferry dock is in the heart of the village, a brief walk from both the hotel and the museum.
Destinations Kinsarvik (1 or 2 hourly; 30min); Kvanndal (1 or 2 hourly; 20min).
**By Hurtigbåt passenger express boat** Express boats use the same dock as the car ferry.

Destinations Eidfjord (May–Oct 1 daily; 2hr); Kinsarvik (May–Oct 1 daily; 25min); Lofthus (May–Oct 1 daily; 40min); Norheimsund (May–Oct 1 daily; 50min); Ulvik (May–Oct 1 daily; 1hr 20min).
**By bus** Buses to Utne pull in beside the ferry dock.
Destinations Bergen, via the Kvanndal ferry (3 daily; 3hr); Jondal (1–3 daily; 1hr); Odda (3 daily; 50min).

### ACCOMMODATION AND EATING

**Utne Hotel** ☎ 53 66 64 00, ⓦ utnehotel.no. Straight opposite the ferry dock, the *Utne Hotel* is a very relaxing spot, its public rooms graced by several fine examples of the painted furniture for which the area was once famous. There are 26 rooms, most in the original building, which dates from 1722, though nine are in the annexe. So far so good, but the walls of the rooms in the main house, which are reached by an unusual spiral staircase, are paper-thin – hard luck if you are billeted next to a champion snorer. The hotel restaurant, a panelled dining room, is first-rate, focusing on local, seasonal ingredients; their three-course set dinner costs around 400kr. **1790kr**, sp/r **1390kr**

## The Folgefonna glacier

Running south of Utne, the jagged peninsula separating the Hardangerfjord from the Sørfjord widens and heightens, its upper reaches holding the **Folgefonna Nasjonalpark**. Remote and mountainous, wild and bleak, the park's 545 square kilometres incorporate Norway's third largest glacier, the tentacular **Folgefonna glacier**. Conditions on the glacier are well-nigh perfect for **summer skiing**, both Alpine and Telemark, as well as snowboarding, best arranged with Folgefonn Sommar Skisenter (see opposite). There's one narrow mountain road up to the glacier from the fjordside hamlet of **Jondal**, 33km southwest of Utne.

### ARRIVAL AND INFORMATION                      THE FOLGEFONNA GLACIER

**By bus** Buses from Utne to Jondal (1–3 daily; 1hr) usually connect with the glacier bus – but check times at your hotel or the nearest tourist office.
**By ferry** There are car ferries across the Hardangerfjord to Jondal from Tørvikbygd (hourly; 20min). Tørvikbygd is on

Highway 49, 12km south of Norheimsund.
**Tourist office** Jondal tourist office is in the centre of the village beside Highway 550 (late June & early Aug daily 9.30am–4pm; July daily 9.30am–5.30pm; ☎ 53 66 85 31, ⓦ visitjondal.no).

### ACTIVITIES

**Summer skiing** For summer skiing on the Folgefonna, the place to head for is the Folgefonn Sommar Skisenter (early May to late Sept daily 9am–4pm; ☎46 80 59 66, ⓦfolgefonn.no), some 20km east of Jondal, on the northern edge of the glacier at 1200m above sea level. The centre offers ski and snowboard rental, a ski school, a café and a ski lift to the slopes. To get there from Utne, head southwest along Highway 550 to Jondal, and then turn east up the signposted mountain road for the bumpy 2km ride up to the Skisenter. At the peak of the season, local bus #982 runs up from Jondal to the Skisenter (late June to mid-Aug 1 daily each way; 45min), giving you just over 5hr up there.

**Glacier hikes and climbs** From Folgefonn Sommar Skisenter, Folgefonni Breførarlag (☎95 11 77 92, ⓦfolgefonni-breforarlag.no) runs a programme of guided glacier hikes and climbs (May to late Aug). The cheaper/ shorter excursions beginning at about 600kr per person including equipment; advance booking – at least the day before – is required.

## Odda

When the carbide factory opened in **ODDA**, about 55km south of Kinsarvik and 45km from Utne, in 1908 it was great news: fjord Norway was impoverished and locals flocked to the plant to secure a decent industrial wage. Other factories followed, not least a hydroelectric station, and within a decade Odda was something of a boom town. Those heady industrial days are long gone, but although the town still bears some of the scars, a sound attempt has now been made to spruce the place up especially along and around the Sørfjord. Perhaps even better, the nearby, 11km-long **Folgefonntunnelen**, which was opened in 2001, bores west beneath the Folgefonna glacier to connect Odda with the region's star historical turn – the Baroniet Rosendal (see p.212).

### ARRIVAL AND INFORMATION                                    ODDA

**By bus** Buses to Odda pull in near the waterfront. Nor-Way Bussekspress operates the Haukeliekspressen (#180) to Utne (2–3 daily; 50min), Bergen (2–3 daily; 3hr 30min) and Oslo (2–3 daily; 7hr).
**Tourist office** Torget (May to mid-June Mon–Fri 10am–5pm; mid-June to Aug daily 9am–7pm; Sept Mon– Fri 10am–5pm; ☎53 65 40 05, ⓦhardangerfjord.com). Down by the fjord, Odda tourist office will supply a comprehensive booklet on the town and the surrounding region.

### ACTIVITIES

**Climbing, hiking and kayaking** The tourist office has details of – and makes bookings for – climbing trips, kayaking and guided walking tours on the nearest nodule of the Folgefonna glacier at Buer, 8km or so from town (approx late June to mid-Aug; advance booking required). The leading local company for outdoor pursuits hereabouts is Flat Earth (☎47 60 68 47, ⓦflatearth.no), who are based in Øvre Eidfjord, but operate most of their trips and expeditions in the Odda area.

### ACCOMMODATION AND EATING

**Tyssedal Hotel** Gamle Oddaveg 3, Tyssedal ☎53 64 00 00, ⓦtyssedalhotel.no. In a distinctive, maroon-painted building in Tyssedal, about 5km north of Odda on Highway 13, this pleasant hotel has 26 large and well-appointed

---

## THE TROLLTUNGA

Much less well known than other, similar vantage points, the **Trolltunga** (troll's tongue) is a narrow ledge of rock that projects out from the mountainside no less than 700m above **Lake Ringedalsvatnet**. Needless to say, the views fair take your breath away. To get there, take Highway 13 north from Odda to **Tyssedal**, where you follow the signs for the 7km journey up into the mountains to **Skjeggedal**, where you can park. The hike starts here in Skjeggedal beside the (currently defunct) funicular Mågelibanen. The path begins on the right-hand side of the funicular, is marked with painted red Ts, takes between eight and ten hours there and back, and involves an ascent of around 1000m. This is tough terrain, so you will need to come properly equipped, and you should check weather conditions at Odda tourist office before you set out – the path is closed when the snows come and is usually open from mid-June to early October. There is no mobile phone coverage along the route.

rooms , though some tend towards the spartan. The hotel benefits from the folksy paintings that grace many of its walls – most are by local artists – and its restaurant is the best in town, featuring local, seasonal ingredients: be sure to try the mountain trout if it's on the menu; mains average 240kr. <u>1300kr</u>, sp/r <u>1000kr</u>

## The Baroniet Rosendal

Hourly guided tours: mid-May to late June & early Aug to mid-Sept daily 11am–3pm; July to early Aug daily 10am–6pm • 100kr, gardens only 50kr • ☎ 53 48 29 99, ⓦ baroniet.no • The Baroniet is a 15min walk from Rosendal jetty

From Odda, it's about 50km west via the Folgefonntunnelen to the hamlet of **ROSENDAL**, at the eastern end of which is the **house and estate of the Baroniet Rosendal**, one of Norway's few country houses – the Norwegian landowning aristocracy has always been too thin on the ground to build more than a hatful. Dating from the seventeenth century, the Baroniet was in private hands until 1927, when the last owner bequeathed the whole lot to the University of Oslo. By comparison with country houses in other European countries, the house is really quite modest, but it does hold a string of period rooms, among which the Baroque library and the Neoclassical "yellow room" are the most diverting. Afterwards, you can stroll out into the surrounding gardens and **park**, with its ponds, bridges and views out across the fjord. Concerts and art exhibitions are a regular feature here too.

### ARRIVAL AND DEPARTURE                                  THE BARONIET ROSENDAL

**By Hurtigbåt passenger express boat** Rodne (ⓦ rodne.no) operates a Hurtigbåt service between Bergen and Rosendal (2 daily; 2hr).

**By bus** There are buses to Rosendal from both Odda (3 daily; 1hr) and Bergen (1 daily; 3hr), from where there are also guided boat tours (see p.202).

**By car** It takes about an hour to drive from Odda to Rosendal via the Folgefonntunnelen. If you are pressing onto Bergen from Rosendal, head north along the road to Odda as far as Årsnes and catch the car ferry over to Gjermundshamn, on Highway 49 (every 30min; 40min). From here, it's another 100km or so to Bergen.

### ACCOMMODATION AND EATING

**Rosendal Turisthotell** Skålagato 17 ☎ 53 47 36 66, ⓦ rosendalturisthotell.no. In a high and handsome old timber building down by the waterfront a 15min walk from the Baroniet Rosendal, this country hotel has benefited from a thoroughgoing refit, its public rooms now neat, trim and very modern. Many of the fourteen rooms have fjord views and all have shared facilities. The hotel's restaurant is the best in the village, with mains around 250kr. <u>900kr</u>

## Lofthus

In a handsome location, **LOFTHUS** strings along the Sørfjord for about 1km with the Folgefonna glacier glinting in the distance. The more northerly part of the village – around the *Hotel Ullensvang* – is somewhat routine, but the southern part is an idyllic place of narrow lanes and mellow stone walls, where a scattering of timber houses sits among the orchards, pinky-white with blossom in the springtime, all to the sound of a stream which tumbles down from the escarpment up above.

### Ullensvang kirke

Late May to mid-June Tues–Fri 10am–2pm; late June to mid-Aug daily 10am–7pm • Free

In the southern part of Lofthus is the village's proudest building, **Ullensvang kirke**, dating from 1250 and named after the district not the village. A good-looking stone structure with immensely thick walls, the church stands just above a pebble beach and a miniature jetty, where the brave propel themselves into the waters of the fjord.

### Hikes on the Hardangervidda plateau

The *Hotel Ullensvang* gives out simple hiking maps indicating both the route to Nosi and other local hikes

Directly behind the *Hotel Ullensvang*, a steep **hiking trail** leads up from Lofthus to the Hardangervidda plateau (see p.215); the upper part of the trail (from 650m above sea level) includes the **Munketreppene**, over six hundred stone steps laid by the monks who farmed this remote spot in medieval times. It takes about two hours to reach the plateau at the **Nosi** (959m) vantage point, and about seven or eight hours to reach the **Stavali** self-service DNT hut.

## ARRIVAL AND DEPARTURE

### LOFTHUS

**By Hurtigbåt passenger express boat** Hurtigbåt boats pull in beside the *Hotel Ullensvang*.
Destinations Eidfjord (May–Oct 1 daily; 1hr 20min); Kinsarvik (May–Oct 1 daily; 15min); Norheimsund (May–Oct 1 daily; 1hr 30min); Ulvik (May–Oct 1 daily; 50min); Utne (May–Oct 1 daily; 40min).

**By bus** Buses stop at the back of the *Hotel Ullensvang*.
Destinations Eidfjord (2–4 daily; 1hr 20min); Kinsarvik (2–4 daily; 15min); Odda (2–4 daily; 40min).

**By car** Lofthus is within easy driving distance of Odda, but

then you're into more rugged terrain with the E134 leading southwest to Haugesund (see p.142) or southeast over the dramatic Haukelifjell to Seljord (see p.177). In the opposite direction, it's just 19km north, via Kinsarvik, to Brimnes, from where a car ferry (1–2 hourly; 10min; ⓦ norled.no) shuttles over to Bruravik, for Ulvik (see p.216) and Voss (see p.218), though the ferry will be replaced by a bridge in June 2013. If you stay on the coastal road, it's another 11km or so east to Eidfjord (see p.214) with the Hardangervidda just behind.

## ACCOMMODATION AND EATING

**Hardanger Vandrerhjem** ⓞ 53 67 14 00, ⓦ hihostels .no. Summer hostel in a substantial and really rather good-looking Folkehøgskule, a residential, rural high school. The hostel has self-catering facilities and a laundry, and is open mid-June to mid-Aug. It's located about 500m up the slope from Highway 13 – just follow the signs. Dorms **300kr**, doubles **700kr**

★ **Hotel Ullensvang** ⓞ 53 67 00 00, ⓦ hotel -ullensvang.no. Spreading out along the Sørfjord, with fine views across to the mountains, this large, family-owned hotel dates back to the 1840s, when an ambitious young lad rowed across from Utne and built himself a boathouse with a loft for guests. Since then, the great and the good have been regular visitors, not least Edvard Grieg, whose stay here is recalled by life-size wooden statues of the composer and his entourage; these stand in the hotel grounds, next to the timber hut where Grieg sat working. The present hotel, which occupies several modern buildings, offers a full basket of facilities, including saunas

and a solarium, a swimming pool, a hairdresser, sports facilities, boat rental and several bars. The decor ranges from the subdued to the almost overpowering with the foyer, where there is an open fireplace and lots of Hardanger bygones, being particularly appealing. There are around 170 guest rooms; the better ones have fjord views for which there is a premium of around 400kr. The hotel restaurant offers an all-you-eat buffet dinner (daily 7–10pm; 495kr). **2300kr**, sp/r **1900kr**

**Ullensvang Gjesteheim** ⓞ 53 66 12 36, ⓦ ullensvang -gjesteheim.no. Appealing guesthouse set within a huddle of antique wooden buildings that roll down towards the fjord from Highway 13 with a cascading stream immediately behind. Has thirteen cosy and unassuming rooms with shared facilities – nothing fancy but perfectly OK. There's a small premium (50kr per person per night) for weekend stays. They also serve dinner (daily 4–9pm) – try the fried mountain trout with sour cream (190kr). Hotel and restaurant open May to mid-Sept. **710kr**

## Kinsarvik

Hugging the Sørfjord, pocket-sized **KINSARVIK**, about 10km from Lofthus, was once an important Viking marketplace. It was just the sort of spot the Vikings liked: the foreshore was gentle, making it easy for them to ground their ships, and it was buried deep in the fjords, making it difficult for any enemy to approach unseen.

### Kinsarvik kirke

Late May to mid-June Tues–Fri 10am–3pm; mid-June to mid-Aug daily 10am–7pm • Free

Nothing now remains from the Viking period period in Kinsarvik, but the sturdy, whitewashed stone **church** lurking on the foreshore dates back as far as the middle of the twelfth century. Those were troubled times, so the church was built with defence in mind – witness the thickness of the walls and the narrowness of the hooped windows – and for several centuries the sails and assorted tackle of the village's *leidangskipet* (defence ship) were stored in its ample loft. Twelfth-century Norwegians knew little of building in stone and it's likely that the church was the work of British masons – though it was clumsily renovated in the 1880s. Inside, the most interesting hints of its medieval past are a series of faint, chalk wall paintings.

## ARRIVAL AND INFORMATION

KINSARVIK

**By car ferry** Ferries dock in the centre of the village metres from the church.

Destinations Kvanndal (1 or 2 hourly; 50min; Utne (1 or 2 hourly; 30min).

**By Hurtigbåt passenger express boat** Hurtigbåt boats use the same dock as the car ferries.

Destinations Eidfjord (May–Oct 1 daily; 1hr 40min); Lofthus (May–Oct 1 daily; 15min); Norheimsund (May–Oct 1 daily; 1hr 15min); Ulvik (May–Oct 1 daily; 1hr); Utne

(May–Oct 1 daily; 25min).

**By bus** Buses pull in beside the ferry dock.

Destinations Eidfjord (2–4 daily; 1hr); Lofthus (2–4 daily; 15min); Odda (2–4 daily; 1hr).

**Tourist office** Opposite the ferry dock (mid-June to mid-Aug daily 9am–7pm; late Aug Mon–Fri 9am–5pm; Sept to mid-June Mon–Fri 8.30am–3.30pm; ☎ 53 66 31 12, ⓦ visitullensvang.no).

## ACCOMMODATION AND EATING

**Best Western Kinsarvik Fjord Hotell** Kinsarvik ☎ 53 66 74 00, ⓦ kinsarvikfjordhotel.com. This well-run, seventy-room hotel occupies a straightforward modern block opposite the ferry jetty. The bedrooms are similarly straightforward, with functional furnishings and fittings,

and the more appealing among them have fjord views. The hotel restaurant is pretty much the only place to eat in Kinsarvik, but fortunately the food is well cooked and prepared – mains average 180kr. **1500kr**

## Eidfjord and around

Given its dramatic location, with the fjords in front and mountains behind, it's hard not to feel that the village of **EIDFJORD**, 11km east of the Brimnes car ferry, should be a tad more inviting – there's nothing wrong with the place, but its modern centre fails to hold the eye. It does, however, boast an unusual attraction in the remote and isolated **Kjeåsen mountain farm**, and it's here that Highway 7 starts its remarkable journey up to the Hardangervidda, weaving and boring its way in a singularly fine feat of engineering. There's been a settlement here at Eidfjord since prehistoric times and for centuries the village prospered as a trading centre at the end of one of the main routes over the Hardangervidda, though this was very much a two-edged sword: traditionally, the villagers were obliged to build and repair foot and cart tracks up to the plateau, forced labour for which they were not paid.

### Kjeåsen mountain farm

Eidfjord's star turn is **Kjeåsen mountain farm**, a lonely complex of old farm buildings, from where you'll be rewarded with spectacular views over the tapering Simadalsfjord. To get there, head northeast from Eidfjord for 7km along the narrow byroad that hugs the Simadalsfjord to reach the tortuous, five-kilometre lane that wriggles up to the farm – it's signed. The lane is much too narrow to take two-way traffic and half the road goes through a tunnel without any lights, but drivers can relax (a little): you can only drive up to the farm on the hour and descend on the half-hour. The byroad is open all the time, but you're asked not to go up after 5pm to respect the privacy of the elderly woman who lives up there on her own.

### Hardangervidda Natursenter

April to mid-June & late Aug to Oct daily 10am–6pm; mid-June to late Aug daily 9am–8pm • 120kr • ☎ 53 67 40 00, ⓦ hardangervidda.org

The **Hardangervidda Natursenter**, in a glassy modern structure in **Øvre Eidfjord**, 7km southeast of Eidfjord along Highway 7, tells you all you ever wanted to know about the Hardangervidda, including its natural history and geology by means of a series of dioramas and a short film. The staff also dispense hiking advice and sell hiking maps.

### Vøringfossen waterfalls

Seventeen kilometres southwest of Eidfjord, past the Hardangervidda Natursenter, Highway 7 passes a large stopping place from where you can view the mighty, 145m-high **Vøringfossen waterfalls**, though the torrent is best viewed from the top at the hamlet/ hotel of **Fossli** a little further on: Fossli is signed from – and about 1km off – Highway 7.

## ARRIVAL AND INFORMATION

**By Hurtigbåt passenger express boat** Hurtigbåt boats dock in the centre of the village a few metres from both Highway 7 and the conspicuous *Quality Hotel & Resort Vøringfoss*.

Destinations Kinsarvik (May–Oct 1 daily; 1hr 30min); Lofthus (May–Oct 1 daily; 1hr 20min); Norheimsund (May–Oct 1 daily; 2hr 50min); Ulvik (May–Oct 1 daily; 40min); Utne (May–Oct 1 daily; 2hr).

**By bus** Buses pull in a few metres from the Hurtigbåt dock. Note that there are no long-distance buses east across the Hardangervidda to Geilo along Highway 7.

## EIDFJORD

Destinations Kinsarvik (2–4 daily; 1hr); Lofthus (2–4 daily; 1hr 15min); Odda (2–4 daily; 2hr).

**Tourist office** Metres from the Hurtigbåt dock (May Mon–Fri 9am–6pm; early June & late Aug Mon–Sat 9am–6pm; mid-June to mid-Aug Mon–Fri 9am–7pm, Sat & Sun 11am–6pm; Sept–April Mon–Fri 9am–4pm; ☎ 53 67 34 00, ⊚ visiteidfjord.no). They will advise on local walks; one popular option is the hour-long haul up to the Hæreid plateau, which has the region's greatest concentration of Viking burial mounds.

## ACCOMMODATION AND EATING

**Quality Hotel & Resort Vøringfoss** Ostangvegen ☎ 53 67 41 00, ⊚ choicehotels.no. There's been a hotel here at the Eidfjord quayside since the 1880s, but the present complex is a large, modern affair built in the general style of its wooden predecessors with mini-towers and decorative gable ends. The 81 rooms are popular with tour groups and decorated in standard chain style, though the pick do have great views over the fjord. There is also a large hotel restaurant. Open March–Dec. **1200kr**

**Vik Pensjonat og Hytter** Simadalsvegen 10 ☎ 53 66 51

62, ⊚ vikpensjonat.com. In the centre of the village, a brief walk from the quayside, this pretty wooden house holds seven rooms, half en suite, and all tastefully decorated in a bright and cheerful manner; the rooms with shared facilities cost 220kr less than the en suite. The same family also rents out two neighbouring cabins (*hytter*) – one for six people (950kr) the other for two (700kr) – and operates a café, where they specialize in local dishes – trout and reindeer for example – with mains averaging 170kr. Café and accommodation from May to Sept. En-suite doubles **1100kr**

## The Hardangervidda plateau

The **Hardangervidda** is Europe's largest mountain plateau, occupying a one-hundred-kilometre-square slab of land east of the Hardangerfjord and broadly south of the Oslo–Bergen railway. The plateau is characterized by rolling fells and wide stretches of level ground, its rocky surfaces strewn with pools, ponds and rivers. The whole plateau is above the tree line, and in places has an almost lunar-like appearance, although even within this elemental landscape there are variations. To the north, in the vicinity of Finse, there are mountains and a glacier, the **Hardangerjøkulen**, while the west is wetter – and the flora somewhat richer – than the barer moorland to the east. The lichen that covers the rocks is savoured by herds of **reindeer**, who leave their winter grazing lands on the east side of the plateau in the spring, chewing their way west to their breeding grounds before returning east again after the autumn rutting season.

Stone Age hunters once followed the reindeer on their migrations, and traces of their presence – arrowheads, pit-traps, etc – have been discovered over much of the plateau. Later, the Hardangervidda became one of the main crossing points between east and west Norway, with horse traders, cattle drivers and Danish dignitaries all cutting across the plateau along cairned paths, many of which are still in use as part of a dense network of **trails** that has been developed – alongside **tourist huts** – by several DNT affiliates. Roughly one-third of the plateau has been incorporated within the **Hardangervidda Nasjonalpark**, but much of the rest is protected too, so hikers won't notice a great deal of difference between the park and its immediate surroundings. The entire plateau is also popular for **winter cross-country, hut-to-hut skiing**. Many hikers and skiers are content with a day on the Hardangervidda, but some find the wide-skied, lichen-dappled scenery particularly enchanting and travel from one end of the plateau to the other, a seven- or eight-day expedition.

## ARRIVAL AND DEPARTURE

**By train** Access to the Hardangervidda can be gained from the Oslo–Bergen train line which calls at Finse (see p.220),

## THE HARDANGERVIDDA PLATEAU

from where hikers and skiers head off across the plateau in all directions.

## THE BATTLE OF THE ORANGES

The Germans invaded Norway on April 9, 1940, and during the next couple of weeks, before the Norwegians threw in the towel, there were several naval skirmishes in the Hardangerfjord. In one of them, the so-called **Battle of Ulvik**, the German navy shelled the centre of the village to smithereens after being shot at from the shore. During the battle, the Norwegian navy, seeing the way things were going, scuttled the *Afrika*, a German merchant ship they had previously captured; the wreck remains in Ulvik harbour today. They also scuttled a neutral ship, the *San Miguel*, which had taken refuge here, thereby – in a true *Whisky Galore* moment – releasing the ship's cargo, thousands of **oranges**, which bobbed around the harbour, much to the amazed delight of the locals, for whom fresh fruit was a real treat.

**By car** Finse is not reachable by road, so motorists mostly use Highway 7, which runs across the plateau between Eidfjord (see p.214) and Geilo (see p.174).

**By foot** You can pick up the plateau's hiking trails at several points along Highway 7, including Dyranut and Halne, respectively 39km and 47km from Eidfjord. Some hikers prefer to walk eastwards onto the Hardangervidda – Lofthus (see p.212) offers the easiest access – while others plump for Rjukan (see p.179), to the southeast of the plateau, where a cable car eases the uphill part of the trek.

**By boat** There are boat trips (late June to early Sept; 1–3 daily; 1hr) from Halne along the Halnefjord, which cuts across the Hardangervidda for around 15km. For times of departure, consult Eidfjord tourist office (see p.215).

**Information** Local tourist offices all carry hiking maps and will advise on hiking routes, as will the Hardangervidda Natursenter (see p.214).

## Ulvik

Tucked away in a snug corner of the Hardangerfjord, the village of **ULVIK** strings prettily along the shoreline with orchards dusting the green, forested hills behind. This is one of the gentlest of fjord landscapes, with little of the harsh beauty of many of its neighbours, and although there's nothing specific to see, strolling the waterfront is a pleasant way to pass the time, and there are plenty of hiking trails in the surrounding hills. Ulvik also has one or two claims to fame: this is the spot where potatoes were first grown in Norway (in 1765) and it was one of the few places in the country to take a real pummelling during World War II (see box above).

### Hikes around Ulvik

Ulvik is an excellent place to unwind, and the favourite pastime is walking. **Hiking trails** lattice the rough uplands behind the village and also explore the surrounding coastline. The tourist office sells a map of the Ulvik area (25kr) describing a dozen, day-long hiking trails, ranging from the easy (2km; 30min) to the more strenuous (8km; 6hr). One of the easiest and most enjoyable is the hour-long, round trip up into the hills to the east of Ulvik, to **Tunheim**, taking in the scant remains of an old Viking burial ground. In the season, from June to August, the tourist office also organizes a daily **cultural walk** (2hr 30min; 250kr), which includes cider tasting: since a change in the law in 2002, local farmers have been allowed to brew their own **cider** – which is precisely what several of them do.

### ARRIVAL AND INFORMATION                                                    ULVIK

**By bus** Buses to Ulvik pull into the centre of the village, metres from the jetty and the waterfront tourist office.
Destinations Bruarvik (3–5 daily; 25min); Voss (3–5 daily; 1hr 15min).

**By Hurtigbåt passenger express boat** Hurtigbåt boats dock next to the tourist office.
Destinations Eidfjord (May–Oct 1 daily; 40min); Kinsarvik (May–Oct 1 daily; 1hr); Lofthus (May–Oct 1 daily; 40min);

Norheimsund (May–Oct 1 daily; 2hr 10min); Utne (May–Oct 1 daily; 1hr 20min).

**Tourist office** Next to the ferry dock (May to mid-Sept Mon–Fri 9am–4pm, plus mid-June to mid-Aug Sat & Sun 11am–3pm; mid-Sept to April Mon–Fri 10am–2pm; ☎56 52 62 80, ⍟hardangerfjord.com). They issue all the usual information, including bus and ferry timetables, sell detailed hiking maps and rent out bikes.

**FROM TOP** ULVIK; ÅLESUND (P.252) >

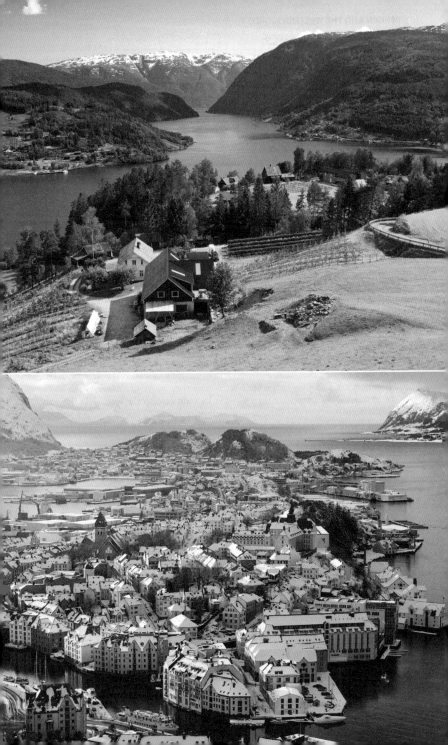

## ACCOMMODATION AND EATING

**Brakanes Hotel** Promenaden ☎ 56 52 61 05, ⓦ brakanes-hotel.no. Hogging the waterfront in the centre of the village, this large, four-storey modern hotel with 143 rooms has all the facilities you might expect, including a fitness centre, and is popular as a conference centre. The rooms are standard-issue chain – wood-laminate floors and so forth – but the better ones do have lovely fjord views and the beds are dead comfy. **2000kr**

**Doktergarden** Tyssevikvegen ☎ 53 50 07 49, ⓦ doktergarden.no. Flanked and fronted by orchards, this enticing B&B overlooks the road – and the fjord – from a small ridge. The house, which dates from the 1920s, started out as a doctor's home and has now been sympathetically renovated to hold five guest rooms with vintage decor. The outside terrace provides grand fjord views and the owners offer aromatherapy too. The B&B is located a 1km walk from the jetty on the east side of the village. No credit cards. **1000kr**

★ **Ulvik Fjord Hotel** Eikjeledbakkjen ☎ 56 52 61 70, ⓦ ulvikfjord.no. This well-maintained and very appealing hotel is situated at the beginning of Ulvik village, an easy 10min walk west from the centre along the waterfront. It has nineteen guest rooms, some in the main house – an attractive, wooden, two-storey building dating from the 1940s – and some in the modern annexe, where most of the rooms have their own outside area beside a babbling brook. It's not a luxury resort – and makes no claim to be so – but it is very comfortable and the family who own and run the place are the friendliest of hosts. Breakfasts are first-rate and home-made evening meals, which come recommended by several of our readers, are available at their café-bar-cum-restaurant; reckon on 160kr for a main course. May to Sept. **950kr**

# Voss

With a population of just 14,000, **VOSS**, 100km from Bergen, is a small town with an attractive lakeside setting and a splendid thirteenth-century church. It is, however, best known as an **adventure-sports and winter-skiing centre**, with everything from skiing and snowboarding through to summertime rafting, kayaking and horseriding. Consequently, unless you're here for a sweat, your best bet is to have a quick look round the town's central shops and cafés – it takes just five minutes to walk from one end of town to the other, though this is still something of a treat if you've been stuck in the tiny hamlets and villages further north – and then move on. There is a caveat, however: Voss is the ideal base for a **day-trip by train** east up the Raundal valley, an especially scenic part of the Bergen–Oslo rail line. The most popular target on this stretch of the line is the Myrdal junction, where you change for the dramatic train ride down to Flåm (see box, p.220).

For centuries, Voss has been a trading centre of some importance, though you'd barely guess this from the modern appearance of the town centre. In 1023, King Olav visited to check that the population had all converted to Christianity, and stuck a big stone cross here to ram home his point, and in the 1270s another king, Magnus Lagabøte, built a church in Voss to act as the religious focal point for the whole region – and this church, the Vangskyrkja, survives today.

## Vangskyrkja

Vangsgata • June–Aug Mon–Sat 10am–4pm, Sun 1–4pm • 20kr • ☎ 56 52 38 80

Guarding the west end of the town centre, the **Vangskyrkja** is Voss's main landmark, its eccentric octagonal spire poking an assertive head high into the sky. Down below, the stone walls of the nave are up to 2m thick, strong enough, as it turned out, to survive the German bombing of the town in 1940. From the outside, the church looks sombre and severe, but the interior is splendid, a surprisingly flamboyant and colourful affair with a Baroque reredos and a folksy rood screen showing a crucified Jesus attended by two cherubs. The ceiling is even more unusual, its timbers painted in 1696 with a cotton-wool cloudy sky inhabited by flying angels – and the closer you get to the high altar, the more angels there are.

## Lake Vangsvatnet

Across the main road from the church, the **Prestegardsalléen** footpath cuts a leafy course along the flat and green shore of lake **Vangsvatnet**. It's a pleasant stroll that leads

## OUTDOOR ACTIVITIES AROUND VOSS

Every **summer**, hundreds of Norwegians make a beeline for Voss on account of its **watersports**. The rivers near the town offer a wide range of conditions, suitable for everything from a quiet paddle to a finger-chewing whitewater ride. In **winter**, **skiing** around Voss starts in mid-December and continues until mid-April – nothing fancy, but good for an enjoyable few days. From behind and above the train station, a **cable car** – the Hangursbanen – climbs 700m to give access to several short runs as well as a series of chairlifts that take you up another 300m. In January and February some trails are floodlit. There's a choice of red, green and black downhill ski routes, and among the greens is a long and fairly gentle route through the hills above town; cross-country skiing here is limited to 20km of tracks.

### SUMMER SPORTS OPERATORS

**Mjølfjell Fjellstove** ☎ 56 52 31 50, ⓦ mjolfjell.no. Up in the hills about 30km east of town, Mjølfjell Fjellstove specializes in mountain horseback riding with guided excursions from one day to a week; a week-long trip costs 4300kr per person.

**Nordic Ventures** ☎ 56 51 00 17, ⓦ nordicventures .com. This operator offers all sorts of kayaking excursions (a day-long trip costs 975kr per person) as well as tandem paragliding and parasailing.

**Voss Rafting Senter** ☎ 56 51 05 25, ⓦ vossrafting .no. Among several rafting operators, this one sets the benchmark. Their whitewater-rafting trips venture out onto two rivers – the Stranda and Raun – with prices beginning at 600kr per person for a 3hr excursion, half of which is actually spent on the water. Other options with the same operator include river boarding (4hr; 1150kr) and waterfall rappelling (4hr; 850kr).

### WINTER SPORTS OPERATORS

**Voss Ski School** ☎ 47 00 47 00, ⓦ vossresort.no. Full equipment for both downhill and cross-country skiing can be rented by the day from this ski school at the upper Hangursbanen station. They also offer lessons in skiing and snowboarding techniques.

**4**

past the town's main campsite to a small bathing area that is itself not far from the point where the River Vosso empties into the lake.

### ARRIVAL AND DEPARTURE
VOSS

**By bus** Buses stop outside the train station at the western end of the town centre, a 5min walk or so from the Vangskyrkja (church). Nor-Way Bussekspress operates the Sognebussen (#450) from Voss to Bergen (4–5 daily; 1hr 50min), Gudvangen (4–5 daily; 50min), Flåm (4–5 daily; 1hr 10min) and Sogndal (4–5 daily; 3hr). Local buses link Voss with Ulvik (3–5 daily; 1hr), Vik (1–2 daily except Sat; 1hr 15min) and Vangsnes (1–2 daily except Sat; 1hr 30min). At Vangsnes, there are connecting ferries over the Sognefjord to Hella for Sogndal and Dragsvik for Balestrand (see p.229).

**By train** Voss train station, which is on the Bergen–Oslo line, stands at the western end of – and a 5min walk from – the town centre. From Voss it's a short haul east by train up the Raundal valley to the Myrdal junction (4–9 trains daily; 40min), where you change for the world-famous train ride down to Flåm on the Flåmsbåna (see p.220). You can, however, choose instead to disembark two stops further down the line at Finse (4 trains daily; 1hr 10min; see p.220), which offers a bevy of hiking and skiing routes amid the stirring scenery of the Hardangervidda mountain plateau. Trains also run to Bergen (4 daily; 1hr 10min), Geilo (4 daily; 1hr 50min) and Oslo (4 daily; 5hr 20min).

**By car** It's a quick and easy 65km north from Voss along the E16 to Flåm (see p.224). The E16 is the main road between Bergen and Oslo and you can dodge most of the traffic by forking off the E16 at Vinje (see p.222) to take scenic Highway 13 down the dales and over the mountains to Vik and Vangsnes (see p.222), from where there are ferries over the Sognefjord. In the opposite direction, you can also drive to the pretty little village of Ulvik (see p.216), about a 30min drive to the south (30km).

### INFORMATION

**Tourist office** Evangervegen 6 (June–Aug Mon–Fri 8am–7pm, Sat 9am–7pm & Sun noon–7pm; Sept–May Mon–Fri 8.30am–3.30pm; ☎ 56 51 94 90, ⓦ visitvoss.no). Opposite the train station, in the conspicuously modern Voss Kulturhuset (Cultural Centre), the tourist office has oodles of information on hiking, rafting, skiing and local touring, the bones of which are detailed in the free *Voss Guide*; they also operate an accommodation booking service.

## ACCOMMODATION AND EATING

**Fleischer's Hotel** Evangervegen ☎ 56 52 05 00, ⓦ fleischers.no. Dating from the 1880s, and standing cheek-by-jowl with the train station, Fleischer's high-gabled and towered facade overlooks the lake. Parts of the hotel, which consists of the original building and a modern wing built in the same style, have the whiff of real luxury – as do many of the bedrooms – but others are more mundane. The restaurant serves the best food in town (mains average 250kr on the à la carte menu) and there's a terrace bar as well. Their all-inclusive food-and-lodging deals offer substantial savings on the normal rate. 1900kr, sp/r 1700kr

**Tre Bør Café** Vangsgata 28 ☎ 56 52 99 25, ⓦ vosscafe .no. Informal, laidback café-restaurant in an old timber house where they serve filling portions from a down-to-earth menu – burgers and so forth. Good cakes and coffee too. Mains average 145kr. Sun–Thurs 9.30am–9pm, Fri & Sat 9.30am to midnight.

**Voss Camping** Prestegardsalléen ☎ 56 51 15 97, ⓦ vosscamping.no. Handily located by the town lake, a short walk south from the Vangskyrkja church, this popular campsite is a straightforward affair, occupying a large, semi-forested site. It's open all year and has a few, two-person cabins. Cabins 600kr, tent pitches from 150kr

**Voss Vandrerhjem** Evangervegen 68 ☎ 56 51 20 17, ⓦ hihostels.no. Voss has lots of inexpensive accommodation to cater for all the visiting sportsfolk, but the best budget option is the excellent, all-year HI hostel, in a modern lodge overlooking the water about 800m west of the train station. The hostel serves good breakfasts and inexpensive evening meals – though these need to be pre-booked – and has self-catering facilities; it also has its own laundry and internet access, and rents out bikes and canoes. Reservations are strongly recommended. To get there, turn right outside the station building and head along the lake away from the town centre – a 10min walk. Dorms 325kr, doubles 930kr

# The Raundal valley, Myrdal and Finse

From Voss, trains – but not cars as there is no road – head east up the **Raundal valley** before climbing up to the bare but eerily beautiful wastes of the Hardangervidda plateau. All trains stop at **Myrdal**, a remote railway junction where you change for the extraordinary train ride down to Flåm (see box below), and then proceed onto **Finse**, just half an hour by train from Myrdal and the highest point on the Bergen–Oslo railway line.

## Finse

A solitary lakeside outpost on the northern peripheries of the plateau, **Finse** comprises nothing more than its station and a few isolated buildings, hunkered down against the howling winds that rip across the Hardangervidda in wintertime. There's snow here from the beginning of November until well into June, and the **cross-country skiing** is

---

### THE FLÅM RAILWAY – THE FLÅMSBANA

The lonely railway junction of **Myrdal**, just forty minutes by train from Voss, is the start of one of Europe's most celebrated branch rail lines, the **Flåmsbana** (ⓦ flaamsbana.no), a 20km, 900m plummet down the Flåmsdal valley to **Flåm** – a fifty-minute train ride that should not be missed if at all possible; it is part of the "Norway in a Nutshell" route (see box, p.207). The track, which took four years to lay in the 1920s, spirals down the mountainside, passing through hand-dug tunnels and, at one point, actually travelling through a hairpin tunnel to drop nearly 300m. The gradient of the line is one of the steepest anywhere in the world, and as the train squeals its way down the mountain, past cascading waterfalls, it's reassuring to know that it has five separate sets of brakes, each capable of bringing it to a stop. The service runs all year round, a local lifeline during the deep winter months. There are ten departures daily from mid-June to late September, between four and eight the rest of the year; Myrdal–Flåm fares are 260kr one-way, 360kr return.

The athletic occasionally undertake the five-hour **walk** from the railway junction at Myrdal down the old road into the valley, instead of taking the train, but much the better option is to disembark about halfway down and walk in from there. **Berekvam** station, at an altitude of 345m, is the best place to alight, leaving an enthralling two- to three-hour hike through changing mountain scenery down to Flåm. **Cycling** down the valley road is also perfectly feasible, though it's much too steep to be relaxing.

particularly enthusiastic, with locals skiing off from the station in every direction. You can rent cross-country ski equipment at the *Finse 1222 Hotel* (see below), but you'll need to reserve. After the snow has melted, cycling (see box below) and **hiking** take over.

### Rallarmuseet

Jan to early Oct Mon–Fri 10am–10pm • 40kr • ☎ 90 50 09 40, ⓦ rallarmuseet.no

Finse may be tiny, but it does have one noteworthy attraction, the **Rallarmuseet** (Navvy Museum), which holds a pictorial record of the planning and construction of the Oslo–Bergen railway, whose final piece of track was laid in 1909. The old black-and-white photos are the most interesting exhibits and a well-earned tribute to the navvies who survived such grim conditions.

### Hikes from Finse

One especially popular hike from Finse is the round trip to the northeast edge of the **Hardangerjøkulen glacier** (4hr). Other, longer hiking trails skirt the glacier to traverse the main body of the Hardangervidda plateau. Alternatively, it's an eleven-hour haul from Finse to Highway 7 at Dyranut (see p.216), so most hikers overnight after around eight hours at the self-catering **Kjeldebu** DNT hut (March to mid-Oct). Finse has scope for more specialist activities too, most notably **guided glacier walks** on the Hardangerjøkulen. These guided walks take place between July and September and last around seven hours (650kr, including equipment rental); they are run by the *Finse 1222 Hotel*.

### ARRIVAL AND DEPARTURE                                                      FINSE  **4**

**By train** The train station is Finse's focal point and it's on the Bergen-Oslo line.
**Destinations** Bergen (4 daily; 2hr 20min); Geilo (4 daily;

50min); Myrdal (4 daily; 30min; change for Flåm); Oslo (4 daily; 4hr); Voss (4 daily; 1hr 10min).

### ACCOMMODATION AND EATING

**Finse 1222 Hotel** ☎ 56 52 71 00, ⓦ finse1222.no. The smarter of Finse's two places to stay, this hotel is a large lodge-style structure with 43 modern rooms, all en suite. It's the setting that appeals most – look outside from any window and it's wilderness as far as the eye can see – but the hotel is comforting and comfortable and even has its own bakery. It also offers expert advice on cycling, hiking and skiing, and

rents out bicycles too. Prices include meals. **1250kr**
**Finsehytta** ☎ 56 52 67 32, ⓦ turistforeningen.no /finsehytta. This fully staffed DNT hut offers frugal lodgings for up to 150, with hikers, skiers, climbers and cyclists in mind. Open early March to early May & July to late Sept. Non-members pay a premium of about 30 percent. Members: dorms **135kr**, doubles **480kr**

---

### CYCLING FROM FINSE: THE RALLARVEGEN

**Cycling** from Finse is made possible by the **Rallarvegen** ("The Navvy Road"; ⓦ rallarvegen .com), which was originally built to allow men and materials to be brought up to the railway during its construction. Now surfaced with gravel and sometimes asphalt, the Rallarvegen begins in **Haugastøl** beside Highway 7, runs west to Finse and then continues to Myrdal, from where you can cycle or take the Flåmsbana down to Flåm. It's 27km by bicycle from Haugastøl to Finse, 37km from Finse to Myrdal and another 16km to Flåm. The Finse-to-Flåm section, which passes through fine upland scenery before descending the Flåmsdal, is the most popular part of the Rallarvegen. Most cyclists travel east to west as Finse is a good deal higher than Myrdal, and the whole journey from Finse to Flåm takes around nine hours; the return trip is usually made by train, with NSB railways transporting bikes for 175kr. Locals reckon that the best time to cycle the Rallarvegen is usually from mid-July to late September. However, snow is not cleared from the route and its highest section – between Finse and Myrdal – can be blocked by snow until very late in summer, so check conditions locally before you set out.
**Mountain-bike rental** is available from the *Finse 1222 Hotel* (see above), but advance reservations are required.

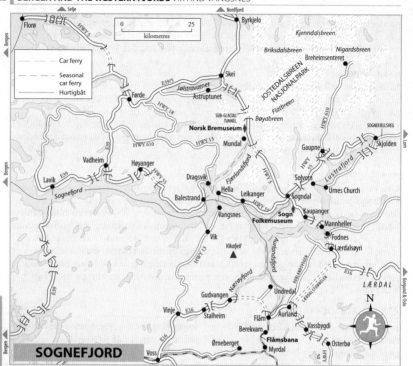

**SOGNEFJORD**

## Vik and Vangsnes

From Voss, it's about 20km north to **Vinje**, where **Highway 13** begins its 60-kilometre trek over to **Vik** and **Vangsnes** on the **Sognefjord**. A quintessential fjordland journey, the road begins by clambering up the Myrkdal valley, passing waterfalls and wild ravines before cutting an improbable route across the bleak and icy wastes of **Vikafjell mountain** – so improbable indeed that the highway is closed in winter, usually from November to April, and snow is piled high on either side of the road until at least the end of May.

### Vik: Hopperstad stave church

Mid-May to mid-June & mid-Aug to mid-Sept daily 10am–5pm; mid-June to mid-Aug daily 9am–6pm • 60kr • ☎ 57 67 88 40, ⓦ stavechurch.com

Sat on a hillock just off Highway 13, about 1500m from the Sognefjord in **VIK**, a rather half-hearted village that sprawls up a wide valley, **Hopperstad stave church** is a reminder of more populous times. The church is well cared for today, but in the 1880s it was about to be knocked down when a visiting architect and his antiquarian chum persuaded the villagers to change their minds. The pair promptly set about repairing the church and they did a good job: Hopperstad is one of the best examples of its type, its angular roofing surmounted by a long and slender tower. The interior has its moments too, with a Gothic side-altar canopy, parts of which may have been swiped from France by the Vikings, and a so-called lepers' window through which the afflicted listened to church services.

### Vangsnes

No more than a handful of houses and a ferry dock, **VANGSNES** is about 11km north of Vik along the Sognefjord. Local farmers must have had a real shock when, in 1913,

Kaiser Wilhelm erected a twelve-metre-high statue of the legendary Viking chief Fridtjof the Bold on the hilltop above their jetty. The **Fridtjovstatuen** still stands, an eccentric and vaguely unpleasant monument to the Kaiser's fascination with Nordic mythology – Fridtjof the Bold was in love with Ingebjorg, daughter of King Bele, whose statue, also commissioned by the Kaiser, is across the fjord at Balestrand (see p.229). You can walk the 500m up from the ferry dock to take a closer look at Fridtjof and there's a wide view of the Sognefjord from here too.

### ARRIVAL AND DEPARTURE VIK AND VANGSNES

**By car ferry** Services run from Vangsnes to Dragsvik (for Balestrand; every 40min–1hr; 30min) and Hella (for Highway 55, including Sogndal; every 40min–1hr; 15min).

**By bus** Buses from Vik (1–2 daily except Sat; 15min) and Voss (1–2 daily except Sat; 1hr 30min) pull in beside the ferry dock.

## Stalheim, Gudvangen and Undredal

At Vinje (see opposite), the **E16** veers east for its dramatic defile down to Flåm (see p.224), passing, after 16km, the scattered hillside hamlet of **Stalheim**. It's here you'll find one of the region's most superbly sited hotels (see p.224), complete with its own folk museum – 24 traditional log buildings and a manor house of 1726, all crammed with ancient artefacts. The byroad to the hotel is actually the **old main road** and this continues past the hotel to zigzag over the mountains before rejoining the E16 a little further on – a fine if mildly hair-raising detour.

### Gudvangen

The mini-port of **GUDVANGEN**, 13km from Stalheim, is a forlorn, shadowy little place at the southern tip of the Nærøyfjord. In the summertime, hundreds of tourists pour through here partly on account of the car-ferry connections to Kaupanger, but mainly because it's on the "Norway in a Nutshell" itinerary (see box, p.207). A modern and singularly unprepossessing complex down by the jetty incorporates souvenir shops, a café and a hotel, whose assorted hut-like structures have turf roofs – an ersatz Vikingarama which you can really do without.

### Undredal

Just beyond Gudvangen, the E16 disappears into an 11km tunnel to emerge just 100m or so from the byroad that leads the 6km north along a boulder-strewn valley to tiny **UNDREDAL**. The village perches right on the edge of the **Aurlandsfjord**, its narrow, meandering lanes overshadowed by the severity of the surrounding mountains. There's been a settlement here since Viking times, and for much of its history the village has been reliant on the export of its goat's cheese, now produced in Undredal's two surviving dairies – there were once a dozen. Undredal has just 80 inhabitants – if you discount the 500 goats – but it is home to a charming **stave church**.

#### Undredal stavkirke

Mid-May to Sept daily 11am–6pm • 40kr • ☎ 95 29 76 68

With its dinky little porch and prim and proper spire, **Undredal stavkirke** is an inordinately pretty country church that dates back as far as the twelfth century, though it was extensively remodelled in the 1720s. A tiny affair – it's one of the smallest churches in the whole of Norway – it's decorated in fine folkloric style, from the floral patterns on the walls through to the crucified Christ above the high altar and the stylized stars and naive figures on the ceiling.

### ARRIVAL AND DEPARTURE STALHEIM, GUDVANGEN AND UNDREDAL

**By boat** Hurtigbåt boats to/from Flåm (May–Sept 3–4 daily; 2hr 10min) and car ferries to/from Kaupanger

(May–Sept 2–3 daily; 2hr 10min) pull in at Gudvangen jetty at the foot of the village.

**By bus** Buses to Gudvangen pull in beside the ferry dock; there's a local, summertime bus service to the *Stalheim Hotel* but no buses to Undredal. Nor-Way Bussekspress operates the Sognebussen (#450) from Gudvangen to Bergen (4–5 daily; 2hr 35min), Flåm (4–5 daily; 20min),

Sogndal (4–5 daily; 2hr) and Voss (4–5 daily; 50min). Local bus #950 (⌨skyss.no) links the *Stalheim Hotel* with Voss (May to late Sept; 2–3 daily; 45min) and Gudvangen (May to late Sept; 2–3 daily; 25min).

## ACCOMMODATION AND EATING

★ **Stalheim Hotel** Stalheim ☎ 56 52 01 22, ⌨stalheim.com. The fourth incarnation of a hotel that was orignally built here on this mini-mountain plateau in the late nineteenth century, today's building – dating from the 1960s – is a large and chunky structure short of grace. All is redeemed inside, however, where the large and spacious public rooms have been kitted out in an endearing version of antique Norwegian style, all heirlooms and bygones plus a few landscape paintings and some fine furniture of classic Scandinavian design probably dating to

the 1970s. The *Stalheim*'s bedrooms are large and modern if a tad plain, but really who's bothered when the highlight is the view – a simply breathtaking vista down along the Nærøydal valley, so stunning, in fact, that David Hockney came and painted it. The hotel serves a top-notch breakfast and an excellent buffet dinner – all you can eat for 400kr – and is popular with tour groups. It's located up a twisty byroad, just 1.5km from the E16 on what was once the main road until they tunnelled through the mountain below. Open May to early Oct. **1700kr**

# Flåm

Fringed by meadows and orchards, **FLÅM** sits beside the Aurlandsfjord, a slender branch of the Sognefjord, with the mountains glowering behind. It's a splendid setting, but otherwise first impressions are poor: the fjordside complex adjoining the train station is crass and commercial – souvenir trolls and the like – and on summer days the place heaves with tourists, who pour off the train, have lunch, and then promptly head out by bus and ferry. But a brief stroll is enough to leave the crowds behind at the harbourside, while out of season or in the evenings, when the day-trippers have all moved on, Flåm is a pleasant spot and an eminently agreeable place to spend the night. If you're prepared to risk the weather, late September is perhaps the **best time to visit**: the peaks already have a covering of snow and the vegetation is just turning its autumnal golden brown. Flåm is also an excellent base for further explorations, whether it be the train ride up to Myrdal on the Flåmsbana (see box, p.220), the dramatic ferry trip over to Gudvangen (see box below) or a day-long hike in the surrounding mountains.

## ARRIVAL AND DEPARTURE                                                    FLÅM

**By train** Flåm train station is adjacent to the jetty, with services on the Flamsbåna to Myrdal, on the Bergen–Oslo line (mid-June to late Sept 10 daily; Oct to mid-June 4–8 daily; 55min).
**By bus** Buses to Flåm pull in beside the ferry dock and train station. Nor-Way Bussekspress operates the Sognebussen (#450) from Flåm to Gudvangen (4–5 daily; 20min), Voss (4–5 daily; 1hr), Bergen (4–5 daily; 3hr), Lærdal (4–5 daily; 50min), Kaupanger (4–5 daily; 1hr

20min) and Sogndal (4–5 daily; 1hr 30min). Fjord1 (⌨fjord1.no) also operates a local, seasonal bus (#23-490) up the Aurlandsdal valley (Highway 50) via Aurland (late May to mid-June & mid- to late Sept 2 daily; mid-June to mid-Sept 4 daily; 10min) to Vassbygdi (late May to mid-June & mid- to late Sept 2 daily; mid-June to mid-Sept 3 daily; 30min), Østerbø (late May to mid-June & mid- to late Sept 2 daily; mid-June to mid-Sept 3 daily; 1hr) and Geilo (late June to mid-Sept 1 daily; 2hr 30min).

---

## FLÅM TO GUDVANGEN: SAILING THE NÆRØYFJORD

Flåm is the starting (or ending) point for one of the most stupendous **ferry trips** in the fjords, the two-hour cruise up the **Aurlandsfjord** and down its narrow offshoot, the **Nærøyfjord** (May–Sept 3–4 daily; 2hr 10min; 275kr one-way, 380kr return; ⌨fjord1.no) to **Gudvangen** (see p.223). The Nærøyfjord is the narrowest fjord in Europe, its high and broody cliffs keeping out the sun throughout the winter, and its stern beauty makes for a magnificent excursion. This forms part of the "Norway in a Nutshell" itinerary (see box, p.207).

**By Hurtigbåt passenger express boat** Hurtigbåt boats pull in at the ever-expanding Flåm jetty at the foot of the village, with services to Balestrand (May–Sept 1–2 daily; 2hr); Bergen (May–Sept 1 daily; 5hr 25min); and Gudvangen (May–Sept 3–4 daily; 2hr 10min).

## INFORMATION

**Tourist office** Flåm's harbourside tourist complex may be modern and ugly, but it is convenient, holding a supermarket, the train station and the tourist office (daily: May & Sept 8.30am–4pm; June–Aug 8.30am–8pm; ✆ 57 63 21 06, ⊚ alr.no), where you can pick up a free and very useful booklet on Aurland, Flåm and Lærdal. They also have details on local hiking routes, sell hiking maps and rent out mountain bikes.

## ACTIVITIES

**Fjord kayaking** Njord (✆ 91 32 66 28, ⊚ njord.as), who operate from the Flåm waterfront, offers an interesting range of tours, the shortest and cheapest of which is their Aurlandsfjord paddle for 490kr per person (3hr); advance reservations are required.

## ACCOMMODATION AND EATING

**Flåm Camping og Vandrerhjem** ✆ 57 63 21 21, ⊚ flaam-camping.no. Handily situated about 300m from the train station towards the back of the village, this well-appointed campsite spreads over a sheltered site beside a stream. Has both tent spaces and dinky little cabins, and also incorporates a small and well-kept HI hostel. April to Sept. Tents (2 people plus tent) __215kr__, dorms __210kr__, doubles __500kr__, cabins from __700kr__

**Flåmsbrygga** ✆ 57 63 20 50, ⊚ flamsbrygga.no. Metres from the train station, this new addition to the Flåm scene includes a real oddity – a bar (daily 11am–5pm, later in summer) built in the style of a Viking long hall: circular, dark, with heavy wooden beams and an open fire. The architecture may be strange, but the beer of the Ægir microbrewey that's based here certainly is not, ranging from the dark and strong Sumbel Porter to the tangy, but equally strong Bøyla Blonde Ale. To the rear of the bar is a modern accommodation block, though here the Vikingarama has not been duplicated and the rooms are cosy and warm with wood-panelled walls and mini-balconies. __1750kr__

★ **Fretheim Hotel** ✆ 57 63 63 00, ⊚ fretheim-hotel .no. Large, rambling hotel with a long pedigree whose attractive older part, with its high-pitched roofs and white-painted clapboard, is now joined to a flashy glass structure that is, in its turn, attached to a matching modern wing. In the early days of fjord tourism, in the 1890s, the Fretheim family, who were local farmers, took a shine to tourism, welcoming foreign hunters and fishermen for whom they subsequently built a lodge then a hotel. Thereafter, it was full steam ahead and, in deference to this family tradition, the rooms in the hotel's older wing have now been restored to an approximation of their original appearance; in this wing also is the immaculately maintained library of Flåm's most notable writer, the poet Per Sivle (1857–1904). The modern rooms in the other wing are more straightforward (and cost around 400kr more), though all are comfortable; the better rooms face the fjord and have mini-balconies. The hotel restaurant is outstanding whether à la carte (mains average 280kr) or at the all-you-can-eat buffet (mid-May to mid-Sept nightly; 450kr). The restaurant features local, seasonal ingredients, many of which come from the family farm, including the cured meats and smoked fish from the smokery. The hotel is a couple of minutes' walk from the train station. Bike rental too. Closed mid-Dec to Jan. __1700kr__

**Heimly Pensjonat** ✆ 57 63 23 00, ⊚ heimly.no. Small guesthouse providing simple but perfectly adequate lodgings in a modern block in a quiet location about 450m east of the train station along the shore; it's a friendly place and the views down the fjord are charming. Bike rental too. __900kr__

# The Aurlandsdal valley

The workaday hamlet of **AURLAND**, just 10km from Flåm, strings along the fjord at the foot of the **Aurlandsdal valley** – and near the entrance to the whopping Lærdal tunnel (see p.227). The valley was once the final part of one of Norway's most celebrated **hikes**, a classic two- or three-day expedition that began at Finse train station (see p.220), from where the trail crossed the northern peripheries of the Hardangervidda plateau before descending the Aurlandsdal, with hikers then pushing on to Flåm to get the train back again. The trail incorporated an extravagant range of scenery, from upland plateau to plunging ravines, and parts of it followed an old cattle-drovers' route that once linked eastern and western

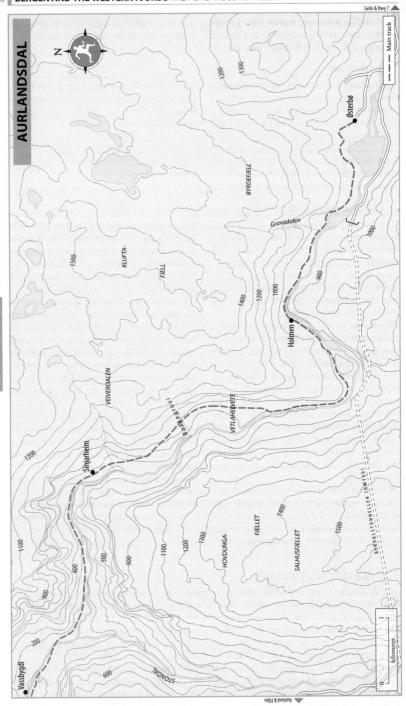

**AURLANDSDAL**

Geilo & Hwy 7

- - - Main track

Østerbø

BYRDEFJELL

Gravadalen

KLUFTA-

FJELL

VEIVERDALEN

Holmen

ROALDKVAM

VETLAHELVETE

Sinjarheim

HOVDUNGA-

FJELLET

SALHUSFJELLET

BLÅDALSTUNNELLEN (HWY 50)

STONDAL

Vassbygdi

kilometre

Aurland & Flåm

4

Norway. The trail lost much of its allure – and some of its beauty – when **Highway 50**, which links Highway 7 near Geilo (see p.174) with Aurland, was rammed through the Aurlandsdal as part of a hydroelectricity generation scheme in the 1970s, but sections of it still provide some excellent hiking. Perhaps the most scenic section today is the 21km stretch between **Østerbø** (820m) and **Vassbygdi** (94m), which takes between six and seven hours to complete (see map opposite). The trail threads its way through the woods and farms of the Aurlandsdal, passing crashing waterfalls and offering handsome valley views as well as one or two tight and steep scrambles. Østerbø, the starting point, comprises a pair of lonely mountain lodges (see below), located about 800m off Highway 50 about 43km from Flåm; Vassbygdi is a dull hamlet where the trail ends at the car park and bus stop.

## ARRIVAL AND DEPARTURE

**By bus** Fjord1 (ⓦ fjord1.no) operates a local seasonal bus (#23-490) up the Aurlandsdal valley (Highway 50) from Flåm to Aurland (late May to mid-June & mid- to late Sept 2 daily; late June to mid-Sept 4 daily; 10min) and then to Vassbygdi (late May to mid-June & mid- to late Sept 2 daily; late June to mid-Sept 3 daily; 20min), Østerbø (late May to mid-June & mid- to late Sept 2 daily; late June to mid-Sept

## THE AURLANDSDAL VALLEY

3 daily; 50min) and Geilo (late June to mid-Sept 1 daily; 2hr 20min). Timetables are such that it is usually possible to catch the bus from Flåm/Aurland to Østerbø, make the hike to Vassbygdi then return by bus the same day, but this means you'll be hiking against the clock. To avoid this, either book a taxi for the return leg or overnight in Østerbø at either of its two privately owned mountain lodges.

## ACCOMMODATION

**Østerbø Fjellstove** Østerbø ☎57 63 11 77, ⓦ aurlandsdalen.com. Nestled in a wide and rocky valley beside Highway 50, this large complex of mountain huts and lodges is a favourite with hikers. On offer are a variety of types of accommodation, from hostel-style beds in some of its lodges through to hotel rooms, which are plain and straightforward but still very comfortable. Full board costs about 300kr on top of the room rate. Late May to Sept.

Dorms 300kr, doubles 1220kr
**Østerbø Turisthytte** Østerbø ☎57 63 11 41, ⓦ osterbo-turisthytte.no. As with the *Fjellstove*, this mountain lodge is popular with hikers and offers a range of accommodation – from four-bunk bedrooms to family cabins and double rooms. They also offer filling evening meals (265kr). Late May to Sept. Dorms 355kr, cabins 540kr, doubles 840kr

# Aurland to Lærdal

Opened in 2000, and linking Aurland with Lærdal, the **Lærdalstunnelen** (Lærdal tunnel) drills its way through the mountains and was the last section of the fast road, the **E16** – from Bergen to Oslo – to be completed. At 24.5km, it's the longest road tunnel in the world, but it only took five years to construct, which is, by any standard, a remarkable achievement. Aware that drivers could become bemused and/or disorientated in the tunnel, three **cave-like** areas have been quarried at 6km intervals and whereas the main tunnel has white lights, the caves have blue lighting with yellow lights at the edges, supposedly to give an impression of sunrise, though the end effect is just surreal. Giant fans draw air in from both entrances, with polluted air driven out through ventilation shafts, and the tunnel also employs its own air treatment plant. The Lærdalstunnelen runs north from just outside the village of Aurland to the **Lærdal valley,** at a point just 6km south of the fjordside village of Lærdalsøyri. The tunnel is, of course, the fastest route from Aurland to Lærdal – and, even better, there are no tolls – but the 48km mountain road the tunnel replaced, the narrow **Aurlandsvegen**, has survived to provide splendid views and some hair-raising moments; it's open from the beginning of June to around the middle of October.

## Lærdalsøyri

Shadowed by a ring of mountains, **LÆRDALSØYRI** – or simply **LÆRDAL** – is an elongated village that lies sandwiched between Highway 5 and the River Lærdalselvi as it gurgles into the fjord. In former times, Lærdalsøyri was a busy port and transit centre, but Norway's road building programme put an end to that – witness the almost total lack of harbour facilities. Nowadays, one part of the village is modern and industrial, the other – known as **Gamle Lærdalsøyri** – comprises a batch of old timber buildings that date back to the late nineteenth century. Strolling through this older part of the village is a pleasant way of spending half an hour or so, and afterwards you can have a cup of tea at the *Lindstrøm Hotell* (see below).

Norsk Villakssenter

May & Sept daily 10am–5pm; June–Aug daily 10am–7pm • 95kr • ☎ 57 66 67 71, ⓦ norsk-villakssenter.no

Lærdalsøyri's showpiece tourist attraction is the **Norsk Villakssenter** (Norwegian Wild Salmon Centre), which occupies a conspicuous – and conspicuously ugly – modern building down by the river on the northern edge of the village, just east of Highway 5. Inside, a film explains the convoluted life cycle of the salmon, which you then observe swimming around in a large tank, and there are displays on salmon fishing.

### ARRIVAL AND INFORMATION                                                      LÆRDALSØYRI

**By bus** Buses pull in beside Highway 5. Nor-Way Bussekspress operates the Sognebussen (#450) to Flåm (4–5 daily; 50min), Voss (4–5 daily; 2hr), Bergen (4–5 daily; 3hr 30min) and Sogndal (4–5 daily; 45min).
**By car ferry** Car ferries from Gudvangen (June–Aug 2 daily; 3hr) and Kaupanger (June–Aug 2 daily; 50min) dock at the jetty at the west end of the village.
**By car** From Lærdalsøyri, it's 8km north along Highway 5

to Fodnes, where a car ferry crosses over the Sognefjord to Mannheller (every 20min, but hourly midnight to 6am; 15min); Mannheller is 18km from Sogndal (see p.232). In the other direction, heading east along the E16, it's about 30km to Borgund stave church (see p.173).
**Tourist office** In the Norsk Villakssenter (daily: June–Aug daily 11am–7pm; Sept 11am–5pm; ☎ 57 66 67 71, ⓦ alr.no).

### ACCOMMODATION AND EATING

**Lindstrøm Hotel** Lærdalsøyri ☎ 57 66 69 00, ⓦ lindstroemhotel.com. In the old part of the village, the *Lindstrøm* occupies five buildings, the oldest of which dates back to the late nineteenth century – witness the fancy

scrollwork. The hotel's 86 rooms are spread among three of these buildings and are modern and functional. Coffee and snacks are served during the day and there's a self-service buffet at night (daily 7–8.30pm). Open May–Sept. **1300kr**

## The Sognefjord

Profoundly beautiful, the **Sognefjord** (ⓦ sognefjord.no) drills in from the coast for some 200km, its inner recesses splintering into half a dozen subsidiary fjords. Perhaps inevitably, none of the villages and small towns that dot the fjord quite lives up to the splendid setting, but **Balestrand** and **Mundal**, on the Fjærlandsfjord, come mighty close and are easily the best bases. Both are on the north side of the fjord which, given the lack of roads on the south side, is where you want (or pretty much have) to be – Flåm (see p.224) apart. Mundal is also near two southerly tentacles of the Jostedalsbreen glacier – **Flatbreen** and easy-to-reach **Bøyabreen**.

Highway 55 hugs the Sognefjord's north bank for much of its length, but at **Sogndal** it slices northeast to clip along the lustrous **Lustrafjord**, which boasts a top-notch attraction in **Urnes stave church**, reached via a quick ferry ride from **Solvorn**. Further north, a side road leaves Highway 55 to clamber up from the Lustrafjord to the east side of the Jostedalsbreen glacier at the **Nigardsbreen nodule**, arguably the glacier's finest vantage point. Thereafter Highway 55 – as the **Sognefjellsveg** – climbs steeply to run along the western side of the **Jotunheimen mountains**, an extraordinarily beautiful journey even by Norwegian standards and one which culminates with the road thumping down to **Lom** on the flatlands beside Highway 15.

### GETTING AROUND                                                           THE SOGNEFJORD

Public transport to and around the Sognefjord is generally excellent, its assorted car ferries, Hurtigbåt express

passenger boats and buses mostly operated by Fjord 1 (ⓦ fjord1.no).

**By bus** Nor-Way Bussekspress (🐧nor-way.no) operates the Sognebussen (#450), which links Bergen with Gudvangen (see p.223), Flåm and Sogndal; and the Sogn og Fjordane Ekspressen (#170), which runs from Florø (see p.240) to Mundal, Sogndal and ultimately Oslo. Local buses shuttle along the northern shore of the Sognefjord to connect Sogndal with Balestrand and, in the summertime only, run north from Sogndal to Turtagrø and Lom via the Sognefjellsveg (Highway 55). A further seasonal service links Sogndal with the Nigardsbreen arm of the Jostedalsbreen glacier.

**By car ferry** There are three main car ferry services on the Sognefjord: Fodnes to Mannheller (for Sogndal); Vangsnes to both Hella and Dragsvik (for Balestrand); and, from May to Sept, Balestrand to Mundal on the Fjærlandsfjord. The last is wonderfully scenic.

**By Hurtigbåt passenger express boat** Express boats link Bergen with Vik, Balestrand, Flåm and Sogndal. There's also a Hurtigbåt between Aurland and Flåm.

## Balestrand

**BALESTRAND**, an appealing first stop on the Sognefjord, has been a tourist destination since the middle of the nineteenth century, when it was discovered by European travellers in search of cool, clear air and picturesque mountain scenery. One of the visitors was Kaiser Wilhelm II, who became a frequent visitor, sharing his holiday spot with the tweeds and bustles of the British bourgeoisie. These days, the village is used as a touring base for the immediate area, as the battery of small hotels above the quay testifies, but it's all very small-scale, and among the thousand-strong population farming remains the principal livelihood.

An hour or so will suffice to take a peek at Balestrand's several low-profile attractions. Lining up along the **harbour** are the old post office, which features temporary displays on the town and its environs; a brace of art galleries; and an aquarium, the Sognefjord Akvarium.

### English church of St Olav

Kong Belesveg • May–Sept daily 10am–10pm • Free

From the harbour, it's a couple of minutes' walk to the **English church of St Olav**, a spiky, brown and beige, wooden structure of 1897. It was built in the general style of a stave church at the behest of a British émigré, a certain Margaret Kvikne, who moved here after she married a local man, Knut Kvikne, the owner of the *Kviknes Hotel* (see p.230). Poor old Margaret actually died from tuberculosis three years before the church was opened, but not before she had climbed a string of local mountains, much to her husband's delight.

### Viking burial mounds

The British interest is recalled by St Olav's church, but the Germans have left their mark too: about 300m south of the church, down beside the fjord, are two humpy **Viking burial mounds**, supposedly the tombs of King Bele and his wife, who both appear in the Sagas. On the larger of them is a statue of the king in heroic pose, plonked there by the Kaiser in 1913 to match the statue of Bele's son-in-law that stands across the fjord in Vangsnes (see p.222).

### Hiking around Balestrand

Several **hiking trails** ascend the rocky, forested slopes immediately to the west of the village, clambering up to the peaks and lakes of the plateau beyond. The tourist office will supply a free map of these hiking trails and advise on their length and difficulty, but perhaps the most appealing is the two-hour jaunt through the woods above the village with fine views over the fjord. For an even wider, view you can make the short detour off the main path up to **Orrabenken** (370m above sea level).

### ARRIVAL AND INFORMATION                                                         BALESTRAND

**By car ferry** Balestrand has a car ferry dock that's right in the centre of the village, but this is only for the boat to the Fjærlandsfjord; otherwise, the nearest you'll get is Dragsvik, 9km north along the fjord on Highway 55. This ferry operates a triangular route between Dragsvik, Hella and Vangsnes. The Fjærlandsfjord ferry is a tourist service, so prices are above the norm (one-way 225kr, return 350kr; car & driver 400kr).

Destinations Dragsvik to Hella (every 40min to hourly; 15min) and Vangsnes (every 40min to hourly; 25min). Balestrand to Mundal, on the Fjærlandsfjord (May–Sept 1–2 daily; 1hr 40min).

**By Hurtigbåt passenger express boat** The Hurtigbåt jetty is in the centre of Balestrand, with boats to Aurland (May–Sept; 1–2 daily; 1hr 45min), Bergen (2 daily; 4hr),

Flåm (May–Sept; 1–2 daily; 2hr) and Sogndal (1 daily; 45min).

**By bus** Buses arrive and depart from beside the ferry dock. Local bus (#14-341) runs from Balestrand to Sogndal bus station (3 daily; 1hr 15min) for onward connections north and south.

**Tourist office** Down by the quayside (May & Sept Mon–Sat 10am–5pm; June–Aug Mon–Sat 8am–6pm, Sun 10am–5pm; ☎ 57 69 12 55, ⊕ visitbalestrand.no). Staff hand out a wide range of fjord leaflets, sell local hiking maps, supply bus and ferry timetables and rent out bicycles.

## ACCOMMODATION AND EATING

### HOTELS

★ **Balestrand Hotell** Kong Belesveg ☎ 57 69 11 38, ⊕ balestrand.com. Small and rather comforting family hotel in a three-storey modern block a 5–10min walk from the ferry dock. Has 30 prim-and-proper guest rooms, all en suite, the pick of which overlook the fjord and have mini-balconies (200kr extra). Mid-May to mid-Sept. **500kr**

**Balestrand Vandrerhjem** Kringsjå Lærargata ☎ 57 69 13 03, ⊕ hihostels.no. Just 150m uphill from the ferry dock, this substantial hostel inhabits an attractive timber building with a long veranda that overlooks the fjord. There are self-catering facilities, a café-restaurant and a laundry plus a neighbouring activity centre geared up for school parties. Late June to mid-Aug. Dorms **265kr**, doubles **820kr**

**Kviknes Hotel** Kviknevegen ☎ 57 69 42 00, ⊕ kviknes .no. The various buildings of this long-established hotel – some old, some new – dominate much of the Balestrand waterfront. Pride of architectural place goes to the original hotel building, an imposing wooden edifice whose balconies and pointy gables look out over the fjord. Inside, its public areas are a treat too, the fittings and furnishings completed in a sort of neo-Viking baronial style, all overseen by a platoon of fine Norwegian land- and seascape paintings. If you do decide to stay here, however, don't take a room without having a gander first: the rooms in the original building vary enormously – some are lovely and distinctly period, others are dowdy and need an overhaul – and you may settle for a room in the modern annexe instead: these are not particularly distinctive, but the best (on the top floors) have wide fjord views and most

have mini-balconies. The hotel restaurant serves up a banquet-sized, help-yourself buffet (500kr) every night – go early to get the pick and be sure to leave room for the ground-moving, earth-shattering mousse. Late April to Sept. **2000kr**

★ **Midtnes Hotel** Kong Belesveg ☎ 57 69 42 40, ⊕ midtnes.no. About 300m from the ferry dock behind the English church, this low-key, pleasantly sedate hotel has a few workaday but spacious rooms in a modern wing adjoining the original clapboard house; make sure to get a room with a fjord view (200kr extra). The *Midtnes* also serves tasty, excellent-value dinners (290kr). Open all year. **990kr**

### CAMPSITE

**Sjøtun Camping** Sjøtunsvegen ☎ 95 06 72 61, ⊕ sjotun.com. The town campsite occupies a treeless field just beyond the Viking burial mounds, 1km or so south of the dock. There are four-person cabins as well as tent and caravan pitches (20kr extra for a vehicle). June to mid-Sept. Tent and two adults **150kr**, cabin **300kr**

### CAFÉ

**Kafé Me Snakkast** Down by the quayside ☎ 91 56 28 42, ⊕ detgylnehus.no. The best café in town, an informal, friendly little place with lots of local art and hand-me-downs on the walls. Their menu emphasizes local ingredients and the soups – troll soup (mushrooms, carrots and onions) for one, fish soup another (12kr) – are filling and tasty. Metres from the ferry dock. Daily: May–Aug 10am–10pm; late April & Sept 10am–5pm.

## Mundal and the Fjærlandsfjord

Most attractively reached by car ferry from Balestrand, the **Fjærlandsfjord** is a wild place, its flanks blanketed by a thick covering of trees that extends down to the water's edge, with a succession of thundering waterfalls tumbling down vast clefts in the rock up above. The village of **MUNDAL** – sometimes inaccurately referred to as Fjærland – matches its surroundings perfectly, a gentle ribbon of old wooden houses edging the fjord, with the mountains as a louring backcloth. It's one of the region's most picturesque places, saved from the developers by its isolation: it was one of the last settlements on the Sognefjord to be connected to the road system, with Highway 5 from Sogndal only being completed in 1986.

## NORWEGIAN BOOK TOWN

Mundal has eschewed the crasser forms of commercialism to become the self-styled "**Den Norske Bokbyen**" (Norwegian Book Town; ⓦ bokbyen.no), with a dozen rustic buildings accommodating antiquarian and secondhand **bookshops**. Naturally enough, most of the books are in Norwegian, but there's a liberal sprinkling of English titles too. The main bookselling season runs from May to late September and the bookshops are usually open daily from 10am to 6pm, though one or two places do hang on into the winter.

### Mundal kirke

June–Sept daily 10am–6pm • Free

Mundal has two good-looking buildings, the *Hotel Mundal* (see p.232) and the adjacent **church**, painted maroon and dating from 1861. The church lacks ornamentation, but it is immaculately maintained and its graveyard hints at the hard but healthy life of the district's farmers – most of them seem to have lived to a ripe old age. One man who didn't make it that far was a German officer, buried here – you'll spot the plinth – after a climbing accident in 1910; his family donated the modest, painted baptismal font.

### Hiking around Mundal

Many locals are still farmers, but in summer precious few of them herd their cattle up to the mountain pastures, as was the custom until the 1960s. The disused tracks to these summer farms (*støls*) now serve as **hiking trails** of varying length and difficulty – the tourist office (see p.232) will advise, but one of the easier routes is the two-hour (each way) hoof west from the village up the country lane that follows **Mundalsdal** to **Fjellstølen**, at 350m. Much easier is the 2.5km stroll north along the quiet byroad that slips prettily along the fjord to link the village with Highway 5. Just before you get to the main road, you'll spy a large **bird hide** that overlooks the protected wetlands at the tip of the Fjærlandsfjord. These wetlands, **Bøyaøri**, attract over one hundred species of bird with mallard, oystercatcher, heron and lapwing, among many others, all making their appearance.

### Norsk Bremuseum

Fjærland • Daily: April, May, Sept & Oct 10am–4pm; June–Aug 9am–7pm • 120kr • ☎ 57 69 32 88, ⓦ bre.museum.no

The **Norsk Bremuseum** (Norwegian Glacier Museum), sitting tight against Highway 5 at the start of the byroad to Mundal, tells you more than you ever wanted to know about glaciers and then some. It features several lavish hands-on displays and screens films about them, and package tourists turn up in their droves. The staff also supply a comprehensive range of information on the **Jostedalsbreen Nasjonalpark**.

### The Jostedalsbreen glacier: Flatbreen

Guided glacier walks 650kr per person, including special equipment • Advance reservations at least a day beforehand are essential via either Mundal tourist office (see p.232) or the Norsk Bremuseum

If you're after a **guided glacier walk** on the Jostedalsbreen, the usual target from Mundal is the **Supphellebreen**, the Jostedalsbreen's nearest hikeable arm, or, to be precise, the part of it called the **Flatbreen**. Beautiful it may be, but it's also challenging and neither is it easy to get to. Flatbreen excursions take between seven and nine hours (with 2–3hr on the ice) and the season runs from late June to early September.

### The Jostedalsbreen glacier: Bøyabreen

It's actually possible to get close to the Jostedalsbreen without breaking sweat. Head north from Mundal on Highway 5 and, after about 10km – just before you enter the tunnel – watch for the signposted, dirt and gravel side road on the right that leads to the **Bøyabreen**, just 800m away. You can drive the first 600m, to the café and car park, and from here it's an easy stroll to the slender glacial lake that is fed by the sooty shank of the Bøyabreen glacier arm up above.

**By bus** Local buses depart from the Mundal ferry dock; long-distance buses pull in beside the Norsk Bremuseum, on Highway 5, about 2.5km from Mundal. Nor-Way Bussekspress operates the long-distance Sogn og Fjordane Ekspressen (#170) to Florø (3 daily; 3hr 10min), Sogndal (3 daily; 30min) and Oslo (3 daily; 7hr 50min). A local bus runs

between Mundal and the Norsk Bremuseum (June to mid-Sept 1–2 daily); it connects with the car ferry from Balestrand.

**By car ferry** Mundal's car ferry dock is at the south end of the village, the briefest of walks from the tourist office, and it has services to Balestrand (May–Sept 1–2 daily; 1hr 40min).

## INFORMATION

**Tourist office** About 300m from the ferry dock (May–Sept daily 10am–6pm; ☎ 57 69 32 33, ⓦ fjaerland.org). They will advise on local hiking routes, sell hiking maps and have bus and ferry timetables. They rent out bicycles too.
**Jostedalsbreen Nasjonalpark** The Norsk Bremuseum

(☎ 57 69 32 88, ⓦ bre.museum.no; see p.231) is one of the Jostedalsbreen Nasjonalpark's three information centres (see box, p.239). The staff supply a comprehensive range of information on the park, including details of Breturar (guided glacier walks) on the nearest negotiable nodule, Flatbreen.

## ACCOMMODATION AND EATING

**Bøyum Camping** ☎ 57 69 32 52, ⓦ fjaerland.org /boyumcamping. Near the Bremuseum, 2km or so from Mundal, this simple and straightforward campsite occupies a large, treeless field. May to Sept. Two-person cabins 730kr, two people and a tent 120kr
**Fjærland Fjordstue Hotell** ☎ 41 00 02 00, ⓦ fjaerland .no. A very well-tended family hotel with sixteen rooms decorated in a frilly, homely manner. Nine of the rooms have views over the adjacent fjord, as does the outside terrace and the sitting room. They offer an evening meal at an extra cost of 380kr. Mid-May to mid-Sept. 1200kr
**Hotel Mundal** ☎ 57 69 31 01, ⓦ hotelmundal.no. This is the obvious choice of the two fjordside hotels in Mundal. It's a splendid, somewhat quirky sort of place whose

cream-painted, nineteenth-century, high-pitched roofs, turrets and verandas overlook the fjord from among the handful of buildings that amount to the village centre. Inside, the public rooms, which date back to 1891, display many original features, from the parquet floors and fancy wooden scrollwork through to the old-fashioned sliding doors of the expansive dining room. The rooms are perhaps a tad frugal, but somehow it doesn't matter much. If you do stay, look out for the old photos on the walls of men in plus-fours and hobnail boots clambering round the glaciers – only softies bothered with gloves. As usual, the overnight rate includes breakfast, but given that Mundal hardly heaves with restaurants, you'll probably want dinner at the hotel too – the four-course set menu costs 550kr. May–Sept. 1700kr

## Sogndal and around

**SOGNDAL**, a short ferry ride and 50km east of Balestrand, is the largest town hereabouts, though, with a population of just under seven thousand, this is hardly a major boast. Neither is Sogndal especially appealing: it has, admittedly, a pleasant fjord setting in a broad valley, sheltered by low, green hills dotted with apple and pear trees, but its straggly centre is a rash of modern concrete and glass. There are, however, a couple of minor attractions within a few kilometres' radius which might detain you.

### De Heibergske Samlinger – Sogn Folkemuseum

May & Sept daily 10am–3pm; June–Aug daily 10am–5pm; Oct–April Mon–Fri 10am–3pm • 70kr • ☎ 47 57 67 82 06, ⓦ dhs.museum.no

Beside Highway 5, 8km from Sogndal, is **De Heibergske Samlinger – Sogn Folkemuseum** (Heiberg Collections of the Sogn Folk Museum), named after a Mr Heiberg, who was an avid collector of – and expert in – old Norwegian agricultural tools. It's hard to say if Mr Heiberg's special interest made him an entertaining dinner guest, but his legacy, this folk museum, is pleasant enough, its thirty-odd relocated buildings, which mostly date from the nineteenth century, rolling down the bumpy hillside. Together, they give something of the flavour of an older rural Norway, especially when the animals are knocking around in the summer months. Speaking of flavours, the staff bake their own cakes and sell them at the **café** – and very tasty they are, too.

### Kaupanger stave church

Early June to mid-Aug daily 9.30am–5.30pm • 50kr • ⓦ stavechurch.com

**KAUPANGER**, 12km along Highway 5 from Sogndal, spreads up the hill from its miniature harbour, the red and white timber houses of the old part of the village inching up towards **Kaupanger stavkirke** (stave church). A much-modified thirteenth-century structure whose dourness is offset by its situation, the church stands amid buttercup meadows with views of the fjord on one side and forested hills on the other. The interior has several unusual features, most memorably a **musical score** painted on one of the walls. No one is quite sure if the score was meant to be purely decorative or had some musical function, but it does appear to be a (rough) copy of a hymn traditionally sung on Ascension Day. The church also has two sad portraits of Danish bailiffs and their families: one is pictured with three stillborn babies, the other with one young son, who has a tiny red cross (for death) above his head.

## ARRIVAL AND INFORMATION

**By Hurtigbåt passenger express boat** Express boats dock on the west side of Sogndal town centre, with services to Bergen (1 daily; 4hr 40min), Balestrand (1 daily; 50min) and Flåm (1 daily; 1hr).

**By car ferry** Ferries from Gudvangen (May–Sept 1–3 daily; 2hr 15min) and Lærdalsøyri (May–Sept 1 daily; 50min) dock at the foot of Kaupanger village, about 15min walk from the stave church.

**By bus** Sogndal bus station is on the west side of the town centre near the end of Gravensteinsgata, the long main drag. Nor-Way Bussekspress operates the Sognebussen (#450) to Bergen (4–5 daily; 4hr 30min), Gudvangen (4–5 daily; 2hr) and Flåm (4–5 daily; 1hr 40min); and the Sogn og Fjordane Ekspressen (#170) to Florø (3 daily; 3hr), the Norsk Bremuseum, near Mundal (3 daily; 30min) and Oslo (3 daily; 7hr 15min). Local buses include the #4-341 to Balestrand (3 daily; 1hr 15min); #23-190 to Lom (late June to late Aug 2

### SOGNDAL AND AROUND

daily; 3hr 30min) and Otta (late June to late Aug 2 daily; 4hr 20min); and the Glacier Bus to Nigardsbreen (late June to late Aug 2 daily; 1hr 30min). There are also several local buses to Solvorn (Mon–Fri 1–2 daily; 30min). Buses to Kaupanger halt near the ferry dock. The Sogn og Fjordane Ekspressen (#170) links Kaupanger with Sogndal (3 daily; 15min).

**By car** From Sogndal, it's about 20km to the Mannheller–Fodnes car ferry (every 20min, but hourly midnight to 6am; 15min).

**Tourist office** Gravensteinsgata, Sogndal (May to mid-June Mon–Fri 10am–4pm; mid-June to mid-Aug Mon–Fri 9am–6pm, Sat 10am–4pm; mid-Aug to Sept Mon–Fri 10am–4pm; ☎ 97 60 04 43, ⓦ sognefjorden.no). In the large and modern Kulturhus beside the main street, staff issue bus and ferry timetables, and have a list of local accommodation. From the tourist office, it's about 600m west to the bus station.

## ACCOMMODATION AND EATING

**Quality Hotel Sogndal** Gravensteinsgata 5 ☎ 57 62 77 00, ⓦ choicehotels.no. A welcome addition to the Sogndal hotel scene, this slick and very glassy modern hotel overlooks the main street at the west end of town. There are 115 rooms here – and smart-chain describes them best. The restaurant offers the best food in Sogndal, with the à la carte menu (daily 3–9pm) doing its best to feature organic ingredients; mains average 220kr. **1430kr**, sp/r **1100kr**

**Sogndal Vandrerhjem** Helgeheimsvegen 9 ☎ 57 62 75 75, ⓦ hihostels.no. HI hostel which actually manages

to feel quite homely despite being housed in a residential rural high school (a Folkehøgskule). Facilities include self-catering and common rooms. Finding the place is straightforward: approaching Sogndal from the southeast on Highway 5, the hostel is clearly signposted from the main drag, just beyond the bridge at the east end of town; in the opposite direction, coming from the bus station, it's about 400m beyond the roundabout at the east end of Gravensteinsgata. Open mid-June to mid-Aug. Dorms **225kr**, doubles **520kr**

## Solvorn and around

**SOLVORN**, around 16km along Highway 55 from Sogndal, is a dainty hamlet of bright-white timber houses clustering the sheltered foreshore of the **Lustrafjord** with the craggy mountains louring behind. Solvorn is a lovely little place and, to make things even better, it possesses a smashing hotel and is only a quick car ferry ride from one of the region's star attractions – Urnes stave church.

### Urnes stave church

May–Sept daily 10.30am–5.30pm • 60kr • ☎ 57 67 88 40, ⓦ stavechurch.com • From the car ferry in Ornes (see p.234), it's a stiff 15min (1.2km) hike up the hill to the church

Magnificently sited across the Lustrafjord from Solvorn, with the hamlet of **Ornes** down below and the mountains in the distance, **Urnes stave church** is the oldest and most celebrated of its kind in Norway. Parts of the building date back to the twelfth century, and its most remarkable feature is its wonderful medieval **carvings**. On the outside, incorporated into the north wall – the remains of an earlier church dating from around 1070 – are several exquisite door panels, alive with a swirling filigree of strange beasts and delicate vegetation. These forceful, superbly crafted panels bear witness to the sophistication of Viking woodcarving – indeed, the church has given its name to this distinctively Nordic art form, found in many countries where Viking influence was felt and now generally known as the "Urnes" style. Most of the interior is seventeenth-century – including some splendidly bulbous pomegranates – but there is Viking woodcarving here too, notably the strange-looking figures and beasts carved on the capitals of the staves and the sacred-heart bench-ends. A small display in the neighbouring house-cum-ticket-office fills in all the details and has photographic enlargements of carvings that are hard to decipher inside the (poorly lit) church.

### ARRIVAL AND DEPARTURE
SOLVORN AND AROUND

**By bus** Buses from Sogndal (Mon–Fri 1–2 daily; 30min) stop beside the ferry dock.

**By car ferry** The jetty is at the foot of Solvorn village, from which a ferry runs across the Lustrafjord to Ornes (for Urnes stave church; May–Sept daily 10am–5pm, hourly; Oct–April Mon–Fri 4–6 daily, no Sat & Sun service; 20min; passengers 32kr, car & driver 87kr; ☏ 91 79 42 11, ⓦ urnesferry.com).

### ACCOMMODATION AND EATING

**Eplet Bed & Apple** Solvorn ☏ 41 64 94 69, ⓦ eplet.net. One of the region's more distinctive places to stay, this combined hostel, hotel and apple juice farm, which inhabits a two-storey modern house, is owned and operated by a one-time long-distance cyclist and traveller who seems to have been just about everywhere. He has created a laid-back, easy-going place with dormitory accommodation and a few neat, plain and modern hotel rooms. You can camp in the grounds too, while mountain-bike rental is free for guests, and there's a self-catering kitchen. They serve breakfast, but otherwise they refer you to the café down at the harbour. The juice factory is in the basement and the house is surrounded by an orchard which has its own complement of sheep. *Eplet* is located in the heart of the village about 300m back up the road from the dock – just watch for the sign. No cards – and there are no ATMs in Solvorn. And, by the way, the apple juice is just fantastic. May–Sept. Tents <u>100kr</u>, dorms <u>200kr</u>, doubles <u>600kr</u>

★ **Walaker Hotell** Solvorn ☏ 57 68 20 80, ⓦ walaker .com. The *Walaker Hotell* has been in the same family for several generations, as witnessed by the old photographs that decorate the dining room-cum-lounge. Nowadays, the hotel divides into two distinct halves, beginning with the old house, a comely, pastel-painted, two-storey building whose porch is supported by a pair of columns – a Neoclassical extravagance that must have once amazed the locals. The rooms in the old house (an extra 250kr) have been attractively decorated in several period styles, from the big and beautiful carved wooden beds through to the floral patterns on the curtains. The annexe is something of a contrast, a one-storey, motel-style structure with modern rooms. At the back of the hotel, an old agricultural building is now used for art exhibitions and at the front is a pretty garden and a gazebo, where you can sit and ponder to the light of a silvery moon. The hotel restaurant is outstanding with a limited but well-chosen menu of beautifully prepared dishes that use local ingredients whenever possible. The hotel is metres from the jetty. May–Sept. Rate includes dinner. <u>1400kr</u>

## Jostedalsbreen Nasjonalpark: the Nigardsbreen

A great rumpled and seamed wall of ice that sweeps between high peaks, the **Nigardsbreen** nodule on the eastern flanks of the **Jostedalsbreen Nasjonalpark** is a magnificent spectacle. Most visitors are satisfied with the short hike up the glacier's shaggy flanks from the jetty on the shore of the icy green lake beneath it, but others plump for a **guided glacier walk** (see p.235): the Nigardsbreen is generally reckoned to have the best glacier walking in the whole of the Jostedalsbreen Nasjonalpark. The season for glacier walking here on this nodule lasts from mid-May to mid-September.

### ARRIVAL AND INFORMATION
JOSTEDALSBREEN: THE NIGARDSBREEN

**By car** Heading northeast from Sogndal on Highway 55, past the turning to Solvorn (see p.233), it's about 35km to Gaupne, where Highway 604 forks north for the delightful 34km trip up the wild, forested river valley to the eastern flanks of the Jostedalsbreen Nasjonalpark, where there's an information centre – the Breheimsenteret (see below). From the centre, it's another 3.5km drive or walk along the toll road (30kr/vehicle) to the lake, where a tiny boat (mid-June to Aug daily 10am–6pm; 40kr return) shuttles across to the bare rock slope beside the Nigardsbreen glacier nodule.

**By bus** The Glacier Bus from Sogndal (late June to late Aug 2 daily; 1hr 30min) stops outside the Breheimsenteret.

**Tourist information** The Breheimsenteret information and exhibition centre was burnt to a cinder in 2011 and while it is being rebuilt, its employees have been moved to temporary accommodation, which has been quickly assembled close to the original site (daily: May to late June & Sept 10am–5pm; late June to Aug 9am–7pm; displays 50kr; ☎57 68 32 50, ⓦjostedal.com). Staff here are experts on all things glacial and will make bookings for guided glacier walks.

## ACTIVITIES

**Guided glacier walks** There is a plethora of guided walks to choose from, beginning with a quick and easy 1–2hr jaunt suitable for children over six (daily July to late Aug; 250kr, children 100kr), through to much tougher 5hr excursions (July to late Aug 4 weekly; 760kr). Prices include

equipment and bookings can be made at the Breheimsenteret (book at least 1hr before departure). Advance reservations for overnight trips must be made at least four weeks beforehand.

## ACCOMMODATION

**Jostedal Hotel** Gjerde ☎ 57 68 31 19, ⓦjostedalhotel .no. In a well-maintained mountain lodge, this family-run hotel has around twenty rooms of the simple and straightforward variety. They serve hot and cold meals too,

with much of the food coming from the family farm. The hotel is about 2.5km south of the Breheimsenteret on Highway 604; the Glacier Bus from Sogndal passes close by. **930kr**

# The Sognefjellsveg

The mountain roads of Norway are some of the most melodramatic in Europe, but the wildest of them all is perhaps the **Sognefjellsveg** (Highway 55; ⓦsognefjellet.com), which runs the 110km from Skjolden, a dull little town at the head of the Lustrafjord, over to Lom (see p.236). Despite the difficulty of the terrain, the Sognefjellsveg – which is closed from late October to May depending on conditions – marks the course of one of the oldest trading routes in Norway, with locals transporting goods by mule or, amazingly enough, on their shoulders: salt and fish went northeast, hides, butter, tar and iron went southwest. That portion of the road that clambers over the highest part of the mountains – no less than 1434m above sea level – was only completed in 1938 under a Great Depression "make-work" scheme, which kept a couple of hundred young men busy for two years. Tourist literature hereabouts refers to the lads' "motivation and drive", but considering the harshness of the conditions and the crudeness of their equipment – pickaxes, spades and wheelbarrows – their purported enthusiasm seems unlikely.

### The route

Beyond **Skjolden**, the Sognefjellsveg weaves its way up the **Bergsdal valley** to a mountain plateau which it proceeds to traverse, providing absolutely stunning views of the jagged, ice-crusted peaks of the **Jotunheimen Nasjonalpark** (see p.163) to the east. En route, the most obvious stopping point is **TURTAGRØ**, just 15km out from Skjolden, which is no more than a handful of buildings – including a hotel (see p.236) – but as good a place as any to pick up one of the several **hiking trails** (see box, p.236) that head off into the mountains.

Beyond Turtagrø, the Sognefjellsveg cuts its wild and windy way across the plateau before clipping down through forested **Leirdal**, passing the old farmstead of **ELVESETER**. Here, about 45km from Turtagrø, a complex of old timber buildings has been turned into a hotel-cum-mini-historical-theme-park, its proudest possession being a bizarre 33-metre-high plaster and cyanite column, the **Sagasøyla**. On top of the column is the figure of that redoubtable Viking Harald Hardrada and down below is carved a romantic interpretation of Norwegian history. Dating from the

### HIKES FROM TURTAGRØ INTO THE SKAGASTØLSDAL VALLEY

One tough hike from the *Turtagrø Hotel* (see below) is the six-hour, round-trip haul southeast along the well-worn (but not especially well-signed) path up the **Skagastølsdal valley** to DNT's self-service **Skagastølsbu hut**, though you can of course make the hike shorter by only going some of the way. The valley is divided into a number of steps, each preceded by a short, steep ascent; the hotel is 884m above sea level, the hut, a small stone affair surrounded by a staggering confusion of ice caps, mini-glaciers and craggy ridges, is at 1758m. The terrain is unforgiving and the weather unpredictable, so novice hikers beware – If you'd rather have a guide, the *Turtagrø Hotel* is a base for mountain guides, who offer an extensive programme of guided mountain walks as well as **summer cross-country skiing** – the hotel will help to sort things out; the season begins at Easter and extends until October.

1830s, the column was brought to this remote place because no one else would have it – not too surprising really.

From Elveseter, it's a short hop over the hills to **Bøverdal**, which runs down into the crossroads settlement of Lom. On the way, you'll pass the start of the narrow, 18km-long mountain road that sneaks up the **Visdal valley** to the *Spiterstulen* lodge (see below).

## GETTING AROUND                                THE SOGNEFJELLSVEG

**By bus** Sogndal bus station is on the west side of the town centre near the end of Gravensteinsgata, the long main drag. Local bus #23-190 runs the length of the

Sognefjellsveg from Sogndal to Lom (late June to late Aug 2 daily; 3hr 30min).

## ACCOMMODATION AND EATING

### TURTAGRØ

⭐ **Turtagrø Hotel** Fortun ☎ 57 68 08 00, �🌐turtagro .no. There's been a hotel here beside the Sognefjellsveg since 1888, but the present structure, a large and attractive red-timber mountain lodge with a sprightly modernist design, was only constructed in 2002, after fire destroyed its predecessor. The interior is very Scandinavian, with spacious public rooms and oodles of pine, and the nineteen guest rooms are in similar vein; as well as the doubles in the main lodge, there are also four- to six-bedded bunk rooms in the older "Swiss chalet" next door and a small campsite. The hotel specializes in all things to do with the surrounding Jotunheim mountains: they sell hiking maps, will advise on local hiking conditions, and will arrange guided walks and climbs; they even have their own "mountain library".

Considering the hotel's solitary location, the restaurant is very good indeed and is strong on local ingredients – try the reindeer. April–Oct. Main lodge 2000kr, dorms 510kr, camping (tent plus two adults) 125kr,

### SPITERSTULEN

**Spiterstulen** Spiterstulen ☎61 21 94 00, ⓦ spiterstulen.no. This mountain lodge complex, high up on the tree line at 1100m, offers a variety of accommodation, from the bunk beds of the youth section to modest double rooms, and there's a café-restaurant too. For part of the season, the lodge becomes an outdoor pursuits centre – the lodge is within a day's hike of no fewer than seventeen peaks. March, April & late May to mid-Oct. Dorms 330kr, doubles 860kr

# Lom

A long-time trading and transport centre, **LOM** benefits – in a modest sort of way – from the farms that dot the surrounding valleys. It also makes a comfortable living from the passing tourist trade, with motorists pausing here before the last thump down Highway 15 to the Geirangerfjord or the dramatic haul up the Sognefjellsveg mountain road. There are a couple of worthwhile attractions too and one particularly enticing place to stay and eat.

## Lom stavkirke

Daily: mid-May to mid-June & mid-Aug to Sept 9am–5pm; mid-June to mid-Aug daily 9am–7pm • 50kr • ☎ 97 07 53 97

Lom's eighteenth-century heyday is recalled by its **stave church**, a strikingly attractive structure perched on a grassy knoll above the river. The original church was built here about 1200, but it was remodelled and enlarged after the Reformation, when the spire and transepts were added and the flashy altar and pulpit installed. Its most attractive features are the dinky, shingle-clad roofs, adorned by dragon finials, and the Baroque acanthus-vine decoration inside.

## Norsk Fjellmuseum

Mid-May to June & late Aug to mid-Sept Mon–Fri 9am–4pm, Sat & Sun 10am–3pm; July to late Aug daily 9am–7pm; mid-Sept to mid-May Mon–Fri 10am–3pm • 70kr • ☎ 61 21 16 00, ⑩ fjell.museum.no

Museum enthusiasts will want to visit Lom's **Norsk Fjellmuseum** (Norwegian Mountain Museum), a modern place just a few metres from the stave church that focuses on the Jotunheimen mountains. It's all here in admirable detail, from the fauna and the flora to the landscapes, farmers and past mountaineers, who scaled the peaks in tweeds and hobnail boots. The Fjellmuseum doubles as Lom tourist office (see below).

## Lom Bygdamuseum

**Buildings** July to mid-Aug daily 11am–4pm • 40kr **Site** open access • Free • ☎ 40 43 84 86

Up behind the Fjellmuseum, in the Skansen area of town, is the town's open-air museum the **Lom Bygdamuseum** (Lom District Museum), a surprisingly enjoyable collection of old log buildings in a forest setting. Norway teems with this type of museum but Lom's is better than most, though you wouldn't think so from the ticket office: it's in what must be the biggest and ugliest late-medieval *storstabburet* (large storehouse) in the country. Persevere, though, as the old wooden buildings in the woods beyond are a delight. One of them, a modest hut known as the **Olavsstugu**, is where St Olav, otherwise King Olav Haraldsson, is said to have spent a night as he beetled his way north to Trondheim. When the museum is closed, you can still wander round the site, though of course all the buildings are locked up.

**4**

### ARRIVAL AND INFORMATION                                     LOM

**By bus** Lom bus station is a few metres west along Highway 55 from the Highway 55/15 crossroads that marks the centre of town. The church, the museums and several hotels are within easy walking distance of the same crossroads. Nor-Way Bussekspress operates the Nordfjordekspressen (#147) to Grotli (3 daily; 1hr), Langvatn (for Gerainger and Åndalsnes, 3 daily; 1hr 10min), Stryn (3 daily; 2hr), Otta (3 daily; 1hr) and Oslo (3 daily; 6hr 40min). There's also local bus (#23-190), which

runs the length of the Sognefjellsveg from Lom to Sogndal (late June to late Aug 2 daily; 3hr 30min).

**Tourist information** In the centre of the village, metres from the main crossroads (mid-May to June & late Aug to mid-Sept Mon–Fri 9am–4pm, Sat & Sun 10am–3pm; July to late Aug daily 9am–7pm; mid-Sept to mid-May Mon–Fri 10am–3pm; ☎ 61 21 29 90, ⑩ visitjotunheimen.com). Staff will advise about hiking in the Jotunheimen mountains, issue bus timetables and sell hiking maps.

### ACCOMMODATION AND EATING

**Fossberg Hotel** ☎ 61 21 22 50, ⑩ fossberg.no. In the centre of Lom, a stone's throw from the main crossroads, this large and modern hotel complex is built in the general style of a mountain lodge. They have stolen a march on many of their rivals by having two pools, a sauna, a solarium and a gym. **1400kr**

★ **Fossheim Turisthotell** ☎ 61 21 95 00, ⑩ fossheimhotel.no. There's been a family-owned hotel here on this site for several generations and although the main lodge has been added to on several occasions, it still has a real mountain-rural feel. The public areas are dotted with bygones and the guest rooms, at the back of the hotel, have timber walls, floors and ceilings. It's all very cosy, and

so are the delightful little wooden cabins that trail up the wooded hillside beside the main building; some of them are very old and all are en suite. In the main lodge also is the hotel restaurant (June–Aug daily noon–3pm & 7–10pm; rest of year daily 1–4pm & 5–10pm), which is outstanding and wherever possible features local ingredients. They serve set meals – three courses 380kr, four courses 525kr – as well as à la carte; try the chicken fricassee in a creamed parmesan sauce. The *Fossheim* is located about 300m east of the village crossroads along Highway 15. Closed Jan & Feb. Cabins **1200kr**; rooms **1600kr**, sp/r **1300kr**

## Nordfjord and the Jostedalsbreen glacier

The inner recesses of the **Nordfjord** (Ⓦ nordfjord.no), the next great fjord system to the north of the Sognefjord, are readily explored along **Highway 60**, which weaves a pleasant, albeit tortuous, course through a string of little towns. Among them, **Loen** is easily the best base for further explorations, though humdrum **Stryn** is larger and more important. Stryn is also where **Highway 15** begins its long journey west along the length of the Nordfjord, with the road dipping and diving along the northern shore in between deep-green reflective waters and bulging peaks. It's a pleasant enough journey, but the Nordfjord doesn't have the severe allure of its more famous neighbours, at least in part because its roadside hamlets lack much appeal – end-of-the-fjord Måløy is unappetizing, though you can loop south to the much more agreeable coastal town of **Florø**. That said – and all in all – you're much better off sticking to Highway 60.

High up in the mountains, dominating the whole of the inner Nordfjord, lurks the **Jostedalsbreen glacier**, a five-hundred-kilometre-square ice plateau that creaks, grumbles and moans out towards the Sognefjord, the Nordfjord and the Jotunheimen mountains. The glacier stretches northeast in a lumpy mass from Highway 5, its myriad arms – or "**nodules**" – nudging down into the nearby valleys, the clay particles of its meltwater giving the local rivers and lakes their distinctive light-green colouring. Catching sight of the ice nestling between peaks and ridges can be unnerving – the overwhelming feeling being that somehow it shouldn't really be there. As the poet **Norman Nicholson** had it:

*A malevolent, rock-crystal*
*Precipitate of lava,*
*Corroded with acid,*
*Inch by inch erupting*
*From volcanoes of cold.*

For centuries, the glacier presented an impenetrable east–west barrier, crossed only at certain points by determined farmers and adventurers. It's no less daunting today, but access is much freer, a corollary of the creation of the **Jostedalsbreen Nasjonalpark** in

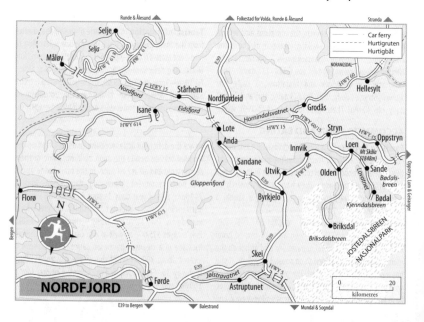

## GUIDED GLACIER WALKS ON THE JOSTEDALSBREEN

Most **guided glacier walks** on the Jostedalsbreen are scheduled between late June and early September, though on some arms of the glacier the season extends from May until October. The walks range from three-hour excursions to five-day expeditions. Day-trip prices start at 500–600kr per person for a four- to six-hour gambol, rising to 700–800kr for six to eight hours. **Booking** arrangements for the shorter glacier walks vary considerably. On some of the trips – for example those at the Nigardsbreen (see p.235) – it's sufficient to turn up at the information centre an hour or two beforehand, but in general it's a good idea to make a reservation at least a day ahead. Sometimes this is best done through one of the information centres (see box below), sometimes direct with the tour operator. In the case of the overnight trips, however, you must reserve at least four weeks beforehand. In all cases, basic **equipment** is provided, though you'll need to take good boots, waterproofs, warm clothes, gloves, hat, sunglasses – and sometimes your own food and drink too.

1991. Since then, roads have been driven deep into the glacier's flanks, the comings (but mostly goings) of the ice have been closely monitored and there has been a proliferation of officially licensed **guided glacier walks** (*breturar*) on its various arms (see box above). If that sounds too energetic and all you're after is a close look at the glacier, then this is possible at several places, with the easiest approach being the stroll to the **Bøyabreen** on the south side of the glacier near Mundal (see p.231). On the west side of the glacier, narrow side roads lead off Highway 60 to two more vantage points, the **Briksdalsbreen**, the most visited of the glacier's nodules, and the **Kjenndalsbreen**, which is much less crowded, far prettier and a twenty-minute walk from the end of the road– a delightful way to spend a morning or afternoon. By contrast, the **Nigardsbreen** (see p.234), on the east side of the glacier, requires more commitment, but the scenery is wilder and, to many tastes, more beautiful.

4

### GETTING AROUND                     NORDFJORD AND THE JOSTEDALSBREEN GLACIER

**By bus** Nor-Way Bussekspress (⬤nor-way.no) operates two particularly useful long-distance bus services in the Nordfjord area. These are the Nordfjordekspressen (#147) linking Stryn with Langvatn (for Geiranger), Lom, Otta and ultimately Oslo; and the Sogn og Fjordane Ekspressen (#170), which runs between Florø, Skei, Mundal, Sogndal and Oslo. Local buses run along the Nordfjord from Stryn to Loen and Olden and some of these continue on to Briksdal (for Briksdalsbreen), but there are no buses to the Kjenndalsbreen.

**By boat** There are two main car ferry services across the Nordfjord: Isane to Stårheim (every 30min; 15min), about halfway along the fjord, and, on the E39, Anda to Lote (every 30min; 20min). The Hurtigruten coastal boat calls at Florø, which is also linked to Bergen by a Hurtigbåt passenger express boat service.

**By car** The most direct way to get from the Sognefjord to the Nordfjord is to travel northwest from Sogndal (see p.232) on Highway 5 as it tunnels beneath an arm of the Jostedalsbreen glacier. Highway 5 then presses on to the Kjøsnes junction, where you turn left for the 11km-long detour to Astruptunet (see p.240). From the junction, it is just a couple of kilometres more to Skei, an important crossroads, where you can turn west for the time-consuming, 100km trip to Florø or head north for the 20km yomp up the valley to the hamlet of Byrkjelo. At Byrkjelo, Highway 60 forks north, cutting a splendid route over the hills on its way to Loen and ultimately Stryn on the Nordfjord. Thereafter, Highway 60 leaves the Nordfjord behind, pressing on north to the Norangsdal valley (see p.243) and Hellesylt on the Geirangerfjord (see p.249).

## JOSTEDALSBREEN NASJONALPARK INFORMATION CENTRES

A comprehensive leaflet detailing all the various walks in Jostedalsbreen is widely available across the region and at the national park's three **information centres**, (⬤jostedalsbre.no). These are the **Norsk Bremuseum**, on the south side of the glacier near Mundal (see p.231); the **Breheimsenteret** on the east side at the Nigardsbreen (see p.235); and the **Jostedalsbreen Nasjonalparksenter** (daily: May & Sept 10am–3pm; June–Aug 10am–6pm; exhibitions 80kr; ☎57 87 72 00) in Oppstryn, 20km east of Stryn on Highway 15. Each of the centres has displays on all things glacial and sells books, souvenirs and hiking maps.

## The Astruptunet

Late May to late June daily 11am–4pm; late June to mid-Aug daily 10am–5pm; mid-Aug to mid-Sept Sat & Sun 11am–4pm • 75kr • ☏ 57
72 67 82, ⓦ astruptunet.com • The Astruptunet is 11km west off Highway 5 from Skei

About 70km north of Sogndal, the **Astruptunet**, the one-time farmstead home and
studio of the artist **Nikolai Astrup** (1880–1928), sits prettily on the steep slope above
the southern shore of Lake Jølstravatnet in the village of **Sandal i Jølster**. Today's huddle
of old turf-roofed timber buildings looks much the same as it did during the artist's
lifetime, though the old barn has been replaced by a modern **gallery**, which is used for
temporary exhibitions of modern art. A versatile artist, Astrup's work included
paintings, sketches, prints and woodcuts, of which a good selection is on display here.
However, the bulk of the collection consists of his beautiful landscape paintings,
characteristically romanticized rural scenes in bright colours, with soft, flowing forms.
Unlike many of his contemporaries, Astrup eschewed Realism in favour of
Neo-Impressionism and, as such, he bridged the gap between his generation of
Norwegian painters and the Matisse-inspired artists who followed.

## Florø

**FLORØ**, Norway's westernmost town, scores high on west-coast commonalities: it has a
blustery island setting, its economy has been boosted by the oil industry, it offers
tourists sea-fishing trips, and its mostly modern centre is wrapped around the
traditional focus of coastal town life, the harbour. It also has one major claim to
historical fame as the birthplace of that redoubtable Viking chieftain **Eric Bloodaxe**
(d.954), who raided far and wide, partly – or so the Sagas suggest – to get away from
his wife, though judging by his name she might not have been too upset by his roving
either. Before the oil, **herrings** were the big economic deal hereabouts, those piscine
times recalled by the townsfolk on one day every June when they assemble a 400m-
long **herring table** (*sildebord*) on the main street, which groans under the weight of that
famous fish served alongside the humble boiled potato.

### The Kystmuseet

Brendøyvegen • Feb to late June & mid-Aug to Dec Mon–Fri 10am–3pm, Sat & Sun noon–3pm; late June to mid-Aug Mon–Fri
11am–6pm, Sat & Sun noon–4pm; closed Jan • 50kr • ☏ 57 74 22 33, ⓦ kyst.museum.no

Florø's only sight of note is the **Kystmuseet** (Coastal Museum), a rambling assortment
of old boathouses and dwellings set around three exhibition buildings, 2km south of
the centre of Florø. These contain a ragbag of local artefacts – tools, fishing tackle,
kitchen utensils etc – supplemented by a model of an oil platform and a small armada
of local wooden boats.

### Kinn

A passenger boat service runs from Florø to Kinn (June–Aug Mon–Fri 1 daily; 30min); boat timetables are available at Florø tourist office

Among the confetti of islands and skerries in the vicinity of Florø, the star turn is **Kinn**,
a rocky little lump whose grassy foreshore holds the stone **Kinnakyrkja** (Kinn church;
open access; free), a much-modified Romanesque structure dating from the twelfth
century with several intriguing carvings and a Baroque altarpiece.

---

**ARRIVAL AND INFORMATION**                                              **FLORØ**

**By bus** Nor-Way Bussekspress (ⓦ nor-way.no) operates
the Sogn og Fjordane Ekspressen (#170; 3 daily) linking
Florø, Skei, Mundal, Sogndal and Oslo.
**By boat** There's an all-year Hurtigbåt passenger express
boat service from Bergen (2 daily; 3hr 30min) and Florø is
also a Hurtigruten port. Boats dock in the main harbour
abutting the town centre.
**By car** The fastest road to Florø is Highway 5 from Sogndal

via Skei. It's also possible to reach Florø via the E39, the
main coastal road, from both Balestrand on the Sognefjord
and from Ålesund, though the latter journey does involve
three short car-ferry trips.
**Tourist office** Strandgata 30 (Mon–Fri 9am–5pm & Sat
10am–4pm, plus June–Sept Sun 11am–3pm; ☏ 57 74 30
00, ⓦ fjordkysten.no).

## ACCOMMODATION AND EATING

**Quality Hotel Florø** Hamnegata 7 ☏ 57 75 75 75, ⓦ choicehotels.no. The best place in Florø, this smart, medium-sized chain hotel sits beside the waterfront and occupies a new building in the style of an old warehouse. The rooms are spick, span and very modern – ask for one with a sea view. The hotel restaurant, *Bryggekanten*, specializes in (local) seafood with mains averaging around 25kr. 1390kr

## The Briksdalsbreen

Local bus (#14-703) runs 3–6 times daily along the Nordfjord from Stryn to the hamlet of Olden (20min), on the Nordfjord, from which another local service covers the 24km to Briksdal (#14-751; 1–3 daily; 30min)

**Briksdal** is s a scattering of mountain chalets that serves as the starting point for the easy and very popular 45-minute (3km) walk to the **Briksdalsbreen glacier arm**. The path skirts waterfalls and weaves up the river until you finally view the glacier, surprisingly blue except for streaks of dirt. Alternatively, you can hop on a twee-looking **battery-driven golf cart** (185kr) at the café area for the twenty-minute drive up to within 500m of the glacier.

## Loen and the Kjenndalsbreen

**LOEN** spreads ribbon-like along the Nordfjord's low-lying, grassy foreshore, with ice-capped mountains breathing down its neck. The village is home to one of Norway's most famous hotels, the outstanding, family-owned *Alexandra* (see p.242), but the handful of dwellings that make up the original village are located about 500m inland.

### Loen kyrkje

Perched on top of a gentle ridge in the old part of the village is **Loen kyrkje** (Loen church), a tidy structure dating from 1837. Its interior is unremarkable, though the folksy furnishings and fittings are pretty enough, but the views from outside over the fjord are delightful. Its churchyard and precincts also hold some items of interest, namely a stone Celtic cross that is at least a thousand years old, and a pair of **memorial plinths** to the villagers who were drowned in the disasters of 1905 and 1936. On both occasions, a great hunk of the Ramnefjell mountain fell into Lake Lovatnet behind the village and the ensuing **tidal wave** swept dozens of local farmsteads away. The second disaster was particularly tragic as the government had only just persuaded many of the villagers to return home after the first trauma.

### The Kjenndalsbreen

From beside the *Hotel Alexandra*, a 21km byroad leads south to the **Kjenndalsbreen** arm of the Jostedalsbreen glacier, whose fissured, blancmange-like blue-and-white folds tumble down the rock face, with a furious white-green river, fed by plummeting meltwater, flowing underneath. If the weather holds, it's a lovely spot for a picnic.

The road to the Kjenndalsbreen starts by slipping up the river valley past lush meadows, before threading along the shore of **Lovatnet**, a long and thin lake of glacial blue. Thereafter, the road scuttles on to the hamlet of **BØDAL**, whose grassy foreshore marks the sight of the village that bore the brunt of the two tidal waves (see above): today's houses perch cautiously on the ridge well above the water. After Bødal, it's a further 3km or so to the start of the toll road (40kr), which culminates in a car park. From here, it's an easy and very pleasant twenty-minute ramble through rocky terrain to the ice.

### Hiking up Mount Skåla

Loen is also the starting point of a popular five-hour hike east up to the plateau-top of **Mount Skåla** (1848m), from where the fjord and mountain views are simply fantastic. The path is clearly marked, but you'll have to be in good physical condition and have proper walking gear to undertake the trek; also, check locally for snow and ice conditions at the summit before setting out. The hike back down again takes about three hours, or you can overnight in the circular stone tower at the summit, the **Skålatårnet**, which serves as a self-service DNT hut with twenty beds and a kitchen. Curiously, the tower was built in 1891 at the behest of a local doctor – one Dr Kloumann – as a recuperation centre for tuberculosis sufferers.

### ARRIVAL AND DEPARTURE

**By bus** Buses to Loen pull in beside the *Hotel Alexandra*. There are no buses from Loen to the Kjenndalsbreen. Local

### LOEN AND THE KJENNDALSBREEN

buses (#14-703) run from Loen to Stryn (3–6 daily; 10min) and Olden (3–6 daily; 10min).

### ACTIVITIES

**Guided glacier walks** From May to Oct, there are guided glacier walks near Bødal on the Bødalsbreen with the main operator being Briksdal Breføring (☎57 87 68 00,

ⓦbriksdal-adventure.com). Their standard offering lasts 5–6hr, including 3hr on the ice, and costs 600kr; there are no guided glacier walks on the Kjenndalsbreen itself.

### ACCOMMODATION AND EATING

★ **Hotel Alexandra** ☎57 87 50 00, ⓦalexandra.no. Something of a fjordland institution, this long-established hotel occupies a capacious and conspicuous modern block looking straight out over the fjord. The expansive foyer sets the tone with its thick carpets, wood panelling and multi-coloured, roughly mortared stone walls – very appealing and very 1960s, as if Britt Ekland might appear in a big hat and shiny white boots at any moment. Beyond, the 200 rooms are spacious, infinitely comfortable and decorated in pastel shades, the better ones equipped with balconies and wide fjord views. Elsewhere, the hotel clocks up a full platoon of facilities, including a pool, a spa, gardens, a solarium, crazy golf plus bike and boat rental. Breakfasts are banquet-like, but the evening buffet (from 7pm; 520kr) is perhaps even better, a wonderful selection that lays fair claim to being the best in the fjords. Closed early Jan. **2600kr**, sp/r **1600kr**

**Hotel Loenfjord** ☎57 87 57 00, ⓦloenfjord.no. On the water's edge opposite – and owned by – the *Alexandra*, this modern, 140-room hotel is a happy cross between a

motel and a lodge, comprising a long and low modern building in a vernacular version of traditional Norwegian style. The rooms are comfortable and kept in prime condition. Closed Oct to May. **1800kr**, sp/r **1600kr**

**Loen Pensjonat** ☎57 87 76 24, ⓦloen-pensjonat .com. Housed in a lodge-like modern building, this pleasant guesthouse has ten guest rooms, each of which is decorated in a homely manner. The *pensjonat* is a few metres from the village church, which is itself about 500m from the *Alexandra*. Great views over the fjord too. Some of the rooms have shared facilities, others are en suite (for an extra 160kr). **520kr**

**Sande Camping** ☎57 87 45 90, ⓦsande-camping .no. One of the best of a string of campsites lining up along the road to the Kjenndalsbreen, with a herd of caravans and tents occupying a narrow slice of open ground right next to the lake. They rent out rowboats, canoes and bikes, and there is a sauna and a café too. Located 4.5km from the *Hotel Alexandra*. Tent with two people and a car **160kr**

## Stryn

**STRYN**, merely 12km around the Nordfjord from Loen, is the biggest town hereabouts, though with a population of just 2300 that's hardly a major boast. For the most part, it's a humdrum modern sprawl straggling beside its long main street, but there is a pleasant pocket of antique **timber houses** huddled round the old bridge, down by the river near the tourist office and just to the south of the main drag; take a few moments to have a look.

### ARRIVAL AND INFORMATION

**By bus** Stryn bus station is beside the river just to the west of the town centre on Highway 15/60. Nor-Way Bussekspress operates the Nordfjordekspressen (#147) to Langvatn (for Geiranger; 3 daily; 45min), Lom (3 daily; 2hr), Otta (3 daily; 3hr) and Oslo (3 daily; 8hr 40min). There are also three especially useful local buses: #14-703 to Loen (3–6 daily; 10min), Olden (3–6 daily; 20min) and Byrkjelo (3–6 daily; 1hr 10min); #14-751 to Briksdal (1–3 daily; 1hr); and #14-781 to Grodås (2–4 daily; 20min) and

### STRYN

Hellesylt (2–4 daily; 1hr).

**Tourist office** Tinggata 3 (June Mon–Fri 9am–6pm, Sat & Sun 10am–5pm; July & Aug Mon–Fri 9am–6pm, Sat & Sun 10am–5pm; Sept–May Mon–Fri 9am–3.30pm; ☎57 87 40 40, ⓦnordfjord.no). In the centre of town, just off the main street – and about 600m east of the bus station – the staff here issue free town maps, have information on (and will make reservations for) guided glacier walks on the Jostedalsbreen, and sell hiking maps.

## ACCOMMODATION AND EATING

**Stryn Camping** Bøavegen 6 ☎ 57 87 11 36, ✆ stryn -camping.no. Handily located, just a couple of hundred metres off the main drag on the east side of the centre, this all-year, four-star campsite occupies a large, partly shaded field. There are 24 cabins plus spaces for caravans and tents. Car and tent plus 2 adults __240kr__, cabins from __650kr__

**Stryn Vandrerhjem** Geilevegen 14 ☎ 57 87 11 06, ✆ hihostels.no. There's no strong reason to overnight in Stryn, but the town does possess a well-sited, all-year HI hostel in a red chalet-meets-barracks building perched high above the centre. The hostel has self-catering facilities and a laundry plus splendid views over Stryn and its

surroundings – compensation for the very steep 1km trek up here. There are small premiums on the basic price during the summertime, from mid-June to Aug, and en-suite doubles are available for 100kr extra. The hostel is signposted from the main drag – north up Bøavegen and keep going. Dorms __250kr__, doubles __650kr__

**Stryn Vertshus** Tonningsgata 19 ☎ 57 87 05 30, ✆ strynvertshus.no. This pleasant, modern café-restaurant in the centre of Stryn, serves tasty salads, sandwiches, quiches and light meals during the day and traditional Norwegian dishes as well as tapas at night, when mains average around 220kr. Mon–Sat 10am–10pm.

## Grodås

It's about 20km northwest from Styrn to the little town of **GRODÅS**, which strings along Highway 60 with the mountains on one side and a lake on the other. The lake, the **Hornindalsvatnet**, is – at 514m – Europe's deepest – not that this deterred the Norwegian telecommunications company Telenor from laying an optical fibre cable along the bottom, rather to the surprise of the townsfolk. Apart from its pleasing lakeside setting, Grodås has one minor attraction, the **Anders Svor Museum**; it is also just 25km from Hellesylt (see p.249), at the western end of the Geirangerfjord, and a little less from the turning to the Norangsdal valley (see below).

### Anders Svor Museum

Late June to mid-Aug daily 11am–5pm; late May to late June & mid-Aug to mid-Sept Sat & Sun noon–3pm • 50kr • ☎ 57 87 97 76, ✆ sfk.museum.no

In the centre of Grodås, the **Anders Svor Museum** inhabits a sweet-looking Neoclassical structure built beside the lake in 1953. Hardly a household name today, Svor (1864–1929) was a local lad, who established something of an international reputation as a sculptor of those highly stylized, romantic figures much admired by the European bourgeoisie of the late nineteenth and early twentieth centuries. Some of the more clichéd pieces on display here, such as *Bøn* (Prayer), *Sorg* (Grief) and *Lita jente* (A Small Girl), are typical of his work, though busts of his family and friends, in particular those of his wife, Brit, and his mother, reveal much more originality and talent. Svor's career was typical of his generation: like other Norwegian artists, he was keen to escape the backwoods, moving to Kristiania (Oslo) in 1881 and four years later to Copenhagen, the start of an extended exile that only ended after Norway won independence in 1905.

## ARRIVAL AND DEPARTURE                                                                      GRODÅS

**By bus** Local bus services run to Stryn (2–4 daily; 20min) and Hellesylt (2–4 daily; 1hr).

## ACCOMMODATION AND EATING

**Best Western Raftevolds** ☎ 57 87 96 05, ✆ www .raftevold.no. There's no strong reason to overnight in Grodås, but the town does possess this agreeable hotel, a modern place, whose well-proportioned concrete and

timber lines overlook the lake. The better rooms, all of which are briskly modern, have mini-balconies with lake views. The hotel also serves up the best food in town, standard Norwegian cuisine with mains averaging 250kr. __1300kr__

# The Norangsdal valley

A century ago, pony and trap took cruise-ship tourists from the Geirangerfjord down through the majestic **Norangsdal valley** to what was then the remote hamlet of **Øye**. By car, it's a simple journey today, but one that looks much the same as it would have done then: steep, snow-tipped peaks rise up on either side of a wide, boulder-strewn and scree-slashed

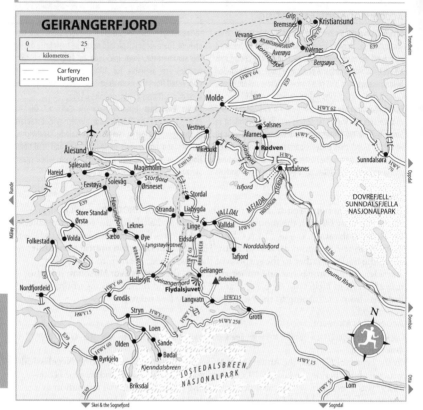

valley, dented by a thousand rockfalls – all in all some of the wildest scenery imaginable. What's more, this wonderful scenery is home to one of the region's most original hotels and abuts the ferocious-looking peaks flanking and fringing the **Hjørundfjord**.

### Highway 655 to Øye

Branching off Highway 60 at the east end of the Norangsdal, **Highway 655** inches its way along the valley, beginning by slipping through the mountain pastures, where local women once spent every summer with their cows. Nobody bothers to herd the cows up here today, but, after about 10km, you'll spy a surviving set of the simple, turf-roofed **cabins** where the cowgirls spent their summers – watch for the roadside plaque, which fleshes out the details of life on these mountain pastures.

Some 3km further along, the road runs besides lake **Lyngstøylvatnet**, created when a large rock-slide dammed the valley's stream in 1908; the lake covers the remains of a group of shacks and the water is so clear that you can still make out their outlines – again, you will spot the plaque. Thereafter, the road dips down into **ØYE**, whose scattering of farmhouses is flanked by green fields with the glassy-green waters of the Norangsfjord straight ahead.

### Leknes and the Hjørundfjord

No more than a handful of houses and a ferry dock, the minuscule port of **LEKNES**, about 8km west of Øye, occupies a magnificent location at the point where the Norangsfjord meets the **Hjørundfjord**, whose blue-black waters stretch away to the north hemmed in by jagged, pyramid-shaped peaks. Only 40km long, the Hjørundfjord is one of the most visually impressive fjords in the whole of the country, a stirringly melancholic place of almost intimidating beauty. Perhaps appropriately, it takes its name from the terrible times when the Black Death swept Norway, leaving the fjord with just one inhabitant, a woman called **Hjørund**, who wandered its peaks crying out at the heavens.

## ARRIVAL AND DEPARTURE

**By car ferry** There's a fairly frequent ferry across the Hjørundfjord from Leknes to Sæbo (every 1–2hr; 15min), but the best way to see more of the fjord is to leave your car at Leknes and take a round trip on the ferry that shuttles along the fjord, visiting several of its tiny settlements, including Store Standal (1–3 daily; 1hr); the whole trip takes a couple of hours. All these ferries are operated by Fjord1 (🌐 fjord1.no).

**By Hurtigbåt passenger express boat** There's a Hurtigbåt service from Leknes to Ålesund (April–Oct 1 daily; 1hr 30min; ☎ 70 11 44 30, 🌐 62.no); advance reservations are required.

**By bus** A patchy local bus services (#15-133) links Øye with Hellesylt (late June to late Aug 1 daily; 30min) and the

## THE NORANGSDAL VALLEY

Leknes ferry dock (Mon–Fri only 2–4 daily; 15min), but the timetable is such that it does not link all three together.

**By car** From the Leknes ferry dock, it's about 28km east to Hellesylt on the Geirangerfjord (see p.249). In the other direction, it's 25km west from Sæbo to Ørsta, on the E39, the main coastal highway, which runs from Bergen to Ålesund. From Ørsta, it's a further 35km to the Festøya–Solevåg ferry (every 30min; 20min) and then 20km onto Ålesund (see p.252). The driving is straightforward, but there is a shorter and more scenic route from Leknes to Festøya: take the Leknes ferry to Store Standal (1–3 daily; 40min), from where it's 14km north along the west shore of the Hjørundfjord to the Festøya–Solevåg ferry.

## ACCOMMODATION AND EATING

★ **Hotel Union** Øye ☎ 70 06 21 00, 🌐 unionoye.no. Øye's pride and joy is this splendid hotel, whose handsome, high-gabled exterior of 1891 was designed to appeal to touring gentry. Neither is the exterior betrayed by what's inside, for every room is crammed with period antiques seemingly hunted down from every corner of the globe. Each of the 27 bedrooms is individually decorated in elaborate, period style and most celebrate the famous people who have stayed here, like King Hakon VII and

Kaiser Wilhelm II, not to mention the Danish author Karen "*Out Of Africa*" Blixen. It's a great place to spend the night and the food is first-rate, too. None of the rooms have telephones or TVs, which is inducement enough to sit on the terrace and watch the weather fronts sweeping in off the Norangsfjord, or have a day's fishing – the hotel sells licences and dispenses advice; they also offer bike rental and will arrange guided mountain walks. April to mid-Dec. __1950kr__

# The Geirangerfjord

The **Geirangerfjord** is one of the region's smallest fjords, but also one of its most breathtaking. A convoluted branch of the Storfjord, it cuts deep inland and is marked by impressive waterfalls, with a village at either end of its snake-like profile – **Hellesylt** in the west and **Geiranger** in the east. Of the two, Geiranger has the smarter hotels as well as the tourist crowds, Hellesylt is tiny and not very interesting, but it is but a troll's throw from the magnificent **Norangsdal valley** (see p.243).

## ARRIVAL AND DEPARTURE

**By car** There are two roads to the Geirangerfjord. In the west, Highway 60 passes through Hellesylt on its way between the Nordfjord and Ålesund; in the east, Highway 63 forks off from Highway 15 to thread its way over the mountains to Geiranger and then continues north to Åndalsnes via the melodramatic Trollstigen (Trolls' Ladder; see p.251). Note, however, that Highway 63 between Highway 15 and Geiranger as well as the Trollstigen north of Geiranger are closed when the snows come.

**By car ferry** There are no roads between Hellesyt and

## THE GERAINGERFJORD

Gerainger, but there is a car ferry service during the season (see box, p.246).

**By bus** There are reasonably frequent bus services between Ålesund and both Hellesylt and Gerainger, and a special tourist bus on the so-called "Golden Route" between Langvatn, on Highway 15, Geiranger and Åndalsnes – but only from late June to Aug (see p.250). At Langvatn, there's a once-daily connection in each direction with the long-distance Nordfjordekspressen (#147) operated by Nor-Way Bussekspress; the Nordfjordekspressen runs from Oslo to Måløy; check connections before you set out.

## GEIRANGER TO HELLESYLT: THE FINEST FERRY TRIP IN THE FJORDS?

With every justification, the **car ferry** trip between Hellesylt and Geiranger is one of the most celebrated journeys in the whole of Norway (May–Sept 4–8 daily; 1hr; passengers 150kr one-way, 200kr return; car & driver 300kr each way; Ⓦ fjord1.no). With rearing cliffs to either side, the ferry follows the S-shaped profile of the fjord, whose cold waters are about 300m deep and fed by a series of plunging waterfalls up to 250m in height. The falls are all named, and the multilingual commentary aboard the ferry does its best to ensure that you become familiar with every stream and rivulet. More interesting are the scattered ruins of **abandoned farms**, built along the fjord's sixteen-kilometre length by fanatically optimistic settlers during the eighteenth and nineteenth centuries. The cliffs backing the fjord are almost uniformly sheer, making farming of any description a short-lived and back-breaking occupation – and not much fun for the children either: when they went out to play, they were roped to the nearest boulder to stop them dropping off.

## Geiranger

Any approach to **GEIRANGER** is spectacular. Arriving by ferry reveals the village tucked away in a hollow at the eastern end of the fjord, while approaching from the north by road involves thundering along a fearsome set of switchbacks on the **Ørnevegen** (Highway 63) for a first view of the village and the fjord glinting in the distance. Similarly, the road in from Highway 15 to the south squeezes through the mountains before squirming down the zigzags to arrive in Geiranger from behind, passing two celebrated vantage points, **Flydalsjuvet** and **Dalsnibba**, on the way.

There can be little argument that Geiranger boasts one of the most magnificent settings in western Norway and the village itself negotiates the steepest of hillsides, its scattering of houses built on a series of narrow shelves. The only fly in the ointment is the excessive number of tourists at the peak of the season, though, to be fair, the congestion is limited to the centre of the village, and it's easy enough to slip away to appreciate the true character of the fjord, hemmed in by sheer rock walls interspersed with hairline waterfalls, with tiny-looking ferries and cruise ships bobbing about on its blue-green waters.

### Norsk Fjordsenter

Jan to April daily 10am–3pm; May–Aug daily 10am–6pm; Sept to mid-Dec Mon–Sat 10am–3pm • 100kr • ☎ 70 26 38 10, Ⓦ geiranger.no

Geiranger's principal man-made attraction is the **Norsk Fjordsenter** (Norwegian Fjord Centre), opposite the *Union Hotel*, a stiff ten-minute walk south up the hill from the waterfront along the main road. The centre follows the usual pattern of purpose-built museums, with separate sections exploring different aspects of the region's history from communications and transportation through to fjord farms and the evolution of tourism. Perhaps the most interesting display examines the problem of fjordland **avalanches** – whenever there's a major rockfall into a fjord, the resulting tidal wave threatens disaster.

### Hiking trails

M/S *Geirangerfjord*: mid-to late May & Sept 1 daily; June–Aug 4–6 daily • 230kr return • Advance reservations are advised either in person at the tourist office or online (Ⓦ geirangerfjord.no)

A network of **hiking trails** lattices the mountains that crimp and crowd Geiranger: some make their way to thundering waterfalls, others visit abandoned mountain farmsteads or venture up to vantage points where the views over the fjord are exhilarating if not downright scary. One popular and very enjoyable excursion involves both a boat ride and a four-hour hike. It begins with a short cruise along the fjord on the M/S *Geirangerfjord* to a small jetty, from where it's a steep, one-hour hike up to the

## EARLY TOURISM TO GEIRANGER

No one bats an eyelid when the **cruise ships** nudge their way up the Geirangerfjord today, but the first one to arrive – in 1869 – gave the Norwegians a spiritual shock: it was packed with **Quakers** bearing tracts and bent on saving souls at a time when the locals thought themselves good Lutheran Christians already. The Quakers may not have had much luck as missionaries, but they were certainly taken with the beauty of the Geirangerfjord and spread the word on their return home: within twenty years the village was receiving a regular supply of visitors. Seizing their chance, local farmers mortgaged, sold and borrowed anything they could to buy **ponies and traps**, and by the end of the century tourists were being carted up from the jetty to the mountains by the score. In 1919, the horse was usurped when a group of farmer-cum-trap-owners clubbed together to import **cars**, which they kitted out with a municipal livery – the region's first taxi service. The present owner of the Hotel Union (see opposite) has restored a dozen or so of these **classic cars**, including a 1922 Hudson, a 1932 Studebaker and a 1931 Nash, and garaged them at the hotel: hotel guests can sometimes admire them for free – ask at reception.

mountain farm of **Skageflå**, followed by either a three-hour trek back to Geiranger or a return by boat.

### Flydalsjuvet and Dalsnibba

Geiranger has two famous viewpoints. There's a short but precarious trail to the nearer of them, the **Flydalsjuvet**, an overhanging rock high above the fjord that features in a thousand leaflets. To get there, drive south from the Geiranger jetty on Highway 63 and watch for the sign after about 5km; the car park offers extravagant views, but the Flydalsjuvet is about 200m away, out at the end of a slippery and somewhat indistinct track.

A second famous viewpoint, **Dalsnibba**, at 1476m, is another 12km or so to the south along Highway 63 and then up a clearly signed, 5km mountain toll-road (100kr/vehicle). There's a large car park at the plateau-summit as well as a café; buses on the so-called "Golden Route" between Highway 15 and Geiranger (see below) detour up here too.

### ARRIVAL AND INFORMATION
**GEIRANGER**

**By boat** Car ferries from Hellesylt (May–Sept 4–8 daily; 1hr) dock at the heart of the village next to the bus stops and the tourist office. In the summertime, the Hurtigruten coastal boat calls in at Geiranger as it heads north (but not south). The Hurtigruten is too large a vessel to pull into the village jetty, so it anchors a little offshore and passengers transfer to smaller boats for the last bit of the journey.
**By bus** Buses stop at and leave from the foot of the village, a stone's throw from the ferry terminal. There are several services, most notably the summer-only "Golden Route" bus (W fjord1.no), which runs north from Langvatn, where you change for long-distance buses running both east and west (see p.245), to Geiranger and ultimately Åndalsnes via the Trollstigen (Trolls' Ladder; see p.251); most of these

buses also detour up to the Dalsnibba viewpoint.
Destinations Ålesund (2–4 daily; 3hr 40min); Åndalsnes (late June to Aug 3 daily; 3hr); Dalsnibba (late June to Aug 2 daily; 45min); Langvatn (late June to Aug 2 daily; 1hr 15min).
**Tourist office** On the waterfront, beside the ferries (daily: May to early June 9am–5pm; early June to Aug 9am–7pm; early Sept daily 10am–5pm; ☎ 70 26 30 99, W visitalesund -geiranger.com). Staff here issue bus and ferry timetables, sell hiking maps and supply free village maps, which usefully outline local hiking routes. They also promote boat tours of the fjord, though the car ferry to/from Hellesylt is perfectly adequate.

### ACCOMMODATION AND EATING

Considering its popularity, Geiranger doesn't have many **hotels**, so vacant rooms are at a premium during the high season, when you should always reserve ahead.

**Geirangerfjorden Feriesenter** ☎ 95 10 75 27, W geirangerfjorden.net. The better of two neighbouring

campsites located by the fjord a couple of kilometres north of the village on the road to Eidsdal – and next to the

*Grande Fjordhotell*. The campsite's assorted caravans, cars and tents hunker down on a small field with a batch of cabins on the edge. The cabins come in various sizes, housing between 4 and 6 people, Cabins mid-April to Sept; camping late April to Sept. Tent, car and two adults <u>200kr</u>, cabins from <u>950kr</u>

**Grande Fjordhotell** ☎70 26 94 90, ⓦgrandefjordhotel.com. Ultramodern, timber-built hotel in the style of a traditional mountain lodge. The 48 guest rooms have few surprises – they are resolutely modern – but the place does have a handsome fjordside location about 2km north of the centre on the Eidsdal road, adjacent to the *Geirangerfjorden Feriesenter*. <u>1100kr</u>

★ **Hotel Union** ☎70 26 83 00, ⓦunion-hotel.no. Cream of the hotel crop, this large and lavish hotel perches high on the hillside about 500m up the road from the jetty. There's been a hotel here since 1891, and although the present building is firmly modern, it's an attractive structure and the public rooms are spacious and eminently

comfortable, plus there is a spa and a pool. The bedrooms are pleasantly furnished in modern style and the best have fjord-facing balconies; those on the fourth floor are the pick. The hotel restaurant offers a magnificent, help-yourself buffet dinner for 515kr, as well as an à la carte menu with mains costing around 260kr; check with the hotel to see when things get started as it's best to get there early before the munching starts in earnest. At both, look out for the fish and meat prepared at the hotel's own smokery. Open Feb to mid-Dec. <u>2500kr</u>, sp/r <u>2100kr</u>

**Hotell Utsikten** ☎70 26 96 60, ⓦhotellutsikten.no. On the south side of Geiranger, high up on the hill beside the main approach road, the *Utsikten* offers simply wonderful views across the fjord and its surrounding mountains. The hotel has thirty-odd guest rooms, each decorated in a simple, modern manner with the pick looking out over the fjord. Incidentally, the plinth and the plaque outside the front door commemorates the visit of a youthful Kaiser Wilhelm II. Open May–Sept. <u>1400kr</u>

## Hellesylt

Tiny, inconsequential **HELLESYLT** is now little more than a stopoff on tourist itineraries, with most visitors staying just long enough to catch the car ferry down the fjord to Geiranger (see box, p.246) or scuttle off along Highway 60. For daytime entertainment, there is a tiny **beach** and bathing jetty (*bådehus*) beyond the mini-marina near the ferry quay, the prelude to some very cold swimming, or you can watch the **waterfall** crashing down the cliffs a few metres from the dock. Otherwise, the place seems more than a little down-at-the-mouth: the main dampener has been Mount Åknes, a great chunk of which is eroding away from the rest of the mountain, threatening to collapse into the Storfjord and create a tsunami which will hit Hellesylt in six minutes; experts are monitoring the mountain closely, but of course no one knows if or when it will go, but it's a very real danger – as evidenced at Tafjord (see p.250).

### Peer Gynt Galleriet

May–Aug daily 10am–4pm • 50kr • ☎70 26 38 80, ⓦvisitalesund-geiranger.com

Occupying a substantial modern building a couple of hundred metres from the ferry dock, the **Peer Gynt Galleriet** (Peer Gynt Gallery) is an idiosyncratic art gallery jam-packed with a set of kitsch-meets-Baroque woodcarvings illustrating Ibsen's *Peer Gynt*. The carvings are the work of a certain Oddvin Parr from Ålesund and although it's all rather strange, it's good(ish) fun all the same. The tourist office (see below) is in the same building.

### ARRIVAL AND INFORMATION                                                    HELLESYLT

**By bus** Local buses to/from Øye (late June to late Aug 1 daily; 30min) stop at the Hydro Texaco petrol station off Highway 60, as do long-distance buses: Nor-Way Bussekspress operates the Fjordekspressen (#431) to Ålesund (2–3 daily; 3hr) and Stryn (2–3 daily; 1hr). Note there are no buses from Hellesylt direct to Leknes.

**By car ferry** Car ferries to/from Geiranger (see box, p.246) dock in the centre of the village, a couple of minutes' walk from the tourist office.

**Tourist office** On the waterfront, 200m or so from the ferry dock (mid-June to mid-Aug daily 10am–4pm; ☎94 81 13 32, ⓦvisitalesund-geiranger.com).

### ACCOMMODATION

**Hellesylt Vandrerhjem** ☎70 26 51 28, ⓦhihostels .no. On a miniature plateau just above the harbour, and

beside Highway 60, this HI hostel has a grand location looking out over the fjord. There's a self-catering kitchen and a laundry, but no café per se and facilities are a little rudimentary. Beds, most of which are in small cabins, attract a small premium on the basic price during the summertime, from June to Sept. En-suite doubles cost 100kr extra. May to Sept. Dorms **260kr**, doubles **640kr**

## Geiranger to Åndalsnes: the Golden Route

Promoted as the "**Golden Route**", the 120-kilometre journey from the village of Langvatn (see p.245) to **Geiranger and Åndalsnes** along Highway 63 is famous for its mountain scenery – and no wonder. Even by Norwegian standards, the route is of outstanding beauty, the road bobbing past a whole army of austere peaks whose cold severity is daunting. The journey also incorporates a ferry ride across the **Norddalsfjord**, a shaggy arm of the Storfjord, and can include a couple of brief but enjoyable detours – one west along the Norddalsfjord from Linge to **Stordal**, home to an especially fine church, the other east from Valldal to the intriguing village of **Tafjord**. Yet, the most memorable section is undoubtedly the **Trollstigen** (Troll's Ladder), a mountain road that cuts an improbable course between the Valldal valley and Åndalsnes, the northern terminus of the dramatic Rauma train line (see box, p.165), though be aware that the Trollstigen closes when the snows come.

### GETTING AROUND                    GEIRANGER TO ÅNDALSNES: THE GOLDEN ROUTE

**By bus** There's a summer-only bus service (ⓦ fjord1.no) from Geiranger to Åndalsnes (late June to August 3 daily; 3hr) over the Trollstigen. At the top of the Trollstigen, the bus pauses for a half-hour sightseeing break. Ticket prices are higher than usual for bus travel: Åndalsnes to Geiranger costs 250kr.

**By car** Drivers should note that the Trollstigen is generally closed from early Oct to mid-May – earlier/later if the snows have been particularly heavy.

**By taxi** Åndalsnes Taxisentral (☎71 22 15 55) in Åndalsnes charge 1000kr for a brief scoot down the Trollstigen.

### The Ørnevegen and Valldal

Heading north from Geiranger, the first part of the Golden Route is the 26-kilometre jaunt up and over the **Ørnevegen** (Highway 63) mountain road to **Eidsdal** on the Norddalsfjord. From here, a **car ferry** (every 20–45min; 10min) shuttles over to the **Linge jetty**, from where it's just 4km east to **VALLDAL**, a shadowy, half-hearted village that straggles along the fjord at the foot of the Valldal valley, which marks the start of the Trollstigen (see opposite).

### Stordal's Rosekyrkja

Late June to mid-Aug daily 11am–4pm • 40kr • ⓦ visitstordal.no

Northwest from Linge (see above), it's a 21km detour off the Golden Route along Highway 650 to **STORDAL**, a workaday furniture-making town in a genial valley setting. The town itself may not fire the soul, but it does possess the remarkable **Rosekyrkja** (Rose Church), standing right beside the main road. Dating from the 1780s, the church has a modest exterior, with oodles of whitewashed clapboard, but the interior is awash with beautiful floral decoration, which swirls round the pillars, across the ceiling and down the walls. There's an intensity of religious feeling here that clearly demonstrates the importance of Christianity to Norway's country folk, an effect amplified by a whole series of naive, almost abstract paintings with biblical connotations.

### Tafjord

At Valldal, a narrow byroad branches off Highway 63 to follow the fjord round to the remote, back-of-beyond village of **TAFJORD**, just 14km away to the east. Ignore the old power station at the entrance to the village, but keep going over the river to the pint-sized **harbour**, notable only for its complete lack of old buildings: they were swept away in 1934, when a great hunk of mountain dropped into the Norddalsfjord, creating a sixteen-metre tidal wave that smashed into the place, killing 23 locals in the process.

Safe just 400m up the slope from the harbour, the upper part of Tafjord did survive and, unlike most of its neighbours, seems to have dodged postwar development almost completely. Here, a string of old houses and barns, with cairn-like chimneys, picket fences and clapboard walls, ramble round twisty lanes demonstrating what these fjord villages looked like as late as the 1950s; it makes for a fascinating hour or so's wander.

## The Trollstigen

The alarming heights of the **Trollstigen** (Troll's Ladder), a trans-mountain route between Valldal and Åndalsnes, are equally compelling in either direction. The road negotiates the mountains by means of eleven hairpins with a maximum gradient of 1:12, but it's still a pretty straightforward drive until, that is, you meet a tour bus coming the other way – followed by a bit of nervous backing up and repositioning. Drivers (and cyclists) should also be particularly careful in wet weather.

From Valldal, the southern end of the Trollstigen starts gently enough with the road rambling up the **Valldal valley**. Thereafter, the road swings north, building up a head of steam as it bowls up the **Meiadal valley** bound for the barren mountains beyond. Now the road starts to climb in earnest, clambering up towards the bleak and icy plateau-pass, the **Trollstigplatået** (see below), which marks its high point. Beyond the Trollstigplatået, the sheer audacity of the road becomes apparent, zigzagging across the face of the mountain and somehow managing to wriggle round the tumultuous, 180-metre **Stigfossen falls**. Beyond the hairpins, on the northern part of the Trollstigen, the road resumes its easy ramblings, scuttling along the **Isterdal** to meet the **E136** just 5km short of Åndalsnes.

### Trollstigplatået

Mid-May to Sept daily 9am–9pm • Free

The clutter of old huts that once patrolled the **Trollstigplatået** have recently been cleared away and replaced by a slick and modern **visitor centre**, which incorporates a café and a modest exhibition on the Trollstigen. More importantly, the visitor centre marks the start of a newly constructed walkway, which leads over the fast-flowing river that rushes off the plateau to barrel down the mountain below to several vantage points beyond. From the main **Utsikten** (viewing point), there is a simply magnificent panorama over the surrounding mountains and valleys. Clearly visible to the west are some of the region's most famous mountains with Bispen and Kongen (the "Bishop" and the "King") being the nearest two, at 1462m and 1614m respectively.

| ACCOMMODATION | THE TROLLSTIGEN |
|---|---|

★ **Juvet Landscape Hotel** Valldal ☎ 95 03 20 10, ⓦ juvet.com. Arguably the most spellbinding place to stay in the country, this new property is set 15km east along the Trollstigen from Valldal (Sylte) in the middle of a canyon, with views to the Valldøla River below and spectacular Alstadfjellet peaks above. The seven singular, freestanding rooms feature deep, dark woods, playful chartreuse bathrooms and unique Japanese-Norwegian designed Stokke Tok recliners perched voyeuristically to gaze out at the world. Excellent spa and on-site restaurant, as well as plenty of available wilderness excursions led by hotel owner and adventureman Knut Slinning. Perfect for nature lovers. May–Sept. **1250kr**

# Åndalsnes

At the end of the splendid Rauma train line from Dombås (see box, p.165), the small town of **ÅNDALSNES** is for many travellers their first – and sometimes only – contact with the fjord country, a distinction that it really does not deserve. It's true that Åndalsnes boasts a fine setting between lofty peaks and the chill waters of the Isfjord, but the centre is humdrum in the extreme and the café-restaurant scene is really rather dire. That said, there is a first-rate HI hostel on the outskirts of town as well as an excellent campsite; plus Åndalsnes is also within easy hiking and driving distance of some wonderful mountain scenery and a charming **stave church**. The most popular

---

### HIKING AROUND THE TROLLSTIGEN

The Trollstigen road was completed in 1936 to replace the **Kløvstien**, the original drovers' track that cut an equally improbable course over the mountains. Much of the track has disappeared, but you can pick it up at **Slettvikane**, from where it's a one-hour walk north across a barren mountain plateau to the Trollstigplatået (see p.251). The Kløvstien then proceeds down the mountains as far as **Bøsetra**, passing the Stigfossen falls on the way; although this stretch only takes an hour or two, it's very steep and exposed, with chains to assist. Both of these hikes are, of course, linear, which is one reason why most hikers prefer to undertake less demanding, circular outings among the peaks and mountain lakes to the west. By contrast, the mountains to the east are part of the **Trollveggen** mountain wall and remain the preserve of climbers. As usual, prospective hikers should come properly equipped and watch for sudden weather changes. It's best to plan your itinerary in advance: hiking maps and advice are available from the tourist offices at both Geiranger and Åndalsnes.

---

hike hereabouts is the six-hour haul to the **Romsdalseggen**, from where there are panoramic views; information is available from the tourist office.

### Rødven stavkirke

Rødven • May to mid-Aug daily 11am–4pm • 50kr • ⓦ stavechurch.com • Take Highway 64 east; after 24km take a signed turning, from which it's a further 10km to the church

In an idyllic setting amid meadows, by a stream and overlooking a slender arm of the Romsdalsfjord a half-hour drive from Åndalsnes, **Rødven stavkirke** (stave church) dates from around 1300, though its distinctive wooden supports may have been added in 1712 during the first of several subsequent remodellings. Every inch a country church, the place's creaky interior holds boxed pews, a painted pulpit and a large medieval crucifix, but it's the bucolic setting that most catches the eye.

### ARRIVAL AND INFORMATION                                   ÅNDALSNES

**By train** Åndalsnes train station is down by the waterfront at the foot of the town. Services run to Dombås (2–4 daily; 1hr 20min) and Oslo (2–4 daily; 5hr 30min).

**By bus** Buses to Åndalsnes stop and leave from outside the train station. "Golden Route" buses run from late June to Aug to Gerainger (3 daily; 3hr) and Langvatn (2 daily; 4hr 30min). Nor-Way Bussekspress operates the Dag og Natt Ekspressen (#142) to Ålesund (2 daily; 2hr 10min).

**Tourist office** Outside the train station (mid-June to mid-Aug daily 9am–8pm; mid-Aug to mid-June Mon–Fri 9am–3pm; ☎71 22 16 22, ⓦ visitandalsnes.com). Staff here provide bus and train timetables, issue regional guides and have details of local day-long hikes and guided climbs. They also sell hiking maps and have details of various fixed-rate sightseeing expeditions, including one by taxi along the Trollstigen (see p.251).

### ACCOMMODATION

**Åndalsnes Camping og Motell** Gryttenveien ☎71 22 16 29, ⓦ andalsnes-camping.com. This combined campsite and motel has a fine riverside setting about 3km from the town centre – follow the route to the youth hostel (see below) but turn first left immediately after the river. It's a well-equipped site with cabins and bunk-bedded rooms, from dorms through to doubles. There is bicycle and boat rental too. Camping 185kr, cabins from 375kr, doubles 750kr

**Åndalsnes Vandrerhjem** Setnes ☎71 22 13 82, ⓦ hihostels.no. This delightful HI hostel has a pleasant

semi-rural setting with open views down to the fjord. Its simple, spartan rooms, set in a group of antique wooden buildings, are extremely popular, making reservations pretty much essential. The buffet-style breakfast, with its fresh fish, is one of the best hostellers are likely to get in the whole country, but note that the hostel doesn't do evening meals – there are however self-catering facilities, along with cycle storage, common rooms and a laundry. The hostel is located a 2km hike west out of town on the E136. Late May to Aug. Dorms 290kr, doubles 710kr

# Ålesund

The fishing and ferry port of **ÅLESUND**, on the coast at the end of the E136, about 120km west of Åndalsnes, is immediately – and distinctively – different from any other

Norwegian town. Neither old clapboard houses nor functional concrete and glass is much in evidence in the old centre, but instead there's a proud conglomeration of stone and brick, three-storey buildings, whose pastel-painted facades are lavishly decorated and topped off by a forest of towers and turrets. There are dragons and human faces, Neoclassical and mock-Gothic facades, decorative flowers and even a pharaoh or two, the whole ensemble ambling round the town's several harbours. Ålesund's architectural eccentricities sprang from disaster: in 1904, a dreadful **fire** left ten thousand people homeless and the town centre destroyed, but within three years a hectic reconstruction programme saw almost the entire area rebuilt in an idiosyncratic **Art Nouveau** style, which borrowed heavily from the German *Jugendstil* movement. Many of the Norwegian architects who undertook the work had been trained in Germany, so the *Jugendstil* influence is hardly surprising, but this was no simple act of plagiarism: the Norwegians added all sorts of whimsical, often folkloric flourishes to the Ålesund stew. The result was – and remains – an especially engaging stylistic hybrid, and Kaiser Wilhelm II, who footed the bill, was mightily pleased.

Ålesund is a lovely place to spend a couple of days, especially as there are several first-rate hotels, and it bolsters its charms with a couple of other mild attractions – principally the nautical comings and goings of its main **harbour** and the open-air **Sunnmøre Museum**. The town also makes a good base from which to day-trip to the bird cliffs of the island of **Runde** (see box, p.257).

## Jugendstil Senteret

Apotekergata 16 • June–Aug daily 10am–5pm; Sept Mon–Sat 11am–4pm, Sun noon–4pm; Oct–May Tues–Sat 11am–4pm, Sun noon–4pm • 70kr including KUBE (see p.254) • ☎ 70 10 49 70, ⓦ jugendstilsenteret.no

To get better acquainted with Ålesund's architectural peccadilloes, you might begin by visiting the **Jugendstil Senteret** (Art Nouveau Centre), bang in the centre of town. The centre occupies one of the town's proudest Art Nouveau buildings, the old **Apothek**

**4**

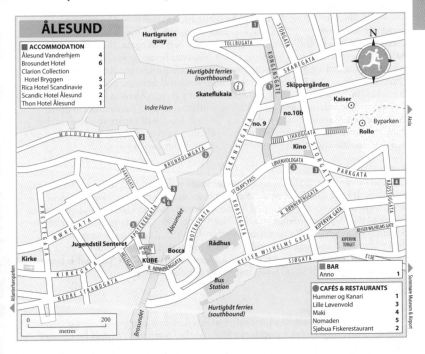

(pharmacy), whose spiky tower and heavy-duty stonework lend it a decidedly neo-baronial appearance. Inside, the ground floor is dominated by the ornate wood display cabinets of the former pharmacy and here also is a rather gimmicky "Time Machine" in which visitors are "beamed back" to 1904 to watch a short film on the fire that ripped through Ålesund and the reconstruction that followed. As the film explains, the fire happened when Norway's construction industry was in the doldrums, so skilled men turned up here looking for work from all over the country. This pleased the city's burghers no end, but they were frightened half to death when these same men turned out to be unionized, demanding a fair wage for a fair day's work – very different from the more placid country folk who made up the local workforce beforehand.

Up above the "Time Machine" – and approached via a handsome corkscrew staircase – the centre's first floor holds an assortment of Art Nouveau pieces – tapestries, silverware, vases, plates, furniture, jewellery and so forth – plus a magnificent, panelled dining room original to the house. Also on this floor two fifteen-minute films are shown in rotation, one on Art Nouveau per se, the other providing its international and sociopolitical context. An underground links the Centre with the KUBE art gallery.

## KUBE

Apotekergata 16 • June–Aug daily 10am–5pm; Sept–May Tues–Sat 11am–4pm, Sun noon–4pm • 70kr, including Jugendstil Senteret (see p.253) • ☎ 70 10 49 70, ⓦ kunstmuseetkube.no

Next door to the Jugendstil Senteret, in what was formerly a bank, is the town's main art gallery, **KUBE**, whose temporary displays, spreading over three small floors, focus on contemporary art, architecture and design with Norwegian artists to the fore. The gallery also displays a modest and regularly rotated sample of nineteenth-century Norwegian paintings drawn from its permanent collection.

## Ålesund kirke

Kirkegata • June–Aug Tues–Sun 10am–2pm • Free

The town's finest building, **Ålesund kirke** (church), was completed in 1909 to a decidedly Romanesque design, from its hooped windows through to the roughly dressed stone blocks and clunky tower. It presides over **Kirkegata**, the town's most harmonious street, where a long line of Art Nouveau houses is adorned with playful gables, turrets and towers altogether reminiscent of a Ruritanian film set. Inside the church, the high altar is flanked by the most wonderful frescoes, a blaze of colour that fair takes the breath away. They were the work of a certain **Enevold Thømt** in the 1920s and are both keenly religious and startlingly original in their amalgamation of Art Nouveau and Arts and Crafts influences. The left-hand wall carries an image of the birth of Christ, the right the Ascension, while the vaulting of the arch above displays a variety of religious symbols – for baptism, communion, and so forth.

## Kongensgate

Ålesund's main drag, pedestrianized **Kongensgate** is flanked by a string of Art Nouveau buildings. It's the whole ensemble that impresses most, but one or two are of special note, beginning with the whimsical medieval tower, hooped windows and geometrical friezes of the **Skippergården**, at no. 18. Nearby, **no. 10b** is the narrowest house in Ålesund, its rough neo-Romanesque stonework contrasting with the smooth tiles, dinky tower and wrought-iron grilles of **no. 9** just across the street. There's more ersatz medievalism round the corner on Løvenvoldgata, where the **Kino** (cinema) is housed in a large and lugubrious stone tower topped by a cutesy cupola.

## Byparken

Lihauggata • Daily dawn to dusk • Free

The town park, **Byparken**, is a pretty slice of greenery at the top of Lihauggata, which runs up from Storgata. It's a surprise to find monkey puzzle and copper beech trees here, as well as a large statue of **Rollo**, a Viking chieftain born and raised in Ålesund, who seized Normandy and became its first duke in 911. Rollo was an ancestor of William the Conqueror, the epitome of the Norman baron and thus evidence of the speed with which the Vikings were absorbed into their host communities. Near to Rollo, up two short flights of steps on top of a mini hillock, is a rough, stone column whose bronze plaque commemorates the town's benefactor, the **Kaiser**, looking suitably proud and equipped with his trademark moustache. From the park, several hundred steps lead to the top of the **Aksla hill**, where the view out along the coast and its islands is nothing short of fabulous.

### The Sunnmøre Museum

Borgundvegen • Late May to late June & late Aug to early Sept Mon–Fri 11am–4pm, Sun noon–4pm; late June to late Aug Mon–Sat 11am–5pm, Sun noon–5pm; early Sept to late May Mon–Fri 11am–3pm, Sun noon–4pm • 80kr • ☎ 70 17 40 00, 🌐 sunnmore .museum.no

The **Sunnmøre Museum**, about 4km east of the town centre just off the E136, is one of the region's more ambitious heritage museums. It may not be especially large, but everything is well presented and the location is really striking, spreading as it does over the lightly wooded hills of a tiny headland with water to either side. Inside the main building, a series of displays explores various aspects of local life from medieval times onwards, and moored outside is an assortment of old and replica **boats** typical of vessels used hereabouts from the seventh century onwards. From beside the main building, a walking trail heads off over the hills to thread its way past fifty-odd antique **timber buildings** moved here from other parts of the Sunnmøre district. The buildings include assorted cowsheds, storehouses, stables and dwellings, as well as a row of eighteenth-century *kyrkjebuer* (church shacks), where local country folk once holed up before attending Sunday service. By law, Norwegians had to go to church, and as this involved many of them in long and arduous journeys, *kyrkjebuer* were built next to parish churches so the peasantry could rest and change into their Sunday best. The *kyrkjebuer* also played a romantic role: it was here that many a Norwegian caught the eye of their future wife or husband.

### The Atlanterhavsparken

Tueneset • June–Aug Mon–Fri & Sun 10am–7pm, Sat 10am–4pm; Sept–May Mon–Sat 10am–4pm, Sun 11am–6pm • 140kr • ☎ 70 10 70 60, 🌐 atlanterhavsparken.no

In the **Atlanterhavsparken** (Atlantic Sea Park), Ålesund possesses one of those prestige tourist attractions so beloved of development boards and local councillors. It comprises a large-scale re-creation of the Atlantic marine environment, including several enormous fish tanks; there's also an outside area with easy footpaths and bathing sites. The sea park is on a low-lying headland 3km west of the town centre.

### ARRIVAL AND INFORMATION                                    ÅLESUND

**By air** Ålesund airport is 15km north of the town centre on the island of Vigra. The airport bus runs from here to the city centre (hourly; 25min; 80kr each way).

**By bus** Ålesund bus station is beside the waterfront on the southern edge of the town centre, which is about 700m from top to bottom; there are no trains. Nor-Way Bussekspress operates the Fjordekspressen (#430/#431) to Bergen (1–2 daily; 9hr 10min), Hellesylt (1–2 daily; 2hr 45min) and Stryn (2–3 daily 3hr 20min). The Mørelinjen (#630) runs to Molde (1–2 daily; 2hr 30min) and Trondheim (1–2 daily; 7hr 20min); the Dag og Natt Ekspressen (#142) to Åndalsnes (2 daily; 2hr 10min). Local buses run to Leknes

on the Hjørundfjord (April–Oct 1 daily; 1hr 30min) and Geiranger (2–4 daily; 3hr 40min).

**By Hurtigruten** The Hurtigruten (see box, p.30) docks on the northern edge of the town centre. Note that the 13hr cruise south along the coast to Bergen is a fine way to see this mountainous, fjord-shredded stretch of coastline.

**By Hurtigbåt passenger express boat** Most Hurtigbåt boats arrive and depart from the Skateflukaia quay. Destinations include Leknes (April–Oct 1 daily; 1hr 30min; ☎ 70 11 44 30, 🌐 62.no); advance reservations are required.

**By car** The main coastal road, the E39, covers some fine coastal scenery on its long journey between Bergen,

Ålesund and Trondheim; if you are heading south, watch out for one particularly handsome stretch of road between Folkestad and Nordfjordeid. There are four ferry crossings on the E39 between Ålesund and Bergen; be sure to pick up ferry timetables from Ålesund tourist office before you set out.

**Tourist office** Skateflukaia quay (June–Aug daily

8.30am–6pm; Sept–May Mon–Fri 9am–4pm; ☏ 70 15 76 00, ⓦ visitalesund.com). They operate an accommodation booking service, supply free town brochures, issue a free if somewhat unrevealing leaflet describing Ålesund's architectural attractions, and coordinate guided walking tours of the centre (mid-June to mid-Aug 1 daily; shoulder seasons 1 weekly; 1hr 30min; 90kr).

## ACCOMMODATION

One of Ålesund's real pleasures is the quality of its downtown **hotels** and **guesthouses**. If your wallet is showing signs of strain, however, there are other, less expensive options too, most economically an HI **hostel**.

**Ålesund Vandrerhjem** Parkgata 14 ☏ 70 11 58 30, ⓦ hihostels.no. Small and central HI hostel in a pleasant 1920s building at the top of Rådstugata. Has a laundry and self-catering facilities plus double rooms both with (an extra 90kr) and without en-suite facilities. Dorms 300kr, doubles 700kr

★ **Brosundet Hotel** Apotekergata 5 ☏ 70 11 45 00, ⓦ brosundet.no. Outstanding hotel, one of fjordland's most delightful, where the staff are extraordinarily efficient and every detail shows finesse, from the Bulgari toiletries and the high-spec showers through to the wonderfully comfortable beds. The hotel has 47 rooms – 15 of which have harbour views – occupying a tastefully converted, waterside warehouse by the harbour. The only criticism is that some of the rooms are just a little small. Free bicycles also provided. Advance reservations advised. 1600kr

**Clarion Collection Hotel Bryggen** Apotekergata 1 ☏ 70 10 33 00, ⓦ choicehotels.no. Smart chain hotel in a carefully modernized old waterside warehouse, where the public areas are kitted out with all sorts of nautical knick-knacks. The guest rooms are set out around three internal galleries that overlook the public areas in the manner of a

cruise ship – and it all works very well. 1520kr, sp/r 1120kr

**Rica Hotel Scandinavie** Løvenvoldgata 8 ☏ 70 15 78 00, ⓦ rica.no. Exemplary chain hotel inhabiting a grand Art Nouveau edifice, which has been sympathetically modernized, from the handsome wrought-iron work of the main doors through to the intricate friezes and medallion frescoes beyond. Unlike several of its rivals, however, it is not down by the water. 1200kr, sp/r 900kr

★ **Scandic Hotel Ålesund** Molovegen 6 ☏ 21 61 45 00, ⓦ scandichotels.com. It may be one of a chain and occupy a routine modern block, but there's something very appealing about this relaxed and friendly hotel, not least its sea and harbour views. The breakfasts are excellent, served in a breakfast room that overlooks the ocean, and the rooms are bright and cheerful, each comfortably furnished in contemporary style with the pick – once again – offering charming sea views. 1300kr, sp/r 940kr

**Thon Hotel Ålesund** Kongensgate 27 ☏ 70 12 29 38, ⓦ thonhotels.no. Suffers by comparison with its more atmospheric rivals, but this large modern block of a hotel is right in the centre and the rooms are perfectly adequate. 1400kr, sp/r 1100kr

## EATING AND DRINKING

For a town of just 42,000, Ålesund does well for **cafés and restaurants**, with the pick all within a stone's throw of the main harbour. If it's hot, locals pile down to the harbourside terrace of the *Anno bar*, though several city-centre restaurants also turn into drinking venues once the chefs have gone home.

### CAFÉS AND RESTAURANTS

**Hummer og Kanari** Kongensgate 19 ☏ 70 12 80 08, ⓦ hummerkanari.no. This relaxed café-restaurant serves up a reasonably tasty line in seafood (around 280kr per main course). Also a good place to try a Norwegian favourite, *klippfisk* (salted and dried cod), cooked every which way and costing about 250kr. After the kitchen closes down – at about 9.30pm – the place turns into one of the grooviest bars in town. Mon–Fri 4pm till late, Sat & Sun from 2pm.

★ **Lille Løvenvold** Løvenvoldgata 2 ☏ 70 12 54 00. Grooviest café in town, attracting a mixed but (nearly always) cool crew, who sip away at the best coffee in town.

New Age-meets-lighter-shade-of-Goth decor in a rabbit warren of rooms. Mon–Sat 11am–11pm, sometimes later, Sun 2–11pm.

**Maki** Brosundet Hotel, Apotekergata 5 ☏ 70 11 45 00, ⓦ brosundet.no. Immaculate and intimate restaurant, with views out over the harbour and a short but well-chosen menu featuring local, seasonal ingredients – try, for example, the ling in a red wine sauce. Mains average around 280kr. Mon–Sat 6–11pm.

★ **Nomaden** Apotekergata 10 ☏ 70 12 54 90. Tasty sandwiches, light meals, coffees and cakes in this cosy little café, where the decor is vaguely Edwardian – antique cupboards and so forth – with prints and paintings on the

## BIRDWATCHING ON RUNDE ISLAND

The steep and craggy cliffs on the pocket-sized island of **Runde**, some 70km west along the coast by road and ferry from Ålesund, are the summer haunt of several hundred thousand **sea birds**. Common species include gannet, kittiwake, fulmar, razorbill and guillemot, but the most numerous of all is the **puffin**, whose breeding holes honeycomb the island's higher ground. Most species, including the puffin, congregate here between mid-April and July, though some – like the grey heron and the velvet scoter – are all-year residents. A network of **hiking trails** provides access to a number of birdwatching vantage points, though these invariably involve a fair climb up from the foreshore. One of the more popular hikes is the stiff forty-minute hoof up to the sea cliffs on the island's north shore from the car park at the end of the road: the island is connected to the mainland by bridge and this, its one and only road, slips along both the south and east shores. For more detailed advice about hiking routes on Runde, consult ⓦrunde.no. The easiest way to see Runde's bird cliffs is on one of the **Wildlife Sea Safaris** (late June to mid-Aug; 2 daily; 2hr; 800kr) operated from Ålesund by **62° Nord** (❼70 11 44 30, ⓦ62.no). You can also **drive** there – allow two hours or so: Runde is itself connected to the mainland by bridge, but the journey still involves the car ferry ride from Sulesund to Hareid (every 30min; 25min; passengers 33kr, car & driver 90kr; ⓦnorled.no).

walls. Smooth, jazzy background music too. Great cheesecake; yum, yum. Tues–Sat 11am–4pm.

★ **Sjøbua Fiskerestaurant** Brunholmgata 1 ❼70 12 71 00, ⓦsjoebua.no. Smart, fairly formal restaurant serving an outstanding range of seafood from its harbourside cellar premises. They even have their own lobster tank – something of a rarity in Norway. It's expensive, with main courses hovering around 300kr, but very popular, so reservations are advised. When the kitchen

closes, around 10pm, the place morphs into a bar. Mon–Fri 4pm–1am.

**BAR**
**Anno** Apotekergata 9 ❼71 70 70 77, ⓦannobar.no. Slickest bar in town with touchy-feely lighting, wood floors and leather and cloth banquettes. Outside terrace too. Mon–Thurs 11am–11pm, Fri & Sat 11am–3am, Sun 1–8pm.

# Ålesund to Kristiansund

Ålesund is within easy striking distance of the next major towns north up along the coast – **Molde** and **Kristiansund**, at 80km and 150km respectively. Neither is especially riveting, but Kristiansund does boast a handsome coastal location plus a handful of mildly interesting sights recalling its heyday as a centre of the *klippfisk* (salted, dried cod) industry. The more appealing of the two routes between the two towns incorporates the **Atlanterhavsvegen**, a short but dramatic stretch of highway that hops from islet to islet on the very edge of the ocean (see box, p.259).

## Molde

**MOLDE** is an industrial town that sprawls along the seashore with a ridge of steep, green hills behind. Despite its modern appearance, it's one of the region's older towns, but was blown to pieces by the Luftwaffe in 1940, an act of destruction watched by King Håkon from these very same hills just weeks before he was forced into exile in England.

### Kvernes stavkirke
Late June to late Aug daily 11am–5pm • 50kr • ⓦ stavechurch.com
In the southeast corner of the island of **Averøy**, a rocky lump with a fretted coastline, **Kvernes stavkirke** (stave church) merits a brief detour from Highway 64 (see box, p.259) – it's just 10km south, along the island's eastern shore. Dating from the thirteenth century, the church was built on what had previously been a pagan ceremonial site, as proved by the discovery here of a Viking phallus stone. Much modified over the centuries, the church is a simple barn-like affair distinguished by its biblical wall paintings, added in the 1630s.

---

## POOTLING ROUND KRISTIANSUND HARBOUR

Beginning its journeys at the south end of the main quay, a small passenger boat, the **Sundbåten** (2 hourly: Mon–Fri 7.30am–7pm, Sat 9.30am–4.30pm; 20kr one-way ticket, day ticket 50kr) crisscrosses Kristiansund's whopping harbour, linking its three islands and modest tourist attractions. The service was once crucial for getting around town, but the islands are now connected by bridge and the boats are, essentially, an exercise in nostalgia.

---

## Kristiansund

Straddling three rocky islets and the enormous channel-cum-harbour that they create, **KRISTIANSUND** has a splendid coastal setting, but it somehow conspires to look quite dull: the Luftwaffe is at least partly to blame as it polished off most of the old town in 1940, and, although Kristiansund dates back to the eighteenth century, precious little remains from prewar days. One minor exception is the handful of antique clapboard houses that string along **Fosnagata**, immediately to the north of the main quay, but otherwise the gridiron of streets that now serves as the town centre – just up the slope to the west of the main quay – is resolutely modern. There is, however, a more forceful nod to the past in the **klippfiskkjerring statue** of a woman carrying a fish standing at the south end of the main quay. The statue recalls the days when salted cod was laid out along the seashore to dry, producing the *klippfisk* that was the main source of income in these parts until well into the 1950s.

### Norsk klippfiskmuseum

Gornalandet • Mid-June to mid-Aug daily noon–5pm • 70kr • ☎ 71 58 70 00, Ⓦ nordmore.museum.no

Kristiansund's piscine days are best recalled at the **Norsk klippfiskmuseum** (Norwegian Klipfish Museum), housed in an old and well-worn warehouse, the **Milnbrygga**, across the harbour to the east of the main quay. The museum's displays tell you all you could ever want to know about salted cod – how it was prepared, where it came from and where it went.

### Gamle Byen

One of Kristiansund's more noteworthy targets is the handful of venerable timber houses that make up the **Gamle Byen** (Old Town), situated on the smallest of the three islets, **Innlandet**, which lies south across the harbour from the main quay. Look out here also for the distinctive **Lossiusgården**, a large and handsome house that belonged to an eighteenth-century merchant; unfortunately, you can't go inside.

### Grip

The M/S *Gripexpressen* (June to mid-Sept 1–2 daily; 300kr return; ☎ 91 80 76 66, Ⓦ gripexpressen.no) leaves for Grip from the south end of the main town quay; reserve at the tourist office

Kristiansund's most popular attraction is **Grip**, a tiny, low-lying islet just 14km offshore. Grip is dotted with brightly painted timber homes, has an appealing assortment of antique boathouses, and comes complete with a much-modified medieval church, where the islanders once took refuge whenever they were threatened by a storm, as they often were – indeed, when you look at the place, it's amazing anyone ever lived here at all: there's a real touch of claustrophobia on the islet even on a calm day, and when the weather's up the effects can be quite overpowering. There are no permanent residents now – the last ones left in 1964 – but in the summertime fishermen dock in the sliver of a harbour.

---

### ARRIVAL AND INFORMATION

**By bus** Buses pull in beside the Nordmørskaia quay metres from the Hurtigbåt jetty. Nor-Way Bussekspress operates the Mørelinjen (#630) from Ålesund to Molde (1–2 daily; 2hr), Bergsøya (1–2 daily; 3hr 20min) and Trondheim (1–2

## BY CAR: ÅLESUND TO KRISTIANSUND

From Ålesund, it's a circuitous yomp over hill and down dale to the southern shore of the Moldefjord, where the **Vestnes ferry** (every 30min–1hr; 35min) scuttles over to **Molde** (see p.257). There are two possible routes north from Molde to Kristiansund. The quicker, but less interesting, option is the **E39**, which begins with a fifty-kilometre canter northeast to a massive suspension **bridge**, which spans the straits between the mainland and the islet of **Bergsøya**. Here, **Highway 70** spears north for the 25-kilometre trip onto Kristiansund – whereas the E39 presses on to Trondheim, another 170km away to the east (see p.266).

The second, and far more picturesque route, is to take **Highway 64**, which forks north off the E39 just to the east of Molde. This tunnels through the mountains before rounding the head of the slender Malmefjord. Then it rattles down the valley and along the edge of the **Kornstadfjord** to reach the coast at the start of the **Atlanterhavsvegen** (Atlantic Highway), some 50km from Molde. A spirited piece of engineering, the Atlanterhavsvegen is a scenic eight-kilometre stretch of road that negotiates the mouth of the Kornstadfjord, manoeuvring from islet to islet by a sequence of bridges and causeways. In calm conditions, it's an attractive run, but in blustery weather it's exhilarating with the wind whistling round the car, the surf roaring and pounding but a stone's throw away. On the far side of the Kornstadfjord is the island of **Averøy**, where you'll find Kvernes stave church (see p.257), while sticking to Highway 64, it's a few kilometres to the **Bremsnes car ferry** over to Kristiansund (every 30min–1hr; 20min).

daily; 7hr 30min). You change at Bergsøya for the 45min bus trip onto Kristiansund – but check the connection before you set out.

**By Hurtigbåt passenger express boat** Hurtigbåt boats from Trondheim (3 daily; 3hr 15min) dock at the Nordmørskaia quay at the north end of the main town quay.

**By Hurtigruten coastal boat** The Hurtigruten docks at Holmakaia, a few metres to the east of the bus station.

**Tourist office** Kongens plass (late June to late Aug Mon–Fri 9am–6pm, Sat 9am–3pm, Sun noon–5pm; late Aug to late June Mon–Fri 9am–3.30pm; ☎71 58 54 54, ⓦvisitkristiansund.com). Staff here provide bus and train timetables, issue regional guides and have details of local boat trips. The office is located a short stroll up Kaibakken from the main town quay.

### ACCOMMODATION AND EATING

**Rica Hotel Kristiansund** Storgata 41 ☎71 57 12 00, ⓦrica.no. In a large, grey and white high-rise block, this chain hotel has a quiet location a short walk south from the main town quay. The rooms on its upper floors have harbour views. <u>1500kr</u>, sp/r <u>1050kr</u>

**Smia** Fosnagata 30 ☎71 67 11 70, ⓦsmia.no. Housed in a converted boat shed metres from the north end of the town quay, this excellent restaurant stands head and shoulders above its competitors. It serves superb fish dishes and, as you're here in Kristiansund, you should really try the *klippfisk* with bacon and carrots (260kr). Mon–Fri 4–11pm, Sat & Sun 2–11pm.

# Trondheim to the Lofoten islands

LOFOTEN ISLANDS

# 5

# Trondheim to the Lofoten islands

Demarcating the transition from the rural south to the blustery north is the 900-kilometre-long stretch of Norway that extends from Trondheim to the island-studded coast near Narvik. Easily the biggest town hereabouts is Trondheim, Norway's third city, a charming place of character and vitality, and a definitive cultural hub for the midriff of the country. The city is readily accessible by train, plane and bus from Oslo, but push on north and you begin to feel far removed from the capital and the more intimate, forested south. Distances between settlements grow ever greater, travelling becomes more of a slog, and as Trøndelag gives way to the province of Nordland the scenery becomes ever wilder and more forbidding – "Arthurian", thought Evelyn Waugh.

North from the modest little industrial town of Mosjøen and nearby **Mo-i-Rana**, is the **Arctic Circle** (see box, p.341) – one of the principal targets for many travellers – at a point where the cruel and barren scenery seems strikingly appropriate. Beyond the Arctic Circle, the mountains of the interior lead down to a fretted, craggy coastline, and even the towns, the largest of which is the port of **Bodø**, have a feral quality about them. The iron-ore port of **Narvik**, in the far north of Nordland, has perhaps the wildest setting of them all, and was the scene of some of the fiercest fighting between the Allied and Axis forces in World War II. To the west lies the offshore archipelago that makes up the **Vesterålen** and **Lofoten islands**. In the north of the Vesterålen, between **Harstad** and **Andenes**, the coastline of this island chain is mauled by massive fjords, whereas to the south, the Lofoten islands are backboned by a mighty and ravishingly beautiful mountain wall – a highlight of any itinerary. Among a handful of idyllic fishing villages in the Lofoten the pick is the tersely named **Å**, though **Henningsvær** and **Stamsund** come a very close second.

As for accommodation, the region has a smattering of strategically located **hostels**, and all the major towns have at least a couple of **hotels**, though advance reservations are strongly recommended in the height of the season. In addition, the Lofoten islands offer inexpensive lodgings in scores of atmospheric **rorbuer** (see box, p.314), small huts/cabins once used by fishermen during the fishing season.

BAKKLANDET, TRONDHEIM

# Highlights

**❶ Nidaros Domkirke, Trondheim**
Scandinavia's largest medieval building makes a
stirring focal point for the city. **See p.268**

**❷ Bakklandet** The bars, cafés and restaurants of
this attractive old district in Trondheim are a great
place for a cosy, studenty night out. **See p.274**

**❸ Ofotbanen railway** A dramatic train ride
from Narvik over the Swedish border through
ravishing mountain scenery. The adventurous
can walk back. **See p.299**

**❹ Whale-watching, Andenes** From late May
to mid-September, whale-watching safaris from
this remote port practically guarantee a
sighting. **See p.308**

**❺ Sailing the Lofoten archipelago** From late
winter to early spring, you can board a sailing rig
and spend a week navigating the Lofotens' east
coast, mooring in harbours along the way and
heading up a mountain on skis. **See p.320**

**❻ Henningsvær** One of Lofoten's most
picturesque fishing villages, with brightly
painted red wooden houses framing the
dinkiest of harbours. **See p.320**

**❼ Norwegian Fishing Village Museum, Å**
Maritime history combines with a stunning
fjordside setting at Northern Norway's most
engaging coastal museum. **See p.326**

HIGHLIGHTS ARE MARKED ON THE MAP ON PP.264–265

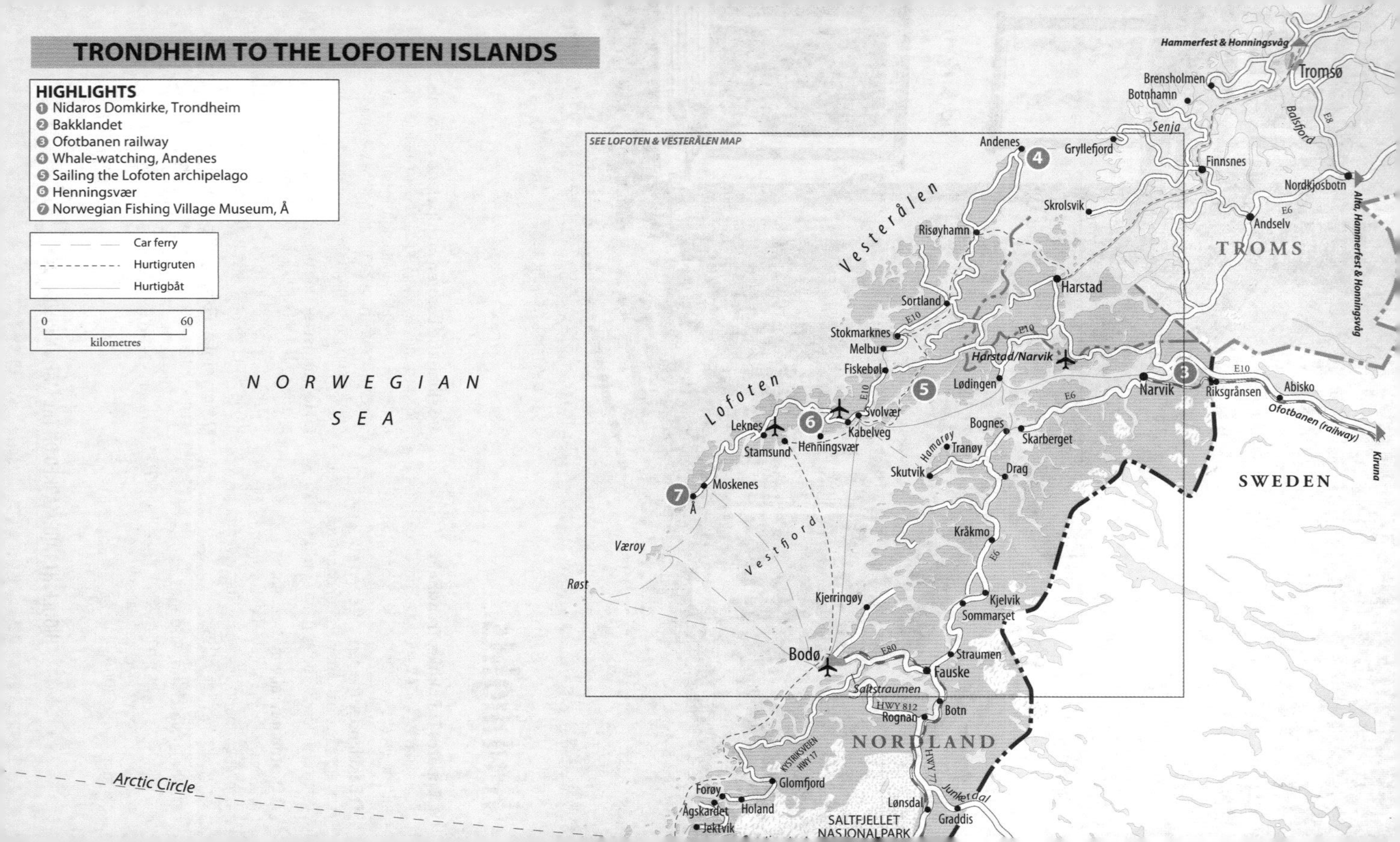

# TRONDHEIM TO THE LOFOTEN ISLANDS

## HIGHLIGHTS
1. Nidaros Domkirke, Trondheim
2. Bakklandet
3. Ofotbanen railway
4. Whale-watching, Andenes
5. Sailing the Lofoten archipelago
6. Henningsvær
7. Norwegian Fishing Village Museum, Å

Car ferry
Hurtigruten
Hurtigbåt

0    kilometres    60

SEE LOFOTEN & VESTERÅLEN MAP

Kiruna

SWEDEN

Alta, Hammerfest & Honningsvåg

Tromsø
Balsfjord
TROMS
E8

Hammerfest & Honningsvåg

Brensholmen
Botnhamn
Senja
Finnsnes
Andselv
Nordkjosbotn
E6
E8
E10
Abisko
Ofotbanen (railway)
Riksgränsen
Narvik

Gryllefjord
Skrolsvik
Harstad

Andenes
4
Risøyhamn
Vesterålen

Sortland
Stokmarknes
Melbu
Fiskebøl
Svolvær
Kabelvåg
Henningsvær
Lofoten
Leknes
Stamsund
Moskenes
Å
7

Skarberget
Drag
Bognes
Tranøy
Hamarøy
Skutvik
Kråkmo
Kjelvik
Sommarset
Straumen
Fauske
Botn
Rognan
Saltstraumen
Bodø
Kjerringøy
Vestfjord
Værøy
Røst

NORDLAND
E6
HWY 77
HWY 812
SALTFJELLET NASJONALPARK
Lønsdal
Graddis
Junkerdal
Glomfjord
Holand
Kilboghavn
Jektvik
Ågskardet

NORWEGIAN

SEA

Arctic Circle

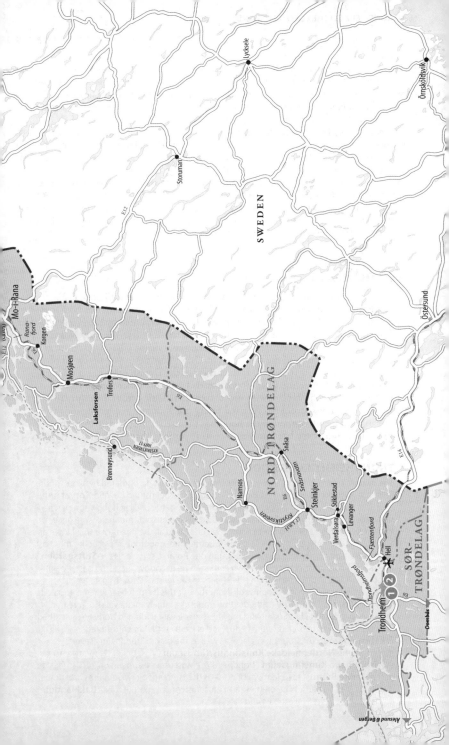

**5**

## GETTING AROUND

**By plane** There are frequent, quick and often inexpensive flights from Trondheim to Bodø with SAS (ⓦflysas.com) and from Bodø on to Lofoten with DAT (ⓦdat.dk).

**By train** The train network reaches as far north as Fauske and nearby Bodø, from both of which buses connect with Narvik, which is the terminal of a separate rail line – the Ofotbanen – that runs the few kilometres to the border and then south through Sweden.

**By bus** The bus network up here is good, which is just as well given the isolated nature of much of the region. The only real problem is likely to be time: it's a day or two's journey from Trondheim to Fauske, and another day from there to Narvik. In fact, unless you've several days to spare, you should think twice before venturing further north: the travelling can be arduous, and is really pretty

## TRONDHEIM TO THE LOFOTEN ISLANDS

pointless if done at a hectic pace.

**By boat** The Hurtigruten coastal boat stops at all the major settlements on its route up the Norwegian coast from Bergen to Kirkenes, while the islands are accessed by a variety of car ferries and Hurtigbåt passenger express boats.

**By car** The E6, or "Arctic Highway", is the main road north from Trondheim: it's kept in excellent condition, though in summer motorhomes and caravans can make the going frustratingly slow. Slower still, but stunningly scenic, the coastal Highway 17, or "Kystriksveien", utilizes road, tunnels, bridges and seven ferries to run the 700km from Steinkjer, just north of Trondheim, up to Bodø, though its most picturesque stretch by a long chalk is north of Mo-i-Rana.

# Trondheim

An atmospheric city with much of its nineteenth-century centre still intact, **TRONDHEIM** was known until the 1500s as Nidaros ("mouth of the river Nid"), its importance as a military and economic power base underpinned by the excellence of its harbour and its position at the head of a wide and fertile valley. The early Norse parliament, or Ting, met here, and the cathedral was a major pilgrimage centre at the end of a route stretching all the way up from Oslo. A fire destroyed almost all of medieval Trondheim in 1681 and, at the behest of the Danish governor, a military engineer from Luxembourg, a certain Caspar de Cicignon, proceeded to rebuild Trondheim on a gridiron plan, with broad avenues radiating from the centre to act as firebreaks. Cicignon's layout has survived pretty much untouched, giving today's city centre an airy, open feel, though the buildings themselves mostly date from the commercial boom of the late nineteenth century. Among them are scores of doughty

## TRONDHEIM: ORIENTATION

The historic centre of Trondheim sits on a small triangle of land bordered by a loop of the River Nid, with the sweep of the long and slender Trondheimsfjord beyond. **Torvet** is the main city square, a spacious open area anchored by a statue of Olav Tryggvason perched high atop a granite column. The broad avenues that radiate out from here were once flanked by long rows of wooden buildings, which served all the needs of a small town and administrative centre. Most of these older structures are long gone, replaced for the most part by uninspiring modern buildings, though one notable survivor is the **Stiftsgården**, a fine timber mansion erected in 1774, while the tangle of narrow alleys and pastel-painted clapboard frontages that fill out the side streets to the west of Prinsens gate are an atmospheric spot for an afternoon stroll. Nonetheless, this is small beer when compared with the **Nidaros Domkirke** (cathedral), an imposing, largely medieval structure that is the city's architectural high point and the finest medieval building in Norway. The cathedral dominates the southern part of the centre and close by is the much-restored **Erkebispegården** (Archbishop's Palace) as well as the pick of Trondheim's several museums, the **Nordenfjeldske Kunstindustrimuseum** (Museum of Decorative Arts) and the **Trondheim Kunstmuseum** (Trondheim Art Museum). Near here too, on the far side of the **Gamle Bybro** – the old town bridge – is the clutter of old warehouses and timber dwellings that comprises the prettiest and most fashionable part of town, **Bakklandet**, home to some of its liveliest bars and cafés.

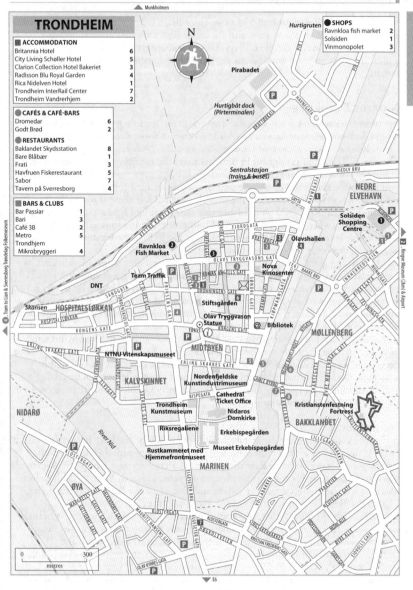

▲ Munkholmen

# TRONDHEIM

## ■ ACCOMMODATION
| | |
|---|---|
| Britannia Hotel | 6 |
| City Living Schøller Hotel | 5 |
| Clarion Collection Hotel Bakeriet | 3 |
| Radisson Blu Royal Garden | 4 |
| Rica Nidelven Hotel | 1 |
| Trondheim InterRail Center | 7 |
| Trondheim Vandrerhjem | 2 |

## ● CAFÉS & CAFÉ-BARS
| | |
|---|---|
| Dromedar | 6 |
| Godt Brød | 2 |

## ● RESTAURANTS
| | |
|---|---|
| Baklandet Skydsstation | 8 |
| Bare Blåbær | 1 |
| Frati | 3 |
| Havfruen Fiskerestaurant | 5 |
| Sabor | 7 |
| Tavern på Sverresborg | 4 |

## ■ BARS & CLUBS
| | |
|---|---|
| Bar Passiar | 1 |
| Bari | 3 |
| Café 3B | 2 |
| Metro | 5 |
| Trondhjem Mikrobryggeri | 4 |

## ● SHOPS
| | |
|---|---|
| Ravnkloa fish market | 2 |
| Solsiden | 1 |
| Vinmonopolet | 3 |

stone structures that were built to impress and a handsome set of old timber warehouses that line up along the river. Together, they provide a suitably expansive setting for the **cathedral**, one of Scandinavia's finest medieval structures.

Trondheim is also the capital of the **Trøndelag** province, whose sweeping valleys are – by Norwegian standards at least – very fertile and profitable: indeed the region's landowners acted as a counterweight to the power of the south for hundreds of years and, when the country regained its independence in 1905, it seemed logical for the new dynasty to hold their coronations here in Trondheim.

**5**

With a population of around 175,000, Trondheim is Norway's third city, but the pace of life here is slow and easy, and the main **sights** are best appreciated in leisurely fashion over a couple of days. Genial and eminently likeable, Trondheim is a pleasant place to wave goodbye to city life before heading for the wilds of the north.

## Nidaros Domkirke

Kongsgårdsgata 2 • **Cathedral** early June to mid-Aug Mon–Fri 9am–6pm, Sat 9am–2pm, Sun 1–4pm; mid-Aug to early June Mon–Sat 9am–2pm, Sun 9–4pm • Guided tours: May to mid-Sept 4 daily; 30min • **Tower** mid-June to mid-Aug Mon–Fri 10am–5pm, Sat 10am–12.30pm, Sun 1–3.30pm • 60kr, combined ticket with Erkebispegården 120kr • ⓦ nidarosdomen.no

The goal of Trondheim's pilgrims in times past was the rambling **Nidaros Domkirke**, Scandinavia's largest medieval building, whose copper-green spire and multiple roofs lord it over the south end of Munkegata. Gloriously restored following several fires and the upheavals of the Reformation, the cathedral, which is dedicated to St Olav (see box opposite), remains the focal point of any visit to the city and is best explored in the early morning, when it's reasonably free of tour groups. In the summertime, there are free English-language **guided tours** and you can climb the cathedral tower for a panoramic view over the city and its surroundings.

The crowning glory of this magnificent blue- and green-grey soapstone edifice is its west facade, a soaring cliff-face of finely worked stone sporting a magnificent rose window, rank after rank of pointed arches, biblical, religious and royal figures by the dozen and a fancy set of gargoyles. The west facade and the nave behind may look medieval, but date from the nineteenth century: the originals were erected in the early Gothic style of the early thirteenth century, but they were destroyed by fire in 1719 and what you see today is a painstakingly accurate reconstruction. The fire did not, however, raze the Romanesque transepts, whose heavy hooped windows and dog-tooth decoration were the work of English stonemasons in the twelfth century. English workmen also lent a hand in the thirteenth-century choir, where the arches, flying buttresses and intricate tracery are the epitome of early Gothic – and are reminiscent of contemporaneous churches in England.

### The interior

Inside the cathedral, the gloomy half-light hides much of the lofty decorative work, but it is possible to examine the strikingly ascetic early twentieth-century **choir screen**, whose wooden figures are the work of Gustav Vigeland (see p.86). Vigeland was also responsible for the adjacent soapstone **font**, a superb piece of medievalism sporting four bas-reliefs depicting Adam and Eve, John the Baptist baptizing the Christ, the Resurrection and a beguiling Noah and the Ark: Noah peers apprehensively out of his boat, not realizing that the dove, with the telltale branch, is up above. The other item of particular interest is a famous fourteenth-century **altar frontal** (front panel of an altar painting) displayed in a chapel off the ambulatory, directly behind the high altar. At a time when few Norwegians could read or write, the cult of St Olav had to be promoted visually, and the frontal is the earliest surviving representation of Olav's life and times. In its centre, Olav looks suitably beatific holding his axe and orb; the top left-hand corner shows the dream Olav had before the Battle of Stiklestad (see p.281), with Jesus dropping a ladder down to him from heaven. In the next panel down, Olav and his men are shown at prayer before the battle and, in the bottom right-hand corner, Olav meets a sticky end, speared and stabbed by three cruel-looking soldiers. The final panel shows church officials exhuming Olav's uncorrupted body and declaring his sainthood.

What you won't see now is the object of the medieval pilgrims' veneration: St Olav's silver casket-coffin was taken to Denmark and unceremoniously melted down to be made into coins in 1537.

## ST OLAV

**5**

Born in 995, **Olav Haraldsson** followed the traditional life of a Viking chieftain from the tender age of 12, "rousing the steel-storm" as the saga writers put it, from Finland to Ireland. He also served as a mercenary to both the duke of Normandy and King Ethelred of England, and it was during this time that he was converted to Christianity. In 1015, he invaded Norway, defeated his enemies and became king, his military success built upon the support of the more prosperous farmers of the Trøndelag, an emergent class of yeomen who were less capricious than the coastal chieftains of Viking fame. However, Olav's zealous **imposition of Christianity** – he ordered the desecration of pagan sites and the execution of those who refused baptism – alienated many of his followers and the bribes of Olav's rival Knut (Canute), king of England and Denmark, did the rest: Olav's retainers deserted him, and he was forced into exile in 1028. Two years later, he was back in the Trøndelag, but the army he had raised was far too weak to defeat his enemies, and Olav was killed near Trondheim at the **Battle of Stiklestad** (see p.281).

Olav might have lost his kingdom, but the nationwide Church he founded had no intention of losing ground. Needing a local **saint** to consolidate its position, the Church carefully nurtured the myth of Olav, a process of sanctification assisted by the oppressive rule of Olav's successor, the "foreigner" Knut. After the Battle of Stiklestad, Olav's body had been spirited away and buried on the banks of the River Nid at what is today Trondheim. There were rumours of miracles in the vicinity of the grave, and when the bishop arrived to investigate these strange goings-on, he exhumed the body and found it, lo and behold, perfectly uncorrupted. Olav was declared a saint, his body placed in a silver casket and when, in 1066, Olav Kyrre, son of Olav's half-brother Harald the Fair-Haired, became king of Norway, he ordered work to begin on a grand church to house the remains in appropriate style. Over the years the church was altered and enlarged to accommodate the growing bands of medieval pilgrims; it achieved cathedral status in 1152, when Trondheim became the seat of an archbishopric whose authority extended as far as Orkney and the Isle of Man.

# Erkebispegården

Kongsgårdsgata

Behind the cathedral stands the heavily restored **Erkebispegården** (Archbishop's Palace), a courtyard complex that was originally built in the twelfth century for the third archbishop, Øystein, though two stone-and-brick wings are all that survive of the medieval quadrangle – the other two wings were added later. After the archbishops were kicked out during the Reformation, the palace became the residence of the Danish governors. It was subsequently used as the city armoury, and many of the old weapons are now displayed in the **west wing** in the **Rustkammeret med Hjemmefrontmuseet**, though the museum's most interesting displays deal with the German occupation of World War II. Next door, also in the west wing, the Norwegian crown jewels are exhibited in the **Riksregaliene**, not that there's actually much to see, while the south wing chips in with the medieval sculptures of the **Museet Erkebispegården**.

After you've finished with the museums, you can leave the Erkebispegården to the south, strolling out onto the grassy **lawns** which flank the River Nid. A trio of earthen bastions are reminders of the military defences that once protected this side of town, but they have worn low with time, and you'll soon reach the dignified old tombstones and wild flowers of the cathedral **graveyard**, just to the east of the church's main entrance.

## The Riksregaliene

May to early June & early Aug to mid-Sept Mon–Sat 10am–3pm, Sun noon–4pm; early June to early Aug Mon–Fri 10am–5pm, Sat 10am–3pm, Sun noon–4pm; mid-Sept to April Tues–Sat 11am–2pm, Sun noon–4pm • 85kr, combined ticket for cathedral & Erkebispegården 120kr

Norway's crown jewels, the **Riksregaliene** (National Regalia), are displayed in the basement of the first part of the Erkebispegården's west wing. At the end of the

**5**

Napoleonic Wars, Britain and her allies forced Denmark to cede Norway to Sweden. The Swedish king was himself new to the throne – oddly enough he had previously been one of Napoleon's generals, Jean-Baptiste Bernadotte – and although he received Norway as a welcome bonus, he was deemed to be a ruler of two kingdoms rather than one. Sweden already had its own crown jewels, but Norway, which hadn't been independent for centuries, had nothing at all. As a consequence, Bernadotte, now Karl IV Johan, scuttled around Stockholm ordering a new set of crown jewels in preparation for his coronation in Trondheim. The results are on display here, principally a crown, a sceptre, an orb and a tiny anointing horn, all made in the 1810s. Another set of ceremonial gear was made for the queen, but it's still a very thin collection and the Sword of State was actually recycled: it had originally been given to Bernadotte by Napoleon in return for military services rendered. The last Norwegian coronation took place here in Trondheim cathedral in 1906 on the accession of Håkon VII, but his successors – Olav V and Harald V – elected for benedictions instead, in 1958 and 1991 respectively.

### Rustkammeret med Hjemmefrontmuseet

June–Aug Mon–Fri 10am–4pm, Sat & Sun noon–4pm • Free • ⓦ forsvaretsmuseer.no

The museum inside the extensive **Rustkammeret** (Armoury) spreads over two main floors. The **first floor** gives the broad details of Norway's involvement in the interminable **Dano–Swedish Wars** that racked Scandinavia from the fifteenth to the nineteenth centuries. As part of the Danish state, Norway was frequently attacked from the east along the Halden–Oslo corridor, the most memorable incursions being by the bellicose Swedish king, Karl XII. Much to the Danish king's surprise, Karl came a cropper in Norway: it was here that he was defeated for the first time and, when he came back for more, shot (possibly by one of his own men) while besieging Fredriksten fortress in 1718 (see p.109).

Of more general interest, the Resistance section on the **second floor** describes the German invasion and occupation of **World War II**, dealing honestly with the sensitive issue of collaboration. In particular, you can hear **Vidkun Quisling**'s broadcast announcing – in a disarmingly squeaky voice – his coup d'état of April 9, 1940. There are also some intriguing displays on the daring antics of the Norwegian Resistance, notably an extraordinary – perhaps hare-brained – attempt to sink the battleship *Tirpitz* as it lay moored in an inlet of the Trondheimsfjord in 1942 (see box, p.280). This escapade, like so many others, involved **Leif Larsen**, the Resistance hero who is commemorated by a statue on the Torget in Bergen. Larsen worked closely with the Royal Navy, organizing covert operations in occupied Norway from the RN base in the Shetlands. Supplies and personnel were transported across the North Sea by Norwegian fishing boats – a lifeline known, in that classically understated British (and Norwegian) way, as the "Shetland bus"; the book of the same name by David Howarth (see p.416) tells the tale of this remarkable enterprise.

### Museet Erkebispegården

May to early June & mid-Aug to mid-Sept Mon–Sat 10am–3pm & Sun noon–4pm; early June to mid-Aug Mon–Fri 10am–5pm, Sat 10am–3pm, Sun noon–4pm; mid-Sept to April Mon–Sat 11am–2pm, Sun noon–3pm • 60kr, combined ticket for cathedral & Erkebispegården 120k

The **south wing** of the old Archbishop's Palace holds the **Museet Erkebispegården** (Archbishop's Palace Museum), which is largely devoted to a few dozen medieval statues retrieved and put away for safekeeping during the nineteenth-century reconstruction of the cathedral's nave and west facade. Many of the statues are too battered and bruised to be engaging, but they are well displayed and several are finely carved. In particular, look out for a life-sized sculpture of **St Denis**, his head in his hands (literally) in accordance with the legend that he was beheaded, but then proceeded to irritate his executioners no end by carrying his head to his grave. Downstairs in the basement, an assortment of artefacts unearthed during a lengthy 1990s archeological investigation of the palace demonstrates the economic power of the archbishops: they employed all manner of skilled artisans – from glaziers and shoemakers to rope-makers, armourers and silversmiths – and even minted their own coins.

## Trondheim Kunstmuseum

Bispegata 7b • June to late Aug daily 10am–5pm; Sept–May Tues–Sun 11am–4pm; all year Weds open until 9pm • 20kr • ⓦ tkm.museum.no

Metres from the cathedral, the **Trondheim Kunstmuseum** (Trondheim Art Museum) is perhaps best known for its temporary exhibitions of contemporary art. The downside is that these exhibitions often leave little space for the museum's permanent collection, which features a particularly enjoyable selection of Norwegian paintings from 1850 onwards. Highlights of the permanent collection include several works by Johan Dahl and Thomas Fearnley, the leading figures of nineteenth-century Norwegian landscape painting, as well as the Romantic canvases of Hans Gude and his chum Adolph Tidemand. The museum also owns the first overtly political work by a Norwegian artist, *The Strike* (*Streik*), painted in 1877 by the radical Theodor Kittelsen (1857–1914), who is better known for his illustrations of the folk tales collected by Jorgen Moe and Peder Asbjørnsen. Additionally, the museum possesses a substantial selection of Munch woodcuts, sketches and lithographs, including several of those disturbing, erotically charged personifications of emotions – *Lust, Fear* and *Jealousy* – that are so characteristic of his oeuvre. However, after the theft of the Munch paintings in Oslo (see p.79), the museum has become notably wary about displaying its Munch pieces, so you'll never see many at any one time.

## Nordenfjeldske Kunstindustrimuseum

Munkegata 5 • June to late Aug Mon–Sat 10am–5pm, Sun noon–5pm; late Aug to May Tues–Wed, Fri & Sat 10am–3pm, Thurs 10am–5pm, Sun noon–4pm • 80kr • ⓦ nkim.no

The delightful **Nordenfjeldske Kunstindustrimuseum** (National Museum of Decorative Arts) has a vast (and diverse) permanent collection spanning textiles, furniture, metalwork and other elements of material production, as well as an ambitious programme of special exhibitions. Start in the **basement**, where the historical collection illustrates bourgeois life in Trøndelag from 1500 to 1900 by means of an eclectic assemblage of furniture, faïence, glassware and silver. The modern collection follows on, featuring a small but well-chosen international selection of Arts & Crafts and Art Nouveau pieces, from glass, ceramics and textiles through to furniture – there's even an immaculate William Morris chair. The domestic theme is developed on the **ground floor**, where one small space has been kitted out with early 1950s furnishings and fittings by the Danish designer Finn Juhl and a second room does the same with the work of the Belgian designer and architect **Henri van de Velde** (1863–1957).

On the **first floor**, fourteen wonderful tapestries by **Hannah Ryggen** occupy an entire room. Born in Malmö in 1894, Ryggen moved to the Trondheim area in the early 1920s and stayed until her death in 1970. Her tapestries are classically naive, the forceful colours and absence of perspective emphasizing the feeling behind them. This is committed art at its best, railing in the 1930s and 1940s against Hitler and Fascism, later moving on to more disparate targets such as the atom bomb and social conformism. But Ryggen still made time to celebrate the things she cherished: *Yes, we love this country* (tapestry no. 11) is as evocative a portrayal of her adopted land as you're likely to find.

## NTNU Vitenskapsmuseet

Erling Skakkes gate 47 (the entrance is at the side of the building, a few metres along Gunnerus gate) • May to mid-Sept Mon–Fri 9am–4pm, Sat & Sun 11am–4pm; mid-Sept to April Tues–Fri 9am–2pm, Sat & Sun noon–4pm • 25kr • Ⓦ ntnu.no/vitenskapsmuseet

Located several blocks northwest of the cathedral, the **NTNU Vitenskapsmuseet** (Museum of Natural History and Archeology) has several engaging collections cobbled together by the university. In the large building at the front, you'll find a substantial rocks-and-minerals section, a nature display full of stuffed animals, and a series of temporary exhibits devoted to all things Norwegian. Rather more interesting, however, is the **Middelalder i Trondheim** (medieval exhibition), in the old **suhmhuset** (hay storehouse), a low, long building to the rear of the main entrance. This tracks the development of Trondheim from its foundation in the tenth century to the great fire of 1681. The thoroughly researched, multilingual text is supported by an excellent range of archeological finds, and departs from the predictable "Kings and Queens" approach, investigating everything from sanitary towels and reliquary jars to popular games and attitudes to life and death. One of the more remarkable exhibits is the **Kulisteinen** (Kuli stone), which is carved with both a Christian cross and a runic inscription. Found near Trondheim and dating from around 1034, it's a very rare illustration of the transitional period between a pagan and a Christian Norway.

### Kirkeutstilling

One of the most interesting exhibitions in the NTNU Vitenskapsmuseet is the **Kirkeinventar og kirkekunst** (church art exhibition) in the building across from the main entrance, though it's normally kept locked and you'll need to ask at reception to gain access. Among the assorted ecclesiastical knick-knacks, there are pulpits and fonts, processional crosses and statues of the saints, plus religious paintings galore. By and large, the workmanship is crude and the painting garish, but there is a raw, naïve vitality to many of the earlier pieces which is really rather delightful. Highlights include several fancily carved stave-church portals and an idiosyncratic, seventeenth-century *Adam and Eve*, whose belly buttons look like eyes.

## Torvet

Set in the dead centre of the city at the crossroads of Munkegata and Kongens gate is the main city square, or **Torvet**, a spacious open area anchored by a statue of **Olav Tryggvason** (c.968–1000), who founded Trondheim in 997. Perched on a tall stone pillar like some medieval Nelson, Tryggvason is kitted out in a full set of chain mail with helmet and sword, and has one arm outstretched presenting an orb, the symbol of

### TRONDHEIM'S TACITURN VIKING

One of the most spectacular Vikings of his time, **Olav Tryggvason** is surrounded by myth and legend. The most plausible account of his early days has his mother fleeing Norway with her son when he was about three years old, ending up in exile in Sweden and ultimately Russia. Thereafter, Tryggvason cut his Viking spurs in a series of piratical raids, before leading a large fleet in an attack on England in 991. The English bought him off, then again three years later, and the two payments of this "Danegeld" made him extremely rich. Part of the deal for the second payment was that he become a Christian and, against all expectations, the Viking chieftain seems to have taken his new faith seriously. Tryggvason then hot-footed it back to Norway, where he quickly wrested control of most of the country and founded Trondheim in 997. His brutal imposition of Christianity, however, infuriated many of his subjects – the Tronders, in particular, were determined to hang onto their pagan gods and were especially hacked off by Olav's bloody attempts to force them to be Christians. Few mourned when, after just five years as king, Tryggvason was ambushed and killed.

**5**

monarchical power. He is depicted looking very laconic, which is apt when you consider the Tronders' reputation for taciturnity. An old joke about two Tronder brothers rowing from Trondheim to Bergen sums up the reputed pithy nature of the locals: getting aboard in Trondheim, one of the brothers fell into the water. "I fell in", he exclaimed. Jumping ashore in Bergen, some five hundred kilometres down the coast, the other brother fell in. "I too", he said.

## Kongens gate's medieval church ruins

Kongens gate 1 • Ruins accessible during library opening hours Mon–Thurs 10am–7pm, Fri 10am–4pm & Sat 11am–4pm; also Sept–March Sun noon–4pm • Free

Trondheim's modern **bibliotek** (library) was built on top of some **medieval church ruins**, which are now in full view. A twelfth-century relic of the days when Trondheim had fifteen or more religious buildings, the ruins are thought to be those of a chapel dedicated to St Olav, although the evidence for this is a bit shaky. Excavations revealed nearly five hundred bodies in the immediate area, which was once the church graveyard, and a pair of skeletons are now neatly displayed under glass.

## Stiftsgården

Munkegata 23 • June to late Aug Mon–Sat 10am–4pm, Sun noon–4pm • Guided tours every hour on the hour till 1hr before closing • 60kr • Ⓦ nkim.no/stiftsgarden

One conspicuous remnant of old timber-town Trondheim survives in the city centre – the **Stiftsgården** (Royal Residence) which stretches out along Munkegata just north of Torvet. Built in 1774–78, this handsome yellow structure is among the largest wooden buildings in northern Europe. These days it serves as an official royal residence with some 140 rooms, a marked ascent of the social ladder from its original function as the home of the provincial governor. Inside, a long string of period rooms illustrates the genteel tastes of the mansion's late eighteenth- to early nineteenth-century occupants. The rooms are decorated in a wide range of styles, from Rococo to Biedermeier, but it's the fanciful Italianate wall paintings that steal the show. The obligatory anecdotal guided tour brings a smile or two – but not perhaps 60kr wide.

## Nedre Elvehavn

Northeast of the city centre, a slender footbridge spans the River Nid to link Havnegata with **Nedre Elvehavn**, home of the city's former shipyard. Today, it has been turned into a leisure and shopping complex that trundles along beside the old quays, and is one of the busiest parts of the city, thronged with revellers every summer weekend. From here, you can stroll along the east side of the river down to the next bridge along, Bakke bru.

## Bakklandet

Beyond the Bakke bru bridge, tiny **Bakklandet** is Trondheim's own "Left Bank", a one-time working-class district of brightly painted timber houses that now holds a battery of quaint cafés and restaurants, including some of Trondheim's best. Bakklandet abuts the **Gamle Bybro** (Old Town Bridge), a quaint wooden structure offering splendid views over **Kjøpmannsgata**'s eighteenth-century gabled and timbered warehouses, now mostly restaurants and offices.

## Kristianstenfestning fortress

Dide Halsess gate 6 • Open access • Free

The small road of Brubakken leads up the hill from Bakklandet to Kristianstensbakken and the **Kristianstenfestning fortress**, dating from 1681 and providing wide views back over Trondheim. The earth and stone fortifications have survived in reasonably good condition here as have several of the old buildings. During the war, this was where the Germans tortured their prisoners, many of whom had been betrayed by Arthur Rinnan, a clever and sadistic Norwegian collaborator who was executed in 1947.

## Around Trondheim

All Trondheim's key attractions are neatly packed within walking distance of each other, on or around the city's central island, but there are nevertheless one or two additional sights that may lure you out of the centre. The historic **Munkholmen island** is an easy ten-minute ferry ride away, while a couple of museums – the **Ringve**, to the northeast of the centre, and the **Sverresborg Trøndelag Folkemuseum** in the southwest – both have merit.

### Munkholmen island

Hourly on the hour: late May & late Aug to early Sept 10am–4pm; June to mid-Aug 10am–6pm • 70kr return • Boats leave from the Ravnkloa jetty

Poking up out of the Trondheimsfjord just 2km offshore, the tiny islet of **Munkholmen** has had an eventful history. In Viking times it was used as the city's execution ground, and St Olav went to the added trouble of displaying the head of one of his enemies on a pike here, which must have made approaching mariners a tad nervous. In the eleventh century, the Benedictines founded a monastery on the island – hence its name – but it was not one of their more successful ventures: the archbishop received dozens of complaints about, of all things, the amount of noise the monks made, not to mention alleged heavy drinking and womanizing. After the Reformation, the island was converted into a prison, which doubled as a fortress designed to protect the seaward approaches to the city; later still it became a customs house. The longest-serving prisoner was the Danish count **Peder Griffenfeld** (1635–99), who spent eighteen years cooped up here until his eventual release in 1698. One of the most powerful men in Denmark, Griffenfeld played a leading role in the assumption of absolute power by King Frederik III (see p.390), but was outmanoeuvred and imprisoned by his rivals after the king's death.

### The fortress

Guided tours hourly from late May to early Sept; 30min • 30kr

Sturdy stone walls encircle almost the entire island, and behind them, sunk in a circular dip, is a set of quaint, almost cottage-like, **prison buildings** surrounding a cobbled courtyard. There are guided tours of the central part of the **fortress**, a cheerful romp through its galleries and corridors. The tour includes a visit to the spacious cell occupied by Griffenfeld, and a glimpse of the gun emplacement the Germans installed during World War II. After the tour you can wander over to the **café**, see some exhibitions of local arts and crafts in the old caretaker's house or scramble along outside the walls and round the rocks beneath to either of a couple of rough, pebbly beaches.

### Ringve Museum

Lade alle 60 • April & mid-Sept to early Nov Sun 11am–4pm; May to late June & first two weeks of Sept daily 11am–4pm; late June to Aug daily 11am–5pm • 90kr • ⓦ ringve.no • Bus #3 or #4 from Munkegata to Lade

The **Ringve Museum** occupies a delightful eighteenth-century country house and courtyard complex on the hilly Lade peninsula, some 4km northeast of the city centre. Devoted to musical history and to musical instruments from all over the world, the museum is divided into two sections. In the main building, the collection focuses on antique European instruments in period settings, with several demonstrations included in a lengthy – and obligatory – guided tour. The second section, in the old barn, contains an international selection of musical instruments and offers a self-guided zip

**5**

through some of the key moments and movements of musical history. There are themes like "the invention of the piano" and "pop and rock", as well as the real humdinger, "the marching band movement in Norway". Immaculately maintained, the surrounding **botanical gardens** (daily; free) make the most of the scenic setting.

## Sverresborg Trøndelag Folkemuseum

Sverresborg Allé 13 • June–Aug daily 11am–6pm; 100kr; Sept–May Mon–Fri 11am–3pm, Sat & Sun noon–4pm; 55kr • ⓦ sverresborg .no • Bus #8 (direction Stavset) from Dronningens gate

Three kilometres southwest of the city centre, the **Sverresborg Trøndelag Folkemuseum** (Trøndelag Folk Museum) is one of Norway's best folk museums. In a pleasant rural setting, with views over the city, the museum's indoor section kicks off with some well-presented displays tracing everyday life in the Trøndelag from the eighteenth century onwards. Outside, you'll see sixty relocated Trøndelag timber buildings, including a post office, grocery store, stave church and all sorts of farmhouses and outhouses, built for a variety of purposes from curing meat to drying hay. Finally, it's worth staying for lunch here to sample some traditional Norwegian dishes at the museum's *Tavern* (see p.278).

---

**ARRIVAL AND DEPARTURE**                                     **TRONDHEIM**

**By plane** Trondheim airport is 35km northeast of the city centre at Værnes. From here, Flybussen (Mon–Fri 4am–8.50pm every 15min; Sat 4am–6pm every 30min; Sun 4am–9pm every 15–30min; 45min; 100kr) run to Sentralstasjon and various points in the city centre, including the *SAS Royal Garden Hotel*.

**By train** The city's combined bus and train terminal, Sentralstasjon, is on the northern edge of the centre, a 10min walk from the main square, Torvet. Inside, an information kiosk (☎177) deals with all local transport enquiries. The main train services (ⓦnsb.no) run between Trondheim and Bodø (2 daily; 10hr); Fauske (2 daily; 9hr); Lønsdal (2 daily; 8hr; request stop); Mo-i-Rana (3 daily; 6hr 30min); Mosjøen (3 daily; 5hr 15min); Oslo (4 daily via Dombås, Lillehammer and Oslo Gardermoen airport; 6hr 30min–7hr 45min); Oslo via Røros (1 daily; 7hr 45min; change at Hamar); Røros (2–3 daily; 2hr 30min); Steinkjer (hourly; 2hr); Stockholm (2 daily; 12hr); and Verdal (hourly; 1hr 40min).

**By bus** Buses arrive at and depart from the combined bus and train terminal, Sentralstasjon (see above). Principal Nor-Way Bussekspress bus services (ⓦnor-way.no) serve Ålesund (3–4 daily; 7hr); Bergen (1 daily; 14hr); Loen (2 daily; 8hr–11hr); Lom (2 daily; 5hr 40min); Oslo (1–3 daily;

8hr 30min); Otta (1 daily; 4hr 345in); and Stryn (1 daily; 7hr 30min).

**By boat** The all-year Kystekspressen (ⓦkystekspressen .no) passenger express boat from Kristiansund (1–3 daily; 3hr 15min) docks at the Pirterminalen, from where it's a dull 15min walk south to Sentralstasjon. The quay for the Hurtigruten coastal boat (ⓦhurtigruten.no) is near the Pirterminalen, another 300m or so away to the north. Local buses #2 and #46 run from the Pirabadet swimming pool, in between the two quays, to Sentralstasjon. Ferries for Munkholmen (see p.275) leave from the Ravnkloa jetty at the end of Munkegata.

**By car** Trondheim is on the E6 highway, a 7–8hr drive (500km) from Oslo. In the city centre, on-street parking during restricted periods (Mon–Fri 8am–8pm, Sat 8am–3pm) is expensive (22kr/hr) and hard to find, but is otherwise free with spaces commonplace. During restricted periods, you're best off heading for a car park: try the handy Torget P-hus, in the centre at Erling Skakkes gate 16 (Mon–Fri 7am–9pm, Sat 7am–7pm); or the Bakke P-hus, east across the bridge from the centre at Nedre Bakklandet 60 (Mon–Fri 6.30am–11pm, Sat 6.30am–9pm). Car park rates are 15kr per hour up to a maximum of 150kr in any 24hr period.

---

**GETTING AROUND**

**On foot** The best way to explore the city centre is on foot – it only takes about 10min to walk from one end to the other.

**By bus and tram** If you want to travel outside the city centre, to one of the outlying museums or the hostel for example, you'll need to use a city tram or bus. These are operated by Nett Buss (☎177, ⓦnettbuss.no), with flat-fare one-way tickets, purchased from the driver, costing 33kr (exact change only). There's also an unlimited 24hr bus ticket,

the *døgnbillet*, which costs 70kr, which can also be bought from the driver. The hub of the system are the bus stops around the Munkegata/Dronningens gate intersection. There's also a Nettbuss Trondheim travel office, which sells tickets and provides information, in the city centre at Dronningens gate 40 (Mon–Fri 8am–6pm, Sat 10am–3pm).

**By car** Car rental is available from Avis, Kjøpmannsgata 34 (☎67 25 56 00) and at the airport (☎67 25 56 10); Europcar, Leangen Alle 8 (☎73 82 88 50) and at the airport

(☎ 74 82 67 00); or Hertz, Innherredsveien 103 (☎ 73 50 35 00) and at the airport (☎ 74 80 16 60).

**By bike** Trondheim has a summertime public bike scheme with ninety bikes in twelve bike racks dotted across the city centre (May–Oct 6am to midnight). The bikes are released just like supermarket trolleys, when you insert your access card, which you can buy at the tourist office for 70kr (plus a deposit of 200kr). This gives you unlimited use of the bikes for 24 hours.

**By taxi** There are eight ranks in and around the city centre including ranks at Torvet, Sentralstasjon and the *Radisson SAS Royal Garden Hotel*; or call Trønder Taxi (☎ 073 73).

## INFORMATION

**Tourist office** Munkegata 19, on the edge of Torvet (mid-June to late June Mon–Fri 9am–6pm, Sat & Sun 10am–4pm; late June to July Mon–Fri 8.30am–8pm, Sat & Sun 10am–6pm; Aug to late Aug Mon–Fri 8.30am–10pm, Sat & Sun 10am–8pm; late Aug to mid-June Mon–Fri 9am–4pm, Sat 10am–2pm; ☎ 73 80 76 60, ⓦ trondheim .no). Staff here issue the free and very useful *Trondheim Guide* (also available from information racks at Sentralstasjon) as well as a wide range of other tourist literature, including a cycle map of the city and its surroundings. They also sell hiking maps, change money and have a limited supply of private rooms (see below).

**DNT** Trondhjems Turistforening, just west of the centre at Sandgata 30 (Mon–Fri 10am–5pm; ☎ 73 92 42 00, ⓦ tt .no), is DNT's local branch, offering advice on the region's hiking trails and huts. It also organizes a variety of guided walks and cross-country skiing trips, with activities concentrated in the mountains to the south and east of the city. There are one-day excursions and longer expeditions to suit different levels of skill and fitness.

## ACCOMMODATION

Accommodation is plentiful in Trondheim, with a choice of private rooms, two hostels, and a selection of reasonably priced hotels. What's more, most of the more appealing places are dotted round the city centre, which is precisely where you want to be. The exception is the **private rooms** booked via the tourist office, which are usually out in the suburbs. These private rooms are good value at around 500–600kr per double per night (400–500kr single), plus a small booking fee.

**Britannia Hotel** Dronningens gate 5 ☎ 73 80 08 00, ⓦ britannia.no. Right in the middle of town, this long-established hotel was built in the nineteenth century with a bright-white facade. Inside, a couple of the public rooms have splendid wood panelling and the breakfast room comes complete with a Moorish fountain, Egyptian-style murals and Corinthian columns. The well-appointed bedrooms manage to be both unfussy and cosy with browns and creams to the fore. **1290kr**

**City Living Schøller Hotel** Dronningens gate 26 ☎ 73 87 08 00, ⓦ cityliving.no. Economy chain hotel above some shops in the centre of the city. The modern rooms are spick-and-span verging on the spartan, but the price is right. **630kr**

**Clarion Collection Hotel Bakeriet** Brattørgata 2 ☎ 73 99 10 00, ⓦ choicehotels.no. With a central location, this competent chain hotel is in an intelligently revamped former bakery in the trendy part of town. The guest rooms, which were once occupied by the bakery workers, are kitted out in standard modern style. **820kr**

**Radisson Blu Royal Garden** Kjøpmannsgata 73 ☎ 73 80 30 00, ⓦ radissonblu.com/hotel-trondheim. Full marks to the architects here, who have designed this large, modern, riverside hotel in the style of the old timber warehouses it replaced. Lots of glass – indeed the interior of the hotel looks a bit like a series of enormous greenhouses – but be sure to ask for a room in the newer, more modern wing. Banquet-like breakfasts. **995kr**

★ **Rica Nidelven Hotel** Havnegata 1–3 ☎ 73 56 80 00, ⓦ rica.no. Large and flashy chain hotel nudging out into the river with lots of glass to maximize views. The public areas are bold and expansive – modernism at its most decisive – though the guest rooms are not perhaps quite as distinctive as they could be. Comes with all mod cons. **1095kr**

**Trondheim InterRail Center** Elgeseter gate 1 ☎ 73 89 95 38, ⓦ tirc.no. Bargain-basement lodgings in the unusual, big, red and round building – the Studentersamfundet (university student centre) – that stands just over the bridge at the south end of Prinsens gate, a 5min walk from the cathedral. Offers basic mixed-dorm accommodation with breakfast served in the downstairs café. No curfew, internet access and an extremely lively crowd. Open early July to mid-Aug only. Dorms **180kr**

**Trondheim Vandrerhjem** Weidemannsveien 41 ☎ 73 87 44 50, ⓦ trondheim-vandrerhjem.no. This large, well-equipped hostel is mostly parcelled up into four-bed dorm rooms, only a few of which are en suite. Looks more like a hospital than somewhere you'd want to stay from the outside, but the interior is pleasant enough – especially the comfortable, newer rooms. It has self-catering facilities, a laundry and a canteen. A 20min, 2km hike east of the centre: cross the Bakke bru (bridge) onto busy Innherredsveien (the E6) and walk uphill; turn right onto Wessels gate and hang a left at the fourth crossroads. To save your legs, take any bus up Innherredsveien and ask the driver to let you off as close as possible. Open all year. Dorms **245kr**, doubles **660kr**

## EATING, DRINKING AND NIGHTLIFE

As befits Norway's third city, Trondheim has a good selection of first-rate restaurants serving a variety of cuisines, though the Norwegian places almost always have the gastronomic edge. In particular, there's a couple of especially fine restaurants in the **Bakklandet** district, by the eastern end of Gamle Bybro, and a third at the south end of neighbouring Kjøpmannsgata. Bars are dotted all over the city centre, but the weekend scene is at its liveliest on and around Brattørgata and in the **Nedre Elvehavn** district, where the former municipal shipyard has been turned into a large leisure complex of shops, bars and restaurants. Finally – if needs must – the city's mobile fast-food stalls are concentrated around Sentralstasjon and along Kongens gate, on either side of Torvet.

### CAFÉS AND CAFÉ-BARS

★ **Dromedar** Nedre Bakklandet 3 ☎73 50 25 02, ⓦdromedar.no. Laidback, cosy-cramped coffee bar in antique wooden premises a few metres north of the Gamle Bybro. One of a small chain, it serves the best coffee in town plus snacks and light meals – filled bagels, sandwiches, etc – at bargain prices. Mon–Fri 7.30am–7pm, Sat 10am–6pm, Sun 10.30am–6pm.

**Godt Brød** Thomas Angells gate 16 ☎73 53 61 40, ⓦbakeverksted.no. The aroma of baking bread, rolls and pastries, all organic, wafts around this cosy little café-cum-bakery, where the coffee is good and the breads and pastries even better. Sandwiches made to order too. Daily except Sun 6am–6pm.

### RESTAURANTS

★ **Baklandet Skydsstation** Øvre Bakklandet 33 ☎73 92 10 44, ⓦskydsstation.no. Friendly, intimate former coaching inn with a warren of homely dining rooms and a small courtyard. The reasonably priced menu with mains from as little as 200kr features home-cooked staples such as that old Norwegian favourite, *bacalao* (dried and salted cod fish), and an earth-moving cheesecake. Daily: June–Aug 10am–1am; Sept–May 11am–1am.

**Bare Blåbær** Innherredsveien 16, Nedre Elvehavn ☎73 53 30 33, ⓦbarebb.no. The excellent-value, stone-baked pizzas at this fast-moving café-restaurant make it very popular with a youthful clientele. Pizzas from 90kr. Mon–Thurs 11am–1.30am, Fri & Sat 11am–2.30am, Sun 11am–1.30am.

**Frati** Munkegata 25 ☎73 52 57 33, ⓦfrati.no. Much favoured by locals, this traditional, family-run Italian restaurant above a bar serves all the classic dishes in generous and authentic portions. Main courses start at 138kr. Mon–Fri 3–11pm, Sat & Sun 2–11pm.

★ **Havfruen Fiskerestaurant** Kjøpmannsgata 7 ☎73 87 40 70, ⓦhavfruen.no. In an old and cleverly revamped riverside warehouse, this smart and extremely popular seafood restaurant is one of the best in town. Main courses – cod, coalfish, char and so forth – average around 270kr, or you can push the boat out with the five-course menu for 665kr. Mon–Sat 4–11.30pm.

★ **Sabor** Øvre Bakklandet 66 ☎40 61 88 04, ⓦsabor .no. Just metres from the Gamle Bybro, this polished tapas spot serves very good Spanish grilled meals. In addition to

standard tapas dishes such as grilled asparagus (35kr), Ibérico de Bellota ham (109kr), you can choose from cheeses such as *manchego*, *mahón* and *cabrales* and a number of great chorizo and pork plates (from 139kr). Mon–Sat 4–11pm.

**Tavern på Sverresborg** Sverresborg allé 7 ☎73 87 80 70, ⓦtavern.no. In business since 1739, this restaurant-tavern is in the Sverresborg Folkemuseum (see p.276). Its low-ceilinged timber rooms are furnished in appropriate period style and the food is traditional Norwegian *husmannskost* (working-class fare) at its best: the *Kjøttkaker i brun saus med erterstuing* (meatballs in brown gravy served with pea stew) is hard to beat, as is the *spekemat* (cured meat), the *rømmegrøt* (sour-cream porridge) and the *fiskekaker* (fishcakes). Mains from 120–335kr. Bus #8 from Dronningens gate. Mon–Fri 4pm–midnight, Sat & Sun 2pm–midnight; kitchen shuts 2–3hr before closing time.

### BARS AND CLUBS

**Bar Passiar** Innherredsveien 16 ☎92 60 62 00, ⓦbarebb.no. Managing to straddle that fine line between trendy and pretentious, this is the pick of the bars along the Nedre Elvehavn dockside strip. The sister of the neighbouring *Bare Blåbær* restaurant (see above), it has house and electro DJs spinning till late, as well as fresh fruit cocktails and outdoor seating. Tues–Thurs 3pm–1.30am, Fri 3pm–2.30am, Sat noon–2.30am.

**Bari** Munkegata 26 ☎73 60 60 24, ⓦbari.no. Smooth and polished bar-restaurant, all dark-stained wood and soft lighting. Attracts an older/smarter crew, who sip wine and cocktails (rather then downing litres of ale). Below the *Frati* restaurant (see above). Mon–Thurs 10.30–1am, Fri & Sat 10.30–2am.

**Café 3B** Brattørgata 3b ☎73 51 15 50, ⓦcafe3b.no. Rock and roll and indie club-cum-bar, where you can drink well into the wee hours. One of the grooviest places in town. Daily 6pm–2.30am.

**Metro** Kjøpmannsgata 12 ⓦgaytrondheim.com. Trondheim's principal gay and lesbian bar, tastefully decorated and with DJs playing at the weekend. Attaracts an international crowd, and drinks are remarkably affordable compared to most other spots in town. There's often a cover charge at weekends. Wed 9pm–1am, Fri & Sat 10pm–2am.

**5**

**Trondhjem Mikrobryggeri** Prinsens gate 39 ☎ 73 51 75 15, ⊛tmb.no. Mainstream bar in a pleasant little courtyard just off Prinsens gate. It serves its own microbrewery brews, as well as plates of filling pub food. Mon 5pm–midnight, Tues–Fri 3pm–2am, Sat noon–2am (kitchen closes at 10pm).

## ENTERTAINMENT

**Nova Kinosenter** Cicignons plass ☎73 80 88 00, ⊛trondheimkino.no. Shows all the movie blockbusters on its eleven screens.

**Olavshallen** Kjøpmannsgata 44 ☎73 99 40 50, ⊛olavshallen.no. The city's main concert hall, offering everything from opera to rock, comedy and musicals. It's also home to the city's symphony orchestra.

## SHOPPING

**Ravnkloa fish market** The fish market is on the jetty at the north end of Munkegata. Mon–Fri 10am–5pm, Sat 10am–4pm.

**Solsiden** Beddingen 10 ⊛solsidensenter.no. Shopping mall with scores of shops and boutiques selling clothing, accessories and homeware. Mon–Fri 10am–9pm, Sat 10am–6pm.

**Vinmonopolet** Olav Tryggvasons gate 28. One of several city-centre branches of the government-run liquor and wine store. Mon–Fri 10am–6pm, Sat 10am–3pm.

## DIRECTORY

**Banks and exchange** ATMs are liberally distributed across the city centre. The main post office (see below), most banks and the tourist office change currency.

**Consulates** UK, Beddingen 8 ☎73 60 02 00.

**Dentists** Dental emergencies ☎73 50 55 00.

**Emergencies** Ambulance ☎113; fire ☎110; police ☎112.

**Internet** There's free internet access at the library, Kongens gate (Mon–Thurs 10am–7pm, Fri 10am–4pm, Sat 11am–4pm; also Sept–March Sun noon–4pm).

**Pharmacy** Vaktapoteket St Olav, Solsiden, Beddingen 4 (Mon–Sat 8.30am–midnight, Sun 10am–midnight; ☎73 88 37 37). Vitusapotek Løven, Olav Tryggvasonsgate 28 (Mon–Fri 9am–6pm, Sat 9am–3pm; ☎73 83 32 83).

**Post office** Main office at Dronningens gate 10 (Mon–Fri 9am–5pm, Sat 10am–3pm, though hours are reduced somewhat in the summer).

# North from Trondheim to Bodø

North of Trondheim, it's a long haul up the coast to the next major places of interest: Bodø, the main ferry port for the Lofoten, and the gritty but likeable transport-hub port of Narvik – respectively 720km and 910km distant. Fortunately, there are several pleasant places to stop en route, beginning with **Steinkjer** and **Snåsa** in the province of Trøndelag. Steinkjer is a modest little town with a couple of good hotels, Snåsa, a relaxed – and relaxing – village, again with somewhere good to stay. Further north, in Nordland, the next province up, **Mosjøen** and **Mo-i-Rana**, two rejigged and revamped former industrial towns, make pleasant pit stops, with Mo-i-Rana serving as a handy starting point for a visit to the **Svartisen glacier**, crowning the coastal peaks close by. The glacier is on the western rim of the **Saltfjellet Nasjonalpark**, a wild and windswept mountain plateau that extends east towards the Swedish border. The E6 and the railway cut through the park, giving ready access, but although this is a popular destination for experienced hikers, it's too fierce an environment for the novice or the lightly equipped.

### ARRIVAL AND DEPARTURE

NORTH FROM TRONDHEIM TO BODØ

**By train** The easiest way to make the bulk of the trip is by train, a rattling good journey on the Nordlandsbanen (Nordland Line) with the scenery becoming wilder and bleaker the further north you go – and you usually get a blast from the whistle as you cross the Arctic Circle – but be sure to sit on the left of the carriage going north as the views are much better. The train takes 9hr to reach Fauske – you can do the journey overnight by sleeper – where the line reaches its northern limit and turns west for the final 60km dash to Bodø. There's precious little to detain you in Fauske, but there are bus connections north to Narvik, a 5hr drive away, and many travellers take an overnight break here, though in fact nearby Bodø makes a far more pleasant stopover; there are buses to Narvik from here too.

**5**

**By road** If you're driving, you'll find the main highway, the E6, which runs all the way from Trondheim to Narvik and points north, too slow to cover more than 300–400km comfortably in a day. The main alternative to the E6 is the coastal Highway 17, the Kystriksveien (ⓦrv17.no), an ingenious and extremely scenic cobbling together of road, tunnel, bridge and car ferry that negotiates the shredded shoreline from Steinkjer, just north of Trondheim, all the way up to Bodø, a distance of nigh on 700km. It's a slow route – there are no fewer than seven ferry crossings – but if you can't spare the time or money to do the whole thing, you could join Highway 17 to the west of Mo-i-Rana, cutting out five ferries and the first 420km, yet still taking in the most dramatic part of the journey, including fabulous views of the Melfjord and the Svartisen glacier.

## Hell

The busy rail junction of **Hell** has nothing to recommend it except its name, though paradoxically *hell* in Norwegian means good fortune: don't despair, the locals still sell postcards of the train station's freight depot tagged "Hell – Gods-Expedition" (an archaic Norwegian spelling of the phrase for "cargo handling" or "freight service"). The only reason you may find yourself in Hell is to change trains from the main line north onto the branch line that heads east to the Swedish frontier, 70km away.

### LEIF LARSEN AND THE ATTACK ON THE TIRPITZ

Commissioned in 1941, the German battleship **Tirpitz** spent most of its three-year existence hidden away in the **Fjættenfjord**, a narrow inlet of the Trondheimsfjord 20km north of Hell, where it was protected from air attack by the mountains and from naval attack by a string of coastal gun emplacements. With the fjord as its base, the *Tirpitz* was able to sally forth to attack Allied convoys bound for Russia and as such was a major irritant to the Royal Navy, who dreamt up a remarkable scheme to sink it. The navy had just perfected a submersible craft called the **Chariot**, which was 6m long, powered by electric motors, and armed with a torpedo. A crew of two volunteer divers manned the craft, sitting astride it at the rear – which must amount to some kind of definition of bravery.

The plan was to transport two of these Chariots across from Shetland to Norway in a Norwegian fishing boat and then, just before the first German checkpoint, to hide them by attaching them to the outside of the boat's hull. Equipped with false papers and a diversionary load of peat, the fishing boat would, it was thought, stand a good chance of slipping through the German defences. Thereafter, as soon as the boat got within reasonable striking distance, the Chariots could be launched towards the *Tirpitz* and, once they got very close to the ship, their torpedoes would be fired.

The boat selected was the *Arthur*, skippered by the redoubtable **Leif Andreas Larsen**, a modest man of extraordinary courage, who, over the course of the war, ran over fifty trips to Norway from the Shetlands. The *Arthur* had a crew of four Norwegian and six British seamen – four to pilot the Chariots and two to help them get into their diving suits. At first the trip went well. As soon as they reached Norway's coastal waters, the crew moved the Chariots from their hiding place in the hold and attached them to the hull. They then fooled the Germans and were allowed into the Trondheimsfjord, but here the weather deteriorated and the Chariots broke loose from the boat, falling to the bottom of the ocean before they could be used. There was, therefore, no choice but to abort the mission, scuttle the *Arthur* and row ashore in the hope that the crew could escape over the mountains to neutral Sweden. They divided into two parties of five, one of which made it without mishap – except for a few lost toes from frostbite – but the other group, led by Larsen, ran into a patrol. In the skirmish that ensued, one of the Englishmen, a certain A.B. Evans, was wounded and had to be left behind; the Germans polished him off.

On September 11, 1944, the *Tirpitz* was caught napping in the **Kåfjord** (see p.346) by Allied bombers, which flew in from a Russian airfield to the east, screened by the mountains edging the fjord. The *Tirpitz* was badly damaged in the attack and although it managed to limp off to Tromsø the warship was finally sunk just outside that city on November 12 by a combined bombing-and-torpedo attack.

# Stiklestad

**5**

One of Norway's most celebrated villages, **STIKLESTAD** was where **Olav Haraldsson**, later St Olav (see p.269), was killed in battle in 1030. A descendant of Harald Hårfagre (the Fair-Haired), Haraldsson was one of Norway's most important medieval kings, a Viking warrior turned resolute Christian monarch whose misfortune it was to be the enemy of the powerful and shrewd King Knut of England and Denmark. It was Knut's bribes that did for Olav, persuading all but his most loyal supporters to change allegiance – as a Norse poet commented in the cautionary *Håvamål* (the Sayings of Odin), "I have never found a man so generous and hospitable that he would not take a present." Dislodged from the throne, Olav returned from exile in Sweden in 1030, but was defeated and killed here at the **Battle of Stiklestad**. His role as founder of the Norwegian Church prompted his subsequent canonization, and his cult flourished at Trondheim until the Reformation.

## Stiklestad Nasjonale Kultursenter

Leksdalsveien 1 • Daily 7am–9pm • 140kr • ☎ 74 04 42 00, ⓦ stiklestad.no

The Norwegian government has spent millions of kroner developing the **Stiklestad Nasjonale Kultursenter** (Stiklestad National Culture Centre) to commemorate the death of Olav Haraldsson. This collection of assorted museums is spread out over a pastoral landscape, and includes an open-air amphitheatre, a folk museum and a Viking longhouse.

### The Kulturhus

The broad-beamed **Kulturhus** houses a pleasingly melodramatic **museum** that uses shadowy dioramas and a ghoulish soundtrack to chronicle the events leading up to Olav's death. Nonetheless, the dioramas contain few artefacts of note, other than one or two bits of armour and jewellery dating from the period, and neither is the text particularly revealing, which is a pity, since something more could have been made of Olav's position in medieval Christian folklore. One such tale, passed down through the generations, relates how Olav spent the night on a remote Norwegian farm, only to discover the family praying over a pickled horse's penis. Expressing some irritation – but no surprise – at this pagan ceremony, Olav threw the phallus to the family dog and took the opportunity to explain some of the finer tenets of Christianity to his hosts. There's a second display on St Olav upstairs in the museum, focusing on his cult and how it spread across Western Europe.

### The kirke

The centre's **kirke** lies across from the Kulturhus in a much-modified, twelfth-century stone building, which reputedly marks the spot where Olav was stabbed to death. Claims that the stone on which the body was first laid out had been incorporated into the church's high altar were abandoned during the Reformation, in case of damage by Protestants.

## The amfiteater and folkemuseum

The open-air **amfiteater** (amphitheatre) lies just up the hill from the Kulturhus, a five-minute walk away, and is where the colourful Olsokspelet (St Olav's Play), a costume drama, is performed each year as part of the **St Olav Festival**. This is held over several days either side of the anniversary of the battle, July 29, and thousands of Norwegians make the trek here; tickets need to be booked months in advance via the Kultursenter website. The amphitheatre also adjoins an open-air **folk museum**, containing a few indoor exhibits, and some thirty seventeenth- to nineteenth-century buildings moved here from all over rural Trøndelag.

## Stiklastadir

ⓦ stiklestad.no

The pride of the site is the medieval **Stiklastadir** (longhouse), which was opened in 2009. This stately, 36m-long building consists of a living space and large banqueting

**5**

hall, where the resident chieftain would hold receptions and meetings. During the summer, there are plenty of activities and games put on for children, as well as exhibitions, dramatized tours and Viking heritage theatre performances.

### ARRIVAL AND DEPARTURE STIKLESTAD

**By train** Stiklestad is difficult to reach without your own transport. A twice-daily train from Trondheim runs to Verdal, 6km away, from where you have to walk, or use one of the taxis that usually wait outside the station. During the

St Olav Festival, however, special trains and buses take visitors to the site from Trondheim – ask for details from the Trondheim tourist office.

### ACCOMMODATION

**Stiklestad Hotel** Leksdalsveien 1 ☎ 74 04 42 00, ⓦ stiklestad.no. Set in the main building of the cultural centre, this is one of the snazziest spots to stay in the area. Despite its focus on business and conference clientele, the

rooms here have oodles of character, with colourful blankets and pillows, lovely hardwood floors and art on the walls. The hotel also has a decent, informal, white-tablecloth restaurant. **1050kr**

## Steinkjer

The pleasant, unassuming town of **STEINKJER** sits in the shadow of wooded hills, at the point where the river that gave the place its name empties into the fjord. The Germans bombed the town to bits in 1940 because it was the site of an infantry training camp, and the modern replacement is a tidy, appealing ensemble that fans out from the long main street, Kongens gate.

### Egge Museum

Fylkesmannsgården • Early June to mid-Aug daily 11am–4pm • 70kr • ☎ 74 13 44 90, ⓦ eggemuseum.no

Set in the grounds of the one-time county governor's mansion, 2km northwest of Steinkjer's centre, the open-air **Egge Museum** consists of a nineteenth-century farmstead with eleven original farm buildings to explore. There are farm animals for children to pet as well as displays of agricultural tools and vehicles, and locals dressed in period costume giving demonstrations of old farming practices and techniques.

### ARRIVAL AND INFORMATION STEINKJER

**By train** The train station is at Strandveien in the southwest of Steinkjer, a 5-min walk from the tourist office with trains from Bodø (2 daily; 7hr 45min) and Trondheim (hourly; 2hr).

**By bus** Steinkjer's bus station is next to the train station, with regular services from Trondheim (3 daily; 2hr).

**Tourist office** In the town centre on highway E6 opposite the Amfi Shopping Centre (mid-June to mid-Aug Mon–Fri 9am–8pm, Sat 10am–7pm & Sun noon–7pm; mid-Aug to mid-June Mon–Fri 9am–4pm; ☎ 74 40 17 16, ⓦ visitinnherred.com).

### ACCOMMODATION

**Best Western Tingvold Park Hotel** Gamle Kongeveg 47, 1km from Steinjker centre ☎ 74 14 11 00, ⓦ tingvoldhotel.no. Central spot offering homely rooms that, while perfectly acceptable, could do with a little updating. Rate includes breakfast and evening buffet of waffles and coffee. **1195kr**

**Quality Hotel Grand Steinkjer** Kongens gate 37 ☎ 74 16 47 00, ⓦ choicehotels.no. Right in the centre of town across from the train station, this hotel occupies a clumpy modern tower block, though the rooms on the upper floors more than redeem matters with their splendid views out along the coast. **980kr**

### EATING AND DRINKING

**Brod & Circus** Kongens gate 40 ☎ 74 16 21 00. A bright and inviting branch of the small local chain where a range of bread is freshly baked on the premises. For something more substantial, there's also a Mediterranean-inspired menu with main courses from 140kr. Mon–Tues 11am–5pm,

Wed–Fri 11am–10pm, Sat noon–midnight.

**Café Madam Brix** Kirkegata 7 ☎ 74 16 74 60, ⓦ madambrix.no. Among the best of Steinkjer's assorted cafés and restaurants, this cosy spot takes its name from the redoubtable widow who founded an inn here in 1722.

In addition to good coffee and cakes, they serve simple meals such as waffles (40kr) and *smørrebrød* (from 40kr), as well as a few wines. Mon–Thurs 11am–10pm, Fri 11am–3am, Sat 11am–3am.

## Snåsa

At the top end of the long and slender Lake Snåsavatn, the sleepy, scattered hamlet of **SNÅSA** is a fine example of a Trøndelag rural community. It looks as if nothing much has happened here for decades, but there is one sight of note, a pretty little hilltop **church** of softly hued grey stone, dating from the Middle Ages and very much in the English style.

### ACCOMMODATION          SNÅSA

**Snåsa Hotell Leiråmoen** ☎ 74 15 10 57, ⓦ snasahotell.no. This modern place on the village's western side, and 6km from the E6, is in a lovely setting overlooking the lake: its decor is somewhat dated, but the 38 bedrooms are more than comfortable. The hotel also operates a small year-round campsite, with nine cabins as well as spaces for tents and caravans. There's a restaurant too, serving humdrum but filling Norwegian staples, though if you're likely to arrive after 7pm, you should telephone ahead to check it will still be open. Doubles 1070kr, tents 120kr, cabins 400kr

## The Laksforsen waterfalls

The harsh landscape of Nordland province, with its bleak plateaux and rangy river valleys, is home to the **Laksforsen waterfalls**, a well-known beauty spot where the River Vefsna takes a 17-metre tumble. The café here offers a grand view of the falls, which were once much favoured by British aristocrats for their salmon fishing. To get here, turn off the E6 about 190km beyond Snåsa, down a short (700m) signposted side road.

## Mosjøen

Although its setting is handsome enough, wedged between fjord, river and mountain, the town of **MOSJØEN** does not immediately impress, as it's dominated by a huge aluminium plant, which hogs the north side of the waterfront. It's worth persevering, however, for Mosjøen was a small-time trading centre long before the factory arrived, and **Sjøgata**, down by the river just to the south of the plant, is lined by attractive old timber dwellings, warehouses and shops dating from the early nineteenth century. It's an appealing streetscape, especially since the buildings are still in everyday use.

### Vefsn Museum

Sjøgata 31 • Mon–Fri 10am–3pm • 30kr • ☎ 75 11 01 10, ⓦ helgelandmuseum.no

The mildly diverting **Vefsn Museum** offers displays on life in old Mosjøen and exhibits some interesting work by contemporary Nordland artists, including some very good photographic work. Nearby is a collection of a dozen or so rural buildings from previous centuries, which can only be viewed from the outside, and the mid-1700s-era Dolstad church (ask at the museum ticket office for entry).

### ARRIVAL AND INFORMATION       MOSJØEN

**By train** Mosjøen train station is beside the E6 on the north side of town in front of the aluminium plant. From here, it's a 1km, well-signed walk to the east end of Sjøgata.

**By bus** Mosjøen bus station is on Strandgata, about 100m beyond the west end of Sjøgata.

**Tourist office** Austerbygdveien 20, a few hundred metres south of the train station (late June to July Mon–Fri 9am–6pm, Sat & Sun 11am–4pm; early Aug Mon–Fri 9am–5pm; late Aug to late June Mon–Fri 10am–3pm; ☎ 75 01 80 00, ⓦ visithelgeland.com).

**5**

## THE E6: A SCENIC ROUTE VIA KORGFJELLET AND KORGEN

Beyond Mosjøen, the E6 cuts inland to weave across the mountains of the interior, while the railway stays glued to the seashore down below. Either way, it's an enjoyable journey, though the E6 has the scenic edge even if it now tunnels through the flanks of **Korgfjellet** rather than going over the top. The old road is, however, still open, offering panoramic views, its highest point marked by a motel and a monument honouring the 550 Yugoslav prisoners of war who built this section of the road during World War II. Just beyond Korgfjellet is the village of **Korgen**, sitting pretty beneath the mountains in the bend of a river. From here, the E6 slips down a river valley and sidles along the fjord to Mo-i-Rana, 90km from Mosjøen.

### ACCOMMODATION

**Fru Haugans** Strandgata 39 ☎ 75 11 41 00, ⓦ fruhaugans.no. Just metres from the tourist office, this is the pick of town's hotels. There has been an inn here since the eighteenth century – it's the oldest hotel in the north of Norway – and the present building is a well-judged amalgamation of old and new. The 93 rooms vary greatly in style, from traditional to modern, and breakfast is served at waterside tables outside. <u>**1395kr**</u>

**Gjestehusene i Sjøgata** Sjøgata 22–24 ☎ 75 17 27 60, ⓦ alrunen.no. Run by a local heritage organization, this guesthouse rents out rooms in several newly renovated old wooden houses around the block. They also run a charming old-fashioned café in their main building, serving coffee and traditional Nordland pastries. <u>**1100kr**</u>

### EATING AND DRINKING

**Ellenstuen** Fru Haugans hotel, Strandgata 39 ☎ 75 11 41 00, ⓦ fruhaugans.no. Hotel restaurant that serves up tasty, mainly Norwegian, dishes from a seasonal menu that makes the most of local ingredients; main courses start at around 240kr. Mon–Sat 5–10.30pm.

**Lille Torget** Strandgata 24 ☎ 75 17 04 14. The liveliest spot in town is this pretty little terrace pub-café, with a great Art Nouveau interior. It's the best place in Mosjøen to meet a local, and the coffee they brew here is among Norway's best. Mon–Sat 10am–1am.

## Mo-i-Rana and around

Hugging the head of the Ranfjord, **MO-I-RANA**, or more usually "Mo", was known in Old Norse records as *Móar*, or grass lowland. Until World War II, it functioned as a minor port and market town, after which its fortunes, and appearance, were transformed by the construction of a steel plant. The plant dominated proceedings until the 1980s, when there was some economic diversification and the town began to clean itself up: the fjord shore was cleared of its industrial clutter and the E6 re-routed to create the pleasantly spacious, surprisingly leafy town centre of today. A predominantly modern town, Mo is also home to a statue by British sculptor, **Antony Gormley**, the large and stern-looking figure, **Havmannen** (Man of the Sea), which gazes determinedly down the fjord. The main reason to come to Mo, however, is as a base for visiting the east side of the **Svartisen glacier** and for exploring the region's caves, such as the **Grønligrotta**, as well as its lakes, fjords and mountains.

### Mo kirke

Kirkegate 10 • Late June to Aug Mon–Fri 8–10pm • At other times ring ☎ 75 12 33 25 to have the church opened

With a high-pitched roof and onion dome perched on a hill on the eastern edge of the centre the 1832-era **Mo kirke** breaks the monotony of some of the town's more modern

## ART IN NORDLAND

Dotted across the province of Nordland are 33 open-air **sculptures** by some of the world's leading contemporary sculptors, including Dorothy Cross, Anish Kapoor, Antony Gormley and Inge Mahn. Together these sculptures comprise the **Skulpturlandskap** (ⓦ skulpturlandskap .no) and although many of the sculptures are in remote, even obscure locations, others – like Gormley's *Havmannen* in Mo-i-Rana (see above) – are more accessible.

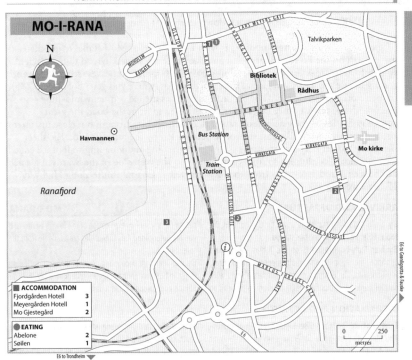

buildings. Enclosed by a mossy stone wall, the well-tended graveyard contains a communal tomb for unidentified Russian prisoners of war and the graves of six Scots Guards killed hereabouts in May 1940. In front of the church is a bust commemorating Thomas van Westen, an eighteenth-century evangelist-missionary who spearheaded early attempts to convert the Sámi.

## The Grønligrotta

Guided tours hourly from mid-June to mid-Aug daily 10am–6pm; 35min • 125kr • ⓦ gronligrotta.no

The limestone and marble mountains to the north of Mo are pocked by caves. The most accessible is the limestone **Grønligrotta**, 25km north of Mo, where an easy guided tour follows a subterranean river and takes in a 400-metre-long underground chamber. Grønligrotta is lit by electric lights – it's the only illuminated cave in Scandinavia – and it's located 25km from Mo: head north out of town along the E6 and follow the signs along the same minor road that leads to the most accessible part of the Svartisen glacier.

## Svartisen glacier

**Boats** mid-June & late Aug 2 daily (depending on the ice); late June to mid-Aug hourly 10am–4pm; 20min each way • 90kr return
**Guided tours** Nordland Turselskap (☎ 90 63 60 86, ⓦ nordlandturselskap.no) and Explore Nordland (☎ 99 23 49 72, ⓦ explorenordland .no) can arrange tours to the west side of Svartisen Glacier from Bodø; excursions start from 800kr (see p.291)

Norway's second largest glacier, **Svartisen** – literally "Black Ice" – covers roughly 375 square kilometres of mountain and valley between the E6 and the coast to the northwest of Mo. The glacier is divided into two sections – east and west – by the Vesterdal valley, though this cleft is a recent phenomenon: when it was surveyed in 1905, the glacier was one giant block, about twenty-five percent bigger than it is today; the reasons for this change are still obscure. The highest parts of the glacier lie at

**5**

around 1500m, but its tentacles reach down to about 170m – the lowest-lying glacial arms in mainland Europe.

One of the glacier's **eastern nodules** is within easy reach of Mo-i-Rana: to get there, drive north on the E6 for about 12km and then take the signed byroad to the glacier, a straightforward 23-kilometre trip running past the Grønligrotta caves (see p.285) and ending beside the ice-green, glacial lake **Svartisvatnet**, where you get a boat (see p.285), though note that services can't begin until the ice has melted – usually mid-June – so check with the tourist office before setting out. Viewed from the boat, the great convoluted folds of the glacier look rather like bluish-white custard, but close up, after a stiff three-kilometre hike past the rocky detritus left by the retreating ice, the sheer size of the glacier becomes apparent – a mighty grinding and groaning wall of ice edged by a jumble of ice chunks, columns and boulders. The **west side** of the Svartisen glacier can be seen – and accessed – from the "Kystriksveien" Coastal Route along Highway 17 (see box below).

### ARRIVAL AND DEPARTURE                                  MO-I-RANA

**By train** Mo's train station is down by the fjord on Ole Tobias Olsens gate, near the bus station.

**By bus** Mo's bus station is on Ole Tobias Olsens gate opposite the foot of the main pedestrianized drag, Jernbanegata. The compact town centre lies a short walk east of here. Local bus services, however, are much too

patchy for any serious exploration of the town's environs: if you are determined, bus timetables are available from the tourist office.

**By car** There are a couple of outlets in town, including Hertz, in the town centre at Gjennomgangen 9 (❶ 75 15 22 55): cars cost around 750kr a day.

### INFORMATION AND ACTIVITIES

**Tourist office** Ole Tobias Olsens gate 3 (mid-June to mid-Aug Mon–Fri 9am–8pm, Sat 9am–4pm & Sun 1–7pm; mid-Aug to mid-June Mon–Fri 10am–3pm; ❶ 75 13 92 00,

ⓦ arctic-circle.no). At the tourist office, about 300m to the south of the bus and train stations, you can pick up the usual local leaflets, free town maps and a free booklet

---

### THE KYSTRIKSVEIEN COASTAL ROUTE ON HIGHWAY 17

Branching off the E6 just beyond Steinkjer (see p.282), the tortuous **Kystriksveien** (ⓦ rv17.no) – the **coastal route** along Highway 17 – threads its way up the west coast, linking many villages that could formerly only be reached by sea. This is an obscure and remote corner of the country, but apart from the lovely scenery there's little of special appeal, and the seven ferry trips that interrupt the 688-kilometre drive north to Bodø (there are no through buses) make it expensive and time-consuming in equal measure. A free booklet describing the route can be obtained at tourist offices throughout the region – including Mo – and it contains all Highway 17's car-ferry timetables.

Conveniently, the stretch of Highway 17 between Mo-i-Rana and Bodø takes in most of the **scenic highlights**, can be negotiated in a day, and cuts out five of the ferry trips. To sample this part of the route, drive 35km west from Mo along Highway 12 to the Highway 17 crossroads, from where it's some 60km north to the **Kilboghamn–Jektvik** ferry (June–Aug every 1–2hr, Sept–May 3–5 daily Mon–Fri & Sun; 1hr; driver and car 158kr; ⓦ hurtigruten.no) and a further 30km to the ferry linking **Ågskardet** with **Forøy** (roughly every hour; 10min; driver and car 63kr). On the first ferry you cross the Arctic Circle with great views down and along the beautiful **Melfjord**, and on the second, after arriving at Forøy, you get a chance to see a westerly arm of the Svartisen glacier (see p.285), viewed across the slender Holandsfjord.

For an even closer look at the glacier, stop at the information centre in **Holand**, 12km beyond Forøy, and catch the **passenger boat** (late May to early Sept Mon–Fri 8am–9pm, Sat & Sun 11am–5.30pm, every 1hr–1hr 30min; 10min; 60kr return; ❶ 99 40 30 00), which zips across the fjord to meet a connecting bus; this travels the kilometre or so up to the **Svartisen Turistsenter** (❶ 75 75 11 00, ⓦ svartisen.no), from where it's another 2km to the glacier. The Turistsenter has a café, rents cabins from 990kr a night, and is the base for four-hour guided **glacier walks** (mid-June to mid-Aug only; prior booking is essential; 600kr).

From Holand, it's 140km to the Saltstraumen (see p.294) and 30km more to Bodø (see p.289).

detailing the Highway 17 Coastal Route (see box opposite). They can arrange a shared taxi ride to the Svartisen glacier (see p.285) and will check that the boats that give access to the glacier are running.

**Outdoor activities** Staff at the tourist office will make reservations for a wide range of guided excursions, from rafting, kayaking and fishing through to caving, climbing and trekking. The tourist office rents bicycles, though you have to be pretty fit to reach most local points of interest – and just forget it altogether if it's raining.

### ACCOMMODATION

**Fjordgården Hotell** Søndre gate 9 ☎75 13 81 00, ⓦrica.no. A summertime-only hotel, and a popular stop with tour groups. It's run by the *Meyergården Hotell* and costs more or less the same, though the rooms have less charm. **1190kr**

★ **Meyergården Hotell** Fridtjof Nansensgate 28, off Ole Tobias Olsens gate ☎75 13 40 00, ⓦmeyergarden.no. Much of this 143-room Rica hotel, a short walk north of the train station, is modern, but

the original lodge has survived and its 15 rooms (most of which have shared baths) are maintained in period style, with stuffed animal heads on the wall and elegant panelled doorways. **1190kr**

**Mo Gjestegård** Elias Blix gata 5 ☎75 15 22 11, ⓦmo -gjestegaard.no. Tucked away in the backstreets near the church, this family-run guesthouse is a little heavy on the pine finishings, but it's quiet and peaceful and the rooms are pleasant and homely. **900kr**

### EATING

**Abelone** Ole Tobias Olsens gate 6 ☎75 15 38 88. This small, cosy spot is done up in faux ski lodge style and serves good food, including competent pizzas and steaks from around 170kr. Daily 2–9pm.

**Søilen** Meyergården Hotell, Fridtjof Nansensgate 28

☎75 13 40 80, ⓦmeyergarden.no. Hotel restaurant serving an excellent range of Norwegian dishes made from local ingredients. Main courses here average around 220kr, while the *koldtbord smorgasbord*, with roast beef, ham, smoked salmon, salad and more, costs 245kr. Daily 1–10pm.

# The Arctic Circle

Given its appeal as a travellers' totem, and considering the amount of effort it takes to get here, crossing the **Arctic Circle**, about 80km north of Mo, comes as quite a disappointment. Uninhabited for the most part, the landscape up here is undeniably bleak, and disfigured by a giant building plonked by the roadside that houses an ugly visitors' centre.

## Polarsirkelsenteret

Daily mid-May to Sept 8am–10pm • ☎75 12 96 96, ⓦpolarsirkelsenteret.no

Inside the large lampshade-shaped building, the **Polarsirkelsenteret** (Arctic Circle Centre) is stuffed with every sort of tourist bauble imaginable including an obligatory (for some) "Polarsirkelen" certificate and specially stamped postcards, as well as a small Arctic exhibition. Less tackily, there are poignant reminders of crueller times back outside, where a couple of simple stone memorials pay tribute to the Yugoslav and Soviet POWs who laboured under terrible conditions to build the Arctic railroad – the Nordlandsbanen – to Narvik for the Germans in World War II.

# Saltfjellet Nasjonalpark

The louring mountains in the vicinity of the Polarsirkelsenteret are part of the **Saltfjellet**, a vast mountain plateau whose spindly pines, stern snow-tipped peaks and rippling moors extend west from the Swedish border to the Svartisen glacier. The E6 and the railway cut inland across this range between Mo-i-Rana and **Rognan**, providing access to the cairned hiking trails that lattice the Saltfjellet, part of which – to the immediate west of the E6 – has been protected as the **Saltfjellet Nasjonalpark**. You can also reach the trails from Highway 77, which forks east off the E6 down the **Junkerdal**, a remote and rather unwelcoming river valley that leads to the Swedish border. The region is, however, largely the preserve of experienced hikers: the trails are not sufficiently clear to dispense with a compass, weather conditions can be treacherous

**5**

and, although there's a good network of DNT-affiliated huts, none is staffed, nor do any of them supply provisions. Keys to these huts (most of which are owned by BOT, Bodø's hiking association; see p.291) are available locally, but clearly you have to arrange this with BOT before setting off.

Among several possible bases for venturing into the Saltfjellet, **LØNSDAL**, around 100km north of Mo and 20km beyond the Arctic Circle, is the most accessible, with some good **hiking trails** leading off into the Saltfjellet. One of the more manageable options is the four-hour hike east (away from the national park) to **GRADDIS**, a tiny hamlet situated beside Highway 77, 18km east of the E6.

### ARRIVAL AND DEPARTURE

### SALTFJELLET NASJONALPARK

**By train** Lønsdal is easily reached by train from Trondheim, Mo or Bodø (1–3 daily, but some trains only stop here by request; check with the conductor).

### ACCOMMODATION

**Graddis Fjellstue og Camping** Røkland ☎75 69 43 41, ✉graddis@c2i.net. This guesthouse and campsite has rudimentary cabins, as well as tent pitches all on a farmstead on the wooded slopes of the Junkerdal. Despite its gloominess, the Junkerdal is a favourite spot from which to explore the Saltfjellet, not least because it's easy to reach by road from Sweden. Open March to mid-Sept. Tents **250kr**, cabins **400kr**

**Polarsirkelen Høysfjellshotell** Lønsdal ☎75 69 41 22, ⊕polarsirkelenhotell.no. Set in a long wooden building in a sheltered location, with a cosy modern interior. This small hotel has basic but modern rooms with a touch of class, and the only restaurant for miles around. Located down a kilometre-long road off the E6 on the way to Lønsdal's lonely train station. **990kr**

## The Krigskirkegården

Signposted from **Botn**, a kilometre-long road leads up to the **Krigskirkegården**, truly one of Nordland's most mournful and moving places. Buried here, in a wooded glade high above the fjord, are the Yugoslav prisoners of war and their German captors who died in the district during World War II. The men are interred in two separate graveyards – both immaculately maintained, though, unlike the plainer Yugoslav cemetery, the German graveyard is entered by a sturdy granite gateway. Mostly captured Tito partisans, the Yugoslavs died in their hundreds from disease, cold and malnutrition, as well as torture and random murder, during the construction of the **Arctic railroad** to the iron-ore port of Narvik. When the Germans occupied Norway in 1940, the railway ended at Mosjøen, but they soon decided to push it north so that their cargo ships might avoid the dangerous voyage along the coast. This line, the **Nordlandsbanen**, involved the labour of 13,000 POWs, but the Germans failed to complete it, and it was not until 1962 that the railway finally reached Bodø.

## Fauske

Aside from a brief stretch of line from Narvik into Sweden, **FAUSKE** marks the northernmost point of the Norwegian rail network and is, consequently, an important transport hub. There's certainly no strong reason to linger here – nearby Bodø is a much more palatable place to stay, never mind Narvik – though it's still a handy place to break your journey. The town's main drag, **Storgata**, doubles as the E6, running parallel to the fjord and holding the handful of shops that passes for the town centre.

### ARRIVAL AND DEPARTURE

### FAUSKE

**By bus** Fauske's long-distance bus station is beside the train station on Jernbanegata, a 5–10min walk from the town centre. It is a departure point for the twice-daily express bus service to Narvik, where you change for either the bus to Tromsø or the next leg of the journey up to Alta (for Honningsvåg and Nordkapp). It takes about 5hr 30min from Fauske to Narvik, a gorgeous run with the E6 careering round the mountains and along a series of blue-black fjords, but if you are aiming for Alta, you'll have to overnight in Narvik (see p.297). Tickets can be purchased from the driver or in advance at any bus station. The main bus services are run by Nobina (ⓦ 777nordland.no) to Bodø

(2–3 daily; 1hr 10min); Lødingen (2 daily; 4hr); Narvik (2 daily; 5hr 30min) and Sortland (2 daily; 5hr).

**By train** Fauske's train station is at Jernbanegata 19, a 5–10min walk uphill from Storgata and the centre of town.

## ACCOMMODATION

**Fauske Hotel** Storgata 82 ☎75 60 20 00, ⓦ fauskehotell.no. This hotel is a chunky square block whose interior is made slightly sickly by a surfeit of salmon-coloured streaky marble. Quarried locally, the marble is exported all over the world, but is something of an acquired taste. Aside from this, the hotel rooms are comfortable enough, and the breakfasts are large and tasty. 1125kr

**Lundhøgda Camping** Lundveien ☎75 64 39 66, ⓦ lundhogdacamping.no. This congenial campsite occupies a splendid location about 3km west of the town centre, overlooking the mountains and the fjord: head out of town along the E80 (the Bodø road), then turn down a signposted country lane, ablaze with wild flowers in the summertime and flanked by old timber buildings. May–Sept. Tents 110kr, cabins 595kr

# Bodø and around

Some 65km west of Fauske along the E80, the town of **BODØ** was founded in 1816. However, it wasn't until the herring boom of the 1860s that it really began to thrive, with the town's harbourfront crowded with the net-menders, coopers, oilskin-makers and canneries that kept the fleet at sea. Later, it accrued several industrial plants and became an important regional centre, but was heavily bombed during World War II, and there's precious little left today of the proud, nineteenth-century buildings that once flanked the waterfront. Nonetheless, Bodø manages a cheerful moder nity, a bright and breezy place whose harbour looks out onto a batch of rugged, treeless hills. The small settlement rambles over a low-lying peninsula that pokes out into the Saltfjord, its long and narrow centre concentrated along two parallel streets, Sjøgata and Storgata.

Bodø has long been a regular stop for the Hurtigruten coastal boat route, and is also within comfortable striking distance of the old trading post of **Kjerringøy**, one of Nordland's most delightful spots. Perhaps most important of all, however, it's much the best place from which to hop over to the choicest parts of the Lofoten islands (see p.312).

## Norsk Luftfartsmuseum

Olav V gate • Mid-June to mid-Aug daily 10am–6pm; mid-Aug to mid-June Mon–Fri 10am–4pm, Sat & Sun 11am–5pm • 110kr • ⓦ luftfart.museum.no

Easily Bodø's most popular attraction, the **Norsk Luftfartsmuseum** (Norwegian Aviation Museum), 2km southeast of the centre, is a large and imaginative exhibition that tracks through the general history of Norwegian aviation. It adopts an imaginative approach to the subject and even the building itself is constructed in the shape of a two-bladed propeller: one "blade" houses air force and defence exhibits, the other civilian displays. The spot where the two blades meet straddles the ring road – Olav V gate – and is topped by part of the old Bodø airport control tower. Among the planes to look out for are a Spitfire, a reminder that two RAF squadrons were manned by Norwegians during World War II, and a rare Norwegian-made Hønningstad C-5 Polar seaplane. Bodø was used by the US Air Force throughout the Cold War, and you can also see one of their U2 spy planes.

## Nordlandsbadet

Plassmyrveien • Mon, Wed & Thurs 3–9pm, Tues & Fri 6.30am–9pm, Sat & Sun 10am–6pm • Adults Mon–Thurs 120kr, Fri–Sun 140kr; children aged 10–15 90/110kr; children aged 3–9 70/95kr; chidren under 3 30kr • ☎75 59 15 00, ⓦ bodospektrum.no

Opposite the Norwegian Aviation Museum, **Nordlandsbadet**, Norway's most modern indoor water park has enough activities to entertain the kids for a full day,

# BODØ

**■ ACCOMMODATION**
Bodø Hotell — 2
Bodøsjøen Camping — 5
City Hotell — 1
Radisson BLU Hotel Bodø — 3
Thon Hotel Nordlys — 4

**● CAFÉS & RESTAURANTS**
Bjørk — 2
En Kopp — 3
Løvolds kafé — 1
Sjøsiden — 3

**■ BARS & CLUBS**
Avenue — 1
Top 13 — 2

N

Saltstraumen

0 — metres — 500

KIRKEVEIEN HWY. 834

Kjerringøy

RØNVIKVEIEN

Hurtigruten Coastal Steamer

Lofoten Ferry

Train Station

DNT

Glasshuset (Shopping Mall)

Hurtigbåt quay & Long-distance Bus Station

Local buses

DNT

SENTRUM

Nyholmsundet

Saltfjord

Moskenes, Værøy & Røst

Trondheim (southbound) & Sarnsund (northbound)

E80

OLAV V GATE

City Nord Shopping Centre

Nordlandsbadet

GAMLE RIKSVEI

PLASSMYRA

Norsk Luftfartsmuseum

Bodin kirke

BODØGÅRD

Galleri Bodøgaard

GAMLE RIKSVEI

SJØGATA

BANKGATA

DRONNINGENS GATE

PRINSENS GATE

STORGATA

TORVGATA

DRONNING CHRISTINES GATE

HÅLOGALANDSGATA

BANKGATA

DRVGATA

PORTINDGATA

HÅLOGALANDS GATA

HAAKON VII GATE

OLAV V GATE

HAAKON VII GATE

PARKVEIEN

PRINSENS GATE

BERNTSENS GATE

BJØRNSONS GATE

Airport

OLAV V GATE

and a big enough spa to do the same for adults. There are several water areas, including diving, wave, therapy and exercise pools, as well as fountains, grottoes, chutes, jacuzzis and saunas.

## Bodin kirke

Storgata 29, 1km from Gamle riksvei roundabout • Late June to mid-Aug Mon–Fri 10am–3pm • Free

Dating from the thirteenth century, the onion-domed **Bodin kirke** is a pretty little stone church sitting snugly among clover meadows. The church was modified after the Reformation by the addition of a tower and the widening of its windows – the Protestants associated dark, gloomy churches with Catholic superstition. It is, however, the colourful seventeenth-century fixtures that catch the eye, plus the lovingly carved Baroque altarboard and pulpit, both painted in the eighteenth century by an itinerant German artist called Gottfried Ezechiel.

## Galleri Bodøgaard

Skeidalen 2 • Tues–Fri 9am–3pm, Sat–Sun noon–4pm • 50kr • ☎ 90 72 08 43, ⓦ bodogaard.no

Set in the grounds of an old Russian prisoner of war camp, the medium-sized **Galleri Bodøgaard** holds the largest private collection of ethnographic goods in northern Norway. Its displays include tools, boating equipment and hunting, fishing and agricultural implements dating from the eighteenth and nineteenth centuries, as well as a collection of some 150 Russian, Polish and Greek religious icons. The highlight, however, is a marvellous copy of the New Testament in Russian dating from 1791 and once belonging to the family of Catherine the Great.

### ARRIVAL AND DEPARTURE

### BODØ

**By plane** Bodø airport is 2km south of the town centre, with regular connections to and from other cities on the mainland as well as the Lofoten. From the airport, there are hourly buses to the local bus station in the centre of Bodø (10min; 30kr one-way).

**By train** Bodø is the terminus of the Trondheim train line. The train station is just off the long main street, Sjøgata, 700m east of the tourist office.

**By bus** Bodø's long-distance bus station is at the Hurtigbåt quay, behind the tourist office (see below) and is the starting point of the express bus heading north. The main services, run by Boreal (ⓦ boreal.no), go to Fauske (2–3 daily; 1hr 10min); Lødingen (2 daily; 6hr); Narvik (2 daily; 6hr 30min); and Sortland (2 daily; 7hr).

**By boat** At the back of the tourist office (see below) is the quay for local ferries, most usefully the Hurtigbåt passenger express boat to Svolvær (1 daily; 344kr; ⓦ torghattennord. no). The southern Lofoten ferry (to and from Moskenes plus the islets of Værøy and Røst) and the Hurtigruten coastal boat use the docks 400m and 600m respectively northeast along the waterfront from the train station. The main car ferries, run by Torghatten Nord (ⓦ torghattennord.no), go to Moskenes (June–Aug 5–6 daily; Sept–May 1–2 daily except Sat; 3hr 45min); Røst (June–Aug 1–2 daily; Sept–May 4 weekly; 4hr 45min); Værøy (June–Aug 1–2 daily except Sun; Sept–May 4 weekly; 6hr 30min). Hurtigruten passenger express boats (ⓦ hurtigruten.no) run to Svolvær (1 daily; 3hr 30min).

### INFORMATION

**Tourist office** Sjøgata 3, a few metres from the bus station (June–Aug Mon–Fri 9am–8pm, Sat 10am–6pm & Sun noon–8pm; Sept–May Mon–Fri 9am–3.30pm; ☎ 75 54 80 00, ⓦ visitbodo.com). They give out information on connections to the Lofoten islands, rent out bikes and also issue a detailed town and district guide.

**DNT** For advice about the region's hiking trails and cabins, you can contact the DNT hiking organization at Bodø og Omegns Turistforening (BOT), at Sandgata 3 (Tues & Wed noon–3pm, Thurs noon–5pm; ☎ 75 52 14 13, ⓦ bot.no).

### TOURS

**Glacier tours** The tourist office coordinates tours to Norway's second largest glacier, Svartisen, some 160km south of Bodø in Holand (see p.286). Most tours last around 12hr, include bus and ferry transport but not food, and cost in the region of 600kr. Reservations are advised – at least a day ahead – as is bringing warm clothing. Local specialist Nordland Turselskap (☎ 90 63 60 86, ⓦ nordlandturselskap .no), runs longer trips from 800kr excluding transport.

**5**

## ACCOMMODATION

**Bodø Hotell** Professor Schyttes gate 5 ☎ 75 54 77 00, ⊛ bodohotell.no. This mid-range spot offers acceptable accommodation in a five-storey block right in the centre of town. The rooms have a modicum of class – exposed wood floors and the odd Persian carpet is about as chic as it gets here – and there are all the usual mod cons. 950kr

**Bodøsjøen Camping** Båtstøveien 1 ☎ 75 56 36 80, ⊛ bodocamp.no. This year-round lakeside campsite is roughly 3km southeast of the centre, not far from the Bodin kirke. Flanked by a ridge of evergreens are 45 cabins of various shapes and sizes, some consisting of just a single small room with two beds. Cabins 250kr, tents 130kr

**City Hotell** Storgata 39 ☎ 75 52 04 02, ⊛ cityhotellbodo.no. There are nearly two dozen simple, unassuming en-suite rooms at this bargain-price hotel-cum-guesthouse. It's just a few blocks west of the train station, so it's good for transiting. Free wi-fi. 750kr

★ **Radisson Blu Hotel Bodø** Storgata 2 ☎ 75 51 90 00, ⊛ radissonblu.com/hotel-bodo. The largest hotel in town occupies a modern concrete-and-glass tower: the rooms are comfortable and decorated in three colourful styles which make them feel less corporate then many chain hotels. Those on the upper floors have great views out to sea. 1495kr

**Thon Hotel Nordlys** Moloveien 14 ☎ 75 53 19 00, ⊛ thonhotels.no. This smart, very modern chain hotel is right on the harbourfront, and most of the 147 guest rooms have some kind of sea view. The accommodation isn't anything special, and there is little doubt you're in a soulless chain property – it's largely marketed at businesspeople – but the location is about as good as it gets. Free internet access. 1195kr

## EATING AND DRINKING

### CAFÉS AND RESTAURANTS

**Bjørk** Glashuset Shopping Centre, Storgata 8 ☎ 75 52 52 50, ⊛ restaurantbjork.no. Pizza, pasta, sandwiches, steaks, catch of the day – even sushi; this is one of those places that tries to do it all. Though its reputation as one of nothern Norway's best restaurants might seem a bit hard to swallow, they do make quite decent seafood dishes, and the place actually pulls off its modern rustic-style interior fairly well. Large dinner mains start at 255kr; lunches cost around 170kr. Reservations recommended. Mon–Sat 10am–10pm, Sun 3–10pm.

**En Kopp** Radisson Blu Hotel, Storgata 2 ☎ 75 51 90 00. This hotel café serves the best coffee you'll find in Bodø, as well as good breakfasts and lunches – and even beer. Daily 11am–11pm.

**Løvolds Kafé** Tollbugata 9. A quayside eatery that serves traditional and inexpensive Norwegian canteen-style dishes, many of which are made from local ingredients.

Main courses average around 120kr. Mon–Fri 9am–6pm, Sat 9am–3pm.

**Sjøsiden** Radisson Blu Hotel, Storgata 2 ☎ 75 51 90 00. The hotel's upstairs restaurant is an upmarket, wood-panelled place that serves a good line in local fish dishes: main courses average 250–300kr. Daily 5–11pm.

### BARS AND CLUBS

**Avenue** Tollbugata 13b ☎ 46 54 00 00, ⊛ clubavenue .no. Bodø's largest nightclub, spread across two floors with a capacity of 550. It's a fully-fledged Euro club playing loud local and international house, hip-hop and drum'n'bass DJs, as well as the occasional live band. Fri & Sat 11pm–3.30am.

**Top 13** Radisson Blu Hotel, Storgata 2 ☎ 75 51 90 00. Rooftop bar with the best view in Bodø. As it holds about 100 people with just a few vinyl couches and chairs, it can get quite crowded here at the weekend. Mon–Thurs 6pm–12.30am, Fri 4pm–2.30am, Sat 11am–2.30am.

## Kjerringøy trading post

Mid-May to Aug daily 11am–5pm • 90kr • Guided tours hourly on the hour; 40kr extra • ☎ 75 55 77 41, ⊛ kjerringoy.no

The **Kjerringøy trading post**, 40km north of Bodø, has a superbly preserved collection of nineteenth-century timber buildings set beside a slender, islet-sheltered channel. This was once the domain of the **Zahl family**, merchants who supplied the fishermen of Lofoten with everything from manufactured goods and clothes to farmyard foodstuffs in return for fish. It was not, however, an equal relationship: the Zahls, who operated a local monopoly until the 1910s, could dictate the price they paid for the fish, and many of the islanders were permanently indebted to them. This social division is still very much in evidence at the trading post, where there's a marked distinction between the guest rooms of the main house and the fishermen's bunk beds in the boat- and cookhouses. Indeed, the **family house** is remarkably fastidious, with its Italianate busts and embroidered curtains – even the medicine cabinet is well stocked with formidable

**5**

Victorian remedies like the bottle of "Sicilian Hair Renewer". Also of interest is the old barn, the Zahlfjøsen, where there is a display on the life and work of the novelist Knut Hamsun (see p.296).

There are enjoyable, hour-long **guided tours** around the main house throughout the summer, and afterwards you can nose around the reconstructed general store, drop in at the café and stroll the fine sandy beach. Taken altogether, it's an especially peaceful and picturesque spot and one that filmgoers may recognize from the movie *I am Dina*, based on *Dina's Book*, by the Norwegian author Herbjørg Wassmo, which was filmed here.

### ARRIVAL AND DEPARTURE                                          KJERRINGØY TRADING POST

**By bus** A day-trip from Bodø bus station is possible on Saturdays: pick up a combined bus-and-ferry timetable at Bodø tourist office.

**By car/ferry** Getting here from Bodø by car is easy enough – a straightforward coastal drive north along

Highway 834 with a ferry ride from Festvåg to Misten (every 30min–1hr 30min, less frequently on Sat & Sun; 10min; passengers 26kr, car & driver 63kr; ☎ 177, ⊚ 177nordland.com).

### ACCOMMODATION AND EATING

**Kjerringøy Havn Bryggehotell** ☎ 76 30 38 22, ⊚ kjerringoybrygge.no. Plush little hotel within the trading post with just a handful of swanky rooms. It also has a small restaurant on site that serves great, but pricey, seafood meals as well as simpler plates such as hamburgers and salads. **1450kr**

**Kjerringøy Prestegård** ☎ 75 51 11 14, ⊚ kjerringoy .no. This former vicarage, 700m north of the trading post along the main road, has simple double rooms in its main building and some slightly more pleasant ones in the renovated cowshed next door. Doubles **500kr**, dorms **300kr**

## Saltstraumen

The **Saltstraumen** maelstrom, which lies 33km east of Bodø round the bay on Highway 17 – just under an hour by car – is a dramatic, and much-publicized, phenomenon whereby billions of gallons of water are forced through a narrow, 150m-wide channel four times a day at speeds of up to 10 knots. It is caused by this part of the country having a huge variation in high and low tides, which sends an absurdly high volume of water – some 400 million tonnes – through the fjords. This produces the Saltstraumen Eddy, the world's strongest tidal current maelstrom, which can reach to 10m in diameter and 5m in depth. The vibration of the massive whirlpools can at times produce an uncanny yelping sound. The whirling creamy water is at its most turbulent at high tide, and its most violent when the moon is new or full: a timetable is available from Bodø tourist office.

Although the scenery hereabouts is, in Norwegian terms at least, flat and dull, and the view from the bridge which spans the channel unexciting, there are other things to occupy visitors. For one, the fauna around these parts includes fox, otter, moose, ferret and the largest concentration in Europe of fish eagles – all are most visible during the colder months. **Fishing** enthusiasts, too, will be impressed by the force of the water which pulls in all sorts of fish: cod, catfish and coalfish are common catches – one coley caught here weighed a remarkable 22.7 kilos (or so they say).

### ARRIVAL AND DEPARTURE                                                        SALTSTRAUMEN

**By bus** Local buses leave from regularly from Bodø bus station (Mon–Sat 4–6 daily, Sun 1 daily; 1hr; ⊚ nbuss.no), though their times won't necessarily coincide with high tide.

**By taxi** A taxi (☎ 07550 or ☎ 98 21 45 10, ⊚ bodotaxi.no) from Bodø centre to the Saltstraumen will cost around 700kr.

## INFORMATION AND ACTIVITIES

**Information** For more information on the area, visit
ⓦ destinasjon-saltstraumen.com.
**Fishing** Rods can be rented at several places, including

Saltstraumen Brygge (ⓞ 75 58 77 91, ⓦ saltstraumen
-brygge.no).

## EATING

**Kafé Kjelen** ⓞ 75 58 75 29, ⓦ kafekjelen.no. This little
red café on the west side of the bridge has a terrace with
great views over the maelstrom. It serves soups, salads and
large fish and meat dishes (3-course menu from 285kr). Try

their *møsbrømlefse*, a traditional, burrito-like pancake
stuffed with a mix of sweet brown-cheese sauce, sour
cream and melted butter (65kr).

# North from Fauske to Narvik

The 240-kilometre journey north from Fauske to Narvik is spectacular, with the **E6**
rounding the fjords, twisting and tunnelling through the mountains and rushing over
high, pine-dusted plateaux. The scenery is the main event hereabouts, and there's little
to merit a stop, with two notable exceptions – the fascinating old farmstead at **Kjelvik**,
where the hardship of rural life in Norway is revealed in idyllic surroundings, and the
remote former trading post of **Tranøy**, a thirty-kilometre detour west of the E6 via
Highway 81. This part of the world has strong connections with the writer Knut
Hamsun, whose childhood home was on the island of **Hamarøy**, and who liked to hang
out in nearby Kråkmo. At the end of the journey, **Narvik** is an eminently likeable
industrial town that witnessed some especially fierce fighting during the German
invasion of 1940. It's a good place for an overnight stop and a useful launching pad for
the long haul to the far north, or a visit to the Vesterålen and Lofoten islands.

## Kjelvik farmstead

Guided tours late June to mid-Aug daily 11am–5pm · 40kr · ⓦ saltenmuseum.no

The old **farmstead** of **KJELVIK**, 56km from Fauske, is a beautiful spot, where a
scattering of old wooden buildings, including a cottage, woodshed, forge and mill,
nestle in a green, wooded valley. Tenant farmers worked the land here until 1967,
when they finally gave up their battle against the harsh isolation. They had no
electricity, or water, the soil was thin, and the only contact with the outside world
was by boat – supply vessels would come up the Leirfjord to the Kjelvik jetty, from
where it was a steep two-kilometre hike to the farm, 200m above the fjord. Today,
there's **open access** to the farm, which is kept in good condition, and wandering

### FERRIES TO LOFOTEN, VESTERÅLEN AND NARVIK

En route between Fauske and Narvik, the E6 presents two opportunities to catch a **car ferry** to
Lofoten – one at Skutvik, the other at Bognes. The more southerly of the two is **Skutvik**, 35km
to the west of the E6, with ferries to Svolvær (see p.314; 2–4 daily; 2hr; passengers 89kr, car &
driver 304kr; reservations advised: ⓞ 177 in Nordland, otherwise ⓞ 75 77 24 10,
ⓦ torghattennord.no). At **Bognes**, where the E6 is interrupted by the Tysfjord, there's a choice
of ferries. One sails to **Lødingen** on the Vesterålen islands, where you can pick up the E10 to
Lofoten (see p.312; late June to mid-Aug roughly hourly, mid-Aug to late June every 1–2 hours;
1hr; passengers 58kr, car & driver 187kr; ⓦ torghattennord.no), while a second hops across the
Tysfjord to **Skarberget** to pick up the E6, just 80km south of Narvik (see p.297; hourly; 25min;
passengers 34kr, car & driver 92kr; ⓦ hurtigruten.no). The ferries from Bognes work on a
first-come, first-served basis, and in summer, it's worth arriving two hours before departure to
be sure of a space.

**5**

around is a delight: you can also follow the old footpath down to the Kjelvik jetty. **Guided tours** of Kjelvik are available in the summer and, on the last Saturday of the season, the **Kjelvik festival** sees the old buildings put to their original uses. Griddle-cakes are cooked on the wood stove, and dollops of sour cream and porridge are doled out to visitors.

## Hamarøy

The island of **Hamarøy**, about 15km off the E6, is noteworthy as the boyhood home of the writer **Knut Hamsun** (1859–1952). Long a leading literary light, Hamsun blotted his Norwegian copybook with his admiration for Hitler and the Nazis before and during the occupation, though his culpability has been the subject of much heated debate. Whatever the truth, Hamsun remained something of a hate figure for several decades and only recently has there been a degree of rehabilitation – as witnessed by the opening of several Hamsun-related sites on this, his home island, including his boyhood home, the tiny and very modest **Hamsuns barndomshjem** (late June to late Aug daily 11am–6pm; 35kr) in the hamlet of **Hamsund.**

### Hamsunsenteret

Presteid • June to mid-Aug daily 11am–6pm & mid-Aug to May Tues–Fri 10am to 3.30pm, Sat & Sun 11am–5pm • 90kr • ⓦ hamsunsenteret.no

By far the most impressive Hamsun site is the **Hamsunsenteret** (Knut Hamsun Centre), 5km from the centre of Hamarøy. This smashing new museum, built by American architect Stevan Holl, was opened in 2009, on the 150th anniversary of Hamsun's birth. The handsome timber and concrete tower rises out of the forest and houses several well-curated exhibits on the author's life and work, as well as a library. In early August, an annual festival is held here celebrating Hamsun's life and works.

## Tranøy

The old trading post of **TRANØY** sits in stern and bleak surroundings on Tranøy island's northern shore. To get there, you have to cross onto the island of Hamarøy first on Highway 81, then take the side road that cuts north to make the fourteen-kilometre journey to Tranøy. For more information on the island, visit ⓦ tranoy.info.

### Hamsungalleriet på Tranøy

Tranøy town • Mid-June to mid-Aug 11am–5pm • 40kr

Located in the old general store where Hamsun worked as a youth, **Hamsungalleriet på Tranøy** (Hamsun Gallery) concentrates on Hamsun-related paintings. More impressive, however, is the permanent open-air exhibition out on the rocks just a short stroll from the gallery, showing nature-related pictures in a stunning setting.

| **ACCOMMODATION, EATING AND DRINKING** | **TRANØY** |
|---|---|

**Edvardas hus** At the end of the road off the E6 ☎ 75 77 21 82, ⓦ edvardashus.no. A hotel occupying two old buildings set a couple of hundred metres apart – one is a merchant's house dating back to the 1910s, the other a former bank built a decade later. There are nine impeccably stylish, extremely comfortable bedrooms here and the food is outstanding – both at breakfast and at the pocket-sized restaurant, where reservations are strongly advised. Mid-June to mid-Aug. **750kr**

**Svolværingen** Tranøy town. The best spot for a drink in Tranøy is this old whaling-boat-turned-pub, overlooking the harbour. They also serve very good fish dishes, with seating both outside and inside. Open mid-June to mid-Aug. 10am–1am.

**Tranøy Fyr** 3km outside Tranøy town ☎ 90 60 46 95, ⓦ tranoyfyr.no. This mid-nineteenth-century lighthouse is one of the most atmospheric places you can stay around these parts. It has a dozen straightforward rooms in the old lighthousemen's quarters, as well as a newer annexe building, and there's a good small café-restaurant, with outdoor seating in the summer. Open mid-June to mid-Aug. **900kr**

**Tranøy Galleri** Tranøy town ☎ 47 02 92 08, ⓦ tranoy -galleri.com. Right next to a small seaside art gallery selling the work of local artists, this comfortable, well-decorated apartment has a small kitchen and an indoor sauna. **800kr**

# Narvik

A relatively modern town, **NARVIK** was established just a century ago as an ice-free port to handle the iron ore brought here by train from the mines in northern Sweden. The town's first modern settlers were the navvies who built the railway line, the **Ofotbanen** (see box, p.299), to the mines in Kiruna, over the border in Sweden at the end of the nineteenth century – a herculean task now commemorated every March by a week of singing, dancing and drinking, when the locals dress up in period costume. The town grew steadily up until World War II, when it was demolished during ferocious fighting for control of the harbour and its iron-ore supply. Today, the place makes no bones about what is still its main function: the **iron-ore docks** are immediately conspicuous, slap-bang in the centre of town, the rust-coloured machinery overwhelming much of the waterfront. Yet, for all the mess, the industrial complex is strangely impressive, its cat's cradle of walkways, conveyor belts, cranes and funnels oddly beguiling and giving the town a frontier, very Arctic, feel. Perhaps inevitably, the rebuilt town centre rather lacks appeal – it's the sort of place where the main street (Kongens gate) doubles as the highway (E6) – with modern concrete buildings replacing the prewar wooden houses, but it still musters a certain breezy northern charm. Of late, Narvik has had a fair old

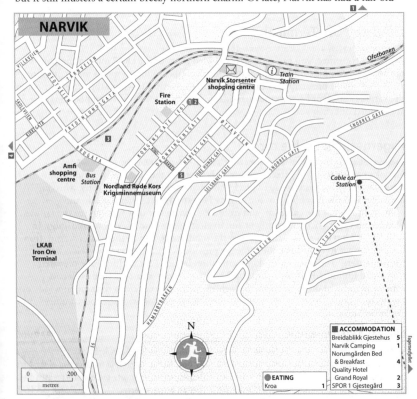

**5**

stab at reinventing itself as an **adventure sports** centre, becoming a popular destination for skiers, paraglidlers and scuba-divers – and developing a good range of guesthouses to match.

## Nordland Røde Kors Krigsminnemuseum

Torget • Late May to early June & late Aug to mid-Sept Mon–Sat 10am–4pm, Sun noon–4pm; early June to late Aug Mon–Sat 10am–9pm, Sun noon–6pm; mid-Sept to late May Mon–Fri 11am–3pm • 75kr • ⓦ warmuseum.no

Run by the Red Cross, the fascinating **Nordland Røde Kors Krigsminnemuseum** (Red Cross War Memorial Museum), just down from the tourist office, documents the wartime German saturation bombing of the town, and the bitter and bloody sea and air battles in which hundreds of foreign servicemen died alongside a swathe of the local population. It was a complicated campaign, with the German invasion of April 1940 followed by an Allied counterattack spearheaded by the Royal Navy. The Allies actually recaptured Narvik, driving the Germans into the mountains, but were hurriedly evacuated when Hitler launched his invasion of France. The fight for Narvik lasted two months and the German commander wrote of the sea change among his Norwegian adversaries, who toughened up to become much more determined soldiers, and skilled ones at that: many were crack shots from their hunting days and all could ski. In the short term, this change of attitude prefigured the formation of the Resistance; in the long term it pretty much put paid to Norway's traditional isolationism. The museum gives a thoroughly moving and thoughtfully presented account of the battle for Narvik and then tracks through the German occupation of Norway until liberation in 1945.

## LKAB Iron Ore Terminal

Mid-June to mid-Aug daily at 3pm • Guided tours organized by the tourist office • 50kr

At the tourist office, you can sign up for guided tours of the **LKAB mining company's ore-terminal complex**, interesting if only for the opportunity to spend ninety minutes amid such giant, ore-stained contraptions. After its arrival by train, the ore is carried on the various conveyor belts to the quayside, from where some thirty million tons of it are shipped out each year.

## Fagernesfjellet cable car

Skistuveien 7 • Daily: early June & Aug 1–9pm; mid-June to July 1pm–1am • 80kr single, 100kr return • ⓦ narvikfjellet.no

Narvik's **cable car**, a stiff fifteen-minute walk up from the town centre and behind the train station, is the easiest way to reach the town's mountainous environs, whisking passengers up the first 650m of the mighty **Fagernesfjellet**. There's a café and viewing point at the top of the cable car, and from here, on a clear day, you can see the Lofoten islands and experience the midnight sun in all its glory (end of May to mid-July). In addition, **hiking trails** delve further into the mountains, and in the winter season, from late November to early May, the cable car provides a shuttle service for **skiers and snowboarders**. The network of skiing amenities includes six ski lifts, nine prepared slopes and unlimited off-piste skiing, with some floodlit areas; for further details contact the tourist office or check the website. The cable car stops running in windy or foggy conditions, so you might want to check it's operating with the tourist office before setting out.

### ARRIVAL AND DEPARTURE

NARVIK

**By train** The train station is at Stasjonsveien 1, at the north end of town. Ofotbanen trains from Narvik operated by SJ (ⓦ sj.se) run to Kiruna, Sweden (2–3 daily; 3hr); Luleå, Sweden (2–3 daily; 6hr 30min–7hr 15 min); and Riksgränsen, Sweden (2–3 daily; 50min).

**By bus** The bus station is in the basement of the Amfi shopping centre, on Brugata, to the west of the main drag. Principal Boreal bus services (ⓦ boreal.no) run to Å (1–2

5

## THE OFOTBANEN

One of the real treats of a visit to Narvik is the **train ride** into the mountains that rear up behind the town and spread east across the Swedish border. Completed in 1903, this railway line – the **Ofotbanen** – was, by any standard, a remarkable achievement and the hundreds of navvies that made up the workforce endured astounding hardships during its construction. The line passes through some visually stunning scenery, slipping in between hostile peaks before reaching the rocky, barren and loch-studded mountain plateaux beyond. The Swedish national rail service (SJ; **w** sj.se) now operates the Ofotbanen and trains arrive at and depart from **Narvik train station** two or three times daily, shuttling to and from Kiruna, three hours away in northern Sweden. The timings of the trains mean that a short day-trip into the mountains behind Narvik is easy enough, and the obvious target is **RIKSGRÄNSEN**, a pleasant hiking and skiing centre just over the border in Sweden – so take your passport. The journey from Narvik to Riksgränsen takes fifty minutes and costs 39kr each way. Most train travellers nose around Riksgränsen for a few hours before returning to Narvik, but the more adventurous can **hike** at least a part of the way back on the **Rallarveien**, the old and refurbished trail originally built for the railway workers. This extends west for 15km from Riksgränsen to the **Rombaksbotn**, a deep and narrow inlet where the navvies once started their strenuous haul up into the mountains; the trail also heads east deeper into Sweden, to Abisko and Kiruna. A favourite option is to walk from Riksgränsen back towards the coast, picking up the return train at one of the several Norwegian stations on the way.

The area around the Ofotbanen isn't nearly as remote now that the E10 crosses the mountains to the north of the railway, but the terrain is difficult and weather unpredictable, so hikers will need to be well equipped. For details of other **trails** hereabouts, as well as **cabins**, contact Narvik tourist office and/or the DNT affiliate Narvik og Omegn Turistforening (**w** narvikfjell.no). Hiking **maps** are also available from the tourist office.

daily except Sat; 7hr 50min); Alta (2 daily except Sat; 9hr 30min); Bodø (2 daily; 6hr 30min); Fauske (2 daily; 5hr 30min); Gullesfjordbotn (2 daily; 3hr); Kabelvåg (1 daily; 4hr 30min); Leknes (2 daily; 6hr); Lødingen (2 daily; 2hr 30min); Svolvær (2 daily; 4hr 20min); and Tromsø (2–3 daily; 4hr).

### INFORMATION

**Tourist office** At the train station (late June to mid-Aug Mon–Fri 9am–7pm, Sat & Sun 10am–5.30pm; late Aug to Sept Mon–Fri 9am–4pm; Oct–May Mon–Fri 10am–3pm; **☎** 76 96 56 00, **w** destinationnarvik.com). The staff here issue free town maps, provide lots of information on outdoor pursuits and have the full range of bus and ferry timetables; they will also assist with ferry and activity reservations.

### ACTIVITIES

**Adventure sports** A number of operators offer adventure sports ranging from from hang- and paragliding through to mountain climbing, caving, canoeing and glacier walking. Most operators will also rent out the appropriate specialist tackle – but check when you reserve. Some good activity companies to try include Sipas Adventures (**☎** 90 69 09 55, **w** sipasadventures.no); Arctic Harley (**☎** 76 92 74 00, **w** arcticharley.no); and Arctic Ranch (**☎** 99 59 04 34, **w** arcticranch.no). **Scuba diving** Divenarvik (**☎** 99 51 22 05, **w** divenarvik .com) runs scuba diving trips amid the wreck-studded waters around Narvik.

### ACCOMMODATION AND EATING

**Breidablikk Gjestehus** Tore Hunds gate 41 **☎** 76 94 14 18, **w** breidablikk.no. The smart rooms in this pleasant, unassuming guesthouse have a certain modern charm. Those on the upper floors have attractive views over town, and a good, hearty breakfast is included in the room rate. It's located at the top of the steps at the end of Kinobakken, a side road leading east off Kongens gate, just up from the main town square. **1195kr**

**Narvik Camping** Rombaksveien 75 **☎** 76 94 58 10, **w** narvikcamping.com. A reasonably convenient year-round campsite, 2km north of the centre on the E6, that is very family-oriented: it has thirty cabins of various sizes as well as fifty tent pitches. Tents **200kr**, cabins **300kr**

★ **Norumgården Bed & Breakfast** Framnesveien 127 **☎** 76 94 48 57, **w** norumgaarden.na rviknett.no. Lavish but good-value B&B in a 1920s timber villa offering copious amounts of charm and

**5**

character. The Germans used the place as an officers' mess during the war and today, tastefully restored, it holds three large guest rooms, two of which have kitchenettes. Antiques are liberally distributed across the house and breakfast is included. **800kr**

**Quality Hotel Grand Royal** Kongens gate 64 ☏ 76 97 70 00, ⓦ choicehotels.no. While some of Narvik's hotels have seen better days, the *Grand*, by contrast, is well kept and well maintained; its public rooms are wood-panelled and appealing, while the bedrooms are perfectly adequate albeit in standard chain style. Its small restaurant, *Kroa*, is a member of the Arctic Menu scheme, specializing in dishes featuring local ingredients: main courses average around 200kr (Mon–Fri 11am–11pm, Sat noon–11pm, Sun 4–9pm). Just down from the train station. **795kr**

**SPOR 1 Gjestegård** Brugata 2a ☏ 76 94 60 20, ⓦ spor1.no. This spick-and-span place, just below the main town bridge, is the pick of the budget/backpacker options with clean if spartan modern rooms. In a creatively recycled former railway building, it's a simple one-storey block that has doubles, quads and a larger dorm plus kitchen facilities, a sauna and a bar. Dorms from **300kr**, doubles **600kr**

# The Vesterålen islands

A raggle-taggle archipelago nudging into the Norwegian Sea, the **Vesterålen islands**, and their southerly neighbours the Lofoten, are like western Norway in miniature: the terrain is hard and unyielding, the sea boisterous and fretful, and the main – often the only – industry is fishing. The weather is temperate but wet, and the islanders' historic isolation has bred a distinctive culture based, in equal measure, on Protestantism, the extended family and respect for the ocean.

Somewhat confusingly, the Vesterålen archipelago is shared between the counties of **Troms** and **Nordland**: the northern Vesterålen islands are in Troms, while the southern half of the Vesterålen and all the Lofoten islands are in Nordland. The Vesterålen islands are the less rugged of the two groups – greener, gentler and less mountainous, with more of the land devoted to agriculture, though this gives way to vast tracts of peaty moorland in the far north. The villages are less immediately appealing too, often no more than narrow ribbons straggling along the coast and across any available stretch of fertile land. Consequently, many travellers simply pass by on their way to Lofoten, a definitive mistake when considering the small fishing port of **Andenes**, which beckons with a strange but enthralling back-of-beyond charm and for a litany of **whale-watching** expeditions. In summer, Andenes also has the advantage of being linked by ferry to Gryllefjord, on the island of Senja. Other Vesterålen highlights are the magnificent but extremely narrow **Trollfjord**, where cruise ships and the Hurtigruten perform some nifty manoeuvres, and **Harstad**, a comparative giant with a population of 23,000 and the proud home to a splendid medieval church.

### Brief history

The archipelago was first settled by semi-nomadic hunter-agriculturalists some 6000 years ago, and it was they and their Iron Age successors who chopped down the birch and pine forests that once covered these coasts. It was boatbuilding, however, which brought prosperity: by the seventh century, islanders were able to build ocean-going

5

vessels, a skill that enabled them to join in the Viking bonanza. Local clan leaders became important warlords, none more so than the eleventh-century chieftain **Tore Hund**, one-time liegeman of Olav Haraldsson, and one of the men selected to finish Olav off at the Battle of Stiklestad (see p.281) – the fulfilment of a blood debt incurred by Olav's execution of his nephew. In the early fourteenth century, the islanders **lost their independence** and were placed under the control of Bergen: by royal decree, all the fish the islanders caught had to be shipped to Bergen for export. This may have suited the economic interests of the Norwegian monarchy and the Danish governors who succeeded them, but it put the islanders at a terrible disadvantage. With their monopoly guaranteed, Bergen's merchants controlled both the price they paid for the fish and the prices of the goods they sold to the islanders – a **truck system** that was to survive, increasingly under the auspices of local merchants, until the early years of the twentieth century. Since World War II, improvements in fishing techniques and, more latterly, the growth in tourism and the improvement and extension of the roadway infrastructure have all combined to transform and improve island life.

## ARRIVAL AND DEPARTURE                    THE VESTERÅLEN ISLANDS

Getting to the Vesterålen islands by **public transport** is easy enough, with car ferries making the crossing from several points on the mainland, as well as bus services from Bodø and Fauske, and a speedy passenger boat service from Tromsø.

### BY CAR FERRY

**From Bognes** The principal car ferry from the mainland to the Vesterålen islands departs from the jetty at Bognes, on the E6 between Fauske and Narvik, and sails to Lødingen (late June to mid-Aug 16 daily; mid-Aug to late June 13 daily; 1hr; passengers 58kr, car & driver 187kr; ⓦ torghattennord.no). From Lødingen, it's just 4km to the E10 at a point midway between Harstad and Sortland.

**From Gryllefjord** A seasonal, car ferry runs from remote Gryllefjord, 110km west of the E6 well to the north of Narvik, to Andenes at the northern tip of the Vesterålen (late May to mid-June & early to late Aug 2 daily; mid-June to early Aug 3 daily; 2hr; passengers 170kr; car & driver 425kr; ☎ 76 14 12 03, ⓦ senjafergene.no). The route is operated by the ferry company Senjafergene, and reservations are strongly advised by email or phone.

**From Fiskebøl** A third car ferry links the Vesterålen islands with Lofoten, running across the Hadselfjord between Melbu and Fiskebøl, both of which are on the E10 (daily 6.20am–10.10pm, roughly hourly; 30min; passengers 34kr, car & driver 95kr; ☎ 177 in Nordland or ☎ 51 56 41 00, ⓦ boreal.no).

### BY HURTIGRUTEN

**North from Bodø** Heading north, the Hurtigruten coastal boat (ⓦ hurtigruten.no) leaves Bodø daily at 3pm and threads a scenic route through the Vesterålen islands, where it calls at Stokmarknes and Sortland in the south, Risøyhamn in the north and Harstad in the east. The journey time from Bodø to Stokmarknes is 10 hours, 3hr 30min more to Risøyhamn and another two hours to Harstad.

**South from Tromsø** Cruising southwards from Tromsø, the boat leaves daily at 1.30am, and follows the same itinerary, but in reverse; the sailing time from Tromsø to Harstad is 6hr 30min.

**The Raftsundet** Scenically, the highlight of the Hurtigruten cruise through the Lofoten and Vesterålen islands is the Raftsundet, a long and narrow sound between Svolvær and Stokmarknes, off which branches the magnificent Trollfjord. Unfortunately, the northbound Hurtigruten leaves Svolvær for Vesterålen at 10pm and so the Raftsundset is only visible during the period of the midnight sun (late May to mid-July); in the opposite direction, however, boats leave Stokmarknes for the three-hour trip to Svolvær at a much more convenient 3.15pm.

**Fares** The passenger fare from Bodø to Risøyhamn is 991kr in summer, 591kr in winter (a car is 468kr), 991/591kr to Harstad and 1235/785kr to Tromsø. The all-year fare for transporting a car from Bodø to Harstad is 480kr, 626kr to Tromsø. The passenger fare for the Svolvær/Stokmarknes trip is 391kr in summer, 241kr in winter; cars cost an extra 374kr throughout the year. For vehicles, advance reservations are essential, and can be made either online or by phoning the ship – ask down at the harbour or at the port's tourist office for assistance.

### BY HURTIGBÅT PASSENGER EXPRESS BOAT

Hurtigbåt boats provide a speedy alternative to the car ferries and the Hurtigruten. The main Hurtigbåt service from the mainland to the Vesterålen runs from Tromsø to Harstad (2–4 daily; 2hr 30min; 550kr; ⓦ tromskortet.no). There's also an especially useful Hurtigbåt boat to the

Riksgränsen ▲    ▲ Riksgränsen

## LOFOTEN & VESTERÅLEN

Car ferries
Hurtigruten
Hurtigbåt

**TROMS**

**NORDLAND**

**NORWEGIAN SEA**

*Vesterålen*

E6/E10

Rombaksbotn

Ofotbanen

Narvik

Harstad/Narvik

E6

Skarberget

Bognes

HWY 83

Harstad

E10

Lødingen

*Hinnøya*

Gullesfjordbotn

HWY 82

Raftsundet

LOFAST

Trollfjord

Andenes

Bleik

Stave

*Andøya*

Nordmela

Risøyhamn

HWY 82

*Langøya*

Sortland

E10

E10

Stokmarknes

*Hadseløya*

Melbu

Fiskebøl

*Austvågøya*

E10

N

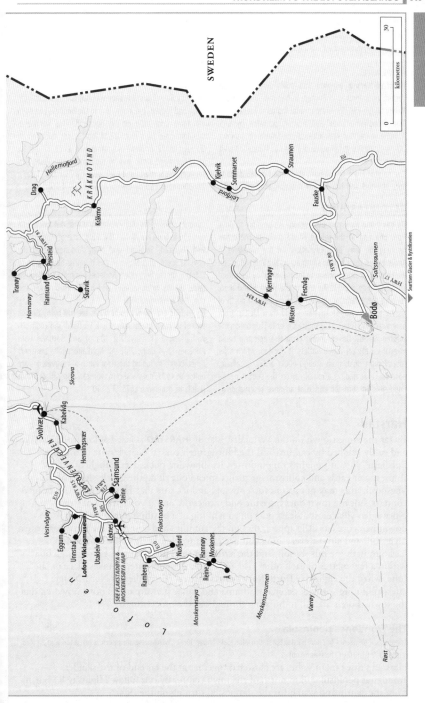

SWEDEN

Svartisen Glacier & Kystriksveien

0            30

kilometres

**5**

Lofoten: Bodø to Svolvær (1 daily; 3hr 30min; 344kr; ⓦ torghatten-nord.no). In both cases, advance reservation – most easily done online – is a good idea.

### BY PLANE

**Harstad/Narvik airport** The main airport for the Vesterålen is located in Evenes, in between Harstad and Narvik on the E10. There are regular flights to Evenes from Oslo, Trondheim, Bodø and Tromsø, operated by SAS, Norwegian and Widerøe airlines. A good airport bus service (☎ 78 40 70 00, ⓦ flybussen.no) runs to Harstad, Narvik and Sortland.

**Car rental** From the airport, it's a good hour's drive to both Harstad and Narvik. Car rental is available at the

airport – both Avis (☎ 76 98 21 33) and Hertz (☎ 41 58 22 28) have outlets here. If you reserve in advance (which is almost essential in high season), the price can drop to about 600kr a day.

### BY BUS

Nor-Way Bussekspress (ⓦ nor-way.no) runs services from Bodø and Fauske (1–2 daily; 1hr) to the Bognes–Lødingen car ferry and then on to Sortland. This service is supplemented by a number of local buses operated by Boreal (☎ 177 in Nordland, otherwise ☎ 75 77 24 10, ⓦ 177nordland.com): two of its most useful Vesterålen services link Sortland and Lødingen with Harstad (1 daily; 2hr 30min) and Sortland with Andenes (2–4 daily; 2hr).

### GETTING AROUND

**By car** If you have your own vehicle it's possible to drive from one end of the whole island chain to the other, catching the ferry from Gryllefjord on the mainland to Andenes and then driving south across the Vesterålen and the Lofoten islands to return to the mainland by ferry from Moskenes (see p.291). The E10 is the main island road, running the 240km or so west from the E6 just north of Narvik to Sortland, Stokmarknes and then Melbu; from here a car ferry (see p.311) shuttles over to Fiskebøl on the Lofoten islands. Drivers intent on a less epic trip could investigate the car rental outlets at Harstad, which offer special short deals from around 600kr a day. Be aware, however, that finding a rental car on the spot is nearly impossible in summer and that advance reservation is

strongly advised. No single itinerary stands out, but the E6 and E10 in from Narvik has the advantage of simplicity – with Harstad, Sortland and then Andenes being the obvious route, plus Stokmarknes if you're heading on to Lofoten. On the Vesterålen, Andenes has most to offer as a base, thanks to its whale- and birdwatching trips and choice of accommodation.

**By public transport** Local buses are run by by Boreal: two of its most useful routes link Sortland and Lødingen with Harstad (1 daily; 2hr 30min) and Sortland with Andenes (2–4 daily; 2hr). All Nordland public transport timetables – including those for much of Vesterålen – are online at ⓦ 177nordland.com; you can also call ☎ 177 in Nordland, otherwise ☎ 75 77 24 10.

## Harstad

By far the largest town on the Vesterålen islands, **HARSTAD** is just 130km from Narvik and easily reached by car, bus and the Hurtigruten coastal boat. Home to much of northern Norway's engineering industry, its sprawling docks are a tangle of supply ships, repair yards and cold-storage plants spread out along the gentle slopes of the Vågsfjord. This may not sound too enticing, and it's true that Harstad wins few beauty contests, but the town does have the odd attraction, and if you're tired of sleepy Norwegian villages, it at least puts on something of a bustling interlude. The downtown core has little appeal, though the comings and goings of the ferry boats are a diversion, and almost everything you need is conveniently clustered around the harbour, with the bus station, and the jetties for the Hurtigbåt and Hurtigruten **boats** within a few metres of each other. The only other spark of interest takes place in late June, when the eight-day **North Norway Arts Festival** (Festspillene i Nord-Norge; ⓦ festspillnn.no) provides concerts, drama and dance performances; note, however, that the town's hotels are full to bursting throughout the proceedings.

### The Trondenes peninsula

Take the local "Trondenes" bus from Harstad bus station (Mon–Sat 1 hourly; 10min), which passes the church, or take a taxi from the town centre (☎ 77 04 10 00, ⓦ harstadtaxi.no)

Harstad's three main sights are clustered together at the far end of the slender **Trondenes peninsula**, 3km north of the town centre. By car, follow Highway 83 north from the centre and watch for the signposted turning on the right.

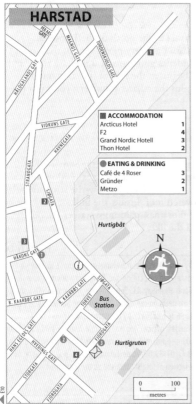

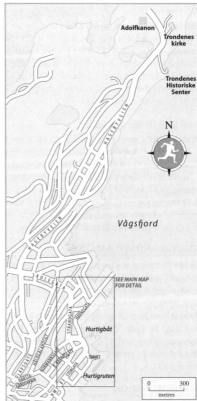

## Trondenes kirke

Opening times vary • Free • Guided tours mid-June to mid-Aug daily at 5pm; 40kr

Harstad's historical pride and joy is **Trondenes kirke** in a lovely leafy location beside the fjord. The original wooden church was built at the behest of King Øystein (of *rorbuer* fame; see box, p.314) at the beginning of the twelfth century and had the distinction of being the northernmost church in Christendom for several centuries. Øystein (c.1088–1123) was one of the more constructive rulers of the period, spending time and effort developing the economy of his domain, building a number of churches like this one in Harstad and, perhaps most unusual of all, refusing to conspire against his brother and co-ruler, Sigurd, when he joined the First Crusade. The stone church that survives today was erected in the 1300s, its thick walls and the remains of its surrounding ramparts reflecting its dual function as a church and fortress, for these were troubled, violent times.

After the stern exterior, the church's warm and homely **interior** comes as a surprise. Here, the dainty arches of the rood screen lead into the choir, where a late medieval, bas-relief wooden triptych surmounts each of the three altars. Of the trio, the middle triptych is the most visually appealing: the main panel, depicting the holy family, is fairly predictable, but down below is a curiously cheerful sequence of biblical figures, each of whom wears a turban and sports a big, bushy and exquisitely carved beard. Back outside, the churchyard is bordered by a dry-stone wall and holds a Soviet memorial to the eight hundred prisoners of war who died hereabouts in World War II at the hands of the Germans.

**5**

## Adolfkanonen

Guided tours mid-June to mid-Aug daily at 11am, 1pm & 3pm; late Aug daily at 3pm • 60kr • ⓦ adolfkanonen.no

Perched on a hilltop in the middle of the peninsula to the north of the **Trondenes** church, is the **Adolfkanonen** (Adolf Gun), a massive artillery piece. One of the largest shore-based weapons of World War II, the Trondenes gun is inside a military zone, and can only be visited on a guided tour. The tour begins at the gate of the compound, 1km from the gun, and takes in the gun itself plus the adjacent **bunkers**: you must have your own vehicle to visit.

## Trondenes Historiske Senter

Trondenes veien 122 (along the fjord from the church, back towards the town centre) • Mid-June to mid-Aug daily 11am–5pm; mid-Aug to mid-June Mon–Fri 10am–2pm, Sun 11am–4pm • 80kr • ⓦ tdm.no

The third sight on the Trondenes peninsula is the **Trondenes Historiske Senter** (Trondenes Historical Centre), a plush modern complex containing exhibitions on some 2000 years of history in the locality. The museum itself is a low-rise structure, half buried beneath the ground, with a sod-covered roof. Inside, the bulk of the material centres around the medieval era, with dioramas, paintings, statues, mood music as well as incidental Viking artefacts and the like.

### ARRIVAL AND INFORMATION                                    HARSTAD

**By bus** The bus station is located just south of the tourist office on Sjøgata. The Lofotenekspressen runs services between Harstad and Å (1 daily; 7hr 15min); Lødingen (2 daily; 1hr 30min); and Svolvær (2–4 daily; 3hr 45min).

**By boat** Hurtigbåt passenger express boats run to Tromsø (2–3 daily; 2hr 45min; ⓦ torghattennord.no), while the Hurtigruten (ⓦ hurtigruten.no) sails north for Tromsø at 8am and south for points in the Vesterålen and Lofoten islands at 8.30am.

**By car** If you're travelling along the E10, Harstad is something of a cul-de-sac, involving a 30km detour north along Highway 83. Several firms in Harstad offer short-term deals on car rental: try Europcar, Samagata 33 (ⓣ 77 01 86 10), or Hertz, by the harbour (ⓣ 77 06 13 46).

**Tourist office** Sjøgata 1b (mid-June to mid-Aug daily 10am–6pm; mid-Aug to mid-June Mon–Fri 8am–3.30pm; ⓣ 77 01 89 89, ⓦ destinationharstad.no). It has a wide selection of tourist literature on the Vesterålen.

### ACCOMMODATION

**Arcticus Hotel** Havnegata 3 ⓣ 77 04 08 00, ⓦ choice .no. The best rates in town by far at this good-value hotel, with breakfast and dinner buffets included in the price. It's a short walk from the Torvet, with recently revamped rooms in retro-chic style. `1250kr`

**F2** Fjordgata 2 ⓣ 77 00 32 00, ⓦ f2hotel.no. This large,

recently renovated hotel has 88 smart rooms with good amenities and all mod cons, plus a modern indoor spa. It also rents out bikes (100kr/day). `1130kr`

**Grand Nordic Hotell** Strandgata 9 ⓣ 77 00 30 00, ⓦ nordic.no. A good choice, though perhaps a bit too conference-orientated for some, this large hotel occupies a

---

### A SCENIC DRIVE: FROM HARSTAD TO ANDENES

The drive between Vesterålen's two main settlements is one of Northern Norway's most atmospheric, its wild and isolated coasts evoking both desolation and surpreme awe. Although Andenes lies northwest of Harstad, it's reached by heading south out of town along the E10, then it's 50km southwest along the fjord to the turning for the Lødingen ferry (see p.301) and a further 50km to the bridge that spans the sound over to Sortland (see p.311). On the near side of this Sortland bridge, **Highway 82** begins its 100-kilometre trek north, snaking along the craggy edge of Hinnøya island before crossing a second bridge over to humdrum **Risøyhamn**, the only Hurtigruten stop on **Andøya**, the most northerly of the Vesterålen islands. Beyond Risøyhamn, the scenery is much less dramatic, as the mountains give way to hills in the west and a vast, peaty moor in the east. Highway 82 strips across this moorland and, despite offering panoramic views of the mountains back on the mainland, it's an uneventful journey on to Andenes. If you have time to spare, consider taking the more scenic route along the west coast of Andøya, branching off from Highway 82 just past Risøyhamn to pass through a series of tiny villages like Nordmela, Stave and Bleik (see p.310).

modern block near the Torvet. The rooms are neat and trim although the interior is well in need of a makeover. **890kr**
**Thon Hotel** Sjøgata 11 ☎ 77 00 08 00, ⓦ thonhotels .no. Stylishly decorated with a marine theme that complements the view over the Vågs fjord and harbour. Its 141 rooms are fairly standard chain-hotel style, with bright wood flooring, while the waterfront terrace is a great spot for an early evening drink. **950kr**

**5**

## EATING AND DRINKING

★ **Café de 4 Roser** Torvet 7a ☎ 92 04 04 44. A first-rate French-influenced restaurant upstairs with the best bar in town below. The downstairs café-bar serves light meals during the day – fish burgers, salads and pasta – before switching to fresh-fruit cocktails after 6pm. Mon–Sat 10am–10pm.
**Gründer** Fjordgata 2 ☎ 77 02 32 80, ⓦ nordic.no. This traditional, affordable chain restaurant has nautical relics on the walls, with wraps, tapas and salads – and really great burgers – on the menu. After hours, it turns into a happening bar and nightclub. Mon–Thurs 11am–midnight, Fri & Sat 11am–3.30am.
**Metzo** Strandgata 12 ☎ 77 07 58 58. Newly opened, this popular daytime and evening hangout is good for its many coffee varieties, simple wok dishes for lunch and dinner, and DJs at the weekend (there's even a piano). It also has a heated terrace to help with the Nordic temperatures. Mon–Sat 10am–1am, Sun 1pm–10pm.

# Andenes

"It is the fish, and that alone, that draws people to Andenes – the place itself has no other temptations," said the writer Poul Alm when he visited the old fishing port of **ANDENES** in 1944. While this is too harsh a judgement today, the main emphasis does indeed remain firmly nautical, with lines of low-slung buildings leading up to a clutter of wooden warehouses and mini boat-repair yards that demarcate the harbour and its prominent breakwaters. Even Andenes' long and straight main drag, Storgata, ends abruptly at the seafront, and the town's main *raison d'être* today is as a field station and research centre for marine biologists studying whales: indeed, among Scandinavians, Andenes is best known for its **whale-watching safaris**. The town is also an excellent place for **gull watching** – large numbers of glaucous and Iceland gulls, white-billed divers and purple sandpipers frequent its environs – as well as being Norway's most southerly wintering area for common and king eider ducks. In late winter, the world's Arctic cod population migrates south from the Barents Sea to spawn in the waters around Andenes – a natural movement that attracts millions of sea birds to the area on the lookout for food.

## Hvalsenter

Late May to mid-June & mid-Aug to mid-Sept daily 8.30am–4pm; mid-June to mid-Aug daily 8.30am–7pm • 60kr; accepts 140kr discount ticket (see p.310)

A visit to the Andenes' **Hvalsenter** (Whale Centre), metres from the harbour in an old warehouse building, is included at the beginning of all whale safaris (see p.308) and, indeed, it does provide a good explanation of what you're likely to witness on the open ocean. That said, the centre's incidental displays on the life and times of the animal hardly fire the imagination, and neither does the massive – and deliberately dark and gloomy – display of a whale munching its way though a herd of squid. However, the enormous 16m-long sperm-whale skeleton, which was washed up on an Andenes beach, gives a clear idea of the sheer scale of the creatures.

## Hisnakul Natural History Centre

Hamnegata 1 • Mid-June to Aug daily 10am–6pm; Sept to mid-June daily 10am–4pm • 50kr, or included on the 140kr discount ticket (see p.310) • ⓦ hisnakul.no

In a refurbished timber warehouse near the Whale Centre, the diverting **Hisnakul Natural History Centre** explores various facets of Andøya life. Although it is short on historical artefacts, it does contain some imaginative displays such as the two hundred facial casts of local people made in 1994 and an assortment of giant replica bird-beaks.

**5**

## Nordlyssenteret

Hamnegata 1 • Late June to late Aug daily 10am–6pm • 40kr, or included on the 140kr discount ticket (see p.310) • ⓦ hisnakul.no

Andenes is a particularly good place from which to view the northern lights (see box, p.341), and the **Nordlyssenteret** (Northern Lights Centre) provides a comprehensive explanation of the phenomenon, illustrated by first-class photographs and a slide show. Upstairs from the main exhibition are two other floors with various hands-on scientific games, experiments and instruments related to the Aurora.

## Andenes fyr

Hamnegat • Mid-June to Aug daily noon–4pm; guided tours hourly on the hour • 35kr, or included on the 140kr discount ticket

The striking red **Andenes fyr** (Andenes lighthouse) is a 40m-high structure dating from the late 1850s and offering wide views over the town from its top, though you'll have to muster the energy to make it up the 148 steep steps. Although the lighthouse was recently sold to a private buyer, it is still in use today – albeit with an automated light, rather than its original candlepower.

## Polarmuseet

Havnegate • Mid-June to mid-Aug daily 10am–6pm • 30kr, or included on the 140kr discount ticket (see p.310)

A modest little building with a pretty wooden porch, the **Polarmuseet** (Polar Museum) lies a brief stroll south of the lighthouse. Inside, its main exhibit is a giant stuffed polar bear that gazes at you from a frightening height; it was allegedly shot by accident on a recent expedition to Spitsbergen. The rest of the interior is mostly dedicated to the Arctic knick-knacks accumulated by a certain Hilmar Nøis, an Andøy man who wintered on Svalbard no fewer than 38 times. Unfortunately all the labelling is in Norwegian, but the helpful staff are willing to translate.

## Whale-watching safaris

Whale safaris (4–5hr) leave from the Andenes Whale Centre, or direct from the harbour (late May and mid-Sept 1–5 daily, subject to demand) • 870kr (children 5–13 years 550kr); includes guided tour of the Whale Centre (see p.307) • Not recommended for children under 5 as the sea can get rough; warm clothing and sensible shoes are essential • Reserve at least a day in advance through the tourist office, or direct on ⓣ 76 11 56 00, ⓦ whalesafari.no

Andenes is famous for its popular **whale-watching safaris**, with a marine biologist on board to point out whales, such as pilots, minkes, humpbacks and sperm, as well other sea creatures like dolphins and porpoise. Operators claim – with every justification – a ninety-five percent chance of a whale sighting, and many will reimburse the price of your ticket if you don't see any. The Vesterålen islands are a stone's throw from the

---

### WHALING IN NORWAY

To many foreigners at least, Norway has an unenviable reputation as one of the few countries in the world still **hunting whales** for commercial purposes. In so doing, the Norwegians ignore the worldwide **ban** on commercial whaling adopted by the International Whaling Commission in 1986. While Japan claims to kill whales for scientific reasons, Norway does not disguise its main reason for hunting – human consumption – and its fisheries department works out its own quota. In 2012, this was 1286 minke whales – the largest catch in a quarter of a century. Whale meat (*hval*) is considered a delicacy by many Norwegians and can still be found on many (north) Norwegian menus, though opinion polls indicate that about one in four Norwegians under thirty oppose the hunt. The method of killing the animals is also subject to bitter debate. Norwegian whalers invented the exploding harpoon and they still use it today. Activists claim there's no humane way to kill a whale, but many abhor this particular method: one in five harpooned whales suffer a long and painful death. Ironically enough, the waters where thousands of tourists venture out on whale-watching safaris are the same as those used by the whale hunters. Indeed, in 2006 a whale was shot and dragged aboard a whaler right in front of a whaling safari boat, causing a real brouhaha.

**5**

continental shelf, which is closer to land here than anywhere else in Norway: deep water and a nutrient-rich food supply such as squid make the area an essential feeding ground for sperm whales, though as they can dive down as deep as 3000m to feed, you're unlikely to glimpse the same whale twice on a single trip.

The tours, which support the research and protection of offshore whale colonies, take place aboard small vessels and use hydrophone technology to pick up the sounds of the whales – essential for locating the mammals without disturbing them. Taking an evening safari during the midnight-sun period can be especially rewarding, as the calmer sea makes it easier to spot the surfacing sperm whales, and the light is simply enchanting.

### Puffin safaris

Puffin safaris leave from the jetty at Bleik, 7km southwest of Andenes; local buses from Andenes often coincide with sailings • June to mid-Aug 1–2 daily • 1hr 30min • 350kr, children 150kr • Reserve through the tourist office or direct ☎ 97 19 52 75, ⓦ puffinsafari.no

Vesterålen is known for its sheltered bays and sandy shores, which are rich in bird life. The highly recommended **puffin safaris** head off round the bird island of **Bleiksøya**, a pyramid-shaped hunk of rock populated by some 80,000 pairs of puffins, as well as kittiwakes, razorbills and, sometimes, white-tailed eagles. There's so much activity out here that you're likely to find puffins flying a few feet in front of you above the waves, dipping down to pull up small fish, or gannets filling their beaks with the day's catch as they struggle to haul more out of the water.

### ARRIVAL AND DEPARTURE

ANDENES

**By bus** The bus station is a few metres east of Storgata, just back from the seafront. Boreal buses (☎ 177 in Nordland, otherwise ☎ 75 77 24 10, ⓦ 177nordland.com) run to Risøyhamn (2–4 daily; 1hr) and Sortland (2–4 daily; 2hr).

**By car and ferry** Heading north to Tromsø (see p.336), the seasonal Senjafergene car ferry (☎ 76 14 12 03, ⓦ senjafergene.no) links Andenes with Gryllefjord on the mainland (late May to mid-June & early to late Aug 2 daily;

mid-June to early Aug 3 daily; 2hr; passengers 170kr; car and driver 425kr; advance reservations strongly advised). From Gryllefjord, it's about 220km to Tromsø via Highway 86 to Finnsnes, then along the scenic Highway 861 to Botnhamn, where a second Senjafergene car ferry crosses over to Brensholmen (May–Aug 5–7 daily; 45min; passengers 70kr, cars 175kr); from Brensholmen it's 70km or so on to Tromsø.

### INFORMATION

**Tourist office** On the harbour, in the same building as the Nordlyssenteret (mid-June to Aug daily 9am–6pm; Sept to mid-June daily 8am–3pm; ☎ 76 14 12 03, ⓦ andoyturist .no). It has a comprehensive range of local information and sells the 140kr all-inclusive discount ticket that gives

admission to all the town's museums and sights. It can make reservations for bird-island boat trips, whale safaris and the car ferry to Gryllefjord (see p.301). It also has details of local bicycle rental and of hiking trails in the surrounding district, as well as free wi-fi.

### ACCOMMODATION AND EATING

Andenes has a fair sprinkling of inexpensive accommodation and several households offer private rooms – look out for the signs – but, considering how isolated a spot this is, you'd be well advised to make a reservation before you get here. Food options are fairly limited.

**Andenes Rorbu Hotel** At the harbour ☎ 76 14 14 99, ⓦ andenesrorbuhotel.no. Opened in 2010, this contemporory hotel is a superb addition to the otherwise very rural accommodation here. As well as modern rooms, they have two green-timbered seafront *sjøhus* that have been divided into several apartments: both have good views over the water. The hotel restaurant, *Sørvesten*, is excellent, with reasonably priced main courses – such as whale steak (conscience permitting) – averaging 175kr. Rooms **600kr**, apartments **1200kr**

★ **Fargeklatten Veita** Sjøgata 38 ☎ 97 76 00 20, ⓦ fargeklatten.no. This stylishly decorated guesthouse near the harbour is easily the nicest place to stay in town. It's housed in a cluster of eighteenth- and nineteenth-century buildings that also includes a small museum showing fishermen's odds and ends and an art gallery. May–Sept. **850kr**

**Havhusene Bleik** Bleik, 9km southwest along the coast from Andenes ☎ 76 14 12 22, ⓦ andrikkenhotell.no. This handful of *sjøhus* containing modern double rooms and apartments (from 700kr) in the pretty village of Bleik are built a few metres from a sandy beach among some craggy hills. The clapboard houses have three bedrooms, spacious living rooms with a dining area and a small kitchenette. There's a pub and a shop a short walk away. **600kr**

**Jul. Nilsens Bakeri & Konditerei** Kong Hansgate 1 ☏ 76 14 10 18. A small bakery-café by the bus station that

is great for cakes and freshly baked goods. Mon–Wed 8am–1pm, Thurs 10am–3pm & 7–8pm, Fri 7am–3pm & 8–9pm, Sun 2–6pm.

**Stave Camping** Stave Beach, 8km south of Bleik in Stave ☏ 76 14 65 62, ⓦ stavecamping.no. Modest cabins with a sea view plus six king-sized hot pools set on a hill overlooking the ocean. Cabins **430kr**, tents **150kr**

# Stokmarknes

The main settlement on the island of **Hadseløya** is **STOKMARKNES**, an unremarkable little town whose mediocrity is partly relieved by its pleasant coastal setting on the island's northern shore. It lies about 30km south of the transport hub of **Sortland**, where you may well have to change bus.

## Hurtigrutemuseet

Markedsgata 1 • Daily: mid-May to mid-June & mid-Aug to mid-Sept noon–4pm; mid-June to mid-Aug 10am–6pm; mid-Sept to mid-May 2–4pm • 90kr • ⓦ hurtigrutemuseet.no

As well as being a stop on the Hurtigruten route, Stokmarknes is also home to the **Hurtigrutemuseet**, which is entirely devoted to the history of the boat, with a genuine 1950s ferry, the M/S *Finnmarken*, parked up outside on the quayside, looking very much its age. Also on the quayside is a statue of Richard With, the skipper responsible for streamlining the coastal ferry service in the 1890s. Before With, long-distance coastal boats did not stick to a rigorous timetable and anchored up during darkness; With changed all that and became something of a folk hero hereabouts as a result.

## The Trollfjord

The Hurtigruten cruise from Stokmarknes to Svolvær leaves daily at 3.15pm and takes a little over 3hr; 291kr per passenger in winter, 391kr in summer; cars 400kr all year. It's also possible to visit the Trollfjord on special boat trips from Svolvær (see p.317 )

Museum aside, the main reason to stop off in **Stokmarknes** is to catch the **Hurtigruten coastal boat** south to Svolvær via the **Trollfjord**, a majestic tear in the landscape just 2km long. The boats down the **Raftsundet**, the narrow sound separating the harsh, rocky shanks of Hinnøya and Austvågøya. Towards the southern end of the sound, the ship usually slows to a gentle chug. It then inches up the narrow gorge, smooth stone towering high above and blocking out the light. At the head of the Trollfjord, it then effects a nautical three-point turn and then crawls back to rejoin the main waterway. It's very atmospheric, and the effect is perhaps even more extraordinary when the weather is up. Note that the Hurtigruten will not enter the Trollfjord when there's the danger of a rockfall, but pauses at the fjord's mouth instead. Check locally before embarkation, though you're only likely to miss out, if at all, in spring.

### ARRIVAL AND INFORMATION                                    STOKMARKNES

**By bus** Buses to Stokmarknes pull in near the harbourfront tourist office.

**By car and ferry** From Stokmarknes, it's 15km south along the E10 to Melbu, from where a car ferry leaves for Fiskebøl on Lofoten (daily 6.20am–10.10pm, roughly hourly; 30min; passengers 34kr, car & driver 95kr; ☏ 177 in

Nordland or ☏ 51 56 41 00, ⓦ boreal.no).

**Tourist office** At the harbour (late May to mid-Aug Mon–Fri 10am–5pm, Sat & Sun 10am–3pm; ☏ 76 16 46 60). Has details of what little local accommodation there is in and around town.

### ACCOMMODATION

**Turistsenteret** At the harbour ☏ 76 15 29 99, ⓦ hurtigrutenhus.com. This brassy, modern hotel-cum-conference centre has 21 double rooms and a dozen wooden-style *rorbuer* with magnificent views of the

Hurtigruten as it makes its way into Stokmarknes harbour. Plonked down on Børøya islet some 15min walk from the museum, at the far end of the first of two bridges back towards Sortland. **840kr**

**5**

# The Lofoten islands

A skeletal curve of mountainous rock stretched out across the Norwegian Sea, the **Lofoten islands** have been the focal point of northern Norway's winter fishing from time immemorial. At the turn of the year, cod migrate from the Barents Sea to spawn here, where the coldness of the water is tempered by the Gulf Stream. The season only lasts from February to April, but fishing impinges on all aspects of island life and is impossible to ignore at any time of the year. At almost every harbour stand the massed ranks of wooden racks used for drying the cod, burgeoning and odiferous in winter, empty in summer like so many abandoned climbing frames.

Sharing the same history, but better known and more beautiful than their neighbours the Vesterålen, the Lofoten islands have everything from sea-bird colonies in the south to beaches and fjords in the north. The traditional approach is by boat from Bodø and this brings visitors face to face with the islands' most striking feature, the towering peaks of the **Lofotenveggen** (Lofoten Wall), a 160-kilometre stretch of mountains, whose jagged teeth bite into the skyline, trapping a string of tiny fishing villages tight against the shore. The mountains are set so close together that on first inspection there seems to be no way through, but in fact the islands are riddled with straits, sounds and fjords.

The Lofoten have their own relaxed pace, and are perfect for a simple, uncluttered few days. For somewhere so far north, the weather can be exceptionally mild: summer days can be spent sunbathing on the rocks or hiking and biking around the superb coastline, and when it rains – as it frequently does – life focuses on the *rorbuer* (fishermen's huts), where freshly caught fish are cooked over wood-burning stoves, stories are told and time gently wasted. If that sounds rather contrived, in a sense it is – the way of life here is to preserve Lofoten's thriving tourist industry – but it's rare to find anyone who isn't less than completely enthralled by it all.

## ARRIVAL AND DEPARTURE | THE LOFOTEN ISLANDS

### BY CAR
You can drive on a ferry-free route from Evenes (Harstad/Narvik) airport to Svolvær in 2hr 30min via the Lofast, a stretch of road built in 2007 that connects between Gullesfjordbotn and Fiskebøl.

### BY CAR FERRY
**From Bodø** The traditional approach to the Lofoten from the mainland is by car ferry from Bodø. There are three destinations to choose from, all on the southern peripheries of the archipelago: Moskenes, a tiny port just a few kilometres from the end of the E10, and the islets of Værøy and Røst. The ferry route varies, but there's almost always one ferry a day (and sometimes more) to Moskenes throughout the year, with marginally less frequent services to the two islets; Moskenes is often the first port of call. The trip from Bodø to Moskenes takes about 4hr; allow a further 2hr to Værøy, and two more for Røst, and be prepared for a rough crossing. The fare from Bodø to Moskenes is 168kr for passengers, 604kr for a car and driver. All these ferries are operated by Torghatten Nord (🌐 torghatten-nord .no) on a first-come, first-served basis, so it's a good idea to turn up a couple of hours before departure. Note, however, that in the summertime (June–Aug) advance

reservations are permitted – and are strongly recommended. Torghatten Nord also operates the shortest car-ferry service to the Lofoten, which links Skutvik, 35km west of the E6 midway between Fauske and Narvik, with Svolvær (1 daily; 2hr; passengers 89kr; car & driver 304kr). Again, given the infrequency of the service, advance reservations are strongly advised.

**From the Vesterålen** Heading for the Lofoten from the Vesterålen, you can either use the Lofast road (see opposite) or take the Melbu–Fiskebøl car ferry (daily 6.20am–10.10pm, roughly hourly; 30min; passengers 34kr, car & driver 95kr; ☎ 177 in Nordland or ☎ 51 56 41 00, 🌐 boreal.no).

### BY HURTIGRUTEN
The northbound Hurtigruten leaves Bodø daily at 3pm calling at two ports in the Lofoten islands – Stamsund (7.30pm) and Svolvær (10pm) – before nudging through the Raftsundet en route to Stokmarknes (1am) and Sortland (3am), on Vesterålen. Heading south, the departure times are as follows: Sortland (1pm); Stokmarknes (3.15pm); Svolvær (8pm); Stamsund (10pm); Bodø (4am).

**Fares** The passenger fare for the cruise from Bodø to Stamsund (4hr 30min) is 491kr in summer, 391kr in winter, and cars cost 374kr all year; the journey to Svolvær (6hr) costs 541/391kr, cars 400kr.

**Reservations** Advance reservations for cars are essential, and can be made online (@ hurtigruten.no) or by phoning the main office in Narvik (@ 810 03 030) – ask down at the harbour or at the port's tourist office for assistance.

### BY HURTIGBÅT

A Hurtigbåt passenger express boat service runs from Bodø to Svolvær (1 daily; 3hr 30min; 344kr; @ 90 62 07 00, @ torghattennord.no). Advance reservation is advised.

### BY BUS

The long-distance Lofoteneekspressen (@ 177 in Nordland, otherwise @ 75 77 24 10, @ 177nordland.com) provides the main bus service from the mainland to the Lofoten. It leaves Narvik twice daily to run along the E6 and then the E10, calling at Evenes airport and Lødingen before taking the Lofast highway to Fiskebøl in the Lofoten; it then proceeds on to Svolvær, where one bus daily continues on to Kabelvåg and Leknes, or you change for the once-daily bus to Leknes and Å. As an example of journey times, Narvik to Leknes takes 6hr, just under 8hr to Å. This long-distance bus service

is supported by a number of somewhat intermittent local buses operated by Boreal (@ boreal.no).

### BY PLANE

**Flights** Flights leave Bodø for the Lofoten airports – or rather airstrips – at Svolvær and Leknes 4–7 times a day. The operator is DAT (@ dat.dk), and tickets can be purchased online or any travel agent; fares from Bodø to the islands vary enormously, but a standard summer return ticket costs in the region of 780kr, half that one-way. Note also that whereas Svolvær airport is merely 5km from town (a 200kr taxi ride), Leknes airport is miles from anywhere you might want to visit, and the onward taxi will cost an arm and a leg.

**Car rental** There is car rental at both airports: Svolvær has Avis (@ 76 07 11 40) and Hertz (@ 76 07 07 20) outlets, as does Leknes – Avis (@ 76 08 01 04) and Hertz (@ 76 08 18 44). Good-value short-term deals abound – from around 600kr/day, though you may find better prices at Svolvær's two locally run rental companies such as Lofoten Sykkel-og bilutleie (@ 99 69 14 20) or Rent a Car Lofoten (@ 47 64 35 60, @ rentacar-lofoten.com); the latter also rents out scooters and motorcycles.

### GETTING AROUND

The E10 weaves a scenic route across Lofoten, running the 170km from Fiskebøl in the north to Å in the south, hopping from island to island by bridge and causeway and by occasionally tunnelling through the mountains and under the sea. The highway passes through or within a few kilometres of all the islands' main villages, Henningsvær, Å and Stamsund. If you have your own vehicle, village-hopping is easy and quick, but it's only when you leave the car and head off into the landscape that the real character of Lofoten begins to reveal itself; allow time for at least one walk or sea trip. Conversely, if you don't have a vehicle and want to reach the islands' remoter spots, it's worth considering renting a car, an inexpensive option if a few people share the cost (see p.316).

**By bus** Public transport is thin on the ground. What local bus services there are stick almost exclusively to the E10, the islands' only main road, and are run by Boreal (@ 177 in Nordland, otherwise @ 75 77 24 10, @ 177nordland.com). Two of Boreal's more useful offerings are Svolvær to

Kabelvåg and Henningsvær (4–10 daily) and Leknes to Stamsund (1–6 daily).

**By bike** Bike rental is available at most hostels, hotels and guesthouses, and the detailed *Cycling in Lofoten* booklet, which includes route maps, is sold at all tourist offices.

### INFORMATION

There's comprehensive **tourist information** on @ lofoten.info, though @ lofoten-info.no covers two of the more southerly islands, Moskenesøya and Flakstadøya, in greater detail.

### ACTIVITIES

**Water activities** The breathtakingly beautiful towns of Henningsvær, Stamsund and Å all make great bases for explorations by boat. Indeed, there's an abundance of marine activity with everything on offer from island cruises, sea-rafting and fishing excursions through to birdwatching trips. Scores of places also rent out fishing boats and equipment, although, because of the strong currents, you should always seek advice about local conditions.

**Hiking** Although the islands don't have a well-developed network of huts and hiking trails, the byroads, where you'll

rarely see a car, provide mile after mile of excellent walking as they delve deep into the heart of the landscape. There's good walking and yet more solitude on mountainous Værøy and flatter, more agricultural Røst, a pair of inhabited islands to the south of Å, reachable by ferry from Moskenes and Bodø.

**Mountaineering** There's plenty of scope for mountaineering on the Lofoten: Austvågøya has the finest climbing, with some of the best ascents in Norway, and there's a prestigious climbing school at Henningsvær.

**5**

## STAYING IN A RORBU OR SJØHUS

All across Lofoten, **rorbuer** (fishermen's shacks) are rented out to tourists for both overnight stays and longer periods. The name *rorbu* is derived from *ror*, "to row" and *bu*, literally "dwelling" – and some older islanders still ask "Will you row this winter?", meaning "Will you go fishing this winter?" *Rorbuer* date back to the twelfth century, when King Øystein ordered the first of them to be built round the Lofoten coastline to provide shelter for visiting fishermen who had previously been obliged to sleep under their upturned boats. Traditionally, *rorbuer* were built on the shore, often on poles sticking out of the sea, and usually coloured with a red paint based on cod-liver oil. They consisted of two sections, a sleeping and eating room and a smaller storage area.

At the peak of the fisheries in the 1930s, some 30,000 men were accommodated in *rorbuer*, but during the 1960s fishing boats became more comfortable and since then many fishermen have preferred to sleep aboard. Most of the original *rorbuer* disappeared years ago, and, although a few have survived, visitors today are much more likely to stay in a modern version, mostly prefabricated units churned out by the dozen with the tourist trade in mind. At their best, they are comfortable and cosy seashore cabins, sometimes a well-planned conversion of an original *rorbu* with bunk beds and wood-fired stoves; at their worst, they are little better than prefabricated hutches in the middle of nowhere. Most have space for between four and six guests and the charge for a hut averages around 1000kr per night – though some can cost as little as 600kr, while others rise to around 2500kr. Similar rates are charged for the islands' **sjøhus** (literally sea-houses), originally the large quayside halls where the catch was processed and the workers slept. Most of the original *sjøhus* have been cleverly converted into attractive apartments with self-catering facilities, a few into dormitory-style accommodation – and again, as with the *rorbuer*, the quality varies enormously. A full list of *rorbuer* and *sjøhus* is given in the *Lofoten Info-Guide*, a free pamphlet that you can pick up at any local tourist office and on ⓦ lofoten.info.

### ACCOMMODATION

As regards accommodation, the Lofoten islands have a sprinkling of **hotels**, a few of which are first-rate, though some are blandly modern, as well as three HI **hostels**, numerous **campsites** and the local speciality, the *rorbuer* (see box above).

## Svolvær

Fly into **SVOLVÆR** from mainland Norway and you'll immediately notice a quiet, quaint and more isolated vibe. The town strings over and around several headlands and bays on the southeast coast of **Austvågøya**, the largest of the Lofoten islands, and while it is far from the most attractive of the archipelago's settlements, the harbour's picturesque red wooden buildings do have a certain charm. The region's administrative and transport centre, it has all the bustle but little of the atmosphere of the other island towns, though it does have more accommodation and better restaurants than its neighbours and – to be fair – its surroundings are suitably mountainous. The central **Torget** (square) is the site of most of the town's facilities, including the tourist board, bus station, Hurtigruten quay and several restaurants.

### Lofoten Krigsminnemuseum

Hurtigruten quay • June–Sept Mon–Fri 10am–4pm, Sat 11am–3pm, Sun noon–3pm; by appointment out of season • 50kr • ⓦ lofotenkrigmus.no

Scandinavia's most engaging museum on World War II, the **Lofoten Krigsminnemuseum** (War Museum) chronicles the British commando raids on Lofoten (see box, p.316) by means of photographs and original artefacts such as uniforms, weapons, epaulets and other small wartime objects. While the collection might feel a bit like bric-a-brac, the displays do a very good job of conveying the life of a soldier during the war.

## SVOLVÆR

**■ ACCOMMODATION**

| | |
|---|---|
| Anker Brygge | 3 |
| Rica Hotel Svolvær | 4 |
| Svinøya Rorbuer | 2 |
| Svolvær Sjøhus | 1 |
| Thon Hotel Svolvær | 5 |

**● EATING & DRINKING**

| | |
|---|---|
| Bacalao | 3 |
| Børsen Spiseri | 1 |
| Du Verden | 2 |

## Magic Ice

Fiskergata 36 • Mid-June to late Aug daily noon–11pm; late Aug to mid-June daily 6–10pm • 95kr • ⓦ magicice.no

The quayside **Magic Ice** gallery depicts Lofoten life in winter by means of giant ice sculptures of local figures and outdoor activities – fishermen, yachts and trawlers sailing the seas, birds and fish in their habitats, as well as trolls, wood nymphs and other mythical creatures. The temperature is permanently below zero inside the gallery, so warm jackets and boots are issued free, and there's an on-site ice bar that serves pricey drinks once you've looked round the displays.

## Nordnorsk Kunstnersenter

Torget • Mid-June to late Aug daily 10am–6pm; late Aug to mid-June Mon 6–10pm, Tues–Sun 10am–4pm & 6–10pm • 30kr • ⓦ nnks.no

Located across the bridge from the centre of town on the islet of Svinøya, the **Nordnorsk Kunstnersenter** (Northern Norwegian Art Centre) is an interesting gallery with some fine paintings by Gunnar Berg (1863–93), including the *Battle of the Trollfjord*. It also

**5**

## THE BRITISH COMMANDO RAIDS OF 1941

The Germans occupied Norway in April 1940, but it wasn't until a year later that the British prepared their response: it took the form of a **commando raid** on Lofoten. The aims were threefold: firstly, it was thought that a successful attack would boost British morale; secondly, it was a way of tying German troops down to garrison duty along the Norwegian coast; and thirdly, the British wanted to destroy as much of Lofoten's plentiful supply of herring oil as they could, to prevent the Germans using it as a raw material in the manufacture of their explosives.

In April 1941, the first commando raid hit Svolvær, Stamsund and Henningsvær, while a second, a few months later, attacked Reine and nearby Sørvangen at the southern end of Lofoten. The first was the more successful, bagging two thousand prisoners and destroying hundreds of barrels of oil, but the Germans extracted a bitter revenge by burning down the houses of all those Norwegians deemed to have been sympathetic to the invaders.

puts on temporary exhibitions featuring work across a range of media (oil painting, ceramics, sculpture, etc) by contemporary Norwegian and international artists.

### ARRIVAL AND DEPARTURE
SVOLVÆR

**By bus** The bus station is around the corner from the tourist office on Fiskergata. The main Boreal bus services (⚙ 177nordland.no) run to Å (1–2 daily; 3hr 15min); Harstad (2–4 daily; 3hr 45min); Kabelvåg (15 daily; 10min); Leknes (3–6 daily; 1hr 30min); Narvik (2 daily; 4hr 25min); Sortland (1–3 daily; 2hr 15min); and Stokmarknes

(1–4 daily; 1hr 45min).

**By boat** Car ferries to Svolvær dock about 1km west of the town centre, while the Hurtigruten and Hurtigbåt boats dock in the centre, a short walk from the bus station.

**By car** Svolvær is a good place to rent a car: Europcar has an outlet at Sivert Nilsens Gate 43 (☏ 76 07 00 00).

### INFORMATION

**Tourist office** Just off the main town square near the harbour (late May to mid-June Mon–Fri 9am–4pm, Sat 10am–2pm; mid- to late June Mon–Fri 9am–8pm, Sat 10am–2pm, Sun 4–8pm; late June to early Aug Mon–Fri 9am–10pm, Sat 9am–8pm, Sun 10am–8pm; early Aug to

late Aug Mon–Fri 9am–8pm, Sat 10am–2pm; Sept to mid-May Mon–Fri 9am–3.30pm; ☏ 76 06 98 07, ⚙ lofoten .info); they have maps, accommodation lists and public transport details.

### ACCOMMODATION

While Svolvær isn't exactly short of accommodation, finding a room in high season can be a real pain. Consequently, advance reservation is highly recommended – especially if you want to avoid the town's clutch of mundane, mini-high-rise hotels. The nicest places to stay are in **rorbuer** cabins, which are chock-full of charm.

★**Anker Brygge** Lamholmen ☏ 76 06 64 80, ⚙ anker-brygge.no. Easily the town's smartest and most desirable accommodation, in a prime location on the tiny islet of Lamholmen, at the end of a causeway in the middle of the harbour. It consists of 22 spacious and gorgeously decorated *rorbuer* (all with full kitchen): number 228 is the swankiest, a two-bedroom suite with dual balconies. The staff are extremely friendly and knowledgeable, and there are wonderful views. **1490kr**

**Rica Hotel Svolvær** Lamholmen ☏ 76 07 22 22, ⚙ rica .no. This well-above-average chain hotel has an attractive modern design, its acres of glass perched on top of timber piles. The rooms are small but comfortable, and some come with a balcony. On the islet of Lamholmen in the middle of the harbour. **910kr**

**Svinøya Rorbuer** Gunnar Bergs vei 2, Svinøya ☏ 76 06 99 30, ⚙ svinoya.no. At the northeast end of town, a

causeway crosses over to the long and slender island of Svinøya, which is home to this set of *rorbuer*. They range from the plain and simple to the deluxe, and there are standard hotel-style rooms as well as apartment-sized suites (2000kr). *Rorbuer* **1050kr**, doubles **1550kr**

**Svolvær Sjøhus** Parkgata ☏ 76 07 03 36, ⚙ svolver -sjohuscamp.no. There are thirteen modest rooms, some with bunk beds, at this long-established place by the seashore. A few of the rooms share a kitchen, while others have self-contained kitchenettes. To get here from the Torget, turn right up the hill along Vestfjordgata and it's to the right, past the library. **590kr**

**Thon Hotel Svolvær** O.J. Kaalbøes gate 5 ☏ 76 04 90 00, ⚙ thonhotels.no. Smart, recently revamped chain hotel right in the centre of town. Thirty neat, efficient and contemporary bedrooms that don't look or feel as if they are part of a chain. **1195kr**

## EATING AND DRINKING

**Bacalao** Havnepromenaden 2 ☏76 07 94 00, ⓦbacalaobar.no. Down on the quay, this spacious café-restaurant mixes Mediterranean and Norwegian cuisine with flair and imagination. Lunches and evening main courses hover around 160kr. The service is snappy, and they serve excellent coffee too. At night it turns into the town's liveliest bar, jam-packed at the weekend. Mon–Thurs 10.30am–1am, Fri & Sat 10.30am–2.30am, Sun noon–1am.

★ **Børsen Spiseri** Svinøya Rorbuer, Gunnar Bergs vei 2, Svinøya ☏76 06 99 30, ⓦsvinoya.no. Lofoten's most atmospheric – and possibly best – restaurant is in a gorgeous old waterfront building dating from 1828, and adorned with maritime paraphernalia such as skin kayaks and primitive fishing gear. Its speciality is stockfish, served in a number of ways – try it steamed with potatoes and carrots (279kr), or grilled and served in bacon on a bed of truffle oil-flavoured risotto (299kr). The smoked whale roll appetizer (114kr), with horseradish and victory onion, served with red beet syrup, is a winner. Also look out for the "krambua", or general store, a museum of sorts, with old wares and shop equipment from days of yore. Reservations recommended. Daily 6–10pm; closed Mon–Wed in winter.

★ **Du Verden** Torget 15 ☏76 07 09 75, ⓦduverden .net. In the central square, this is one of the north's best restaurants, presided over by chef Roy Magne Berglund, who has won pretty much every culinary award there is in Norway. His creative menu features the freshest ingredients

---

## SVOLVÆR ACTIVITIES AND EXCURSIONS

Svolvær's dramatic environs merit exploration, either by climbing one of the local peaks, or by taking a boat trip out to the surrounding fjordlands – though you'll only really find the full range of excursions on offer in the summertime. Out of season, tours will go out once a week, at best.

### BOAT TRIPS TO THE TROLLFJORD

Every day throughout the summer boats leave from the quay alongside the Torget in Svolvær for the **Trollfjord** (2 times daily; return trip 3hr; 450kr; buy tickets on board; ⓦlofoten-charter boat.no), an impossibly narrow, two-kilometre-long stretch of water that's also on the Hurtigruten itinerary (see p.30). The intrepid might also consider making the same excursion by **speedboat** (3 times daily; return trip 2hr; 650kr; ⓦlofoten-explorer.com) – heavy jackets and goggles are included.

### FERRIES TO SKROVA

For the best and most scenic walks in the area, take a ferry to the pretty islet of **Skrova**, just offshore from Svolvær. Perfect for an afternoon seascape stroll, Skrova's only settlement trails along a slender rocky spit, its harbour dominated by the country's largest whaling station. The village is attached by a causeway to the main body of the island, which is dominated by the steep Mount Høgskrova (258m). Before you leave, pick up the makings of a picnic at one of the shops in Svolvær and prepare to enjoy it in splendid isolation. **Ferries** run from the quay in Svolvær (2–5 ferries daily; 30min; 38kr each way) to Skrova, while both the express boats from Svolvær to Bodø/Narvik, and the car ferry between Svolvær and Skutvik also call in there.

### CLIMBING SVOLVÆRGEITA

Svolvær boasts one of the archipelago's most famous **climbs**, the haul up to the top of the **Svolværgeita** (the "Svolvær Goat"), a twin-pronged peak that rises high above the E10 to the northeast of town. The lower slopes of the mountain are hard enough, but the last 40m – up the horns of the "Goat" – require considerable expertise. Daring-daft mountaineers complete the thrill by jumping from one pinnacle to the other.

### LOFOTEN POLARLYSSENTER

For the best introduction to the **northern lights**, take an excursion to the **Lofoten Polarlyssenter** (Polar Light Centre; ☏91 12 46 68, ⓦpolarlightcenter.com). This rural science centre is run by a friendly Dutch couple with a collection of astronomic instruments that determine exactly when the Aurora is about to strike. In addition to a lecture on the science of the lights – and how to photograph them – they also provide an SMS alert service, which sends out messages during your stay in Norway that advise when Aurora activity is getting stronger. Located in **Laukvik**, approximately 45 minutes by car from Svolvær; they can arrange transport if you do not have a car.

**5**

in dishes that range from sushi to pizza to classic seafood plates that average around 250kr. If you're considering splashing out on lunch, this is definitely the place.

Mid-May to Aug Mon–Thurs 11am–1am, Fri & Sat 11am–12.30am, Sun 11am–1am; Sept to mid-May Mon–Fri 11am–10pm, Sat 11am–midnight.

## Kabelvåg

With its pretty wooden centre draped around the shore of a narrow and knobbly inlet, **KABELVÅG** is immediately more appealing than Svolvær, just 6km away. The most important village on Lofoten from Viking times until the early years of the twentieth century, Kabelvåg was founded by King Øystein, who ruled Norway until 1123. It was once the centre of the coastal fishery industry and home to the country's first *rorbuer*, built in 1120, as well as one of its first inns, which dates from 1792. The town's charming little square has oodles of character, and on a winter's day is simply magical. The neighbouring, smaller settlement of **Storvågan**, 2km south, also has a few galleries, museums and a statue commemorating Øystein.

### Vågan kirke

Villaveien 9 • May–Aug Mon–Fri 10am–6pm, Sun noon–6pm • 30kr

The late nineteenth-century **Vågan kirke**, also known as the Lofot Cathedral, is a big and breezy timber church that rests alongside the E10 on the eastern edge of the village. A reminder of Lofoten's busier days, the church's hangar-like interior was built to accommodate a congregation of over a thousand, and is the second largest timber religious structure in the country.

### Lofotmuseet

May Mon–Fri 9am–3pm, Sat & Sun 11am–3pm; June to mid-Aug daily 10am–6pm; mid-Aug to late Aug Mon–Fri 9am–3pm, Sat & Sun 11am–3pm; Sept Mon–Fri 9am–3pm & Sun 11am–3pm; Oct–April Mon–Fri 9am–3pm • 70kr, or 180k with a Storvågan multi-ticket that includes the gallery and aquarium • ⓦ lofotmuseet.no

The **Lofotmuseet** (Lofoten Museum), 1.5km west of Kabelvåg by the seashore in Storvågan, is one of Lofoten's best museums. In an old house and country store dating from the 1800s, it traces the history of the islands' fisheries, boats and *rorbuer*, and displays the definitive collection of maritime equipment and other cultural paraphernalia. It also houses a great little gift shop.

### Galleri Espolin

Storvågan • March & April Sun–Fri 10am–3pm; May daily 11am–3pm; early June & late Aug daily 10am–6pm; mid-June to mid-Aug daily 10am–7pm; Sept–Feb Mon–Fri & Sun 11am–3pm • 70kr or 180k with a Storvågan multi-ticket that includes the musuem and aquarium • ⓦ galleri-espolin.no

This small art gallery, innovatively built into a hillside, features Norway's largest collection of paintings and sketches by **Kaare Espolin Johnson** (1907–94), a renowned Norwegian artist of Romantic inclination, who specialized in Arctic images and imagery. The artist's haunting, almost three-dimensional style is distinguished by its use of watercolour, oil, lead and soot – he was forced to experiment with techniques due to his extremely poor vision during much of his life. Two of the gallery's halls exhibit Johnson's works, while a third is used for temporary exhibitions.

### Lofotakvariet

Storvågan • Feb–April & Sept–Nov Mon–Fri & Sun 11am–3pm; May daily 11am–3pm; June–Aug daily 10am–6pm • 110kr, or 180k with a Storvågan multi-ticket that includes the gallery and museum • ⓦ lofotakvariet.no

Displaying a wide variety of Atlantic species, the indoor and outdoor **Lofotakvariet** (Aquarium) has a number of exhibits on the fauna of the Norwegian coast. The most engaging part of the visit, however, is watching the regular feeding times of various live sea creatures, including otters and seals.

**5**

**By bus** Buses from Svolvær and Henningsvær (3–12 daily) drop passengers right in the centre of Kabelvåg.

### ACTIVITIES

For skiing, hiking and climbing, the best operator in town is Northern Alpine Guides, Havnegata 3 (☎94 24 91 10, ⓦalpineguides.no). Run by expert American climber Seth Hobby, it organizes a range of challenging activities year-round including day hikes and ski outings, rock- and ice-climbing courses and week-long sail-and-ski excursions up the Lofoten coast. Prices for most activities start from 100kr/day. Lofoten Aktiv, Rødmyrveien 26 (☎99 23 11 00, ⓦlofoten-aktiv.no), specializes in sea-kayaking courses, but also runs fishing, cycling, trekking and skiing trips as well.

### ACCOMMODATION AND EATING

**Kabelvåg Sommerhotell** East of Kabelvåg centre, 500m from the E10 ☎76 06 98 80, ⓦlofotensommerhotell.no. Kabelvåg's spartan HI hostel is based in a school building: its facilities have been recently overhauled into sleek and clean (if somewhat IKEA-esque) modern digs. Great big breakfasts included. June to mid-Aug. Dorms 275kr, doubles 650kr

**Tyskhella Rorbuferie** Sjøgata 24 ☎76 07 45 00, ⓦlofotferie.no. Built in 1905, these twelve old tackle buildings are some of Lofoten's most modernized *rorbuer* – yet they still manage to retain some real charm. The largest of them can sleep up to ten people. Laundry facilities. 1200kr

**Nyvågar Rorbuhotell** Storvågan ☎76 06 97 00, ⓦnyvaagar.no. By far the most luxurious choice hereabouts, comprising a scattering of smart four-bedded *rorbuer*. The rooms are squeaky clean and effectively modern apartments, so lack a little Nordic rustic charm. However, the nicest are on the waterfront, with secluded terraces overlooking the water, and make a very scenic spot to enjoy a glass of wine. A large wooden hot-tub outside hosts some festive get-togethers, and there is cycle (55kr/day) and boat rental (200kr/hr) too. The on-site restaurant, *Lorchstua* (daily mid-June to Aug 5–11pm*)* is recommended, too. *Rorbu* for four 2100kr

★ **Præstengbrygga Pub** Kaiveien 9 ☎76 07 80 60, ⓦprestengbrygga.no. Right in the centre of the village overlooking the dock, this lively, all-wood spot is the heart of the Kabelvåg social scene. They serve enormous, excellent-value sandwiches, salads and pizzas from 80kr, have a popular bottomless-cup-of-coffee deal, and feature a locally famous fish soup in autumn and winter and the best *bacalao* you'll taste in summer. The owner is a whisky connoisseur and they have hundreds of bottles to choose from. Free wi-fi. June–Aug Sun–Thurs 11am–1am, Fri & Sat 10am–2.30am; Sept–May Mon–Tues 11am–4pm, Wed & Thurs 11am–1pm, Fri & Sat 11am–2.30am, Sun noon–3pm.

**Sandvika Sjøcamping** Ørsvågveien 45 ☎76 07 81 45, ⓦlofotferie.no. The better of Kabelvåg's two fjordside campsites, with modern cabins that come in various sizes, a small beach and motorboats for rent (200kr/hr). Cabins from 950kr, tents 145kr

## Henningsvær

One of Lofoten's most picturesque and beguiling of headland villages, **HENNINGSVÆR** is a cobweb of cramped and twisting lanes lined with brightly painted wooden houses. These frame a tiny inlet that literally cuts the place in half, forming a sheltered, picture-postcard harbour. The town is well supplied with accommodation, eating establishments and excursion options, and almost inevitably, coach parties are wheeled in and out, despite the narrowness of the two high-arched bridges into the village. For all its hustle and bustle, Henningsvær richly deserves at the very least an overnight stay.

### Galleri Lofotens Hus

Hjellskjæret • March Fri–Sun 10am–5pm, April daily 5–7pm, May daily 10am–7pm, June–Aug daily 9am–7pm • 80kr • ☎91 59 50 83, ⓦgalleri-lofoten.no

Set in a former fish-processing plant, the **Galleri Lofotens Hus** is one of the town's main draws, exhibiting (and selling) the work of the contemporary Norwegian artist Karl Erik Harr. Also on display is a competent selection of late nineteenth- and twentieth-century Lofoten paintings by artists such as Einar Berge, Adelsteen Normann, Gunnar Berg and Otto Sinding – you can't miss the latter's whopping *Funeral in Lofoten* of 1886 – plus historic and contemporary photographs and slides mostly of the islands.

**5**

## COD FISHING FROM HENNINGSVÆR

For hundreds of years fishermen have gathered in the waters off Lofoten to catch the **cod** that have migrated here from the Barents Sea to spawn. The fish arrive in late January or early February and the season lasts until April. There are tremendous fluctuations in the number of cod making the journey; although the reasons for this variation are not fully understood, relative water temperatures and, more recently, over-fishing are two key components. Sometimes the cod arrive packed together, at other times they are thinly spread, their distribution dictated by water temperature. The fish prefer a water temperature of about 5°C, which occurs here off Lofoten between the warm and salty bottom current and the colder surface waters: sometimes this band of water is thick, sometimes thin; sometimes it's close to the shore, sometimes it's way out to sea, all of which affect the fishing. If you fancy trying your hand at fishing, you can take an organized trip (see below).

## Engelskmannsbrygga

Dreyersgt 1 • Late Feb to early June & mid-Aug to Dec Fri–Sun noon–4pm; mid-June to early Aug daily 10am–8pm • Free • ☎ 76 07 52 85, ⓦ engelskmannsbrygga.no

Henningsvær's Arctic light, combined with the might of the mountains, has long attracted Norwegian painters, making it something of an arts centre. **Engelskmannsbrygga** ("Englishman's Wharf"), on the main square, is a gallery run by a collective of artists, whom you can watch at work. It's a good place to purchase, or simply admire, the art, plus ceramics and glassware.

### ARRIVAL AND DEPARTURE
### HENNINGSVÆR

**By bus** The Lofotenekspressen bus (see p.313) does not detour off the E10 to Henningsvær, but there is a local bus service from Svolvær and Kabelvåg (7 daily).

**By car** It's 11km to Henningsvær from Kabelvåg on the E10, then a further 8km-long drive off that.

### ACTIVITIES

**Fishing** Lofoten Opplevelser, Hjellskjæret (☎ 76 07 50 01, ⓦ lofoten-opplevelser.no), organizes cod-fishing trips (2hr) from the middle of March to the end of the season at a cost of 750kr per person.

**Mountaineering** The intrepid should make a beeline for Lofoten's best mountaineering school, Nord Norsk Klatreskole (☎ 90 57 42 08, ⓦ nordnorskklatreskole.no), who operate a range of all-inclusive climbing holidays in the mountains near Henningsvær, catering for various

degrees of fitness and experience. Prices vary depending on the trip, but summer climbing tends to run in the region of 2000kr per person per day, including equipment and food.

**Sea-eagle safaris** Lofoten Opplevelser, Hjellskjæret (☎ 76 07 50 01, ⓦ lofoten-opplevelser.no) runs sea-eagle trips, which depart daily at 2:30pm throughout the summer (500kr).

### ACCOMMODATION

**Den Siste Viking** Misværveien 10 ☎ 90 57 42 08, ⓦ nordnorskklatreskole.no. Run by the island's mountaineering school, these frugal, unadorned lodgings are pleasant enough and located right in the centre. One of the rooms is where author Johan Bojer penned his masterpiece *The Last of the Vikings* – though the room retains little of its nineteenth-century charm today. **600kr**

**Henningsvær Bryggehotell** Hjellskjæret ☎ 76 07 47 50, ⓦ henningsvaer.no. This attractive modern building right on the quayside is the town's smartest hotel, with thirty rooms done out in traditional style. It can be popular with larger groups, and use of the sauna is included in the price. It has a very good restaurant on site, *Den Blå Fisk*. **1500kr**

**Henningsvær Hotell** Dreyers gate 8 ☎ 76 07 07 77,

ⓦ henningsvaer-hotell.no. The rooms in this cheerful hotel are themed, with different colour schemes and quirky, characterful furnishings (a heart-shaped bed lamp, say, or freestanding bathtubs). There's also a spacious restaurant on the premises that specializes in halibut, codfish and *bacalao*. **1295kr**

**Henningsvær Rorbuer** Banhammaren 53 ☎ 76 06 60 00, ⓦ henningsvar-rorbuer.no. This stylish, well-kept place consists of 26 recently restored and well-equipped *rorbuer* of various shapes and sizes at the far end of the town: some have outdoor seating and loft beds and you can use a giant wooden hot-tub and sauna nearby. You can also rent boats from 80kr/hr: the more expensive ones come with outboard motors. **1150kr**

**5**

## EATING AND DRINKING

**Fiskekrogen** Dreyersgate 19 ☎ 76 07 46 52. This very classy restaurant is set at the waterside, and most tables offer great views right of the fjord. The chef's seafood dishes in general, and the fish soup (85kr) in particular, are simply superb. Mains such as cod, monkfish and mussels cost around 250kr. Mid-May till mid-Aug daily noon–11pm; mid-Aug to mid-May Tues–Sun noon–6pm.

**Klatrekafeen** Den Siste Viking, Misværveien 10 ☎ 90 57 42 08, ⊛ nordnorskklatreskole.no. A solid range of Norwegian stand-bys from 100kr are served here, along with soup and salads and some killer chocolate cupcakes,

all washed down with first-rate coffee. Climbing relics and candlelight gives the place oodles of atmosphere. Feb to mid-May & Sept–Nov Wed 8pm–1am, Fri 9pm–2am, Sat noon–4pm & 9pm–2am, Sun noon–4pm; mid-May to Aug Mon–Thurs 11am–1am, Fri–Sat 11am–2am, Sun 11am–1am.

**Lysstøperi** Gammelveien 2 ☎ 90 55 18 77. One of the more unusual places to eat in Norway must certainly be the café inside this local candle shop, where they serve *kanelsnurr* and *skolebolle*, both sweet treats designed to test your dental work. Wed–Sun 11am–4pm.

## Vestvågøy

The island of **Vestvågøy**, which lies southwest of Austvågøya, is one that captivates many travellers to Lofoten – in particular the charming town of **Stamsund**. Fans of wild scenery, however, should head out to Vestvågøy's blustery **northwest coast**, where a few hardy fishing villages struggled on until they were finally abandoned to the birds, the wind and the sea in the 1950s – give or take the occasional summer resident.

### ARRIVAL AND DEPARTURE       VESTVÅGØY

**By plane** The island's airport is located 15km west of Stamsund in the dull administrative centre of Leknes, from where there are several flights daily to Bodø.

**By bus** Lofotenekspressen (see p.313) runs services from Svolvær to Stamsund (Mon–Sat 3–4 daily). The bus service along the E10 is reasonable, but there are no regular buses off it to the northwest coast

**By boat** The Hurtigruten (see p.30) calls at Stamsund on its way north from Bodø.

**By car** The quickest way to Stamsund from Svolvær is to turn south off the E10 down Highway 815, a scenic 40km coastal drive. This coast is accessed by a series of turnings off the E10 as it slices across Vestvågøy's drab central valley.

### Stamsund

There is a certain laidback charm to **STAMSUND**, whose older buildings string along the rocky, fretted seashore in an amiable jumble of crusty port buildings, wooden houses and *rorbuer*. It's also home to the modern art **Galleri 2** (June–Aug Tues–Sun noon–4pm & 7–9.30pm; 20kr; ⊛ galleri2.no), 100m from the Hurtigruten dock, which is worth a look for its small canvases and lithographs of local scenes, and textile and ceramic work.

### ACCOMMODATION AND EATING       STAMSUND

**Skjærbrygga** Hjellskjæret ☎ 76 05 46 00, ⊛ skjaerbrygga.no. This stylishly decorated and intelligently revamped old *rorbu* is located right in the centre of Stamsund by the harbour. The old *Skjærbrygga sjøhus* has been attractively renovated too, and now contains a café and an excellent restaurant, which features fresh local ingredients: main courses at the restaurant go for around 250kr, though the attached café is rather more affordable. Prices drop somewhat outside of high season. *Rorbu* **1250kr**

★ **Stamsund Vandrerhjem** Svarholt, 1km down the road from the port ☎ 76 08 93 34, ⊛ hihostels.no. This

popular and easy-going HI hostel consists of several *rorbuer* and a *sjøhus* perched over a bonny little bay: it has a washing machine and tumble drier, as well as self-catering facilities. You can rent bikes here (100kr a day), and the warden is very knowledgeable on everything about Vestvågøy, from cycling through to hiking and fishing. The fishing is first-class too; you can borrow the hostel's rowing boats and lines to take out on the (usually still) water. Afterwards you can barbecue your catch and eat alfresco on the veranda overlooking the bay. March to mid-Oct. Dorms **160kr**, doubles **460kr**

### Utakleiv

The old village of **UTAKLEIV** sits on the edge of a wide and windy bay surrounded by austere cliffs. It's remarkably flat, with grazing sheep and cows dotting the pastureland,

**5**

### A HIKE FROM UNSTAD TO EGGUM

A popular nine-kilometre **trail** with mountains and lakes on one side and the surging ocean on the other, runs east from the village of **Unstad** to the tiny hamlet of **Eggum**. The scenery is stern around Unstad, a huddle of houses in a diminutive river valley set beneath the mountains and with wide views out to sea. The main draw here is the ocean: this is by far the best **surfing** spot on the island with a great and stable swell. The trail passes the remains of a radar station built by the Germans during World War II, en route to Eggum, an especially pretty spot, its handful of houses clinging on to a precarious headland dwarfed by the mountains behind and with a whopping pebble beach in front. Both Unstad and Eggum can be reached by turning off the E10.

#### ACCOMMODATION

**Unstad Camping** Unstadt ☏ 76 08 64 33, ⓦ unstadcamping.no. The only accommodation in Unstad also rents out surf gear (480kr/day) and runs four-hour surf clinics (695kr). May–Sept. Cabins 590kr, tents 180kr

and there are two crisp white beaches where you can **camp** for 100kr per night. To get here, turn north from Leknes along the E10 for the three-kilometre journey to the first signposted byroad, which leads for 10km over the hills, along the seashore and through a narrow tunnel to the village.

### Lofotr Vikingmuseum

Prestegårdsveien 59, Bøstad (14km from Leknes) • May & mid-Aug to mid-Sept daily 11am–5pm; June to mid-Aug daily 10am–7pm; mid-Sept to April Wed & Sun noon–5pm • 140kr • ⓦ lofotr.no

This interesting archeological museum was set up after the accidental discovery of the remains of a Viking chieftain's house by a local farmer in 1981. The exhibits are housed within a reconstructed 83-metre Viking house, with flickering lights, wood-tar smells and so forth all adding to the atmosphere. There's also a permanent exhibition of Viking artefacts found in the vicinity, and the boathouse contains a full-sized replica of the Gokstad ship displayed in Oslo (see p.84).

## Flakstadøya and Moskenesøya

By any standard, the next two islands of the archipelago, **Flakstadøya** – known to the Vikings as "Vargfot", or wolf's paw, on account of its shape – and **Moskenesøya**, are extraordinarily beautiful. As the Lofoten taper towards their southerly conclusion, the rearing peaks of the Lofotenveggen crimp the sea-shredded coastline, providing a thunderously scenic backdrop to a necklace of tiny fishing villages. The E10 travels along almost all of this shoreline, leaving Leknes to tunnel west under the sound separating Vestvågøy from Flakstadøya.

### Nusfjord

An extravagantly picturesque fishing village in a tight and forbidding cove, **NUSFJORD** lies about 20km from Leknes, down an improbable byroad that somehow wiggles for 6km through the mountains to the village. Unlike many *rorbuer* elsewhere in Lofoten, the ones here are the genuine nineteenth-century article, and the general store, with its wooden floors and antique appearance, fits in nicely too. Perhaps inevitably, it's tourism that keeps the local economy afloat and indeed the village is now so popular with day-trippers that there's a 50kr fee to get in. Don't let that deter you: some of the buildings, like the cod-liver refinery, the smithy and the sawmill, have been attractively restored and in the evening, when the crowds have disappeared, Nusfjord is truly beguiling.

## FLAKSTADØYA & MOSKENESØYA

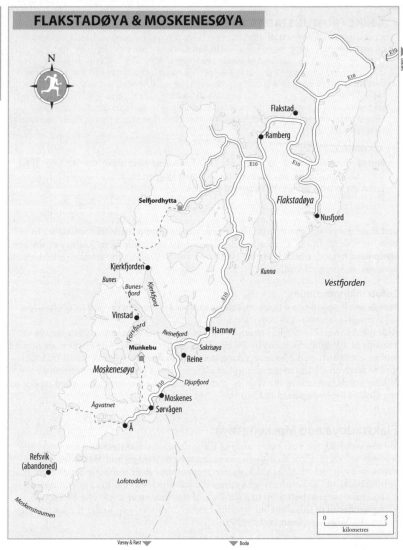

N

Flakstad

Ramberg

E10

E10

E10

Flakstadøya

Selfjordhytta

Nusfjord

Kjerkfjorden

Bunes

Bunes-
fjord

Kjerkfjord

Kunna

Vestfjorden

Vinstad

Forsfjord

Reinefjord

Hamnøy

E10

Munkebu

Sakrisøya

Moskenesøya

Reine

E10

Djupfjord

Ågvatnet

Moskenes

Sørvågen

Å

Refsvik
(abandoned)

Lofotodden

Moskenstraumen

0       5
kilometres

Værøy & Røst ▼      ▼ Bodø

### ACTIVITIES

NUSFJORD

**Diving** If you're certified, you can go deep-sea diving with Aqua Lofoten, in the centre of Nusfjord by the Statoil petrol station (☎ 99 01 90 42, ⍵ aqualofoten.no; 550kr for one dive), who also rent out apartments.

### ACCOMMODATION

**Nusfjord Rorbu Holidays** Nusfjord harbour ☎ 76 09 30 20, ⍵ nusfjord.no. Various types of comfortably refurbished *rorbuer,* ranging from simple, standard versions sleeping up to four people, to luxurious two-bedroom affairs that cost an arm and a leg; advance reservations are strongly advised. They also rent out cycles (185kr/day), kayaks (420kr/day) and boats (500kr/day), as well as fishing gear (no charge). <u>1300kr</u>

## Flakstad kirke

On the E10, on the outskirts of Ramberg • Late June to early Aug 11am–3pm • ☎ 76 09 31 45

**5**

With its distinctive onion-dome, the red timber **Flakstad kirke** was built in 1780. The church's ornate pulpit was painted by the itinerant German artist Gottfried Ezechiel, as was the painting above the altar, whose main motif is the Last Supper. The church lies on the outskirts of Ramberg, Flakstadøya's administrative centre that strings along the sandy beach, with a smattering of services (garage, supermarket and suchlike).

## Hamnøy

In an impossibly picturesque setting on the island of **Moskenesøya**, the fishing village of **HAMNØY** sits on the north side of the Reinefjord inlet. At the mouth of the Reinefjord, the island of Sakrisøya is linked to Hamnøy by the E10, which runs over a series of bridges.

### ACCOMMODATION AND EATING                                                          HAMNØY

**Hamnøy Rorbuer** In the centre of Hamnøy by the jetty ☎ 76 09 23 20, ⓦ lofoten-info.no/hamnoy. Ten plain, functional *rorbuer*, with access to laundry facililties as well as cycle and boat rental. Also has a quaint summertime restaurant, serving good traditional Norwegian cuisine – try the cod tongues, an island delicacy. **800kr**

★ **Sakrisøy Rorbuer** On Sakrisøya midway between Hamnøy and Reine ☎ 76 09 21 43, ⓦ lofoten.ws. The pick of the places to stay hereabouts, these cosy, ochre-coloured restored *rorbuer*, located in a collection of original 1870 cabins, come with kitchenettes, radio and wood stoves. They rent out bikes for a small charge and will lend you rowboats for free. The owners also run the fishmongers opposite, where they dish out delicious home-made fish burgers and sell freshly caught fish. **975kr**

## Reine

On the far side of the Reinefjord inlet, **REINE** keeps a fabulous location, ambling along a tiny islet connected to the rest of Moskenesøya by a narrow causeway that branches off the E10. It's the departure point for a variety of **boat trips**, including the trip to Vinstad (see below), midnight-sun cruises, coastal voyages, fishing expeditions and trips to the Moskenstraumen (see p.327): for further information, ask around locally or contact the Moskenes tourist office (see p.326). Reine is also a superb spot for seeing the northern lights.

### Eva Harr Gallery

Reine kultursenter, next to the boat dock • Late May to late Aug daily 10.30am–6pm • 60kr • ☎ 76 09 10 10, ⓦ evaharr.no

Reine is also home to the **Eva Harr Gallery**, which is devoted to this Harstad-born contemporary artist's work. Her expressive paintings of Lofoten are displayed alongside a selection of her graphic work.

---

### A HIKE FROM VINSTAD TO BUNES

An eerily deserted village with just one permanent inhabitant and a few holiday homes, the settlement of **Vinstad** is the starting point for the ninety-minute hike over to Moskenesøya's northwest coast. The first thirty minutes of the hike, along an old dirt trail, are not especially enjoyable, but things improve thereafter as you proceed along the west shore of the narrow and very steep Bunesfjord with jagged mountains rearing up in every direction. The dirt trail ends abruptly just past the cemetery and you have to make a sharp left, continuing up a steep grass path that takes you over a ridge between the mountains. An hour or so on from here, you'll reach the sandy cove of **Bunes**, the epitome of isolation and a smashing place to watch the midnight sun. It isn't a difficult hike, but given that this last section can get very slippery and the weather can change in minutes, you'll need to be properly equipped.

To get to Vinstad from Reine, pick up one of the small passenger ferries that run up the Reinefjord to Vinstad (2–3 daily; 50kr each way; ☎ 99 49 18 05).

**5**

**Reine Rorbuer** On the harbour ☎76 09 22 22, ⓦreinerorbuer.com. Once the local police station, these 22 recently renovated *rorbuer* and three apartments are the best place to stay in town. An on-site restaurant (May–Aug) occupies the old general store and offers top-notch seafood risottos, local lamb and marinated salmon with a terrace overlooking the harbour; mains from 180kr. **1400kr**

## Moskenes

The town of **MOSKENES**, 5km south of Reine, is the island's main port to and from Bodø. There's not much to it, aside from the boat jetty, a helpful tourist office and a handful of houses dotted round a horseshoe-shaped bay.

**Tourist office** At the jetty (March–April & Sept Mon–Fri 10am–2pm; May Mon–Fri 10am–5pm; mid-June to mid-Aug daily 9am–7.30pm; early June to mid-June and mid-Aug to late Aug daily 10am–5pm; ☎98 01 75 64, ⓦlofoten-info.no).

**Moskenes Camping** 150m from the ferry in Moskenesvågen ☎99 48 94 05. A very basic waterside (and mostly gravel) campsite, with a small patch of grass to pitch a tent. May–Aug. Tents **120kr**

## Å

The tersely named **Å** is one of Lofoten's most delightful villages, its huddle of old buildings rambling along a foreshore that's wedged in tight between the grey-green mountains and the surging sea. It's located five kilometres south of Moskenes, where the road abruptly ends.

### Norsk Fiskeværsmuseum

Sørvågen • Late June to late Aug daily 10am–6pm; late Aug to late June Mon–Fri 10am–3.30pm • 60kr • ⓦ lofoten-info.no /nfmuseum

Thanks to so much of Å's heritage being preserved, the engaging **Norsk Fiskeværsmuseum** (Norwegian Fishing Village Museum), is largely successful in its attempt to re-create life here at the end of the nineteenth century. There are about fifteen buildings to explore here, including a boathouse, forge, cod-liver-oil processing plant, *rorbuer*, and the houses of both the traders who dominated things hereabouts and the fishermen who did their bidding. According to the census of 1900, Å had 91 inhabitants, of whom ten were traders and their relatives, 18 servants, and 63 fishermen and their dependants. It was a rigidly hierarchical society underpinned by terms and conditions akin to serfdom: the fishermen did not own any land and had to pay rent for the ground on which their houses stood. Payment was made in the form of unpaid labour on the merchant's farmland during the summer harvest and, to rub salt into the wound, the fishermen couldn't control the price of the fish upon which they were reliant – no wonder Norwegians emigrated in their thousands. The museum has a series of **displays** detailing every aspect of village life – and very well presented it is too.

### Tørrfiskmuseum

Early to late June Mon–Fri 11am–4pm; late June to late Aug daily 10am–5.30pm • 40kr

If you're interested in extending your knowledge of all things fishy, head to is the **Tørrfiskmuseum** (Stockfish Museum) at the harbour – stockfish being the air-dried fish that served as the staple diet of most Norwegians well into the twentieth century. Presided over by a gregarious curator, the museum provides more information than you ever wanted to know about the history of this very typical Norwegian foodstuff.

**5**

## EDGAR ALLAN POE ON THE MOSKENSTRAUMEN

There are other places to see similar phenomena in Norway – Bodø's Saltstraumen springs to mind – but the **Moskenstraumen** is the most dramatic of the country's maelstroms and was described by **Edgar Allan Poe** in his short story *A Descent into the Maelstrom*:

*Even while I gazed, this current acquired a monstrous velocity. Each moment added to its speed – to its headlong impetuosity. In five minutes the whole sea … was lashed into ungovernable fury… Here the vast bed of the waters seamed and scarred into a thousand conflicting channels, burst suddenly into frenzied convulsion – heaving, boiling, hissing…*

### ARRIVAL AND DEPARTURE — Å

**By bus** The Lofoten Ekspressen (w 177nordland.com) runs to Leknes (1–4 daily; 1hr 45min) and Reine (2–7 daily; 30min). Note that bus times do not usually coincide with ferry sailings to and from Moskenes, meaning that you'll either have to walk between the two towns – it's an easy 5km – or take a taxi.

### ACTIVITIES

**Boat trips** Every day between May and Sept, boat trips depart Å's jetty for day-long fishing expeditions (500kr per person), coastal cruises (3hr; 500kr), and, weather and tides permitting, cruises to the abandoned fishing village of Refsvik and the Moskenstraumen (5hr; 800kr), the dramatic maelstrom at the southern tip of Moskenesøya (see box above). *Å-Hamna Rorbuer* (☎ 76 09 12 11 or ☎ 91 15 05 60) runs a great 2–4hr "Fisherman for a Day" excursion.

**Hikes** While Å may not offer too much in the way of hiking trails, there is an enjoyable route leading west from the village to the other side of the island. This begins by skirting the south shore of Lake Ågvatnet, before climbing over a steep ridge and then pushing on to the sea cliffs of the exposed west coast. The hike takes a whole day, and shouldn't be attempted in bad weather.

### ACCOMMODATION

**Å Rorbuer** In the centre of Å by the jetty ☎ 76 09 11 21, w lofoten-rorbu.com. This collection of buildings in town feature *rorbuer* of various shapes and sizes – some of the nicest have some great period furnishings – though many of the bathrooms are shared. **1175kr**

**Hostel Å** In the centre of Å by the jetty ☎ 76 09 12 11, w hihostels.no. This quaint hostel has an assortment of smart one- to eight-bedded *rorbuer* around the dock, as well as the adjacent *sjøhus*, which offers comfortable and equally smart hotel-standard rooms. Open year round. Dorms **200kr**, doubles **420kr**, rorbu from **850kr**

### EATING

**Brygga** In the centre of Å by the jetty ☎ 76 09 11 21, w lofoten-rorbu.com. In one of Å's newer buildings is a cosy bar, with seagull-egg bar snacks, and the town's only restaurant to speak of. It serves very good seafood, with lunch specials for 125kr, and dinner main courses significantly pricier. June–Aug daily 6–10pm.

**Gammelgården Bakery** Sørvågen ☎ 76 09 14 88. Built in the late nineteenth century with a gabled slate roof, this is where the temporary fishery workers were housed in season. Now, it is possibly Lofoten's best bakery, cooking excellent cinnamon buns right in an original, vintage oven. Daily mid-June to mid-Aug Mon–Sun.

# Værøy

The second most southerly of the Lofoten islands, **VÆRØY** is just 8km long, with a slender, lightly populated, grassy-green coastal strip that ends suddenly in the steep, bare mountains that backbone the island. The weather out here in Lofoten's remote isles is uncommonly mild throughout the year, potential **hiking routes** are ubiquitous, and the occasional beach glorious and deserted. Værøy's few kilometres of roads primarily connect the farmsteads of the plain, but one squeezes through the mountains to wiggle along a portion of the west coast. The island is, however, best explored on foot, either along the steep (and sometimes dangerous) footpaths of the mountains, or on the easier and clearer paths that lead out along the Nupsneset promontory.

**5**

### THE PUFFIN DOGS OF MÅSTAD

The inhabitants of Måstad, on Værøy, varied their fishy diet by catching puffins from the neighbouring sea cliffs, then curing the bird meat in salt. They were assisted in this arduous task by specially bred dogs known as puffin dogs, or **Lundehund**. In order to improve their stability and traction on the steep cliffs, these small (32–38cm high) and innocuous-looking dogs developed several distinctive features, including being six-toed (as opposed to the usual four), which helps them to grip on slippery skerries and wriggle themselves through small spaces. They are also extremely flexible, with legs that bend outwards to the extent that the dog can lay completely prone on its chest (reindeer can perform similar manoeuvres). They can also close their ears against dust and moisture and can bend their heads right round onto their backs. Once reduced to only five remaining dogs, the breed was brought back from near-extinction in the 1960s and now numbers well over a thousand, a quarter of whom live in the United States.

On **Nordland**, the northern section of the island, you can visit a handful of **Viking burial sites**, as well as the oldest church in Lofoten: the wooden, domed **Værøy Kirke** with its fifteenth-century alabaster altarpiece, was transplanted here in 1799 from its original location in Kabelvåg.

The island is well known for its **bird colonies**: Mount Måstadfjell (at 435m) hosts well over one million puffins, eiders and gulls that breed in the summer months, as well as cormorants, terns, kittiwakes, guillemots, rare sea eagles and more recent immigrants like the fulmar and gannet. Værøy's most important **bird cliffs** occupy the southwest corner of the island, but they are much too steep and slippery to approach on foot, so the best bet is to take a **boat trip** (see below).

#### ARRIVAL AND DEPARTURE                                      VÆRØY

**By plane** Flying, of course, is the quickest way to get here: Værøy can be reached from Bodø by the world's most northerly helicopter service (1–2 daily; 25min; ☎ 77 60 83 00, ⌨ lufttransport.no), which costs 827kr one-way.
**By car/ferry** Værøy is one of the most time-consuming of the Lofoten islands to reach: indeed, unless you're careful, the irregular ferry schedules can leave you stranded here for a couple of days. Hurtigruten boats (☎ 90 62 07 00, ⌨ torghattennord.no) dock at Værøy's southeastern tip,

about 800m from the tourist office. From Bodø to Værøy, the fare is 156kr per person and 558kr for a car and driver; from Moskenes it takes under 2hr and costs 168/604kr. The 2hr journey between Værøy and Røst, costs 87/300kr. From June to Aug advance ferry reservations are advised, but for the rest of the year the ferries are first-come, first-served, so it's a good idea to turn up at least an hour before departure.

#### INFORMATION

**Tourist office** Inside the Husfliden shop in the centre of Værøy's main settlement (mid-June to mid-Aug Mon–Fri 9.30am–3pm; mid-Aug to mid-June Mon–Fri 9am–2pm; ☎ 75 42 06 14). They can advise on boat tours and

accommodation – though you would be foolhardy not to arrange this beforehand, especially as the maps they hand out here are absurdly outdated.

#### ACTIVITIES

**Bike rental** Cycles can be rented next to the supermarket in the centre of Værøy town.
**Boat trips** Several island operators run birdwatching boat trips: for a 3hr excursion expect to pay between 350kr and 450kr. You can book at the tourist office, or just ask around to see which boats are going out.

**Hikes** The most popular walk on the island is the hiking trail that leads along the west coast from the end of the road about 6km north of Sørland along the Isthmus of Eidet to the isolated village of Måstad, abandoned in the 1950s; it's a tricky walk which takes 2–3hr each way.

#### ACCOMMODATION AND EATING

**Gamle Prestegård** Værøy harbour ☎ 76 09 54 11, ⌨ prestegaarden.no. Set on the northern side of the

island, this very well-kept guesthouse ("The Old Vicarage") has eleven rooms, several of which are singles that share a bath. The nicest rooms are in the "Hønsehuset" building, done out from top to bottom in local pine. There's a similarly rustic restaurant on site with exposed beams and the original nineteenth-century decor. **690kr**

**Lofoten Værøy Brygge** Værøy harbour ✆ 76 09 50 10, ⊛ lvb.no. Choose from spacious, modern but rather soulless rooms built in 2009, or more rustic accommodation in half a dozen large red cabins in the nearby *Kornelius Kro*.

The suite-type cabins are big, but with small bathrooms, or go for the "Barbecue cabin", which can sleep an extended family and features a burbling wood-fired seawater hot-tub. There's a modern seafood restaurant on site that offers an evening buffet for 250kr, though service is somewhat lacking. Rooms **1350kr**, cabins **1240kr**, barbecue cabin **3500kr**

# Røst

With a population of just 750, the island of **RØST** is even smaller than neighbouring Værøy, its smattering of lonely farmsteads dotted over a flat, marshy landscape interrupted by dozens of tiny lakes. This is about as remote as you can get along the Norwegian coast and it is the most southerly island in the Lofoten archipelago. It was here in 1431 that the lifeboat of a shipwrecked Italian nobleman, Pietro Querini, was washed up after weeks at sea. Querini, and his fellow Venetians, stayed the winter and his written account is one of the few surviving records of everyday life in Nordland in the Middle Ages. This connection might in part explain why today over ninety percent of the island's air-dried cod is exported to Italy (Røst is said to produce the best stockfish in Lofoten). The church on the north side of the island, consecrated in 1900, features one of the five altar triptychs – restored several times over – which was given to Norway by Princess Elizabeth of the Netherlands in 1520.

## ARRIVAL AND DEPARTURE                                          RØST

**By plane** Røst has a tiny airstrip with flights from Bodø, which take just 30min (1–2 daily; around 390kr one-way; ⊛ dat.dk).

**By ferry** Ferries dock at a tiny, craggy outcrop on the island's southwest corner, 3km from the main village. Torghatten Nord (✆ 90 62 07 00, ⊛ torghattennord.no), runs car ferries from Bodø once or twice daily, calling at Moskenes: the fare from Bodø to Røst is 190kr (688kr with a car).

## INFORMATION AND TOURS

**Tourist office** By the jetty (late June to late Aug Mon–Sat 10am–1.30pm & usually when the boat comes in; ✆ 76 05 05 15).

**Island tour** For an informative, informal tour (150kr; 45min) of the island, contact Steinar Greger (✆ 92 68 56 01, ✉ sjgreger@johngreger.no), a gregarious local who runs his family's stockfish company and knows all Værøy's nooks and crannies.

## ACCOMMODATION AND EATING

**Kårøy Rorbucamping** Kårøy harbour ✆ 76 09 62 38, ⊛ karoy.no. Originally built as *rorbu* for the fishermen of the stockfish factory, these plain and inexpensive lodgings have 2-, 4- and 6-bed rooms, all with shared showers, toilets and kitchens. There's also a small campsite. Located on Kårøy island, a few minutes' boat ride from Røst harbour: the campsite will organize transport over from Røst. Open May–Aug. Tents **150kr**, rooms **500kr**

**Røst Bryggehotell** At the Kårøysundet pier ✆ 76 05 08 00, ⊛ rostbryggehotell.no. This small hotel has sixteen plain rooms with the ocean and the mountains as your closest neighbours. They rent out boats (600kr/day), kayaks (400/day) and cycles (100kr/day), as well as organizing boat trips to the sea-bird colonies on the jagged islets to the southwest of Røst. There's also an outdoor wood-heated jacuzzi on the quayside, which you can book for several hours for 750kr. **1090kr**

**Skomværkroa** At the harbour ✆ 92 68 56 01. Great little café serving coffee and waffles. Opening hours vary.

# North Norway

MIDNIGHT SUN, SVALBARD

# North Norway

Karl Baedeker, writing a hundred years ago about Norway's remote northern provinces of Troms and Finnmark, observed that they "possess attractions for the scientific traveller and the sportsman, but can hardly be recommended for the ordinary tourist" – a comment that isn't too wide off the mark even today. These are enticing lands, no question: the natural environment they offer is stunning in its extremes, with the midnight sun and polar night further defamiliarizing the often lunar-like terrain. But the travelling can be hard going, the individual sights geographically disparate and, once you do reach them, rather subdued in their appeal.

**6**

The intricate, fretted coastline of **Troms** has shaped its history since the days when powerful Viking lords operated a trading empire from the region's islands. And while half the population still lives offshore in dozens of tiny fishing villages, the place to aim for first is **Tromsø**, the so-called "Capital of the North" and a lively university town where King Håkon and his government proclaimed a "Free Norway" in 1940, before fleeing into exile. Beyond Tromsø, the long trek north and east begins in earnest as you enter **Finnmark**, a vast wilderness covering 48,000 square kilometres, but home to just two percent of the Norwegian population. Much of this land was laid to waste during World War II, the combined effect of the Russian advance and the retreating German army's scorched-earth policy, and it's now possible to drive for hours without coming across a building much more than sixty years old.

The first obvious target in Finnmark is **Alta**, a sprawling settlement – relatively speaking, of course – and an important crossroads famous for its prehistoric rock carvings. From here, most visitors make straight for the steely cliffs of **Nordkapp** (the North Cape), ostensibly but not actually Europe's northernmost point, with or without a detour to the likeable port of **Hammerfest**, and leave it at that; but some doggedly press on to **Kirkenes**, the last town before the Russian border, where you feel as if you're about to drop off the end of the world.

The main alternative from Alta is to travel inland across the eerily endless scrubland of the **Finnmarksvidda**, where winter temperatures can plummet to -35°C. This high plateau is the last stronghold of the **Sámi**, northern Norway's indigenous people, some of whom still live a semi-nomadic life tied to the movement of their reindeer herds. You'll spot Sámi in their brightly coloured traditional gear all across the region, but most notably in the remote towns of **Kautokeino** and **Karasjok**, strange, disconsolate places in the middle of the plain.

Finally, and even more adventurously, there is the **Svalbard** archipelago, whose icy mountains rise out of the Arctic Ocean over 800km north of mainland Norway. Once

ZODIAC EXCURSION ON ISFJORDEN, SVALBARD

# Highlights

**❶ Emmas Drømmekjøkken, Tromsø** Try the Arctic specialities – reindeer and char for instance – at this exquisite Tromsø restaurant. **See p.342**

**❷ Alta's prehistoric rock carvings** Follow the trail round northern Europe's most extensive collection of prehistoric rock carvings. **See p.347**

**❸ Juhls' Silver Gallery, Kautokeino** The first and foremost of Finnmark's Sámi-influenced jewellery-makers and designers. **See p.349**

**❹ Repvåg** An old fishing station with traditional red-painted wooden buildings on stilts, framed by a picture-postcard setting. **See p.358**

**❺ The Hurtigruten** Cruise around the tippity top of the European continent and across the Barents Sea – the most remote and spectacular section of this long-distance coastal boat trip. **See p.362**

**❻ End of the World Guesthouse** Wonderful, charming new B&B set right out at the region's most northerly stretches in laconic, iconic Gamvik. **See p.364**

**❼ Wildlife safaris on the Svalbard archipelago** Take a snowmobile or Zodiac boat out in this remote archipelago to find over one hundred species of migratory birds as well as seals, walruses, whales, arctic foxes, reindeer and polar bears. **See p.374**

HIGHLIGHTS ARE MARKED ON THE MAP ON P.334

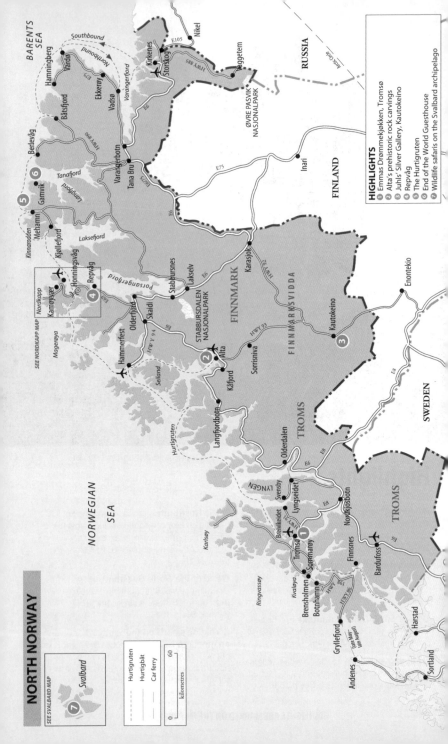

# NORTH NORWAY

## SEE SVALBARD MAP

Svalbard ⑦

- - - - Hurtigruten
——— Hurtigbåt
——— Car ferry

0 ⎯⎯ 60
kilometres

### HIGHLIGHTS

① Emmas Drømmekjøkken, Tromsø
② Alta's prehistoric rock carvings
③ Juhls' Silver Gallery, Kautokeino
④ Repvåg
⑤ The Hurtigruten
⑥ End of the World Guesthouse
⑦ Wildlife safaris on the Svalbard archipelago

BARENTS SEA

Hamningberg
Vardø
Vadsø
Ekkerøy
Vadsø
Båtsfjord
Berlevåg ⑥
Gamvik ⑤
Mehamn
Kjøllefjord
Kinnarodden
Kvalsund
Honningsvåg
Repvåg ④
Nordkapp
Kamøyvær
Magerøya
SEE NORDKAPP MAP
Hammerfest
Seiland
Langfjordbotn
Hurtigruten

NORWEGIAN SEA

Karlsøy
Ringvassøya
Kvaløya
Brensholmen
Botnhamn
Tromsø
Sommarøy
Breivikedet
Svensby
Lyngseidet
LYNGEN
Olderdalen
Skaidi
Olderfjord
Stabbursnes
STABBURSDALEN NASJONALPARK
Alta ②
Kåfjord
Sortisniva

Gryllefjord
(late May–
late August)
Andenes
Finnsnes
Bardufoss
Nordkjosbotn
TROMS

Harstad
Sortland

FINNMARK

FINNMARKSVIDDA

Karasjok
Kautokeino ③

Lakselv
Stabbursnes
Porsangerfjord
Laksefjord
Tanafjord
Tana Bru
Varangerbotn
Varangerfjord

Kirkenes
Storskog
Nikel
Riggetem
RUSSIA

ØVRE PASVIK NASJONALPARK

FINLAND

Inari
Enontekio
Enontekio

SWEDEN

Southbound
Northbound

the exclusive haunt of trappers, fishermen and coal miners, Svalbard now makes a tidy income from adventure tourism, offering everything from guided glacier walks to hard-core snowmobile excursions and husky riding: journeys that will take you out to places as remote and wild a spot as you're ever likely to get in your life. You can fly there independently from Tromsø and Oslo at surprisingly bearable prices, though most people opt for a package tour.

As for **accommodation**, all the major settlements have at least a couple of hotels and the main roads are sprinkled with campsites. If you have a tent and a well-insulated sleeping bag, you can, in theory, bed down more or less where you like, but the hostility of the climate and the ferocity of the summer mosquitoes, especially in the marshy areas of the Finnmarksvidda, make most people think (at least) twice. There are HI **hostels** at Alta, Karasjok, Kirkenes, Honningsvåg, Mehamn, Harstad, Senja, Skibotndalen and Tromsø.

**6**

## GETTING AROUND
NORTH NORWAY

Public transport in the provinces of Troms and Finnmark is by bus, the Hurtigruten coastal boat and plane – there are no trains to speak of. For all but the most truncated of tours, the best idea is to pick and mix these different forms of transport – for example by flying from Tromsø to Kirkenes and then taking the Hurtigruten back, or vice versa – in order to experience this part of Norway in as many ways as you can. What you should try to avoid is endless doubling-back on the E6, though this is often difficult as it is the only road to run right across the region. To give an idea of the distances involved, from Tromsø it's 400km to Alta, 640km to Nordkapp and 970km to Kirkenes.

### BY PLANE
**Airports** The region has several airports, including those at Alta, Hammerfest, Honningsvåg, Kirkenes, Tromsø and Longyearbyen, on Svalbard.

**Airlines** SAS (ⓦflysas.com) and its subsidiary, Widerøe (ⓦwideroe.no), have the widest range of flights to northern Norway – including a twice-daily route to and from Svalbard – but Norwegian Airlines (ⓦnorwegian.com) chips in too, flying regularly to Tromsø, Alta, Kirkenes, Harstad/Narvik, Bardufoss and Lakselv.

**Fares** Standard return fares are usually expensive, but discounts are frequent and Norwegian Airlines are most economical.

### BY BUS
**Routes** Torghatten Nord (ⓦtorghattennord.no) runs buses north from Bodø and Fauske to Alta in three segments: Bodø to Narvik via Fauske (2 daily; 6hr 15min); Narvik to Tromsø (1–3 daily; 4hr 20min); and Tromsø to Alta (1 daily; 6hr 30min). To get from Narvik to Alta you must change buses at Balsfjord and then Nordkjosbotn. Passengers heading to Nordkapp overnight at Alta, before proceeding on the next leg of the journey north to Honningsvåg, where – from early June to late Aug – they can change onto the connecting bus to Nordkapp. Alta is also where you can pick up local buses to Hammerfest, Kautokeino, Karasjok and Kirkenes.

**Timetables and tickets** Bus timetables are available at most tourist offices and bus stations; they are also available online – Nobina covers Tromsø and its environs (ⓣ177, ⓦtromskortet.no) and Boreal the whole of Finnmark (ⓣ177, ⓦboreal.no). On the longer rides, it's a good idea to buy tickets in advance, or turn up early, as buses fill up fast in the summer.

### BY BOAT
**Hurtigruten coastal boat** A leisurely way to cross the region is on the daily Hurtigruten coastal boat (ⓦhurtigruten.no; see p.30), which takes 40hr to cross the huge fjords between Tromsø and Kirkenes. En route, it calls at eleven ports, mostly remote fishing villages but also Hammerfest and Honningsvåg, where northbound ferries pause for 4hr so that special buses can cart passengers off to Nordkapp and back.

Car and boat travel One especially appealing option, though this has more to do with comfort than speed, is to travel by land and sea. Special deals on the Hurtigruten can make this surprisingly affordable and tourist offices at the Hurtigruten's ports of call will make bookings. If you are renting a car, taking your vehicle onto the Hurtigruten may well work out a lot cheaper than leaving it at your port of embarkation (see p.336).

**Hurtigbåt passenger express boat** At the other end of the nautical extreme, the region has various Hurtigbåt passenger express boat services to some of the smaller settlements in Finnmark, as well as one main one between Tromsø and Harstad, which operates 3–4 times daily (twice at weekends).

### BY CAR
**Driving** Though the E6 and some other main roads are kept open throughout the winter (as far as possible), conditions are not necessarily straightforward: drivers will find the going a little slow as they have to negotiate some pretty

tough terrain, and ice and snow can make the roads treacherous, if not temporarily impassable, at any time. You can cover 250–300km in a day without any problem, but much more and it all becomes rather wearisome. Keep an eye on the fuel indicator too, as petrol stations are confined to the larger settlements and they may be 100– 200km apart. Car repairs can take time since workshops are scarce and parts often have to be ordered from the south. Note also that if you are renting a car, one-way drop-off charges in Norway are invariably exorbitant, often exceeding 1000kr.

**Summer** Be warned that in July and August the E6 north of Alta can get congested with caravans and motorhomes on their way to Nordkapp. You can avoid the crush by starting early or, for that matter, by driving overnight – an eerie experience when it's bright sunlight in the wee hours of the morning.

**Winter** If you're not used to driving in winter conditions, don't start here – especially during the polar night (late Nov to late Jan), which can be extremely disorientating. If you intend to use the region's minor, unpaved roads, be prepared for the worst and take food and drink, warm clothes and a mobile phone.

# Tromsø

Located at the northern end of the E8 some 260km north of Narvik, **TROMSØ** has been referred to, rather farcically, as the "Paris of the North", and while even the tourist office doesn't make any explicit pretence to such grandiose titles today, the city is without question the de facto social and cultural capital of northern Norway. Easily the region's most populous town, its street cred harks back to the Middle Ages and beyond, when seafarers made use of its sheltered harbour, and there's been a church here at least since the thirteenth century. Tromsø received its municipal charter in 1794, when it was primarily a **fishing port** and trading station, and flourished in the middle of the nineteenth century when its seamen ventured north to Svalbard to reap rich rewards hunting arctic fox, polar bears, reindeer, walrus and, most profitable of all, seal. Subsequently, Tromsø became famous as the jumping-off point for a string of Arctic expeditions, its celebrity status assured when the explorer **Roald Amundsen** flew from here to his death somewhere on the Arctic icecap in 1928. Since those heady days, Tromsø has grown into an urbane and likeable small city with a population of 68,000 employed in a wide range of industries and at the university. It's become an important port too, for although the city is some 360km north of the Arctic Circle, its climate is moderated by the Gulf Stream, which sweeps up the Norwegian coast and keeps its harbour ice-free. Give or take the odd museum, the city may fall somewhat short on top-ranking **sights**, but its amiable atmosphere, fine mountain-and-fjord setting, and clutch of lively **restaurants and bars** more than compensate. Scenesters here remain extremely proud of locally grown electro-emo heroes Röyksopp, and the Tromsø's DJ culture is consequently alive and kicking.

The compact centre slopes up from the eastern shores of the hilly island of Tromsøya, connected to the mainland by bridge and tunnel. A five-minute walk from one side to the other, the busiest part of the city centre spreads south from **Stortorget**, the main square, along Storgata, the main street and north–south axis, as far as Kirkegata and the harbourfront.

## Domkirke

Kirkegata 7 • June–Aug Tues–Sat noon–4pm, Sun 10am–4pm; Sept–May Tues–Sat noon–4pm, Sun 10am–2pm • Free

Completed in 1861, the beige Lutheran **Domkirke** (Cathedral), bang in the centre on Kirkegata, bears witness to the prosperity of the town's nineteenth-century merchants, who became rich on the back of the barter trade with Russia. They part-funded the cathedral's construction, the result being the large and handsome structure of today, whose slender spire and dinky little tower pokes high into the sky above the neo-Gothic pointed windows of the nave. The building is now the only wooden cathedral in the country.

## Nordnorsk Kunstmuseum

Sjøgata 1 • Mid-June to mid-Aug daily 11am–6pm; rest of year Mon–Fri 10am–5pm, Sat & Sun noon–5pm • Free • Ⓦ nnkm.no

In a sizeable old building a block east of the cathedral, the **Nordnorsk Kunstmuseum** (Art Museum of Northern Norway) is not a large ensemble, but the second-floor displays of the permanent collection were overhauled when the museum turned 25 in 2010, modernizing the place somewhat. The collection now covers all of Norway's artistic bases, beginning in the nineteenth century with the ingenious landscapes of Thomas Fearnley and Johan Dahl (see p.68) and several Romantic peasant scenes by Adolph Tidemand

6

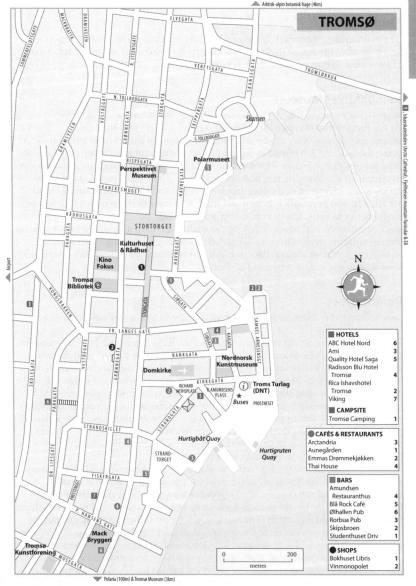

TROMSØ

▲ Arktisk-alpin botanisk hage (4km)

N

| ▮ HOTELS | |
|---|---|
| ABC Hotel Nord | 6 |
| Ami | 3 |
| Quality Hotel Saga | 5 |
| Radisson Blu Hotel Tromsø | 4 |
| Rica Ishavshotel Tromsø | 2 |
| Viking | 7 |

| ▮ CAMPSITE | |
|---|---|
| Tromsø Camping | 1 |

| ● CAFÉS & RESTAURANTS | |
|---|---|
| Arctandria | 3 |
| Aunegården | 1 |
| Emmas Drømmekjøkken | 2 |
| Thai House | 4 |

| ▮ BARS | |
|---|---|
| Amundsen Restauranthus | 4 |
| Blå Rock Café | 5 |
| Ølhallen Pub | 6 |
| Rorbua Pub | 3 |
| Skipsbroen | 2 |
| Studenthuset Driv | 1 |

| ● SHOPS | |
|---|---|
| Bokhuset Libris | 1 |
| Vinmonopolet | 2 |

▼ Polaria (100m) & Tromsø Museum (3km)

(1814–76). There are lots of north Norway landscapes and seascapes here too, including several delightful paintings by Kongsberg-born Otto Sinding (1842–1909) – look out for his *Spring Day in Lofoten* – as well as a whole battery of paintings by the talented and prolific Axel Revold (1887–1962), whose work typically maintains a gentle, heart-warming lyricism. By contrast, Willi Midelfarts (1904–75) was clearly enraged when he painted his bloody *Assault on the House of Karl Liebknecht*, a reference to the murder of one of Germany's leading Marxists in 1919. The museum also owns a handful of minor works by Edvard Munch, including a handsome portrait entitled *Parisian Model*.

## Stortorget

The main square, **Stortorget**, is the site of a daily open-air **market** selling flowers and knick-knacks. The square nudges down towards the waterfront, where fresh fish and prawns are sold direct from inshore fishing boats throughout the summer.

## Perspektivet Museum

Storgata 95 • June–Aug Tues–Sun 11am–5pm; Sept–May Tues–Fri 11am–3pm, Thurs till 7pm • Free • ⓦ perspektivet.no

At the **Perspektivet Museum** the emphasis is on all things local, with a lively programme of temporary exhibitions concerning Tromsø and its inhabitants. In recent years, the museum has turned to focusing on its **photographic collections** – which now total some 400,000 images – even commissioning new works from local photographers to document the changing face of modern Tromsø. The building itself, dating from 1838, is also of interest as the one-time home of the local writer **Cora Sandel** (1880–1974), who was born Sara Fabricius and lived in Tromsø from 1893 to 1905, before shipping out to Paris. Sandel's important works include the *Alberte Trilogy*, a set of semi-autobiographical novels following the trials and tribulations of a young woman as she attempts to establish her own independent identity. The museum has a small section on Sandel on the first floor, but it is confined to a few of her knick-knacks and several photos of her on walkabout in Tromsø.

## Polarmuseet

Søndre Tollbodgate 11 • Daily: March to mid-June & mid-Aug to Sept 11am–5pm; mid-June to mid-Aug 10am–7pm; Oct–Feb 11am–4pm • 50kr • ⓦ polarmuseum.no

Down by the water, an old wooden warehouse holds the city's most engaging museum, the **Polarmuseet** (Polar Museum). The collection begins with a less-than-stimulating series of displays on trapping in the Arctic, but beyond is an outstanding section on Svalbard, including archeological finds retrieved in the 1980s from an eighteenth-century **Russian whaling station**. Most of the artefacts come from graves preserved by permafrost and, among many items, there are combs, leather boots, parts of a sledge, slippers and even – just to prove illicit puffing is not a recent phenomenon – a clay pipe from a period when the Russian company in charge of affairs forbade trappers from smoking. Two other sections on the first floor focus on **seal hunting**, an important part of the local economy until the 1950s.

Upstairs, on the second floor, a further section is devoted to the exploits of one **Henry Rudi** (1889–1970), the so-called "Isbjørnkongen" (Polar Bear King), who spent 27 winters on Svalbard and Greenland, bludgeoning his way through the local wildlife, killing 713 polar bears in the process. Rather more edifying is the extensive display on the polar explorer **Roald Amundsen** (1872–1928), who spent thirty years searching out the secrets of the polar regions (see box opposite). The museum exhibits all sorts of oddments used by Amundsen and his men – from long johns and pipes through to boots and ice picks – but it is the photos that steal the show, providing a fascinating insight into the way Amundsen's polar expeditions were organized and the hardships he and his men

**ROALD AMUNDSEN**

One of Norway's most celebrated sons, **Roald Amundsen** (1872–1928) was intent on becoming a polar explorer from his early teens. He read everything there was to read on the subject, even training as a sea captain in preparation, and, in 1897, embarked with a Belgian expedition upon his first trip to Antarctica. Undeterred by a winter on the ice after the ship broke up, he was soon planning his own expedition. In 1901, he purchased a sealer, the *Gjøa*, in Tromsø, leaving in June 1903 to spend three years sailing and charting the **Northwest Passage** between the Atlantic and the Pacific. The *Gjøa* (now on display in Oslo; see p.84) was the first vessel to complete this extraordinary voyage, which tested Amundsen and his crew to the very limits. Long searched for, the Passage had for centuries been something of a nautical Holy Grail and the voyage's progress – and at times the lack of it – was headline news right across the world.

Amundsen's next target was the North Pole, but during his preparations, in 1909, the American admiral and explorer Robert Peary got there first. Amundsen immediately switched his attention to the **South Pole**, and in 1910 set out in a new ship, the *Fram* (also exhibited in Oslo; see p.84), for the Antarctic, which he reached on December 14, 1911, famously beating the British expedition of Captain Scott by just a couple of weeks.

Neither did Amundsen's ambitions end there: in 1926, he became one of the first men to fly over the North Pole in the airship of the Italian Umberto Nobile, though it was this last expedition that did for Amundsen: in 1928, the Norwegian flew north out of Tromsø in a bid to rescue the stranded Nobile and was never seen again.

6

endured. Amundsen clearly liked having his picture taken, judging from the heroic poses he struck, his derring-do emphasized by the finest set of eyebrows north of Oslo.

Finally, there's another extensive section on Amundsen's contemporary **Fridtjof Nansen** (1861–1930), a polar explorer of similar renown who, in his later years, became a leading figure in international famine relief. In 1895, Nansen and his colleague Hjalmar Johansen made an abortive effort to reach the North Pole by dog sledge after their ship was trapped by pack ice. It took them a full fifteen months to get back to safety, a journey of such epic proportions that tales of it captivated all of Scandinavia.

## Tromsø Kunstforening

Musegata 2 · Wed–Sun noon–5pm · Free · ⓦ tromsokunstforening.no

Just to the south of the town centre, at the upper end of Muségata, the **Tromsø Kunstforening** (Tromsø Art Society) occupies part of a large and attractive Neoclassical building dating from the 1890s. The cultural organization puts on imaginative temporary exhibitions of Norwegian contemporary art with the emphasis on the work of northern Norwegian artists.

## Polaria

Hjalmar Johansens gate 12 · Daily: mid-May to mid-Aug 10am–7pm; mid-Aug to mid-May 11am–5pm · 105kr · ⓦ polaria.no · The complex is 200m south of Tromsø Kunstforening along Storgata

A lavish waterfront complex, **Polaria** deals with all things Arctic. There's an aquarium filled with Arctic species, a 180-degree cinema showing a film on Svalbard shot from a helicopter and several exhibitions on polar research. Parked outside in a glass greenhouse is a 1940s sealing ship, the **M/S Polstjerna**.

## Arktisk-alpin botanisk hage

Breivika · Year-round dawn to dusk · Free · ⓦ uit.no/botanisk · Bus #42

Located next to the University of Tromsø's Breivika campus in the centre of the island 4km north of the centre, the **Arktisk-alpin botanisk hage** (Arctic-Alpine Botanical

Gardens) are the world's most northerly botanical gardens, spanning some five acres of land. There are plants from all continents, with particular strong representation from Siberia, the Himalayas and the Rockies; they all tend to bloom from May to October.

## Tromsø Museum

Lars Thørings veg 10 • June–Aug daily 9am–6pm; rest of year Mon–Fri 9am–4.30pm, Sat noon–3pm, Sun 11am–4pm • 30kr • ⓦ uit.no/tmu • Bus #37 from the centre (every 30min; ⓦ nobina.no)

About 3km south of the centre, near the southern tip of Tromsøya, the **Tromsø Museum** is a historical and ethnographic museum run by the university. It's a varied collection, featuring nature and the sciences downstairs, and culture and history above. Pride of place goes to the **medieval religious carvings**, naïve but evocative pieces retrieved from various northern Norwegian churches. There's also an enjoyable section on the Sámi featuring displays on every aspect of Sámi life – from dwellings, tools and equipment through to traditional costume and hunting techniques. Meanwhile, the aurora borealis exhibit gives a particularly good explanation on exactly why and how the phenomenon exists.

## Ishavskatedralen

Hans Nilsens veg 41 • Mid- to late May daily 3–6pm; June to mid-Aug Mon–Sat 9am–7pm, Sun 1–7pm; mid-Aug to mid-May daily 3/4–6pm • 35kr • ⓦ ishavskatedralen.no • Bus #20, #24 or #28

A few minutes' walk east from the centre, across the spindly, cantilevered Tromsøbrua bridge, rises the desperately modern **Ishavskatedralen** (Arctic Cathedral). Completed in 1965 – and recently renovated – the church maintains a strikingly white, glacier-like appearance, achieved by means of eleven immense triangular concrete sections, representing the eleven Apostles left after the betrayal. The entire east wall is formed by a huge stained-glass window, one of the largest in Europe, and the organ is unusual too, built to represent a ship when viewed from beneath – recalling the tradition, still seen in many a Nordic church, of suspending a ship from the ceiling as a good-luck talisman for seafarers.

## Fjellheisen mountain funicular

Daily every 30min: Feb & March 10am–4pm; April to late May & Sept 10am–5pm; late May to early Aug 10am–1am; Aug 10am–10pm; Oct–Dec 1am–4pm; • 120kr • ⓦ fjellheisen.no • Bus #26 from the city centre or a 15min walk southeast of the Ishavskatedralen

Every half-hour the **Fjellheisen mountain funicular**, 3km from the centre across the bridge, whisks up to 27 passengers up to the top of **Mount Storsteinen**. From the 421m summit, the views of the city and its surroundings are extensive and it's a smashing spot to catch the midnight sun; there's even a café at the top. Note that mountain funicular services are suspended during inclement weather.

### ARRIVAL AND DEPARTURE
### TROMSØ

**By plane** The airport is 5km west of the centre on the other side of Tromsøya. Frequent Flybussen (Mon–Fri 5.30am–midnight every 15min–1hr, Sat 5.30am–4.40pm roughly hourly, Sun 10.20am–midnight hourly; 60kr) run into the city, stopping at the *Rica Ishavshotel* on Sjøgata and at most central hotels. A taxi to the centre will cost between 120–150kr.

**By bus** Long-distance buses pull in at the stops on Prostneset, metres from the Hurtigruten quay. Torghatten (ⓦ tromskortet.no) services run to Alta (1–2 daily; 6hr 30min) and Narvik (2–4 daily; 4hr 15min).

**By boat** The Hurtigruten coastal boat (ⓦ hurtigruten.com)

docks in the town centre beside the Prostneset quay at the foot of Kirkegata, while Hurtigbåt services (ⓦ tromskortet .no) arrive at the jetty about 150m to the south. Northbound, the Hurtigruten leaves Tromsø for Hammerfest daily at 6.30pm (11hr); southbound it sails at 1.30am, arriving in Harstad 6hr 30min later. The main Hurtigbåt passenger express boat service, meanwhile, links Tromsø with Harstad (2–5 daily; 2hr 45min). For Lofoten, it's quickest and easiest if you take the Hurtigbåt to Harstad, then the bus.

**By car** Cars in Tromsø can be rented from Europcar, Alkeveien 5, and at the airport (☎ 77 67 56 00); Hertz, Fridtjof Nansenplass 3c, and at the airport (☎ 48 26 20 00).

# ARCTIC PHENOMENA

On and above the **Arctic Circle**, an imaginary line drawn round the earth at latitude 66.5 degrees north, there is a period around midsummer during which the sun never makes it below the horizon, even at midnight – hence the **midnight sun**. On the Arctic Circle itself, this only happens on one night of the year – at the summer solstice – but the further north you go, the greater the number of nights without darkness: in Bodø, it's from the first week of June to early July; in Tromsø from late May to late July; in Alta, from the third week in May to the end of July; in Hammerfest, mid-May to late July; and in Nordkapp, early May to the end of July. Obviously, the midnight sun is best experienced on a clear night, but fog or cloud can turn the sun into a glowing, red ball – a spectacle that can be wonderful but also strangely uncanny. All the region's tourist offices have the exact dates of the midnight sun, though note that these are calculated at sea level; climb up a hill and you can extend the dates by a day or two. The converse of all this is the **polar night**, a period of constant darkness either side of the winter solstice; again the further north of the Arctic Circle you are, the longer this lasts.

The Arctic Circle also marks the typical southern limit of the **northern lights**, or **aurora borealis**, though this extraordinary phenomenon has been seen as far south as latitude 40 degrees north – roughly the position of New York or Ankara. Caused by the bombardment of the atmosphere by electrons, carried away from the sun by the solar wind, the northern lights take various forms and are highly mobile – either flickering in one spot or travelling across the sky. At relatively low latitudes hereabouts, the aurora is tilted at an angle and is often coloured red – the sagas tell of Vikings being half scared to death by them – but nearer the pole, they hang like gigantic luminous curtains, often tinted greenish blue. Naturally enough, there's no predicting when the northern lights will occur. They are most likely to come out during the darkest period (between November and February) – though they can be seen as early as late August and as late as mid-April. On a clear night the fiery ribbons can be strangely humbling.

## GETTING AROUND

**By bus** For Tromsø's outlying attractions you'll need to catch a municipal bus (☎177, ⊚tromskortet.no). The standard, flat-rate fare is 28kr.

**By taxi** Tromsø Taxi ☎77 60 30 10 (24hr).

**By bike** Bikes can be rented from Tromsø Natur og Fritid, Sjøgata 14 (⊚tromsonaturogfritid.no), which has touring cycles from 230kr/day.

## INFORMATION

**Tourist office** Kirkegata 2, a few paces from the Prostneset quay (mid-May to Aug Mon–Fri 9am–7pm, Sat & Sun 10am–4pm; rest of year Mon–Fri 9am–4pm, Sat 10am–4pm, plus Jan & Feb Sun 11am–3.30pm; ☎77 61 00 00, ⊚visittromso.no). It issues free town maps, has a small list of B&Bs (see p.342), and provides oodles of local information, including details of bus and boat sightseeing trips around neighbouring islands.

## OUTDOOR ACTIVITIES

**Diving and sea rafting** Dykkersenteret AS, Stakkevollveien 72 (☎77 69 66 00, ⊚dykkersentret.no), organizes guided diving tours to local wrecks in the surrounding fjords. Also runs fishing and midnight-sun excursions and offers equipment rental.

**Hiking** Troms Turlag, next door to the tourist office at Kirkegata 2 (Wed noon–4pm, Thurs noon–6pm, Fri noon–2pm; ☎77 68 51 75, ⊚turistforeningen.no/troms), is a DNT affiliate with bags of information on local hiking trails and DNT huts.

**Wilderness tours** Among several wilderness-tour specialists, Tromsø Villmarkssenter (Tromsø Wilderness Centre; ☎77 69 60 02, ⊚villmarkssenter.no) offers a wide range of activities from guided glacier walks, kayak paddling and mountain climbing in summer to ski trips and dog-sled rides in winter. Overnight trips staying in a *lavvo* (a Sámi tent) can also be arranged. It is run by Tove Sorensen and Tore Albrigtsen – and their several hundred Alaskan huskies – Norway's most experienced dog-sled racers. The centre is located about 6km from downtown Tromsø at Straumsvegen 603, beyond the airport on the island of Kvaløya.

## ACCOMMODATION

Tromsø has a good supply of modern, central **hotels**, though the majority occupy chunky concrete high-rises whose exterior may or may not be indicative of what lies await inside. Less expensive – and sometimes more distinctive – are the

**6**

town's **guesthouses**; there's also a rudimentary HI **hostel**. In addition, the tourist office has a small list of **B&Bs**, but most are stuck out in the suburbs. Tromsø is a popular destination, so advance reservation is recommended, especially in the summer.

## HOTELS
**ABC Hotel Nord** Parkgata 4 ☎77 66 83 00, ⓦhotellnord.no. Though Tromsø no longer has an HI hostel, this budget hotel is aimed at backpackers and students (with discounts for the latter), and offers an unbeatable central location three blocks west of the cathedral on Storgata. Rooms feature free calls to Norwegian landlines, and there is free parking and use of the well-appointed kitchen. Cycle rental 150kr/day. **875kr**
**Ami** Skolegata 24 ☎77 62 10 00, ⓦamihotel.no. With seventeen simple rooms offering significantly more style than other spots in this price range, this guesthouse/hotel is set in a period wooden villa behind the town centre and offers wide views over the city from the hillside. Wi-fi access and breakfast included in price. **750kr**
**Quality Hotel Saga** Richard Withsplass 2 ☎77 60 70 00, ⓦchoicehotels.no. Although there has been some Ikea-ization at this mid-sized, 1960s chain hotel, renovated in 2010, the public areas remain reassuringly old-fashioned with lots of pine (rather than chipboard), while most of the 103 rooms have at least a bit of pizzazz. Ask for a room on a high floor for views right onto the Domkirke. Set smack in the centre of town. **1295kr**
**Radisson Blu Hotel Tromsø** Sjøgata 7 ☎77 60 00 00, ⓦradissonblu.com. The largest hotel in town – and a very popular one – occupying two large ten-storey towers at the harbour. The rooms, which had a refit a few years ago, have been kitted out in two styles, Arctic (calming white, orange and green finishes) and Chilli (somewhat warmer red

tones); the Superior ones (as well as the gym and sauna) have cracking views of the harbour. Ultra-efficient service, and free wi-fi to boot. Downstairs is the lively and well-known (to Norwegians, at least) *Rorbua* pub, which occasionally features live music. **1195kr**
★ **Rica Ishavshotel Tromsø** Fr. Langes gate 2 ☎77 66 64 00, ⓦrica.no. Perched on the harbourfront a few metres from the Hurtigruten dock, this imaginatively designed hotel is partly built in the style of a ship, complete with a sort of crow's-nest bar. Lovely rooms – half of them are singles, thanks to such a big trade in business travellers here – and unbeatable views over the harbour with the mountains glinting behind make it the best setting in town. Fourth-floor bar has some breathtaking views. **1495kr**
**Viking** Grønnegata 18 ☎77 64 77 30, ⓦviking-hotell.no. The 24 bright and modern rooms at this breezy guesthouse have considerably more energy than most other places in town. They also have several contemporary apartment-style rooms with full kitchens and large living spaces. Centrally located near the Mack brewery. **980kr**

## CAMPSITE
**Tromsø Camping** Elvestrandvegen ☎77 63 80 37, ⓦtromsocamping.no. Reasonably handy waterside site about 2km east of the Arctic Cathedral (Ishavskatedralen), on the mainland side of the main bridge, with 55 modern and "rustic" cabins. Open year-round. Take bus #20 or #24. Cabins from **1049kr**, tent pitches for two people from **130kr**

## EATING, DRINKING AND NIGHTLIFE
With a clutch of first-rate **restaurants**, several enjoyable **cafés** and a great supply of late-night **bars**, Tromsø is at least as well served as any comparably sized Norwegian city. The best of the cafés and restaurants are concentrated in the vicinity of the Domkirke, and most of the livelier bars – many of which sell Mack, the local brew – are in the centre, too.

## CAFÉS AND RESTAURANTS
★ **Arctandria** Strandtorget 1 ☎77 60 07 20, ⓦskarven.no. Some of the best food in town. The upstairs restaurant serves a superb range of fish, with the emphasis on Arctic species, and there's also reindeer, whale and seal; main courses start at around 245kr (or 195kr if you're going vegetarian). If you've come on an empty stomach, try their five-course Mack Menu (595kr), with every course cooked in some capacity with local beer. Prices are somewhat cheaper downstairs at the café-bar *Vertshuset Skarven*, where there's a slightly less varied menu. Mon–Sat 4pm–midnight.
**Aunegården** Sjøgata 29 ☎77 65 12 34 ⓦaunegarden.no. Cosy and popular café-restaurant within the listed late

nineteenth-century Aunegården building, which was set up as a butcher in 1830. All the standard Norwegian dishes are served, including stockfish, at moderate prices (mains 108–157kr), and the triad of rather more controversial dishes – whale, seal and shark – also make an appearance. Still, these are nothing when compared with the cakes – wonderful confections, which are made at their own bakery. Weep with pleasure as you nibble at the cheesecake – then weep with pain as you realize that pleasure just cost you a dear 69kr. Mon–Sat 10.30am–11pm, Sun noon–6pm.
★ **Emmas Drømmekjøkken** Kirkegata 8 ☎77 63 77 30, ⓦwww.emmasdrommekjokken.no. Much praised in the national press as a gourmet treat, "Emma's dream

**6**

kitchen" lives up to its name, with an imaginative and wide-ranging menu focused on Norwegian produce. The grilled arctic char with gorgonzola sauce and cowberries is a treat as is the delicious Tana reindeer fillet with port sauce and roasted garlic. Excellent service in smart premises. Main courses are 335kr and up. Reservations recommended. Mon–Sat from 6pm; closed Sun.

**Thai House** Storgata 22 ☎77 67 05 26, ⊛thaihouse .no. Decent Thai cooking with the welcome inclusion of some excellent fish and vegetable dishes; the Thai spicy salads are especially good, as are the soups, though prices aren't cheap, with mains from around 220kr). Daily noon–11pm.

## BARS

**Amundsen Restauranthus** Storgata 42 ☎77 68 52 34, ⊛arh.no. Named after the Norwegian explorer who stayed in this building when he lived in Tromsø, this trendy, colourfully decorated bar is Tromsø's most gay-friendly nightspot. Mon 3pm–midnight, Tues–Thurs 1pm–1.30am, Fri & Sat 11am–3am, Sun 3–11pm.

**Blå Rock Café** Strandgata 14 ☎77 61 00 20, ⊛blarock .no. Definitely the place to go for loud rock music. Also features regular live acts, plus the best burgers in town (try the amazing blue-cheese Astroburger). They serve several dozen beers, most priced at around 60kr. Mon–Thurs 11.30am–2am, Fri & Sat 11.30am–3.30am, Sun 1pm–2am.

**Ølhallen Pub** Storgata 4 ☎77 62 45 80, ⊛olhallen.no. Solid (some might say stolid) basement pub adjoining the Mack brewery, whose various ales are its speciality. It's the first pub in town to start serving – and the earliest to close – and so only pulls in the serious drinkers. Mon–Thurs 9am–5pm, Fri 9am–6pm, Sat 9am–3pm.

**Rorbua Pub** Søren Fløttmanns plass ☎77 75 90 86,

⊛rorbuapub.no. Known all over the country thanks to its long-time home as a popular weekly talk show, *Du skal høre mye* ("You'll Hear a Lot"). Presided over by a mammoth stuffed polar bear, this timbered spot calls to mind a drunken fisherman's cabin from times of yore.

**Skipsbroen** Rica Ishavshotel, Fr. Langes gate 2 ☎77 66 64 00, ⊛rica.no. Inside the *Rica Ishavshotel* (see p.342), this smart little bar overlooks the waterfront from on high – it occupies the top of a slender tower with wide windows and sea views. Relaxed atmosphere but lots of tourists. Mon–Thurs 6pm–1.30am, Fri & Sat 3pm–3am; closed Sun.

**Studenthuset Driv** Søndre Tollbodgate 3b ☎77 60 07 76, ⊛driv.no. Built in the early 1900s as a fisherman's warehouse, and now dining out on its exposed beams and planking, this three-tiered student hangout never wants for its share of barflies. Wed & Thurs there are live concerts (cover from 30–160kr), while Fri & Sat the disco (cover 40kr) crowd takes over. Come early to snag a seat on the benches outside; come late to watch the pick-up games begin. Mon–Thurs noon–2am, Fri & Sat noon–3.30am.

## ENTERTAINMENT

**Kino Fokus** ☎90 88 99 00, ⊛tromsokino.no. The main cinema is where you'll find many students and sober locals looking to catch up on some culture. They tend to feature Hollywood box office hits side by side with a surprising number of domestically produced cinematic fare. The odd European art-house flick is added in from time to time for good measure.

**Kulturhuset** Erling Bangsunds plass 1 ☎77 79 16 66, ⊛kulturhuset.tr.no. The principal venue for cultural events of all kinds, this large space beside Grønnegata tends to focus on live Nordic music groups, though there are also touring dance troupes and the odd musical revue as well.

## SHOPPING

**Bokhuset Libris** Storgata 86 ☎77 68 30 36, ⊛libris.no. Hardly the biggest bookshop in Norway, but this family-owed franchise of the big chain is Tromsø's best, with a very good selection of English-language publications. Mon–

Thurs 9am–6pm, Fri 9am–4.30pm, Sat 10am–4pm.

**Vinmonopolet** Grønnegata 64. Effectively the only place in town to pick up hard liquor; also stocks Tromsø's largest selection of wines. Mon–Fri 10am–6pm, Sat 10am–3pm.

## DIRECTORY

**Internet** Free access at Tromsø Bibliotek, on Grønnegata near Stortorget (Mon–Thurs 9am–7pm, Fri 9am–5pm, Sat 11am–3pm, Sun noon–4pm).

**Pharmacy** Vitusapotek Svanen, opposite the *Radisson SAS*

*Hotel* at Fr. Langes gate 9 (Mon–Fri 8.30am–4.30pm, Sat 10am–2pm).

**Post office** Main office at Strandgata 41 (Mon–Fri 8am–6pm, Sat 10am–3pm).

# West from Tromsø: Kvaløya and Sommarøy

Heading west from Tromsø towards Andenes (see p.307), Highway 862 crosses the Sandnessundet straits to reach the mountainous island of **Kvaløya**, whose three distinct parts are joined by a couple of narrow isthmuses. On the far side of the straits, the highway meanders south offering lovely fjord and mountain views en route to the Brensholmen–Botnhamn car ferry (see below), about 60km from Tromsø. From Botnhamn, it's a further 160km to Gryllefjord, where a second car ferry (see below) takes you across to Andenes on Vesterålen (see p.307). The pretty route makes a great little journey in itself, and breaking up the trip on the tiny islet of **Sommarøy**, linked to Kvaløya by a causeway that branches off Highway 862 a few kilometres short of Brensholmen, is a good option, where you can stay at a fetching little waterside *hytte* at the *Sommarøy Arctic Hotel*, then hop into one of their wooden outdoor hot-tubs for a Nordic jacuzzi session.

**6**

### ARRIVAL AND DEPARTURE            WEST FROM TROMSØ: KVALØYA AND SOMMARØY

**Car ferries** Senjafergene (☎99 48 57 50, ⓦsenjafergene .no) operate the Brensholmen–Botnhamn (May–Aug 5–7 daily; 45min) and Gryllefjord–Andenes (late May to mid-June & mid- to late Aug 2 daily; mid-June to early Aug 3 daily; 1hr 40min; reservations advised) car ferries.

### ACCOMMODATION AND EATING

**Sommarøy Arctic Hotel** Sommarøy ☎77 66 40 00, ⓦsommaroy.no. This relaxing hotel offers accommodation in the main building, plus high-quality, well-equipped seashore cabins for up to ten people (2600kr/day). The restaurant is excellent too, particularly its Arctic specialities, and there are two traditional *badestamp* – wooden hot-tubs seating up to ten people – one inside and one outdoors, next to the ocean. Rooms **1090kr**, six-berth cabins **1590kr**

# The road to Finnmark

**Beyond Tromsø**, the vast sweep of the northern landscape slowly unfolds, with silent fjords cutting deep into the coastline beneath ice-tipped peaks which themselves fade into the high plateau of the interior. This forbidding, elemental terrain is interrupted by the occasional valley, where those few souls hardy enough to make a living in these parts struggle on – often subsisting by dairy farming. Curiously enough, one particular problem for the farmers here has been the abundance of Siberian garlic (*Allium sibiricum*): the cows love the stuff – it tastes much more like a chive than garlic – but if they eat a lot of it, the milk they produce tastes of onions.

Slipping along the valleys and traversing the mountains in between, the **E8** and then the **E6** follow the coast pretty much all the way from Tromsø to Alta, some 410km – and about a seven-hour drive – to the north. Drivers can save around 100km (although not necessarily time and certainly not money) by turning off the E8 25km south of Tromsø onto **Highway 91** – a quieter, even more scenic route, offering extravagant fjord and mountain views. Highway 91 begins by cutting across the rocky peninsula that backs onto Tromsø to reach the **Breivikeidet–Svensby car ferry** (see below), a magnificent twenty-minute journey over to the glaciated Lyngen peninsula. From the Svendsby ferry dock, it's just 24km over the Lyngen to the **Lyngseidet–Olderdalen car ferry** (see below), by means of which you can rejoin the E6 at Olderdalen, some 220km south of Alta. This route is at its most spectacular between Svendsby and Lyngseidet, with the road nudging along a narrow channel flanked by the imposing peaks of the Lyngsalpene, or Lyngen Alps. Beyond Olderdalen, the E6 eventually enters the province of **Finnmark** as it approaches the hamlet of **Langfjordboten**, at the head of the long and slender Langfjord. Thereafter, the road sticks tight against the coast en route to Kåfjord.

### GETTING AROUND                                      THE ROAD TO FINNMARK

**Car ferries** Breivikeidet–Svensby car ferry (hourly; Mon– Fri 6.30am–10.30pm, Sat 8.10am–8.10pm, Sun 8.10am–9.55pm; 25min; 87kr car and driver; ☎77 71 14 00, ⓦbjorklid.no); Lyngseidet–Olderdalen car ferry (hourly; Mon–Fri 7.20am–9.05pm, Sat 9.05am–7.20pm, Sun 9.05am–9.05pm; 40min; 122kr car and driver; ☎77 71 14 00, ⓦbjorklid.no).

## Kåfjord

Some 60km from Langfordboten is the tiny village of **KÅFJORD**, whose sympathetically restored nineteenth-century **church** was built by the English company who operated the area's copper mines until they were abandoned as uneconomic in the 1870s. The Kåfjord itself is a narrow and sheltered arm of the Altafjord, which was used as an Arctic hideaway by the *Tirpitz* and other German battleships during World War II.

## 6 | Alta

Some 20km from Kåfjord, **ALTA**'s primary claim to fame is the most extensive area of **prehistoric rock carvings** in northern Europe, which are impressive enough to have been designated a UNESCO World Heritage Site. At first blush, however, the view of the town is somewhat less than encouraging. With a population of around 20,000, it comprises a string of unenticing modern settlements that spread along the E6 for several kilometres. The ugliest part is **Alta Sentrum**, now befuddled by a platoon of soulless concrete blocks. World War II polished off much of the local Sámi culture that used to thrive here, as well as destroying all the old wooden buildings that once clustered together in Alta's oldest district, **Bossekop**, where Dutch whalers settled in the seventeenth century.

That being said, the settlement is an excellent place to base oneself in for explorations out to the Finnmark plateau. The area around here gets very green in the summer months, and hiking, canyoning and riverboat safaris are all on offer. In the wintertime, the stable (if very cold) climate allows for plenty of **outdoor activities**, including dog-sledding, snowmobiling, cross-country skiing and chasing the northern lights. Additionally, Europe's largest dog-sled race, the **Finnmarksløpet** (🌐 finnmarkslopet.no), is put on here in mid-March, complemented by a big week-long cultural celebration, the Borealis Winter Festival.

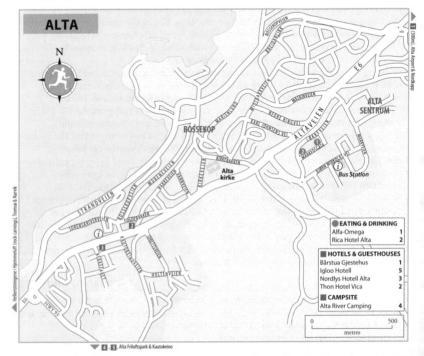

## Alta's prehistoric rock carvings and the Alta Museum

Altaveien 19 • May to mid-June daily 8am–5pm; mid-June to Aug daily 8am–8pm; Sept–April Mon–Fri 8am–3pm, Sat & Sun 11am–4pm • 90kr • ⓦ alta.museum.no • A limited local bus service – *bybussen* – runs from the bus station south to Bossekop and the museum (Mon–Sat every 30min–1hr; 10min); alternatively call Alta Taxi (☎ 78 43 53 11)

Accessed along the E6, Alta's prehistoric rock carvings, the **Helleristningene i Hjemmeluft**, form part of the **Alta Museum**. Count on at least an hour to view the carvings and appreciate the site. A visit begins in the museum building, 5km from town, where there's a wealth of background information on the carvings in particular and on prehistoric Finnmark in general. It also offers a potted history of the Alta area, with exhibitions on the salmon-fishing industry, copper mining and so forth.

The **rock carvings** themselves extend down the hill from the museum to the fjordside along a clear and easy-to-follow footpath and boardwalk that stretches for just under 3km. On the trail, there are a dozen or so **vantage points** offering close-up views of the carvings, recognizable through highly stylized representations of boats, animals and people picked out in red pigment (the colours have been retouched by researchers). They make up an extraordinarily complex tableau, whose minor variations – there are **four identifiable bands** – in subject matter and design indicate successive historical periods. The carvings were executed between 2500 and 6000 years ago, and are indisputably impressive: clear, stylish, and touching in their simplicity. They provide an insight into a prehistoric culture that was essentially settled and largely reliant on the hunting of land animals, who were killed with flint and bone implements; sealing and fishing were of lesser importance. Many experts think it likely the carvings had spiritual significance because of the effort that was expended by the people who created them, but this is the stuff of conjecture.

## Around Alta: Sorrisniva

☎ 78 43 33 78, ⓦ sorrisniva.no • Call for details about shuttle transfers from Alta

Aside from the rock carvings, the only real reason to linger hereabouts is the **Alta Friluftspark**, 20km to the south of town off Highway 93, beside the river in Storelvdalen. Here, all manner of Finnmark experiences are on offer, from snowmobile tours, dog-sled trips, ice-fishing and reindeer racing in winter, to summer boat trips along the 400m-deep **Sautso canyon**, Scandinavia's largest.

### ARRIVAL AND DEPARTURE                                      ALTA

**By bus** Alta is something of a transport hub. Long-distance buses pull into the bus station just off the E6 at Alta Sentrum. To reach Nordkapp, passengers must change – and overnight – in Honningsvåg (see p.359). The following bus companies run onward services:

Boreal (ⓦ boreal.no) to: Hammerfest (1–4 daily; 2hr 30min); Honningsvåg (1–2 daily; 4hr); Karasjok (1–2 daily except Sat; 5hr); Kautokeino (1–3 daily except Sat; 2hr 15min); Kirkenes (3 weekly; 11–13hr).

Torghatten Nord (ⓦ tts.no) to: Honningsvåg (1–2 daily; 4hr); Narvik (1 daily; 9hr 25min); Tromsø (1 daily; 7hr).

### INFORMATION

**Tourist office** Bjorn Wirkolas vei 11, in the same building as the bus terminal (June & Aug daily 9am–6pm; July daily 9am–8pm; Sept–May Mon–Fri 9am–3.30pm, Sat 10am–3pm; ☎ 78 44 50 50, ⓦ visitalta.no); near the Coop supermarket, Bossekop shopping centre (mid-June to mid-Aug only Mon–Fri 10am–6pm; same number). Both branches of the tourist office issue free town maps, will advise on hiking the Finnmarksvidda (see p.352) and help with finding accommodation. The latter is a particularly useful service if you're dependent on public transport – the town's hotels and motels are widely dispersed – or if you're here at the height of the season.

### ACCOMMODATION

#### HOTELS AND GUESTHOUSES

**Bårstua Gjestehus** Kongleveien 2a ☎ 78 43 33 33, ⓦ baarstua.no. Of Alta's several guesthouses, this is the most appealing, located just off the E6 on the north side of town. The eight rooms here are large and pleasant enough and all of them have kitchenettes. **830kr**

**Igloo Hotell** Sorrisniva ☎ 78 43 33 78, ⓦ sorrisniva.no. Sorrisniva boasts a 100-bed, 1100-square-metre hotel built entirely out of ice and snow, including the beds and the glasses in the bar. It's set near the riverside, and while staying in an ice hotel seems gimmicky, it's a (erm) cool – and memorable – way of avoiding the bland Ikea decor and amenities of the chain hotels. As the hotel is fantastically popular, advance reservations are essential. Late Jan to early April only. <u>3990kr</u>

**Nordlys Hotell Alta** Bekkefaret 3 ☏ 78 45 72 00, ⊛ nordlyshotell.no. Located just opposite the Bossekop tourist office, this Best Western hotel sports a rather uninviting mishmash of styles, but offers large, comfortable if somewhat spartan rooms. <u>1095kr</u>

**Thon Hotel Vica** Fogdebakken 6 ☏ 78 48 22 22, ⊛ thonhotels.com. Among Alta's several hotels, this is one of the more appealing. Occupying a wooden building that started out as a farmhouse a couple of minutes' walk from the Bossekop tourist office, it's a small, cosy place with two dozen smart, modern rooms. Also has a suntrap of a terrace and free wi-fi. <u>1045kr</u>

### CAMPSITE

**Alta River Camping** ☏ 78 43 43 53, ⊛ alta-river -camping.no. The best of the campsites around Alta, this well-equipped, four-star site is set on a large green plot right on the Alta River. They have tent spaces here as well as hotel-style rooms and cabins, some of which have en-suite baths (others share), plus a sauna right on the water. Located about 5km out of town along Highway 93, which branches off the E6 in between Bossekop and the rock paintings. Open year-round. Tents <u>170kr</u>, doubles <u>400kr</u>, cabins <u>600kr</u>

### EATING AND DRINKING

**Alfa-Omega** Markedsgata 16 ☏ 78 44 54 00, ⊛ alfaomega-alta.no. *Omega* is the continental eatery; *Alfa* is the no-holds-barred bar, whose vaguely Cuban aesthetic manages to attract more than its share of fortysomethings. Mon–Wed 8pm–midnight, Thurs 7pm–1am, Fri 6pm–2.30am, Sat noon–2.30am.

**Rica Hotel Alta** Løkkeveien 61 ☏ 78 48 27 00. Large, smart hotel restaurant that's part of the Arctic Menu scheme (see box, p.300), specializing in regional delicacies – cloudberries, reindeer and the like. Mains cost around 200kr. Open daily noon–11.30pm.

# The Finnmarksvidda

Venture far inland from Alta and you enter the **Finnmarksvidda**, a vast mountain plateau which spreads southeast up to and beyond the Finnish border. Rivers, lakes and marshes lattice the region, but there's nary a tree, let alone a mountain, to break the contours of a landscape whose wide skies and deep horizons are nevertheless eerily beautiful. Distances are hard to gauge – a dot of a storm can soon be upon you, breaking with alarming ferocity – and the air is crystal-clear, giving a whitish lustre to the sunshine. A handful of roads cross this expanse, but for the most part it remains the preserve of the few thousand semi-nomadic **Sámi** (see box, p.350) who make up the majority of the local population. Many still wear traditional dress, a brightly coloured, wool and felt affair of red bonnets and blue jerkins or dresses, all trimmed with red, white and yellow embroidery. You'll see permutations on this traditional costume all over Finnmark, but especially at roadside souvenir stalls and, on Sundays, outside Sámi churches.

Despite the slow encroachments of the tourist industry, lifestyles on the Finnmarksvidda have remained remarkably constant for centuries. The main occupation is **reindeer herding**, supplemented by hunting and fishing, and the pattern

## EASTER FESTIVALS IN THE FINNSMARKSVIDDA

As neither of the Finnmarksvidda region's two principal settlements, Karasjok and Kautokeino, is particularly appealing in winter, **Easter** is without question the best time to be here, when the inhabitants celebrate the end of the polar night and the arrival of spring. There are folk-music concerts, church services and traditional sports, including the famed **reindeer races** – not, thank goodness, reindeers racing each other (they would never cooperate), but reindeer pulling passenger-laden sleds. Details of the Easter festivals are available at any Finnmark tourist office.

of Sámi life is still mostly dictated by the biology of these animals. During the winter, the reindeer graze the flat plains and shallow valleys of the interior, migrating towards the coast in early May as the snow begins to melt, and temperatures inland begin to climb, even reaching 30°C on occasion. By October, both people and reindeer are journeying back from their temporary summer quarters on the coast. The long, dark winter is spent in preparation for the great **Easter festivals** (see box opposite), when weddings and baptisms are celebrated in the region's two principal settlements, **Karasjok** and – more especially – **Kautokeino**. Summer visits, on the other hand, can be rather disappointing, culturally speaking at least, since many families and their reindeer are kicking back at coastal pastures and there is precious little activity in either town. Still, your best bet for spotting small herds are along the road to Hammerfest and in the area around Nordkapp.

The best time to **hike** the Finnmarksvidda is in late August and early September, after the peak mosquito season and before the weather turns cold. For the most part the plateau vegetation is scrub and open birch forest, which makes the going fairly easy, though the many marshes, rivers and lakes often impede progress. There are a handful of clearly demarcated **hiking trails** as well as a smattering of appropriately sited but unstaffed huts; for detailed information, ask at Alta tourist office (see p.347).

## ARRIVAL AND DEPARTURE                                    THE FINNMARKSVIDDA

**By bus** Operated by Boreal (❶ 177, ⓦ boreal.no), bus services across the Finnmarksvidda are patchy: except on Sat, there are 1–2 buses a day from Alta to Kautokeino (just over 2hr) and to Karasjok (5hr), but nothing between Kautokeino and Karasjok. Some Alta–Karasjok buses continue to Kirkenes (12hr), while a further service links Karasjok with Hammerfest (Mon–Fri 3–4 daily, Sat & Sun 1–2 daily; 3hr).

**By car** From Alta, the only direct route into the Finnmarksvidda is south along Highway 93 to Kautokeino, a distance of 130km. Just short of Kautokeino, about 100km from Alta, Highway 93 connects with Highway 92, which travels the 100km or so northeast to Karasjok, where you can rejoin the E6 (but well beyond the turning to Nordkapp).

# Kautokeino

It's a two-hour drive or bus ride from Alta across the Finnmarksvidda to **KAUTOKEINO** (Guovdageaidnu in Sámi), the principal winter camp of the Norwegian Sámi and their reindeer, who are kept in the surrounding plains. The Sámi are not, however, easy town dwellers and although Kautokeino is very useful to them as a supply base, it's still a desultory, desolate-looking place straggling along Highway 93 for a couple of kilometres, with the handful of buildings that pass for the town centre gathered at the point where the road crosses the Kautokeinoelva River.

## Juhls' Silver Gallery

Galaniitoluodda • Daily: June to early Aug 9am–8pm; early Aug to May 9am–6pm; ring in winter to confirm hours on ❶ 78 48 43 30 • Regular guided tours (30min; free) • ⓦ juhls.no

Though it lacks obvious appeal, Kautokeino has become something of a tourist draw on account of the **jewellers Frank and Regine Juhls**, who braved all sorts of difficulties to set up their workshop here in 1959. It was a bold move at a time when the Sámi were very much a neglected minority, but the Juhls had a keen interest in nomadic cultures and, although the Sámi had no tradition of jewellery-making, they did adorn themselves with all sorts of unusual items traded in from the outside world. The couple was much influenced by this Sámi style of self-adornment, repeating and developing it in their own work, and their business prospered – perhaps beyond their wildest dreams.

## THE SÁMI

The northernmost reaches of Norway, Sweden and Finland, plus the Kola peninsula of northwest Russia, are collectively known as **Lapland**. Traditionally, the indigenous population were called "Lapps", but in recent years this name has fallen out of favour and been replaced by the term **Sámi**, although the change is by no means universal. This more commonly used term comes from the Sámi word *sámpi* referring to both the land and its people, who now number around 70,000 scattered across the whole of the region. Among the oldest peoples in Europe, the Sámi most likely descended from prehistoric clans who migrated here from Siberia by way of the Baltic. Their **language** is closely related to Finnish and Estonian, though it's somewhat misleading to speak of a "Sámi language" as there are, in fact, three distinct versions, each of which breaks down into a number of markedly different regional dialects. All share many common features, however, including a superabundance of words and phrases to express variations in snow and ice conditions.

Originally, the Sámi were a semi-nomadic people, living in small communities (*siidas*), each of which had a degree of control over the surrounding hunting grounds. They lived off hunting, fishing and trapping, preying on all the edible creatures of the north, but it was the wild reindeer that supplied most of their needs. This changed in the sixteenth century when the Sámi moved over to **reindeer herding**, with communities following the seasonal movements of the animals.

The contact the Sámi have had with other Scandinavians has almost always been to their disadvantage. In the ninth century, they paid significant fur, feather and hide taxes to Norse chieftains. Later, in the seventeenth century, they faced colonization and moves to **dislocate their culture** from the various thrones in Sweden, Russia and Norway. The frontiers of Sámiland were only agreed in 1826, by which point hundreds of farmers had settled in "Lapland", to the consternation of its native population. By that point, Norway's Sámi had kowtowed to Protestant missionaries and accepted the **religion** of their colonizers – though the more progressive among them did support the use of Sámi languages and even translated hundreds of books into their language. In the nineteenth century, the government's aggressive Social Darwinist policy of "**Norwegianization**" banned the use of indigenous languages in schools, and only allowed Sámi to buy land if they could speak Norwegian. Only in the 1950s were these policies abandoned and slowly replaced by a more considerate, progressive approach.

1986 was a catastrophic year for the Sámi: the **Chernobyl nuclear disaster** contaminated much of the region's flora and fauna, which effectively meant the collapse of the reindeer export market. While reindeer herding is now the main occupation of just one-fifth of the Sámi population, expressions of Sámi **culture** have expanded. Traditional arts and crafts are now widely available in all of Scandinavia's major cities and a number of Sámi films – including the critically acclaimed *Veiviseren* (The Pathfinder) – have been released. Sámi music (*joik*) has also been given a hearing by world-music, jazz and even electronica buffs. Although their provenance is uncertain, the rhythmic song-poems that constitute *joik* were probably devised to soothe anxious reindeer; the words are subordinated to the unaccompanied singing and at times are replaced altogether by meaningless, sung syllables.

Since the international anti-colonial struggles of the 1960s, the Norwegians have been obliged to thoroughly re-evaluate their relationship with the Sámi – initially by amending the national constitution to include social, cultural and linguistic rights for them in 1988, then a year later establishing a Sámi Parliament, the **Sameting**, in Karasjok. Certain deep-seated problems do remain – issues such as land and mineral rights and the identity of Sámi both as an indigenous, partly autonomous people and as citizens of a particular country – but at least Oslo is asking the right questions.

As further testimony to the Juhls' commercial success, the plain and simple workshop they first built has been replaced by an extensive complex of low-lying **showrooms and workshops**. Exquisitely beautiful, high-quality silver work is made and sold here alongside a much broader range of classy craftwork. The complex's interior is intriguing in its own right, with some rooms decorated in crisp, modern pan-Scandinavian style, others done out in an elaborate version of Sámi design. The gallery is located on a ridge above the west bank of the Kautokeinoelva, 2.5km south of the town centre – follow the signs.

## Kautokeino kirke

Goahtedievva 2 • June to mid-Aug daily 9am–9pm • Free

This delightful wooden **Kautokeino kirke** (Kautokeino church), located just south of the centre on the east bank of the Kautokeinoelva River and visible from everywhere in town, is decorated in bright, typically Sámi colours; it looks particularly appealing when the Sámi turn up here in their Sunday best (Easter is a good time of the year for lots of activity as many Sámi prefer to get married around then). The church, which seats three hundred, was originally built by the Swedes in 1701, and then rebuilt following German bombing in 1944. It sports a ridged turret over the entrance – typical of churches built in the 1950s.

## Kautokeino Bygdetun og Museum

Mid-June to mid-Aug Mon–Sat 9am–7pm, Sun noon–7pm; mid-Aug to mid-June Mon–Fri 9am–3pm • 30kr

The small **Kautokeino Bygdetun og Museum** (Guovdageaidnu Gilisillju or Kautokeino Parish Museum) holds a history of the town inside and a number of draughty-looking Sámi dwellings outside. You'll spot the same little turf huts and tents (known as *lavvo*) all over Finnmark, occasionally housing souvenir stalls.

### ARRIVAL AND DEPARTURE
### KAUTOKEINO

**By bus** Buses stop at the *Thon Hotel* and the Statoil petrol station. Boreal (ⓦ boreal.no) run services to Alta (1–2 daily except Sat; 2hr 5min) and Karasjok (1 daily; 2hr–2hr 30min). Note that buses to and from Karasjok operate on Tues and Thurs during the school year, and Fri and Sun all year round.

### INFORMATION AND TOURS

**Tourist office** The tourist office (daily: late June to early Aug 9am–4pm; July 9am–8pm; ☎78 48 65 00, ⓦ kautokeino.no) is located in a different location pretty much every year. It provides town maps and has details of local events and activities, from fishing and hiking through to "Sámi adventures", which typically include a boat trip and a visit to a *lavvo* ("tent") where you can sample traditional Sámi food and listen to *joik* (rhythmic song-poems) for around 350kr.

**Tour operators** One leading local tour operator is Cavzo Safari (☎78 48 75 88, ⓦ cavzo.no), located on the road between Alta and Kautokeino.

### ACCOMMODATION AND EATING

#### HOTELS

**Kautokeino Villmarkssenter** Hannoluohka 2 ☎78 48 76 02, ⓦ www.mamut.net/vmsenter. Located across the highway from the tourist office, this modest and modern spot has seventeen rooms, one apartment for four and eight separate cabins. The rooms and apartment are fairly soulless, modern digs, but the cabins are much more atmospheric (and rustic) – log-cabin-style huts with four bunked beds and shared bath and shower. Cabins **500kr**; rooms **750kr**; apartment **1200kr**

**Thon Hotel Kautokeino** Biedjovaggeluodda 2 ☎78 48 70 00, ⓦ thonhotels.no/kautokeino. The largest hotel in Kautokeino, this fortress-like modern structure north of the river just off Highway 93 is set on a small hillside overlooking the town. The 65 guest rooms are decorated in a bright and breezy style, with walls decorated by photos shot by a local artist. **795kr**

#### RESTAURANT

**Duottar** Thon Hotel Kautokeino, Biedjovaggeluodda 2 ☎78 48 70 00. The *Thon's* passable restaurant specializes in local dishes with a modern twist – reindeer soup, baked salmon and sea crab, for example – with mains that range between 150kr and 300kr.

### ENTERTAINMENT

**Kautokeino Kulturhus** Bredbuktnesveien 50 ☎78 48 44 60, ⓦ beaivvas.no. Winner of various architectural awards, the Kautokeino Kulturhus (Guovdageaidnu Kulturviessu or Cultural Centre) houses the only state-sponsored Sámi theatre in Norway. Though not much to see on its own, if there's anything going on in town entertainment-wise, this is where you'll find it.

## Karasjok

Apart from Kautokeino, the only other settlement of any size on the Finnmarksvidda is **KARASJOK** (Kárásjohka in Sámi), 130km east from Kautokeino, 270km south of Nordkapp, 220km southeast of Hammerfest, and 330km west of Kirkenes. Norway's Sámi capital straddles the E6 on the main route from Finland to Nordkapp – and consequently sees plenty of tourists. Spread across a wooded river valley, the town has none of the desolation of Kautokeino, yet it still conspires to be fairly mundane despite the presence of the Sámi Parliament and the country's best Sámi museum.

### Sápmi Park

Early June to mid-Aug daily 9am–7pm; rest of year Mon–Fri 9am–4pm • 100kr • ☎ 78 46 88 00, ⓦ eng.sapmi.no

Incorporated within the tourist office (see p.354) is **Sápmi Park**, a miniature Sámi theme park, which offers a fancy multimedia introduction to the Sámi in the Stálubákti ("Magic Theatre") and a performance of the *joik*, the Samis' yodel-like singing tradition. Here also are examples of traditional Sámi dwellings, Sámi shops and a restaurant plus displays of various ancient Sámi skills with the obligatory reindeer brought along as decoration or to be roped and coralled.

### De Samiske Samlinger

Early June to mid-Aug daily 9am–6pm; mid-Aug to early June Tues–Fri 9am–3pm • 75kr • ⓦ rdm.no • Walk 200m from the tourist office north along the Nordkapp road to Museumsgata, then turn right

The small collection at **De Samiske Samlinger** (Sámiid vourká dávvirat or Sámi Collections) does a great job of providing an overview of Sámi culture and history, with the outdoor exhibits comprising an assortment of old dwellings that illustrate the frugality of Sámi life. Inside, a large and clearly presented collection of incidental bygones includes a colourful sample of folkloric Sámi costumes.

### Gamle kirke

June–Aug daily 8am–9pm • Free

The **Gamle kirke** (old church) was the only building left standing in Karasjok at the end of World War II (which necessitated the rebuilding of the town's primary church in 1958). Of simple design, it dates from 1807, making it easily the oldest-surviving church in Finnmark. It is set on the south side of the river, just off Highway 92.

### Samisk Kunstnersenter

Jeagilvarmadii 54 • Tues–Fri 10am–4pm, Sat & Sun 1–4pm • Free • ⓦ samiskkunstnersenter.no

This unassuming gallery (Sámi daiddaguovddás or Sámi Artists' Centre) showcases the work of contemporary Sámi artists, but don't expect folksy canvases – Sámi artists are a diverse bunch and as likely to be influenced by postmodernism as reindeer herding. It is located off Highway 92 – take the next major right after the church.

---

### HIKES INTO THE FINNMARKSVIDDA

Karasjok is an excellent point of departure for an exploration of the Finnmarksvidda. The region's most popular long-distance **hike** is the five-day haul across the heart of the Finnmarksvidda, from Karasjok to Alta via a string of strategically located huts – gorgeous and invigorating but not for the faint-hearted or inexperienced. More gentle a trek is the 3.5km **Ássebákti nature trail**, which passes more than a hundred Sámi cultural monuments on the way. Clearly signed, the trail begins some 16km west of Karasjok along Highway 92 towards Kautokeino. For information on walks in the region, enquire at either the Karasjok or Alta tourist offices.

---

**6**

## ARRIVAL AND DEPARTURE

**By bus** Buses pull into Karasjok bus station, on Storgata, from where it's a signposted 5–10min walk west to the tourist office (see below). There is limited bus service with Boreal (ⓦboreal.no) from Karasjok to and from Alta, Kautokeino, Hammerfest and Kirkenes, and schedules occasionally make it possible to spend a couple of hours here before moving on – enough to see the sights, but

hardly long enough to get the true flavour of the place. Note that buses to and from Kautokeino operate on Tues and Thurs during the school year, and Fri and Sun all year round.

Destinations Alta (1–2 daily except Sat; 5hr); Hammerfest (1–2 daily except Sat; 4hr); Kirkenes (3–4 weekly; 11hr–13hr).

## INFORMATION AND TOURS

**Tourist office** Sápmi, on the north side of the river beside the E6 and Highway 92 crossroads (early June to mid-Aug daily 9am–7pm; rest of year Mon–Fri 9am–4pm; ☎78 46 88 00, ⓦsapmi.no). The busiest place in town, for all intents and purposes, the tourist office is the centre of town. Staff here issue free town maps, book overnight accommodation and organize

authentic(ish) Sámi expeditions.

**Tours** The tourist office has information on dog-sledging, visits to a Sámi camp, a boat trip on the Karasjokka River, cross-country skiing and even gold-panning. One group to contact is Kirsten Berit Siida (ⓦkb-siida.no), which run various Sámi reindeer-related excursions.

## ACCOMMODATION AND EATING

★ **Engholm's Husky Lodge** 7km west of Karasjok on Highway 92 ☎78 46 71 66, ⓦengholm.no. This fantastic all-year HI-accredited lodge features a number of home-made cabins of various shapes and sizes. The lodge offers self-catering facilities, a sauna and Arctic dinners, where guests sit on reindeer skins around an open fire. The owner, the illustrious Sven, is an expert dog-sled racer and keeps about forty huskies; he uses them on a variety of guided winter tours and in summer organizes everything from fishing trips and guided wilderness hikes to horseback riding. No dorms, but HI members get a ten percent

discount. Pick-up from Karasjok costs 150kr. Full-board from 2200kr. Cabins from **500kr**

**Rica Hotel Karasjok** ☎78 46 88 60, ⓦrica.no. Though much less atmospheric than *Engholm's*, this breezy modern establishment set in a large chalet-like building, a short stroll north of the tourist office along the E6, is the best option for staying in the town centre. The hotel also boasts the summertime *Storgammen* restaurant, a set of turf-covered huts where a limited selection of Sámi-style meals, such as reindeer or salmon with cloudberries and cream, are served. Reckon on 220kr for a main course. **1100kr**

# Hammerfest

Situated on the western shore of the rugged island of Kvaløya, linked to the mainland by bridge, **HAMMERFEST**, some 150km north of Alta, claims to be the world's northernmost town, though in actuality this prize goes to Longyearbyen on Svalbard. It was, however, the first town in Europe to have electric street-lighting, and is indeed mainland Europe's most northerly settlement. Hardly fascinating facts perhaps, but both give a glimpse of the pride the locals take in making the most of what is, indisputably, an inhospitable location. Indeed, it's a wonder the town has survived at all: a hurricane flattened the place in 1856; it was burnt to the ground in 1890; and the retreating Germans mauled it at the end of World War II. Yet, instead of being abandoned, Hammerfest was stubbornly rebuilt for a third time. Nor is it the grim industrial town you might expect from the proximity of the offshore oil wells, but a bright, cheerful port, which drapes around a horseshoe-shaped **harbour** sheltered from the elements by a steep, rocky hill. Hammerfest also benefits from the occasional dignified wooden building that recalls its nineteenth-century heyday as the centre of the Pomor trade in which Norwegian fish were traded for boat-loads of Russian flour. But don't get too carried away: Bill Bryson, in *Neither Here Nor There*, hit the nail on the head with his description of Hammerfest as "an agreeable enough town in a thank-you-God-for-not-making-me-live-here sort of way". To be sure, it's the general atmosphere of the place that appeals rather than any specific sight.

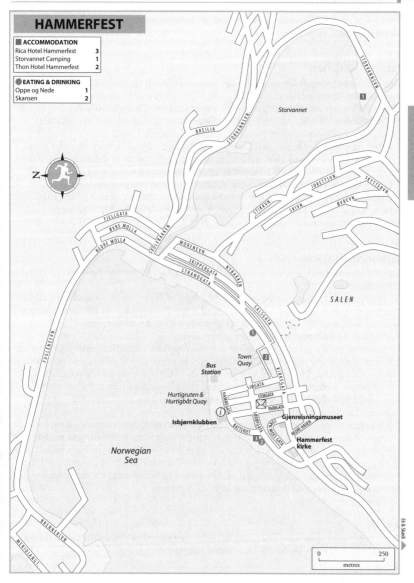

**6**

## Strandgata

Running parallel to the waterfront, **Strandgata**, the town's principal street, is a busy, 500m-long run of supermarkets, clothes and souvenir shops, partly inspired by the town's role as a stopoff for cruise ships on the way to Nordkapp.

## The old town quay

Most of the activity takes place on the **old town quay**, off Sjøgata, with tourists emerging from the liners to beetle around the harbourfront, eat shellfish from the stalls along the wharf or buy souvenirs in the small, summertime Sámi market.

## Isbjørnklubben

Hamnegata 3 • June & July Mon–Fri 6am–6pm, Sat & Sun 6am–4pm; rest of year Mon–Fri 9am–4pm, Sat & Sun 10am–2pm • Free; membership 180kr • Ⓦ isbjornklubb.no

One of Hammerfest's (begrudgingly, for some) renowned attractions is the **Isbjørnklubben** (Royal and Ancient Polar Bear Society), located next to the tourist office. The society's pint-sized museum – filled with stuffed polar bears and seal-skin-covered furniture – tells the story of Hammerfest as a trapping centre for polar bears, eagles and arctic fox, and gives the background to the creation of the society itself in 1963. You could always join 235,000 others and become a member of the society, whose proceeds are put towards Arctic conservation and endangered animals programmes. Whatever you do, be sure to avoid the ceremony of being "knighted" with a walrus's penis bone – not only will it set you back 225kr, but it's sure to make you cringe with embarrassment for weeks on end.

## Gjenreisningsmuseet

Kirkegata 21 • June to mid-Aug Mon–Fri 9am–4pm, Sat & Sun 10am–2pm; mid-Aug to May daily 11am–2pm • 50kr • Ⓦ gjenreisningsmuseet.no

The purpose-built **Gjenreisningsmuseet** (Museum of Reconstruction for Finnmark and Northern Troms), a five-minute walk west of the old town quay up Kirkegata, begins with a fascinating section on the hardships endured by the inhabitants of Finnmark during the **German retreat** in the face of the advancing Russians in late 1944. The Germans ordered a general evacuation and then applied a scorched-earth policy, which left almost all of the region's towns and villages in ruins. Just in case any of his soldiers got the wrong idea, Hitler's orders stipulated that "Compassion for the population is out of place." Refugees in their own country, the Norwegians found shelter wherever they could and several thousand hid out in caves until May 1945, though many died from cold and malnutrition.

Subsequent sections of the museum deal with **postwar reconstruction**, giving a sharply critical account of the central government bureaucracy initially put in charge. Under the weight of complaints, it was disbanded in 1948 and control was passed back to the municipalities. Interestingly, the left-wing Labour Party, who co-ordinated the reconstruction programme, adopted an almost evangelical stance, crusading against dirtiness, inequality and drunkenness in equal measure.

## Salen

For something a little more energetic, take the **footpath** that zigzags up **Salen**, the hill behind town. It takes about fifteen minutes to reach the plateau at the top, from where

---

### SEILAND

Should you get antsy while holed up in Hammerfest, try a day-trip or overnight excursion out to **Seiland**, a nearby island where you can take in any number of activities, including hiking, deep-sea fishing, boating, snowmobiling and hunting. Trips offered by Seiland Explore (❶ 78 41 96 40, Ⓦ seiland-explore.com) range from deep-sea fishing (from 1000kr/day) to a two-day guided excursion to a glacier (from around 7000kr per group). Alternatively, the tourist office has details of local excursions, easily the most popular of which are the fishing trips and the summertime **sea cruises** to local bird cliffs, which seethe and squawk with guillemots, gannets and kittiwakes, among many other types of sea birds.

there are panoramic views out across the town and over to the nearby islands. The footpath begins a couple of minutes' walk from the old town quay on Salsgata, one block south of Strandgata.

## ARRIVAL AND INFORMATION
## HAMMERFEST

**By bus** Hammerfest is some 60km from the E6 along Highway 94. Buses pull into Hammerfest bus station at the foot of Sjøgata. Boreal (☎177, ⓦboreal.no) run services to: Alta (1–3 daily, mid-Dec to late Feb no Sat service; 2hr 30min); Honningsvåg (1–2 Mon–Fri & Sun; 1 Sat early June to late Aug only; 3hr 30min); Karasjok (1–2 daily except Sat; 4hr); Kirkenes (4–5 weekly; 10hr–12hr 40min); and Skaidi (1–3 daily, no Sat service mid-Dec to late Feb; 1hr).

**By boat** The Hurtigruten coastal boat quay is adjacent to the bus station. The boat spends 1hr 30min at Hammerfest, arriving at an unsociable 5.15am on its way north, and at a more palatable 11.15am heading south. Services sail north daily from Hammerfest at 6.45am, reaching Honningsvåg at 11.45am, where it pauses for 3hr 30min, plenty enough

time for special connecting buses to make the return trip to Nordkapp. Southbound it departs at 12.45pm for Tromsø (11hr).

**By car** For those looking to reach Nordkapp, Hammerfest has several car rental companies that frequently offer attractive short-term deals from around 700kr a day unlimited mileage. Try Europcar (☎93 00 44 55) or Hertz (☎78 41 71 66). Comparable rental deals may be available at Honningsvåg (see p.359), 180km north.

**Tourist office** Hamnegata 3 (June & July Mon–Fri 6am–6pm, Sat & Sun 6am–4pm; Aug–May Mon–Fri 9am–4pm, Sat & Sun 10am–2pm; ☎78 41 21 85, ⓦhammerfest-turist.no). In the same building as the Isbjørnklubben, the tourist office issues free town maps and has details of local trips (see box, p.356).

## ACCOMMODATION

★ **Rica Hotel Hammerfest** Sørøygata 15 ☎78 42 57 00, ⓦrica.no. This attractive and well-maintained modern place sits on a grassy knoll a couple of minutes' walk west of the main quay and has excellent sea views, making it the choice stay in town. The spiffy rooms do tend towards the small, but ask for one with views of the harbour and you'll not mind as much. Sprawling breakfast buffet. **1595kr**

**Storvannet Camping** Storvannsveien 103 ☎78 41 10 10, ⓦnafcamp.com. Your best camping option in town, this quiet lakeside site is set a 15min walk from the harbour. Offers a handful of very simple one-room cabins

that get booked up in advance in the summer. June–Sept. Cabins **400kr**, tent pitch for two people **200kr**

**Thon Hotel Hammerfest** Strandgata 2–4 ☎78 42 96 00, ⓦthonhotels.no. Occupying a prime spot just metres from the old town quay, this cosy spot, overhauled in 2011, is housed in a routine modern block but has a handsome, old-fashioned air about it. Smallish rooms are equipped with chunky wooden fittings that (mostly) predate the chipboard mania of today. Those facing the street can get noisy, and not just at weekends. Holds three very lively bars. **895kr**

## EATING AND DRINKING

**Oppe og Nede** Strandgata 22 ☎90 59 29 30, ⓦonhammerfest.blogspot.com. Also known as *ON*, this continental restaurant serves salads, soups, pasta and larger mains (from 115kr). It is better known, however, as the town's hottest nightspot from Tues to Sat, with multiple dancefloors – downstairs for teens (weekends only), upstairs for everyone else. Mon & Fri 10.30am–3pm,

Tues–Thurs 10.30am–1am, Sat 11am–3am, Sun 3–10pm.

**Skansen** Rica Hotel Hammerfest, Sørøygata 15 ☎78 42 57 00, ⓦrica.no. This à la carte hotel restaurant is the best the town has, offering ocean views and delicious seafood. Main courses start at around 220kr. Daily 4–10.30pm.

# Nordkapp and around

At the northern tip of Norway, the treeless and windswept island of **Magerøya** is mainly of interest to travellers as the location of the **Nordkapp** (North Cape), generally regarded as Europe's northernmost point, though it is in fact nothing of the kind (see box, p.358). The development of the Nordkapp as a tourist spot has not been without its critics, who argue that the large and lavish visitor centre – **Nordkapphallen** – is crass and soulless and grossly overpriced; their opponents simply point to the huge number of people who visit. Whichever side you're on, nearly everyone who comes this far north does so to visit Nordkapp, though Magerøya island has other charms too,

**6**

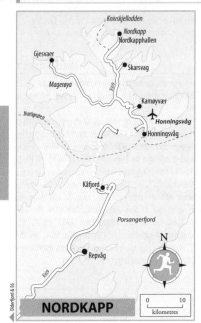

Olderfjord & E6

**NORDKAPP**

0       10
kilometres

N

notably a bleak, rugged beauty that's readily seen from the E69 as it threads across the mountainous interior from Honningsvåg, on the south coast, to Nordkapp, a distance of 34km.

The obvious base for a visit to Nordkapp is the island's main settlement, **Honningsvåg**, an extremely quaint fishing village with an unexpected clutch of chain hotels. More appealing, however, is the tiny hamlet of **Kamøyvær**, nestling beside a narrow fjord just off the E69 between Honningsvåg and Nordkapp, and with a couple of family-run guesthouses. Bear in mind also that Nordkapp is within easy striking distance of other places back on the mainland – certainly the picturesque fishing-station-cum-hotel at **Repvåg**, and maybe even Hammerfest (see p.354) and Alta (see p.346), respectively 210km and 240km away.

## Repvåg

Set about 20 miles down the north shore of the **Porsangerfjord**, a deep and wide inlet flanked by bare, low-lying hills whose stone has been fractured and made flaky by the biting cold of winter, rests the old timber fishing station of **REPVÅG**. The E69 scuttles north along massive monoliths interrupting the coast, but for the most part the scenery in these parts is unusually tame and the shoreline accommodates a string of fishermen's houses – plus the wooden racks used to air-dry their catch. Repvåg makes an ideal base – certainly more quaint than Honningsvåg – from which to reach Nordkapp, though once you're ensconced here, you may settle instead for a fishing tour or, quite possibly, a few days in real solitude.

### ACCOMMODATION AND EATING                                    REPVÅG

★ **Repvåg Fjordhotell og Rorbusenter** Repvåg harbour ☎78 47 54 40, ⓦ repvag-fjordhotell.no. A rare and particularly picturesque survivor from prewar days – it was once a thriving fish packing factory – this year-round complex, painted in traditional red, is perched on stilts on the water's edge, with public areas decked out with authentic nautical tackle and cosy furniture. The main building features simple,

unassuming rooms, while the cluster of eight old fishermen's *rorbuer* (shacks) are very charming places to stay – solitary and scenic in equal proportions. The hotel also offers boat and fishing trips out on the Porsangerfjord, and its restaurant, which specializes in seafood, is very good too. Half- and full-board available. Cabins 900kr, doubles 753kr

---

#### TRUE NORTH?

While umpteen marketing brochures gladly refer to Nordkapp at Europe's northernmost point, in fact the neighbouring **Knivskjellodden peninsula** actually lies 1457m further north. And if it's *mainland* Europe we're talking about, the distinction belongs to **Kinnarodden**, a remote headland about 80km further to the east. Nonetheless, everyone seems to have conspired to ignore this simple latitudinal fact and now, while Nordkapp has become one of the most popular tourist destinations in the country, there isn't even a road to Kinnarodden, which can only be reached on a long and difficult 25km hike from the Hurtigruten port of **Mehamn**.

# Honningsvåg

You'll spy the island of **Magerøya**, a hunk of brown rock looking like an inverted blancmange, long before you get there. It's the site of minor fishing and sea port of **HONNINGSVÅG**, which straggles along the seashore for about 1km. Honningsvåg's jumble of well-worn modern buildings is sheltered from the blizzards of winter by the surrounding crags – though, given the conditions, sheltered is a comparative term. Honningsvåg is officially classified as a city – claiming to be the most northerly in the world – thus maintaining a long-running rivalry with Hammerfest, some 80km southwest, which takes great pains to rob the settlement of this title (it is perhaps incidental that both places actually lose out to Longyearbyen as "northernmost" settlement) – hard luck considering neither is any smaller nor less hardy in the face of adversity than the neighbouring rival.

Honningsvåg has accumulated several chain hotels, which make a steady living from the tourists who stream through bound for the Nordkapp, and is at its prettiest at the head of the **harbour**, where an assortment of timber warehouses, dating back to the days when the village was entirely reliant on fish, makes an attractive ensemble. Draped with fishing nets and tackle, these handsome buildings perch on crusty timber stilts that jut out into the water. They have wide eaves to protect against the snow, and each has its own jetty where fishing smacks are roped in tight against the wind.

## ARRIVAL AND INFORMATION
HONNINGSVÅG

**By air** Widerøe (ⓦ wideroe.no) operates flights from Tromsø, Mehamn and Hammerfest to Honningsvåg airport (☎ 67 03 51 19), a 5min drive due north of town. A taxi (☎ 78 47 22 34) to town costs around 120kr.

**By bus** Buses from the mainland, including the long-distance Nord-Norgeekspressen, pull into the bus station at the southern end of the village. Arriving from Alta and Skaidi (for Hammerfest), Boreal (1–3 daily; ⓦ boreal.no) stops at Honningsvåg, where passengers change for services onto Nordkapp (mid-May to mid-Aug 3 daily; mid-Aug to mid-Sept 2 daily; 45min). Outside of these dates, buses to Nordkapp run on reservation only, to be made by 3pm the day before travel (☎ 78 47 70 30 or ☎ 92 68 10 86). The schedule is such that if you take the first bus from Honningsvåg to Nordkapp, you can spend between 1hr 30min and 2hr there before catching the first bus back. If you take the second bus (which does not run between mid-Aug and mid-May), you'll arrive at Nordkapp at 10.15pm with the return bus departing over 2hr later at 12.30am, which means, of course, that you can view the midnight sun.

**By boat** Hurtigruten coastal boats dock at the adjacent jetty, with northbound boats arriving at 11.45am and departing 3.15pm; southbound, the boats don't overlay here, arriving at 6am and departing 15min later; the northbound service is met by special Nordkapp excursion buses – details on board.

**By car** Buses apart, the best way of proceeding from Honningsvåg to Nordkapp is to rent a car or take a taxi. Cars can be rented from Nordkapp Bilservice (☎ 78 47 60 60, ⓦ nordkappbilservice.no) from 800kr/day, or slightly less expensive for 4hr – plenty of time to head up to North Cape and back. Bear in mind that the last stretch of the Honningsvåg–Nordkapp road is closed by snow in winter, roughly from Nov to early April.

**By taxi** The taxi fare to Nordkapp from the centre of Honningsvåg , including an hour's waiting time after you get there, is about 900kr return, 500kr one-way; contact Nordkapp Taxisentral (☎ 78 47 22 34).

**Tourist office** Nordkapphallen (mid-June to mid-Aug Mon–Fri 8.30am–8pm, Sat & Sun noon–8pm; rest of year Mon–Fri 8.30am–4pm; ☎ 78 47 70 30, ⓦ nordkapp.no).

## BOAT TOURS FROM HONNINGSVÅG

Of the tours offered from Honningsvåg's harbour, Destinasjon 71° Nord's three-and-a-half-hour **king crab safari** (☎ 47 28 93 20, ⓦ 71-nord.no; 995kr), departing several times daily in the summertime, is the most engaging. The Zodiac-based excursion explores the traps in the Sarnesfjorden – the crabs in this region can measure up to 2m in length and weigh some 10kg – before heading to land to prepare what you've caught. Another option is a **bird safari** to the **Gjesværstappan Nature Reserve** located on the opposite side of Magerøya island. The two-hour tour (☎ 41 61 39 83, ⓦ birdsafari.com) departs Honningsvåg for the ten-minute boat ride, from which you'll be able to view one of the country's largest collections of puffins, kittiwakes and other migratory birds who nest up here between April and September. There are between one and three departures daily from May to August.

## ACCOMMODATION

**Honningsvåg Brygge Hotel** Vågen 1 ☎ 78 47 64 64, ⓦ hvg-brygge.no. This tasteful and intelligent conversion of a set of wooden warehouses is perched on one of the old jetties at the harbour's southern cove. The two-dozen-odd rooms are neat and cosy, with lots of exposed wood. Breakfast is included. Advance reservations are strongly advised. **1400kr**

**Nordkapp Camping** Skipsfjorden ☎ 78 47 33 77, ⓦ nordkappcamping.no. This campsite, set roughly halfway between Honningsvåg and Kamøyvær on the road to Nordkapp, is a good bet for camping out in the middle of nowhere. Some small wooden cottages offer 3 or 4 beds, as well as kitchenettes (but no baths), while the larger en-suite bungalows have full kitchens and separate living rooms. Free wi-fi. Open May to mid-Sept. Cabins **585kr**, bungalows **1090kr**, tents **140kr**

**Nordkapp Vandrerhjem** Kobbhullveien 10 ☎ 91 82 41 56, ⓦ hihostels.no/nordkapp. The town's HI hostel is a 20min walk north of Honningsvåg – and just 1km from the end of the tunnel from the mainland. There are self-catering facilities here, but no café or restaurant. Open May–Dec. Dorms **330kr**, doubles **760kr**

**Rica Bryggen** Vågen 1 ☎ 78 47 72 50, ⓦ rica.no. This boxy but smart concrete hotel at the head of the harbour has bright, modern and comfortable rooms, though it's hardly inspiring. Open Feb, March, June to mid-Aug & Oct to mid-Dec. **1595kr**

**Rica Hotel Honningsvåg** Nordkappgata 4 ☎ 78 47 72 20, ⓦ rica.no. A few metres south of the bus station is this routine modern block with nearly 200 acceptable rooms, though some of them have seen better days. The public spaces, which have been through a recent renovation, are slightly more promising. Be wary of the rooms with a "view", most of which consist of a panorama of old warehouse buildings. Open May–Sept. **1595kr**

## EATING AND DRINKING

**Arctico Icebar** Sjøgata 1 ☎ 78 47 15 00, ⓦ articoicebar .com. Opened a decade ago by two transplanted Spaniards, this large storage freezer offers a wintertime Arctic experience in the spring- and summertime ice bar. 135kr entrance, which includes two (non-alcoholic) drinks. April to mid-Oct 9am–9pm.

**Corner** Fiskeriveien 2 ☎ 78 47 63 40, ⓦ corner.no. As you'd expect, this modern bistro serves fresh seafood – try the sautéed cod tongue with remoulade and chilli sauce or the herb-baked king crab symphony (125kr), served on a bed of salad with bread – but also does good burgers and stews. If you're prepared to go out on a limb in terms of political correctness, you might try their whale steak, served with red wine sauce, cranberries and roasted potatoes (229kr). Occasionally puts on theme evenings, such as the well-attended crab nights, and once a week the place turns into the local disco. Daily 10am–11pm (kitchen closes at 9pm).

**Sjøhuset** Honningsvåg Brygge Hotel ☎ 99 44 97 50, ⓦ hvg-brygge.no. Not your average hotel restaurant, this independently run rustic spot dishes up delicious seafood plates from a weekly changing menu, making it the best place to dine in town. Seafood mains such as crab and other shellfish cost from 155kr, while meat-based mains such as locally herded reindeer fillet can run as high as 300kr. Reservations are strongly advised. June to early Aug daily 4–11pm; rest of year every other Fri & Sat for dinner, during which it is only open to hotel guests.

# Kamøyvær

Just 9km from Honningsvåg, 2km off the E69 – accessed by a turning just beyond the conspicuous *Rica Hotel Nordkapp* – **KAMØYVÆR** is a pretty little village of 140 hardy folk tucked in tight between the sea and the hills,. The laconic settlement itself doesn't have much more to offer than its remote, quaint character.

## East of the Sun Gallery

Mid-May to mid-Aug 3–10pm • ☎ 78 47 51 37, ⓦ evart.no

At the small **art gallery** at the harbour, resident German artist Eva Schmutterer exhibits a collection of intriguing, Arctic-inspired paintings and handicrafts. Originals of her multicoloured canvases start from around 1500kr, and there are also several of her illustrated books on sale.

## ACCOMMODATION KAMØYVÆR

**Hotel Árran Nordkapp** Kamøyvær harbour ☎ 78 47 51 29, ⓦ arran.as. Pleasant, family-run hotel, whose fifty guest rooms are distributed among several brightly painted and well-tended houses. They serve seafood dinners here too, though it's best to book ahead. Open mid-May to mid-Sept. **1100kr**

# Knivskjellodden and Nordkapp

North of Honningsvåg, the E69 twists a solitary course up through the hills to cross a high-tundra plateau, the mountains stretching away on either side. It's a fine run, with snow and ice lingering well into the summer and impressive views over the treeless and elemental Arctic terrain. From June to October this is pastureland for herds of reindeer, who graze right up to the road, paying little heed to the passing vehicles unless they wander too close. The Sámi, who bring them here by boat, combine herding with souvenir selling, setting up camp at the roadside in full costume to peddle clothes, jewellery and sets of antlers, which some motorists are daft enough to attach to the front of their vehicles.

## Knivskjellodden

About 29km from Honningsvåg, the E69 passes the start of the well-marked **hiking trail** that leads to the headland of **Knivskjellodden**, stretching about 1500m further north than its famous neighbour. The 18km hike – there and back – takes between two and three hours each way, but though the terrain isn't too severe, the climate is too unpredictable for the novice or poorly equipped hiker.

## Nordkapp

When they finally reach **Nordkapp** (North Cape), many visitors feel desperately disappointed – it is, after all, only a cliff and, at 307m, it isn't even all that high. But for others there's something about this greyish-black hunk of slate, stuck at the end of a bare, wind-battered promontory, that exhilarates the senses. Some such feeling must have inspired the prehistoric Sámi to establish a sacrificial site here, and the Nordkapp certainly stirred the romantic notions of earlier generations of tourists, often inspiring them to metaphysical ruminations. In 1802, the Italian naturalist, Giuseppe Acerbi, author of *Travels through Sweden, Finland and Lapland*, exclaimed: "The northern sun, creeping at midnight along the horizon, and the immeasurable ocean in apparent contact with the skies, form the grand outlines in the sublime picture presented to the astonished spectator". Quite – though the seventeenth-century traveller Francesco Negri wasn't far behind: "Here, where the world comes to an end, my curiosity does as well, and now I can return home content."

### NORTHERN NAVIGATIONS

While the first "official" tourist to visit North Cape was a Franciscan friar, Francesco Negri, who arrived in 1664, the point was named by the English explorer **Richard Chancellor** in 1553, as he drifted along the Norwegian coast in an attempt to find the Northeast Passage from the Atlantic to the Pacific. Chancellor failed, but managed to reach the White Sea, from where he and his crew travelled overland to Moscow, thereby opening a new, northern trade route to Russia. Chancellor's account, published in the geographer Richard Hakluyt's *Navigations*, brought his exploits to the attention of seamen across Europe, but it was to be another three hundred years before the Northeast Passage was finally negotiated by the Swede, Nils Nordenskjøld, in 1879. In the meantime, just a trickle of visitors ventured to the Nordkapp. Among them, in 1795, was the exiled Louis Philippe of Orleans (subsequently king of France), and King Chulalongkorn of Thailand, who had his name carved into a nearby rock. But it was the visit of the Norwegian king **Oscar II** in 1873 that opened the tourist floodgates. Two years later, Thomas Cook sent a tour group of 24 to visit. There were no island roads to the plateau, so the tourists had to be ferried by rowing boat from Gjesvær to Hornvika, at the base of the cliffs, before being instructed to climb the steep crags up to the top. The globe monument that now stands in for the actual cape – famous in postcards all over the country – was erected in 1978.

Nordkapphallen

Daily: mid-May to mid-Aug 11am–1am; mid-Aug to Sept 11am–10pm; Oct to mid-May 11am–3pm • 235kr for 48hr, including parking • Ⓦ visitnordkapp.net

The lavish **Nordkapphallen** (North Cape Hall), cut into the rock of the Cape, entertains hundreds of visitors every day. Fronted by a statue of King Oscar II, the main building contains a new restaurant, café, a post office where you get your letters specially stamped, and a panoramic cinema showing – you guessed it – films about the Cape and the island it lies on. There's a viewing area too, but there's not much to see except the sea – and, weather permitting, the midnight sun from May 12 to July 29.

A **tunnel** runs from the main building to the cliff face. It's flanked by a couple of little side-chambers, in one of which is a chapel where you can get married should you have the inclination, and by a series of displays detailing past events and visitors, including the unlikely appearance of the king of Siam in 1907, who was so ill that he had to be carried up here from his boat on a stretcher. At the far end, the cavernous *Grotten Bar* offers caviar and champagne, long views out to sea through the massive glass wall and (of all things) a mock bird-cliff. Alternatively, to escape the hurly-burly, you may decide to walk out on to the surrounding headland, though this is too bleak a spot to be much fun. The closest place to here to stay is Honningsvåg.

# East to Kirkenes

**Southeast of Nordkapp** the landscape is a relentless expanse of barren plateaux, mountains and ocean. Occasionally a determined village relieves the monotony with commanding views over the fjords that slice deep into the mainland, but generally there is little for the eyes of most visitors. Nor is there much of anything to actually do in what are predominantly fishing and industrial settlements, and there are few tangible attractions beyond the sheer impossibility of the chill wilderness.

The E6 weaves a circuitous course across this vast territory, hugging the Finnish border for much of its length. The only obvious target is the Sámi centre of Karasjok (see p.352), 270km from Nordkapp and 220km from Hammerfest and easily the region's most interesting town. Frankly, there's not much reason to push on further east unless you're intent on picking up the **Hurtigruten coastal boat** as it bobs along the remote and spectacular shores of the Barents Sea. Among the Hurtigruten's several ports of call, perhaps the most diverting is **Kirkenes**, 320km to the east of Karasjok at the end of the E6 and near the Russian frontier: if any European town comes close to defining remoteness then this surely must be it.

Finally, **accommodation** is very thin on the ground, being confined to a handful of the larger communities. Reservations, therefore, are strongly advised. Campsites are more frequent and usually have cabins for rent, but they are mostly stuck in the middle of nowhere.

## South from Nordkapp: Stabbursnes and Tana Bru

Beyond its junction with the E69 Nordkapp road, the E6 bangs along the western shore of the **Porsangerfjord**, a wide inlet that slowly shelves up into the sticky marshes and mud flats at its head. After about 45km, the road reaches Stabbursnes.

### Stabbursnes

The hamlet of **STABBURSNES** lies on the E6 along the western shore of the Porsangerfjord, some 178km south of Nordkapp (and 90km north of Karasjok).

Stabbursnes Naturhus og Museum

Early June daily 11am–6pm; mid-June to mid-Aug daily 9am–8pm; late Aug daily 11am–6pm; Sept–May Tues & Thurs noon–3pm, Wed noon–6pm • 50kr • ⓦ stabbursnes.no

The small but enjoyable **Stabbursnes Naturhus og Museum** (Stabbursnes Nature House and Museum) provides an overview of the region's flora and fauna. There are diagrams of the elaborate heat-exchanger in the reindeer's nose that helps stop the animal from freezing to death in winter, for example, and blow-ups of the warble fly which torments it in summer and various examples of half-hearted taxidermy. There are also examples of traditional Sámi handicrafts and a good section on Finnmark's topography, examining, for example, how and why some of the region's rivers are slow and sluggish, while others have cut deep gashes in the landscape. The museum stands on the eastern periphery of Stabbursdalen Nasjonalpark (see below).

**6**

Stabbursdalen Nasjonalpark

The Stabbursnes Museum is the area's information centre, and sells small guides with some detail on hiking in the park

A large slab of wilderness that contains the world's most northerly pine forest, the **Stabbursdalen Nasjonalpark** covers the slopes of the Stabbursdalen river valley, which runs down from the Finnmarksvidda plateau to the Porsangerfjord. The lower end of the park's valley is broad and marshy, but beyond lie precipitous canyons and chasms – challenging terrain, with a couple of marked **hiking trails**. If that sounds too much like hard work, opt instead for the easy 2.8km stroll east from the museum along the clearly marked nature trail that traverses the thick gravel banks of the Stabbursdalen River where it trickles into the Porsangerfjord. It's an eerily chill landscape and there's a good chance of spotting several species of **wetland bird** in spring and summer: ducks, geese and waders like the lapwing, the curlew and the arctic knot are common. Indeed, these salt marshes and mud flats are such an important resting and feeding area for migratory wetland birds that they have been protected as the Stabbursnes **nature reserve**.

## Tana Bru

Tourist office ☏ 78 92 95 05, ⓦ visittana.no • Buses running between Karasjok and Kirkenes transit at Tana Bru

Some 180km northeast from Karasjok on the E6/E75 along the Finnish border is **TANA BRU**, a Sámi settlement clustered around a suspension bridge over the River Tana. Some 300km long, the Tana, which rattles down to the Tanafjord, an inlet of the Barents Sea, is one of Europe's best salmon rivers – there are regularly catches of up to 250 tons annually. Still, while the fishing is outstanding, it's hedged with restrictions about what you can catch and when; the tourist office will advise.

# Southeast from Nordkapp: Gamvik and Berlevåg

Beyond Nordkapp, the Hurtigruten steers a fine route round the very top of the country, nudging its way between tiny islets and craggy bluffs, and stopping at a series of solitary fishing villages. First stop on the Nordkinn Peninsula (Nordkinnhalvøya in Norwegian; Čorgašnjárga in Sámi) after the quiet Kjøllefjord is the flatlining town of **Mehamn**, though you should skip whatever little life you find here for the 20km drive east to even more remote **Gamvik**.

## Gamvik

**GAMVIK** is a small settlement with a gorgeous little guesthouse (see p.364), Europe's most northerly lighthouse and some excellent outdoor activities on offer. The regional route 888 connects the main towns of Mehamn and Gamvik with the E6, which skirts the base of the peninsula.

## Gamvik Museum

Strandveien 93 • Mid-June to Aug daily 9.30am–4.30pm; Sept to mid-June Mon–Fri 10am–4pm • 50kr • ☎ 78 49 79 49, Ⓦ kystmuseene.no

Covering the history and lives of the people (mostly Sámi) from this area, with a focus on coastal culture and the history of the region's fishing industry, the **Gamvik Museum** is the primary site to visit in town. The several collections cover, for example, the role of women in Finnmark daily life, and also lend themselves to interesting (if small) displays on hunting, trapping, whaling and the Pomor trade.

## Slettnes Fyr

Access by guided tour only; contact Gamvik Museum (☎ 78 49 79 49, Ⓦ kystmuseene.no)

The Gamvik Museum is in charge of mainland Europe's northernmost lighthouse, the red, cast-iron **Slettnes Fyr**, set at the very end of Strandveien. Built in 1905, the lighthouse has since been automated but the museum offers regular guided tours in the summertime. Slettnes also comprises a small nature reserve where you can find sizeable populations of breeding arctic terns, skuas and white-billed divers in the warmer months.

## Berlevåg

Next port of call for the Hurtigruten after Gamvik (or eight hours by land), **BERLEVÅG**, is similarly picturesque, sitting amid a landscape of eerie greenish-grey rock, splashes of colour in a land otherwise stripped by the elements. It's a tiny village, with a population of just 1200, but its cultural traditions and tight community spirit were deftly explored in Knut Jensen's documentary *Heftig og Begeistret* (Cool & Crazy), released in 2001. The film received rave reviews both in Norway and across Europe, a welcome fillip to Berlevåg in general and the subject matter of the film – the local men's choir, the **Berlevåg Mannsangforening** – in particular.

## Berlevåg Harbour Museum

Mid-June to mid-Aug Mon–Fri 10am–6pm, Sat & Sun 1–6pm; mid-Aug to mid-June Mon–Fri 10am–3pm • Free • ☎ 78 98 13 66, Ⓦ kystmuseene.no

Set within an 1950s retrofitted stockhouse, the **Berlevåg Harbour Museum** is the village's main draw. Exhibits here include an old shuttle boat and a less-than-scintillating display on Berlevåg's concrete breakwaters, used to dissipate the extreme force of coastal waves. The museum is also focuses on the history and lives of local fisherfolk.

### ARRIVAL AND DEPARTURE    SOUTHEAST FROM NORDKAPP: GAMVIK AND BERLEVÅG

**By bus** Buses to Gamvik and Berlevåg arrive in the centre of both towns. Boreal Transport (Ⓦ boreal.no) run the following services: Gamvik to Berlevåg (1–2 daily except Sat; 2hr 30min); Berlevåg to Kirkenes (1–2 daily except Sat; 2hr 30min); and Berlevåg to Vadsø (2–5 weekly except Sat, change at Tana Bru; 1hr 10min).

**By boat** On its way north, the Hurtigruten (Ⓦ hurtigruten.com) arrives at 10.30pm; southbound, it docks at 10.15pm. Both boats dock in the harbour for a mere 15min.

### ACCOMMODATION

**Berlevåg Pensjonat og Camping** Havnegata 8, Berlevåg ☎ 78 98 16 10, Ⓦ berlevag-pensjonat.no. This place offers tent pitches and four simple, straightforward guest rooms. Reservations recommended. Pitches 150kr, doubles 750kr

★ **End of the World Guesthouse** Strandveien 43, Gamvik ☎ 90 28 00 38 or ☎ 94 86 85 87, Ⓦ worldendinn .webs.com. Once an overnight spot for sojourning fisherfolk, this clapboard structure has been converted into a small guesthouse by a charming Finnish-Sámi couple. The four simple, rustic, colourful rooms, all with shared bath, look as though a frugal Nordic Martha Stewart has had her way here. Horseriding, ice-hole fishing and king crab safaris are all on offer, and they also rent out skis and cycles. Located on Gamvik's remote coastal road, this is about as back-of-beyond a place to overnight in Norway as you're ever going to find. 600kr

# Vardø and around

Just over five hours on the Hurtigruten from Berlevåg, **VARDØ** is Norway's most easterly town and a busy fishing port of 2500 souls. Like everywhere else in Finnmark, it was savaged in World War II and the modern town that grew up in the 1950s could hardly be described as beautiful, though its geography at least is unusual: Vardø spreads out over two little islets connected by a narrow causeway, which in turn forms the apex of the town's harbour; a tunnel connects Vardø with the mainland, just a couple of kilometres away.

**6**

## Vardøhus Festning

Daily: mid-April to mid-Sept 10am–9pm; mid-Sept to mid-April 10am–6pm • 30kr

One primary reason for a visit to Vardø is the **Vardøhus Festning** (Vardø fortress), a tiny star-shaped fortification located about 600m southwest of the Hurtigruten quay. The site was first built up in 1300, but the present structure dates from the 1730s, built at the behest of King Christian VI. When this singularly unprepossessing monarch toured Finnmark he was greeted, according to one of his courtiers, with "expressions of abject flattery in atrocious verse" – and the king loved it. Christian had the fortress built to guard the northeastern approaches to his kingdom, but it has never seen active service – hence its excellent state of preservation. A small **museum** gives further details of the fort's history.

## Steilneset

Open access • Free

Vardø's newest attraction is the **Steilneset monument**, christened in 2011 by Queen Sonja and commemorating the witches put to death in this region (see box below). Designed by Pritzker Prize-winning Swiss architect Peter Zumthor and the late artist Louise Bourgeois, the monument consists of two structures: a narrow 125m-long building lined with windows – one for each victim of the witch hunts – and a glass building holding a chair with gas flames rising eternally out of it. The memorial is located on the land thought to be the execution site of the witches. During the summer months, an on-site guide provides relevant historical information.

## Vardøhus museum

Mid-June to mid-Aug Mon–Fri 9am–6pm, Sat & Sun 11am–6pm; mid-Aug to mid-June Mon–Fri 9am–3pm • 40kr • ☎ 78 94 04 44

Likely to be housed in a new location by the time you read this, this interesting museum houses a series of well-presented displays covering Vardø's history, with sections devoted to explorers such as Willem Barents and Fridtjof Nansen, plus others examining local flora and fauna. Most interesting of all is the section on the **witch-hunting** fever that gripped Finnmark in the seventeenth century.

---

### DARK TIMES: WITCHFINDING IN FINNMARK

Finnmark was long known to medieval Christians as Ultima Thule – **the end of the world** – and legend has it that the road to hell was a small, unpaved one set out towards the Varanger peninsula, presided over by devils and dark knights. After paganism was outlawed and the Black Death decimated local populations in the late 1300s, the Scandinavian kingdoms exhibited marked intolerance towards anyone harbouring anti-Christian tendencies. Although the Church had long regarded the extremes of Finnmark as the realm of the devil, **witchfinding** only took a hold in the 1620s – half a century or so later than the rest of Europe – when, it was alleged, a coven set up shop in a cave on the edge of Vardø. Over the next sixty years, Norway indicted 135 "witches" found in and around the town, and burned 91 of them alive at the stake – a huge number considering the size of the population.

### Hornøya

Boat trips April to mid-Oct daily; 175kr per person; advance bookings are essential (contact the tourist office; see below)

Of Vardø's outdoor attractions, top of the list is the boat trip that leaves Vardø harbour to cruise round nearby **Hornøya**, a rocky islet that is the country's easternmost protected nature reserve, where thousands of Atlantic puffins, European shags, razorbills, guillemots and great black-backed gulls nest each summer.

### Hamningberg

A byroad threads its way northwest from Vardø along the coast, passing through a lunar-like landscape to reach the (largely) abandoned fishing village of **Hamningberg** after 45km. It's a picturesque spot and scores of locals walk here during Vardø's main festival – Pomordagene (Pomor Days), in early July.

**ARRIVAL AND INFORMATION**                    **VARDØ AND AROUND**

**By bus** Boreal buses (☎ 177, ⊚ boreal.no) run the 75km from Vadsø (see below) to Vardø (1–2 daily; 1hr 35min); sometimes these connect with the service from Varangerbotn, on the Varangerfjord east of Tana Bru (see p.363), to Vadsø service, sometimes they don't – check before you set out.
**By boat** The northbound Hurtigruten reaches Vardø at

4am and leaves just 15min later; southbound it docks at 4pm and leaves 1hr later.

**Tourist office** Havnepromenaden, metres from the Hurtigruten quay (mid-June to mid-Aug Mon–Fri 9am–5.30pm, Sat & Sun 11am–5.30pm; ☎ 78 98 69 07, ⊚ varanger.com).

**ACCOMMODATION**

**Ekkerøy Feriehus** ☎ 90 89 15 58, ⊚ ekkeroy.net. Run by an ecotourism company, these three newly refurbished, freestanding homes outside of town have washing machines and DVD players, as well as access to a wood sauna by the sea, and excellent views out to the Varangerfjord from the rooms. Especially good for birders, who can catch glimpse of sparrows, redshanks,

red-breasted snipes and sanderlings. Located on pretty Ekkerøy peninsula, 20km from Vadsø towards Vardø. Minimum 2 nights. **1300kr**
**Vardo Hotell** Kaigata 8 ☎ 78 98 77 61, ⊚ vardohotel .no. Nothing to write home about, this is effectively the only hotel in town and is appropriately functional. Located a few minutes' walk from the tourist office. **1170kr**

## Vadsø

Four hours by Hurtigruten from Vardø (northbound only) lies the **Varangerfjord**, a bleak, weather-beaten inlet with all its colour and vegetation confined to the northern shore, strewn about with weathered, worn farms and faded fishing boats. The only settlement to speak of hereabouts is **VADSØ**, a once Finnish-speaking town – even now over half the population of 5500 claims Finnish descent. Vadsø's main claim to fame is as the administrative centre of Finnmark, which – to be blunt – isn't a whole heck of a lot to get excited about. Russian bombers and German soldiers between them destroyed a good amount of the town centre during World War II, but there do remain a number of fetching nineteenth-century houses in the northern part of town that comprise the town's museum and are open for visits. If you're arriving by boat, keep an eye out for the **airship mast** used by Roald Amundsen and Umberto Nobile during their North Pole expedition in 1926, placed right where the Hurtigruten docks. Further on, in the centre of town, is the **Innvandrermonumentet** (Immigration Monument), which commemorates the many Finns who migrated here in the eighteenth and nineteenth centuries.

### Vadsø Museum-Ruija Kven Museum

50kr covers all four sites • ☎ 78 94 28 90, ⊚ varangermuseum.no

The **Vadsø Museum-Ruija Kven Museum** documents the culture of the Kven people, ethnic Finns who settled in Norway centuries ago. The museum's "collection" actually comprises the structures and contents of a handful of individual nineteenth-century farmstead buildings.

## Esbensengården and Tuomainen farm

**Esbensengården** Hvistendahlsgata 31 **Tuomainen farm** Slettengata 21 • Both sites mid-June to mid-Aug Mon–Fri 10am–5pm, Sat & Sun 10am-4pm; rest of the year Mon–Fri 10am–3pm

The main building is the **Esbensengården** (Esbensen estate), a late-nineteenth-century home of a well-to-do merchant family that has been decked out with period furnishings. A block away from here is the **Tuomainen farm**, an 1840s-era structure in which the house and barn were combined under the same roof to conserve heat.

## Bietilæ farmhouse

**6**

Havnegata 83 • Sun noon–3pm

Roughly 2km west of town is the newly restored **Bietilæ farmhouse**, a coastal Kven immigrant estate used for farming and fishing. The complex consists of a main house, three barns, a jetty and a slipway. A thorough renovation of the project was completed in 2011, returning the complex to near-original condition.

## Kjeldsen fishing factory

Ekkerøy • Daily noon–6pm

Finally, some 15km east on Ekkerøy is the **Kjeldsenbruket** (Kjeldsen fishing factory), one of the few prewar fishing establishments still intact in Finnmark. Dating from 1911, the complex comprises a jetty, packing house, a grim cod-liver oil steamer, as well as small shacks for baiting the lines and cleaning the fish.

### ARRIVAL AND DEPARTURE                                                        VADSØ

**By bus** Boreal buses (☏ 177, ⊛ boreal.no) from Kirkenes/ Varangerbotn (1–2 daily except Sat; 3hr 30min/50min) as well as Vardø (see p.365) pull into Vadsø bus station on Strandgata, located on a stumpy promontory in the centre of town. From here, it's about 1km to the Hurtigruten dock, over the bridge on Vadsøya island.
**By boat** The northbound Hurtigruten reaches Vadsø at 7.30am and leaves 30min later; the southbound boat does not dock here. From Vadsø, the ship takes nearly 2hr to cross the deep blue-black waters of the

Varangerfjord on the last stage of its journey to Kirkenes. There's snow on the mainland here even in July, which makes for a picturesque chug across the fjord, the odd fishing boat the only sign of life. Note that as the town centre is located 1km across a bridge from the harbour, you're best off catching a taxi over here if you have very limited time.
**Tourist office** At the quay (mid-June to mid-Aug Mon–Fri 9am–5.30pm, Sat & Sun 11am–5.30pm; ☏ 78 98 69 07, ⊛ varanger.com).

### ACCOMMODATION

**Rica Hotel Vadsø** Oscars gate 4 ☏ 78 95 52 50, ⊛ rica.no. A large, modern and really rather pleasant affair in the town centre, with lots of exposed wood in the rooms. Definitely Vadsø's best place to stay, and also holds the town's best restaurant, *Oscar Mat og Vinhus*,

which features daily specials. <u>1045kr</u>
**Vadsø Apartments** Tibergveien 2 ☏ 78 95 44 00, ✉ akloghhe@online.no. These eight modern en-suite single and double rooms have a kitchenette, plus access to a washer/dryer. Set a few minutes from the quay. <u>500kr</u>

# Kirkenes

Used by the Nazis to ship out iron ore from its ice-free port, the mining town of **KIRKENES** was bombed more heavily during World War II than any other place in Europe apart from Malta. The retreating German army torched what was left as they fled in the face of liberating Soviet soldiers, who found 3500 locals hiding in the nearby iron-ore mines. The mines finally closed in 1996, threatening the future of this 4000-strong community, which is now trying hard to kindle trade with Russia to keep itself afloat. The sterling part Kirkenes played in the war is recalled in the Sør-Varanger museum (see p.368) and also by a couple of **monuments** – one dedicated to the town's wartime women in the main square, and a second to the Red Army, plonked on Roald Amundsens gate, just to the east.

Thanks to the bombs, Kirkenes is now almost entirely modern, with long rows of uniform houses spreading out along the Bøkfjord, a narrow arm of the Barents Sea. If that sounds dull, it's not to slight the town, which makes the most of its inhospitable surroundings with some pleasant public gardens, lakes and residential areas – it's just that it seems an awfully long way to come for not very much.

## Sør-Varanger museum

Early June to mid-Aug daily 10am–6pm; mid-Aug to early June Mon–Fri 10am–2pm, Sat & Sun 10am–3.30pm • 50kr • ⓦ varangermuseum.no • The museum is about 1.5km south of the main harbourfront

Set at the end of Solheimsveien (the E6) beside one of the town's several little lakes, is the **Sør-Varanger museum**, one of whose sections – the **Grenselandmuseet** (Frontier Museum) – focuses on the history of the region and its people, and includes a detailed account of the events of World War II, illustrated by some fascinating old photos. In the same building is a display of the work of **John Savio** (1902–38), a local Sámi artist whose life was brief and tragic. Orphaned at the age of three, Savio was ill from childhood onwards and died in poverty of tuberculosis at the age of 36. This lends poignancy to his woodcuts and paintings, with their lonely evocations of the Sámi way of life and the overbearing power of nature.

## Andersgrotta Cave

Presteveien 19–21 • Mid-June to mid-Aug daily 10am–3pm • 100kr • ⓦ andersgrotta.no

In the face of successive waves of Soviet bombing, the **Andersgrotta** air-raid shelter was commissioned by the occupying Germans and blasted out in 1941. After the war, the bunker was strengthened with concrete and continued to be used as a nuclear shelter throughout the Cold War. Stairs lead down to the extensive (but rather cold) space, where you can amble the corridors and catch a very short English-language film about Kirkenes's role during the war.

### ARRIVAL AND INFORMATION                                    KIRKENES

**By plane** Widerøe (ⓦ wideroe.no) flies to Kirkenes from a hatful of north Norwegian towns, including Alta, Hammerfest and Tromsø; a one-way ticket from Kirkenes to Alta can go for as little as 550kr, though 750kr is a more usual fare. SAS (ⓦ flysas.com) and Norwegian (ⓦ norwegian.com) also offer direct flights several times daily. The airport is located 13km west of town just off the E6; Flybussen (2–5 daily; 20min; 85kr one-way) connects the airport with the centre. A taxi (☎ 78 99 13 97) will run in excess of 250kr.

**By bus** The bus station is at the west end of the main harbourfront. Boreal services (ⓦ boreal.no) run to: Alta (1–2 daily except Sat; 11–13hr); Hammerfest (4 weekly; 10hr–12hr 30min); Karasjok (4 weekly; 5hr 20min–5hr 40min); and Vadsø (1–2 daily except Sat; 4hr 40min).

**By boat** Kirkenes is the northern terminus of the Hurtigruten, which arrives here at 10am and departs for points south at 12.45pm. Taking the boat also means that you can avoid the long haul back the way you came – and by the time you reach Kirkenes you'll certainly be heartily sick of the E6. The Hurtigruten uses the quay just over 1km east of the town centre; a local bus shuttles between the two.

**Tourist office** Presteveien 1, roughly 400m east along Kirkegata from the bus station (June–Aug Mon–Fri 10am–6pm, Sat & Sun 10am–4pm; Sept–May Mon–Fri 10am–4pm; ☎ 78 99 80 11, ⓦ kirkenesinfo.no).

### ACCOMMODATION

**Kirkenes Snowhotel** Andrevann ☎ 78 97 05 40, ⓦ kirkenessnowhotel.com. The adventurous set will jump at the chance to experience a night in this unique cosy overnight spot. Rooms, built out of ice and snow, are kept at −5°C and for shuteye, guests jump into expedition-strength, subzero Ajungilak sleeping bags, then lie down on a furry cut of reindeer hide. Set in the Gabba Reindeer Park a few kilometres south of town, so Rudolf is just steps away. Also an excellent place to catch the northern lights. Open mid-Dec to mid-April. Price includes transfer and half-board. **4700kr**

**Rica Arctic** Kongensgata 1 ☎ 78 99 59 00, ⓦ rica.no. It's

a chain all right, but all the way up here who can afford to be picky? The eighty well-appointed rooms occupy a smart modern block in the centre near the town square. Swimming pool and sauna to boot. The restaurant is one of the best in town. **1125kr**

**Thon Hotel Kirkenes** Johan Knudtzens gate 11 ☎ 78 97 10 50, ⓦ thonhotels.com. Opened in 2010, this 144-room spot is set on the fjord in the centre of town. Rooms are thankfully very modern, with some real class and flair to them, making it the best – as well as largest – place to stay in town. Free wi-fi. **995kr**

## EATING

**Gapahuken** Sollia Gjestegård ☎78 99 08 20, ⓦstorskog.no. Set about 10km from town close to the Russian border, this excellent rustic Norwegian restaurant actually looks right into Mother Russia. The whale steak and king crab come highly recommended. They also rent out cabins (from 1050kr) and double rooms (from 900kr). Outside of summer you must reserve a table one day in advance. Mid-June to Aug Tues–Sat 3–10pm, Sun 3–7pm, closed Mon.

**Thon Hotel Kirkenes** Johan Knudtzens gate 11 ☎78 97 10 50, ⓦthonhotels.com. The town's newest restaurant addition, often going by the name of *69 North*, is this competent take on Nordic cuisine. The menu is dominated by local fish and shellfish, with dishes priced at around 200kr/main. In the warmer months, get a seat on the terrace right by the fjord's waterfront. Mon–Sat 11am–4pm & 5–10pm, Sun 4–10pm.

# Øvre Pasvik Nasjonalpark

Hidden away some 120km south of Kirkenes, where the borders of Norway, Finland and Russia intersect, is a ten-by-nine-kilometre parcel of wilderness that comprises the **Øvre Pasvik Nasjonalpark**, a western offshoot of the Siberian taiga. The park's subarctic pine forest covers a series of low-lying hills that make up about half the total area, and below lie swamps, marshes and lakes. Wolverines and bears live in the forest, and there are also traces of the prehistoric Komsa culture, notably the vague remains of pit-traps beside **Lake Ødevatn**. The Kirkenes tourist office has details of guided tours to the park, which are useful as you have to be something of a wilderness-hiker-cum-survivalist expert to delve into the park under your own steam. The absence of natural landmarks makes it easy to get lost, especially as there are no marked footpaths, nor is there any map that can be relied upon.

### ARRIVAL AND DEPARTURE      ØVRE PASVIK NASJONALPARK

**By car** If you have your own vehicle (there's no public transport), then drive south from Kirkenes for about 100km along Highway 885 through the pine forests of the Pasvik river valley as far as Vaggatem. Turn off the main road 1.5km or so further on and then follow the 9km rough forest road south to a lake, Sortbrysttjern (Sortabaetluobbal), from where a footpath takes you into the park at another lake, Ellenvatnet.

## CROSSING INTO RUSSIA

From Kirkenes, it's just 16km southeast along the E105 to **Storskog**, Norway's only official border crossing point with Russia. You can take photographs of the frontier, provided you don't snap any Russian personnel or military installations – which rather limits the options as there's little else to see. The crossing is busy for much of the year, but it's not open for casual day-trippers; in any case, the only convenient settlement nearby is the ugly and heavily sullied Russian mining town of **Nikel**, around 40km further to the south, from where you can – extraordinarily enough – travel by train all the way to Vladivostok. Several Kirkenes travel agents organize day- and weekend tours into Russia, the most worthwhile being those to the Arctic port of **Murmansk**. The trips include both a visa and the fee for the invitation you need to acquire said visa (500kr for one day, 675kr for three), which the agents can arrange in a few hours once they have your passport, a completed visa application form, an extra passport photo and the money; if you do it on your own, reckon on at least one week, possibly two or three. Among these **travel agents**, Pasvikturist, in the centre at Dr. Wesselsgate 9 (☎78 99 50 80, ⓦpasvikturist.no), is as good as any. They have details of trips to Murmansk, both one-night (2900kr per person) and weekend (3200kr) excursions – a return bus trip alone will run you 600kr (or 1750kr in a taxi, which seats three passengers). Incidentally, there is a **Russian consulate** in Kirkenes, at Arbeidergata 6 (☎78 99 37 37, ⓦwww.kirkenes.mid.ru), but they will not shortcut the visa process, which costs 315kr (excluding invitation) and can take between 5 and 10 days. If a Russian jaunt proves impossible, you'll have to be content with the reflection that if you have made it to Kirkenes and the border, you are further east than Istanbul and as far north as Alaska.

6

## ACCOMMODATION

**Øvre Pasvik Café and Camping** ☎ 78 99 55 30, ⓦ pasvik-cafe.no. Located in Vaggatem along the eastern side of Highway 885, this year-round spot offers ten simple wooden huts. All have fridge and cooking facilities, and they also rent out bicycles and small boats. Cabins <u>**500kr**</u>

# Svalbard

**6**

The 62,500-square-kilometre **Svalbard archipelago** is one of the most hostile places on earth. Some 836km north of the Norwegian mainland – and just 1308km from the North Pole – two-thirds of its surface is covered by glaciers, the soil frozen to a depth of up to 500m. Despite the hardships such topography engenders, there are convincing reasons to make a trip. For one, Svalbard's hinterlands make it a devastatingly gorgeous place to visit – whether in summer, autumn or spring when a magical light engulfs a Bergmanesque landscape and the Arctic opens itself up to curious visitors (during winter Svalbard is unconscionably dark). Experiences up here can be otherworldly: hiking a permafrost landscape strewn with antlers and whalebones; donning a massive orange drysuit to float around in icy waters; and dining at a snowy beach on campfire-cooked ox gruel and fjord-chilled champagne.

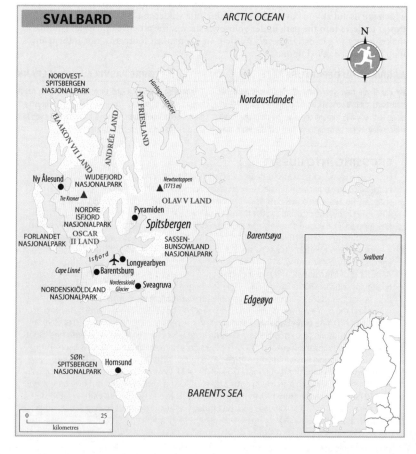

It's not your average place to visit – this is a land where there are double as many polar bears as people – and is a once-in-a-lifetime destination if ever there was one.

**Weather**-wise, things are actually much better than you might expect. The warming Gulf Stream helps keep the coastal waters of this Arctic desert largely ice-free and navigable for much of the year – though the main fjords do tend to freeze over for several months of the winter – and the land is oddly fertile. Between late April and late August there's continuous daylight and, with temperatures bobbing up into the high teens, the snow has all but disappeared by July, leaving the valleys covered in wild flowers. And then there's the **wildlife**, an abundance of Arctic fauna, including over a hundred species of migratory birds, arctic foxes, polar bears and reindeer on land, and seals, walruses and whales offshore. In winter, it's a slighly different story: the polar night, during which the sun remains a full 8° below the horizon, lasts from late October to mid-February. The average temperature in February, Svalbard's coldest month, is -16.2°C, though this has plummeted to a staggering record low of -46°C – and that's not counting wind-chill.

### Brief history

Though the landscape of Svalbard is mentioned in a twelfth-century Icelandic saga, suggesting that the Vikings made it up here several centuries previously, the first recorded discovery of Svalbard's ice shards was by Dutch explorer **Willem Barents** on June 17, 1596. It was the third year in a row that Barents had come in search of the Northeast Passage, and when his Dutch crew saw the icy peaks of Svalbard (whose modern name for which derives from the Old Norse for "land with the cold coast", they actually believed they had arrived at part of Greenland. After a protracted maritime battle with a polar bear, Barents was forced to winter at Bjørnøya just south of the main island, and later died sailing towards the Russian Arctic island of Novaya Zemlya. A decade later, an English ship landed to hunt walrus, followed by French and Danish whalers, Russian polar bear and fox trappers and, at the beginning of the twentieth century, coal miners from all over the place.

Even today, the mythology of early European exploration informs everyday life here, with place names that read like an encyclopedia of imperial Arctic discoverers and explorers. Aside from the Barents Sea, there is Taylorfjellet, a mountain recalling the Victorian editor of *The Scottish Geographical Magazine*, W.A. Taylor; Murraypynten, a cape named after Scottish oceanographer Sir John Murray; and a group of islands named after sixteenth-century merchant and adventurer Thomas Smythe.

After rich **coal** deposits were discovered in 1899 – the geological residue of a prehistoric tropical forest – the first coal mine was opened by an American seven years later and passed into Norwegian hands in 1916. Meanwhile, other countries, particularly Russia and Sweden, were getting into the coal-mining act, and when, in 1920, **Norway's sovereignty** over the archipelago was ratified by international treaty, it was on condition that those other countries who were operating mines could continue to do so. It was also agreed that the islands would be a demilitarized zone, which made them, incidentally, sitting ducks for a German squadron, which arrived here to bombard the Norwegian coal mines during World War II. Today though, only two of the collieries are still in operation – generating enough energy to run Longyearbyen's power station – and Svalbard's role is now primarily as an outpost for Arctic research and a place where tourists come to experience life at the end of the world.

## Spitsbergen

The main island of the Svalbard archipelago, **Spitsbergen**, is the only one with the facilities that make it possible to visit. It is also the only island that is permanently inhabited, with five settlements in total – three Norwegian, one Russian and one Polish – and a total population of roughly 2000. Spitsbergen ("pointed mountains") was named by Willem Barents in 1596, though the appellation was first applied to both the main island and the archipelago as a whole – and in fact Svalbard continues to be known as Spitsbergen in most countries around the world.

## ARRIVAL AND DEPARTURE                                                    SPITSBERGEN

**By air** The simplest way by a long shot to reach Svalbard is to fly to the archipelago's airport at Longyearbyen, on Spitsbergen. SAS operates direct services there from Tromsø and Oslo Gardermoen. A return ticket on the Tromsø–Longyearbyen flight (1hr 40min) without restrictions is a steep 4500kr, though special deals are commonplace, reducing this to 2500–3500kr. Don't count on any of the budget airlines getting a toehold on the Svalbard routes though. Before you book your flight, you'll need to reserve accommodation in Longyearbyen (see opposite) and – unless you're happy to be stuck in your lodgings – you'd be well advised to pre-book any guided excursions you fancy too.

## GETTING AROUND

There are no road connections between any of Svalbard's settlements – snowmobiles, boats and aircraft are the only modes of transport – though there are 43km of road in and around Longyearbyen. Public transport is limited to the airport bus, occasional cargo ships from Longyearbyen to both Barentsburg and Ny Ålesund, and a light-aircraft service from Longyearbyen to Ny Ålesund, though government employees and researchers take priority on these flights.

## Longyearbyen

With just over two thousand year-round inhabitants, the only Norwegian settlement of any size up here is **LONGYEARBYEN**, a comparatively desolate spot that huddles on the narrow coastal plain below the mountains and beside the Adventfjorden, a small bay on the southern side of the Isfjorden, roughly in the middle of the island. It was founded in 1906, when John Munroe Longyear, an American mine-owner, established the Arctic Coal Company here.

From most angles, Longyearbyen is an altogether ramshackle sort of place hunkered and bunkered down against the blast of winter. Strewn about with large containers, transport vehicles and building machinery, it resembles something of a junkyard construction site. The few buildings that pass for the town centre are located about 500m in from the fjord just to the east of the Longyearelva River. Longyearbyen is, however, well equipped with services, including shops, cafés, a post office, bank, swimming pool, several tour companies, a campsite, a couple of guesthouses and half a dozen hotels, though advance reservations are essential for all accommodation.

### Svalbard Museum

Daily: March–Sept 10am–5pm; Oct–Feb noon–5pm • 75kr • Ⓦ svalbardmuseum.no

This vast, newly created space in the town centre is one of northern Norway's best museums. A massive polar bear looms over displays of ethnographic artefacts, documents and dioramas, while there are several multimedia presentations on the history of the region – and some of the issues it is currently facing. It's definitely worth at least an hour

---

### GLOBAL SEED VAULT

Svalbard is home to the **Global Seed Vault**, a "doomsday" bank built in 2008 that stores seeds from thousands of crop varieties and their botanical wild relatives from all over the world. The current total number of seed samples numbers some 250 million (representing 500,000 different varieties), including members of one-third of the world's most important varieties of food crops. The vault is most commonly used in the event that any of the world's thousand-plus collections of diverse crops accidentally lose or destroy samples – not an infrequent occurrence. The structure is about as impervious to an end-of-the-world catastrophe as possible, constructed some 120m inside a sandstone mountain and 130m above sea level, which ensures the site will stay dry even in the event that all the icecaps melt. Seeds are kept in specially constructed four-ply packets and heat-sealed to exclude moisture. For obvious reasons, the vault is closed to visitors unable to prove some specific scientific purpose.

of your time before or after exploring the back of beyond outside of town, and has a great gift shop too selling maps and a large selection of Arctic-related books.

## ARRIVAL AND INFORMATION

**Longyearbyen airport** The airport is 5km west of the town centre and the airport bus links the two, its schedule coinciding with flight arrivals and departures.

**Tourist office** Inside the Svalbard Museum (Daily: May–Sept 10am–5pm; Oct–April noon–5pm; ☎ 79 02 55 50, ⓦ svalbard.net). The tourist office has information on a wide range of day-long and multi-day excursions available,

## LONGYEARBYEN

as well as cultural events such as concerts, art exhibitions and films on in town.

**Listings** *Icepeople* (ⓦ icepeople.net) is a weekly printed and online English-language news and society publication produced every Tues in Longyearbyen.

**Internet** You can get free internet access at the Lompensentret (book on ☎ 79 02 23 70).

## ACCOMMODATION

★ **Basecamp Trapper's Hotel** ☎ 79 02 46 00, ⓦ basecampspitsbergen.com. Possibly the most classically "Arctic" of Longyearbyen's places to stay is this sort of enlarged mock-up of a trapper's cabin, complete with sealskins and a sauna and mostly made from old, recycled lumber; it all feels vaguely kitsch and put-on but great fun all the same – and very convivial. Be sure to visit the upstairs "Cognac attic", where you can sip on an ultra-pricey drink as you gaze out to the mountains from the glass roof. 1050kr

**Longyearbyen Camping** ☎ 79 02 14 44, ⓦ www .longyearbyen-camping.com. While probably not your first choice as a camping destination – for one thing, it's about an hour's walk from town – this 30,000-square-metre tundra coastal plain out by the airport is likely to be the most remote spot you've ever pitched a tent. And if you're brave you can get an official campsite-issued "Longyearbyen Camping Arctic Naked-bathing Certificate", provided someone has seen you do the dirty deed. Open March–Sept. Tents 100kr, doubles 300kr

**Mary Ann's Polarrigg** ☎ 79 02 37 02, ⓦ polarriggen .com. Set a few minutes drive from town and looking right onto the Hjorthfjellet mountain face, "The Rig" opened its doors several decades ago as a small wooden barracks for local labourers. The three buildings have since been converted and done up in Arctic ephemera that is vaguely evocative of what Svalbard was probably like for the miners and trappers who came here a century ago – give or take

the restorative on-site Thai spa. The 41 atmospheric rooms feature exposed beams and rustic amenities, there's a comfy lounge filled with books and curiosities, and the great Thai-inspired restaurant also serves cod tongue, whale tartare and steak of seal – though the beef stew is a real winner too. 895kr

**Radisson BLU Polar Hotel** ☎ 79 02 34 50, ⓦ radissonblu.com. This modern chalet-like affair has nearly a hundred rooms decorated in fairly standard Nordic chain style, the pick of which have views over to the Isfjorden. The hotel is a few minutes' walk from the tourist office. 1610kr

**Svalbard Hotel** ☎ 79 02 46 60, ⓦ svalbardbooking .com. Longyearbyen's newest hotel, opened in 2011, is this sleek, modern and surprisingly soulful wall-to-wall carpeted spot just at the top of the town's main road. The seventeen rooms here have bright and spiffy modern decor, and many feature wall-sized Arctic photographs (of a polar bear, for instance). 1190kr

★ **Spitsbergen Hotel** ☎ 79 02 62 00, ⓦ spitsbergen travel.no. Once housing the CEOs and technical engineers of local mining companies and also known as "Funken", this is the settlement's best mid-level hotel. The 88 rooms offer some classical, nauticalesque atmosphere – rich exposed wood floors, gold-plated fixtures – and it holds a small library, a sauna and an excellent on-site restaurant, *Funktionærmessen*. Located a 10min walk from the town centre on a small ridge. Excellent bargain. 790kr

## EATING AND DRINKING

### CAFÉS AND RESTAURANTS

**Brasseri Nansen** Radisson BLU Polar Hotel ☎ 79 02 34 50, ⓦ radissonblu.com. A good bet for a proper sit-down meal, serving all manner of Arctic specialities from char to reindeer, seal and (like it or not) whale. Burgers and salads start at 113kr, though more local dishes such as the Barents Sea spotted catfish with garlic bok choy, cassava root and king crab wonton of shellfish sauce (247kr), are better. Go for a window table, with great views out to the fjord. The attached, often rowdy bar, *Barentz*, is the place to head in town for a last-ditch pull at 2am. Daily noon–10.30pm.

**Classic Pizza Sentrum** Lompensentret. This simple snack spot serves good burgers (79kr) and better kebabs (99kr). It tends to get the most activity well after midnight, especially when the town's three bars let out. Sun–Thurs 3pm–3am, Fri & Sat 3pm–5am.

**Fruene Kaffe & Vinbar** Lompensentret ☎ 79 02 76 40. This buzzy café has friendly staff and tends to really pack out for lunch. In addition to soups, sandwiches (around 150kr) and great cinnamon buns (25kr), they serve twelve flavours of ice cream in case you happen to need a shot of cold. Daily 10am–5pm.

**6**

## SVALBARD TOURS

Guided tours are big business on Svalbard and you can choose anything from hiking and snowmobiling through to kayaking, ice-caving, dog-sledging, Zodiac boat trips and wildlife safaris, not to mention trips into a former coal mine and stays on a converted Dutch schooner moored in the polar ice. The winter season runs from December to late May, while June to November is the season for "summer" activities. Your first point of contact should be Longyearbyen's official tourist office, **Svalbard Tourism** (see p.373), which presents a fairly thorough overview of everything you can do on the island. Next, select a tour operator – some of the best ones are listed below; prices tend to not vary too much. Note that in addition to the tours below, most of the operators run day-trips to Barentsburg (see p.376) by snowmobile or Zodiac, and some do overnight trips as well, with a stay in the hotel.

You can, of course, book a whole holiday with an operator back home (see p.27) or even take pot luck when you get there, but be warned that wilderness excursions are often fully booked weeks in advance. And finally, note that if you are determined to strike out into the wilderness **independently**, you first have to seek permission from, and log your itinerary with, the governor's office, Sysselmannen på Svalbard, Postboks 633, N-9171 Longyearbyen (📞 79 02 43 00, 🌐 sysselmannen.no) – and they will certainly require you to carry some form of weapon (see box opposite).

### LOCAL TOUR OPERATORS

**Basecamp Spitsbergen** 📞 79 02 46 00, 🌐 basecampspitsbergen.com. Svalbard's most innovative adventure company, whose offerings include an evening snowshoe trip to see the northern lights (590kr), a three-day dog-sledding trip out to a century-old Dutch schooner (now an atmospheric floating hotel) moored in the ice (15,900kr) and five-day skiing expedition to the glacial peaks of Oscar II Land (12,900kr). Also operates the boutique *Isfjord Radio* guesthouse several hours southwest of Longyearbyen (see box, p.376).

**Poli Arctici** 📞 79 02 17 05, 🌐 poliarctici.com. Run by an affable Italian outdoorsman, this smallish specialist operator is one of the best in town, offering snowmobiling, boating and hiking tours from 690kr. They also rent out small apartments in Longyearbyen, and have a cottage out at Van Mijenfjorden, some 65km away, that's available for stays during the winter.

**Spitsbergen Travel** 📞 79 02 61 00, 🌐 spitsbergentravel.no. One of Svalbard's largest outfitters, they run hotels, restaurants, safaris and can even rent out weapons and clothing. Their amazing four-day summer cross-country ski expedition (9700kr) heads out to the north of Spitsbergen, passing through Ny Ålesund.

**Svalbard Husky** 📞 98 87 16 21, 🌐 svalbardhusky .no. A solid dog-sledding group with around 50 huskies based about 10min outside of Longyearbyen in Adventdalen. A 4hr winter husky tour costs from 1090kr. In the warmer months, the dogs pull sledges outfitted with wheels (790kr).

**Svalbard Maxi Taxi** 📞 79 02 13 05, 🌐 taxiguiden .no. This local taxi company offers informative guided tours twice daily of Longyearbyen (275kr per person), which take in the Global Seed Vault, Adventdalen coal mine and Longyearbyen church, among other sights.

**Svalbard Snøscooterutleie** 📞 79 02 46 61, 🌐 scooterutleie.net. Manned by a gang of consummate Norwegian adventurers and maintaining scores of vehicles, this is one of your best options for snowmobiling adventures. A 3hr journey through the polar night starts at 1350kr; an 8hr day-trip to Barentsburg costs from 2050kr.

**Terra Polaris** 📞 79 02 10 68, 🌐 www.terrapolaris .com. One of the most hard-core of Svalbard's adventure companies, this place specializes in extended journeys out to some of the archipelago's more remote spots. Pick from a skiing expedition to Newtontoppen and Atomfjella (15 days; 22,500kr), a tour of Spitsbergen and eastern Greenland (13 days; €4500), or a visit to Franz Josef Land and Novaya Zemlya by Russian ice breaker (12 days; 45,000kr), among many other journeys. Owned by Svalbard expert and guidebook author Andreas Umbreit.

★ **Huset** 📞 79 02 25 00, 🌐 huset.com. Located on the west side of the river at the southern end of town, this outstanding white-tablecloth restaurant specializes in Arctic dishes with main courses at around 250kr, much less if you eat at the attached bar. The difference is the management, the head of whom trained with Gordon Ramsay and it shows: staff have never been more deferential. After hours the place turns into Svalbard's closest approximation to a disco – though the dancing here tends to be pretty low-key. Restaurant daily 7pm–midnight; bar Sun–Fri 4pm–midnight, Sat 2pm–midnight; nightclub 11pm–3am.

**Kroa** ☎ 79 02 13 00, ⓦ kroa-svalbard.no. Built out of the remains of a dilapidated Russian coal mine, this rivals *Huset* in terms of food quality and choice, and the decor is unbeatable for end-of-the-world rustic charm. The sizeable dishes tend towards the "continental" – the seal and whale being two of the few exceptions. Daily 11.30am–2am.

### BARS

★ **Karls-Berger Pub** Lompensentret ☎ 79 02 25 11. Set into a cosy (and often cramped) wooded room, this is Longyearbyen's most atmospheric place to get sauced and chat up a local. While they don't serve draught beers, what they do offer is an astounding 1000 bottles of different whiskies and other top- and bottom-shelf spirits – a 1908 Armagnac, for example, or a Cognac from 1802 (you don't even want to know how much). Six shots of whatever the drink of the day is – more often Jägermeister or something of equal shelf weight – will cost you 219kr. Sun–Fri 5pm–2am, Sat 3pm–2am.

**Svalbar** ☎ 79 02 50 00, ⓦ svalbar.no. With a Les Paul signed by four members of Mötley Crüe and enough Drakkar Noir-wearing Norwegians to film a school reunion reality show, this spacious bar, filled with large vinyl couches, is your best bet for authentic local colour after hours. Also the place to play pool or darts, or catch the football. Carlsberg on draught (44kr), and great burgers too. Mon–Fri 10am–2am, Sat & Sun noon–2am.

### SHOPPING

**Lompensentret** The local indoor mall features a dozen-odd shops and cafés, including Gullgruva, which sells various gold and silver jewellery, silverware and souvenirs. You'll also find a pharmacy and the local library here, the latter offering a great selection of polar-related titles. Mon–Fri 10am–6pm, Sat 10am–3pm; library Mon–Thurs 9am–9pm, Fri 9am–6.30pm, Sat 9.45am–5.30pm.

**Norwegian Polar Institute** ☎ 79 02 26 00, ⓦ npolar .no. Inside the same building as the museum and the governor's office, this place sells a very good collection of topographical and touring maps, as well as handbooks on the Arctic. Mon–Fri 8.30am–4pm.

**Svalbardbutikken** ⓦ svalbardbutikken.no. Also known as Coop Svalbard, this large modern supermarket in the centre of town sells almost any food product you'd find elsewhere in Norway – including freshly baked goods – as well as a good selection of souvenirs. More crucially, though, it contains the only liquor store in town – a popular stop given Svalbard's exemption from Norway's exceedingly high taxes on alcohol. Be sure to bring your airline ticket to prove that you're a visitor. Supermarket Mon–Fri 10am–8pm, Sat 10am–6pm, Sun 3–6pm; liquor store Mon–Fri 10am–6pm, Sat 10am–3pm.

## TO BEAR ARMS

As the world's most northerly settled land, Svalbard easily lends itself to notching up your bedpost with geographic superlatives: most northerly kebab; most northerly naff souvenir shop; most northerly place in the world where you can walk around in a hoodie and carry a **gun** without ever getting a second look from your neighbour. Island law requires everyone of age to carry a firearm anywhere outside of Longyearbyen – most residents travel with a Ruger .30 rifle – as well as a "shocking device", a signal pistol or suchlike, to ward off polar bears. Firearms can be rented from, among other places, Ingeniør G. Paulsen (☎ 79 02 32 00) in town, though you'll need to either show documentation that you have permission to possess a firearm in your home country or apply for a licence with the governor (see box, p.374).

These regulations are a constant reminder that somewhere out there lurks *Ursus maritimus*, the common, hungry **polar bear**. Polar bear attacks up here, while not commonplace, tend to get plenty of press in the international media, which often serves to tarnish Svalbard's good name for a while and result in a few cancelled holiday plans. In 2011, a British teenager was tragically mauled to death and four others injured when a polar bear entered their tent during an expedition sponsored in part by the Royal Geographical Society. Though there have been just five fatal bear attacks on humans since 1971, thirteen bears were shot to death between 2001 and 2011. The root cause of all these deaths – both human and ursine – isn't carelessness, though: it's **global warming**. As the sea ice retreats, the bears, who more commonly hunt seals, are forced to unaccustomedly look inland for sustenance, even targeting such unlikely food sources as the eggs of barnacle geese. As food and proper hunting grounds dwindle, interactions between polar bears and humans are likely to increase, particularly as out of the estimated 3500 polar bears that comprise the Barents Sea population roughly half live on or around Spitsbergen.

**6**

---

### ARCTIC POSH: ISFJORD RADIO

At **Cape Linne** on the Isfjord's southernmost tip is a tiny settlement that has been retrofitted over the past several years into one of Svalbard's premier adventure destinations, Loomed over today by a massive radio tower and a dilapidated satellite dish, the cape's **Isfjord Radio Station** was established in 1933 as the sole telecommunications link between Svalbard and the Norwegian mainland. When underwater fibre optics laid seventy years later outmoded the station overnight, Norwegian adventure company **Basecamp Spitsbergen** (**☎** 79 02 46 00, **Ⓦ** basecampspitsbergen.com; inclusive stays from 7300kr per person) stepped in and re-envisioned the settlement's half-dozen buildings as a remote, rustic-chic base for explorations into the Arctic wilderness. The 23 swish, blue-grey rooms are done up with exposed wood, large comfy beds, goatskin blankets and driftwood sculptures, with high-powered binoculars that await you at the window sills (the station looks out onto a protected bird area).

---

## Around the island

Outside of Longyearbyen you will need your own transport and guide – in almost all cases this will need to be organized by a local operator (see box, p.374). Of the areas covered below, **Isfjorden**, **Barentsberg** and to a lesser extent, **Pyramiden** are the only places with any accommodation to speak of for travellers.

### Isfjorden

Extending west from Longyearbyen into the Arctic Sea, the **Isfjorden** is Svalbard's second longest fjord, and is one of the most common places to head out on organized overland (or water-based) excursions not least as a large chunk is preserved in the **Nordre Isfjorden Nasjonalpark**. Visits include crossings to **Trygghamna**, a quiet, snowy pocket of the fjord that attracted Basque and English whalers during the sixteenth century. Another option is out to the bird cliffs of **Alkhornet**, where the umber land undulates in tussocky patches of arctic poppy, polar willow and saxifrage – flora that take advantage of the long periods of midnight sun to compensate for the polar nights. Here you'll encounter thousands of squawking Brünnich guillemots, fulmars and petrels breaking the Arctic silence high above. The best spot to base yourself for any of these excursions is Basecamp Spitsbergen's *Isfjord Radio* (see box above).

### Barentsburg

The only Russian settlement is the flatlining coal-mining township of **Barentsburg**, a community sold by Norway to Russia in 1932. Today, some 300 Russian and Ukrainian residents eke out a living in coal-mining and cling onto the (not entirely unfounded) hope that one day oil will be found up here. It can be a dire and bleak place, with street lamps lit by coal fire, no small amount of rusty scrap iron and the odd sauced Russian staggering down the street at midday. There isn't a whole heck of a lot to do in town, beyond visiting the ageing Soviet **sports hall** and its filthy swimming pool, or the **chapel** just opposite, built following a tragic 1996 plane crash in Longyearbyen in which 141 Russians were killed – but the staff at the *Barentsburg Hotel* (see below) will walk visitors around town on an English-language tour (80kr per person) for an hour or so.

For logistical and transport reasons, visits to Barentsburg should always be arranged as part of an excursion (see box, p.374). Note that Norwegian kroner, US dollars and euros are accepted for payment on Barentsburg, but not UK pound sterling.

## ACCOMMODATION                                                                                    BARENTSBURG

**Barentsburg Hotel ☎** 79 02 18 14 or **☎** 95 30 68 86. The die-hard can stay overnight in a simple, wood-panelled room at this Soviet-era hotel, which has just come out of a thorough renovation, bringing most of the place up to "modern" European standard. There is a large restaurant serving, in addition to traditional Russian meat-and-potatoes meals, Russian vodka. A small gift shop on the first floor sells not-overpriced Russian and

Soviet-era paraphernalia such as matryoshka dolls and military hats. **600kr**

Pyramiden

A second Russian mining settlement, **Pyramiden**, to the north of Longyearbyen, was abandoned in 2001 when the coal seams ran out – it has the distinct feel of a ghost town where everyone one day just up and left mid-sentence. Since then, there have been lengthy debates as to what to do with it – the establishment of an international science station seems the most popular option. A small handful of Russians are resident here, though this seems to be mostly so that the Russian state avoids forfeiting its claim on the land, which according to legislation must be returned to Norway if it goes uninhabited for ten years.

In recent years, attempts have been made to stimulate tourism to Pyramiden – the *Pyramiden Hotel*, closed in 2000, may well reopen one day, but for now three containers have been set up as very basic **accommodation**. Excursions to Pyramiden can be combined with a visit to the impressive **Nordenskiöld glacier**.

Other settlements

Of Svalbard's other Norwegian settlements, **Ny Ålesund** (25–120 inhabitants, depending on the season), located to the northwest of Longyearbyen, functioned as a mining town until an explosion in the 1960 resulted in its closure and reopening as a polar research centre. **Sveagruva** (or simply "Svea"), home to 300 shift workers, is 44km to the southeast, and comprises the largest of Svalbard's two active mining centres, producing a whopping three million tonnes of mined coal every year. **Hornsund**, the Polish settlement, is the smallest of the five, comprising a research station with just a dozen or so scientists based there.

STAVE CHURCH DETAIL, KULTURHISTORISK MUSEUM, OSLO

# Contexts

# History

For much of its early history, Norway punched well above its international weight. By the tenth century its people had explored – and conquered – much of northern Europe, and roamed the Atlantic as far as the North American mainland. Yet these heady days came to an end when Norway lost its independence in the fourteenth century, coming under the sway of first Denmark and then Sweden: the country then became isolated and poor in equal measure. Independent again from 1905, Norway was propelled into World War II by the German invasion of 1940, an act of aggression that transformed the Norwegians' attitude to the outside world. Gone was the old insularity, replaced by a liberal internationalism exemplified by Norway's leading role in the environmental movement. And then came the money – or rather the oil: since its discovery in the late 1960s, Norway's North Sea oil has made it one of the wealthiest countries in Europe.

## Early civilizations

The earliest signs of human habitation in Norway date from the end of the last Ice Age, around 10,000 BC. In the Finnmark region of north Norway, the **Komsa culture** was reliant upon sealing, whereas the peoples of the **Fosna culture**, further south near present-day Kristiansund, hunted both seals and reindeer. Both these societies were essentially static, dependent upon flint and bone implements. At Alta, the Komsa people left behind hundreds of **rock carvings and drawings** (see p.347), naturalistic representations of their way of life dating from the seventh to the third millennium BC.

As the edges of the ice cap retreated from the western coastline, so new migrants slowly filtered north. These new peoples, of the **Nøstvet-økser culture**, were also hunters and fishers, but they were able to manufacture stone axes, examples of which were first unearthed at Nøstvet, near Oslo. Beginning around 2700 BC, immigrants from the east, principally the semi-nomadic **Boat Axe** and **Battle-Axe peoples** – so named because of the distinctive shape of their stone weapons/tools – introduced animal husbandry and agriculture. The new arrivals did not, however, overwhelm their predecessors; the two groups coexisted, each picking up hints from the other – a reflection of the harsh infertility of the land.

## Into the Bronze Age

These **late Stone Age** cultures flourished at a time when other, more southerly countries were already using metal. Norway was poor and had little to trade, but the Danes and

| 10,000 BC | 4000 BC | 3000BC | 2700 BC |
|---|---|---|---|
| As the ice cap retreats, so hunters and gatherers spread across most of Norway. | Job creation? Locals begin work on the Alta rock carvings. | Norwegians start farming, eking out a living from the country's thin soils. | Animal husbandry gets off to a slow start – chickens yet to arrive. |

---

**RANDOM THOUGHTS FROM NORWAY**

"*Adventure is just bad planning.*" Roald Amundsen

"*Hollywood is loneliness beside the swimming pool.*" Liv Ullmann

"*The burden of disease falls on the poor.*" ex-Norwegian PM Gro Harlem Brundtland

"*We do not regard Englishmen as foreigners. We look on them only as rather mad Norwegians.*" Halvard Lange, Norwegian politician and diplomat

"*I have no fear of photography as long as it cannot be used in heaven and in hell.*" Edvard Munch

---

Swedes exchanged amber for copper and tin from the bronze-making countries of central Europe. A fraction of the imported bronze subsequently passed into Norway, mostly to the Battle-Axe people, who appear to have had a comparatively prosperous aristocracy. This was the beginning of the Norwegian **Bronze Age** (1500–500 BC), which also saw a change in burial customs. In the Stone Age, the Battle-Axe peoples had dug shallow earth graves, but these were now supplanted by **burial mounds** enclosing coffins in which supplies were placed in readiness for the afterlife. Building the mounds involved a substantial amount of effort, suggesting the existence of powerful chieftains who could organize the work, and who may also have been priests. **Rock carvings** became prevalent in southern Norway during this period too – workaday images of men ploughing with oxen, riding horses, carrying arms and using boats to navigate the coastal waters, which were supplemented by drawings of religious or symbolic significance. In general terms, however, the Bronze Age was characterized more by the development of agriculture than by the use of metal, and stone implements remained the norm.

## 500 BC to 200 AD

Around **500 BC** Norway was affected by two adverse changes: the climate deteriorated, and trade with the Mediterranean was disrupted by the westward movement of the Celts across central Europe. The former encouraged the development of settled, communal farming in an attempt to improve winter shelter and storage, with each clan resident in a large stone, turf and timber dwelling; the latter cut the supply of tin and copper and subsequently isolated Norway from the early Iron Age. The country's isolation continued through much of the Classical period. The Greek geographer Pytheas of Marseilles, who went far enough north to note the short summer nights, probably visited southern Norway, but the regions beyond remained the subject of vague speculation. Pliny the Elder mentions "Nerigon" as the great island south of the legendary "**Ultima Thule**", the outermost region of the earth, while Tacitus, in his *Germania*, demonstrated knowledge only of the Danes and Swedes.

The expansion of the Roman Empire in the first and second centuries AD revived Norway's **trading links with the Mediterranean**. Evidence of these renewed contacts is provided across Scandinavia by **runes**, carved inscriptions dating from around 200 AD, whose 24-letter alphabet – the *futhark* – was clearly influenced by Greek and Latin

| 1500 BC | 500 BC | 200 AD | 3rd century AD |
|---|---|---|---|
| Norwegian Bronze Age begins – better tools mean bigger harvests. | Norway gets colder; Norwegians club together to gather winter feed. | Norwegians take up rune carving – patient, time-consuming work with a complicated alphabet. | Roman goods filter their way north to Norway – coins, vessels, glass beakers and buckles are the most common items. |

capitals. Initially, runes were seen as having magical powers and it was to gain their knowledge that the god Odin hung for nine nights on *Yggdrasill*, the tree of life, with a spear in his side; they also turn up in the sagas with Egil, in *Egil's Saga* for instance, destroying a whale bone carved with runes because they contained "Ten secret characters, [which] gave the young girl [the daughter of his friend] her grinding pain." But gradually rune usage became more prosaic, and most of the eight hundred or so runic inscriptions extant across southern Norway commemorate events and individuals: mothers and fathers, sons and slain comrades.

## The Norwegian Iron Age and early medieval Norway

The renewal of trade with the Mediterranean also spread the use of **iron**. Norway's agriculture was transformed by the use of iron tools, and the pace of change accelerated in the fifth century AD, when the Norwegians learned how to smelt the brown iron ore, limonite, that lay in their bogs and lakes – hence its common name, **bog-iron**. Clearing the forests with iron axes was relatively easy and, with more land available, the pattern of settlement became less concentrated. Family homesteads leapfrogged up the valleys, and a class of wealthy farmers emerged, their prosperity based on fields and flocks. Above them in the pecking order were **local chieftains**, the nature of whose authority varied considerably. Inland, the chieftains' power was based on landed wealth and constrained by feudal responsibilities, whereas the coastal lords, who had often accumulated influence from trade, piracy and military prowess, were less encumbered. Like the farmers, these seafarers had also benefited from the **iron axe**, which made boat building much easier. An early seventh-century ship found at Kvalsund, near Hammerfest, was 18m long, its skilfully crafted oak hull equipped with a high prow and stern, prefiguring the vessels of the Vikings.

By the **middle of the eighth century**, Norway had become a country of small, independent kingships, its geography impeding the development of any central authority. In the event, it was the **Yngling chieftains** of southeast Norway who attempted to assert some sort of wider control. Their first leaders are listed in the *Ynglinga Tal*, a paean compiled by the Norwegian *skald* (court poet) Thjodolf in the ninth century. According to Thjodolf, early royal life had its ups and downs: King Domaldi was sacrificed to ensure the fertility of his land; Dag was killed by an accidental blow from a pitchfork; and Fjolnir got up in the night to take a leak, fell into a vat of mead and drowned.

## The Vikings

Overpopulation, clan discord, and the lure of plunder and commerce all contributed to the sudden explosion that launched the **Vikings** (from the Norse word *vik*, meaning creek, and *-ing*, frequenter of), upon an unsuspecting Europe in the ninth century. The patterns of attack and eventual settlement were dictated by the geographical position of the various Scandinavian countries. The Swedish Vikings turned eastwards, the Danes headed south and southwest, while the **Norwegians sailed west**, their longships landing on the Hebrides, Shetland, Orkney, the Scottish mainland and western Ireland. The Pictish population was unable to muster much resistance and the islands were quickly

| 5th century AD | 583 | 8th century |
|---|---|---|
| Norwegians enter the Iron Age: even better tools mean even bigger harvests. | Norwegians start using drinking horns; practice makes perfect; teetotallers concerned. | King Fjolnir drowns in a vat of mead; teetotallers even more concerned. |

overrun, becoming, together with the Isle of Man, the nucleus of a new Norse kingdom that provided a base for further attacks on Scotland and Ireland.

The Norwegians founded Dublin in 836, and from Ireland turned their attention eastward to northern Britain. Elsewhere, Norwegian Vikings settled the Faroe Islands and Iceland, and even raided as far south as Moorish Spain, attacking Seville in 844. The raiders soon became settlers, sometimes colonizing the entire country – as in Iceland and the Faroes – but mostly intermingling with the local population. The speed of their assimilation is, in fact, one of the Vikings' most striking features: **William the Conqueror** (1027–87) was the epitome of the Norman baron, yet he was also the descendant of Rollo, the Viking warrior whose army had overrun Normandy just a century before.

The whole of Norway felt the **stimulating effects** of the Viking expeditions. The economy was boosted by the spoils of war and the population grew in physical stature as health and nutrition improved. Farmland was no longer in such short supply; cereal and dairy farming were extended into new areas in eastern Norway; new vegetables, such as cabbages and turnips, were introduced from Britain; and farming methods were improved by overseas contact – the Celts, for instance, taught the Norwegians how to thresh grain with flails.

### Alfred the Great and Ottar

The Vikings also rigorously exploited the hunting and fishing peoples who roamed the far north of Norway. Detailed information on Finnmark in the late ninth century comes from a surprising source, the court of **Alfred the Great**, which was visited by a Norwegian chieftain named **Ottar** in about 890. Ottar dwelt, so he claimed, "northernmost of all Norsemen", and he regaled Alfred with tales of his native land, which the king promptly incorporated within his translation of a fifth-century Latin text, the *History of the World* by Paulus Orosius. Ottar, who boasted that he owed political allegiance to no one, had a few cows, sheep and pigs and a tiny slice of arable land, which he ploughed with horses, but his real wealth came from other sources. Fishing, whaling and walrus hunting provided both food for his retinue and exportable commodities. He also possessed a herd of six hundred tame reindeer – plus six decoy animals used to snare wild reindeer – and extracted a heavy tribute from the Sámi (see box, p.350), payable in furs and hides.

### Viking religion and art

The Vikings' brand of **paganism** (see p.403), with its wayward, unscrupulous deities, underpinned their inclination to vendettas and clan warfare. Nevertheless, institutions slowly developed which helped regulate the blood-letting. Western Norway adopted the Germanic *wergeld* system of cash-for-injury compensation; every free man was entitled to attend the local *Thing* (*Ting*) or parliament, while a regional *Allthing* made laws and settled disputes. Justice was class-based, however, with society divided into three main categories: the lord, the freeman, and the thrall or slave, who was worth about eight cows. The Vikings were industrious slavers, opening slave markets wherever they went, sending thousands to work on their land back home and supplying the needs of other buyers.

Viking **decorative art** was also pan-Scandinavian, with the most distinguished work being the elaborate and often grotesque animal motifs that adorned their ships, sledges,

| 9th century AD | 836 | 900 | 985 |
|---|---|---|---|
| Vikings are propelled out of Scandinavia, falling on an unsuspecting Europe heavily armed and borne hither and thither by their remarkably seaworthy longships; they do not, however, wear horned helmets. | Norwegian Vikings found Dublin. | Harald Hårfagre becomes Norway's first widely recognized king. | Erik the Red colonizes Greenland. |

## VIKING JEWELLERY

The Vikings were particularly keen on **jewellery**, both as a form of adornment and as a way of showing their wealth. Silver was the primary metal of value, as gold was in desperately short supply and only used by the most privileged. The early Vikings were quite content to wear imported – or indeed looted – jewellery of pretty much any description, but by the tenth century it was the silver- and goldsmiths back home who produced the most valued pieces, decorated with a densely wrought filigree of abstract patterns. Viking gold- and silver-work is categorized into several different periods, beginning with the intricate **Oseberg** and **Borre** styles of the ninth century and culminating in the more sophisticated **Jellinge** and **Urnes** styles of the tenth. However, only the wealthier Vikings could afford gold and silver and most had to make do with bronze jewellery, which was mass-produced in clay moulds. The most common items were bracelets and brooches, armlets and buckles, neck rings and pendants; earrings were unknown and finger rings rare. The two finest collections of surviving Viking silver-work are in Oslo – at the Kulturhistorisk Museum (see p.67), and at the Vikingskipshuset (see p.82).

buildings and furniture. This craftsmanship is seen to good advantage in the **ship burials** of Oseberg and Gokstad, the retrieved artefacts which are on display in Oslo's Viking Ships Museum (see p.82). The Oseberg ship is thought to be the burial ship of Åse, wife of the early ninth-century **Yngling** king, Gudrød Storlatnes. She was also the mother of Halfdan the Black, whose body had a very different fate from her own – it was chopped up, and the bits were buried across his kingdom to ensure the fertility of the land.

## Norway's first kings

It was from the **Ynglings of Vestfold** that Norway's first widely recognized king, **Harald Hårfagre** (Fair-Hair; c.880–930), claimed descent. Shortly before 900 (the exact date is unclear), Harald won a decisive victory at Hafrsfjord (near modern Stavanger), which gave him control of the coastal region as far north as Trøndelag. It sparked an exodus of minor rulers, most of whom left to settle in Iceland. The thirteenth-century *Laxdaela Saga* records the departure of one such family, the Ketils of Romsdal, who would not be "forced to become Harald's vassals or be denied compensation for fallen kinsmen". Harald's long rule was based on personal pledges of fealty and, with the notable exception of the regional *Allthings*, there were no institutions to sustain it; consequently, when he died, Harald's kingdom broke up into its component parts. Harald did, however, leave a less tangible but extremely important legacy: from now on every ambitious chieftain was not content to be a local lord, but strove to be ruler of a kingdom stretching from the Trøndelag to Vestfold.

Harald's son, **Erik Bloodaxe** (d.954), struggled to hold his father's kingdom together, but was outmanoeuvred by his youngest brother, **Håkon the Good** (920–60), who secured the allegiance of the major chieftains before returning home from England where he had been raised (and Christianized) at the court of King Athelstan of Wessex. Erik fled to Northumbria to become king of Viking York. Initially, Håkon was well received, and, although his attempts to introduce Christianity failed, he did carry out a number of far-ranging reforms. He established a common legal code for the whole of

| 990s | 1000 | 1020s | 1030 |
|---|---|---|---|
| Olav Tryggvason attacks his pagan enemies with Christian zeal. | Leif Eriksson reaches the North American mainland (Vinland). | Olav Haraldsson turns Norway Christian; worship of pickled horses' penises banned. | Olav Haraldsson killed at the Battle of Stiklestad. |

Vestfold and Trøndelag, and also introduced the system of *Leidangr*, the division of the coastal districts into areas, each of which was responsible for maintaining and manning a warship.

### Harald Greycloak Eriksson and Håkon Sigurdsson

Håkon's rule was, however, punctuated by struggles against Erik's heirs, who – with the backing of the Danish king Harald Bluetooth – defeated and killed Håkon in battle in 960. Håkon's kingdom then passed to one of Erik's sons, **Harald Greycloak Eriksson** (935–70). This forceful man set about extending his territories with gusto. Indeed, he was, in Bluetooth's opinion, much too successful; keen to keep Norway within his sphere of influence, the Dane slaughtered Greycloak on the battlefield in 970 and replaced him with a Danish appointee, **Håkon Sigurdsson** (d.995), the last genuine heathen to rule Norway. But again Bluetooth seems to have got more than he bargained for. Sigurdsson based himself in Trøndelag, a decent distance from his overlord, and it's believed he soon refused to recognize Danish suzerainty: certainly the Christian Bluetooth would not have sanctioned Sigurdsson's restitution of pagan sacred sites.

### Olav Tryggvason

In 995 the redoubtable **Olav Tryggvason** (c.968-1000), another Viking chieftain who had been baptized in England, sailed to Norway to challenge Sigurdsson, who was conveniently dispatched by one of his own servants before the fighting started. Olav quickly asserted control over the Trøndelag and parts of southern and western Norway. He founded Nidaros (now Trondheim), from where he launched a sustained and brutal campaign against his pagan compatriots – which incidentally secured him the adulation of later saga-writers. Despite his evangelical zeal, Olav's religious beliefs are something of an enigma: he had pagan magicians in his personal retinue, and was so good at predicting the future from bird bones that he was called *Craccaben* (Crowbone). Olav's real problem remained the enmity of the Danish-controlled southeastern regions of Norway, and of Bluetooth's son **Svein Forkbeard** (d.1014), who regarded Norway as his rightful inheritance. In alliance with the Swedish king, Svein defeated Olav at a sea battle in the Skaggerak in 1000, and Norway was divided up among the victors.

## West across the Atlantic

Meanwhile, amid all these dynastic shenanigans, Norwegian settlers were laying the foundations of independent Norse communities in the **Faroes and Iceland**, where they established a parliament, the *Allthing*, in 930. The Norwegian Vikings went on to make further discoveries: Erik the Red, exiled from Norway and then banished from Iceland for three years for murder, set out in 985 with 25 ships, fourteen of which arrived in **Greenland**. The new colony prospered, and by the start of the eleventh century there were about three thousand settlers. This created a shortage of good farmland, making another push west inevitable. The two **Vinland Sagas** (see p.402) provide the only surviving account of these further explorations, recounting the exploits of Leif Eriksson the Lucky, who founded a colony he called Vinland on the **shores of North America** around 1000 AD.

| 1047 | 1066 | 1204 | 1263 |
|------|------|------|------|
| Harald Hardrada, the last of the great Viking chieftains, becomes king of Norway. | Hardrada is killed at the battle of Stamford Bridge in England. | Håkon IV becomes king; Norway's "Period of Greatness" follows. | Magnus the Lawmender, Norway's wisest ruler, becomes king; Norwegians happy. |

Norse settlers continued to secure resources from Vinland for the next few decades, until the native population drove them out. The Viking site discovered at L'Anse aux Meadows in Newfoundland may have been either Vinland itself or the result of one of these further foragings. The Greenland colonists carried on collecting timber from Labrador up until the fourteenth century, when the climate is known to have cooled and deteriorated, making the sea trip too dangerous. Attacks by the Inuit and the difficulties of maintaining trading links with Norway then took their toll on the main Greenland colonies. All contact with the outside world was lost in around 1410, and the last of the half-starved, disease-ridden survivors died out towards the end of the fifteenth century, just as **Christopher Columbus** was eyeing up his "New World".

# The arrival of Christianity

In 1015, **Olav Haraldsson** (995–1030), a prominent Viking chieftain, sailed for Norway from England, intent upon conquering his homeland. Significantly, he arrived by merchant ship with just 100 men, rather than with a fleet of longships and an army, a clear sign of the passing of the Viking heyday. He gained the support of the yeoman farmers of the interior – a new force in Norway that was rapidly supplanting the old warrior aristocracy – and with Svein Forkbeard's son and successor Knut (King Canute of England) otherwise engaged, Haraldsson soon assumed the mantle of king of much of the country.

For twelve years Olav ruled in peace, founding Norway's first national government. His authority was based on the regional *Things* – consultative and broadly democratic bodies which administered local law – and on his willingness to deliver justice without fear or favour. The king's most enduring achievement, however, was to make Norway **Christian**. Olav had been converted during his days as a Viking, and vigorously imposed his new faith on his countrymen. Wherever necessary he executed persistent heathens and destroyed their sacred places. The dominant position of the new religion was ensured by the foundation of the Norwegian Church, whose first priests were consecrated in Bremen in Germany.

## Olav's death and Magnus the Good

It was foreign policy rather than pagan enmity that brought about Olav's downfall. By scheming with the Swedish king against **Knut** (d.1035), who had now consolidated his position as king of Denmark and England, Olav provoked a Danish invasion, whose course was smoothed by massive bribes. The Norwegian chieftains, who had suffered at the hands of Olav, could be expected to help Knut, but even the yeomen failed to rally to Olav's cause, possibly alienated by his imperious ways. In 1028, Olav was forced to flee, first to Sweden and then to Russia, while Knut's young son **Svein** and his mother, the English queen Aelfgifu, took the Norwegian crown. Two years later, Olav made a sensational return at the head of a scratch army, only to be defeated and killed by an alliance of wealthy landowners and chieftains at **Stiklestad**, the first major Norwegian land battle (see p.281).

The petty chieftains and yeoman farmers who had opposed Olav soon fell out with their new king: Svein had no intention of relaxing the royal grip and his rule was at least as arbitrary as that of his predecessor. The rebellion that ensued seems also to have

| 1266 | 1316 | 1349 | 1397 |
|---|---|---|---|
| Magnus sells the Hebrides and the Isle of Man to Scotland. | Norway loses its independence; Norwegians no longer happy. | Black Death ravages Norway. | Sweden, Denmark and Norway united by the Kalmar Union. |

had nationalistic undertones – many Norwegians had no wish to be ruled by a Dane. Svein fled the country, and Olav's old enemies popped over to Sweden to bring back Olav's young son, **Magnus the Good** (1024–47), who became king in 1035.

The chastening experience of Svein's short rule transformed the popular memory of Olav. With surprising speed, he came to be regarded as a heroic champion, and there was talk of miracles brought about by the dead king's body. The Norwegian Church, looking for a local saint to enhance its position, fostered the legends and had Olav canonized. The remains of **St Olav** were then re-interred ceremoniously at Nidaros, today's Trondheim, where the miracles increased in scope, hastening the conversion of what remained of heathen Norway.

### Harald Hardrada

On Magnus's death in 1047, **Harald Hardrada** (1015–66), Olav Haraldsson's half-brother, became king, and soon consolidated his grip on the whole of Norway from the Trøndelag to the Oslofjord. The last of the Viking heroes, Hardrada was a giant of a man, reputedly almost seven feet tall with a sweeping moustache and eccentric eyebrows. He had fought alongside Olav at Stiklestad and, after the battle, he and his men had fled east, fighting as mercenaries in Russia and ultimately Byzantium, where Hardrada was appointed the commander of the Varangians, the Norse bodyguard of the Byzantine emperor.

Back in Norway, Harald dominated the country by force of arms for over twenty years, earning the soubriquet "Hardrada" (the Hard) for his ruthless treatment of his enemies, many of whom he made "kiss the thin lips of the axe" as the saga writers put it. Neither was Hardrada satisfied with being king of just Norway. At first he tried to batter Denmark into submission through regular raiding, but the stratagem failed and he finally made peace with the Danish king, Svein, in 1064.

In 1066, the death of Edward the Confessor presented Harald with an opportunity to press his claim to the English throne. The Norwegian promptly sailed on England, landing near York with a massive fleet, but just outside the city, at **Stamford Bridge**, his army was surprised and trounced by Harold Godwinson, the new Saxon king of England. It was a battle of crucial importance, and one that gave rise to all sorts of legends, penned by both Norse and English writers. The two kings are supposed to have eyed each other up like prize fighters, with Hardrada proclaiming his rival "a small king, but one that stood well in his stirrups", and Harold promising the Norwegian "seven feet of English ground, or as much more as he is taller than other men". Hardrada was defeated and killed, and the threat of a Norwegian conquest of England had – though no one realized it at the time – gone forever. Not that the victory did much good for Godwinson, whose weakened army trudged back south to be defeated by William of Normandy at the **Battle of Hastings**.

## Medieval consolidation

After the Battle of Stamford Bridge, the life of Harald Hardrada's son, **Olav Kyrre** (the Peaceful; d.1093), was spared on condition that he never attacked England again. He kept his promise and went on to reign as king of Norway for the next 25 years. Peace engendered economic prosperity, and treaties with Denmark ensured Norwegian independence. Three native bishoprics were established, and cathedrals built at

| 1410 | 1448 | 1523 | 1536 |
| --- | --- | --- | --- |
| Norway loses contact with Greenland, where the Viking colonists slowly starve to death. | War between Sweden and Denmark – one of many. | Final break-up of the Kalmar Union; Norway in thrall to Denmark. | Denmark breaks with Rome; Lutheran church of Norway founded. |

Nidaros, Bergen and Oslo. It's from this period, too, that Norway's surviving **stave churches** (see box, p.173) date: wooden structures resembling an upturned keel, they were lavishly decorated with dragon heads and scenes from Norse mythology, proof that the traditions of the pagan world were slow to disappear.

The first decades of the twelfth century witnessed the further consolidation of Norway's position as an independent power, despite internal disorder as the descendants of Olav Kyrre competed for influence. Civil war ceased only when **Håkon IV** (1204–63) took the throne in 1240, ushering in what is often called **"The Period of Greatness"**. Secure at home, Håkon strengthened the Norwegian hold on the Faroe and Shetland islands, and in 1262 both Iceland and Greenland accepted Norwegian sovereignty. A year later, however, the king died in the Orkneys during a campaign to assert his control over the Hebrides, and three years later the Hebrides and the Isle of Man (always the weakest links in the Norwegian empire) were sold to the Scottish Crown by Håkon's successor, **Magnus the Lawmender** (1238–80).

Under Magnus, Norway prospered. Law and order were maintained, trade flourished and, in striking contrast to the rough-and-ready ways of Hardrada, the king's court even followed a code of etiquette compiled in what became known as the *Konungs skuggsja* or "King's Mirror". Neither was the power of the monarchy threatened by feudal barons as elsewhere in thirteenth-century Europe: Norway's scattered farms were not susceptible to feudal tutelage and, as a consequence, the nobility lacked both local autonomy and resources. Castles remained few and far between and instead the energies of the nobility were drawn into the centralized administration of the state, a process that only happened several centuries later in the rest of western Europe. Norwegian **Gothic art** reached its full maturity in this period, as construction began on the nave at Nidaros Cathedral and on Håkon's Hall in Bergen.

Magnus was succeeded by his sons, first the undistinguished Erik and then **Håkon V** (1270–1319), the last of medieval Norway's talented kings. Håkon continued the policy of his predecessors, making further improvements to central government and asserting royal control of Finnmark through the construction of a fortress at Vardø. His achievements, however, were soon to be swept away along with the independence of Norway itself.

## Loss of sovereignty

Norway's independence was threatened from two quarters. With strongholds in Bergen and Oslo, the merchants of the **Hanseatic League** had steadily increased their influence, exerting a virtual monopoly on the region's imports and controlling inland trade. They also came to exercise undue influence on the royal household, which grew dependent on the taxes the merchants paid. The second threat was **dynastic**. When Håkon died in 1319 he left no male heir and was succeeded by his grandson, the 3-year-old son of a Swedish duke. The boy, **Magnus Eriksson** (1316–74), was elected Swedish king two months later, marking the virtual end of Norway as an independent country until 1905.

Magnus assumed full power over both countries in 1332, but his reign was a difficult one. When the Norwegian nobility rebelled he agreed that the monarchy should again be split: his 3-year-old son, Håkon, would become Norwegian king (as Håkon VI) when he came of age, while the Swedes agreed to elect his eldest son Erik to the Swedish throne. It was then, in 1349, that the **Black Death** struck, spreading quickly

| 1596 | 1643 | 1660 |
|---|---|---|
| Willem Barents becomes the first known European to land on Svalbard; a motley crew of adventurers, hunters and prospectors are to follow. | Norway enters the literary age with the founding of its first printing press. | Frederik III established an absolute monarchy over Denmark and Norway. |

along the coast and up the valleys, killing almost two-thirds of the Norwegian population. It was a catastrophe of unimaginable proportions, its effects compounded by the way the country's agriculture was structured. Animal husbandry was easily the most important part of Norwegian farming, and harvesting and drying winter fodder was labour-intensive. Without the labourers, the animals died in their hundreds and famine conditions prevailed for several generations.

Many farms were abandoned and, deprived of their rents, the petty chieftains who had once dominated rural Norway were, as a class, almost entirely swept away. The vacuum was filled by royal officials, the **syslemenn**, each of whom exercised control over a large chunk of territory on behalf of a Royal Council. The collapse of local governance was compounded by dynastic toing and froing at the top of the social ladder. In 1380, Håkon VI died and Norway passed into Danish control with **Olav**, the son of Håkon and the Danish princess **Margaret**, becoming ruler of the two kingdoms.

## The Kalmar Union

Despite Olav's early death in 1387, the resourceful **Margaret** persevered with the union. Proclaimed regent by both the Danish and (what remained of the) Norwegian nobility, she engineered a treaty with the Swedish nobles that not only recognized her as regent of Sweden but also agreed to accept any king she should nominate. Her chosen heir, **Erik of Pomerania** (1382–1459), was foisted on the Norwegians in 1389. When he reached the age of majority in 1397, Margaret organized a grand coronation with Erik crowned king of all three countries at Kalmar in Sweden – hence the **Kalmar Union**.

After Margaret's death in 1412, all power was concentrated in Denmark. In Norway, foreigners were preferred in both state and church, and the country became impoverished by the taxes levied to pay for Erik's various wars. Incompetent and brutal in equal measure, Erik managed to get himself deposed in all three countries at the same time, ending his days as a Baltic pirate.

## Union with Denmark

The Kalmar Union was to struggle on until 1523, but long before that it was wracked by dynastic conflict with one or other of Sweden and Denmark trying to break out. The big turning point for Norway came in 1450, when a Danish count, **Christian of Oldenburg**, was crowned king of Norway and Denmark (but not Sweden) after lengthy negotiations between the Swedes and the Danes, neither of whom bothered to consult the Norwegians. Thereafter, Norway simply ceased to take any meaningful part in Scandinavian affairs. Successive monarchs continued to appoint foreigners to important positions, appropriating Norwegian funds for Danish purposes and even mortgaging Orkney and Shetland in 1469 to the Scots. Danish became the official tongue, replacing **Old Norse**, which came to be regarded as the language of the ignorant and inconsequential. Of local institutions, only the **Norwegian Church** retained any power, though this was soon to be squashed by the Reformation, and only once did it look as if Norway might break the Danish stranglehold. This was in 1501, when a Swedish-Norwegian nobleman, **Knut Alvsson**, crossed the border and overran southern Norway, but the Danes rallied and Alvsson was treacherously murdered as he sued for peace.

| 1707 | 1720 | 1727 |
| --- | --- | --- |
| Death of Petter Dass, Lutheran clergyman, hymn-writer and poet. | The naval hero Peter Tordenskiold dies in a duel, four years after inflicting a crushing defeat on the Swedes. | Death of Thomas von Westen, Lutheran clergyman and evangelist to the Sámi. |

The Danish victor, King **Christian II** (1481–1559), imposed a crash programme of "Danicization" on the Norwegians and mercilessly hunted down his opponents, but his attempts to dominate the Swedes led to his forced abdication in 1523. The leaders of the Norwegian opposition coalesced under the archbishop of Nidaros, Olav Engelbrektsson, but their attempt to gain terms from the new king Frederik I failed. The Danish civil war that followed the death of Frederik resulted in the victory of the Protestant **Christian III** (1503–59) and the loss of Norway's last independent national institution, the Catholic Church. In 1536 Christian III declared that Norway should cease to be a separate country and that the Lutheran creed should be established there. Christian even carted the silver casket that had contained the bones of St Olav back to Copenhagen, where he melted it down into coins.

Thereafter, Norway became, to all intents and purposes, simply a source of raw materials – fish, timber and iron ore – whose proceeds lined the Danish royal purse. Naturally enough, the Swedes coveted these materials too, the upshot being a long and inconclusive war (1563–70), which saw much of Norway ravaged by competing bands of mercenaries. Ironically, the Swedish attempt to capture Norway induced a change of attitude in Copenhagen: keen to keep their subjects happy, a degree of decentralization became the order of the day, and the Danes appointed a **Governor-General** (*Stattholder*) to administer justice in accordance with traditional Norwegian law.

### The Reformation

Though slow to take root among the Norwegian peasantry, **Lutheranism** served as a powerful instrument in establishing Danish control. The Bible, catechism and hymnal were all in Danish and the bishops were all Danes too. Thus, the Norwegian **Reformation** was very much an instrument of Danish colonization rather than a reflection of widespread intellectual ferment: the urban apprentices and craftsmen who fired the movement elsewhere in Europe simply didn't exist in significant numbers here in rustic Norway. Neither had the **Renaissance** made much impact here: the first printing press wasn't established in Norway until 1643, and the reading public remained minuscule. However, the country did manage to produce a surprising number of humanist writers and something of the Renaissance spirit arrived in the form of **Christian IV** (1588–1648). Among the Danish kings of the period, he proved the most sympathetic to Norway. He visited the country often, improving the quality of its administration and founding new towns – including Kongsberg, Kristiansand and Christiania (later Oslo) – whose buildings were laid out on a spacious gridiron plan.

At last, in the **late sixteenth century**, the Norwegian economy began to pick up. The population grew, trade increased and, benefiting from the decline of the Hanseatic League, a native bourgeoisie began to take control of certain parts of the economy, most notably the herring industry. But Norwegian cultural self-esteem remained at a low ebb: the country's merchants spoke Danish, mimicked Danish manners and read Danish literature. What's more, Norway was a constant bone of contention between Sweden and Denmark, the result being a long series of **wars** in which competing armies regularly overran its more easterly provinces.

### The beginnings of Danish absolutism

The year **1660** marked a turning point in the constitutional arrangements governing

| 1807 | 1814 | 1828 | 1843 |
| --- | --- | --- | --- |
| British navy bombards Copenhagen during the Napoleonic Wars. | Treaty of Kiel compels the Danes to give Norway to Sweden at the end of the Napoleonic Wars. | Henrik Ibsen born in Skien. | Edvard Grieg born in Bergen. |

Norway. For centuries, the Danish Council of State had had the power to elect the monarch and impose limitations on his or her rule. Now, a powerful alliance of merchants and clergy swept these powers away to make **Frederik III** (1609–70) absolute ruler. This was, however, not a reactionary coup, but an attempt to limit the power of the conservative-minded nobility. In addition, the development of a centralized state machine would, many calculated, provide all sorts of job opportunities for the low-born but adept. As a result, Norway was incorporated into the administrative structure of Denmark with royal authority delegated to the beefed-up office of *Stattholder*, who governed through what soon became a veritable army of professional bureaucrats.

In the event, there were several positive advantages for Norway – the country acquired better defences, simpler taxes, a separate High Court and further doses of Norwegian law – but once again power was exercised almost exclusively by Danes. The functionaries were allowed to charge for their services, and there was no fixed tariff – a swindler's charter for which the peasantry paid heavily. So much so, in fact, that one of the *Stattholders*, **Ulrik Gyldenløve**, launched a vigorous campaign against corruption, his efforts rewarded by a far-reaching series of reforming edicts promulgated in 1684.

## The eighteenth century

The **absolute monarchy** established by **Frederik III** soon came to concern itself with every aspect of Norwegian life. The ranks and duties of a host of minor officials were carefully delineated, religious observances tightly regulated and restrictions were imposed on everything from begging and dress through to the food and drink that could be consumed at weddings and funerals. This extraordinary superstructure placed a leaden hand on imagination and invention. Neither was it impartial: there were some benefits for the country's farmers and fishermen, but by and large the system worked **in favour of the middle class**. The merchants of every small town were allocated exclusive rights to trade in a particular area and competition between towns was forbidden. These local monopolies placed the peasantry at a dreadful disadvantage, nowhere more iniquitously than in the Lofoten islands, where fishermen not only had to buy supplies and equipment at the price set by the merchant, but had to sell their fish at the price set by him too.

The Dano-Norwegian functionaries who controlled Norway also set the **cultural agenda**, patronizing an insipid and imitative art and literature. The writings of **Petter Dass** (1647–1707) stand out from the dross, however – heartfelt verses and descriptions of life in the Nordland where he worked as a pastor. There were liberal, vaguely nationalist stirrings too, in the foundation of the Norwegian Society in Copenhagen twelve years later.

### Missionaries into the north

There was also renewed missionary interest in Norway's old colony of **Greenland**. In part, this was down to the eccentric ethnic obsessions of the clergyman concerned, one **Hans Egede** (1686–1758), who was looking for Inuit with Viking features, but Bergen's merchants went along with Egede on condition that he build them a Greenland fur-trading station. As it happened, this was a poor investment, as the trading

| 1844 | 1852 | 1863 | 1867 |
|------|------|------|------|
| Death of Karl Johan IV, king of Sweden and Norway. | Sámi uprising against the Norwegians breaks out in Kautokeino. | Edvard Munch born in a farmhouse in Hedmark. | Alfred Nobel patents his new invention – dynamite. |

monopoly was given to a Dane. There was also missionary work in **Finnmark**, where a determined effort was made to Christianize the Sámi (see box, p.350). This was a very different undertaking from Egede's, and one that reflected the changing temperament of the Lutheran Church of Norway, which had been reinvigorated by **pietist clergymen**. One of their number, **Thomas von Westen** (1682–1727), learned the Sámi language and led an extraordinarily successful mission to the far north. He was certainly a good deal more popular than many of his fellow pietists down south who persuaded **Christian VI** (1730–46) to impose draconian penalties for such crimes as not observing the Sabbath and not going to church regularly.

### War and peace
In the meantime, there were more wars between Denmark and Sweden. In 1700, **Frederik IV** (1699–1730) made the rash decision to attack the Swedes at the time when their king, **Karl XII** (1682–1718), was generally reckoned to be one of Europe's most brilliant military strategists. Predictably, the Danes were defeated and only the intervention of the British saved Copenhagen from falling into Swedish hands. Undeterred, Frederik tried again, and this time Karl retaliated by launching a full-scale invasion of Norway. The Swedes rapidly occupied southern Norway, but then, much to everyone's amazement, things began to go wrong. The Norwegians successfully held out in the Akershus fortress in Christiania (Oslo) and added insult to injury by holding on to Halden too. Furthermore, a naval commander, one **Peter Tordenskiold** (1691–1720), became a national hero in Norway when he caught the Swedish fleet napping and ripped it to pieces off Strømstad. Karl was forced to retreat, but returned with a new army two years later. He promptly besieged the fortress at Halden for a second time, but while he was inspecting his troops someone shot him in the head – whether it was one of his own soldiers or a Norwegian has been the subject of heated debate (in Scandinavia) ever since. Whatever the truth, Karl's death enabled the protagonists to agree the **Peace of Frederiksborg** (1720), which ended hostilities for the rest of the eighteenth century. Tordenskiold, however, did not benefit from the peace: he was killed in a duel after an argument at the gaming table.

### Trade and religious revival
Peace favoured the growth of **trade**, but although Norway's economy prospered it was hampered by the increasing **centralization** of the Dano-Norwegian state. Regulations pushed more and more trade through Copenhagen, much to the irritation of the majority of Norwegian merchants who were accustomed to trading direct with their customers. Increasingly, they wanted the same privileges as the Danes, and especially, given the chronic shortage of capital and credit, their own national bank. In the 1760s, Copenhagen did a dramatic U-turn, abolishing monopolies, removing trade barriers and even permitting a free press – and the Norwegian economy boomed. Nonetheless, the bulk of the population remained impoverished and prey to famine whenever the harvest was poor. The number of **landless agricultural labourers** rose dramatically, partly because more prosperous farmers were buying up large slices of land, and for the first time Norway had something akin to a proletariat.

Nonetheless, proletariat or not, Norway was one of the few European countries little affected by the French Revolution. Instead of political action, there was a **religious**

| 1898 | 1901 | 1902 | 1905 |
|---|---|---|---|
| Universal male suffrage introduced. | First Nobel peace prize award. Jean Henry Dunant and Frédéric Passy are the recipients. | Criminal law amended to abolish the death penalty in peacetime. | Norway breaks from Sweden to become independent. |

**revival**, with a carpenter by the name of **Hans Nielson Hauge** (1771–1824) emerging as the leading evangelist. The movement's characteristic hostility to officialdom caused concern, and Hauge was imprisoned, but in reality it posed little threat to the status quo. The end result was rather the foundation of a **Christian fundamentalist movement** that is still a force to be reckoned with in parts of west Norway.

## The early nineteenth century: the end of union with Denmark

Denmark-Norway had remained neutral throughout the Seven Years' War (1756–63) between England and France, and renewed that neutrality in 1792, during the period leading up to the **Napoleonic Wars**. Neutrality was good for Norway: overseas trade, especially with England, flourished, and demand for Norwegian timber, iron and cargo-space heralded a period of unparalleled prosperity at least for the bourgeoisie. However, when Napoleon implemented a trade blockade – the **Continental System** – against Britain, he roped in the Danes. As a result, the British fleet bombarded Copenhagen in 1807 and forced the surrender of the entire Dano-Norwegian fleet. Denmark, in retaliation, declared war on England and Sweden. The move was disastrous for the Norwegian economy, which had also suffered bad harvests in 1807 and 1808, and the English blockade of its seaports ruined trade.

By 1811 it was obvious to many Norwegians that the Danes had backed the wrong side in the war, and the idea of a union of equals with Sweden, which had supported Britain, became increasingly attractive. By attaching their coat-tails to the victors, they hoped to restore the commercially vital trade with England. They also thought that the new Swedish king would be able to deal with the Danes if it came to a fight – just as the Swedes had themselves calculated when they appointed him in 1810. The man concerned, **Karl XIV Johan**, was, curiously enough, none other than Jean-Baptiste Bernadotte, formerly one of Napoleon's marshals (see box, p.65). With perfect timing, he had helped the British defeat Napoleon at Leipzig in 1813. His reward came in the **Treaty of Kiel** the following year, when the great powers instructed the Danes to cede to Sweden all rights in Norway (although they did keep the dependencies of Iceland, Greenland and the Faroes). Four hundred years of union were ended at a stroke.

## Union with Sweden (1814–1905)

The high-handed transfer of Norway from Denmark to Sweden did little to assuage the growing demands for greater Norwegian independence. Furthermore, the Danish Crown Prince Christian Frederik roamed Norway stirring up fears of Swedish intentions. The prince and his supporters convened a **Constituent Assembly**, which met in a country house outside Eidsvoll (see p.150) in April 1814 and produced a **constitution**. Issued on May 17, 1814 (still a national holiday), this declared Norway to be a "free, independent and indivisible realm" with Christian Frederik as its king. Not surprisingly, Karl Johan would have none of this and – with the support of the great powers – he promptly invaded Norway. Completely outgunned, Christian Frederik barely mounted any resistance. In exchange for Swedish promises to recognize the Norwegian constitution and the *Storting* (parliament), he abdicated as soon as he had signed a peace treaty – the so-called **Convention of Moss** – in August 1814.

| 1911 | 1914 | 1919 |
| --- | --- | --- |
| Roald Amundsen reaches the South Pole, but complains about the weather. 1913 Universal suffrage introduced. | Norway neutral in World War I, and its merchants make a packet from trading with both Britain and Germany. | A referendum sanctions Prohibition. |

The ensuing period was marred by struggles between the *Storting* and **Karl XIV Johan** over the nature of the union. Although the constitution emphasized Norway's independence, Johan had a suspensive veto over the *Storting*'s actions, the post of *Stattholder* in Norway could only be held by a Swede, and foreign and diplomatic matters concerning Norway remained entirely in Swedish hands. Despite this, Karl Johan proved popular in Norway, and during his reign the country enjoyed a degree of independence. The Swedes allowed all the highest offices in Norway to be filled by Norwegians and democratic local councils were established, in part due to the rise of the peasant farmers as a political force.

### Pan-Scandinavianism
Under both Oscar I (1844–59) and Karl XV (1859–72), however, it was **pan-Scandinavianism** that ruled the intellectual roost. This belief in the natural solidarity of Denmark, Norway and Sweden was espoused by the leading artists of the period, but died a toothless death in 1864 when the Norwegians and the Swedes refused to help Denmark when it was attacked by Austria and Prussia; some of the loudest cries of treachery came from a young writer by the name of Henrik Ibsen, whose poetic drama, *Brand*, was a spirited indictment of Norwegian perfidy.

### The end of the union with Sweden
In the 1850s, domestic politics were transformed by the rise to power of **Johan Sverdrup** (1816–92), who started a long and ultimately successful campaign to wrest executive power from the king and transfer it to the *Storting*. By the mid-1880s, Sverdrup and his political allies had pretty much won the day, though a further bout of sabre-rattling between the supporters of Norwegian independence and the Swedish king **Oscar II** (1872–1907) was necessary before both sides would accept a plebiscite. This took place in August 1905, when there was an overwhelming vote in favour of the **dissolution of the union**, which was duly confirmed by the Treaty of Karlstad. A second **plebiscite** determined that independent Norway should be a monarchy rather than a republic, and, in November 1905, Prince Karl of Denmark (Edward VII of England's son-in-law) was elected to the throne as **Håkon VII** (1872–1957).

### Norway's National Romantic movement
In the meantime, Norway's increasing prosperity had been having important social and cultural implications. The layout and buildings of modern Oslo – the Royal Palace, Karl Johans gate, the university – date from this period, while **Johan Christian Dahl** (1788–1857), the most distinguished Scandinavian landscape painter of his day, was instrumental in the foundation of Oslo's Nasjonalgalleriet (National Gallery; see p.68) in 1836. More importantly, Dahl and other prominent members of the bourgeoisie formed the nucleus of a **National Romantic movement**, which championed all things Norwegian. The movement's serious intent was flagged up by Jens Kraft, who produced a massive six-volume topographical survey of the country, and the poet, prose writer and propagandist **Henrik Wergeland** (1808–45), who decried the civil-servant culture that had dominated Norway for so long in favour of the more sincere qualities of the peasant farmer. Indeed, the movement endowed the Norwegian peasantry with all sorts of previously unidentified qualities, while the **temperance movement** sought to bring

| 1922 | 1923 | 1926 | 1928 |
| --- | --- | --- | --- |
| Vinmonopolet, which still operates a state monopoly of liquor, wine and strong beer, founded in preparation for a relaxation of Prohibition. | Prohibition relaxed. | Prohibition fully repealed. | Amundsen disappears in the Arctic while undertaking a rescue mission; his body is never found. |

## FRIDTJOF NANSEN

One of Norway's most celebrated sons, **Fridtjof Nansen** (1861–1930), was something of a Renaissance man – in fact, his skills and abilities were so wide-ranging that it almost seems unfair. As a teenager, he was a champion skier and ice skater and in his twenties he moved on to **exploration**: in 1888, he led the first expedition across the interior of Greenland and in the 1890s he made a gallant if ultimately unsuccessful attempt to reach the North Pole. He then went on to study zoology, becoming an influential figure in the field of neurology, and, after supporting Norway's break with Sweden in 1905, he was appointed the Norwegian representative in London. The last years of his life were devoted to the **League of Nations**, where he became the High Commissioner for Refugees. Among much else, Nansen struggled manfully to mitigate the effects of the famine in the Soviet Union in 1921 and pioneered the use of the so-called "Nansen passport" for the stateless and dispossessed at the end of World War I. In 1922, he was awarded the Nobel Peace Prize.

them up to these lofty ideals by promoting laws to prohibit the use of small stills, once found on every farm. The government obliged by formally banning these stills in 1844, and by the mid-nineteenth century, consumption of spirits had dropped drastically and coffee rivalled beer as the national drink.

Similarly, the **Norwegian language** and its folklore was rediscovered by a number of academics, helping to restore the country's cultural self-respect. Following on were authors like Alexander Kielland, whose key works were published between 1880 and 1891, and **Knut Hamsun** (1859–1952), whose most characteristic novel, *Hunger*, was published in 1890. In music, **Edvard Grieg** (1843–1907) was inspired by old Norwegian folk melodies, composing some of his most famous music for Ibsen's *Peer Gynt*, while the artist **Edvard Munch** (1863–1944) completed many of his major works in the 1880s and 1890s. Finally, the internationally acclaimed dramatist **Henrik Ibsen** (1828–1906) returned to Oslo in 1891 after a prolonged self-imposed exile.

## Early independence: 1905–39

Norway's **independence** came at a time of further economic advance, engendered by the introduction of hydroelectric power and underpinned by a burgeoning merchant navy, the third-largest after the US and Britain. Social reforms also saw funds being made available for unemployment relief, accident insurance schemes and a Factory Act (1909), governing safety in the workplace. An extension to the franchise gave the **vote** to all men over 25, and, in 1913, to women too. The education system was reorganized, and substantial sums were spent on new arms and defence. This prewar period also saw the emergence of a strong trade-union movement and of a Labour Party committed to revolutionary change.

Since 1814, Norway had had little to do with European affairs, and at the outbreak of **World War I** it declared itself neutral. Its sympathies, though, lay largely with the Western Allies, and the Norwegian economy boomed as its ships and timber were in great demand. Yet, by 1916, Norway had begun to feel the pinch as German submarines took to sinking both enemy and neutral shipping, and by the end of the war Norway had lost half its chartered tonnage and 2000 crew. The Norwegian

| 1940 | 1941 | 1945 |
|---|---|---|
| Germans occupy Norway; Norwegians taken completely by surprise. | Norway's government in exile reinstates the death penalty for torture, treason and murder – and applies the new law after the liberation. | The traitor Vidkun Quisling is executed; few grieve. |

economy also suffered after the Americans entered the war: the US imposed strict trade restrictions in their attempt to prevent supplies getting to Germany, and rationing had to be introduced across Norway. Indeed, the overall price of neutrality turned out to be high: there was a rise in state expenditure, a soaring cost of living and, at the end of the war, no seat at the conference table. In spite of its losses, Norway got no share of confiscated German shipping, although it was partly compensated by gaining sovereignty of **Spitsbergen** and its coal deposits – the first extension of Norwegian frontiers for 500 years. In 1920 Norway also entered the new League of Nations.

### The late 1920s
In the **late 1920s**, the decline in world trade led to decreased demand for Norwegian shipping and raw materials. This led to a prolonged period of economic disarray within Norway during which there was a string of bank failures, wild currency fluctuations and bitter industrial strife, with wage cuts and burgeoning unemployment as the backcloth. A strengthening Norwegian **Labour Party** took advantage of the situation, breaking out of its urban heartlands in the election of 1927 to become the largest party within the *Storting*, but it could not muster an overall majority and the old Liberal-Conservative elite manoeuvred them out of office within a fortnight. Many Norwegians felt cheated and trade disputes and lockouts continued with troops often used to protect scabs.

### The early 1930s
During World War I, **Prohibition** had been introduced as a temporary measure and a referendum of 1919 showed a clear majority in favour of its continuation. But the ban did little to quell – and even exacerbated – drunkenness, and it was completely abandoned in 1926, replaced by the government monopoly on the sale of wines and spirits that remains in force today. The **1933 election** gave the Labour Party more seats than ever. Having shed its revolutionary image, a campaigning, reformist Labour Party benefited from the growing popular conviction that state control and a centrally planned economy were the only answer to Norway's economic problems. In 1935 the Labour Party, in alliance with the Agrarian Party, took power – an unlikely combination since the Agrarians were profoundly nationalist in outlook, so much so that one of their defence spokesmen had been the rabid anti-Semite **Vidkun Quisling** (1887–1945). Frustrated by the democratic process, Quisling had left the Agrarians in 1933 to found **Nasjonal Samling** (National Unification), a fascist movement which proposed, among other things, that both Hitler and Mussolini should be nominated for the Nobel Peace Prize. Quisling had good contacts with Nazi Germany but little support in Norway – local elections in 1937 reduced his local representation to a mere seven seats, and party membership fell to 1500.

The Labour government under **Johan Nygaardsvold** (1879–1952) presided over an improving economy. By 1938 industrial production was 75 percent higher than it had been in 1914 and unemployment dropped as expenditure on roads, railways and public works increased. Social-welfare reforms were implemented and trade-union membership increased. When war broke out in 1939, Norway was lacking only one thing – **adequate defence**. A vigorous member of the League of Nations, the country

| 1946 | 1948 | 1949 |
|---|---|---|
| Norwegian politician Trygve Lie become first Secretary General of the United Nations. | Musk ox reintroduced into Norway; local wildlife confused. | Norway joins NATO – a controversial move among many Norwegians, who want to remain neutral. |

had pursued disarmament- and peace-oriented policies since the end of World War I and was determined to remain **neutral**.

## World War II

Odd as it may seem in hindsight, in **early 1940** the Norwegian government was more preoccupied with Allied mine-laying off the Norwegian coast than the threat posed by Hitler. The Allies mined Norwegian waters in an attempt to prevent Swedish iron ore being shipped from Narvik to Germany, but the Norwegians felt this compromised their neutrality. Indeed, such was Norwegian naivety that they made a formal protest to Britain on the day of the **German invasion**. Caught napping, the Norwegian army offered little initial resistance and the south and central regions of the country were quickly overrun. King Håkon and the *Storting* were forced into a hasty evacuation of Oslo and headed north to Elverum, evading capture by just a couple of hours. Here, at the government's temporary headquarters, the executive was granted full powers to take whatever decisions were necessary in the interests of Norway – a mandate which later formed the basis of the Norwegian government-in-exile in Britain.

The Germans contacted the king and his government in Elverum, demanding, among other things, that Quisling be accepted as prime minister as a condition of surrender. Though their situation was desperate, the Norwegians rejected this outright and instead chose resistance. The ensuing **campaign** lasted for two months and, although the Norwegians fought determinedly with the help of a small force of British regulars, they were no match for the German army. In June both king and government fled to Britain from Tromsø in northern Norway. The country was rapidly brought under Nazi control, Hitler sending **Josef Terboven** to take full charge of Norwegian affairs.

The fascist **Nasjonal Samling** was declared the only legal party and the media, civil servants and teachers were brought under its control. As **civil resistance** grew, a state of emergency was declared: two trade-union leaders were shot, arrests increased and a concentration camp was set up outside Oslo. In February 1942 Quisling was installed as "Minister President" of Norway, but it soon became clear that his government didn't have the support of the Norwegian people. The Church refused to cooperate, schoolteachers protested and trade-union members and officials resigned en masse. In response, deportations increased, death sentences were announced and a compulsory labour scheme was introduced.

### The Resistance

**Military resistance** escalated as the German occupation hardened. A military organization (**MILORG**) was established as a branch of the armed forces under the control of the High Command in London. By May 1941 it had enlisted 20,000 men (32,000 by 1944) in clandestine groups all over the country. Arms and instructors came from Britain, radio stations were set up and a continuous flow of intelligence about German movements was sent back. Sabotage operations were legion, the most notable being the destruction of the heavy-water plant at **Rjukan** (see p.179), foiling a German attempt to produce an atomic bomb. Reprisals against the Resistance were severe and some were carried out by Norwegian **collaborators**, around 15,000 of whom enlisted in the German army.

| 1960 | 1969 | 1972 |
|---|---|---|
| Laws on abortion relaxed – but married women still need the consent of their husbands. | Oil discovered beneath the Norwegian Sea. | Referendum 1: Norwegians decide not to join the EEC. |

The **government-in-exile** in London continued to represent free Norway to the world, mobilizing support on behalf of the Allies. Most of the Norwegian merchant fleet was abroad when the Nazis invaded, and by 1943 the Norwegian navy had seventy ships helping the Allied convoys. With the German position deteriorating, neutral Sweden adopted a more sympathetic policy to its Norwegian neighbours, allowing the creation of thinly disguised training grounds for Resistance fighters. These camps also served to produce the police detachments that were to secure law and order after liberation.

### German surrender

When the Allies landed in Normandy in June 1944, overt action against the occupying Germans in Norway was temporarily discouraged as the US and Britain could not guarantee military supplies. Help was at hand, however, in the form of the **Soviets** who crossed into the far north of Norway in late October, driving back the Germans at double speed. Tragically, the Germans chose to burn everything in their path as they retreated, a scorched-earth policy that inflicted untold suffering on the local population, many of whom hid in the forests and caves. To prevent the Germans reinforcing their beleaguered Finnmark battalions, the Resistance organized a campaign of mass railway sabotage, stopping three-quarters of the troop movements overnight. With their control of Norway crumbling, the Germans finally **surrendered** on May 7, 1945. King Håkon returned to Norway on June 7, five years to the day since he'd left for exile.

Terboven committed suicide and the NS collaborators were rounded up. A caretaker government took office, staffed by Resistance leaders, and was replaced in October 1945 by a majority **Labour government**. The Communists won eleven seats, reflecting the efforts of Communist saboteurs in the war and the prestige that the Soviet Union enjoyed in Norway after the liberation. **Quisling** was shot, along with 24 other high-ranking traitors, and thousands of collaborators were punished with varying degrees of severity.

## Postwar reconstruction

At the end of the war, Norway was on its knees: the far north – Finnmark – had been laid waste, half the mercantile fleet lost, and production was at a standstill. Nevertheless, recovery, fostered by a palpable sense of national unity, was quick and it was only three years before GNP was at its prewar level. In addition, Norway's part in the war had increased her international prestige. The country became one of the founding members of the **United Nations** in 1945, and the first UN Secretary-General, Trygve Lie, was, at the time of his appointment, Norwegian Foreign Minister. With the failure of discussions to promote a Scandinavian defence union, the *Storting* also voted to enter **NATO** in 1949.

Domestically, there was general agreement about the form that **social reconstruction** should take. In 1948, the *Storting* passed the laws that introduced the Welfare State almost unanimously. The 1949 election saw the government returned with a larger majority, and Labour governments continued to be elected throughout the following decade, with the dominant political figure being **Einar Gerhardsen** (1897–1987). As national prosperity increased, society became ever more egalitarian, levelling up rather

| 1978 | 1981 | 1985 |
| --- | --- | --- |
| The Norwegian Labour Party pushes through a law legalizing abortion on demand in the first twelve weeks of pregnancy. | Gro Harlem Brundtland becomes Norway's first woman prime minister. | Norway's a-ha release their debut album; audio delight. |

than down. Subsidies were paid to the agricultural and fishing industries, wages increased, and a comprehensive social security system helped to eradicate poverty. The state ran the important mining industry, was the largest shareholder in the national hydroelectric company and built an enormous steelworks at Mo-i-Rana to help develop the economy of the devastated northern counties. Rationing ended in 1952 and, as the demand for higher education grew, so new universities were created in Bergen, Trondheim and Tromsø.

## Beyond consensus: the 1960s to the 1970s

The political consensus began to fragment in the early 1960s. Following the restructuring of rural constituencies in the 1950s, there was a realignment in centre politics, the outmoded Agrarian Party becoming the **Centre Party**. There was change on the left too, where defence squabbles within the Labour Party led to the formation of the **Socialist People's Party (SF)**, which wanted Norway out of NATO and sought a renunciation of nuclear weapons. The Labour Party's 1961 declaration that no nuclear weapons would be stationed in Norway except under an immediate threat of war did not placate the SF, who unexpectedly took two seats at the election that year. Holding the balance of power, the SF voted with the Labour Party until 1963, when it helped bring down the government over mismanagement of state industries. A replacement coalition collapsed after only one month, but the writing was on the wall. Rising prices, dissatisfaction with high taxation and a continuing housing shortage meant that the 1965 election put a **non-socialist coalition** in power for the first time in twenty years.

Under the leadership of **Per Borten** (1913–2005) of the Centre Party, the coalition's programme was unambitious. Nonetheless, living standards continued to rise, and although the 1969 election saw a marked increase in Labour Party support, the coalition hung onto power. Also that year, **oil and gas** were discovered beneath the North Sea and, as the vast extent of the reserves became obvious, it became clear that the Norwegians were to enjoy a magnificent bonanza – one which was destined to pay a large chunk of the government's annual bills.

Elsewhere, Norway's politicians, who had applied twice previously for membership of the **European Economic Community (EEC)** – in 1962 and 1967 – believed that de Gaulle's fall in France presented a good opportunity for a third application, which was made in 1970. There was great concern, though, about the effect of membership on Norwegian agriculture and fisheries, and in 1971 Per Borten was forced to resign following his indiscreet handling of the negotiations. The Labour Party, the majority of its representatives in favour of EEC membership, formed a minority administration, but when the **1972 referendum** narrowly voted "No" to joining the EEC, the government resigned.

With the 1973 election producing another minority Labour government, the uncertain political pattern of the previous ten years continued. Even the postwar consensus on **Norwegian security policy** broke down on various issues – primarily the question of a northern European nuclear-free zone and the stocking of Allied material in Norway – although there remained strong agreement for continued NATO membership.

### 1987

Political scandal: tongues start wagging across the whole of Norway when a right-wing politician claims to be in receipt of a letter from an immigrant – Mohammad Mustafa – that claims that Norway's Muslims are planning to convert Norway to Islam.

## The 1980s and early 1990s

In 1983, the Christian Democrats and the Centre Party joined together in a non-socialist coalition, which lasted only two years. It was replaced in 1986 by a minority Labour administration, led by **Dr Gro Harlem Brundtland** (b.1939), Norway's first woman prime minister. She made sweeping changes to the way the country was run, introducing seven women into her eighteen-member cabinet, but her government was beset by problems for the three years of its life: tumbling oil prices led to a recession, unemployment rose (though only to four percent) and there was widespread dissatisfaction with Labour's high taxation policies.

At the **general election** in September 1989, Labour lost eight seats and was forced out of office – the worst result the party had suffered since 1930. More surprising was the success of the extremist parties on both political wings – the anti-NATO, leftist Socialist Party and the right-wing, anti-immigrant Progress Party both scored spectacular results, winning almost a quarter of the votes cast, and increasing their representation in the *Storting* many times over. This deprived the Conservative Party (one of whose leaders, bizarrely, was Gro Harlem Brundtland's husband) of the majority it might have expected, the result being yet another shaky minority administration – this time a **centre-right coalition** between the Conservatives, the Centre Party and the Christian Democrats, led by Jan Syse.

The new government immediately faced problems familiar to the last Labour administration. In particular, there was continuing conflict over joining the **European Community** (as the European Union was then known), a policy still supported by many in the Norwegian establishment but flatly rejected by the Centre Party. It was this, in part, that signalled the end of the coalition, for after just over a year in office, the Centre Party withdrew its support and forced the downfall of Syse. In October 1990, Gro Harlem Brundtland was put back in power at the head of a **minority Labour administration**, remaining in office till her re-election for a fourth minority term in 1993. The 1993 elections saw a revival in Labour Party fortunes and, to the relief of the majority, the collapse of the Progress Party vote. However, it was also an untidy, confusing affair where the main issue, membership of the EU, cut across the traditional left-versus-right divide.

## The 1990s: political argy-bargy

Following the 1993 election, the country tumbled into a long and fiercely conducted campaign over **membership of the EU**. Brundtland and her main political opponents wanted in, but despite the near-unanimity of the political class, the Norwegians narrowly rejected the EU in a 1994 referendum. It was a close call (52.5 percent versus 47.5 percent), but in the end farmers and fishermen afraid of the economic results of joining, as well as women's groups and environmentalists, who felt that Norway's high standards of social care and "green" controls would suffer, came together to swing opinion against joining. Afterwards, and unlike the Labour government of 1972, the Brundtland administration soldiered on, wisely soothing ruffled feathers by promising to shelve the whole EU membership issue until at least 2000. Nonetheless, the **1997 election** saw a move to the right, the main beneficiaries being the Christian Democratic Party and the ultra-conservative Progress Party. In itself, this was not enough to remove

| 1989 | 1991 | 1993 |
| --- | --- | --- |
| Sámi Parliament established in Karasjok , bringing some degree of political independence to the indigenous population of the Arctic north. | Harald V of Norway ascends the throne upon the death of his popular father, Olav V. | Norway resumes commercial hunting of the minke whale. |

the Labour-led coalition from office – indeed Labour remained comfortably the largest party – but the right was dealt a trump card by the new Labour leader, **Thorbjørn Jagland**. During the campaign Jagland had promised that the Labour Party would step down from office if it failed to elicit more than the 36.9 percent of the vote it had secured in 1993. Much to the chagrin of his colleagues, Jagland's political chickens came home to roost when Labour only received 35 percent of the vote – and they had to go, leaving power in the hands of an unwieldy right-of-centre, minority coalition. Bargaining with its rivals from a position of parliamentary weakness, the new government found it difficult to cut a clear path – or at least one very different from its predecessor – apart from managing to antagonize the women's movement by some reactionary social legislation whose none-too-hidden subtext seemed to read "A woman's place is in the home". In the spring of 2000, the government resigned and the Labour Party resumed command.

## The 2000s to the present day

The Labour Party administration that took over the reins of government in 2000 didn't last long: in elections the following year, they took a drubbing and the right prospered, paving the way for another ungainly centre-right coalition. This coalition battled on until **late 2005** when the Labour Party, along with its allies the Socialist Left Party and the Centre Party, won a general election, with the politically experienced **Jens Stoltenberg** becoming Prime Minister – as he remains at time of writing. Stoltenberg proceeded to bolt together one of Norway's more secure coalitions with a standard-issue, centre-left political agenda: for instance, a flexible retirement from the age of 62 (it was 67) was introduced in 2010; a careful incomes policy was geared to the needs of both employer and employee; and there were detailed promises on tackling climate change and global warming. As Stoltenberg put it himself at the time of his election victory "Our gains are due to a clear political message about jobs, education, and giving people security in their old age. Our aim is to give this country a stable and predictable government."

In the summer of 2008, however, the wheels began to come off the coalition wagon with arguments about the killing of wolves, corruption, and the state of the health-care system. Stoltenberg's popularity sank, but then came the worldwide **banking crisis** during which Stoltenberg started to look more like a prime minister who could take care of business – and the opinion polls gave him and his Labour Party a much improved rating. He was helped by the soundness of the Norwegian banking system, which had learnt some harsh lessons about capitalization during the country's own banking crisis, which had run from 1988 to 1993. Even so, Stoltenberg was obliged to dip into the country's oil wealth in 2009 to set up two funds totalling 100 billion kroner to bolster its banks and bond market.

Neither was Stoltenberg averse to some political shimmying, conspicuously tightening **immigration** rules to undercut criticism coming from the Progress Party to his political right. The proof was in the electoral pudding of **2009**, when the Labour Party-led coalition won another parliamentary majority, albeit with less of the popular vote than its rivals (47.9% versus 49.5%). Few would argue that Stoltenberg has become a shrewd political operator and aspects of his private life have attracted much

| 1994 | 2000 | 2004 |
| --- | --- | --- |
| Referendum 2: Norwegians decide not to join the EU. | Opening of the Lærdal–Aurland road tunnel, at 24.5km the longest in the world. | Munch's *The Scream* stolen from the Munch-museet in Oslo. Much Norwegian embarrassment. |

sympathetic attention, not least the heroin addiction of his sister Nini. More importantly, Stoltenberg was equal to the task of speaking the nation's grief at a memorial service held in Oslo cathedral after the dreadful events of July 22, 2011, when **Anders Behring Breivik** killed 77 innocents by detonating a bomb in Oslo and then going on a shooting spree at a Labour Party summer camp.

## Into the future

In the long term, quite what Norway will make of its splendid **isolation from the EU** is unclear, though the situation is mitigated by Norway's membership of the European Economic Agreement (EEA), a free-trade deal of January 1994 that covers both Norway and the EU. Whatever happens, and whether or not there is another EU referendum, it's hard to imagine that the Norwegians will suffer any permanent economic harm. They have, after all, a superabundance of natural resources – primarily 0.6% of the world's proven oil reserves and 1.6% of the gas – and arguably the most educated workforce in the world with unemployment at consistently low levels (3 per cent or so). But that doesn't mean the country doesn't collectively **fret**: Norway's Lutheran roots run deep and, if an old joke is to be believed, the low point of the average Norwegian's year is the summer vacation. There's also a vague feeling of (Lutheran) unease about the country's prosperity with no less a figure than Jo Nesbø declaring, in no uncertain terms, that "money has corrupted us".

The Norwegians also fret (and argue) about **environmental** issues, with one hot potato being the country's **road building** programme. A curse afflicting prewar Norway had always been rural isolation and the Norwegians of 1945 were determined to connect (almost) all of the country's villages to the road system. Give or take the occasional hamlet, this has now been achieved and a second phase is underway, involving the upgrading of roads and the construction of innumerable tunnels. Wherever this makes conditions safer, the popular consensus for the programme survives, but there is increasing opposition to the prestige projects so beloved by politicians – the enormous tunnel near Flåm (see p.227) being a case in point. There is, however, precious little internal argument when it comes to **whaling and sealing**, with the majority continuing to support the hunting of these animals as has been the custom for centuries – indeed, for some Norwegians whaling and sealing go some way to defining what they consider to be the national identity. This is inexplicable to many Western Europeans, who point to Norway's eminently liberal approach to most other matters, but the Norwegians see things very differently: why, many of them ask, is the culling of seals and minke seen in a different light from the mass slaughter of farmed animals?

| 2009 | 2009 | 2012 |
|------|------|------|
| Same-sex marriages become legal. | Norway wins the Eurovision Song Contest; country euphoric. | Life expectancy at birth of the average Norwegian hits 80 years. |

# Legends and folklore

Norway has an exceptionally rich body of historical legend and folk tradition – and it plays an important part in the national consciousness even today. Most famous are the sagas, mainly written in Iceland between the twelfth and fourteenth centuries and constituting a vast collection of part-historical, part-fictionalized stories covering several centuries of Norse history. Thanks to the survival of one of these sagas, the *Poetic Edda* (see below), our knowledge of Norse mythology is also far from conjectural. In addition, much that was not recorded in the sagas survived in the country's oral tradition and this was revived from the 1830s onwards by the artists and writers of the National Romantic movement. Some members of this movement also set about collecting the folk tales and legends of the rural regions. The difficulties they experienced in rendering the Norwegian dialects into written form – there was no written Norwegian language per se – fuelled the language movement, and sent the academic Ivar Aasen (1813–96) roaming the countryside to assemble the material from which he formulated *Landsmål* (see p.422).

## Sagas

The Norwegian Vikings settled in **Iceland** in the ninth century and throughout the medieval period the Icelanders had a deep attachment to, and interest in, their original homeland. The result was a body of work that remains one of the richest sources of European medieval literature. That so much of it has survived is due to Iceland's isolation – most Norwegian sources disappeared centuries ago.

All the **sagas** feature real people and tell of events which are usually known to have happened, though the plots are embroidered to suit the tales' heroic style. They reveal much about a Norse culture in which arguments between individuals might spring from comparatively trivial disputes over horses or sheep, but where a strict code of honour and revenge meant that every insult, whether real or imagined, had to be avenged. Thus personal disputes soon turned into clan vendettas. Plots are complex, the dialogue laconic, and the pared-down prose omits unnecessary detail. New characters are often introduced by means of tedious genealogies, necessary to explain the motivation behind their later actions (though the more adept translations render these explanations as footnotes). Personality is only revealed through speech, facial expressions and general demeanour, or the comments and gossip of others.

The earliest Icelandic work, the **Elder** or **Poetic Edda**, comprises 34 lays dating from as early as the eighth century, and they combine to give a detailed insight into early Norse culture as well as pagan cosmogony and belief. It's not to be confused with the **Younger** or **Prose Edda**, written centuries later by Snorri Sturluson, the most distinguished of the saga writers. Also noteworthy are *The Vinland Saga, Njal's Saga* and the *Laxdaela Saga*, tales of ninth- and tenth-century Icelandic derring-do; and *Harald's Saga*, a rattling good yarn celebrating the life and times of Harald Hardrada. English translations of all the above are readily available.

# Norse mythology

The Vikings shared a common **pagan faith**, whose polytheistic tenets were upheld right across Scandinavia. The deities were worshipped at a thousand village shrines, usually by means of sacrifices in which animals, weapons, boats and other artefacts, even humans, were gifted to the gods. There was very little theology to sanctify these rituals; instead the principal gods – Odin, Thor and Frey – were surrounded by mythical tales attributing to them a bewildering variety of strengths, weaknesses and powers.

## Odin and Frigga

The god of war, wisdom, poetry and magic, **Odin** was untrustworthy, violent and wise in equal measure. The most powerful of the twelve Viking deities, the Aesir, who lived at Asgard, he was also lord of the **Valkyries**, women warrior-servants who tended his needs while he held court at **Valhalla**, the hall of dead heroes. As with many of the other pagan gods, he had the power to change into any form he desired. Odin's wife, **Frigga**, was the goddess protecting the home and the family.

## Yggdrasil

At the beginning of time, it was Odin who made heaven and earth from the body of the giant **Ymir**, and created man from an ash tree, woman from an alder. However, **Yggdrasil**, the tree of life that supported the whole universe, was beyond his control; the Vikings believed that eventually the tree would die and both gods and mortals would perish in the **Ragnarok**, the twilight of the gods. Among the Anglo-Saxons, the equivalent of Odin was Woden, hence "Wednesday".

## Thor

One of Odin's sons, **Thor** appears to have been the most worshipped of the Norse gods. A giant with superhuman strength, he was the short-tempered god of thunder, fire and lightning. He regularly fought with the evil Frost Giants in the Jotunheim mountains, his favourite weapon being the hammer, Mjolnir, which the trolls (see p.404) had fashioned for him. His chariot was drawn by two goats – Cracktooth and Gaptooth – who could be killed and eaten at night, but would be fully recovered the next morning, providing none of their bones were broken. It's from Thor that we get "Thursday".

## Loki and Sigyn

A negative force, **Loki** personified cunning and trickery. His treachery turned the other deities against him, and he was chained up beneath a serpent that dripped venom onto his face. His wife, **Sigyn**, remained loyal and held a bowl over his head to catch the venom, but when the bowl was full she had to turn away to empty it, and in those moments his squirmings would cause earthquakes.

## Frey and Freya

The god of fertility was **Frey**, whose pride and joy was *Skidbladnir*, a ship that was large enough to carry all the gods, but could still be folded up and put into his bag. He often lived with the elves (see p.404) in Elfheim. **Freya** was the goddess of love, healing and fertility – and "Friday" was named after her.

## Hel and the Norns

The goddess of the dead, **Hel** lived on brains and bone marrow. She presided over "Hel", where those who died of illness or old age went, living a miserable existence under the roots of Yggdrasil, the tree of life. Representing the past, the present and the future, the **Norns** were the three goddesses of fate, casting lots over the cradle of every newborn child.

## Folk tales and legends

Norway's extensive oral folklore was first written down in the early nineteenth century, most famously by **Peter Christen Asbjørnsen** and **Jørgen Moe**, the first of whose compilations appeared to great popular acclaim in 1842. These tales succoured the country's emergent nationalism, but in fact many of them were far from uniquely Norwegian, sharing characteristics with – and having the same roots as – folk tales across the whole of northern Europe. They were, however, populated by stock characters who were recognizably Norwegian – the king, for example, was always pictured as a wealthy farmer.

There are three types of Norwegian **folk tale**: comical tales; animal yarns, in which the beasts concerned – most frequently the wolf, fox and bear – talk and behave like human beings; and most common of all, magical stories populated by a host of supernatural creatures. The folk tale is always written matter-of-factly, no matter how fantastic the events it retells. In this respect it has much in common with the **folk legend**, though the latter purports to be factual. Norwegian legends "explain" scores of unusual natural phenomena – the location of boulders, holes in cliffs, etc – and are crammed with supernatural beings, again as is broadly familiar right across northern Europe.

The assorted **supernatural creatures** of folk tale and legend hark back to the pagan myths of the pre-Christian era, but whereas the Vikings held them of secondary importance to their gods, in Norwegian folk tales they take centre stage. In post-pagan Norwegian folk tradition, these creatures were regarded as the descendants of children that Eve hid from God. When they were discovered by him, they were assigned particular realms in which to dwell, but their illicit wanderings were legion. Towards the end of the nineteenth century, book illustrations by **Erik Werenskiold** and **Theodor Kittelsen** effectively defined what the various supernatural creatures looked like in the Norwegian public's imagination. As mythologized in Norway, the creatures of the folk tales possess a confusing range of virtues and vices. Here's a brief round-up of some of the more important.

### Giants

Enormous in size and strength, the **giants** of Norwegian folklore were reputed to be rather stupid and capable both of kindly actions and great cruelty towards humans. They usually had a human appearance, but some were monsters with many heads. They were fond of carrying parts of the landscape from one place to another, dropping boulders and even islands as they went. According to the Eddic cosmogony, the first giant, Ymir, was killed by Odin and the world made from his body – his blood formed the sea, his bones the mountains and so on. Ymir was the ancestor of the evil **Frost Giants**, who lived in Jotunheim, and who regularly fought with Thor.

### Trolls

Spirits of the underground, **trolls** were ambivalent figures, able both to hinder and help humans – and were arguably a folkloric expression of the id. The first trolls were depicted as giants, but later versions were small, strong, misshapen and of pale countenance from living underground; sunlight would turn them into stone. They worked in metals and wood and were fabulous craftsmen. They made Odin's spear and Thor's hammer, though Thor's inclination to throw the weapon at them made them hate noise; as late as the eighteenth century, Norwegian villagers would ring church bells for hours on end to drive them away. If the trolls were forced to make something for a human, they would put a secret curse on it; this would render it dangerous to the owner. Some trolls had a penchant for stealing children and others carried off women to be their wives.

### Elves

Akin to fairies, **elves** were usually divided between good-hearted but mischievous white elves, and nasty black elves, who brought injury and sickness. Both lived underground in a world, Elfheim, that echoed that of humans – with farms, animals and the like – but made excursions into the glades and groves of the forests up above. At night, the white elves liked singing and dancing to the accompaniment of the harp. They were normally invisible, though you could spot their dancing places wherever the grass grew more luxuriantly in circular patterns than elsewhere. The black elves were also invisible, a good job considering they were extremely ugly and had long, filthy noses. If struck by a sunbeam, they would turn to stone. Both types of elf were prone to entice humans into their kingdom, usually for a short period – but sometimes forever.

### Wights
In pre-Christian times, the Vikings believed their lands to be populated with invisible guardian spirits, the **wights** (*vetter*), who needed to be treated with respect. One result was that when a longship was approaching the shore, the fearsome figurehead at its prow was removed so as not to frighten the *vetter* away. Bad luck would follow if a *vetter* left the locality.

### Witches
As with **witches** across much of the rest of Europe, the Scandinavian version was typically an old woman who had made a pact with the Devil, swapping her soul in return for special powers. The witch could inflict injury and illness, especially if she was in possession of something her victim had touched or owned – anything from a lock of hair to an item of clothing. She could disguise herself as an animal, and had familiars – usually insects or cats – which assisted her in foul deeds. Most witches travelled through the air on broomsticks, but some rode on wolves bridled with snakes.

### Water spirits
Personifying all those who have died at sea, the **draugen** was a ghostly apparition who appeared as a headless fisherman in oilskins. He sailed the seas in half a boat and wailed when someone was about to drown. Other water spirits included the malicious river sprite, the **nixie**, who could assume different forms to lure the unsuspecting to a watery grave. There were also the shy and benign **mermaids** and **mermen**, half-fish and half-human, who dived into the water whenever they spied a human. However, they also liked to dress up as humans to go to market.

# Viking customs and rituals

The Vikings have long been the subject of historical discussion and debate with accurate and unbiased contemporary accounts being few and far between. A remarkable exception is the annals of Ibn Fadlan, a member of a diplomatic delegation sent from the Baghdad Caliphate to Bulgar on the Volga in 921–922 AD. In the following extracts Fadlan details the habits and rituals of a tribe of Swedish Vikings, the Rus, who dealt in furs and slaves. The first piece notes with disgust the finer points of Viking personal hygiene, the second provides a sober eyewitness account of the rituals of a Viking ship burial.

## Habits and rituals

I saw the Rus when they arrived on their trading mission and anchored at the River Atul (Volga). Never had I seen people of more perfect physique; they are tall as date-palms, and reddish in colour. They wear neither mantle nor coat, but each man carries a cape, which covers one half of his body, leaving one hand free. Their swords are Frankish in pattern, broad, flat and fluted. Each man has (tattooed upon him) trees, figures and the like from the finger-nails to the neck. Each woman carries on her bosom a container made of iron, silver, copper or gold – its size and substance depending on her man's wealth. Attached to the container is a ring carrying her knife, which is also tied to her bosom. Round her neck she wears gold or silver rings; when a man amasses 10,000 *dirhems* he makes his wife one gold ring; when he has 20,000 he makes two; and so the woman gets a new ring for every 10,000 *dirhems* her husband acquires, and often a woman has many of these rings. Their finest ornaments are green beads made from clay. They will go to any length to get hold of these; for one *dirhem* they procure one such bead and they string these into necklaces for their women.

They are the filthiest of god's creatures. They do not wash after discharging their natural functions, neither do they wash their hands after meals. They are as stray donkeys. They arrive from their distant lands and lay their ships alongside the banks of the Atul, which is a great river, and there they build big wooden houses on its shores. Ten or twenty of them may live together in one house, and each of them has a couch of his own where he sits and diverts himself with the pretty slave-girls whom he has brought along to offer for sale. He will make love with one of them in the presence of his comrades, sometimes this develops into a communal orgy and, if a customer should turn up to buy a girl, the Rus will not let her go till he has finished with her.

Every day they wash their faces and heads, all using the same water which is as filthy as can be imagined. This is how it is done. Every morning a girl brings her master a large bowl of water in which he washes his face and hands and hair, combing it also over the bowl, then blows his nose and spits into the water. No dirt is left on him which doesn't go into the water. When he has finished the girl takes the same bowl to his neighbour – who repeats the performance – until the bowl has gone round the entire household. All have blown their noses, spat and washed their faces and hair in the water.

On anchoring their vessels, each man goes ashore carrying bread, meat, onions, milk, and *nabid* [wine], and these he takes to a large wooden stake with a face like that of a human being, surrounded by smaller figures, and behind them tall poles in the ground. Each man prostrates himself before the large post and recites: "O Lord, I have come from distant parts with so many girls, so many furs (and whatever other commodities he is carrying). I now bring you this offering." He then presents his gift and continues "Please send me a merchant who has many dinars and *dirhems*, and who will trade favourably with me without too much bartering." Then he retires. If, after this, business does not pick up quickly and go well, he returns to the statue to present further gifts. If results continue slow, he then presents gifts to the minor figures and begs their intercession, saying, "These are our Lord's wives, daughters and sons." Then he pleads before each figure in turn, begging them to intercede for him and humbling himself before them. Often trade picks up, and he says "My Lord has required my needs, and now it is my duty to repay him." Whereupon he sacrifices goats or cattle, some of which he distributes as alms. The rest he lays before the statues, large and small, and the heads of the beasts he plants upon the poles. After dark, of course, the dogs come and devour the lot – and the successful trader says, "My Lord is pleased with me, and has eaten my offerings."

If one of the Rus falls sick they put him in a tent by himself and leave bread and water for him. They do not visit him, however, or speak to him, especially if he is a serf. Should he recover he rejoins the others; if he dies they burn him. If he happens to be a serf, however, they leave him for the dogs and vultures to devour. If they catch a robber they hang him in a tree until he is torn to shreds by wind and weather …

## The burial

… I had been told that when their chieftains died cremation was the least part of their whole funeral procedure, and I was, therefore, very much interested to find out more about this. One day I heard that one of their leaders had died. They laid him forthwith in a grave, which they covered up for ten days till they had finished cutting-out and sewing his costume. If the dead man is poor they make a little ship, put him in it, and burn it. If he is wealthy, however, they divide his property and goods into three parts: one for his family, one to pay for his costume, and one to make *nabid*. This they drink on the day when the slave woman of the dead man is killed and burnt together with her master. They are deeply addicted to *nabid*, drinking it day and night; and often one of them has been found dead with a beaker in his hand. When a chieftain among them has died, his family demands of his slave women and servants: "Which of you wishes to die with him?" Then one of them says "I do" – and having said that the person concerned is forced to do so, and no backing out is possible. Those who are willing are mostly the slave women.

So when this man died they said to his slave women "Which of you wants to die with him?" One of them answered "I do." From that moment she was put in the constant care of two other women servants who took care of her to the extent of washing her feet with their own hands. They began to get things ready for the dead man, to cut his costume and so on, while every day the doomed woman drank and sang as though in anticipation of a joyous event.

When the day arrived on which the chieftain and his slave woman were going to be burnt, I went to the river where his ship was moored. It had been hauled ashore and four posts were made for it of birch and other wood. Further there was arranged around it what looked like a big store of wood. Then the ship was hauled near and placed on the wood. People now began to walk about talking in a language I could not understand, and the corpse still lay in the grave; they had not taken it out. They then produced a wooden bench, placed it on the ship, and covered it with carpets of Byzantine *dibag* (painted silk) and with cushions of Byzantine *dibag*. Then came an old woman whom they called "the Angel of Death", and she spread these cushions out over the bench. She was in charge of the whole affair from dressing the corpse to the killing of the slave woman. I noticed that she was an old giant-woman, a massive and grim figure. When they came to his grave they removed the earth from the wooden frame and they also took the frame away. They then divested the corpse of the clothes in which he had died. The body, I noticed, had turned black because of the intense frost. When they first put him in the grave, they had also given him beer, fruit, and a lute, all of which they now removed. Strangely enough the corpse did not smell, nor had anything about him changed save the colour of his flesh. They now proceeded to dress him in hose, and trousers, boots, coat, and a mantle of *dibag* adorned with gold buttons; put on his head a cap of *dibag* and sable fur; and carried him to the tent on the ship, where they put him on the blanket and supported him with cushions. They then produced *nabid*, fruit, and aromatic plants, and put these round his body; and they also brought bread, meat, and onions which they flung before him. Next they took a dog, cut it in half, and flung the pieces into the ship, and after this they took all his weapons and placed them beside him.

Next they brought two horses and ran them about until they were in a sweat, after which they cut them to pieces with swords and flung their meat into the ship; this also happened to two cows. Then they produced a cock and a hen, killed them, and threw them in. Meanwhile the slave woman who wished to be killed walked up and down, going into one tent after the other, and the owner of each tent had sexual intercourse with her, saying "Tell your master I did this out of love for him."

It was now Friday afternoon and they took the slave woman away to something which they had made resembling a doorframe. Then she placed her legs on the palms of the men and reached high enough to look over the frame, and she said something in a foreign language, after which they took her down. And they lifted her up again and she did the same as the first time. Then they took her down and lifted her a third time and she did the same as the first and second times. Then they gave her a chicken and she cut its head off and threw it away; they took the hen and threw it into the ship. Then I asked the interpreter what she had done. He answered: "The first time they lifted her she said: 'Look! I see my mother and father.' The second time she said: 'Look! I see all my dead relatives sitting around.' The third time she said: 'Look! I see my master in Paradise, and Paradise is beautiful and green and together with him are men and young boys. He calls me. Let me join him then.'"

They now led her towards the ship. Then she took off two bracelets she was wearing and gave them to the old woman, "the Angel of Death", the one who was going to kill her. She next took off two anklets she was wearing and gave them to the daughters of that same woman. They then led her to the ship but did not allow her inside the tent. Then a number of men carrying wooden shields and sticks arrived, and gave her a beaker with *nabid*. She sang over it and emptied it. The interpreter then said to me, "Now with that she is bidding farewell to all her women friends." Then she was given another beaker. She took it and sang a lengthy song; but the old woman told her to hurry and drink up and enter the tent where her master was. When I looked at her she seemed completely bewildered. She wanted to enter the tent and she put her head between it and the ship. Then the woman took her head and managed to get it inside the tent, and the woman herself followed. Then the men began to beat the shields with the wooden sticks, to deaden her shouts so that the other girls would not become afraid and shrink from dying with their masters. Six men entered the tent and all of them had intercourse with her. Thereafter they laid her by the side of her dead master. Two held her hands and two her feet, and the woman called "the Angel of Death" put a cord round the girl's neck, doubled with an end at each side, and gave it to two men to pull. Then she advanced holding a small dagger with a broad blade and began to plunge it between the girl's ribs to and fro while the two men choked her with the cord till she died.

The dead man's nearest kinsman now appeared. He took a piece of wood and ignited it. Then he walked backwards, his back towards the ship and his face towards the crowd, holding the piece of wood in one hand and the other hand on his buttock; and he was naked. In this way the wood was ignited which they had placed under the ship after they had laid the slave woman, whom they had killed, beside her master. Then people came with branches and wood; each brought a burning brand and threw it on the pyre, so that the fire took hold of the wood, then the ship, then the tent and the man and the slave woman and all. Thereafter a strong and terrible wind rose so that the flame stirred and the fire blazed still more.

I heard one of the Rus folk, standing by, say something to my interpreter, and when I inquired what he had said, my interpreter answered: "He said: 'You Arabs are foolish'". "Why?" I asked. "Well, because you throw those you love and honour to the ground where the earth and the maggots and fields devour them, whereas we, on the other hand, burn them up quickly and they go to Paradise that very moment." The man burst out laughing, and on being asked why, he said: "His Lord, out of love for him, has sent this wind to take him away within the hour!" And so it proved, for within that time the ship and the pyre, the girl and the corpse had all become ashes and then dust. On the spot where the ship stood after having been hauled ashore, they built something like a round mould. In the middle of it they raised a large post of birch-wood on which they wrote the names of the dead man and the king of the Rus, and then the crowd dispersed.

*The above extract, translated by Karre Stov, was taken from* The Vikings *by Johanes Brøndsted, and is reprinted by permission of Penguin Books.*

# Flora and fauna

There are significant differences in climate between the west coast of Norway, which is warmed by the Gulf Stream, and the interior of the country, but these variations prove much less significant for the country's flora than altitude and latitude. With regard to Norway's fauna, wild animals survive in significant numbers in the more inaccessible regions, but have been hunted extensively elsewhere, while the west coast is home to dozens of extensive sea-bird colonies.

## Flora

Much of the Norwegian landscape is dominated by vast **forests of spruce**, though these are, in fact, a relatively recent feature: the original forest cover was mainly of pine, birch and oak, and only in the last two thousand years has spruce spread across the whole of southeast and central Norway. That said, a rich variety of **deciduous trees** – notably oak, ash, lime, hazel, rowan, elm and maple – still flourishes in a wide belt along the south coast, up through the fjord country and as far north as Trondheim, but only at relatively low altitudes. For their part, **conifers** thin out at around 900m above sea level in the south, 450m in Finnmark, to be replaced by a birch zone, where there are also aspen and mountain ash. Norway's deciduous trees contrive to ripen their seeds despite a short, cool summer, and can consequently be found at low altitudes almost as far north as Nordkapp (North Cape) – as can the pine, the most robust of the conifers. At around 1100m/650m, the birch fizzle out to be replaced by willow and dwarf birch, while above the timber line are bare mountain peaks and huge plateaux, the latter usually dotted with hundreds of lakes.

### Berries

Norway accommodates in the region of two thousand plant species, but few of these are native. The most sought-after are the **berrying** species that grow wild all over Norway, mainly cranberries, blueberries and yellow **cloudberries**. Common in the country's peat bogs, and now also extensively cultivated, the cloudberry is a small herbaceous bramble whose fruits have a tangy flavour that is much prized in Norway – and very fashionable today in some of the country's best foodie haunts. In drier situations and on the mountain plateaux, **lichens** – the favourite food of the reindeer – predominate, while in all but the thickest of spruce forests, the ground is thickly carpeted with **moss** and **heather**.

### Wild flowers

Everywhere, spring brings **wild flowers**, splashes of brilliant colour at their most intense on the west coast, where a wide range of mountain plants is nourished by the wet conditions and a geology that varies from limestone to acidic granites. Most of these species can also be found in the Alps, but there are several rarities, notably the **alpine clematis** (*Clematis alpina*) found in the Gudbrandsdal valley, hundreds of miles from its normal homes in eastern Finland and the Carpathian mountains. Another, larger group comprises about thirty **Canadian mountain plants**, found in Europe only in the Dovre and Jotunheim mountains; quite how they come to be there has long baffled botanists.

The mildness of the west-coast winter has allowed certain species to prosper beyond their usual northerly latitudes. Among species that can tolerate very little frost or snow are the star hyacinth (*Scilla verna*) and the purple heather (*Erica purpurea*), while a short distance inland come varieties that can withstand only short icy spells, including the foxglove (*Digitalis purpurea*) and the holly (*Ilex aquifolium*). In the southeastern part of the country, where the winters are harder and the summers hotter, the conditions support species that can lie dormant under the snow for several months a year – for example the blue anemone (*Anemone hepatica*) and the aconite (*Aconitum septentrionale*).

In the far north, certain Siberian species have migrated west down the rivers and along the coasts to the fjords of Finnmark and Troms. The most significant is the **Siberian garlic** (*Allium sibiricum*), which grows in such abundance that farmers have to make sure their cows don't eat too much of it or else the milk becomes garlic-flavoured. Other Siberian species to look out for are the fringed pink (*Dianthus superbus*) and a large, lily-like plant, the sneezewort (*Veratrum album*).

## Fauna

The larger Arctic **predators** of Norway, principally the lynx, wolf, wolverine and bear, are virtually extinct, and where they have survived they are mainly confined to the more inaccessible regions of the north. To a degree this has been caused by the timber industry, which has logged out great chunks of forest. The smaller predators – the arctic fox, otter, badger and marten – have fared rather better and remain comparatively common.

In the 1930s, the **beaver** population had dropped to just 500 animals in southern Norway. A total ban on hunting has, however, led to a dramatic increase in their numbers, and beavers have begun to recolonize their old hunting grounds right across Scandinavia. The elk has benefited from the rolling back of the forests, grazing the newly treeless areas and breeding in sufficient numbers to allow an annual cull of around 40,000 animals; the red deer of the west coast are flourishing too. Otherwise, the Norwegians own about two million sheep and around 200,000 domesticated **reindeer**, most of whom are herded by the Sámi. The last wild reindeer in Europe, some 25,000 beasts, wander the Northern plateau and mountainous provinces; the largest group – some 7,000 animals – can be found on Hardangervidda. There is also a herd of **musk ox** in the Dovrefjell-Sunndalsfjella Nasjonalpark (see p.168), though these prodigious beasts are not native – they were imported from Greenland in the late 1940s.

### Lemmings

Among Norway's rodents, the most interesting is the **lemming**, whose numbers vary over a four-year cycle. In the first three to four years there is a gradual increase, which is followed, in the course of a few months, by a sudden fall. The cause of these variations is not known, though theories are plentiful. In addition to this four-year fluctuation, the lemming population goes through a violent explosion every eleven to twelve years. Competition for food is so ferocious that many animals start to range over wide areas. In these so-called lemming years the mountains and surrounding areas teem with countless thousands of lemmings, and hundreds swarm to their deaths by falling off cliff edges and the like in a stampede of migration (though there is no truth in the idea that they commit mass suicide). In lemming years, predators and birds of prey have an abundant source of food and frequently give birth to twice as many young as normal – not surprising considering the lemmings are extremely easy to catch. More inexplicably, the snowy owl leaves its polar habitat in lemming years, flying south to join in the feast: quite how they know when to turn up is a mystery. The Vikings were particularly fascinated by lemmings, believing that they dropped from the sky during thunderstorms.

## THE PUFFIN

Some 30cm tall, with a triangular, red, blue and yellow striped bill, the **puffin** (*Fratercula arctica*) is the most distinctive of the many sea birds that congregate along the Norwegian coast. It feeds on small fish, and breeds in holes it excavates in turf on cliffs or grassy flatlands, sometimes even adapting former rabbit burrows. When hunting, puffins use their wings to propel themselves underwater and, indeed, are much better at swimming than flying, finding it difficult both to get airborne and to land – collisions of one sort or another are commonplace. Their nesting habits and repetitive flight paths make them easy to catch, and puffin has long been a west-coast delicacy, though hunting them is now severely restricted. In the summer, puffins nest along the whole of the Atlantic coast from Stavanger to Nordkapp, with Værøy (see p.328) and Runde (see p.257) being two of the most likely places for a sighting. In the autumn the puffins move south, though residual winter populations remain on the southerly part of the west coast between Stavanger and Ålesund.

### Birds

With the exception of the raven, the partridge and the grouse, all the **mountain birds** of Norway are **migratory**, reflecting the harshness of winter conditions. Most fly back and forth from the Mediterranean and Africa, but some winter down on the coast. **Woodland** species include the wood grouse, the black grouse, several different sorts of owl, woodpecker and birds of prey, while the country's **lakes and marshes** are inhabited by cranes, swans, grebes, geese, ducks and many types of wader. Most dramatic of all are the coastal nesting cliffs, where millions of **sea birds**, such as kittiwake, guillemots, puffin, cormorant and gull, congregate. What you won't see is the great auk, a flightless, 50cm-high bird resembling a penguin that once nested in its millions along the Atlantic seaboard but is now extinct: the last Norwegian great auk was killed in the eighteenth century and the last one of all was shot near Iceland a century later.

### Fish

The waters off Norway once teemed with **seals** and **whales**, but indiscriminate hunting has drastically reduced their numbers, prompting several late-in-the-day conservation measures. The commonest species of **fish** – cod, haddock, coalfish and halibut – have been overexploited too, and whereas there were once gigantic shoals of them right along the coast up to the Arctic Sea, they are now much less common. The cod, like several other species, live far out in the Barents Sea, only coming to the coast to spawn, a favourite destination being the waters round the Lofoten islands.

The only fish along Norway's coast that can survive in both salt and fresh water is the **salmon**, which grows to maturity in the sea and only swims upriver to spawn and die. In the following spring the young salmon return to the sea on the spring flood. Trout and char populate the rivers and lakes of western Norway, living on a diet of crustacea, which tints their meat pink, like the salmon. Eastern Norway and Finnmark are the domain of **whitefish**, so-called because they feed on plant remains, insects and animals, which keep their flesh white. In prehistoric times, these species migrated here from the east via what was then the freshwater Baltic; the most important of them are the perch, powan, pike and grayling.

# Cinema

For most of its short history, Norwegian cinema has been overshadowed by its Nordic neighbours and has struggled to make any sort of impact on the international scene. In the last decade or so, however, a group of talented film-makers has emerged and they have been responsible for a string of stylish, honest and refreshingly lucid films, often assisted by healthy government subsidies. Cinema receipts speak for themselves: in 2010, Norwegian films were responsible for 23.4 percent of domestic box office sales, which was a record by some margin. For the latest news on Norwegian cinema, consult the Norwegian Film Institute website (@nfi.no).

## 1950s to the mid-1980s

Early Norwegian cinematic successes were few and far between, an exception being *Kon-Tiki*, a 1951 Oscar-winning documentary recording Thor Heyerdahl's journey across the Pacific on a balsa raft (see p.85), though the producer (and Oscar recipient) was a Swede, Olle Nordemar. In 1957, *Nine Lives* (*Ni Liv*), produced and directed by the Norwegian **Arne Skouen** (1913–2003), was widely acclaimed for its tale of a betrayed Resistance fighter, who managed to drag himself across northern Norway in winter to safety in neutral Sweden. Two years later **Erik Løchen**'s *The Hunt* (*Jakten*) was much influenced by the French New Wave in its mixture of time and space, dream and reality, as was the early work of **Anja Breien** (b.1940), whose *Growing Up* (*Jostedalsrypa*) relates the story of a young girl who is the sole survivor from the Black Death in a remote fjordland village. Breien followed this up in 1975 with a successful improvised comedy *Wives* (*Hustruer*), in which three former classmates meet at a school reunion and subsequently share their life experiences. Breien developed this into a trilogy with *Wives Ten Years Later* (*Hustruer ti år etter*) in 1985 and *Wives III* in 1996. She also garnered critical success at Cannes with *Next of Kin* (*Arven*; 1979), and won prizes at the Venice Film Festival with *Witch Hunt* (*Forfølgelsen*; 1982), an exploration of the persecution of women in the Middle Ages.

## Mid-1980s to 2000

**Liv Ullmann** (b.1939) is easily the most famous Norwegian actor, but in Scandinavia she has worked chiefly with Swedish and Danish producers and directors, most famously Ingmar Bergman (with whom she also had a daughter). In 1995, Ullmann brought the popular Norwegian writer Sigrid Undset's medieval epic *Kristin Lavransdatter* to the screen in a three-hour film that attracted mixed reviews. Another Norwegian writer to have had his work made into films is Knut Hamsun (see p.296, p.394 & p.419): in the mid-1990s, the Swedish director Jan Troell filmed the superb biographical *Trial against Hamsun* (*Prosessen mot Hamsun*), while in 1993 Oslo's **Erik Gustavson** directed *The Telegraphist* (*Telegrafisten*), based on a Hamsun story. The success of *The Telegraphist* led to Gustavson being offered the job of bringing Jostein Gaarder's extraordinarily popular novel *Sophie's World* (*Sofies Verden*; 1999) to the screen.

**Nils Gaup**'s debut film *The Pathfinder* (*Veiviseren*; 1987), an epic adventure based on a medieval Sámi legend, was widely acclaimed both in Norway and abroad when it was released, not least because the dialogue was in the Sámi language. Gaup followed it up with a nautical adventure, *Shipwrecked* (*Håkon Håkonsen*; 1990), and then a thriller

*Head Above Water* (*Hodet over vannet;* 1993), which had a pretty woeful Hollywood remake starring Cameron Diaz and Harvey Keitel. Among other Norwegian successes in the 1990s was **Pål Sletaune**'s *Junk Mail* (*Budbringeren;* 1997), a darkly humorous tale of an Oslo postman who opens the mail himself, and **Erik Skjoldbjaerg**'s *Insomnia* (1997), a film noir set in the permanent summer daylight of northern Norway. Stylish and compelling, it impressed Hollywood so much that it was remade in 2002 starring Al Pacino, but the newer version was a big glossy film without the grittiness of the original.

Much praised, too, were **Berit Nesheim**'s *The Other Side of Sunday* (*Søndagsengler;* 1996), the story of a vicar's daughter desperate to escape from her father's oppressive control, and **Eva Isaksen**'s *Death at Oslo Central* (*Døden på Oslo S;* 1990), a moving story of drug abuse and family conflict among the capital's young down-and-outs.

## 2000 to 2005

In 2001, **Knut Erik Jensen**'s surprise hit *Cool and Crazy* (*Heftig og Begeistret*) was a gentle, lyrical documentary about the male voice choir of Berlevåg (see p.364), a remote community in the far north of the country. Much to Jensen's surprise, his film was picked up abroad and became a major hit on the art-house cinema circuit. Similarly successful was **Peter Næss**'s *Elling* (2001), a sort of tragic-comedy that relates the heart-warming/-rending story of Elling, a fastidious and obsessive ex-mental patient who moves into an Oslo flat with one of the other former patients – an odd coupling if ever there was one. Equally idiosyncratic was **Bent Hamer**'s *Kitchen Stories* (*Salmer fra kjøkkenet;* 2003), a comic tale in which a tester for a Swedish kitchen-design company is dispatched to Norway to study the culinary goings-on of Isak, a farmer who lives a solitary life deep in the countryside. The two become friends, but it's a bumpy business with each having to dispense with his prejudices against the other's nationality.

Cinematic highlights of 2005 included **Sara Johnsen**'s *Kissed by Winter* (*Vinterkyss*), a harrowing tale of death, racism and murder in rural Norway, and an ambitious re-working of an Ibsen play, *An Enemy of the People* (*En folkefiende*), by **Erik Skjoldbjaerg**, in which the contamination of the medicinal baths in a small coastal town becomes a moral barometer about who wants to admit the disaster and who wants to cover it up.

## 2006 to the present

In 2006, *The Bothersome Man* (*Den brysomme mannen*), directed by **Jens Lien**, was a hard-edged parable of a man who suddenly finds himself in an outwardly perfect, but entirely soulless world – no points for comparing this dystopia with Norway – whereas **Joachim Trier**'s *Reprise* was a playful, subtle film about love and sorrow, success and failure, creativity and friendship. The same year also saw a cracking Norwegian horror film, **Roar Uthaug**'s *Cold Prey* (*Fritt Vilt*), with Uthaug producing a second offering, *Cold Prey 2* (*Fritt Vilt II*), two years later. 2008 also saw several rather more interesting productions, including *Man of War* (*Max Manus*), based on the wartime exploits of the Resistance fighter Max Manus: something of an epic, it had 1800 extras and a budget that dwarfed any other previous Norwegian film. Even more intriguing perhaps was *The Kautokeino Rebellion* (*Kautokeino-opprøret*) marking a return to cinematic form by Nils Gaup and focusing on the oppression of the Sámi by a deliciously evil Norwegian priest and merchant in Kautokeino in 1852.

The high point of 2010 was certainly **André Øvredal**'s *The Troll Hunter* (*Trolljegeren*), part mockumentary, part farce and part paranoid fantasy in which the Norwegian government hides the existence of trolls from the population. The film "claims", for example, that the musk ox of the Dovrefjell were imported to feed the mountain trolls – a troll larder if you will. At the time of writing, new films by Pål Sletaune and Jens Lien were in production and Headhunters (2011), based on a searingly brutal yarn by Jo Nesbø (see p.420), had been released to wide critical acclaim, much to the delight of its director Morten Tyldum.

# Books

Perhaps surprisingly, precious few travellers have written in English about the joys of journeying around Norway, though you might want to dig out a copy of a vintage *Baedeker's Norway and Sweden*, if only for the phrasebook, from which you can learn such gems as the Norwegian for "Do you want to cheat me?". Neither has Norwegian history been a major preoccupation – with the notable exception of the Vikings, who have attracted the attention of a veritable raft of historians and translators, whose works have often focused on the sagas, a rich body of work mostly written in Iceland between the twelfth and fourteenth centuries (see p.402). Scandinavian fiction is, however, an entirely different matter, with a flood of translations appearing on the market, a literary charge led by the immaculate crime novels of the Swede, Henning Mankell, with the Norwegians following in his slipstream.

Most of the books listed below are **in print and in paperback**, and those that are **out of print** should be easy to track down either in secondhand bookshops or through Amazon's used and secondhand book service (ⓦamazon.co.uk or ⓦamazon.com). Note also that while we recommend all the books we've listed below, we do have favourites – and these have been marked with ★.

## TRAVEL AND GENERAL

**Thor Heyerdahl** *The Kon-Tiki Expedition.* You may want to read this after visiting Oslo's Kon-Tiki Museum (p.85). Heyerdahl's account of the *Kon-Tiki* expedition aroused huge interest when it was first published, and it remains a ripping yarn – though surprisingly few people care to read it today. Heyerdahl's further exploits are related in *The Ra Expeditions* and *The Tigris Expedition* as is his long research trip to Easter Island in *Aku-Aku: The Secret of Easter Island.*

**Roland Huntford** *Scott and Amundsen: The Last Place on Earth.* There are dozens of books on the polar explorers Scott, Amundsen and Nansen, but this is one of the more recent, describing with flair and panache the race to the South Pole between Scott and Amundsen. Also worth a read is the same author's *Nansen*, a doorstep-sized biography of the noble explorer, academic and statesman Fridtjof Nansen.

**Lucy Jago** *The Northern Lights: How One Man Sacrificed Love, Happiness and Sanity to Solve the Mystery of the Aurora Borealis.* Intriguing biography of Kristian Birkeland, who spent years ferreting around northern Norway bent on understanding the northern lights – a quest for which he paid a heavy personal price.

★ **Mark Kurlansky** *Cod: A Biography of the Fish that Changed the World.* This wonderful book tracks the life and times of the cod and the generations of fishermen who have lived off it. There are sections on overfishing and the fish's breeding habits, and recipes are provided too.

Norwegians figure frequently – after all, cod was the staple diet of much of the country for centuries. Published in 1998.

★ **Sven Lindqvist** *Bench Press.* Delightful little book delving into the nature of weight-training – and the Swedish/Scandinavian attitude to it. Wry and perceptive cultural commentary by one of Sweden's wittiest and most impassioned cultural commentators. Published in 2003.

**Eva Maagerø and Birte Simonsen** (ed) *Norway: Society and Culture.* Published in 2008, this ambitious collection of essays attempts to summarize where Norway is sociologically and culturally – and where it has come from. Among much else, there are essays on the Welfare State, Religion, Literature, Art, Music and Language. Some are very good, but others are really rather pedestrian.

**Trygve Mathiesen** Sid's Norwegian romance – *Sex Pistols Exiled to Trondheim 1977.* The curious tale of The Sex Pistols' two-day stay in Trondheim and Sid's tingles and tangles with a Norwegian. If you like it, try the same author's *Sex Pistols Exiled to Oslo 1977.*

**Christoph Ransmayr** *The Terrors of Ice and Darkness.* Clever mingling of fact and fiction as the book's main character follows the route of the doomed Austro-Hungarian Arctic expedition in 1873. A story of obsession and, ultimately, insanity.

**Roger Took** *Running with Reindeer.* A thoughtful account of Took's extended visit to – and explorations of – Russia's

Kola peninsula in the 1990s, with much to say about the Sámi and their current predicaments.

**Paul Watkins** *The Fellowship of Ghosts*. Modern-day musings as Watkins travels through the mountains and fjords of southern Norway. Easy reading, but sometimes over-written – and if that doesn't get you, the barrage of jokes probably will. There again, to be fair, there are lots of useful bits and pieces about Norway and its people.

**Mary Wollstonecraft** *Letters written during a Short Residence in Sweden, Norway and Denmark*. For reasons that have never been entirely clear, Wollstonecraft, the author of *A Vindication of the Rights of Women*, and mother of Mary Shelley, travelled Scandinavia for several months in 1795. Her letters home represent a real historical curiosity, though her trenchant comments on Norway often get sidelined by her intense melancholia.

## HIKING AND CLIMBING

**James Baxter** *Scandinavian Mountains and Peaks over 2000 Metres in the Hurrungane* (Jotunheim). Published in 2005, this specialist text details a series of walks and climbs in the Jotunheim mountains. Detailed text with maps, but you'll still need to invest in a proper hiking map. By the same author, and published in 2012, there's also *Norway: the Outdoor Paradise – A Ski and Kayak Odyssey in Europe's Great Wilderness*. An energetic chap, this James Baxter.

**Anthony Dyer** *Walks and Scrambles in Norway*. English-language books on Norway's hiking trails are thin on the ground. This one describes over fifty hikes and scrambles from one end of the country to the other, though the majority are in the western fjords (as in our Chapter 4). Lots of photographs, and the text is detailed and thoroughly researched, but the maps are only general and you'll need to buy specialist hiking ones to supplement them. Published in 2006.

**Tony Howard** *Climbs, Scrambles and Walks in Romsdal*. Originally published in 1970, but thoroughly updated and revised in 2005, this book – easily the best on its subject – explores the mighty mountains near Åndalsnes (see p.165). Tips, hints and details of 300 climbs, scrambles and walks with some maps and diagrams.

**Tony Howard** *Troll Wall*. It's 1965 and a group of climbers from the north of England are encamped at the foot of the Troll Wall near Åndalsnes (see p.165). The Wall has never been climbed before – but it is now and Howard tells the tale with dramatic panache.

**Bernhard Pollmann** *Norway – South*. This Rother Walking Guide describes fifty suggested hikes in southern Norway. The descriptions are clear and concise, the photos helpful and the maps useful for preparation. The walks themselves range from the short and easy to the long and very strenuous. New, revised edition published in 2009.

## GENERAL HISTORY

**Jack Adams** *The Doomed Expedition* (o/p). Thorough and well-researched account of the 1940 Allied campaign in Norway in all its brave but incompetent detail.

**Martin Conway** *No Man's Land*. Anecdotal and entertaining account of the history of Spitsbergen (Svalbard) from 1596 to modern times. Full of intriguing detail, such as Admiral Nelson's near-death experience (aged 14), when he set out on the ice at night to kill a polar bear. Written in 1906 and published by Kessinger in its "Legacy Reprints" series.

★ **Fredrik Dahl** *Quisling: A Study in Treachery*. A comprehensive biography of the world's most famous traitor, Vidkun Quisling, who got his just deserts at the end of World War II. Well-written and incisive exploration of Quisling's complex character – and one that also sheds a grim light on the nature and extent of Norwegian collaboration. Published by Cambridge University Press.

**Rolf Danielsen et al** *Norway: A History from the Vikings to Our Own Times*. Thoughtful and well-presented account investigating the social and economic development of Norway – a modern and well-judged book that avoids the "kings and queens" approach to its subject, but out of print (o/p) and expensive.

**Tony Griffiths** *Scandinavia: At War with Trolls – A Modern History from the Napoleonic Era to the Third Millennium*.

Engaging title for an engaging, well-written and well-researched book covering its subject in a very manageable 320 pages. First published in 2004.

**Knut Helle et al** *The Cambridge History of Scandinavia* (o/p). Comprehensive history, from the Stone Age onwards, in three whopping (and expensive) volumes. No stone is left unturned, no rune unread. Published in 2003.

★ **David Howarth** *Shetland Bus*. Entertaining and fascinating in equal measure, this excellent book, written by one of the British naval officers involved, details the clandestine wartime missions that shuttled between the Shetlands and occupied Norway in World War II.

**Chris Mann** *Hitler's Arctic War*. An account (2002) of the war that raged across the Arctic wastes of Norway, Finland and the USSR from 1940–45, both on sea and land.

**Alan Palmer** *Bernadotte* (o/p). Biography of Napoleon's marshal, later King Karl Johan of Norway and Sweden, a fascinating if enigmatic figure whom this lively and comprehensive book presents to good effect.

**Geoffrey Parker** *The Thirty Years' War*. First published in the 1980s, this book provides the authoritative account of the pan-European war that so deeply affected Scandinavia in general and Sweden in particular. Superbly written and researched.

**Kathleen Stokker** *Folklore Fights the Nazis: Humor in Occupied Norway 1940–1945*. A book that can't help but make you laugh – and one that also provides a real insight into Norwegian society and its subtle mores. The only problem is that Stokker adopts an encyclopedic approach, which means you have to plough through the poor jokes to get to the good ones. Stokker adopted a similar approach in her comparable *Remedies and Rituals: Folk Medicine in Norway and the New Land*.

**Raymond Strait** *Queen of Ice, Queen of Shadows: The Unsuspected Life of Sonja Henie* (o/p). In-depth biography of the ice-skating gold medallist, film star and conspicuous consumer Sonja Henie, whose art collection was bequeathed to the Oslo museum that bears her name (see p.86). An unpleasant woman by (almost) all accounts, whose alleged obsessions were money and sex, supposedly including affairs with Joe Louis and Tyrone Power.

## THE VIKINGS, NORSE MYTHOLOGY AND FOLK TALES

**Peter Christen Asbjørnsen and Jørgen Moe** *Norwegian Folk Tales*. Of all the many books on Norwegian folk tales, this is the edition you want – the illustrations by Erik Werenskiold and Theodor Kittelsen are superb. A Pantheon book published in 1991, but currently o/p.

**Johannes Brøndsted** *The Vikings* (o/p). Extremely readable account with fascinating sections on social and cultural life, art, religious beliefs and customs: see p.406 for an extract from this book.

**H.R. Ellis Davidson** *The Gods and Myths of Northern Europe*. Classic text, first published over forty years ago, that gives a who's who of Norse mythology, including some useful reviews of the more obscure gods. Importantly, it displaced the classical deities and their world as the most relevant mythological framework for northern and western Europeans.

**Robert Ferguson** *The Hammer and The Cross: A New History of the Vikings*. The latest book on the subject written by a well-regarded Scandinavia expert – see also *Enigma: the Life of Knut Hamsun* (see p.419). Thoroughly researched and well written.

**Paddy Griffith** *The Viking Art of War*. This detailed text examines its chosen subject well. Excellently researched with considered if sometimes surprising conclusions.

**John Haywood** *The Penguin Historical Atlas of the Vikings*. Accessible and attractive sequence of maps charting the Vikings' various wanderings as explorers, settlers, raiders, conquerors, traders and mercenaries. Also *The Encyclopaedia of the Viking Age*, an easy-to-use who's who and what's what of the Viking era. Published in 1996 and 2000 respectively.

★ **Gwyn Jones** *A History of the Vikings*. Superbly crafted, erudite and very detailed account of the Vikings, with excellent sections on every aspect of their history and culture. The same author wrote *Scandinavian Legends and Folk Tales* (see below).

**Gwyn Jones** *Scandinavian Legends and Folk Tales* (o/p). The Oxford University Press commissioned this anthology, whose stories are drawn from every part of Scandinavia and cover many themes – from the heroic to the tragic – and are populated by a mixed crew of trolls, wolves, bears and princelings.

**Magnus Magnusson and Hermann Palsson** (translators) *The Vinland Sagas: The Norse Discovery of America*. These two sagas tell of the Vikings' settlement of Greenland and of the "discovery" of North America in the tenth century. The introduction of this particular edition, which was first published in the 1960s, is an especially interesting and acute analysis of these two colonial outposts. There's also a newer edition in the Penguin Classics series by Leifur Ericksson (2010). See also Snorri Sturluson (below).

**Heather O'Donoghue** *From Asgard to Valhalla: the Remarkable History of the Norse Myths*. Well, the "remarkable" in the title may well have been dreamed up by someone in PR, as what you get here is a well-researched and detailed investigation/exploration of its subject matter. The chapters are arranged by theme – "Creation and Cosmos" and "Heroes and Humans" for example.

**Else Roesdahl** *The Vikings*. A clearly presented, 350-page exploration of Viking history and culture, including sections on art, burial customs, class divisions, jewellery, kingship, kinship and poetry. An excellent introduction to its subject.

**Peter Sawyer** (ed) *The Oxford Illustrated History of the Vikings* (o/p). Published in 2001, this book brings together what was then the latest historical research on the Vikings in a series of well-considered essays by leading experts. Includes sections on religion, shipbuilding and diet.

★ **Jane Smiley et al** *The Sagas of Icelanders*. Easy-to-read translations of all the main sagas – galloping, rip-roaring tales from medieval Iceland. The index makes it an excellent reference book too.

**Snorri Sturluson** *Egil's Saga, Laxdaela Saga, Njal's Saga, and King Harald's Saga*. These Icelandic sagas (for more on which, see p.402) were written in the early years of the thirteenth century, but relate tales of ninth- and tenth-century derring-do. There's clan warfare in the *Laxdaela* and *Njal* sagas, more bloodthirstiness in *Egil's*, and a bit more biography in *King Harald's*, penned to celebrate one of the last and most ferocious Viking chieftains – Harald Hardrada (see p.386). Among those who have worked on translating these sagas was the former UK TV celebrity Magnus Magnusson, long a leading light in the effort to popularize them; see also the *Vinland Sagas* and *The Sagas of Icelanders* above.

## ARCHITECTURE, FILM AND THE VISUAL ARTS

**Ketil Bjørnstad** *The Story of Edvard Munch* (o/p). Precise and detailed biography of the great artist that makes liberal use of Munch's own letters and diaries as well as contemporary newspapers and periodicals. A vivid tale indeed, just a shame that Munch isn't more likeable.

**Angela Cheroux** *Edvard Munch: The Modern Eye*. Published by Tate in 2012, this scholarly work fills something of an artistic hole – and benefits from an especially lavish set of illustrations. Munch revealed in all his enigmatic/unpleasant detail.

**Einar Haugen and Camilla Cai** *Ole Bull: Norway's Romantic Musician and Cosmopolitan Patriot*. A neglected figure, Ole Bull (see p.200), the nineteenth-century virtuoso violinist and utopian socialist, deserves a better historical fate. This biography attempts to rectify matters by delving into every facet of his life, but it's ponderously written and over-detailed. For Bull lovers only.

**J.P. Hodin** *Edvard Munch*. A good general introduction to Munch's life and work, with much interesting historical detail. Beautifully illustrated, as you would expect from a Thames & Hudson publication. Reprinted in 1991.

**Neil Kent** *The Soul of the North: A Social, Architectural and Cultural History of the Nordic Countries 1700–1940*. Immaculately illustrated, erudite chronicle of Scandinavian art and architecture during its most influential periods. Published in 2001.

**Robert Layton** *Grieg*. Clear, concise and attractively illustrated book on Norway's greatest composer. Essential reading if you want to get to grips with the man and his times. Published in 1998.

**Marion Nelson** (ed) *Norwegian Folk Art: The Migration of a Tradition*. (o/p). Lavishly illustrated, specialist book discussing the whole range of folk art, from woodcarvings through to bedspreads and traditional dress. It's particularly strong on the influence of Norwegian folk art in the US, but the text sometimes lacks focus. It's earth-shatteringly expensive too.

**Sue Prideaux** *Edvard Munch: Behind the Scream*. Not a classic biography perhaps, but a thorough (520 pages) and well-researched trawl through the life of a man who fulfilled most of the stereotypes of the alienated and tormented (drunken) artist. Published by Yale University Press.

★ **Tytti Soila et al** *Nordic National Cinemas* and *The Cinema of Scandinavia*. These two books are the best there is on Scandinavian cinema in general and Norwegian cinema in particular. Published in 1998, the first of the two has separate chapters on each of the Nordic countries and each chapter provides a chronological overview. The second book, published in 2005, adopts a more cinematic approach with 24 extended essays on key Scandinavian films – and an intriguing bunch they are too.

## FICTION, DRAMA AND LITERARY BIOGRAPHY

★ **Kjell Askildsen** *A Sudden Liberating Thought* (o/p). Short stories, in the Kafkaesque tradition, from one of Norway's most uncompromisingly modernist writers (b. 1929).

**Paul Binding** *With Vine-Leaves in His Hair: The Role of the Artist in Ibsen's Plays*. Academic title ideal for Ibsen lovers/students.

**Jens Bjørneboe** *The Sharks*. Set at the end of the last century, this is a thrilling tale of shipwreck and mutiny by a well-known Norwegian writer (1920–76), who had an enviable reputation for challenging authoritarianism of any description. Also recommended is his darker

trilogy – *Moment of Freedom*, *The Powderhouse* and *The Silence* – exploring the nature of cruelty and injustice. All of these titles are, however, o/p.

**Johan Bojer** *The Emigrants* (o/p). One of the leading Norwegian novelists of his day, Bojer (1872–1959) wrote extensively about the hardships of rural life. *The Emigrants*, perhaps his most finely crafted work, deals with a group of young Norwegians who emigrate to North Dakota in the 1880s – and the difficulties they experience. In Norway, Bojer is better known for *Last of the Vikings* (o/p), a heart-rending tale of fishermen from the tiny village of Rissa in Nordland, who are forced to row out to the Lofoten winter

## NORWEGIAN LITERATURE

It was **Jostein Gaarder**'s *Sophie's World* that brought **Norwegian literature** to a worldwide audience in the 1990s, though in fact the Norwegians have been mining a deep, if somewhat idiosyncratic, literary seam since the middle of the nineteenth century. From Ibsen onwards, the country's authors – and playwrights – have been deeply influenced by Norway's unyielding geography and stern pietism, their preoccupations often focused on anxiety and alienation. These themes also underpin many of the Norwegian **crime novels** that have proved so internationally popular in the last decade - with Karin Fossum and Jo Nesbø two of the big authorial names. But, to be fair, Norwegian crime has followed in the slipstream of Henning Mankell, a Swede who is undoubtedly Scandinavia's leading crime writer, never mind what fans of Stieg Larsson say.

fishery, no matter what the conditions, to keep from starving. It was first published in 1921.

**Lars Saabye Christensen** *Herman*. Christensen made a real literary splash with *The Half Brother*, an intense tale focused on four generations of an Oslo family in the years following World War II, with the narrator being Barnum, a midget, alcoholic screenplay-writer. It is, however, a real doorstopper of a book and before you embark on such a long read you might want to sample Christensen's *Herman*, a lighter (and much shorter) tale of adolescence with an Oslo backdrop.

**Camilla Collett** *The District Governor's Daughters*. First published in 1854, this heartfelt demand for the emotional and intellectual emancipation of women is set within a bourgeois Norwegian milieu. The central character, Sophie, struggles against her conditioning and the expectations of those around her. An important, early feminist novel.

**Kjell Ola Dahl** *Lethal Investments*. Dahl's first novel, a fast-paced and particularly well-written tale of murder and mystery, seediness and unwholesomeness, set in Oslo. Smart observations and clever dialogue plus an à la mode jaded detective, Inspector Frolich. There's more Frolich in *The Fourth Man* which has the feel of a classic American noir thriller/chiller.

**Thomas Enger** *Burned*. Enger's debut novel where the protagonist – Henning Juul – returns to work as a journalist after a domestic fire which has killed his son. Vulnerable and newly sensitive to death and loss, Juul is put to work on a crime case – with unexpected results.

★ **Per Olov Enquist** *The Visit of the Royal Physician*. Wonderfully entertaining and beautifully written novel, set in the Danish court in Copenhagen at the end of the eighteenth century – a time when Denmark governed Norway.

**Knut Faldbakken** *Adam's Diary* (o/p). Three former lovers describe their relationships with the same woman – an absorbing and spirited novel by one of Norway's more talented writers, born in Hamar in 1941.

**Robert Ferguson** *Enigma: the Life of Knut Hamsun*. Detailed and well-considered biography of Norway's most controversial writer (see p.296). The same author also wrote *Ibsen*, an in-depth biography of the playwright.

★ **Barry Forshaw** *Death in a Cold Climate: A Guide to Scandinavian Crime Fiction*. Right across Europe, Scandinavian crime writing has never been more popular and this outstanding book, published in 2012, summarizes and analyses the nature of the genre and the reasons for its success. Includes extensive – and very apposite – quotes from the likes of Karin Fossum and Jo Nesbø.

★ **Karin Fossum** *Calling out for You; Don't Look Back; Black Seconds; The Caller; The Water's Edge*. Arguably Norway's finest crime writer, Fossum has written a string of superb thrillers in the Inspector Sejer series – and each gives the real flavour of contemporary Norway. These four

novels are the best place to get started – but avoid *When the Devil Holds the Candle*, which is a bit of a dud. Born in Sandefjord, on the south coast of Norway, in 1954, Fossum began her literary career with the publication of a collection of poetry, but it was the sharp brilliance of her crime writing which has made her famous, her taut and tight tales gripping and unpredictable in equal measure. Refreshingly, these are compassionate thrillers examining the motives and emotions of the murderer and the murdered, and how some individuals become outcasts.

**Jostein Gaarder** *Sophie's World*. Hugely popular novel that deserves all the critical praise it has garnered. Beautifully and gently written, with the puff of whimsy, it bears comparison with Hawking's *A Brief History of Time*, though the subject matter here is philosophy, and there's an engaging mystery story tucked in too. Also try Gaarder's comparable *Through A Glass Darkly* and his more recent *The Castle in the Pyrenees*, an elaborate love story, which is – despite the title – set in Norway.

**Janet Garton** (ed) *Contemporary Norwegian Women's Writing*. Wide-ranging anthology, beginning with the directly political works of the 1970s and culminating in the more fantastical tales typical of the 2000s. Fiction, drama and poetry all make an appearance and there are lots of issues too – from prostitution and abuse through to women's empowerment. Published by Norvik Press (ⓦ norvikpress.com).

**Knut Hamsun** *Hunger*. Norway's leading literary light in the 1920s and early 1930s, Knut Hamsun (1859–1952) was a writer of international acclaim until he disgraced himself by supporting Hitler – for which many Norwegians never forgave him. Of Hamsun's many novels, it was *Hunger* (1890) that made his name, a trip into the psyche of an alienated and angst-ridden young writer, which shocked contemporary readers. The book was to have a seminal influence on the development of the modern novel. In the latter part of his career, Hamsun advocated a return to the soil and basic rural values. He won the Nobel Prize for Literature for one of his works from this period, *Growth of the Soil*, but you have to be pretty determined to plough through its metaphysical claptrap. In recent years, Hamsun has been tentatively accepted back into the Norwegian literary fold and there has been some resurgence of interest in his works; there's also been a biographical film, *Hamsun*, starring Max von Sydow.

**William Heinesen** *The Black Cauldron*. It would be churlish to omit the Faroe-islander William Heinesen (1900–91), whose evocative novels delve into the subtleties of Faroese life – and thereby shed light on the related culture of western Norway. This particular book, arguably his best, is rigorously modernistic in approach and style – an intriguing, challenging read, with the circling forces of Faroese society set against the British occupation of the Faroes in World War II. If this whets your appetite, carry on with the same author's *The Tower at the Edge of the World*.

**Sigbjørn Holmebakk** *The Carriage Stone* (o/p). Evil and innocence, suffering and redemption, with death lurking in the background, make this a serious and powerful novel. These themes are explored through the character of Eilif Grotteland, a Lutheran priest who loses his faith and resigns his ministry. Holmebakk (1922–81), who was a leading light in the Ban the Bomb movement, wrote several other excellent novels, but no other has ever appeared in translation.

**Anne Holt** *1222*. The prolific Anne Holt is one of Norway's most popular crime writers, making her debut in 1993 with the first of a series of books that starred a female cop, Hanne Wilhelmsen. *1222* is Wilhelmsen's latest adventure.

★ **Henrik Ibsen** *Four Major Plays*. The key figure of Norwegian literature, Ibsen (see p.66) was a social dramatist with a keen eye for hypocrisy, repression and alienation. Ibsen's most popular plays – primarily *A Doll's House* and *Hedda Gabler* – pop up in all sorts of editions, but this particular collection, in the Oxford World Classics series, contains both these favourites as well as *Ghosts* and *The Master Builder*. What's more, it's inexpensive and translated by one of the leading Ibsen experts, James McFarlane. In print also are several editions of Ibsen's whole oeuvre.

★ **Jan Kjærstad** *The Seducer*. This remarkable novel weaves and wanders, rambles and roams around the life of its protagonist, Jonas Wergeland, in a series of digressions as our hero/anti-hero sits in his flat with his murdered wife lying in an adjoining room. Mysterious and convoluted, pensive and whimsical, it's a truly extraordinary work that won the Nordic Prize for Literature in 2001. Rather surprisingly, it's currently o/p.

★ **Jan Kjærstad (ed)** *Leopard VI: The Norwegian Feeling for Real*. Promoted by the queen of Norway no less, this first-rate anthology of modern Norwegian writers hits all the literary buttons – from boozy nights out in Oslo to the loneliness of rural Norway and small-town envy. Contains 28 short stories plus potted biographies of all the featured writers. Published in 2005.

**Björn Larsson** *Long John Silver*. Larsson, a veteran Swedish sailor with an extensive knowledge of eighteenth-century British sea lore, uses his specialist knowledge to great effect in this chunky but charming novel that provides an extra twist – or two – to Stevenson's original.

**Jonas Lie** *The Seer & Other Norwegian Stories* (o/p). Part of the Norwegian literary and cultural revival of the late nineteenth century, Jonas Lie is largely forgotten today, but this collection of mystical folk tales makes for intriguing reading. It is printed alongside his first great success, the novella *The Seer*, in which a teacher is saved from insanity, born of ancient (pagan) superstitions, by the power of Christianity. Also *Weird Tales from Northern Seas: Norwegian Legends*, a collection much enjoyed by no less than Roald Dahl.

★ **Henning Mankell** *Faceless Killers, Sidetracked*. Cracking yarns from Scandinavia's leading crime writer featuring Inspector Kurt Wallander, a shambolic and melancholic middle-aged police officer struggling to make sense of all the evils washed up into small-town southern Sweden. Hard to beat. The latest in the series, *The Troubled Man*, may/may not be the last time we see the inspector.

**Jo Nesbø** *The Devil's Star; The Redbreast; The Redeemer*. No-holds-barred crime fiction in the sardonic (American) style from Norway's answer to Stieg Larsson – as Nesbø is often billed. Nesbø's star detective, Inspector Harry Hole, is on the case. Grim/scintillating reading, depending on your tastes.

**Per Petterson** *Out Stealing Horses*. Doom and gloom, guilt and isolation deep in the Norwegian woods. Hardly cheerful fare perhaps, but stirring, unsettling stuff all the same. If you like it, try Petterson's *It's Fine by Me*, a tale of troubled adolescence set in 1970s Oslo.

**Cora Sandel** *Alberta and Freedom, Alberta Alone, Alberta and Jacob*. Set in a small town in early twentieth-century Norway, the *Alberta* trilogy follows the attempts of a young woman to establish an independent life/identity. Characterized by sharp insights and a wealth of contemporary detail. For more on Sandel, who lived in Tromsø as a young woman, see p.338.

**Kjersti Scheen** *Final Curtain* (o/p). Fast-paced detective story from one of the country's most popular crime writers. Refreshingly, the detective isn't a middle-aged man, but an Oslo-based woman.

**Amalie Skram** *Under Observation* and *Lucie*. Bergen's Amalie Skram (1846–1905) married young and went through the marital mangle before turning her experiences into several novels and a commitment to women's emancipation, including attempts to regulate prostitution. Published in 1888, *Lucie* was a coruscating attack on bourgeois morality in general, and male sexual hypocrisy in particular, with the eponymous heroine gradually ground down into submission. Inevitably, the novel created a huge furore.

**Dag Solstad** *Shyness & Dignity*. One of the big names of Norwegian literature, Solstad's (b.1941) sombre tale of a middle-aged teacher's psychological collapse is set in a dour Oslo. "What shall become of me?" he complains – yes, what indeed. Solstad's latest novel, *Professor Andersen's Night*, reprises the theme of a mid-life crisis brought on when the eponymous protagonist witnesses a murder on Christmas Eve. Isolation and alienation are given another good Norwegian airing.

**Sven Somme** *Another Man's Shoes*. In World War II, the redoubtable Sven Somme managed to escape the clutches of the Germans and make his escape over the mountains into neutral Sweden. Sixty years later, his two daughters, now resident in England, retraced his steps as described in his memoirs – and this is the result, a combination of the original text and their comments on their own journey. The title comes from the pair of shoes left behind by Sven and (touchingly) kept by one of the families who helped him.

**Sigrid Undset** *Kristin Lavransdatter: The Cross, The Bridal Wreath, The Garland & The Mistress of Husaby.* The prolific Undset (1882–1949), one of the country's leading literary lights, could certainly churn it out. This historical series – arguably encapsulating her best work – is set in medieval Norway and has all the excitement of a pulp thriller, along with subtle plots and deft(ish) characterizations.

**Helene Uri** *Honey Tongues* A former doctor of linguistics at Oslo University, the prolific Uri is one of Norway's most popular contemporary writers, producing everything from novels to children's books. This particular novel exposes malevolent rivalry and manipulation between the (all-female) members of a sewing group when they go on a trip to Copenhagen.

★ **Herbjørg Wassmo** *Dina's Book: A Novel.* Set in rural northern Norway in the middle of the nineteenth century, this strange but engaging tale has a plot centred on a powerful but tormented heroine. Dina is wilful to the point of ruthlessness: she eliminates her husband and takes a new lover, while the funeral is in progress elsewhere. Yet beneath her toughness is a deep sense of betrayal: rejected as a child by her father after she accidentally caused her mother's death, Dina has grown up expecting betrayal. Also *Dina's Son*, again with a nineteenth-century setting, but with intriguing sections focused on the protagonist's move from rural Norway to the city. Both currently o/p.

# Norwegian

There are two official Norwegian languages: *Riksmål* or *Bokmål* (book language), a modification of the old Dano-Norwegian tongue left over from the days of Danish dominance; and *Landsmål* or *Nynorsk* (new Norwegian), which was codified during the nineteenth-century upsurge of Norwegian nationalism and is based on rural dialects of Old Norse provenance. Roughly ninety percent of schoolchildren have *Bokmål* as their primary language, and the remaining ten percent are *Nynorsk* dialect speakers, concentrated in the fjord country of the west coast and the mountain districts of central Norway. Despite the best efforts of the government, *Nynorsk* as an official language is in decline – in 1944 fully one-third of the population used it. As the more common of the two languages, *Bokmål* is what we use here in this guide.

You don't really need to know any Norwegian to get by in Norway. Nearly everyone speaks some English, and in any case many words are not too far removed from their English equivalents; there's also plenty of English (or American) on billboards, the TV and at the cinema. Mastering "hello" or "thank you" will, however, be greatly appreciated, while if you speak either Danish or Swedish you should have few problems being understood. Incidentally, Norwegians find Danish easier to read than Swedish, but verbally it's the other way round.

**Phrasebooks** are fairly thin on the ground, but Berlitz's *Norwegian Phrasebook with Dictionary* has – as you would expect from the title – a mini-dictionary, not to mention a useful grammar section and a menu reader; Dorling Kindersley's *Norwegian Phrasebook* is comparable. There are several **dictionaries** to choose from, all of which include pronunciation tips and so forth. The best is generally considered to be the Collins *English–Norwegian Dictionary*, though this is currently out of print so you might decide to opt for the Berlitz *Norwegian Pocket Dictionary* instead.

## PRONUNCIATION

Pronunciation can be tricky. A **vowel** is usually long when it's the final syllable or followed by only one consonant; followed by two it's generally short. Unfamiliar ones are:

**æ** before an r, as in b**a**d; otherwise as in s**ay**
**ø** as in f**u**r but without pronouncing the r
**å** usually as in s**aw**

**øy** between the ø sound and b**oy**
**ei** as in s**ay**

**Consonants** are pronounced as in English except:

**c**, **q**, **w**, **z** found only in foreign words and pronounced as in the original language
**g** before i, **y** or ei, as in **y**et; otherwise hard
**hv** as in **v**iew

**j**, **gj**, **hj**, **lj** as in **y**et
**rs** almost always as in **sh**ut
**k** before i, y or j, like the Scottish lo**ch**; otherwise hard
**sj**, **sk** before i, y, ø or øy, as in **sh**ut

## WORDS AND PHRASES

### BASIC PHRASES

| | | | |
|---|---|---|---|
| **do you speak English?** | snakker du engelsk? | **do you understand?** | forstår du? |
| **yes** | ja | **I don't understand** | jeg forstår ikke |
| **no** | nei | **I understand** | jeg forstår |

| | |
|---|---|
| please (is near enough, though there's no direct equivalent) | vær så god |
| thank you (very much) | takk (tusen takk) |
| you're welcome | vær så god |
| excuse me | unnskyld |
| good morning | god morgen |
| good afternoon | god dag |
| good night | god natt |
| goodbye | adjø |
| today | i dag |
| tomorrow | i morgen |
| day after tomorrow | i overmorgen |
| in the morning | om morgenen |
| in the afternoon | om ettermiddagen |
| in the evening | om kvelden |

## SOME SIGNS

| | |
|---|---|
| entrance | inngang |
| exit | utgang |
| gentlemen | herrer/menn |
| ladies | damer/kvinner |
| open | åpen |
| closed | stengt |
| arrival | ankomst |
| police | politi |
| hospital | sykehus |
| cycle path | sykkelsti |
| no smoking | røyking forbudt |
| no camping | camping forbudt |
| no trespassing | uvedkommende forbudt |
| no entry | ingen adgang |
| pull/push | trekk/trykk |
| departure | avgang |
| parking fees | avgift |

## QUESTIONS AND DIRECTIONS

| | |
|---|---|
| where? (where is/are?) | hvor? (hvor er?) |
| when? | når? |
| what? | hva? |
| how much/many? | hvor mye/hvor mange? |
| why? | hvorfor? |
| which? | hvilken/hvilket? |
| what's that called in Norwegian? | hva kaller man det på norsk? |
| can you direct me to ...? | kan du vise meg veien til ...? |
| it is/there is (is it/is there) | det er (er det?) |
| what time is it? | hva er klokken? |
| big/small | stor/liten |
| cheap/expensive | billig/dyrt |
| early/late | tidlig/sent |
| hot/cold | varm/kald |

| | |
|---|---|
| near/far | i nærheten/langt borte |
| good/bad | god/dårlig |
| vacant/occupied | ledig/opptatt |
| a little/a lot | litt/mye |
| more/less | mer/mindre |
| can we camp here? | kan vi campe her? |
| is there a youth hostel near here? | er det et vandrerhjem i nærheten? |
| how do I get to ...? | hvordan kommer jeg til ...? |
| how far is it to ...? | hvor langt er det til ...? |
| ticket | billett |
| one-way/return | en vei/tur-retur |
| can you give me a lift to ...? | kan jeg få sitte på til ...? |
| left/right | venstre/høyre |
| go straight ahead | kjør rett frem |

## NUMBERS

| | |
|---|---|
| 0 | null |
| 1 | en |
| 2 | to |
| 3 | tre |
| 4 | fire |
| 5 | fem |
| 6 | seks |
| 7 | sju |
| 8 | åtte |
| 9 | ni |
| 10 | ti |
| 11 | elleve |
| 12 | tolv |
| 13 | tretten |
| 14 | fjorten |
| 15 | femten |
| 16 | seksten |
| 17 | sytten |
| 18 | atten |
| 19 | nitten |
| 20 | tjue |
| 21 | tjueen |
| 22 | tjueto |
| 30 | tretti |
| 40 | førti |
| 50 | femti |
| 60 | seksti |
| 70 | sytti |
| 80 | åtti |
| 90 | nitti |
| 100 | hundre |
| 101 | hundreogen |
| 200 | to hundre |
| 1000 | tusen |

## DAYS

| | |
|---|---|
| Sunday | søndag |
| Monday | mandag |
| Tuesday | tirsdag |
| Wednesday | onsdag |
| Thursday | torsdag |
| Friday | fredag |
| Saturday | lørdag |

## MONTHS

| | |
|---|---|
| January | januar |
| February | februar |
| March | mars |
| April | april |
| May | mai |
| June | juni |
| July | juli |
| August | august |
| September | september |
| October | oktober |
| November | november |
| December | desember |

(Note: days and months are never capitalized)

## MENU READER

### BASICS AND SNACKS

| | |
|---|---|
| appelsin, marmelade | marmalade |
| brød | bread |
| eddik | vinegar |
| egg | egg |
| eggerøre | scrambled eggs |
| flatbrød | crispbread |
| fløte | cream |
| grønsaker | vegetables |
| grøt | porridge |
| iskrem | ice cream |
| kaffefløte | single cream for coffee |
| kake | cake |
| kaviar | caviar |
| kjeks | biscuits |
| krem | whipped cream |
| melk | milk |
| mineralvann | mineral water |
| nøtter | nuts |
| olje | oil |
| omelett | omelette |
| ost | cheese |
| pannekake | pancakes |
| pepper | pepper |
| potetchips | crisps (potato chips) |
| pommes-frites | chips (French fries) |
| ris | rice |
| rundstykker | bread roll |
| salat | salad |
| salt | salt |
| sennep | mustard |
| smør | butter |
| smørbrød | open sandwich |
| sukker | sugar |
| suppe | soup |
| syltetøy | jam |
| varm pølse | hot dog |
| yoghurt | yoghurt |

### MEAT (KJØTT) AND GAME (VILT)

| | |
|---|---|
| dyrestek | venison |
| elg | elk |
| kalkun | turkey |
| kjøttboller | meatballs |
| kjøttkaker | rissoles |
| kylling | chicken |
| lammekjøtt | lamb |
| lever | liver |
| oksekjøtt | beef |
| postei | pâté |
| pølser | sausages |
| reinsdyr | reindeer |
| ribbe | pork rib |
| skinke | ham |
| spekemat | dried meat |
| stek | steak |
| svinekjøtt | pork |
| varm pølse | frankfurter/hot dog |

### FISH (FISK) AND SHELLFISH (SKALLDYR)

| | |
|---|---|
| ål | eel |
| ansjos | anchovies (brisling) |
| blåskjell | mussels |
| brisling | sprats |
| hummer | lobster |
| hvitting | whiting |
| kaviar | caviar |
| krabbe | crab |
| kreps | crayfish |
| laks | salmon |
| makrell | mackerel |
| ørret | trout |
| piggvar | turbot |
| reker | shrimps |
| rødspette | plaice |
| røkelaks | smoked salmon |
| sardiner | sardines (brisling) |
| sei | coalfish |

| | |
|---|---|
| sild | herring |
| sjøtunge | sole |
| småfisk | whitebait |
| steinbit | catfish |
| torsk | cod |
| tunfisk | tuna |

## VEGETABLES (GRØNSAKER)

| | |
|---|---|
| agurk | cucumber/gherkin/pickle |
| blomkål | cauliflower |
| bønner | beans |
| erter | peas |
| gulrøtter | carrots |
| hodesalat | lettuce |
| hvitløk | garlic |
| kål | cabbage |
| linser | lentils |
| løk | onion |
| mais | sweetcorn |
| nepe | turnip |
| paprika | peppers |
| poteter | potatoes |
| rosenkål | Brussels sprouts |
| selleri | celery |
| sopp | mushrooms |
| spinat | spinach |
| tomater | tomatoes |

## FRUIT (FRUKT)

| | |
|---|---|
| ananas | pineapple |
| appelsin | orange |
| aprikos | apricot |
| banan | banana |
| blåbær | blueberries |
| druer | grapes |
| eple | apple |
| fersken | peach |
| fruktsalat | fruit salad |
| grapefrukt | grapefruit |
| jordbær | strawberries |
| multer | cloudberries |
| pærer | pears |

| | |
|---|---|
| plommer | plums |
| sitron | lemon |
| solbær | blackcurrants |
| tyttbær | cranberries |

## COOKING TERMS

| | |
|---|---|
| blodig | rare, underdone |
| godt stekt | well done |
| grillet | grilled |
| grytestekt | braised |
| kokt | boiled |
| marinert | marinated |
| ovnstekt | baked/roasted |
| røkt | smoked |
| saltet | cured |
| stekt | fried |
| stuet | stewed |
| sur | sour, pickled |
| syltet | pickled |

## DRINKS

| | |
|---|---|
| akevitt | aquavit |
| appelsin | orange squash |
| brus | fizzy soft drink |
| eplesider | cider |
| fruktsaft | sweetened fruit juice |
| kaffe | coffee |
| melk | milk |
| mineralvann | mineral water |
| øl | beer |
| saft/juice | juice |
| sitronbrus | lemonade |
| te med melk/sitron | tea with milk/lemon |
| vann | water |
| varm sjokolade | hot chocolate |
| vin | wine |
| søt | sweet |
| tørr | dry |
| rød | red |
| hvit | white |
| rosé | rosé |
| skål | cheers |

## GLOSSARY OF NORWEGIAN TERMS

**allting** Parliament or public gathering
**apotek** chemist
**bakke** hill
**bokhandel** bookshop
**bre** glacier
**bro/bru** bridge
**brygge** quay or wharf
**dal** valley/dale
**DNT (Den Norske Turistforening)** nationwide hiking organization whose local affiliates maintain hiking paths across almost all the country.
**Domkirke** Cathedral
**drosje** taxi
**E.kr** AD
**elv/bekk** river/stream
**ferje/ferge** ferry
**fjell/berg** mountain
**Flybussen** Airport bus (literally "plane bus")

**F.kr** BC
**foss** waterfall
**gågate** urban pedestrianized area
**gate (gt.)** street
**Gamle byen** literally "Old Town"; used wherever the old part of town has remained distinct from the rest (eg Fredrikstad). Also spelt as one word.
**hav** ocean
**havn** harbour
**Hurtigbåt** passenger express boat; usually a catamaran
**Hurtigruten** literally "quick route", but familiar as the name of the boat service along the west coast from Bergen to Kirkenes.
**hytte** cottage, cabin
**innsjø** lake
**jernbanestasjon** train station
**kirke/kjerke** church
**Kfum/kfuk** Norwegian YMCA/YWCA
**klokken/kl.** o'clock
**klippfisk** salted whitefish, usually cod
**moderasjon** discount or price reduction
**Moms or mva** sales tax – applied to almost all consumables
**museet** museum
**NAF** nationwide Norwegian automobile association. Membership covers rescue and repair.

**øy/øya** islet
**rabatt** discount or price reduction
**rådhus** town hall
**rorbu** originally a simple wooden cabin built near the fishing grounds for incoming (ie non-local) fishermen. Many cabins are now used as tourist accommodation, especially in the Lofoten (see box, p.314).
**Sámi** formerly called Lapps, the Sámi inhabit the northern reaches of Norway, Finland and Sweden – Lapland.
**sentrum** city or town centre
**sjø** sea
**sjøhus** harbourside building where the catch was sorted, salted, filleted and iced. Many are now redundant and some have been turned into tourist accommodation.
**skog** forest
**slott** castle, palace
**Stavkirke** Stave church
**Storting** Parliament
**tilbud** special offer
**torget** main town square, often home to an outdoor market; sometimes spelt Torvet
**Vandrerhjem** Youth hostel
**vann/vatn** water or lake
**vei/veg/vn.** road

## GLOSSARY OF NORWEGIAN MOTORING TERMINOLOGY

**avgiftsvei** toll road
**bensinstasjon** petrol station
**bilutleie firma** car rental agency
**blyfri bensin** unleaded petrol
**bomstasjon** toll
**innkjorsel** entrance
**motorolje** motor oil

**motorvei** highway
**omkjonng** detour
**parkering** parking
**politi** police
**politistasjon** police station
**sykehus** hospital
**utkjorsel** exit

## GLOSSARY OF ENGLISH ART AND ARCHITECTURAL TERMS

**Ambulatory** Covered passage around the outer edge of the choir in the chancel of a church.
**Art Deco** Geometrical style of art and architecture popular in the 1930s.
**Art Nouveau** Style of art, architecture and design based on highly stylized vegetal forms. Particularly popular in the early part of the twentieth century.
**Baroque** The art and architecture of the Counter-Reformation, dating from around 1600 onwards, and distinguished by extreme ornateness, exuberance and the complex but harmonious spatial arrange-ment of interiors.
**Classical** Architectural style incorporating Greek and Roman elements – pillars, domes, colonnades, etc – at its height in the seventeenth century and revived, as Neoclassical, in the nineteenth century.

**Fresco** Wall painting – made durable through applying paint to wet plaster.
**Gothic** Architectural style of the thirteenth to sixteenth centuries, characterized by pointed arches, rib vaulting, flying buttresses and a general emphasis on verticality.
**Misericord** Ledge on a choir stall on which the occupant can be supported while standing; often carved with secular subjects (bottoms were not thought worthy of religious ones).
**Nave** Main body of a church.
**Neoclassical** Architectural style derived from Greek and Roman elements – pillars, domes, colonnades, etc – popular in Norway throughout the nineteenth century.
**Renaissance** Movement in art and architecture developed in fifteenth-century Italy.

**Rococo** Highly florid, light and graceful eighteenth-century style of architecture, painting and interior design, forming the last phase of Baroque.

**Rood screen** Decorative screen separating the nave from the chancel.

**Romanesque** Early medieval architecture distinguished by squat forms, rounded arches and naive sculpture.

**Stucco** Marble-based plaster used to embellish ceilings, etc.

**Transept** Arms of a cross-shaped church, placed at ninety degrees to nave and chancel.

**Triptych** Carved or painted work on three panels. Often used as an altarpiece.

**Vault** An arched ceiling or roof.

# Small print and index

## A ROUGH GUIDE TO ROUGH GUIDES

Published in 1982, the first Rough Guide – to Greece – was a student scheme that became a publishing phenomenon. Mark Ellingham, a recent graduate in English from Bristol University, had been travelling in Greece the previous summer and couldn't find the right guidebook. With a small group of friends he wrote his own guide, combining a highly contemporary, journalistic style with a thoroughly practical approach to travellers' needs.

The immediate success of the book spawned a series that rapidly covered dozens of destinations. And, in addition to impecunious backpackers, Rough Guides soon acquired a much broader readership that relished the guides' wit and inquisitiveness as much as their enthusiastic, critical approach and value-for-money ethos.

These days, Rough Guides include recommendations from budget to luxury and cover more than 200 destinations around the globe, as well as producing an ever-growing range of eBooks and apps.

Visit **roughguides.com** to see our latest publications.

## Rough Guide credits

**Editors**: Edward Aves, Amanda Tomlin
**Layout**: Anita Singh
**Cartography**: Rajesh Mishra
**Picture editor**: Natascha Sturny
**Proofreader**: Karen Parker
**Managing editor**: Monica Woods
**Assistant editor**: Dipika Dasgupta
**Production**: Gemma Sharpe
**Cover design**: Nicole Newman, Anita Singh
**Editorial assistant**: Eleanor Aldridge

**Photographer**: Roger Norum
**Senior pre-press designer**: Dan May
**Design director**: Scott Stickland
**Travel publisher**: Joanna Kirby
**Digital travel publisher**: Peter Buckley
**Reference director**: Andrew Lockett
**Operations coordinator**: Becky Doyle
**Publishing director (Travel)**: Clare Currie
**Commercial manager**: Gino Magnotta
**Managing director**: John Duhigg

## Publishing information

This sixth edition published September 2012 by
**Rough Guides Ltd**,
80 Strand, London WC2R 0RL
11, Community Centre, Panchsheel Park,
New Delhi 110017, India
**Distributed by the Penguin Group**
Penguin Books Ltd,
80 Strand, London WC2R 0RL
Penguin Group (USA)
375 Hudson Street, NY 10014, USA
Penguin Group (Australia)
250 Camberwell Road, Camberwell,
Victoria 3124, Australia
Penguin Group (NZ)
67 Apollo Drive, Mairangi Bay, Auckland 1310,
New Zealand
Penguin Group (South Africa)
Block D, Rosebank Office Park, 181 Jan Smuts Avenue,
Parktown North, Gauteng, South Africa 2193
Rough Guides is represented in Canada by Tourmaline
Editions Inc. 662 King Street West, Suite 304, Toronto,
Ontario M5V 1M7
Printed in Singapore

MIX
Paper from
responsible sources
FSC
www.fsc.org    FSC™ C018179

## Help us update

We've gone to a lot of effort to ensure that the sixth
edition of **The Rough Guide to Norway** is accurate and
up-to-date. However, things change – places get "discovered", opening hours are notoriously fickle, restaurants
and rooms raise prices or lower standards. If you feel we've
got it wrong or left something out, we'd like to know, and
if you can remember the address, the price, the hours, the
phone number, so much the better.

Please send your comments with the subject line
**"Rough Guide Norway Update"** to @mail
@uk.roughguides.com. We'll credit all contributions and
send a copy of the next edition (or any other Rough Guide
if you prefer) for the very best emails.
Find more travel information, connect with fellow
travellers and book your trip on ⓦroughguides.com

## ABOUT THE AUTHORS

**Phil Lee** A one-time deckhand in the Danish merchant navy, Phil Lee has been writing for Rough Guides for well over twenty years. His other books in the series include Canada, Amsterdam, Norfolk & Suffolk, Mallorca and Belgium & Luxembourg. He lives in Nottingham, where he was born and raised.

**Roger Norum** Since his studies in Nordic literature and linguistics at the University of Tromsø, Roger has authored Rough Guides to Denmark, Finland and Scandinavia and contributed to a dozen more. Based between New York and Oxford, he now writes and photographs regularly on travel, food, cars and social anthropology for a good range of publications. ⓦrogernorum.com

## Acknowledgements

**Phil Lee** would like to thank his editor, Ed Aves, for his careful implementation of the new Rough Guide design in the preparation of this new edition of the *Rough Guide to Norway*. I would also like to express my appreciation to my ever-helpful co-author, Roger Norum. Special thanks also to Helen Siverstøl of Fjord Norway; Annett Brohmann of Visit Oslo; Nils Henrik Geitle of De Historiske – historic hotels and restaurants; Linn Kjos Falkenberg of the Bergen Tourist Board; Anne Randi Farnes of Destination Balestrand; Torunn Dyrkorn of Destination Molde & Romsdal; Lene Wiese of Destination Sogndal & Luster; Sindre Mjelva of the *Hotel Union*; Geir Steinar Vik of Destination Ålesund; Cathrin Åkre of Destination Geiranger; Beate Hauge of Destination Stryn & Nordfjord; Elizabeth Bakken of the *Hotel Alexandra*; Ole Henrik Walaker of the *Walaker Hotell*; Mette Bakketun of the *Fretheim Hotel*; Andreas Meinheit and Hans Jørgen Andersen of Destination Hardangerfjord; and Wenche Berger of NSB railways.

**Roger Norum** would like to thank the hospitable, generous and always hilarious Hanne Knudsen at Innovation Norway for extensive and invaluable help organising research

logistics and for being the best travelling companion ever to the far north on several occasions. Eva-Britt Kornfeldt at Visit Oslo was also very helpful with helping organise visits and supplying information, advice and tips on the capital. General assistance, hospitality and insight was also offered by a range of tourist officials, press officers, curators, hoteliers and restaurateurs across the country, including Sonja Louise Birch-Olsen, Lucy Moss, Knut Slinning, Knut Hansvold, Kjersti Norås, Marit Løvhaug, Bree Sims, Morten Moe, Anne Karin Braut, Piers Crocker, Gøril Ovesen, Evgenia Egorova, Anne Haga, Lisbeth Fallan, Rigmor Myhre, Solveig Claussen, Monica Kristensen, Kirsten Toft, Maria Anttila, Kate Utsi, Constance Andersen and Marie and Jarle Sølverud. Great thanks is also due to Damien, Kieh and Turner Dunn-Christopherson and the Australian Embassy in Kathmandu for desk space, a comfy bed and plenty of comic relief during the final throes of writing. My gratitude goes to my family in Connecticut, who rarely question why I do what I do (or even ask what it is), and to SKM, who was inspirational in more ways than she knows.

## Readers' letters

Thanks to all the readers who have taken the time to write in with comments and suggestions (and apologies if we've inadvertently omitted or misspelt anyone's name):

Tommy Andreasen; Katy Ball; Simon Barton; Gavin Bell; Natalie Birk; Ross Brown; Noel Cooper; Stephen Dodd; Simon Frayers; Guro; Trine Grønn Iversen; Lindsay Jack; Alan Kraus; Niall and Jenny Martin; Raymond Maxwell; Greg Minshall; Bob Morris; Birgit Myrie; David Paul; Daniel Payne; Siri Pedersen; Per Persson; Bill Pike; Michael Plunkett; Ian Robins; Peter Rollason; Stacey Ross; Bogdan Solga; Anthony Stern; Alan Tait; Alan and Sally Thornber; Ingrid Tønneberg; Yanni Vikan.

## Photo credits

All photos © Rough Guides except the following:
(Key: t-top; c-centre; b-bottom; l-left; r-right)

**p.1** Corbis: Douglas Pearson
**p.2** visitnorway.com: Johan Wildhagen
**p.5** visitnorway.com: Casper Tybjerg
**p.9** visitnorway.com: Christopher Hagelund (t, b); Corbis: Jon Hicks (c)
**p.10** visitnorway.com: CH
**p.11** Terje Borud (t); Pal Bugge (c); visitnorway.com: Johan Wildhagen (b)
**p.12** Corbis: Jochen Schlenker/Robert Harding World Imagery
**p.13** Corbis: Douglas Pearson (t)
**p.14** visitnorway.com: Terje Rakke/Nordic Life
**p.15** Tim Davis (tr); Corbis: Jose Fuste Raga (c); Morten Rakke/rakke.no (b)
**p.16** visitnorway.com: Nancy Bundt (tl); Per Eide (tr); Sónia Arrepia Photography (b)
**p.17** visitnorway.com: Frithjof Fure (b)
**p.18** Getty Images: Jens Kuhfs (t); visitnorway.com: Anders Gjengedal (b)
**p.19** Jens Henrik (tl); visitnorway.com: Andrea Giubelli (tr)
**p.20** Jan Olav (t); visitnorway.com: Bård Løken (b)
**p.21** Corbis: Scanpix Norway/Reuters (tl); visitnorway.com: Anders Gjengedal (c); CH (b)
**p.22** visitnorway.com: Kurt Hamann (l); Per Eide (c); Terje Rakke/Nordic Life (r)
**p.24** visitnorway.com: Kurt Hamann
**p.97** Tom Sivesind (tr); Tom Henning Bratlie (br)

**p.131** Corbis: Christian Kober (b)
**p.144** Corbis: Marco Cristofori
**p.147** Heidal Rafting: Outdoor Photo
**p.167** visitnorway.com: Morten Helgesen
**p.182** Getty Images: Age Fotostock RM
**p.185** visitnorway.com: Per Eide
**p.197** visitnorway.com: CH (t)
**p.217** Corbis: Douglas Pearson (t); visitnorway.com: Terje Borud (b)
**p.247** Corbis: Arctic-Images
**p.260** visitnorway.com: Sonia Arrepia Photography
**p.263** visitnorway.com: TerjeRakke/Nordic Life
**p.273** Johan Berge (t); visitnorway.com: CH (bl)
**p.293** Getty Images: Johner (t); visitnorway.com: Avani (b)
**p.309** visitnorway.com: CH (t); Terje Rakke/Nordic Life (b)
**p.319** visitnorway.com: CH
**p.343** Johan Wildhagen (t); visitnorway.com: CH (c); Kurt Hamann (b)
**p.353** visitnorway.com: Terje Rakke/Nordic Life (t, bl)
**p.378** Corbis: Werner Forman

**Front cover** Reine, Lofoten islands © Maurizio Rellini/SIME/4Corners
**Back cover** Skiing in Austvågøy, Lofoten islands © visitnorway.com: Kristin Folsland Olsen (t); Stavanger harbour © Pal Bugge (bl); Urnes stave church © visitnorway.com: Per Eide (br)

# Index

Note that the Norwegian alphabet has three more letters than its English counterpart. These are Æ, Ø and Å. In Norwegian dictionaries, words beginning with these two letters appear at the back after "Z". However in this index we follow conventional English alphabetical order, so Æ is listed with "AE", Ø with "O" and Å with "A".
Maps are marked in grey

# Map symbols

The symbols below are used on maps throughout the book

| | |
|---|---|
| ▬▬▬ ▪ | International boundary |
| ▬▬▬ ▪ | County boundary |
| ▬▬ ▬ ▪ | Chapter division boundary |
| ▭▭▭▭ | Road |
| ▭▭▭▭ | Pedestrianized road |
| ) ▭▭▭ ( | Tunnel |
| ▪ ▪ ▪ ▪ ▪ | Unpaved road/track |
| ▬ ▬ ▬ ▬ | Footpath |
| ▭▭▭▭ | Steps |
| ▬▬▬▬ | Railway |
| )▭ ▬ ▬ ( | Railway tunnel |
| ▬▬▬▬ | Castle/fortress wall |
| ●▬ ▬ ▬● | Cable car |
| ▬ ▬ ▬ | Ferry route |

| | |
|---|---|
| ⋉ | Bridge |
| ✈ | Airport |
| ★ | Bus stop/taxi stand |
| Ⓣ | T- Bane |
| 🅿 | Parking |
| @ | Internet café/access |
| ✉ | Post office |
| ⓘ | Tourist office/information |
| ⊞ | Hospital |
| ◆ | Place of interest |
| ⊙ | Statue |
| ⵔ | Lighthouse |
| 🏛 | Country house |
| ⚘ | Viewpoint |

| | |
|---|---|
| ⚥ | Waterfall |
| ⋀⋀ | Mountain range |
| ▲ | Mountain peak |
| ⌂ | Mountain lodge/hut |
| ✝ | Church (regional map) |
| ⛷ | Ski resort/ski centre |
| ▨ | Building |
| ▢ | Market |
| ▥ | Church (town map) |
| ◯ | Stadium |
| ▢ | Park/gardens |
| ▢ | Beach |
| ▣ | Cemetery |
| ▢ | Glacier |

## Listings key

| | |
|---|---|
| ■ | Accommodation |
| ● | Eating |
| ■ | Drinking and nightlife |
| ● | Shopping |

# MAKE THE MOST OF YOUR TIME IN BRITAIN

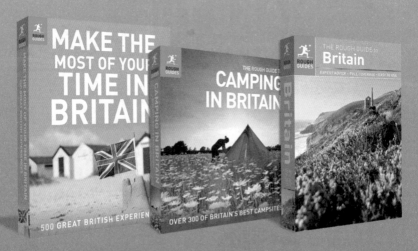

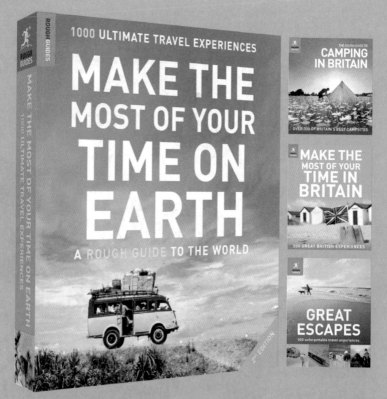

ROUGH GUIDES

# WE GET AROUND

**ONLINE** start your journey at roughguides.com

**EBOOKS & MOBILE APPS**

**GUIDEBOOKS** from Amsterdam to Zanzibar

**PHRASEBOOKS** learn the lingo

**MAPS** so you don't get lost

**GIFTBOOKS** inspiration is our middle name

**LIFESTYLE** from iPads to climate change

## ...SO YOU CAN TOO

BOOKS | EBOOKS | APPS